From Deference to Defiance

Charlestown,
Massachusetts
1629–1692

From Deference to Defiance

Charlestown, Massachusetts 1629–1692

Roger Thompson

NEW ENGLAND HISTORIC
GENEALOGICAL SOCIETY
2012

ISBN-13: 978-0-88082-258-9 (hardcover)
    978-0-88082-261-9 (softcover)
Library of Congress Control Number: 2011934670

On the cover: Detail of "An exact draught of Bostone harbour with a survey of most
of the islands about it, 1711," as reproduced in *A Topographical and Historical Description of Boston* by Nathaniel B. Shurtleff (Boston: City Council, 1890).
Design by Carolyn Sheppard Oakley
Printed in the United States of America

NEW ENGLAND HISTORIC GENEALOGICAL SOCIETY
Boston, Massachusetts
www.AmericanAncestors.org

Contents

List of Maps

to
Sandra and Colin
Patricia and Alec

The best of friends

Abbreviations and Sources

ANB—J. A. Garraty and M. C. Carnes, eds., *American National Biography* (Oxford: Oxford University Press, 1999)

Aspinwall—*Aspinwall Notarial Records* (Boston: Record Commission, vol. 32, 1903)

Assistants—John Noble and John T. Cronin, eds., *Records of the Court of Assistants,* 3 vols. (Boston: County of Suffolk, 1901–18)

Bailyn, *Merchants*—Bernard Bailyn, *New England Merchants in the 17th Century* (New York: Harper, 1964)

Brenner, *Merchants & Revolution*—Robert Brenner, *Merchants and Revolution: Commercial Change, Political Conflict and London's Overseas Traders, 1550–1653* (Cambridge: Cambridge University Press, 1993)

CSMP—*Colonial Society of Massachusetts Publications* (Boston: The Society, 1795–)

CSPCol—*Calendars of State Papers Colonial* (London: Public Record Office)

CSPD—Ibid., *Domestic*

CTR—MS Charlestown Town Records, 1634–92, Boston Public Library, Microtext Department, Reels 1 & 2. CTR 1A: Munro transcription 1634–64

CTrR—MS Charlestown Treasury Records, 1634–92, 3 vols., Boston Public Library, Rare Books Department

***Charlestown VR*—**R. D. Joslyn, ed., *Vital Records of Charlestown to 1850* (Boston: NEHGS, 1984)

Coldham—P. W. Coldham, *English Adventurers and Emigrants,* 3 vols. (Baltimore: Genealogical Publishing, 1984, 1985, 2002).

Dunn—Richard S. Dunn, James Savage and Laetitia Yeandle, eds., *The Diary of John Winthrop* (Cambridge: Harvard University Press, 1996)

Doc.—Document Number in MxCC D&O, 1 (photostats)

Emerson, *Letters*—Everett Emerson, ed., *Letters from New England* (Amherst: University of Massachusetts Press, 1976)

Essex CC—G. F. Dow, ed., Records and Files of the Quarterly Court of Essex County, 1636–86, 9 vols. (Salem: Perley, 1911–75)

Frothingham—Richard Frothingham, *The History of Charlestown* (Boston: Little & Brown, 1845)

GDMNH—S. Noyes, C. T. Libby, and W. G. Davis, *Genealogical Dictionary of Maine and New Hampshire* (Baltimore: Genealogical Publishing, 1972)

GM—Robert Charles Anderson, George F. Sanborn Jr., and Melinde Lutz Sanborn, *The Great Migration,* Vols. 1 & 2 (Boston: NEHGS, 1999–2001); Anderson, Vols. 3–6 (2003–2009)

GMB—Robert Charles Anderson, *The Great Migration Begins,* 3 vols. (Boston: NEHGS, 1995) pagination continuous

Hammond, Diary—Diary of Lawrence Hammond, 1678–94, 2 *MHSP,* 7 (1892) 144–72

Hotten—J. C. Hotten, ed., Original [Shipping] Lists of Persons of Quality (Baltimore: Genealogical Publishing, 1974)

Hull Diary John Hull, Diary, *Transactions of American Antiquarian Society,* 3 (1857)

Hull Letter Book—Typescript transcription of originals at the American Antiquarian Society, Worcester, Mass.

Hunnewell—J. F. Hunnewell, ed., *Records of the First Church of Charlestown 1632–1789* (Boston: privately printed, 1880)

Johnson—Edward Johnson, *Wonder-Working Providence of Sion's Saviour (WWPSS),* ed. J. F. Jameson (London, 1654)

Lechford—E. E. Hale, ed., *Note-book kept by Thomas Lechford...1638–41* (Cambridge: Wilson, 1885)

Magnalia—Cotton Mather, *Magnalia Christi Americana,* 2 vols. (New York: Russell and Russell, 1967)

MA— Massachusetts Archives, 220 Morrissey Boulevard, Columbia Point, Boston, MA 02125

Mass Archives— MHS Photostats of Massachusetts Archives and other documents, arranged chronologically, 1508

MHS—Massachusetts Historical Society

MHSC—*MHS Collections* (1792–), preceded by decadal series number

MHSP—*MHS Proceedings* (1791–), preceded by decadal series number

MR—Nathaniel B. Shurtleff, ed., *Records of the Governor and Company of Massachusetts Bay, 1628–86,* 6 vols. (Boston: White, 1853–54)

MxD—Middlesex Registry of Deeds, vols. 1–10, County Courthouse, East Cambridge

MPR—Middlesex Probate Registers, vols. 1–5, at MA; subsequent volumes on microfilm at Middlesex Probate Registry, County Courthouse, East Cambridge

MW—Microfilm of Middlesex Wills, Inventories and Administrations, series 1, 1648–1871, at MA

MxCC RB—Middlesex County Court, Record Books, 1, 3, 4, transcribed by David Pulsifer, originals, transcriptions and microfilms at MA

MxCC D&O—Middlesex County Court, Folios of Depositions and Orders, originals and five microfilm reels at MA; photostats of vol. 1 (1649–63) also at Harvard Law School Library (Special Collections)

Morison, *Founding*—Samuel Eliot Morison, *The Founding of Harvard College* (Cambridge: Harvard University Press, 1935)

Morison, 17th Century—Samuel Eliot Morison, *Harvard College in the Seventeenth Century,* 2 vols. (Cambridge: Harvard University Press, 1936)

NEHGS—New England Historic Genealogical Society, 99–101 Newbury St., Boston, MA 02116-3007

NEQ—*New England Quarterly*

NYGBR—*New York Genealogical and Biographical Record*

OED—James A. H. Murray et al., eds., *Oxford English Dictionary*, 11 vols. (Oxford: Clarendon, 1933)

ODNB—Colin Matthew & Brian Harrison, eds., *The Oxford Dictionary of National Biography*, 60 vols. (London: Oxford University Press, 2001–4)

Possessions—*Report of Boston Record Commissioners containing Charlestown Land Records 1638–1802* (Boston: Rockwell & Churchill, 1883)

R—*New England Historic Genealogical Register*

Rodgers—Robert H. Rodgers, *Middlesex County Records of Probate and Administration 1649–76*, 3 vols. (Boston: NEHGS, 1999, 2001; Rockport, Maine: Picton, 2005)

Savage—James Savage, *Genealogical Dictionary of the First Settlers of New England*, 4 vols. (Baltimore: Genealogical Publishing, 1965) pagination continuous

Sewall—M. Halsey Thomas, ed., *The Diary of Samuel Sewall, 1674–1729*, 2 vols. (New York: Farrar, Straus and Giroux, 1973)

Sibley—John Langdon Sibley, *Biographical Sketches of Graduates of Harvard University, 1642–89*, 3 vols. (Cambridge: Harvard University Press, 1873–85)

Sfk CCR—S. E. Morison, ed, *Records of the Suffolk County Court, 1671–80*, 2 vols. (Boston: CSMP, vols. 29–30,1933)

Sfk Deeds—John T. Hassam, ed. *Suffolk Deeds,* 14 vols. (Boston: Rockwell and Churchill, 1880–1906)

Sfk Wills—Judith McGhan, compiler, *Suffolk County Wills* (Baltimore: Genealogical Publishing, 1984)

s.n.—Under the name of, in Index

TAG—*The American Genealogist.*

Test. Testimony of

Thompson, *Cambridge Cameos*—Roger Thompson, *Cambridge Cameos* (Boston: NEHGS, 2005)

Thompson, *Divided*—Roger Thompson, *Divided We Stand: Watertown 1630–80* (Amherst: University of Massachusetts Press, 2001)

Thompson, *Mobility & Migration*—Roger Thompson, *Mobility and Migration: East Anglian Founders of New England 1629–1640* (Amherst: University of Massachusetts Press, 1994)

Thompson, *Sex*—Roger Thompson, *Sex in Middlesex: Popular Mores in a Massachusetts County* (Amherst: University of Massachusetts Press, 1986)

Torrey—Clarence Almon Torrey, *New England Marriages Prior to 1700*, 3 vols. (Baltimore: Genealogical Publishing, no date)

Venns—John and J.A. Venn, *Alumni Cantabrigiae, Part I (From Earliest Times to 1751)*, 4 vols. (Cambridge: Cambridge University Press, 1922–27)

VCH*—Victoria County Histories*

WMQ*—William and Mary Quarterly*

***WJ*—**John Winthrop, *Journal: "History of New England,"* ed. J. K. Hosmer, 2 vols. (New York: Scribners, 1908)

***WP*—**Allyn Forbes and Francis J. Bremer, eds., *Winthrop Papers*, 6 vols. (Boston: MHS, 1925–92)

Wyman— Thomas B. Wyman, *Charlestown Genealogies and Estates* (Boston: Clapp, 1879)

Note: Years began on March 25 in the seventeenth century; here, dates have been adjusted to New Year's Day on January 1. In quotations, spelling has been modernized and some punctuation added for clarity's sake.

Preface

In September 1994, as early reviews of my book *Mobility and Migration* began to appear, I embarked on a research fellowship at that Ali Baba's Cave for scholars, the Newberry Library in Chicago. I was intrigued about the New England experiences of some of the East Anglians whose roots and interrelationships I had traced. These residents of the Stour Valley region had joined Rev. George Phillips and Sir Richard Saltonstall to found Watertown, Massachusetts in 1630. *Divided We Stand*, my history of Watertown's early years, appeared in 2001. Another group of Eastern Counties migrants had joined with fellow devotees of Rev. Thomas Shepard to settle in Newtown, Massachusetts, during the second half of the 1630s. Having recently retired, I moved on to a similar investigation of the first three generations of inhabitants in the town we know as Cambridge. *Cambridge Cameos* came out in 2005.

One of the bases of my research had been the manuscript Middlesex County Court Records, which I had first used for *Sex in Middlesex* in the early 1980s. I had realized then that the busy port of Charlestown was very different in its mores from the upriver or inland towns of the county. I decided to investigate its seventeenth-century development more closely without reiterating the case studies in *Sex in Middlesex*; *From Deference to Defiance* is the fruit of that research.

Divided We Stand was predominantly a traditional town study with sections on landscape, immigrant origins, founding the town, farming, religion, welfare, Native Americans, and change over time; it was arranged topically, with illustrative examples from the various records interspersed. At the end, I included a few particularly striking case studies (including one of a pedophile, who turned out to be the forebear of one of my in-laws!).

Cambridge Cameos has quite a long analytical introduction, but is then entirely composed of case studies, arranged chronologically. Many of these are included in order to convey vivid depictions of early colonial ways of life, thought, belief, speech, hopes and fears. Others, such as a pleading letter written by Thomas Danforth to the king's representative as he sails back to report (negatively) to Whitehall, are hooks on which to hang a broader account of Anglo-Massachusetts relations after the royal restoration of 1660 and other evolving themes.

From Deference to Defiance is a hybrid. It is mainly composed of case studies, but they are arranged topically, as was *Divided We Stand*. The core of the book is the section on "The Sea," deriving from the wealth of material about Charlestown's maritime interests and involvement in the Atlantic economy. The section on "Peopling" looks at the very different origins of the settlers and their effects on the town's development. The one or two East Anglian families there must have felt like strangers.

This book completes my studies of the three founding towns on the north bank of the Charles River, and of present-day Middlesex County. The final chapter tries to pull together the lessons from three very distinct communities, evaluating both their contrasts and their similarities.

When I first began serious work on the colonial period in the 1960s, town studies were all the rage. The names of Demos, Grayson Allen, Greven, Lockridge, Powell, Rutman, Warden, and Zuckerman were celebrated and their work influential. Since the 1970s, other interests have taken the limelight, notably feminist, black and Native American histories. Recently, however, two striking new community analyses have appeared: Brian Donahue's *Great Meadow,* about the sustainable economy of the town of Concord, Massachusetts; and Barry Levy's *Town Born,* a reassertion of the importance of the administrative unit of the town as a crucial organizer of its group political economy. Concurrently, the early modern local historians of England have produced an invaluable range of books, articles and collections on county, town, and parish communities. This book is intended as a modest addition to both these enterprises.

Acknowledgments

I am most grateful for help and advice from the following: Ann and Harry Booth, Jessica Collins, Richard Crockatt, Laurel Damashek, Colin Davis, David Dearborn, Brian Donahue, Peter Drummy, Janice Duffy, Bettina and Herwig Friedl, David Hall, Richard Hogg, Doris Jones-Baker, Tim Lang, Michael Leclerc, Barry Levy, Lisa Lieberman, Susan Maycock, Barbara Melone, Ginevra Morse, Eric and Megan Ross, Pamela Ross, Scott Sanford, Steve Csipke, D. Brenton Simons, Penny Stratton, Charles Sullivan, Oriel Thompson, Conrad Wright.

My thanks also for generous assistance from members of the staff of the following institutions: American Antiquarian Society; Bedford Record Office; Boston Parks Commission (Historic Burying Grounds); Boston Public Library (Rare Book and Microtext Departments); British Library; Bunker Hill Memorial Museum; Cambridge Public Library; Dorset Record Office; Guildhall Library London; Harvard University Library System (Andover-Newton, Archives, Business School, Houghton, Law School, Lamont, Maps, Tozzer, Widener); London Metropolitan Archives; Massachusetts Archives; Massachusetts Historical Society; Middlesex Registry of Deeds; New England Historic Genealogical Society; Society of Genealogists, London; Somerville Public Library (Manuscript and Research Departments); University of East Anglia Library.

Introduction

"Charlestown: what does the name mean to you?" I have asked Americans I have met over the last few years.

"Capital of South Carolina?" is the response from the over-eager, ill-informed, or hard of hearing.

"*Town*," and it's in Massachusetts.

"Oh! Bunker Hill!" say the Revolutionary War buffs, and tourists who have done *all* the Freedom Trail, climbed the obelisk and visited the new Memorial Museum. They also remember visiting the old Navy Yard and the USS *Constitution*.

"Wasn't there trouble over school busing?" ask older New Englanders and readers of J. Anthony Lukas's evocative *Common Ground*.

"And crime!" say those who have seen such movies as *Mystic River* or *The Town*, which opens with the claim that Charlestown is the home of more armored car and bank robbers than anywhere else in the United States.

People who haven't been there for a long time recollect a run-down place, with a large Irish blue-collar population and two fine but soot-stained Roman Catholic churches, all blighted by the traffic on Interstate 93 thundering overhead.

Occasionally a genealogist has come up with some ancestral names: Sprague, Russell, Sedgwick, Frothingham, Edes, or Tufts. Gradually jigsaw pieces build up a picture, but the picture is usually post-revolutionary.

Since the completion of Boston's grand construction project the "Big Dig," Charlestown has been transformed and gentrified. When I have asked recent visitors whether they have seen any survivals from before the War of Independence, they mention the new City Park. This has the foundation lines of the 1629 Great House, which became the famous

Three Cranes Tavern, and small display stands with photographs of archeological discoveries unearthed during the Big Dig. The Harvard Mall memorializes the most famous, if short-lived, early resident. A wanderer down side streets might have spotted the Phipps Street Burying Ground, off Main Street. Gravestone fanciers will have heard of the pioneering "Charlestown Stonecutter." Visitors to Tufts University or Davis Square may have lighted on the old Powder House in outer Somerville, built about 1703 as a windmill on the spinal ridge ending at Bunker Hill and Breed's Hill. In those days Somerville was still part of the "Main[land]" of Charlestown. Apart from the twists and turns of its street plan, and its surviving records, these few remnants–site of first dwelling with archaeological finds, cemetery, and mill–are all that remain of colonial Charlestown. The Battle of Bunker Hill on 17 June 1775 not only cost hundreds of lives, it also destroyed the town.[1]

This book seeks to recreate the lost world of seventeenth-century Charlestown. The town started as a proud and independent rival of Boston, just across the mouth of the Charles River, rather than a mere neighborhood of the city, to which it was annexed in 1874. As the oldest town after Salem in the original Massachusetts Colony, it seems to have been intended as the capital–hence the Great House. Within a few years its inhabitants had not only established houses and barns, planting grounds, a mill, a meetinghouse, an inn, a marketplace, and a street plan, they were also exploring their Atlantic coastline and its river systems for trading opportunities in fish, furs, and timber. Rapidly thereafter they were embarking on more ambitious ocean voyages: to England, the Azores, Spain, the Caribbean, and the Chesapeake. They built warehouses, wharves, docks, shipyards, ropewalks, shops, and eventually the colonies' first dry dock in 1677–78. This is an inspiring achievement, especially using premodern technology.

Recovering the lives and work of the first three generations of townspeople depends primarily on the surviving records. Four nineteenth-century antiquarians have made this task much easier. The first was Richard Frothingham Jr. (1812–80), a descendant of one of the founding families and married to a Blanchard, whose irritating forebears we will soon meet.

---

[1] The Phipps Street Burying Ground is a useful source of dating and kinship research; it has about 100 gravestones of people who lived in the seventeenth century. The identity of the Charlestown Stonecutter is unknown, but his successors, especially four generations of the Lamson family, carried the art of slate carving to aesthetic heights. R. L. Tucker, "Lamson Family Gravestone Carvers," *Markers,* 10 (1993), 150-–218; A. I. Ludwig, *Graven Images* (Hanover, N.H.: University Press of New England, 1999), 107, 160, 168, 287, 295, 300, 308, 309.

Frothingham was "Mr. Charlestown" of the mid-1800s: proprietor and managing editor of the *Boston Post*, local leader of the Democratic Party, second mayor from 1851 to 1853, elected to the Massachusetts House of Representatives, treasurer of the Massachusetts Historical Society, and historian of the Battle of Bunker Hill. He was familiar with town and colony records, and his *History of Charlestown* published in 1845 contains many excerpts, particularly lists of land grantees, censuses of inhabitants, and documents covering the turbulent divisions of the Glorious Revolution in the town from 1689 to 1692. His account is divided into civil and ecclesiastical chapters, and it is presented in the form of annals, year-by-year events. No detailed history of the early town has been written since Frothingham's.

In 1880, his kinsman, merchant and author James Frothingham Hunnewell (1832–1910), published his edition of the records of the First Church, founded in 1632, though it had been combined with Boston's since the summer of 1630. This invaluable source lists baptisms, admissions to church membership, and the disciplinary cases against errant brothers and sisters. A prolific writer, Hunnewell also published *A Century of Town Life: A History of Charlestown 1775–1887*, which includes a chapter on "The Village in 1638," with a plotting of the houselots of the earliest settlers around the marketplace and Windmill Hill (see Map 3). A "very early" plot of Line Field, published by George A. Gordon of Somerville in 1894, and John Winthrop's 1637 sketch map of his Ten Hills Farm adjoining Charlestown's grazing common are the only seventeenth-century maps to have survived. A pertinacious grant plotter like the late Robert Nylander of Cambridge is sorely needed to delineate the spaces of the whole Charlestown domain.[2]

Meanwhile, an "eccentric bachelor," Thomas Bellows Wyman (1817–78), another cousin of Frothingham's, was combing the town clerk's documents, the County Court vaults, the great books in the Registry of Middlesex Deeds, the recently published *Records of the Governor and Company of Massachusetts Bay*, and other archival material for his monumental dictionary: *The Genealogies and Estates of Charlestown*, published

---

[2] Hunnewell, *Century* (Boston: Little Brown, 1888); in 1880, Hunnewell published (privately) a *Bibliography of Charlestown History*; memoir of Hunnewell's life: *R*, 65 (1911) Alxiii–iv. Gordon: *R*, 48 (1894) 56–-58; Ten Hills: *WP*, 4: 416. Maps: the best pre-Revolution map of Charlestown and environs is the English military map of 1775, at the Bunker Hill Museum; Frothingham and Wyman reprint the Peter Tufts Survey of 1818; the 1830 Hales Survey of Charlestown is at the Charlestown Historical Society in the Museum building; the Matthew Draper map of Somerville of 1852 is at Somerville Public Library. Other maps, at the Boston Public Library, are the Pelham Map of 1777 and the Plan of Charlestown of December 1794.

a year after his death, under the management of his disciple H. H. Edes. Although plenty of new material has been discovered in the intervening thirteen decades, much of it gathered in Robert Charles Anderson's magisterial *Great Migration Project*, Wyman's compilation remains a reliable and highly detailed source for historians of early Charlestown.[3]

The fourth nineteenth-century historical midwife was the businessman and archivist Henry Herbert Edes (1849–1922). He was responsible for recovering and editing the Charlestown town records. Some important work was already being done, most notably the transcription of John Greene Jr.'s 1664 copy of the earliest records. The 1868 transcriber was Frederic Munro, a fine, accurate penman. At the same time Edes was bringing order to the records, separating sets of bound papers into topic volumes, like the Treasury Series, and printing brief bibliographic introductions to each volume of documents. Many of the seventeenth-century minutes and accounts were completed by him in 1873, though none was published, except for the *Book of Possessions* in 1883. What had prompted Edes's rummaging in the bottom of barrels and disturbing the dust on the upper shelves of the town clerk's office was Charlestown's second disappearance. The town had already lost Somerville at its incorporation in 1842. As we have seen, the remaining Charlestown peninsula was annexed to Boston in 1874. This explains why the records are now held by the Boston Public Library. Harry Edes's sorting, recovering, and ordering make the exploration of the town's first six decades far more straightforward and logical than it would otherwise have been. To all four pioneers, the colonial researcher owes a great debt.[4]

I was tempted to follow the example of my former colleague Diane Purkiss, author of *The English Civil War*, and call this book "A People's History," since most of its sources highlight the activities (often nefarious) of individuals. Court records, like the voluminous files of the Middlesex County Court, rarely celebrate the better sides of human nature, and there are well-known shortcomings in their reliability. I have presented such evidence with, I hope, a strong dash of skepticism, and, where available, it is supported by alternative documentation, such as letters, petitions, probate papers, and town or colony records. One of the huge advantages of court records, however, is their quirky and vibrant vividness. Often

---

[3] *Records:* ed. N. B. Shurtleff, see *MR.* Wyman's notebooks are in NEHGS. His career is celebrated in *R*, 33 (1879) 450--52.

[4] Both Edes and Frothingham Papers are at MHS. On Edes's life, *R*, 77 (1923) 83–87. Records: see "Town" below.

unconsciously, a witness, petitioner, confessor, or defendant will give us unexpected and revealing slants on seventeenth-century attitudes and expectations.[5]

Among many others, we will meet Ursula Cole, cheesemaker and alewife, who opined that she would rather hear a cat mew than either of her ministers preach. A free Cuban, Katherina Sims, jealously guarded certificates of her non-slave status and successfully asserted her rights to appeal to the governor and the courts. The unappreciated pastor Zechariah Symmes (who had once compared a witness to a blindfolded boy held down in a children's game) comes colorfully to life as a harrier of dissent—antinomian and antipaedobaptist. He interrupted a Baptist leader's self-defence with a cry of "He lies!" His critics were equally quick on the draw. When Symmes dismissed a scriptural quotation with "Aye, it may be in your Bible," magistrate Richard Russell shot back "Yea, and in yours too, if you'll look into it." When the impatient minister tried to hustle through an admonition, a layman reminded him that he needed to have the consent of the church members.

Our imaginations are whetted by the Mousall family's coming home to find their property vandalized—bed curtains and mattress slashed, chests prized open—and by Sarah Lowden, cowering in a neighbour's inglenook, terrified of her drunken brute of a husband. We follow a pair of young Charlestown thieves on their increasingly inebriated and belligerent crawl round Boston pubs, or Sarah Largin as she sports with foreign seamen in haylofts and stays out with a boyfriend until 3 a.m. We hear the servant who prefers "the church of the pint pot" to the church of the hourglass (in the pulpit), and Dr. Thomas Starr saying he would eat a firebrand if anyone could cure his patient's leg. The talk of the town was often by turns boastful, caustic, skeptical, or provocative.

Many incidents occur on voyages, like Captain Richard Martin's "smiting us [crew] with his cane, and kicking us with his foot…Nothing of the mention of God unless it was cursing and banning," and his subsequent bloody nose from the galled ship's carpenter. Captain William Marshall, eager to sail from Surinam, had to search on shore for his missing boatswain. He found him in a bordello, rocking "in a hammock with a Spanish woman, which is a Miss to a Jew," chased him with his rapier, and

---

[5]   Purkiss: *The English Civil War: Papists, Gentlewomen, Soldiers, and Witchfinders in the Birth of Modern Britain* (London: Harper, 2006). Shortcomings: L. Gowing, *Domestic Dangers* (Oxford: Clarendon, 1996), Ch. 1. I have not indulged in much statistical analysis, but have reproduced raw material that is amenable to such processing.

"so terrified the bosun that he was forced [to climb] the tops [topmast]." Many seadogs behaved like petty tyrants with their seamen.

In the early decades of the Middlesex Court records, the 1650s and 1660s, those convicted would often plead or petition for leniency. Formerly insolent drunks, raucous tarts, or seditious gossips addressed the bench with abject apologies to God and man, self-flagellating promises of amendment, and tears and groans of sorrow at their past sins (and possible sentences). How genuine was their craven deference to authority, we may often doubt. However, they rehearsed the rituals of a hierarchical community, and in so doing, reinforced its values.

The obdurate suffered humiliating and savage punishment. Mistress Mansfield, poverty-stricken, her twins in foster care, lashed out at her wealthy, upper-class neighbor Mistress Russell. For this outrage, she received ten lashes on her bare back. This too would be the fate of poor single mothers if they could not raise a £2 fine. If the birch or whip was not "well laid on," then the constable responsible could find himself in the dock. Moral offenses could be punished by forcing the miscreant to stand on a stool in front of the congregation during Lord's Day services. Insolent militiamen would have to crave forgiveness on parade "at the head of the company." Seamen who displeased their skippers would be summarily flogged at the mainmast by the ship's mate. Thus was due deference maintained, if personal submission had been insufficiently internalized.

However, as we shall see on a range of issues, this instinctive obedience, acceptance of inferior status, and kowtowing to one's "betters" began to evaporate during the tense and divisive 1670s and 1680s. During the early 1670s, clergy, magistrates and deputies were at loggerheads with each other, and the General Court was paralyzed by turmoil. This and later conflict within the ruling class, lay and clerical, inevitably tore their seamless superiority. During King Philip's War (1675–76), several incidents involving Charlestown troops were either mutinous or in defiance of orders. Clergy and magistrates who attempted to protect friendly Indians were threatened with death. Hierarchy was imploding.

After the war, the Charlestown church was embattled by fierce arguments about ministerial appointments, which culminated in the lordly Dr. Thomas Graves stamping out of one of many fractious meetings, refusing to give reasons for his (minority) position. This fight was far more bitter and drawn-out than previous disagreements about the treatment of dissenters. It pitted a group of men like Graves, who assumed that their superior birth and education privileged them to dictate to their neighbors, against those neighbors who had different and equally valid preferences.

Despite clerical leaders' bemoaning the lack of respect and the moral laxity among the lesser sort, crews subjected to violent and arbitrary commanders started questioning and resisting the unreasonable dictates of the quarterdeck. We shall meet two masters who were reduced to impotence by concerted crew reactions to their behavior. These uprisings continued in the courts after their vicious voyages were over.

This defiance of self-appointed or autocratic authority came to a head in the late 1680s and early 1690s, in association with the loss of the first charter in 1684 and the Glorious Revolution against royal dictatorship. The decision of the proprietors to enclose their individual holdings on the huge stinted common led to a mini-revolution among excluded "young beginners" and craftsmen deprived of raw materials. The authority of the selectmen was flouted in demonstrations to assert the "moral economy" of the whole commonwealth. Ill feelings from these confrontations carried over to the 1689–92 inter-charter period, when members of the militia train band mutinied against commanders who had accepted royal commissions, when a Harvard-educated resident was forced to assume his fair share of the administrative load in what he regarded as the lowly office of constable, and when the wishes of other "betters" were put to the vote and resolutely defeated. Again, the ruling elite was divided, with some notables preferring the popular resistance to the royalism of their colleagues. Even Charlestown's minister was outspoken in his support of popular consent and elective office. He had recently fled from England, and knew of what he spoke.

Charlestown had become a very different place from the early oligarchy. By the time the new charter arrived in 1692, bending of the knee and touching of the forelock were going out of fashion. We have only to read the outraged letters and petitions of the unseated top men to appreciate how much deference had given way to defiance in Charlestown after the "glorious" revolution.

Part 1
Peopling

Origins

The "Great Migration" of as many as 20,000 people to New England during the 1630s was, in its long-term effects, the most important event in English seventeenth-century history. It has been depicted as a farther-reaching extension of an already mobile English population, though I have argued elsewhere that many emigrants to New England came from long-settled backgrounds. What distinguished the Great Migration was its family nature, as compared to the settling of the Chesapeake or the Caribbean, where individual young men predominated (among mobile sections of the English population). Moreover, many arrivals in Salem, Charlestown, or Boston were members of "companies"—interrelated clans, or followers of gentlemen or ministers. This chapter presents a collection of such companies from various English catchment areas; others in this section exemplify other early Charlestown inhabitants: loners, agents, involuntary arrivals, and incomers from other colonial towns.[1]

People's origins had a huge influence on whether and whither they emigrated. Non-Puritan venturers rapidly learned that there was little point in going to Massachusetts. They would not be welcome. Some Puritan emigrants with enough money for return fares decided England, for all its faults, might be preferable to deprivation, disillusion, and death in New England. Well-endowed conventional gentlemen or yeomen living in large swaths of England not "infected" with "fanaticism" would have felt no urge to depart; nor would large numbers of modest husbandmen, settled laborers, cottagers, or artisans without the assets or sponsors for even one-way family fares.

In the new world, newly arrived "companies" or individual families would seek out the kind of landscape similar to that which they had left

---

[1] Thompson, *Mobility and Migration.*

behind. They needed sufficient variety to support the sustainable mixed-farming economy familiar and vital to them. If there was a dominant specialist group, they might additionally seek a site that could serve their interests. Considerable shuffling around might follow initial perching, as families or companies prospected for ideal plantations. The attractions of a site might change over time. Initial compulsions for fresh water, shelter, and defense might gradually recede, and other attractions emerge for development.

Though many planters in Charlestown were husbandmen or yeoman farmers, the early settlement of the Mishawum peninsula was dominated by five companies involved in trade and industry. Four of these companies were small but nonetheless extremely influential. The first two comprised West Countrymen from a region of England long associated with North Atlantic trade and discovery.

DORSET

Among the first arrivals of the Great Migration to Mishawum were the three Sprague brothers: Ralph, a fuller; Richard, a merchant; and William, a yeoman. They had sailed in April 1629 on the *Lion's Whelp* and landed at Naumkeag (later Salem). This was the bridgehead established by survivors of the unsuccessful fishing settlement at Cape Ann, ten miles northeast, and by the advance party of what would become the Massachusetts Bay Company under John Endicott, who had arrived 6 September 1628. The Spragues preferred what they saw at Mishawum, where Thomas Graves the company surveyor was laying out Governor Matthew Craddock's farm up the Mystic and constructing the Great House for future settlement leaders. He parceled out lots for the Spragues and their seven companions, who set about constructing rough shelters against the winter. As we shall see, the three brothers and their progeny would be important town officials and grow in wealth not only in Charlestown, but also in the daughter town of Malden and in Hingham, across the bay.[2]

The Spragues' origins connect them with the Cape Ann project, and with the powerful West Country transatlantic fishing and colonizing impulse. Upwey, their birthplace, was a village on the main road between Dorchester, county town (county seat) of Dorset, and, eight miles to the south, Weymouth, its major port, from which fleets of up to eighty vessels sailed each year to the cod banks of Newfoundland and the North

---

[2]   See below, "People Trafficking," and "Keeping Up with the Spragues."

Atlantic. The main promoter of the Dorchester Company and its 1624–27 settlement at Cape Ann (now Gloucester, Massachusetts) was Rev. John White, one of the most vigorous Puritan moral and civic reformers of the early Stuart era. The Spragues were personal friends of White and may have been related to others in the 1629 group. Anthony Eames, from their village, arrived in Charlestown in 1634. He was already related, because Alice Sprague had married his kinsman Richard Eames. The ties were soon strengthened when William Sprague married Eames's eldest daughter, Millicent. The Spragues were distinct from the West Dorset company that sailed in the *Mary and John* in March 1630 from Plymouth. They "sat down" at Dorchester, Massachusetts, before moving to Windsor, Connecticut, in 1635. Richard and Mary (Sharpe) Sprague were childless, and William moved to Hingham in 1636, so the Sprague line north of the Charles derived from Ralph and Joan (Warren) Sprague's six surviving offspring.[3]

BRISTOL

The second company came from Bristol, "the metropolis of the west" and England's second port. "Peninsulated" by the confluence of the Rivers Avon and Frome, it was strategically situated near the Severn Estuary; it served as the distribution nexus for a large area of western England and South Wales, from Minehead in Devon to Hereford near the Welsh border, via the Upper Severn and the Warwick Avon to the West and Central Midlands. This huge area was developing fast in the early modern period.[4]

Bristol had long been a pioneer of transatlantic discovery and investment. Explorers John Cabot (1497) and Martin Pring (1603) both sailed from there. The Elizabethan promoter of expansion Richard Hakluyt was appointed Prebend of Bristol in 1585. Early projectors (investors) like John Popham and Ferdinando Gorges had close connections with the port. Its ships were engaged in the North Atlantic fisheries from 1400, and their dried

---

[3]   Frank Thistlethwaite, *Dorset Pilgrims* (London: Barrie & Rockliffe, 1989), 26–44; *GMB*, 3: 1728–39; the Spragues were also identified with Fordington St. George. Richard's wife Mary was the sister of Charlestown's Mary Rand. 1629 group: John Meech, Nicholas Stowers, Samuel Hoyt, Abraham Palmer, Walter Palmer, Rev. Francis Bright, John Stickline. "Early Charlestown Records," Alexander Young, *Chronicles of the First Planters* (Baltimore: Genealogical Publishing, 1975), 373–77. The unreliable C. E. Banks, *Topographical Dictionary* (Baltimore: Genealogical Publishing, 1957) claims that Walter Palmer originated in Yetminster, about ten miles north of Dorchester; there is no evidence of kinship between the two Palmers.

[4]   C. G. A. Clay, *Economic Expansion and Social Change* (Cambridge: Cambridge University Press, 1984), 1: 179; D. H. Sacks, *The Widening Gate* (Berkeley: University of California Press, 1991) is a fine account of Bristol's growth from 1450–1700. Cf. Joan Vanes, ed., "Overseas Trade of Bristol," *Bristol Record Society*, 31 (1979), 5–25.

cod proved a vital element in the town's predominant overseas trade with Spain, Portugal, and the Mediterranean. In 1630 the *Lyon* of Bristol–Captain Pierce, master–arrived in New England waters ahead of the Winthrop Fleet. This ship, sent back to its home port for supplies, saved the starving colonists in February 1631. Bristol ships regularly carried emigrants to New England, and investors from the town sank money into the early development of the Piscataqua Basin and the Maine fisheries. After the 1640s, Bristolians carried thousands of indentured servants to the Chesapeake and the West Indies, returning with cargoes of tobacco and sugar.[5]

Up to 1642, Bristol's hierarchical society was controlled by an oligarchy of "mere merchants," wealthy wholesale merchant venturers, enriched by their Iberian and Mediterranean monopoly. This dominance was emphasized by a new charter for their Society from Charles I in 1639, which threatened to exclude retailers, such as drapers, from the lucrative import-export business. Furthermore, as conflict loomed, leading venturers favored both the elaborate rituals demanded by Archbishop Laud and the royalist cause in politics. The prospect for young, more radical freemen was ominous.[6]

Two such young family men settled in Charlestown and clustered around Sconce (Fort) Point by the water: James Carey, a draper from a leading commercial family who arrived in 1639; and Richard Russell, woolen draper and son-in-law of the famous Alderman William Pitt (1640). Russell brought his sister-in-law Mary (Pitt) Newell, wife or widow of Andrew, "merchant of Bristol," and her two sons (1647). From the upstream Severn Valley town of Tewkesbury came Barnabas Davis (1639) after several brief visits on behalf of English investors. Both the Careys and the Newells were generously favored in Russell's legacies of 1674. Russell's will also shows that he maintained close contacts with Bristol, where two of his sisters, Elizabeth Corbett and Sarah Russell, continued to live. The Russell-Carey-Newell group would prove extremely influential, Russell as a magistrate and chairman of selectmen, Carey and Newell as town clerks and executive officers [7]

---

[5] Sacks, 35–36, 49, 251–52. Mark Kurlansky, *Cod* (New York: Penguin, 1997), 26–30, 52; Dunn, 100, 151–52, 187; *WP,* 2: 265. S. Hornsby, *British Atlantic, American Frontier* (Lebanon, NH: University Press of New England, 2005), 14.

[6] Sacks, "Corporate Towns and the English State: Bristol's 'Little Businesses,' 1625–41," *Past and Present,* 110 (1986), 69–105. On religious radicalism in Bristol: Joseph Fletcher, *History of the Revival and Progress of Independency,* 4 vols. (London: Snow, 1847–48), 3: 191–98; R. Hayden, ed., "Records of the Church of Christ [Broadmead] 1640–87," *Bristol Record Society,* 27 (1974), 72–88.

[7] Carey: Patrick McGrath, ed., "Records relating to the Society of Merchant Venturers of the City of Bristol," *Bristol Record Society Publications,* XVII (1952), xliii, 32, 48, 61, 91, 95, 295; Sacks,

Another useful citizen first visited Charlestown in 1635. Nicholas Shapleigh was master of the *George* of Bristol when she set sail for New England in the late summer. She just escaped wrecking on the Isles of Shoals, and limped into the Charles on 7 November. In 1637 he was back, in command of the *Bristol Merchant*; he was in business with Edward Gerrish of Bristol, whose family settled in Newbury before his son Doctor William Gerrish moved to Charlestown. Shapleigh "set down" among fellow Bristolians on Sconce Point in 1646, though he continued seafaring. He was admitted to the church in 1652 and served the town as a surveyor and town clerk until his death in 1663. Richard Russell was the first-named overseer of his estate.[8]

A Bristolian who settled on the Mystic in 1635 was Robert Pennoyer, who had been baptized in St. Thomas's parish in 1614. He was a turner by trade, and the brother of William Pennoyer, who became a leading merchant in London and was a radical politician during the Puritan Revolution. William, of the Puritan St. Stephen's Coleman Street, traded in partnership with both transatlantic magnate Maurice Thompson, investing in Cape Anne fishing, and with his former master, Matthew Craddock, first governor of The Massachusetts Bay Company. Robert was associated with Craddock's plantation at Medford, and in 1639 was accused of trying to seduce Lydia, wife of Josiah Dastin of Charlestown. He was whipped and soon removed to New Amsterdam.[9]

Widening Gate, 328–40. Newell: Mary Pitt Newell became a church member in 1647, see below "Women and the Churches;" the only possible reference to Andrew Newell ("Nooll") that I have found in Massachusetts Records is in *GM,* 2: 220, s.n. Courser. However, Wyman dates the birth of younger son Joseph Newell to 1651, seventeen years after his brother John; his mother would have been aged 45. Davis: *GM,* 2: 289–92, and below, "Travels and Travails" and "Sharecropping Conflict." Russell will: D&O, 4: Folio 96; MPR, 5: 461–63; see below, "Godly Merchants." Bristol: Russell's colleague Daniel Gookin had been baptized at Bristol, and in 1635 Richard Mather had embarked there for New England in disguise. Russell was trading with Bristol during the 1650s, Patrick M. McGrath, ed., "Merchants and Merchandise in 17th-Century Bristol," *Bristol Record Society Publications,* XIX (1955), 243. McGrath's introduction to this volume has an excellent account of Bristol's merchant community and its trade with the New World.

[8]   B. J. L. Berry, *Shapleigh Families* (Baltimore: Gateway 1993), 134–49 disentangles Charlestown's Nicholas from his namesake, son of Alexander Shapleigh of Kittery, Maine. Our man was at Somers Island in 1648, *WP,* 5: 225; two years later he returned in the *Dolphin* from Barbados with 15,812 lb. of good merchantable, well-cured muscovado sugar, Berry, 137. John Oliver, linen-draper of Bristol, also emigrated to Newbury; William Gerrish married his widow in 1645. Boston merchant Robert Knight was also a Bristolian, as was Walter Price of Salem. Aspinwall, *Notarial Records,* 45, 82, 107.

[9]   *GM,* 5: 429–37; Brenner, *Merchants and Revolution,* 135–37, 190. William's interests extended to India, the Levant, Virginia, and the West Indies. R. H. Lounsbury, *The Pennoyer Brothers* (Philadelphia: Dorrance, 1971). The Pennoyer Scholarships are still awarded at Harvard.

DUNSTABLE

The third mercantile group came from the Dunstable area of Bedford-shire; they were followers of Rev. Zechariah Symmes, who sailed on the *Griffin* in 1634. Mrs. Anne Hutchinson was another passenger, as was the nonconformist minister Rev. John Lathrop of Eastwell, Kent, Southwark and Wapping, London. Symmes was born to a clerical family in Canter-bury, Kent, and his father William had ministered in the radical Kentish port of Sandwich, "famous for its patronage of godliness." He was a gradu-ate of Emmanuel College Cambridge, and from 1621–25 lecturer at the Puritan preachers' training ground St. Antholin's, in the heart of the City of London.

Symmes was the first beneficiary of the Puritan campaign to acquire appointments to "hot Protestant" congregations in important market towns, the "Feoffees for the Purchase of Impropriations" (1625–33). He had taken up the enhanced curacy of Dunstable only a few months before the devastating plague of 1625–26 struck the town, a busy wool and grain center on the north slope of the Chiltern Hills where the Roman Watling Street, the major northwesterly route from London to Chester, crossed the Icknield Way, an equally ancient ridgeway. It had not taken the infec-tion long to travel the 33 miles from the capital. Symmes and his new wife Sarah immediately endeared themselves to their parishioners at the great Norman crossroads church of St. Peter's by their care and dedication. Their emigration was doubtless prompted both by the suppression of the Feoffees in 1633, and by William Laud's translation to the Archbishopric of Canterbury and campaign against the Puritan-tolerating Bishop of Lin-coln, John Williams.[10]

---

[10]   Symmes was a close friend of the famous Puritan preacher Jeremiah Burroughs, *Magnalia*, 460; Zechariah and Sarah (Baker) were married for 49 years and seven months; ibid., 236–37. On Sarah: Johnson, 100, "Southwark," and "Women and the Churches" below. On Sandwich: Peter Clark, *English Provincial Society from the Reformation to the Revolution: Religion, Politics and Society in Kent 1500–1640* (Hassocks: Harvester, 1977), 302, 305, 307, 319, 322, 323, 327, 332, 335, 340, 350, 362, 371, 372, 381, 386, 393, 402; Jacqueline Eales, "Rise of Ideological Poli-tics 1568–1640," Michael Zell, ed., *Early Modern Kent* (Maidstone: Kent County Council, 2000), 279–313. On the Feoffees, four ministers, four merchants and four lawyers, and their involve-ment in Puritan colonization, Isabel M. Calder, *Activities of the Puritan Faction of the Church of England 1625–33* (London: Society for Promoting Christian Knowledge, 1957), xi–xx; Calder, "17ᵗʰ-Century Attempts to Purify the Anglican Church," *American Historical Review*, 53 (1948); Christopher Hill, *Economic Problems of the Church* (Oxford: Clarendon, 1963), 252–271. South-wark: Rev. Henry Jacobs's voluntary/separatist congregation had been a center of Puritan radical-ism at the south end of London Bridge since 1616; this was the group that sought refuge under Lathrop in Wapping, *GM*, 4: 345–51; in 1627, a local merchant gave the Feoffees the huge sum of £700 to found a new church in the parish, Calder, xii; Thompson, *Divided*, 65. St. Antholin's had

Further members of the Dunstable company were the families of Thomas Lynde (1634), Robert Long (1635), George Bunker (1634) and his brother-in-law William Johnson (1634). This group provided Charlestown with its first expert innkeeper in Long, proprietor of the Three Cranes; a deacon, deputy, and wealthy maltster/landowner in Lynde; and a brickmaker and mason in Johnson. An affiliate of this influential group was the famous historian Captain Edward Johnson, probably William's brother. He had been born in Canterbury the same year as Symmes, 1599, and in his *Wonderworking Providence of Sion's Saviour* referred admiringly to Symmes's father as an anti-prelatist and Puritan leader in the county. Johnson went on from Charlestown to help establish Woburn, and at the founding of its church, Symmes preached and prayed for nearly five hours.[11]

In turn, the Long, Lynde, and Johnson families with their similar backgrounds provided sea captains, innkeepers, merchants, and shipwrights to later generations. Johnsons and Longs intermarried; William Symmes became Charlestown's leading surveyor and allotter. His father's arrival in the town and appointment as Teaching Elder of the church stabilized that rather vulnerable gathering and gave it long-term leadership. The Dunstable company gave a disproportionate thrust to Charlestown's religious and commercial development.[12]

---

previously been a full Genevan-rite Huguenot refugee church; its minister was Charles Offspring, one of the four ministerial Feoffees. In 1628, 198 London Puritans had contributed £1555 to support six early morning lecturers at St. Antholin's. The Feoffees spent £350 for ministerial nomination at St. Peter's, Dunstable, and paid Symmes £20 a year over and above his local income. On the radical tradition at St. Peter's: Joyce Godber, *History of Bedfordshire* (Bedford: Bedfordshire County Council, 1969), 193, 249, 269. On emigration: Ross Lee, "Bedfordshire in the Civil War," *Bedfordshire Historical Society Publications*, 65 (1986) 21–25, 37.

[11]   Johnson, Long and Lynde: *GM*, 4: 84–90, 316–20, 369–78. Long: licensee of one of eleven inns along Watling Street in Dunstable; a John Long of Dunstable had made his will in 1545/6, Godber, 202. A Henry Lynde is mentioned in a 1546 will as resident at Dunton, Beds., 20 miles northeast of Dunstable. Margaret McGregor, ed., "Bedfordshire Wills 1383–1548," *Beds Hist Soc Pubs*, 58 (1979), 172, 176. Bedfordshire clay was, and still is, famous for brickmaking. The relationship between William and Edward Johnson is derived from the will of Matthew Johnson of Woburn, MW: 12726. George Bunker came from Odell, Bedfordshire, at the opposite end of the county, but Elizabeth Bunker, probably his sister, had married William Johnson at Dunstable in 1630. Odell emigrants usually settled in Concord with their minister Peter Bulkeley. Bunkers were resident from at least the 1400s, Godber, 168, and still are, *Beds Hist Soc Pubs*, 78 (1999). Francis Norton, of Southwark, had been born at Markyate, four miles from Dunstable, his mother's birthplace; see below, "Southwark," and "Captain Francis Norton's Estate."

[12]   Three other families emigrated from parishes within ten miles of Dunstable: the Sweetzers, from Tring, Hertfordshire (1637), the Felts, from Leighton Buzzard, Bedfordshire (1633), and the Whittemores, from Hitchin, Hertfordshire (1639). The Puritans of Leighton Buzzard had clubbed together to finance a lecturer, because their vicar was a Laudian. In 1634, the parishioners of Hitchin were presented for "gadding from their own church by troops to other churches" to hear

STEPNEY

By far the most influential company in the founding and successful expansion of Charlestown arrived from the huge London East End parish of Stepney (along with many other planters). Until the 1500s, the marshy flats on the north bank of the River Thames between the Tower of London at the eastern wall of the city and the River Lea three miles to the east, including the southward peninsula known as the Isle of Dogs, was a bleak and sparsely peopled wasteland of only about two thousand inhabitants. There were some dwellings along the Mile End Road and Ratcliffe Highway, and the church of St. Dunstan stood in a small huddle of houses on the edge of Stepney Green, but the riverside was liable to flooding and treacherously boggy; the terrain gave its name to Wapping Marsh, Stepney Marsh, and East Marsh. Shadwell, a hamlet on the riverside, was virtually empty. The parish's main products were hay and marsh grass, as well as lime burnt at the kilns at Limehouse Field.[13]

By the time of the Great Migration of the 1630s, these vacant pastoral and watery outskirts had changed out of all recognition. The burgeoning population bursting London's seams and the dynamic expansion of the city's overseas trade were two major causes of the transformation of Stepney, especially Thames-side. The soggy river's edge had been embanked with walls effective against high tides in the sixteenth century, and districts like Wapping, Shadwell, Ratcliffe, Limehouse, Poplar, and Blackwall rapidly acquired landing places, wharves, forges, and small shipyards and mast-yards along the river. Off the main roads were murky side alleys and warrens of jerry-built wooden shacks, workshops, and rooming houses "swarming with seafarers and shipwrights, caulkers and coopers, scavelmen, boatmakers,

---

more Puritanical sermons and lectures. Two Charlestown families originated from Sandwich, Kent: the Isaac Coles (1635) and the Matthew Smiths (1637). Zechariah Symmes and Edward Johnson were born in the same parish of Canterbury; the wives of Symmes and Edward Johnson Jr. shared the same maiden name of Baker.

[13] Main sources for early modern Stepney: John Stow, *Survey of London*, ed. C.L. Kingsford (Oxford: Clarendon, 1971), 2: 70–71, 367; G. W. Hill & W. H. Frere, eds., *Memorials of Stepney Parish: Vestry Minutes 1579–1662* (Guildford: Billings, 1890–91), vii–xiv; D. Morris & K. Cozens, *Wapping 1600–1800* (London: East London History Society, 2009); J.F. Merritt, ed., *Imagining Early Modern London* (Cambridge: Cambridge University Press, 2001); Roy Porter, *London, A Social History* (Cambridge MA: Harvard University Press, 1994); Patricia E. C. Croot, "Stepney", T. F. T. Baker, ed., *Victoria County History of Middlesex: Ossulstone Hundred* (London: Institute of Historical Research, 1998), 1–81; Norman G. Brett-James, *The Growth of Stuart London* (London: London and Middlesex Archeological Society, 1935), 189–212; Michael J. Power, "East London Housing in the 17th Century," in Peter Clark & Paul Slack, eds. *Crisis and Order in English Towns 1500–1700* (London: Routledge, 1972), 237–262, and "Shadwell: Development of a London Suburban Community in the 17th Century," *London Magazine*, 4 (1978), 29–48.

plumbers, pumpmakers and pitchbeaters."[14] These were joined by refugees from rising rents in London: "a great number of dissolute, loose and insolent people harboured in . . . noisome and disorderly houses . . . poor cottages and the habitations of beggars and people without trades, stables, inns, alehouses, taverns, garden houses converted to dwellings, ordinaries, dicing houses, bowling alleys and brothel houses."[15] Built-up Shadwell averaged 50 habitations per acre. In 1598, John Stow lamented the loss of fields and avenues of stately elms, replaced by filthy strait passages and dingy courts inhabited by sailors' victuallers. He conceded that "shipwrights and the other marine men have builded large and strong houses for themselves" on higher ground north of Ratcliffe Highway and along the river wall, but his general picture was of ramshackle squalor.[16]

As trade and population burgeoned in the early seventeenth century, the pressure increased. In 1620, the Pool of London below London Bridge exhibited a "forest of masts upon your river for traffic." By the time Wenceslaus Hollar etched his "Long View of London" from Southwark in 1647, this "forest" had spread downstream as far as his eye could see. From the 1530s, the Royal Navy used moorings at Blackwall and Ratcliffe, and in 1614 the East India Company (founded 1600) built a dockyard at Blackwall. Between 1624 and 1654, seventeen great ships were built in Wapping yards. John Graves of Limehouse, Warden of the Shipwrights' Company, managed to launch a ship of 250 tons or more annually from 1625–1637. 400–500 ton merchantmen anchored off Limehouse awaiting lighters to offload them and carry their cargo up to the "Legal Quays" above the Tower. The rise of trade around the coast, to Europe, the Mediterranean, the Atlantic, and the Indian Oceans, added crafts and businesses to the already seething waterfront. Along with anchorsmiths, carpenters, bakers, brewers, tanners, slaughtermen, lightermen, boatmen, dockers, ropemakers, and sailmakers were tobacconists, coal and sugar merchants.[17]

---

[14] Stow, 2: 70–72.

[15] Ibid., 367, 368.

[16] Porter, 140; Merritt, 14–15; Croot, 14, 16, 17; Power, "Shadwell," 38; Vanessa Harding, "Population of London 1550–1700," *London Journal*, 15 (1990), 112, gives the city's numbers as 200,000 in 1600 and more than half a million by 1700, most of this increase being in the suburbs, which by 1660 accounted for more than half of the population. The Navy Victualling Office was north east of the Tower, and provisioners "hugged Wapping riverside."

[17] Pool: Bishop of London addressing merchants at St. Paul's, Porter, 73; East India Company: by 1618, 232 employees were working at Blackwall, Brett-James, 197; coal: by 1650, 325,000 tons a year were brought to London from Newcastle, Porter, 139. Trade and population: Brian Dietz, "Overseas Trade and Metropolitan Growth," in A. L. Beier & Roger Finlay, eds., *London 1500–1700: Making of the Metropolis* (London: Longman, 1986), 115–40; Graves: ibid., 127, 139; Finlay & B. Shearer, "Population Growth and Urban Expansion," ibid., 37–59; East London Population

Accommodation was urgently needed. As successful merchants erected solid brick houses, illegal buildings were thrown up around marshy patches, on laystalls (refuse dumps), and near the waterfront: two hundred in Pease Close, Wapping in 1626 alone. More than six hundred wooden shacks reared up around the mudflats of Shadwell in the 1630s and 1640s. In 1638, another 250 houses were illegally erected in Wapping, some overnight. During the 1630s more pews and galleries had to be installed at St. Dunstan's. By 1662, the Bishop of London acknowledged "the vast number of inhabitants in the parish of Stepney." The population of the parish would rise from two thousand in 1550 to thirteen thousand in 1610 to forty thousand by 1665. In the whole century it would more than quadruple.[18]

The clean and healthful air that Stow had nostalgically celebrated from his youth was polluted by smell and noise. The stench from burning urine at the Wapping alum works was exacerbated by stinking tanneries and the "soil" of multitudes of defecators in middens, channels, and on the foreshore exposed at low tide. Droves of cattle left their dung on through roads to the nearby Smithfield meat market. Many Londoners believed that the frequent early visitations of plague spread out from the "crowded and insanitary" eastern suburbs. An observer described Stepney waterfront as "a detestable exhibition of the worst outskirts of London."[19]

Vice, drunkenness, riot, and degradation thrived in these cramped and ill-lit conditions. In 1617 the apprentices in their annual Shrove Tuesday tumult destroyed seven or eight brothels in Wapping and defaced another five. At least three of these bawdy houses were run by sailors' wives while their husbands were at sea. In 1626 after the disastrous expedition to the Ile de Rhé, off La Rochelle, unpaid sailors rioted and had to be billeted in Stepney until money could be found in 1628. In 1630 there were thirty-seven taverns in Wapping, even after twenty-six illegal grog shops had been suppressed. By 1650 the tiny hamlet of Shadwell had forty-four pubs. During the 1630s, the arrival of press gangs led to street fights and organized resistance to impressments into the Royal Navy. In October 1632, respectable parishioners petitioned the Privy Council about "the great numbers of people . . . especially the

Studies Group, "Population of Stepney in the early 17th century," *Local Population Studies*, 3 (1976), 39–53; D. Cressey, "Occupations, Migration and Literacy in East London, 1580–1640," ibid., 5 (1978) 53–60.

[18] Brett-James, 203–208; Porter, 91–92; Power, "Shadwell," 29; Power, "Housing," 237; V. Harding, "Changing Shape of London," in Merritt, 139; "Population of Stepney," 41.

[19] Porter, 43, 44, 119; Brett-James 202–3, 205.

poorer sort . . . beggars and other loose persons swarming about the City who were harboured in these outplaces." Such God-fearing petitioners bemoaned the collapse of order and civility in their parish.[20]

Amid this hectic boom town there were indeed islands of "solid bourgeois prosperity," even some "merchant princes" who wished to be "near their businesses."[21] Within these respectable groups, traditions of religious dissent were often long-held and deep-seated. East End mariners and traders were "exposed to new ideas abroad" in Calvinist ports of France, the Netherlands, North Germany, and the Baltic. Religious refugees from Catholic persecution found safe havens in Spitalfields, Whitechapel, and Stepney. The extramural freedom of the large parish allowed separatist gatherings of Brownists in the 1580s and 1590s. In 1633, Rev. John Lathrop's separatist group crossed the river from Southwark to Wapping. The following year Lathrop was forced to emigrate and sailed with Zechariah Symmes on the *Griffin*.[22]

Other Stepney parishioners had later affiliations with New England. One of the leading vestrymen at St. Dunstan's until his death from plague in 1625 was merchant John Vassall, whose sons Samuel and William were among the founders of Massachusetts. The pressing population prompted the foundation of subsidiary chapels to ease accommodation problems in the churches of St. Dunstan and St. Mary Matfelon, Whitechapel (immediately to the west of Stepney). Three other men with Massachusetts connections engineered the 1617 creation of the chapel of St. John in Wapping: Rowland Coytmore, master of the East Indiaman *Royal James*, husband of Katherine and father of Thomas, both later Charlestown residents; Robert Bourne, whose eldest son Nehemiah became a leading Boston shipbuilder; and its first curate/lecturer, Rev. Richard Sedgwick. He was a Peterhouse, Cambridge graduate often in trouble with the Anglican authorities for his nonconformist beliefs and refusal to use the prescribed Book of Common Prayer. His fellow alumnus, the famous London Puritan preacher Stephen Egerton, uncle of John Winthrop's wife Margaret, had previously found private or overseas posts for Sedgwick, who from

---

[20]   Brett-James, 195, 204, 205; Croot, 19; Paul Griffiths, *Lost Londons* (Cambridge: Cambridge University Press, 2008), 1, 77–9, 113, 182, 403–7; wives: Robert Ashton, "Popular Entertainment," *London Magazine*, 9 (1983), 14.

[21]   Brett-James, 195.

[22]   Ibid., 194; Porter, 92; Croot, 32, 74; *GM*, 4: 348–50; Hill & Frere, vii, xiii–xv. In 1633, some former conventiclers with Lathrop celebrated the first Particular Baptist rebaptism in Wapping, W. T. Whitley, "Records of the Jacob-Lathrop-Jessey Church," *Transactions of the Baptist Historical Society*, 1 (1908–9) 189.

now on ministered to the Puritans of Wapping until his death in 1643. Robert Sedgwick, merchant, soldier and leading citizen of Charlestown, may well have been a kinsman.[23]

The parish of Stepney, and particularly its riverine southern districts, provided not only a vibrant spirit of industry, enterprise, and exploration, but also a strong Puritan base and long godly tradition. From what so recently had been a kind of eastern wilderness, its adaptable and ambitious, yet disciplined and devoted emigrants ventured down the Thames during the 1630s to attempt to tame a "wilderness" in the west.

Twenty-one East London families, most of them seafaring, artisanal, or trading, made the hazardous journey to Charlestown during the 1630s and 1640s. When pioneer minister Francis Higginson wrote home from Salem in July 1629 to his "Friends in Leicester" where he had preached during the 1620s, he advised that "if any be of the mind to buy a ship, my cousin Nowell's counsel would be good. Also one Mr. [Thomas Beecher] a very godly man and master of the ship [*Talbot*] we went in, and likewise one Mr. Graves, the master's mate dwelling in Wapping, may herein stand you in good stead." Increase Nowell was the leading figure in the establishment of Charlestown. His surname would have been instantly recognizable in the City thanks to his uncle Alexander Nowell, the famous Puritan catechist and dean of St. Paul's who served from 1560 to 1602. During the late 1620s, Increase lived in a house on Philpot Lane once owned by Sir Thomas Smythe, governor of the East India Company and treasurer of the Virginia Company. In the first two decades of the seventeenth century, the house served as the City headquarters of the East India Company and was thronged with shareholders, seamen, or their needy wives. Philpot Lane was in the parish of St. Benet, Gracechurch Street, dominated by wealthy Puritan merchants.

Nowell's far-flung family connections formed a Wapping "clan-company" among his neighbors in the New World. Captain Beecher was a "cousin" like Higginson, and Mrs. Christian Beecher was the widow of another mariner, Thomas Cooper of Wapping. The wife of Increase Nowell (1593–55)

---

[23] Vassall: *GMB*, 3: 1871–75; chapel: Brett-James 195; Bourne, Egerton: *ODNB*; Sedgwick: Paul Seaver, *Puritan Lectureships* (Palo Alto, CA: Stanford University Press, 1970), 185–86, 233. Prior to his appointment to Wapping, Richard Sedgwick was "our preacher here in Hamburg," whose church was "fully reformed." He was one of three trustees of the 1615 £1,000 legacy by Hamburg merchant William Jones to "poor preachers in England." Nicholas Tyack, "Fortune's English Puritan," Dr. Williams's Library, 1990, 7. Robert Sedgwick provided a London link to the Bedfordshire company; he had been baptized at Woburn, Bedfordshire, on 6 May 1613, the son of William, gentleman of London and Elizabeth (Howes). His brother William became a leading Puritan preacher in Essex, *ODNB*. See below, "Godly Merchants."

was Parnell, daughter of Katherine (Gray) Coytmore and stepdaughter of Rowland Coytmore, the East India skipper and founder of Wapping Chapel. Other daughters of Katherine had married Boston merchant William Tyng and the Thomas Graves of Higginson's letter, who served as pilot of the *Arbella* in 1630 and master on frequent transatlantic voyages during the 1630s and 1640s. Thomas was the son of John Graves, a Limehouse shipwright who sold his extensive premises to William Graves in 1637. Thomas became an inhabitant of Charlestown about 1639, but was often back in Wapping during the 1640s. On one such voyage he managed to overpower a predatory Dutch privateer in the English Channel; a grateful Parliament appointed him to the rank of Vice Admiral. He died aged 48 in 1653 in battle off Scheveningen during the First Dutch War, but his son Nathaniel and step-grandson Thomas Adams carried on the family seafaring tradition. Another son, Thomas, would become a leading third-generation citizen of Charlestown. [24]

Katherine and Rowland Coytmore's son Captain Thomas emigrated from Wapping to Charlestown in 1636; his widowed mother joined her Wapping clan in New England two years later at the age of 62. She lived in Charlestown for a further twenty-one years, but Thomas was tragically drowned off the Spanish coast in 1644. Two other Wapping emigrant families were connected to this clan: the Rainboroughs and the Harrises. Not only was Thomas's wife Martha a Rainborough, but her mother had been a Coytmore who married the rising Levant merchant William Rainborough. Martha had two brothers, Thomas and William Jr.; the latter briefly settled in Charlestown in 1639, and bought the original meetinghouse. His father's death and the start of the Civil War in 1642 led to his return to Wapping. Many New Englanders who went back to fight for Parliament in the War served in Colonel Thomas Rainborough's regiment. William rose to the rank of major in another regiment of Cromwell's New Model Army and took the Leveller side in the Army's Putney Debates about a future constitution, but then turned to the religious radicalism of the "Ranters." He was in Stepney in 1661, but had returned to Boston by his death in 1673. Rowland Coytmore's first wife had been the widow of William Harris, merchant of

---

[24] Higginson: Emerson, 25–27, *GMB*, 2: 933–37; Higginson died in 1630. Beecher: GMB, 1: 145–46. Nowell: *GMB*, 2: 1342–46, *ODNB*; M. J. Leclerc, "Sarah (Parker) Williams," *TAG*, 82 (2007) 172-77 reveals other relationships. Tyng: his family mercantile connections are analyzed in Bailyn, *New England Merchants*, 136–38. Graves: Frothingham, 139; Croot, 24; Wyman 232–33; Hill & Frere, 60, seq; Savage. His voyages can be followed in *WP*, 5: 2, 7, 8, 14, 21, 144, 219, 244, and *WJ*, 1: 31, 65, 80, 102, 103, 104, 152, 153; 2: 157. Winthrop described him as "a discreet man." Admiral Graves is not to be confused with "Engineer" Graves, who built the Great House and laid out the early town before returning to England., *GMB*, 2: 805–807.

Wapping. Two Harris stepsons of Katherine Coytmore, John and William, emigrated to Boston, where they intermarried with another famous emigrant Wapping family, the Bournes, and engaged in trade.[25]

Subsequent members of this kinship group continued the Charlestown-Wapping connection. Three of "cousin" Francis Higginson's sons were resident in Stepney Parish by the 1650s. Nowell children married into seafaring or transatlantic trading families like the Ushers, the Longs, the Winslows, and the Hiltons. Mehitabel (Nowell) Hilton's second husband, Deacon John Cutler, had Stepney connections. The will of Nowell Hilton, the Deacon's stepson—a mariner who died in London during a voyage in 1687—left his personal estate to his kinsman Nathaniel Cutler, sawyer of Stepney. Members of this Nowell-Coytmore-Graves-Rainborough extended family, often leading figures in the commerce and religion of Stepney parish, carried across their authority, wealth, discipline and devotion to Charlestown.[26]

In 1635 Captain Thomas Graves had sailed down east to explore the Isle of Sable off Nova Scotia with another skipper from Wapping and Limehouse, John Hodges, who had sailed from London to Virginia in 1631 and settled in Charlestown in 1633. Somewhat less "discreet" than Graves, this hard-drinking, foul-mouthed and indolent seadog had several brushes with authority during his twenty-one-year residence in Charlestown. His widow, related to the mercantile Davison family, married a Boston shipbuilder, and the next generation allied with Lyndes, Haymans, and Phillipses: all mercantile families. Similarly, the litigious Captain John Trumbull, son of Robert, mariner of Wapping, wed the daughter of a ship's captain. They in turn married their daughter in Charlestown to Captain Richard Martin, commander of the *Blossom*. A grandson, John Baxter, also took to sea, making the fourth generation of sailors in one family.[27]

Trade associations linked two more East London immigrants to the Graves family. Francis Willoughby, Wapping shipwright, arrived in 1638. His distinguished career as merchant, English Republican naval administrator, Massachusetts deputy governor, and Charlestown leader is told

---

[25]   Coytmore, Harris: *R*, 106 (1952), 15–17. Bourne, *WP*, 5: 243–45, *ODNB*. Rainborough: W. R. D. Jones, *Thomas Rainborow* (Woodbridge: Boydell, 2005). Stephen Winthrop married Judith Rainborough, sister of Martha, whose second husband was John Winthrop Sr. See below, "Wealthy Women."

[26]   Hilton: Wyman, 504.

[27]   Hodges: *GMB*, 2: 962–64; Mary (Miller) Hodges was sister to Joanna (Miller) Davison, wife of merchant Nicholas, who arrived in Charlestown from London in 1639. He was a leading citizen until 1658, when he and his family moved to Pemaquid. Trumbull: *R*, 49 (1896), 148–52, 322–32, 417–26; Martin: Thompson, *Sex*, 182–85.

below. The second shipbuilder, from Whitechapel, adjacent to Wapping, was Thomas Hawkins. He too diversified after his arrival in Massachusetts in 1636, when he was granted a lot in Charlestown. He skippered two ships he had built in New England, but both were wrecked: the first in 1644, the second two years later. Thomas Coytmore drowned in the first sinking. Hawkins traded with Maine, the West Indies, England, and the Mediterranean. He died a wealthy man, on a passage from London to New England in 1648.[28]

Nicholas Trerice was a young mariner with a Cornish name but a Wapping address. He became an inhabitant of Charlestown in 1636, but was annually employed in transatlantic voyages. His owners and backers in London included such famous New transatlantic investors as Maurice and George Thompson, Joshua Foote, George Foxcroft, Richard Hill, Robert Rich, and William Hibbins. Trerice also sailed to Virginia, the Caribbean, Spain, the Azores, and Madeira.[29]

A pair of Charlestown families had interesting links with the parish of Stepney. After the death of Dr. Richard Palgrave in 1651, his widow Anne is next found in Stepney. Two of her daughters, Elizabeth and Lydia, married Stepney men and seem to have remained there, though their mother returned to New England by 1665. We shall later encounter the touching welcome written by Charlestown widow Arrald Cole to her new daughter-in-law Ruth, who had married mariner James Cole in Stepney in the mid-1650s. James soon died, and Ruth's second husband was Henry Mudd of Stepney. A Peter Mudd, who had a house in Charlestown, was involved in the fishing industry until his death in 1656, as was James Cole's brother John.[30]

Little is known of the backgrounds or kinship connections of the eight other families of East London origin who settled in Charlestown. Listed in the *Planter* in 1635 were Nicholas Davis and family, including William Lock, aged six, son of William Lock of Wapping, mariner. Glover George Hepburn arrived from Stepney in 1636 with his wife Hannah, two children and two servants. They were followed in 1637 by Captain James Garrett and pregnant wife Deborah from Wapping and Phillip Knight, cooper, aged 20, from Stepney. John March and wife Rebecca emigrated

---

[28] Willoughby: see below, "Godly Merchants," and "Wealthy Women." Hawkins: *R*, 27 (1873), 28; W. H. M. Wilcox, "Thomas Hawkins," ibid., 151 (1997), 193–216. See below, "Charlestown and the Atlantic World."

[29] *R*, 143 (1990), 26–35; *R*, 159 (2005), 235–36.

[30] *GMB*, 1: 426–29. 3: 1373–76. Peter Mudd witnessed a bond in Charlestown on 4 September 1647. Aspinwall, 85

from Shadwell in 1638 with four children, including cause of future trouble and expense 13-year-old Theophilus. In the same year, Nathaniel Hadlock of Wapping, mariner, was admitted an inhabitant of Charlestown. In 1645 Robert Chalkley, a weaver, arrived with wife Elizabeth from the textile district of Spitalfields, bordering Stepney. Finally, the shadowy figure of Edward Payne was admitted to Charlestown in 1638; after his death his son went home to Wapping in 1649 to reclaim family property there.[31]

SOUTHWARK

The last group brings us across London Bridge to London's southern suburbs, the South Bank communities of Southwark and its neighbours Bermondsey and Lambeth. A 1630s satirist compared London to a pregnant woman, "always with child, for she grows greater every day." As we have seen with the flood of people to the East End, the old city had burst at the seams; part of the excess population swelled the low-lying former ecclesiastical estates of the South Bank parishes around the foot of London Bridge, by 1600 "one of the largest centers of population in England." [32]

Indeed, the main road south from the foot of the bridge, known as Long Southwark or the Borough, was a rough dividing line between the two main parishes: St. Saviour's, west or upstream of the Bridge, and St. Olave's (Olaf's), east or downstream. Since London Bridge was a barrier to large vessels, the two parishes had developed different cultures. St. Saviour's included "Bankside," a center of various disreputable and suspect activities such as

---

[31]   All these families are briefly noted in Wyman. Charlestown citizens with known London roots are: Abraham Pratt, Southwark/St. Brides, *R*, 143 (1989), 35; Abraham Palmer, London, *GMB*, 3: 1376–79; James Hayden, St. Dunstan in the East, a mariner from a strongly mercantile Thamesside parish, *GM*, 3: 277–80; William Learned, Bermondsey, wife Southwark, *GMB*, 2:1164–66; William Smith, London, Wyman, 872. Payne was a sea captain from Wapping, who had married Margery Fell in 1633, Ferguson, 230. He commanded the *Susan and Helen* in 1638, and was building a new vessel in 1640. He addressed Governor Winthrop as his "loving friend," and bought and sold land in Charlestown and in Suffolk. He imprudently lent £300 to Nathaniel Eaton, the rascally first head of Harvard, *WP*, 4: 204–5, 248–49, 430, 435; CTR, 1A: 68; Aspinwall, 15.

[32]   Satirist: Donald Lupton, *London and the Country Carbonardoed* (London: Okes, 1632; reprinted, Edinburgh: Aungervylle Society, 1883), 59. Southwark: D. J. Johnson, *Southwark and the City* (London: Corporation of London, 1969); Martha Karlin, *Medieval Southwark* (London: Hambledon, 1996); J. Boulton, *Neighbourhood and Society* (Cambridge: Cambridge University Press, 1987); William Rendle, *Old Southwark and its People* (Southwark: Drewett, 1878); R. C. Carrington, *Two [Southwark] Schools* (Orpington: privately printed, 1971); J. A. Browner, "The Wrong Side of the River," *Essays in History*, 36 (1994) 34–56. Brett-James, *Growth of Stuart London*, Johnson, Boulton, and Rendle have excellent maps; Carrington contains some fine prints. Population: by 1631, the population of Southwark was said to be 25,718: larger than Norwich, the second city of the kingdom. Boulton, 19–29, Johnson, 273.

theaters, bull- and bear-baitings, entertainments, pleasure gardens, taverns, gambling houses, and brothels, including the notorious Holland's Leaguer. The same satirist described Paris Garden at the western end of the parish as "a foul den of idle base persons that want [lack] employment, the swaggering roarer, the cunning cheater, the rotten bawd, the swearing drunkard, and the bloody butcher . . . as many civil religious men [are here] as saints in hell." As with most of the seventeenth-century metropolis, the southern suburbs suffered from the insistent problem of "rogues, beggars, idle and vagrant persons . . . marauding bands of vagrants [swelled by] demobilized soldiers and sailors." However, St. Saviour's (often known as the Borough or Boroughside) was also a major center of trade with its four weekly markets and its inns catering to travellers to and from Kent, Surrey, Sussex and the south coast. Its economy was also supported by processing foodstuffs, especially preparing fresh fish, butchering cattle, and milling grain.[33]

By contrast, St. Olave's, with its thoroughfare Tooley Street (Short Southwark) leading to the grazing land of Horsleydown and Bermondsey to the east, was open to seagoing vessels. The rectory stood "so close to the waterside that the decks of ships moored there were within three or four feet of the house."[34] Rombout van den Houte's print of 1632 shows two large vessels tied up and another coming in. St. Olave's wharves, like Sellinger's, Goodchepe's and Woodmongers'; the City Garners (granaries) and ovens in case of bread shortages in London; the Bridge House with its office and stores for maintaining the Bridge; and several major breweries lined Tooley Street and its tributary lanes and alleyways. Some brewhouses had been built by recent refugees from European persecution, but Southwark ales had been renowned since Chaucer's time. Other "strangers" brought to the parish expertise as silk workers, dyers, jewelers, hatters, weavers, potters and glassblowers. Among the parish's many inns, the White Lion and the Walnut Tree were opposite St. Olave's church, the Ram's Head nearby on the bank downstream, and Falstaff's Boar's Head just around the corner. As well as custom from local artisans such as leather processors, weavers, feltmakers, and metalworkers, these pubs were a favorite resort of sailors. In 1628, a mob of sailors rioted outside the White Lion Prison demanding the

---

[33] Lupton, 75; R. Ashton, "Popular Entertainment and Social Control," *London Magazine,* 9 (1983) 3–19; taverns: in 1631 Surrey J. Ps. reported 228 alehouses in Southwark and Kentish Street, ibid., 11; brothels: R. Thompson, *Unfit for Modest Ears* (London: Macmillan, 1979), 63, 73, 135, 141, 147, 177; Carrington, 52; trade: Boulton, 266, Johnson, 309, Brett-James, 57; fish: Lupton, 81. Vagrancy: P. Griffiths, *Lost Londons* (Cambridge: Cambridge University Press, 2007); Johnson, 325–26. "Borough:" this name came from pre-Norman defensive works south of the bridge; Southwark was not a municipal borough during the 1600s.

[34] Karlin, 86.

release of some of their mates. Though the Bridge House Trust donated an annual £20 towards the poor of St. Olave's, living conditions for many were increasingly crowded and insanitary. In 1625 and 1636, the plague struck with particular ferocity.[35]

One reason that persecuted refugees from Europe flocked to Southwark was its reputation for religious radicalism. Its parishes often had "hot Protestant" incumbents, whose fiery Sabbath sermons were matched by weekday lectures from "factious" (inspired) preachers. Both St. Saviour's and St. Olave's congregations were "heated" by a series of Puritans in their pulpits from Elizabeth's reign to the 1660 Restoration. Not only would regular communicants refuse, in the precisian tradition, to receive the bread and wine kneeling at the altar, but this "stronghold of nonconformity" also nurtured separatist and semi-separatist congregations, Baptist groups, and Independents; the most famous of these was Henry Jacob's conventicle founded in 1616. It came as little surprise that, during the Long Parliament's campaign against Archbishop Laud, the mob of 500 that attacked his palace at Lambeth in 1641 had marched east from Southwark.[36]

Along with religious radicalism went political opposition. Two leading anti-royalists in the 1640s had Southwark connections. Isaac Pennington, galvanizer of popular demonstrations, was Southwark's alderman; its member of Parliament after 1646 was the equally radical transatlantic trader George Snelling. In 1647, when the Parliament sought to exclude Thomas Fairfax's less conciliatory army from marching into London, it was the citizens of Southwark who opened the Bridge gates to let the troops in. Among the inhabitants, apprentices in the Southwark parishes had a reputation for riotousness, particularly the numerous trainee feltmakers. This busy, mixed, and seething suburb proved a source of important migrants to Charlestown.[37]

---

[35] Moored: Karlin, 86; Houye: Carrington, 37; brewers: e.g., Leake, Webling and Goodyer, Rendle, 265, Carrington, 33, 50; strangers: as early as 1568, 916 aliens had sought refuge in Southwark. Ida Darlington, "Reformation in Southwark," *Proceedings of the Huguenot Society of London,* 19 (1915) 65–81; Rendle, 265; artisans: ibid., 241; sailors: Johnson, 336, Boulton, 71, 98; the poor: Johnson, 128; plague: ibid., 235–36; Boulton, 28, 66.

[36] Hot Protestants: Boulton, 143, 275, Boulton, "Limits of Formal Religion," *London Magazine,* 10 (1984) 136–54, Darlington, "Reformation," Rendle, 250, Carrington, 54; Brenner, *Merchants and Revolution,* 502, 514; Jacob: see below; Lambeth Palace: B. Manning, *English People and the English Revolution* (Harmondsworth: Penguin, 1978), 44–57; M. Braddick, *God's Fury, England's Fire* (London: Allen Lane, 2008), 93–97.

[37] Pennington, Snelling: Johnson, 146–52; Pennington, Lord Mayor from 1642–43, was not resident in Southwark; Brenner, *Merchants,* 502. Fairfax: Braddick, 501–02; Browner, "Wrong Side," 38; feltmakers: ibid., 56.

The most illustrious of the Southwark emigrants was undoubtedly Rev. John Harvard (1607–38), who arrived in Charlestown in 1637 with his young bride, Ann (Sadler).

The plague had scythed through the Harvard family in St. Saviour's, killing father Robert, a successful wholesale butcher, mother Katherine (Rogers), rich stepfather, and several of his eight siblings, so that John, the survivor, was worth some £2,000, a huge fortune, when he was elected teacher of Charlestown church in November 1637. He survived only thirteen months in his new home before dying of consumption on 14 September 1638. His wealth had been enhanced by large land grants from the town. Since his marriage was childless, he left some £800, including his library of 400 books, to the college that bears his name (established in 1636 as New College). Ann was remarried to John's ministerial successor, Rev. Thomas Allen, and in 1651 returned with him to England. John Harvard was linked to many early clergy, including Pastor Symmes, by his attendance at Emmanuel College, Cambridge. A geographical link between Harvard and Symmes was provided by Mistress Symmes. She was the daughter of the well-endowed Southwark merchant Humphrey Baker, and married Zechariah in 1622 at St. Saviour's. He was then one of the Lecturers at St. Antholin's, Budge Row, near St. Paul's. The first head of Harvard College, Nathaniel Eaton, was John Harvard's contemporary at Emmanuel.[38]

Two other influential Charlestown wives originated in Southwark. Deputy Governor Willoughby's second wife, Margaret (Lock), was the granddaughter of Roger Cole of St. Saviour's, Southwark. She brought to the marriage considerable inherited property from the South Bank parishes. One of the masters of the *Arbella* fleet in 1630 was Captain Nicholas Hurlston of the *Jewel*, sent out by Matthew Craddock, former governor of the Massachusetts Bay Company. Three years before, his kinswoman Rebecca Hurlston of the small parish of St. George's Southwark had married young Wapping mariner Nicholas Trerice. Though he named his new ship *Rebecca* in 1643, marital relations were sometimes fraught. Mrs. Trerice kept a shop in Charlestown, and after Nicholas died in 1653 she remarried wealthy fuller and merchant Thomas Lynde. The Trerices' only son, John, became a sea captain; their three surviving daughters all married merchants or skippers.[39]

---

[38] Outstanding article by C. E. Wright in *ODNB*. Sarah (Baker) Symmes: see below, "Women and the Churches."

[39] Lock: see "Wealthy Women," below. Hurlston: *R*, 143 (1990), 26–35; *R*, 159 (2005), 235–36; Trerice: marriage: MxCC D&O, 1: doc 361; shop: CTR, 1: 652B; children: Elizabeth, baptized Stepney 1629, married merchant Thomas Kemble; Rebecca married Capt. Thomas Jenner; Sarah married Capt. John Goose. Hurlston: *WJ*, 1: 24. Frances, daughter of St. Saviour's Grammar

Three sets of South Bank emigrants were connected by kinship ties. The will of the colony's first surgeon, "Londoner" Abraham Pratt (ca. 1580–1644), another victim of the sinking of Captain Hawkins's *Sea Fort* off Cadiz at the end of 1644, suggests a relationship to Rebecca Hurlston Trerice. His wife Jane (Charter) also drowned. Ironically, they were returning to England because "he feared that he should fall in want in his old age and therefore would needs go back to England (for surgeons were then in great request there by reason of the [civil] wars." William Learned, who was a founding settler of Charlestown, had lived in Bermondsey, and married a Southwark woman in 1606 at St. Olave's. His eldest daughter Sarah married two emigrants: the first was Thomas Ewer at Bermondsey in 1624, and the second, in Charlestown, was Thomas Lathrop, son of Rev. John Lathrop of Lambeth, Wapping, the ecclesiastical prison of the Court of High Commission for nearly two years; in 1634 he escaped to Charlestown and then moved to Scituate. The younger Lathrop's brother Benjamin, a cooper, moved to Charlestown in the late 1650s. The elder Lathrop had taken over Rev. Henry Jacob's semi-separatist Southwark conventicle in 1624. Ministry of this radical group was assumed by Rev. Henry Jessey, Winthrop's friend and correspondent. The Jacob-Lathrop-Jessey Southwark gathering have been seen as precursors of Independent, non-separating Congregationalist and Particular Baptist strains.[40]

The third and most important Southwark clan in Charlestown was linked by the Houghton family. Robert Houghton, the patriarch, was a wealthy brewer, merchant, and investor of St. Olave's. His wife was the sister of entrepreneur Major Robert Sedgwick of Charlestown. Robert Houghton's sister Mary's second husband was Francis Norton, haberdasher of St. Olave's and another Charlestown merchant grandee. Houghton was a major investor in the Massachusetts ironworks, and a partner with his two brothers-in-law in the fishing industry and other transatlantic enterprises. Houghton's interest in New England may well have been stirred by a fellow St. Olave's brewer, Richard Tuffnal, who had invested £50 in the Massachusetts Bay Company in 1629. This kinship group was one of the most vibrant mercantile partnerships of the 1640s and 1650s.[41]

School head 1644–48, Hezekiah Woodward, married emigrant minister John Oxenbridge. Carrington, 61.

[40] Pratt: *GMB*, 1504–7; *WJ*, 2: 248–49. Learned: ibid., 1164–65. Lathrop: *GM*, 4: 345–51. Conventicle: W.T. Whitley, "Records of the Jacob-Lathrop-Jessay Church," *Transactions of the Baptist Historical Society*, 1 (1908–9), 203–56; influence: Stephen Brachlow, *The Communion of Saints* (Oxford: Oxford University Press, 1988). Another member of the conventicle, Mr. Richard Brown, became ruling elder of Watertown church in 1630. Thompson, *Divided We Stand*, 65.

[41] See below, "Godly Merchants" and "Captain Francis Norton's Estate." Tuffnal: F. Rose-Troup, *The Massachusetts Bay Company* (New York: Grafton, 1930), 155.

A final and delayed Southwark-Charlestown connection, cementing the radical Protestant tradition of both places, involves the latter's seventh minister. Charles Morton's father Nicholas had been recruited in 1630 from his remote Cornish post to the hustle and factionalism of the parish of St. Saviour's, Southwark, when Charles was three. There he remained until his death in 1640, ministering to a congregation of distinctly Puritanical bent.

Although our knowledge of the backgrounds of many members of these founding companies of Charlestown is often scanty or nonexistent, the better-documented families exhibit important common characteristics. The first is age: many of the early emigrants were in their 20s or 30s. Sometimes they were recently married, like the Nowells, the Coytmores, the Russells, the Harvards, or the Hodges. Settlement in New England was a fresh start in more senses than one. Sometimes a parent had recently died, releasing family assets and also the necessity for care. This was the case with Thomas Graves, John Harvard, and Thomas Coytmore, and was a frequent pattern among emigrants generally.[42]

Early modern London was a powerful magnet for enterprising and ambitious young people. Many metropolitan emigrants came originally from provincial families. Increase Nowell's parents were probably Warwickshire people (like William Shakespeare's). Trerice was a Cornish name, Hepburne Scottish. Katherine Coytmore was born in East Suffolk and her first husband lived in the Essex port of Harwich. Elizabeth King, the wife of John Trumbull, was the daughter of an Ipswich ship's carpenter. Robert Sedgwick had been baptized in Woburn, Bedfordshire, though he grew up in London. Francis Norton had come to London as an apprentice from the Bedfordshire-Hertfordshire border. Both ministers Symmes and Lathrop came from Kent; the availability of lectureships in London drew them to the capital. The later London emigrant Nicholas Davison had Norfolk roots. The mercantile interests of most of these families help explain their mobility; their shallow roots in the "wild east"or the "unsolid south" of the city may have made transatlantic relocation a little more feasible.[43]

The expanding town of Bristol also radiated attraction to a broad hinterland. Richard Russell had been born in Hereford forty miles to the north, and Barnabas Davis in Tewkesbury the same distance to the northeast. A

---

[42]   Thompson, *Mobility*, 24–26.

[43]   Nowell: *GMB*, 1342–46; *ODNB*. Coytmore: *R*, 106 (1952), 15–17. Sedgwick: *ODNB*. Norton: see "Captain Norton's Estate," below. King: Suffolk Probates, Ipswich Record Office, England, William King will, 30 March 1655. Davison: Rodgers, 2: 230.

different kind of pull was exerted by religious zeal. The Bedfordshire group, and perhaps some Kentish emigrants, were drawn to the preaching and leadership of Zechariah Symmes; likewise with John Lathrop. Such was Symmes's reputation that some of his followers came from quite distant towns, such as Odell, forty miles to the north. "Gadding to sermons" of sympathetic preachers was a common Puritan trait.[44]

Other families had been settled for longer in their ports of emigration. The sisters Mary and Maud Pitt, wives of Andrew Newell and Richard Russell, came from an established leading Bristol family, as did James Carey. The Lyndes had been long resident in Bedfordshire. Graves, Coytmore, Cole, and Trumbull families had lived in London since Elizabeth's reign.[45]

Among those whose probate inventories have survived, leading members of these companies had amassed (and probably brought with them) considerable wealth. Francis Willoughby left the huge fortune of £4813 in 1671; Richard Russell £3505 in 1676; Richard Sprague £2398 in 1668; Nicholas Davison £1896 in 1664; Thomas Lynde £1709 in 1671; John Harvard £1600 in 1638; Thomas Graves £1054 in 1653; and the thirty-two-year-old Thomas Coytmore £1255 after only eight years in Charlestown. Minister Zechariah Symmes had accumulated £681 after nearly forty years in the town, and his English parishioner the innkeeper Robert Long £602 after three decades. Even the Widow Coytmore had £665 to bequeath when she died at the age of 83 in 1659. These founders were people of substance who committed their wealth to the New World and often multiplied it through hard work and skill.[46]

Most company members from Dorset, Bristol, Bedfordshire and London were devout believers, but a few mariners betrayed less savory attitudes from their port and seafaring lives. John Hodges was a foul-mouthed boozer; the daughter of quarrelsome John Trumbull, Elizabeth, became embroiled in sexual scandal and his son-in-law Richard Martin would emerge as a hot-tempered, violent bully. Nicholas Trerice had a

---

[44]   Russell: Wyman, 829–31; Davis, *GM*, 2: 286–92. Symmes company: see above. Gadding: Thompson, *Divided*, 26–28.

[45]   Pitt: Frothingham, 94; McGrath, "Merchants and Merchandise," 4, 210, 237. Graves, Coytmore, Trumbull: see above. Cole, of Southwark: see Margaret Lock Willoughby, above.

[46]   Inventories: Russell: MPR, 5: 461–63; Davison: RR, 2: 229; Graves: Wyman, 432–33; Lynde: *GM*, 4: 373; T. Coytmore: Mass Archives: 16 Nov 1647; Symmes: Wyman; Long: Rodgers, 2: 210–15; K. Coytmore: Rodgers, 1: 417–21. Average of five inventories for the Nowell cousinage from total of £4051: £810. Four Bristol families total £4044, average of £1011, driven up by Russell's wealth. The Dunstable Company of five left £3613, averaging £723. The total assets at death of twenty-six of these first-generation townspeople whose probate inventories survive were £16,177, an average of £622; in the seventeenth century this represented serious wealth. For a full list, see "Charlestown Immigrants" below.

reputation for slippery untrustworthiness, perhaps a cause of his later marital and financial problems. Robert Pennoyer was a sexual predator. Seafarers often combined a fearful superstition at sea with roistering recklessness ashore. Even among the first generation, this would present problems to authority.[47]

Dorset's small company of four families comprised sixteen individuals. Fifty-seven people emigrated in the twenty-one East London families during the 1630s, and sixteen from five South Bank families. Fourteen people in six families came from the Bristol area, and forty-eight from eight families came from Dunstable and its environs. Including eighteen possible Symmes followers from Kent, the total from these dominant sources was forty-six families, or 151 men, women and children. These would produce most of the leaders of the community's first thirty or forty years. Their immigrant children, and those born during the first decade of settlement, would provide successors who would have to grapple with increasing threats to Charlestown's integrity, independence, and safety in the late 1670s and 1680s.

---

[47]   On Hodges, Trumbull, and Martin, see above; Trumbull later proved a fearless and well-versed defender of the Charlestown Baptists, see below, "Thomas Gould and the Baptist Debates." Trerice: see above.

Charlestown Immigrant Origins, 1630–40

DORSET

Upwey/Fordington:

1629   Ralph Sprague, 4 people in party, he aged 34, wife's age unknown, by trade in England: fuller, estate at death £742

1629   Richard Sprague, 2, 33, w[48] 33, merchant, £2398.

1629   William Sprague, 1, 20, yeoman, [real: £94]

1634   Anthony Eames, 9, 42, yeoman

BRISTOL

1635   Nicholas Shapleigh, 3, 36, ship captain, £560

1635   Robert Pennoyer, 1, 31, turner

1639   James Carey, 2, ca. 39, w 22, draper, £219

1639   from Tewkesbury, Barnabas Davis, 4, 40, w 36, tallow chandler, £96

1640   Richard Russell, 2, 29, draper, £3505

1640?   Mary Newell, 2, 33, widow of mariner, £224

DUNSTABLE

1634   Zechariah Symmes, 7, 35, minister, £681

1634   Thomas Lynde, 5, 40, maltster, £1709

1634   George Bunker, 7, 35, £314

---

[48]   Wife or widow.

1634	William Johnson, 3, 26, brickmaker, £307
1635	Robert Long, 12, 45, w 30, innkeeper, £602
1633	from Leighton Buzzard, George Felt, 1, 23, mason, £556
1637	from Tring, Seth Sweetzer, 5, 31, shoemaker, £270
ca.1639	from Hitchin, Thomas Whittemore, 8, ca. 43, £286

Stepney

1630	Increase Nowell, 2, 37, w 27, gentleman/official, £592
1630	Thomas Beecher, 2, ca. 30, ship captain, £485
1630	Thomas Graves, 4, 25, w 25, ship captain, £1054
1636	Thomas Coytmore, 2, ca. 24, ship captain, £1266
1638	Katherine Coytmore, 1, 62, widow, £665
1639	William Rainborough, 1, ca. 22
1630	Richard Palgrave, 5, 37, w 36, physician, £313
1633	John Hodges, 2, 25, ship captain
1635	Nicholas Davis, 4, 40, tailor, £103
1636	Nicholas Trerice, 3, 38, w 30, ship captain, £147
1636–55	Cambridge, Charlestown, John Trumbull, 2, 28, w 26, ship captain, £237
1636	Thomas Hawkins, 2, 27, shipwright, £919
1636	George Hepburne, 6, 44, w 47, glover, £110
1637	James Garrett, 2, ship captain
1637	Phillip Knight, 1, 20, cooper
1637	Robert Cutler?, 5, blacksmith, £602
1638	Francis Willoughby, 3, 33, shipwright, £4813
1638	John March, 4, £213
1638	Nathaniel Hadlock, 2, mariner
1638	Edward Payne, 2, ship captain
1639	Nicholas Davison, 2, 28, merchant, £1896

Southwark

1630	from Bermondsey, William Learned, 6, ca. 49
1635	from Southwark, Robert Sedgwick?, 2, 22, merchant
1636	Abraham Pratt, 2, 50, surgeon
1637	Francis Norton, 4, 35, w 37, haberdasher, assets: £623, liabilities: £1368
1637	John Harvard, 2, 30, minister, £1600

KENT

1635   from Sandwich, Isaac Cole, 4, 28, carpenter, £120

1637   Matthew Smith, 2, 27, shoemaker, £52

1637   from Canterbury, Edward Johnson, 12, 39, joiner, £1297

OTHER KENT EMIGRANTS

1634   from Dover, William Bachelor, 4, 37, victualler, £262

1635   from Faversham, Thomas Brigden, 4, ca. 31, cooper, £244

1635   from Herne Hill, Phillip Drinker, 4, 39, w 32, potter, £109

1635   from Strood, Thomas Ewer, 6, 42, tailor (son-in-law of
W. Learned, Southwark)

1637   from Faversham, Thomas Call, 6, 39, tilemaker, baker

24 emigrants from five families.

Suffolk Loner:
Stephen Fosdick

Not all early settlers in Charlestown were from the six major English catchment areas. Some immigrants from other parts of the old country were attracted to Charlestown by the inhabitants' need for their skills or by their idiosyncrasies and resultant isolation. Both seem to have played a part in the settlement of the Fosdick family in the town.

The patriarch Stephen (1583/4–1664) came from the village of Great Wenham six miles southwest of Ipswich, the major port of Suffolk; his first marriage was registered in 1612 at the neighbouring town of Hadleigh. In 1635 Stephen received his first land grant in Charlestown. By 1637, after a year's return to England, he brought second wife Sarah (?Wetherell) to the town with six children aged from five to nineteen. [49]

Both Wenham and Hadleigh were important Puritan centers. The vicar of Great Wenham from 1612 to 1634 was Rev. James Hopkins, who had studied and taught at Peterhouse, Cambridge. He was a friend and correspondent of John Winthrop. In a letter of 25 February 1633, he wrote: "Sir, I am so well affected to your plantation that if I cannot enjoyce (sic) my liberty upon God's terms as I have done, I have a purpose to make myself a member of your plantation, and when I come I hope I shall not come alone." His accustomed liberty would be rapidly curtailed with William Laud's elevation to the Archbishopric of Canterbury that year. Though Hopkins died before he could emigrate, his will of 25 December 1634 reveals his commitment. He left his six children (including the fanatical

---

[49]   The family background is based on *GM*, 2: 545–51; since the name does not appear on any shipping list, it is possible that Stephen's return was to collect some or all his family after establishing a bridgehead. The six children were all by his first marriage. His second marriage took place probably about 1630.

"Witchfinder-General" Matthew Hopkins) 100 marks each (£33-13-4d) at age twenty-two. Second son Thomas was to be sent by his mother Mary "over the seas to such our friends in New England as she shall think fit, and there abide" until he reached twenty-two, when he would receive his legacy. If he failed to stay, then he would receive nothing. New England would have been much discussed in the Fosdicks' hometown.[50]

One of the overseers of Hopkins's will was Mr. John Gurdon of Great Wenham, who had sent his love to Winthrop and his wife in the vicar's letter. Gurdon (1595–1675) was the eldest child of Winthrop's close friend Brampton Gurdon of Assington, Suffolk, who had himself seriously considered emigration in the mid-1630s. John had attended the radical Emmanuel College, Cambridge, and emerged an ardent Puritan, "a man so hot for his zeal to set a kingdom on fire." He championed the Parliamentary cause in the English Civil Wars and was a member of the Council of State in 1650. His younger brother Edmund (ca. 1616–) emigrated to New England in 1635 (the same year as Stephen Fosdick), followed by his sister Muriel Gurdon Saltonstall in June 1636. In this party were the Gurdons' Assington vicar Rev. Nathaniel Rogers and three local families. Sarah Fosdick's brother John Wetherell also travelled to Massachusetts about 1638. The Gurdon-Rogers exodus proved quite considerable. The Fosdicks were part of an emigrant company.[51]

The cloth-making town of Hadleigh had been a Puritan shrine since the fiery 8 February 1555 martyrdom of its rector Dr. Rowland Taylor on Aldham Common during the reign of Catholic "Bloody Mary" Tudor. Taylor's career and last words at the stake were celebrated in Foxe's *Book of Martyrs,* as were the nine townsmen who escaped persecution by fleeing to Switzerland. Five families, including the wealthy Paine brothers, left from this town, which had books on navigation in its parish library. Dozens more came from its satellite villages, though the Fosdicks were the only emigrant family from Wenham. It is no surprise, then, that the names of these two Puritan hotbeds should also migrate; Wenham, Massachusetts, was founded in 1637 between Salem and Ipswich and developed by a group of Suffolk immigrants. Hadley in western

---

[50] Cambridge: Venns. Letter: *WP,* 3: 105–107. The will is in the probate papers of the Norwich Consistory Court, 1604–1686, in the Norfolk and Norwich Record Office, Norwich, filed as 233 Playford. It has been transcribed by George Knowles, for his study of Matthew Hopkins, at www.hulford.co.uk/matthew.html.

[51] John Gurdon: *ODNB;* B. G. Blackwood, *Tudor and Stuart Suffolk* (Lancaster: Carnegie, 2001), 141, 186, 188, 226, 335. Brampton Gurdon: *WP,* 3: 244. Edmund Gurdon and other migrants: *WP,* 3: 295.

Massachusetts became home to a group of dissidents from Hartford, Connecticut, in the late 1650s.[52]

Suffolk people flocked to New England during the 1630s, but were rare in Charlestown. Stephen's skills as a carpenter and housewright probably encouraged the town to invite him to settle. He and Sarah were admitted to membership in the Charlestown church in 1638, and he became a freeman of the colony. About that time, their eldest daughter Hannah married a Tingley; three years later her sister Martha married Watertown carpenter Richard Holden, another Suffolk man. Their brother Samuel (ca. 1618–49) embarked on his career as a ship's carpenter; Thomas (ca. 1623–50) was a woodworker too; and the youngest boy John (ca. 1625–1716) began learning the rudiments of the building trade. In these years of constructing permanent housing and infrastructure, the Fosdicks would have represented a valuable asset.[53]

There may have been an ideological motive behind Stephen Fosdick's separation from the rest of his Suffolk company. In 1643, he was excommunicated from Charlestown church amid bitter acrimony. All we know about the cause was that it involved some disagreement about the church covenant. Stephen contumaciously "neglected to hear the church in their dealings with" him. Like some Watertown neighbors, he may have been attracted to Baptist ideas. Whatever the grounds, excommunication was a rare and draconian punishment only inflicted after much soul-searching. The victim was not only exiled from the circle of the godly elect, those judged by their peers likely to be saved and heaven-bound, but also deprived of all except the most necessary communication with church members. This social ostracism was made worse in 1647 by a huge £20 fine levied by the General Court. In the same year, a family house worth £15 that had been attached by the authorities burned to the ground.

The body blows continued. In 1649, eldest son Samuel died on board the *Fortune* at the age of thirty-one, on a voyage to Guinea and Barbados. The next year, Thomas, about four years younger, followed him to the grave after only two years of marriage, leaving his young wife with two babies. In the same year, youngest son John was named father of a child born to Ann Shapleigh, who was newly married to Henry Branson. The

---

[52]   W. A. B. Jones, *Hadleigh through the Ages* (Ipswich: 1977), 29–37.

[53]   Thomas was ordered on 19 March 1650 to supply a gatepost or pay a fine for felling the tree upon which hung the gate to the militia training ground, ChTR, 677. On 15 August 1661 the authorities attached lime, limestone and a lime[burning] house belonging to John. With Nathaniel Frothingham, he was employed by the town in 1675 to rebuild three galleries in the meetinghouse for £45. Frothingham, 187.

1640s had not been kind to the family; the weight of these misfortunes fell particularly heavily on the shoulders of the paterfamilias, himself returned to loner status.[54]

Stephen only made his peace with Charlestown church in 1664, shortly before his final exit aged eighty on 21 May. He came in from the cold of separation that seems to have affected much of his life in New England, and perhaps even old England. In his will, he left houses and lands in Charlestown and Malden worth £260 to his grandsons and their heirs, "never to go out of the generation of the Fosdicks for ever." His movable property included a lathe and many carpenter's tools, including a felling axe made by Goodman Cutler, the blacksmith, which he left to his wife. Matriarch Sarah had brought up six stepchildren and looked after her husband for over 30 years. That caring had been mutual. Only after Stephen's death did John Wetherell of Watertown seek assistance: "His loving brother Stephen Fosdick hath left behind him an aged infirm crazy wife being about 75, lame of her feet, going on crutches." Unsung contributions like hers over the years had been vital to the health and development of the town; they help to explain the extraordinary survival and success of early Massachusetts.[55]

---

[54] *GM,* 2: 545–46, 548; Baptists: *Divided We Stand,* 68–71. By 1667, Ann Shapleigh Branson was listed as Ann Fosdick; she was by then the mother of five Fosdick children. Branson was a shadowy figure. *GM,* 2: 550. Paterfamilias: see various court actions he had to pursue, MxCC RB, 1: 14, 61–62, 186; Rodgers, 1: 185–87; 2: 216–17.

[55] Will & inventory: Rodgers, 2: 215–17. Stephen was still splitting felled trees at the age of seventy-five, MxCC D&O, 1: doc. 1363. Sarah: *GM,* 2: 550–51, Thompson, *Divided,* 137. "Crazy" here probably means unsteady on her feet. The origins of many first-generation settlers in Charlestown remain unknown. Some other "loners," mostly artisans like Fosdick, were: in 1633, James Brown, glazier, from Colchester, Essex; in 1637, Thomas Jones butcher from Elsing, Norfolk and Peter Tufts, from Wilby, Norfolk; in 1638, William Sargent, hatter and preacher, from Northampton; and in 1639, Gawdy James, cordwainer, from Winfarthing, Norfolk. See "Travels and Travails of Barnabas Davis" below.

The Travels and Travails of
Barnabas Davis, 1635–41

Barnabas Davis of Tetbury and Tewkesbury, Gloucestershire, had thought about emigrating to the New World since the early 1630s, and by 1635 was actively implementing the move. About Easter, however, he was diverted from transporting his wife and family up to London to embark by Mr. William Woodcock, the "husband" or managing director of the Providence Island Company and a major London importer of tobacco from Virginia. Woodcock retained Davis (who later reported) "to come over to New England to look to his affairs here." These affairs involved the building of a house, and the impaling (fencing) of 400 acres on the Connecticut River by a team of carpenters and servants led by Francis Stiles. Davis would become the manager of the spread, and stock it with sheep or cattle. Woodcock's estate would be near the "park" Stiles was to set out for Sir Richard Saltonstall, and was part and parcel of the aristocratic-mercantile project led by the Puritan Earl of Warwick, Lord Saye and Sele, and Lord Brooke, to colonize the "Warwick Patent" in the Connecticut Valley with a series of cattle "ranches."[56]

For the next four years, the retainer was sent on a wild goose chase at his employers' behest. At the very least, he travelled 16,760 miles, including five transatlantic voyages. Having tramped on his first mission, from Boston to the Connecticut River in the heat of summer of 1635, Davis found that Stiles and his gang had only built themselves a house, and Stiles had then returned to England. Thither Davis followed him, armed with accounts by Thomas

---

[56] Documents: Lechford, 367–72, 381–83, 396–401, 407. Woodcock: Brenner, *Merchants and Revolution*, 158; project: ibid., 92–112; Davis's prior relationship to Woodcock is unknown. Saltonstall, *ODNB*. The Providence Island Company was a 1630s Puritan enterprise to colonize an island off the coast of Honduras. K. O. Kupperman, *Providence Island, 1630–41: The Other Puritan Colony* (Cambridge: Cambridge University Press, 1993).

Hooker to Woodcock and Lord Saye and Sele, and another complaint to Sir Richard Saltonstall, about Stiles's shortcomings. Arriving back in March 1636 after a midwinter voyage, Davis had about a month in England and a quick dash to Tewkesbury to see (and impregnate) his aptly named wife Patience, before he was dispatched back to New England to ensure Stiles's fulfilled his contract. Back in Connecticut, Davis took Hooker the six miles up from Hartford to Windsor, where they and local minister John Warham found that Stiles had again "dealt ill with Mr. Woodcock in not procuring the 400 acres of land to be laid to the house and impaling it." He had hardly pocketed Hooker's letters to Woodcock and Saye before "he was taken for a soldier against the Pequods."[57] It was not until August 1637 that he was free to return to England to report. There he was required by his employer "to ride from Tewkesbury to London nine or ten times, and from London to Essex about twelve times, and from London to Dunstable & from London to Bristol, and after to and fro upon his occasions . . . near a year and three quarters." At this point, early in 1639, William Woodcock died. His brother John took over both the enterprise and the retainer; in June 1639 Davis was back in New England for the third time. In Connecticut he successfully sued Stiles for £300 and exchanged the young breeding cattle he had previously bought for draft beasts that could earn income by ploughing and carting. He kept careful accounts of the £150 William Woodcock had previously entrusted him for cattle, and managed the property.[58]

We would know nothing of Barnabas Davis's odyssey but for the failure of either Woodcock to pay him, and John Woodcock's 1640/41 counter-demand for return of earnings, damages, assets, and accounts. In New England, Davis had to retain the services of Thomas Lechford, a Boston notary, and sought letters to corroborate his account from Richard Lygon, "Lords Saye's gentleman"; from Lord Brooke's secretary, Mr. Coventry; from his

---

[57] Pequod War 1637 between a tribe centered around the borders of Rhode Island and Connecticut and the colonies of Massachusetts and Plymouth. A. T. Vaughan, *New England Frontier: Puritans and Indians, 1620-75* (Norman: University of Oklahoma Press, 1995), Ch. 3.

[58] Stiles, one of four brothers from Millbrook, near Ampthill, Bedfordshire, first arrived in Boston on the barque *Christian* on 16 June 1635 with 20 servants. His task was exacerbated by the prior arrival at Windsor, Connecticut, of an advanced party of squatters under Roger Ludlow from Dorchester MA, and by the presence of a Plymouth trading post. Stiles had a 45 acre lot at the north end of Windsor by the ferry which led to Saltonstall's 350 acres on the east side of the Great River. Davis's movements have been dated in *GM*, 2: 291–92; his first crossing was in the *Blessing* which sailed from London on 13 July 1635, when he was aged 35. Letter to Saltonstall: *WP*, 3: 217–18; Lord Brooke was induced by William Woodcock to write to his Saybrook, Connecticut agent, John Winthrop Jr., about the obstructiveness of the Dorchester men, ibid., 218–19. On the Dorchester migration, see F. Thistlethwaite, *Dorset Pilgrims* (London: Barrie & Jenkins, 1989), 89, 100–111, 135, 139, 141, 144, 163. On the Stiles family, *GM*, 6: 513–33.

father- and brother-in-law; from Mr. Robert Bridges of Anster and Captain Babb of the *Blessing*; from Mr. Archbold of the ships' clerks office; and from Mistress Washburne, administratrix of the estate of William Woodcock (and probably his widow). When the case came to court in 1641, the jury found that Woodcock should receive his money, goods, and cattle in New England, and that Davis should be paid his long-awaited due (claimed to total £64-10-10) as decided by auditors. Although Lechford wrote a persuasive seven-point opinion on 26 May 1641 justifying Davis's cause, the case dragged on and its outcome is unknown. The Civil War in England and the economic crash in New England undermined the chances of an equitable settlement.[59]

Barnabas Davis had been a minor actor in the dramatic expansion of transatlantic investment. He was known not only to local worthies in Connecticut like Thomas Hooker and Eleazer Holyoke, but also to great English Puritan lords like Saye and Brooke, and to wealthy investors like Saltonstall and Woodcock. This was a very different kind of enterprise than the settlement of a town like Charlestown. It resembled the estate at Medford granted to Matthew Craddock, first governor and major financial backer of the Massachusetts Bay Company. The Puritan lords had bridled at the absence of aristocratic privilege in Massachusetts, and had little intention of permanent settlement. Sir Richard Saltonstall had returned from Watertown on the first ship in 1631. They and their merchant collaborators were more interested in large-scale extractive enterprise operated by paid servants like Stiles or Davis, rather than the sustainable cultivation and long-term international partnerships of the Bay Colony.

After his four-year run-around, Davis had finally settled in Charlestown in 1639. He had "lost divers advantages for himself having yet no land to plant for himself, and his wife and his four children and family." He brought a strikingly different experience than that of his neighbors, and the reason for his choice of home remains unclear. His welcome appears to have been pretty chilly. He was never admitted to church membership, and only appointed to one minor office. Nonetheless, he stayed put in Charlestown until his death in 1685, aged eighty-six. He traded as a tallow chandler, and raised a daughter and six sons (some of whom proved troublesome). Despite his experience as a colonial agent, he and his family never integrated into the community, or prospered. He left the very modest estate of £77. Every town had its share of sore thumbs.[60]

---

[59] Lechford, see above.

[60] *GM*, 2: 287–89. Troublesome: MxCC RB, 1: 196, James, assault; D & O, 1, doc. 1076, Samuel

People-Trafficking:
Sprague v. Collins, 1671

Most immigrants to seventeenth-century Charlestown were volunteers for the new world, but some came under duress. The most notorious were the Scottish prisoners of war, captured after Cromwellian victories at Dunbar (3 September 1650) and Worcester (3 September 1651). Among over 500 transported to Massachusetts as servants in 1652 on the *Sarah and John* and other vessels were several who were taken on by Charlestown masters and stayed on as inhabitants after the Restoration of 1660. Their initial impact resembled a squadron of Hell's Angels gatecrashing a prayer meeting. By the end of our period, 1691, a handful of black servants, as they were still called, also worked in the households of some of the wealthiest families. New England also played reluctant host to an indeterminate number of servants "stolen" or "spirited" from English ports, like the gullible defendant in this pitiful story.[61]

In the summer of 1670, young Robert Collins, suffering from "weakness and infirmity," was in London, probably in the East End, where trans-

fornication; doc. 1651, Samuel bad workmanship, see "Sharecropping Conflicts" below; doc. 2182, Barnabas Jr. disturbance of peace; RB, 3: 144, John drunkenness.

[61]   Mass Archives, 11 November 1651, has the names of prisoners to be embarked on the *Sarah and John*. Three Charlestown Scots were convicted as sexual predators: John Roy, soap boiler, seduced a resident's daughter, and after a hasty marriage fathered eight more Novanglo-Scots, MxCC RB, 1: 285, 11 June 1663; Nicholas Wallace was ordered to marry a serving maid he had impregnated, ibid., 81, 90, 26 December 1655; Henry Marr, Widow Wallace's second Scottish husband, took her to Woburn where he was convicted of abusing four-year-old John Wallace, ibid., 240, 17 December 1661; Robert Montgomery, the lecherous miller's assistant, repeatedly propositioned women customers; Thompson, *Sex in Middlesex*, 76, 81, and below "A Damned Whore." Alexander Stewart's alcoholism is also described below, "Drink and Violence." Black servants: see "Katherina Kidnapped" below, Thompson, *Sex in Middlesex*, 106, 221, and Thompson, *Cambridge Cameos*, 271–76.

atlantic shipping anchored. He was picked up by a man who claimed to be the boatswain of the New England ship *Arrabella* (Captain Richard Sprague, master; owned by Thomas Knights). This "subtle fellow" asked Collins "if he would go to sea . . . he should have 18s. as soon as he came on board . . . and also 18s. a month otherwise until he came to New England." Swayed by the boatswain's promise to "be a friend to him all the said voyage," Collins "through ignorance, condescended." The boatswain clung to his new recruit like a barnacle, hailed the *Arrabella's* boat, and promising to follow "immediately, sent him on board." Several days later, the "pretended boatswain" had still not appeared. When Collins asked the seamen, they "laughed at [him] and told him that he had been catched by the kidnapper . . . deluded, spirited by the mansteadler." He was a virtual prisoner on board; during the five weeks at anchor he was allowed ashore once, at Gravesend on the south shore of the Thames Estuary. However, he had "3 or 4 to look after [care for] him and that in such blind corners and uncouth places that he knew not which way to go [even] if he had been at liberty." His one hope of escape was the Searchers (inspectors of passengers). When they came on board, Collins "did refuse to give them his name and told positively that he was not willing to go the voyage . . . to New England to be a servant to Mr. Sprague or to be disposed of." No one could be under any illusion that he "utterly misliked his coming." The skipper's response was "that he would strip him naked and turn him ashore and Collins did then express himself willing to go ashore though stripped but the said Master would not suffer him." Somehow, the Clerk of the Passengers was persuaded by Sprague to enter Collins's name, and the *Arrabella* set sail. She called at Torbay at the western end of the English Channel, before heading out into the Atlantic. Torbay was Collins's last chance, and "he would have gone ashore there; [however] upon the manifestation thereof, [Captain] Sprague made him strip himself naked, and when his clothes were off, the said Mr. Sprague would not suffer him to go ashore notwithstanding all the seamen told the said Collins with the passengers that if they were not willing to go the voyage . . . they might be cleared."[62]

---

[62] *Sfk CCR*, 18–20: Collins "Answer to Sprague's Reasons for Appeal," 4 March 1671; test. William Hearsy, aged 21; case heard 3 October 1671. I have found nothing about Knights, the owner. On 21 August 1670, Hull reported Sprague's arrival, "Letter Book," 1; Sprague sailed for the Canary Islands on 29 July 1671, ibid., 25. He was represented by the wealthy mast-merchant Peter Lidget. Searchers were notoriously ineffective since the system was not compulsory for servants, A. E. Smith, *Colonists in Bondage* (New York: Norton, 1971), 73–4.

The reason we know this sad story is that once in New England, Sprague sued Collins on behalf of the owner Thomas Knights for "absenting himself from the service of the said Knights." Three times the plaintiffs were "cast [by the jury] upon clear and just evidence; and yet they rest unsatisfied, witness their present appeal." Sprague tried to persuade the court that Collins had initially announced himself on board as "willing to be a servant in New England." He had accepted £3 7s. 0d.worth of "meat drink and lodging in the ship . . . for five weeks before she sailed from Gravesend." Collins's name was on the Searchers' Passenger List. Rather than being snared in a "trap and circumvented by fraud" and "brought as a captive," Collins was a cynical freeloader. Three juries and three benches were unconvinced, as was the court on 31 October 1671. Perhaps the clear proof that Sprague had "paid 40s. to the kidnapper for sending the said man" swayed them. Despite this fourth defeat, Sprague would not give up and sued Collins for his £13 passage money and other expenses in January 1672. He lost.[63]

In the same year as this case of Sprague v. Collins, William Haverland was convicted before Justice Morton [in London] of being a 'spirit' [kidnapper], and to save himself turned king's evidence, giving a great deal of interesting testimony. He told, for instance, of John Steward, of St. Katherine's Parish [East London], who had been spiriting persons for twelve years at the rate of 500 a year. Steward used to give twenty-five shillings to anyone who would bring him a victim, and could then sell immediately to a merchant for forty shillings. A shoemaker of East Smithfield had also been in business for twelve years, and in one year had transported 840 persons. Robert Bayley had his headquarters sometimes in St. Giles and sometimes in St. Katherine's, and made his entire living by the trade. Haverland named sixteen persons who were spirits: a haberdasher, a hostler, a waterman, two victuallers, a seaman, a brewer's servant, and so on, all of whom had been conducting their activities for at least two years.[64]

In 1664, the English attorney-general had reported "that the mischiefs of spiriting were indeed very great and frequent, and that there was scarcely a voyage to the plantations without some persons being illegally carried away."[65]

---

[63] *Sfk CCR*, 43; the jury were quite clear that Collins had been kidnapped, as was the bench.

[64] Smith, *Colonists in Bondage*, 74. Haverland is the subject of John Wareing's London University Ph.D. thesis of 2000; cf. his "Violently Taken Away or Cheatingly Duckoyed," *London Journal*, 26 (2001) 1–22.

[65] Ibid., 73. In 1664 the servant trade was ordered to be regulated by registration. However, the need for a subsequent bill of 1671 "to prevent stealing children and other persons" demonstrates its ineffectiveness. Wareing quotes the Journal of Edward Barlow recounting the frequency of seductions and captivities like Collins's. "Not one in a hundred can get away; they keep them on board, will not let them land, nor send the least note to friends to come and get them clear." Basil

Our "pretended boatswain" was part of a thriving human-trafficking racket, and Sprague was not so unusual in his cruelty. However, surviving evidence suggests that most manstealing, or "kidnabbing," was for the Southern and West Indian plantations, and that such behavior was rare for New England skippers. Equally unusual was for Massachusetts juries to favour servants or laborers against the employing class, of which jurymen were members. Nor, in theory, should they have doubted Sprague's oft-repeated conviction that he was in the right. Why were they so unsympathetic?[66]

Richard Sprague had been one of the first children born in Charlestown. The son of Ralph and Joan Sprague, later of Malden, he inherited a major part of the huge fortune of his childless uncle Richard, a Charlestown merchant, who died in 1668, shortly before the outward voyage of the *Arrabella*. Richard Jr. was about forty when Collins was kidnapped, but he was not yet married and not a church member. He had held no office in Charlestown, though this may have been because of his uncle's civic dominance until shortly before. Towns usually avoided the over-weighting of influence by two generations of the same family. Certainly, Sprague's treatment of Collins was that of a petty tyrant, and his repeated reversals in court suggest that juries were repelled by his behavior.[67]

Sprague's subsequent behavior was not particularly endearing either. His house in Charlestown was enviably large. He would second his brother Samuel in his exorbitant suit against Captain William Foster, and suggest that his crew should be charged for compensation. During the Dominion period he would collaborate with James II's absolutist regime, and make himself profoundly unpopular by questioning the colony government after the Glorious Revolution in Massachusetts. He would favor representation of towns by the rich rather than by local deputies. His funeral in 1703 would be extravagantly lavish, costing the enormous sum of £147-16-0. Since both his marriages were child-

---

Lubbock, ed., *Barlow's Journal 1659–1703* (London: Hurst and Blackett, 1934), 2 vols., 1: 26–28.

[66] Sprague's is the only New England case noted by Smith; in MCC RBs, the only Charlestown case is that of a free black woman. See below, "Katherina Kidnapped." 210,000 servants are estimated to have gone to the American colonies between 1630 and 1700, Wareing, 4. However, Alexander Gordon records similar blandishments from Watertown's John Cloyse in 1653, Thompson, *Divided We Stand*, 230–31; cf. Stephen Maddock, 1641, ibid., 103.

[67] *GMB*, 3: 1728–35. Richard Sr. left £2,398. Offices: Sprague was later a selectman from 1679–87, a deputy annually after 1681, a commissioner for small causes from 1681, and captain of the second Charlestown militia company formed in 1680. On generations: Thompson, *Divided We Stand*, 122.

less, and his second wife had predeceased him, his fortune was liberally bequeathed to good causes: the poor, the ministry, Charlestown Free School (£50), and Harvard College (£400). Sewall reports many scholars at his burial.[68]

Sprague comes across as one of the new breed of merchant-mariner, rather arrogant and class-conscious, less swayed by divine providence than by his individualistic assertiveness, more self-centered than communally driven. His outlook foreshadowed that of the "Tories" who made themselves so unpopular in eighteenth-century Massachusetts and were mob targets in the run-up to the American Revolution. It is ironic that his ship had virtually the same name as Winthrop's, laden with eager emigrants in 1630; Captain Richard Sprague had moved a long way from the daily loving neighborliness of the "Model of Christian Charity."[69]

---

[68] See below, "The Ordeals of Captain Foster," "Keeping up with the Spragues," and "The Glorious Revolution in Charlestown." Fortune: £1000 in real estate, Wyman, 892. Burial: Sewall, *Diary*, 492. Deputies: ibid., 374.

[69] The new breed of post-Restoration merchants is analyzed in Bailyn, *Merchants*, chapters 5–7.

Incomer: Phineas Pratt

As well as immigrants from England, Scotland, and the West Indies who were either Puritan citizens upon a hill seeking to develop the "wilderness," or involuntary "servants," some Charlestown residents arrived after living in other settlements. Sometimes their motives can be discovered—marriage into a Charlestown family, inheritance of property, or the hope of greater economic opportunities. For many, however, no reasons have survived. They simply appear in the town records as new inhabitants.[70]

Such was Phineas Pratt (ca. 1593–1680) who had lived for 25 years in Plymouth before his 1648 arrival in Charlestown with wife Mary (Priest) (ca. 1609–1689) and their six children aged from 15 to three. He sold up his land in Plymouth and bought one of George Bunker's dwellings and garden in Charlestown. There he set up business as a joiner. He received town grants of woodland and meadow on Mystic Side in 1658, 350 acres of wilderness land from the Massachusetts General Court in 1662, and

---

[70] Some servants came over voluntarily, either with their masters' families or as indentured servants, but compared to the Chesapeake colonies or the early West Indies, their numbers were negligible. See below, "Land: Introduction." Other incomers: Thomas Blanchard, from Braintree, 1650: purchases Rev. John Wilson's farm beyond the Neck, Wyman, 88. William Bullard, from Dedham, ca. 1658: marries Widow Mary Griswold, *R*, 146 (1992), 279–80, and 154 (2000), 172–78. Edward Burt, from Lynn, 1653: marries Elizabeth Bunker, *GM*, 1: 501–02. John Founell, from Cambridge, ca. 1650: investment and employment in town tide mill, Wyman, 366. George Fowle, from Concord, 1648: buys land for tannery near Penny Ferry, Wyman, 367. John Guppy, from Weymouth, 1662: exchanges Weymouth land with Nathaniel Blanchard, MxCC D&O, 3: folio 65, Wyman, 450. Thomas Lord, from Ipswich, ca. 1660: marries Alice Rand. Aaron Ludkin, from Braintree, 1651: marries Widow Anna (Hepburn) Sally ca. 1651, after his father's death in 1648, *GM*, 4: 358–59. John Mansfield, from Boston, 1647: marries Mary Gove, see below "Mary Mansfield and the Jarndyce Effect." Luke Perkins, from Hampton, 1663: after 1654 apprenticeship to Samuel Carter, marries Widow Hannah (Long) Cookery, 1663, Wyman, 738, W. G. Davis, *Ancestry of Dudley Wildes* (Portland, ME: Athoensen, 1959), 89. John Trumbull, from Cambridge, 1655: buys deceased Augustine Walker's land, Rodgers, 1: 180–83.

another 350 acres of unbroken land from Plymouth General Court two years later. These broad acres were remote and almost valueless; the Pratts sold the Plymouth grant in 1672.[71]

By this time, Phineas was about seventy-nine and "in a low condition." He had already received the first instalment of "what he needs" from Charlestown's constable on 25 January 1669. The selectmen's and treasurer's records thereafter list sporadic grants to "Father Pratt" for "necessities." In 1678, Goodwife Pratt joined the town welfare roll and payments became pretty regular. By June 1687 she was being lodged at John Mousall's house. Their eldest son, waterman Joseph Pratt, had served in King Philip's War, but in December 1681, he too was in financial difficulties: he was nearly a decade overdue with mortgage repayments. When he died in 1712, he was worth only £39, £2 less than his father: not a hugely helpful boost to his five children.[72]

In most circumstances, a needy incomer would have been a resented presence, reluctantly supplied by his neighbors' rates. Yet Phineas Pratt had a heroic past as the savior of their neighbouring South Shore Plantation of Plymouth. His 350 acres of wilderness "East of the Merrimack River" was Massachusetts's recognition of his bravery, and a reward for his writing one of the most remarkable plebeian accounts of the early settlement of New England.

His "Decliration of the Afaires of the Einglish Peaople [that first] Inhabited New Eingland," with minimal punctuation and phonetic spelling ("Roome" for Rome, "prodastance" for Protestants, etc.) was presented to the Massachusetts General Court in 1662. The somewhat damaged three folio sheets tell the story of the Plymouth Pilgrims' early sufferings from fear of Indian attack, cold, famine, and disease. In 1622, Thomas Weston, London merchant and colonial investor, sponsored a second settlement; Pratt was a planter sent out in the *Sparrow*, which reached the South Shore in May. About 60 men set about creating a defended settlement at Wessaguscassett, later Weymouth, between the future Hingham and Braintree. The defenses were essential, because "the savages pretended to be good friends with us while they feared us, but when they see famine prevail, they begun to insult." Their local sachem boasted to Pratt how he and his warriors had starved to death one group of shipwrecked Frenchmen, and had lured the crew of another French trading ship with cheap beaver, "and when [the chief] give the word thrust your knives [hidden under their loin cloths] in

---

71   *GMB*, 1514–15. The Massachusetts grant was in the future town of Dunstable.

72   CTR, 3: 25, 205; 4: 2, 16, 17, 56, 83, 89, 92; CTrR: 77–78. Joseph: MW, 17902; *GMB*, 1516.

the French men's bellies . . . we killed them all . . . and divided their goods and fired their ship."[73]

As the planters' supplies dwindled and the weather chilled, relations with the surrounding Indians worsened. They were outraged when one settler started stealing corn from their stores. By March 1623, sinister Indian warrior gatherings, the coming and going of messengers from afar, flaunting of knives, "throwing dust in our faces," and threats of white annihilation all along the coast, terrified the surviving Weymouth men. Pratt continued:

> When we understood that their plot was to kill all English people in one day when the snow was gone, I would have sent a man to Plymouth, but none were willing to go. Then I said if Plymouth men know not of this treacherous plot, they and we are all dead men; therefore, if God willing, tomorrow I will go. [After eight days delay] I said to our company "Now is the time to run to Plymouth. Is there any compass to be found?" They said, "None but them that belong to the ship." I said "They are too big. I have borne no arms of defence these 7 or 8 days. Now if I take my arms they will mistrust me." Then they said "The savages will pursue after you & kill you & we shall never see you again." Thus with other words of lamentation we parted.
>
> Then I took a hoe and went to the Long Swamp nearby their [Indian] houses and digged on the edge as if I had been looking for groundnuts, but seeing no man, I went in [to the swamp], and ran through it. Then looking about me, I run southward till 3 of the clock, but the snow being in many places, I was the more distressed because of my footsteps. The sun being beclouded, I wandered, not knowing my way; but at the going down of the sun, it appeared red; then hearing a great howling of wolves, I came to a river; the water being deep and cold and many rocks, I passed through with much ado. Then was I in great distress—faint from want of food, weary with running, fearing to make a fire because of them that pursued me. Then I came to a deep dell or hole, there being much wood fallen into it. Then I said in my thoughts, this is God's providence that here I may make a fire. Then having made a fire, the stars began to appear and I saw Ursa Major and the pole. [So he came next day to Duxbury, where he encountered a visiting Englishman] coming in the path before me. Then I

---

[73] R. Frothingham, ed., "Phinehas Pratt's Narrative," 4*CMHS*, 4 (1858), 476–91; quotations: 479–80.

sat down on a tree and rising up to salute him said, "Mr. Hamden, I am glad to see you alive." He said "I am glad and full of wonder to see you alive; let us sit down, I see you are weary." I said, "Let [damaged] eat some parched corn."

Plymouth sent Captain Miles Standish with a militia company by sea up to Weymouth, and he fell upon the Indian warriors. Thus were Plymouth and Weymouth saved. Pratt moved to Plymouth in 1623, and observed the early hopes and rapid collapses of a series of other underfinanced ventures up and down the coast. These "gentlemen were wise men" and blamed human error for their failures, "not considering that God plants and pulls up, builds and pulls down, and turns the wisdom of wise men into foolishness."[74]

Pratt's powerful narrative is laced with dialogue between English and Indians, examples of divine interventions, and tricks used by the planters to conceal their vulnerability, like propping armed invalids against trees to pretend stronger defensive manpower, or sprinkling corn on top of non-edibles in a chest to imply copious supplies. Before his epic unarmed, unguided race to Plymouth, Pratt had lulled suspicious Native American watchers into carelessness by eight days of inaction. He describes the naming of two distrusted Indian hostages as "Wat Tyler" and "Jack Straw" after "two of the greatest rebels that ever were in England." It may not be too fanciful to imagine the lame old "father" regaling younger neighbors with the dangers and terrors faced by the first New England settlers.

The honour in which this particular incomer was held is suggested by the raising of a tombstone over his grave in Charlestown's Old Burying Ground.

FUGIT HORA

HERE LIES THE BODY OF PHINEHAS

PRATT AGED ABOVE 90 YEARS. DECEASED APRIL

THE 19, 1680

& WAS ONE OF THE FIRST ENGLISH

INHABITANTS OF THE MASSACHUSETTS COLONY[75]

---

74 Ibid., 483–85, spelling and punctuation modernized. Cf. Nathaniel Philbrick, *Mayflower* (New York: Viking, 2006), 147–48.

75 "Narrative," 476; Frothingham copied the inscription on 26 March 1858. Joshua Pratt (ca. 1605–1652/56) who came to Plymouth in the *Anne* in 1623, was almost certainly Phineas's brother, *GMB*, 1510–13.

Numbers

Here we explore Charlestown's population numbers during the period from 1629 to 1691. Even the first Great Migration pioneers in 1629 were denied "virgin land." Not only were Native Americans in residence, but some survivors of previous colonizing ventures were also living in and around Mishawum, like Thomas Walford, blacksmith, with his family, singularly un-Puritan forerunners who wisely relocated. After the ten male members of the 1629 advance party had spent an uncomfortable winter on the peninsula, Winthrop and his company came and went (to Boston), leaving Increase Nowell's company, five families numbering about nineteen individuals, and 16 other families from the *Arbella* fleet. By the end of 1630 the town's population consisted of about forty-five families. We do not know how many wives, children, and servants had accompanied these pioneers. If all had arrived by the end of 1630, we can estimate the total population to have been around 180. Against this must be set the mortality of the newly landed passengers, often suffering from scurvy and insufficiently prepared for this strange new world.[76]

The first list in the town records appears on folio 17 of John Green's transcription for 1633, and has the names of 58 families, or some 232

---

[76] Native Americans: see below, "Land." Walford: *GMB*, 1902–6; the Walfords almost immediately brushed with authority, and were banished in 1631. As survivors of an expedition sent out by Sir Ferdinando Gorges, ibid., 794–95, the five of them moved to the Piscataqua, where the Gorges family had claims. Advanced party: as well as the Spragues in "Origins," Thomas Graves, the surveyor, had two servants and maybe his wife and five children, ibid., 806; Abraham Palmer ?and wife; Walter Palmer, with party of six; Nicholas Stowers with five, and John Strickland, with three, an eventual total of thirty-five. Sixteen other families: Frothingham, 59. Mortality: Johnson, *Wonderworking*, 65–66; the most famous deaths were those of Isaac and Lady Arbella Johnson. For these early years I have used the conservative multiplier of four per household. In 1632, when Charlestown founded its own church, separating from Boston, thirty-five church members were dismissed (i.e., transferred) on 11 October. However, twelve families never left the Boston First Church, Mary Macmanus Ramsbottom, "Religious Society and the Family in Charlestown, Massachusetts, 1630–1740" (PhD diss., Yale University, 1987), 26.

individuals. By January 1636, 72 households are recorded, or about 288 inhabitants. However, 19 additional families and individuals are known to have arrived in 1635, bringing the households to 91 and population to around 364. Between 1635 and 1637, a total of 95 households arrived in Charlestown and as a result, the selectmen decided to sharply reduce admissions to a community feeling the strains of subsistence. These measure were reinforced during the next three years, 1638 to 1640. Pressure was felt on the town's common grazing land, and when stinting, or rationing, was introduced in 1637, 113 inhabitants were named. In the 23 April 1638 division of lots on Mystic Side, 108 families are included. The total, using the higher 4.5 multiplier to take account of the increasing child population, would be between 478 and 509. This number of households towards the end of the 1630s is corroborated by the 119 names listed in the 1638 *Book of Possessions,* six of whom were either non-residents or duplicates. By the end of the decade, the hectic mid-30s inrush had been diverted elsewhere.[77]

During the 1640s, some easing of the population pressure on the land took place. Three factors contributed. Immigration slowed down from a torrent to a trickle in 1640, the year of the calling of the Short and Long Parliaments and the consequent end of Charles I's personal rule and of the unchecked dominance of Archbishop Laud. The creation of two daughter towns on the edges of Charlestown's domain further reduced demand. Woburn, founded in 1640, attracted thirty-two Charlestown households northwards, probably a reduction of about 144 mouths needing feeding. Malden, on Mystic Side, had at least twenty-eight families from the mother hive, representing about 126 more people by 1651, three years after its foundation. A few other families moved out to new pastures or wharves, like the Gibbonses, the Hodges and the Kembles to Boston. During the 1640s and 1650s, others returned to the English Civil War and Republic: Rainboroughs, Paines, Graveses, Willoughbies, Sedgwicks and the Thomas Allens. Thus was the town's equilibrium preserved.[78]

---

[77]   Green: Frothingham, 83; Jan. 1636 and additions, ibid., 84–85; ninety-five households: Ramsbottom, 63, reinforced, ibid. 75. *Book of Possessions,* 40. R. J. Crandall and R. J. Coffman, "From Emigrants to Rulers: The Charlestown Oligarchy in the Great Migration," *R,* 131 (1977), 21–27, 121–32, 207–13, tabulate 257 families and individuals associated with Charlestown during the 1630s, of whom 216 were admitted residents. However, many of these were "perchers" who quickly moved on from "New England's haven town" to more permanent settlement elsewhere, as indicated in Crandall and Coffman's Appendix.

[78]   On Woburn emigrants, see ibid., Appendix. Malden: the ten founders on 1 January 1648: Joseph Hills, Ralph Sprague, Edward Carr, Thomas Squire, Jonathan Wade, James Green, Abraham Hill, Thomas Osborne, John Lewis and Thomas Call, D. P. Corey, *The History of Malden*

Nonetheless, despite these quantitative easings of population pressure, the natural increase of the town quickly made up for the emigrants. Two town lists have survived from the late 1650s. In early 1658, 4,603 acres of town wood and common land on Mystic Side were proportioned out to 192 families. Seventeen absentee landowners, young adults, poor artisans, and the schoolmaster received only token grants. However, the 16 October 1658 tax list from the town's Treasury Records provides a more complete census. To pay the £70-14-6 town expenditures, 195 resident "Heads" of households are named. This hitherto unpublished list also reveals the town's pecking order through the level of individual family rates. The number of adults in each household is also valuable. Using rather conservative multipliers again, this list suggests that the population of Charlestown was approaching a thousand, with a total of around 878.[79]

The next authoritative town listing I have found was compiled twenty years later. The carnage and devastation of King Philip's War were, as we shall see, attributed by an influential group of ministers and civic leaders to God's wrath at the backsliding and declension of His chosen people in New England. Though Charlestown was spared many war deaths, it was battered by the smallpox storm of 1677–78, losing at least 130 residents, including its minister. To expiate for these fatal shortcomings, the Massachusetts General Court ordered that every town should appoint tithingmen responsible for supervising the behavior of ten neighboring households. The 10 March 1678 list of these groups totals 256 families, roughly 1,132 souls. This represents a very modest rise over the two decades.[80]

Our numbers thus suggest three waymark totals:

At the end of the 1630s, about 500 residents;

by 1660, about 1,000;

by 1680, about 1,200.

Although several of the household lists are reliable, notably the 1630s land grant lists, the 1658 rating list and the 1678 tithingmen's list, the

---

(privately printed, 1899), 107; the 28 family names belong to the women petitioners to the General Court in favour of Rev. Marmaduke Matthews, their beleaguered minister, ibid., 146. No town or church records for Malden survive before 1678.

[79] Proprietors: Frothingham, 152–54; on the Stinted Common, see below, "Common Land." Tax list: CTrR, 1: 59v–61r, see below.

[80] Frothingham, 182–84. War: see below, "Mass Violence"; smallpox: see below, "The Ordeals of Captain William Foster" and "Captain Jenner's Journeys." We may compare this list with a "list of freemen [i.e., full church members] in Charlestown taken on 27 April 1677" with 81 names, including three war refugees, ibid. 181. War records list 119 militiamen credited with £308 15s. 6d. on 27 August 1676 in the dying days of King Philip's War. Not all the town's train band was listed, however, so the usual 5.3 multiplier, producing total population of 620, is plainly incomplete. G. M. Bodge, *Soldiers of King Philip's War* (Boston: privately printed, 1891), 312–13.

computing of total population by using multipliers is a source of considerable argument. The comparatively early age of marriage for New England women, the high average birth rate of about 44:1,000, and the longevity of many townspeople has encouraged some demographers to advocate the doubling of town populations every generation. A 1688 tax list, only discovered during the proof stage of publication, suggests a total population between 1,600 and 1,850. This could align with a twofold increase of our second waymark total of about 1,000; at least it would point to rapid growth since the smallpox epidemic of 1678.[81]

Against this exuberant view of exceptional colonial natural increase should be set certain special factors in Charlestown's case. Many of its male citizens were mariners, fishermen, or sea-going merchants. As we shall see, these were the most dangerous careers in the seventeenth-century colonies and claimed many lives. These deaths, or even long absences, exposed families to suffering and further mortalities. Ports were also particularly vulnerable to seaborne diseases, most notably smallpox. The rapid growth rate could have been significantly slowed by the loss of unusual numbers of young males. As an early settlement, Charlestown was comparatively straitened for land. The impetus upon the younger generation of farmers to move to newer, more generous townships was that much stronger. All we can reliably say about the town's population is that it grew from 10 families, a possible 35 people, in 1629 to 256 families in 1678. By 1691, it is probable that the town's population totaled nearly 2,000 people. Natural increase rather than heavy immigration accounted for the quadrupling of the 500 settlers who had arrived by the end of the 1630s, an extraordinary colonial achievement.

---

[81] These claims are discussed in Thompson, Divided We Stand, 116–17, 235. Ramsbottom, 205, quotes Gary Nash's Urban Crucible (Cambridge: Harvard University Press, 1979), 54–55, as estimating Charlestown's population at 2,000 compared to Boston's 6,000 in 1690. The 1688 Town Rate was first published as a communication by W. L. Jeffries, R. 34 (1880) 269–76. To the recorded total of 319 heads should be added 59 extras listed, the households of the four constables and that of the minister. A multiplier of five, to allow for higher post-epidemic birth rate as well as additional white, black, and native servants, would produce a population of 1,850. On smallpox, see "Captain Jenner's Journeys" below.

Charlestown Tax List: 16 November 1658

Heads

Will Stilson 2	0-18-6
Tho Adams 1	0-3-6
Mr Richard Russell	0-0-0 A
Rand Nicholls 3	1-0-0
Ed Wilson 1	0-5-0
Marke King 1	0-5-8
Jno Drinker 1	0-2-9
Mr Will Roswell 2	0-8-4
Mr Jos Phillips 1	0-2-6
Jno Lawrence 1	0-2-8
Capt Shaplay 1	0-10-0
Steeven Fosdick 1	0-6-10
Jno Fosdick 1	0-2-4
Abe Bell 1	0-3-0
*Capt. Lushers	0-9-0
[wife's land]	
Jno Downing 1	0-2-6
Mych Long 1	0-3-3
*G. Drapier	0-0-6
Mr Bradly 2	0-4-4
Jno Trumble 2	0-16-0
Rich Martyn 1	0-1-8
Tho Mousall 1	0-8-10 ob
Will Foster 1	0-8-0
Tho Sheppye 2	0-6-0
Wid Stubbs	0-0-0
Nic Wallis	0-0-0
Jno Smyth 1	0-6-3
Tho Brigden jun 1	0-3-11
Sam Adams 1	0-16-10 ob
Ben Lothrop 1	0-3-6
Jno Clough 1	0-3-0
Will Clough 1	0-3-0

Heads

*Good [Miles] Nutt.1	0-4-0
Sol fippes 1	0-16-0
Mr Carey 1	0-5-0
Goodm[Walt] Allen 1	0-14-8
Jno Coale 1	0-3-0
Isaac Coale 1	0-2-6
Thomas Rann 1	0-9-3
Josh Tid 1	0-9-0
Lawr Douse 1	0-6-2
Math Smyth 1	0-2-6
Wid Stowers 1	0-4-0
Joseph Stowers 1	0-1-8
Jno Penticost 2	0-10-0
Wid Nash	0-0-0
Peet Nash 1	0-2-3
Tho Lyne 1	1-5-2
George Hutchinson 2	0-12-0
Tho Kemble 1	0-4-0
Tho Horton 1	0-2-6
Mr Browne 1	0-4-6
Rob Hale 3	0-10-9
Zach Long 1	0-8-2
Ed Johnson 2	0-4-0
Tho Brigden sen 1	0-3-6
Mris Terrise	0-9-0
Tho Jenner 1	0-1-6
Tho Hett 3	0-8-2
Mris Graves	0-16-8
Nath Graves 1	0-1-8
Rich Templer 1	0-4-6
Jno Scott 1	0-5-5
Jno Whiteman 1	0-5-0
Mr Mansfield	0-0-0

heads

Josh Edmunds 1	0-8-0
Fer? Hadden 1	0-1-8
Tho Carter 1	0-6-4
George Hybburne 1	0-3-4 ob
Aaron Ludkin 1	0-3-0
Will Dady 2	0-17-0
Dan Edmunds 2	0-14-0
Wid Coale	0-2-6
*Will Moris 1	0-3-6
Will Johnson 2	0-9-2
Wid Carter	0-2-0
G. [Phineas] Pratt	0-0-0
Will Goose 1	0-1-8
Jno Larkins 1	0-4-0
Benj Wilson 1	0-2-0
Jno Knight 1	0-4-0
Jno Myricke 1	0-2-8
Ed Carrington 3	0-12-6
Rob Cutler 2	0-18-8
*Jno Laieforge 2	0-4-0
Jacob Greene 2	0-16-4
Jno Phillips 1	0-5-0
Mr [Nic] Davyson 2	1-0-0
James Parker 1	0-2-0
[WM} Bollard 1	0-2-0
Ed Burtt 2	0-4-0
James Hayden	0-0-0
Capt Allen 2	1-0-0
Jno Patefield 2	0-5-0
*Maior Sedgwick to	
C Norton	
John Call 1	0-2-0
Faythfull Rouse 1	0-10-0
Will Batchelor 1	0-5-0
Dan King 1	0-2-0
Capt Norton 3	2-10-0
Jno Newell 1	0-2-0
Mr. Spencer 1	0-8-4
Jno Baxter 1	0-5-0
Ed Wyer 2 his man	0-4-0
Alex Steward 1	0-2-0
Rich Austin 1	0-2-6
*Jno Everell 1	0-1-8
Mr [Tom] Shepheard in	
Mris Coytmoors house	
Mr [Zac] Symes.	0-0-0
Math Prise 1	0-4-0
Steeven Georr 1	0-1-8
Allen ye currier 1	0-2-0
Mr [Chris] Belvill 1	0-12-0
Mris Nowell	0-4-0
Rich Pritchett 1	0-5-0
Haringtons new house.	0-0-6

heads

Mr [Jon] Willoby to	
North Cape	
Fayntnot Wines 1	0-4-8
Mris Greene	0-0-0
Tho Joanes 1	0-15-2
Mr Rob Long 2	0-8-0
John Long 2	0-8-2
Mris Kempthorne	0-1-6
Sam Carter 3	0-12-9
Elias Roe 2	0-4-0
Mr Cookry 1	0-3-0
Will Hurry 1	0-2-5
Tho Starr 1	0-5-2
Jno Burrage 2	0-6-6
	60
Jno Johnson 2	0-4-6
Jno Fownall 2	0-12-7
Wid Farn[roth]ingham 1	0-12-0
Rich Lowden 3	0-12-0
Jno Cloyse 2	0-4-4
Roger Else…	0-0-0
Rich Spragg 3	1-12-0
George Bunker 2	0-19-3
Will Crouch 1	0-3-0
Biknalls house	0-
Alex Bow 1	0-3-4
Her Courser 1	0-2-0
Xtopher Goodwin 1	0-4-0
George Fowle 3	0-16-0
Jno Harris 2	0-4-0
Wid Mousall	0-15-0
Jno Mousall 1	0-10-0
G Biknall 1	0-6-0
Tho Osburne 1	0-3-0
Will Joanes 1	0-7-0
Jno Palmer 1	0-6-0
Jno Roaper 1	0-5-0
G Leach 1	0-10-0
Jno Foskett 1	0-3-0
Tho Wilder 1	0-9-7
Tho Gould 3	0-8-0
Jno George 1	0-2-6
Mr Winthrops farme	1-7-9
Ban Davis 2	0-17-0
Sam Warde 2	0-15-0
Hen Harbertt 1	0-12-0
Mr Davysons farme	0-
G. Brasier 1	0-2-0
Tho Welch 1	0-7-9
Sam Davis 1	0-4-0
Morris house	0-
G Bullard 1	0-6-9
Tho Pearce 1	0-7-8

heads

Hen Salter 1	0-1-8
Jno Cutler 1	0-6-0
Math Griffin 1	0-3-0
James Browne 2	0-8-4
Jno March 2	0-8-4
Rob Chalkley 3	0-8-0
Josiah Wood 1	0-3-0
Sergt Kettle 3	0-9-1
Mr Morly 1	0-4-0
Ben Switzer 1	0-4-0
Tho Fillebrowne 1	0-2-6

15-11-00

*Will Russell 1	0-1-2
*Tho Littell 1	0-5-10
g. Browne 1	0-4-11
Jno Gould 2	0-18-10
*Zacheus Curtis 1	0-3-5
*Jno Greenland 2	0-9-5
Tho Witamoore 2	0-7-3
George Felt 2	0-8-0
Rich Dexter 3	0-13-0
Rich Stowers 2	0-9-0
*James Barrett 1	0-6-1
Steeven Payne 2	0-16-0
*Will Egere 1	0-1-8
*Will Bucknam 1	0-3-2 ob
*Mich Smyth 1	0-2-0
Sam Blancher 1	0-8-0
George Blancher 1	0-8-5
Nath Blancher 1	0-6-7
G Adams misticke side	0-0-3
*Tho Line	0-0-1
*Ralph Shepheard	0-0-7
*Wid Larnett	0-0-2
Tho Grover	0-0-4
*Phil Atwood	0-1-0
*James Lane	0-0-4
*Wid Moulton	0-1-4
George Knower	0-1-6
*Rich Cooke	0-0-4
*Pet Tuffe	0-0-3
G. Switser 1	0-5-0
*Rob Burden	0-0-6
*Tho Mytchell 1	0-2-2
?Tho Cory…	0-0-4
Jno Blanchard 2	0-12-0

70-1-6

g Brackenbury
Mris Coytmoore
Jno Berbean

heads

Tho White 1	0-12-0
Ab Smyth	0-8-6
Will Baker 1	0-6-0
Benanuel Boweres 1	0-7-6
Mris Cogin	0-4-0
G Leasing…menatomyes	0-13-4
*Ens Winchip	0-0-6
*G Fishington	0-1-0
*G With…	0-1-0
*G Cooke	0-0-8
*G Cutter	0-2-4
*G Hall	0-0-4
*Hen Swann	0-0-4
*G Bull…	0-0-6
*Mr Broughtons mill	0-12-6
*G Adams	0-0-4
----s-nes…	0-18-0

	16:9:9d
mr Trymbals proportion comes to	34:6:11d
bro Scotts proportion comes to	£62:3s:id
Constable Blanchers comes to	£11:00s:09d

Notes:
Figures after names presumably refer to
number of dwellings.
The list has no heading in the original.
It is in Edward Burt's hand.
* = non-residents
* A = Assistant (in text)

Total number of Charlestown residents:	195.

Why They Came

Why most people went to Charlestown we can only guess. Individuals were usually far too occupied during preparation, emigration and plantation to record their reasons for undertaking this life-threatening ordeal. We can only adduce possible factors from the heart-searchings of such (hardly typical) migrants as Governor Winthrop, and from the prevailing conditions in emigrant areas of England.

In previous studies of Charlestown's neighbors Watertown and Cambridge, I have analysed religious, economic, political and cultural spurs to removal, and the attractions of Massachusetts as a destination. The leadership of both these plantations was predominantly East Anglian, from the two valleys of the Stour and the Colne, Northern Essex and Southern Suffolk. This was a major cloth-producing area. During the late 1620s and the 1630s, the industry suffered a severe depression that dragged down the whole regional economy. Though the cloth exports of Bristol (Richard Russell was a draper) were hit by war, piracy and reduced Mediterranean markets, and the weaving districts of Dorset (Ralph Sprague was a fuller) would feel the pinch, other English suppliers of settlers would have been less immediately affected commercially.[82]

Striving young Bristolians and Londoners were linked, however, by a need to escape the frustrating exclusion from profitable business openings by monopolistic mercantile groups in close financial cahoots with the early Stuart monarchy. Historians of early seventeenth-century London and Bristol emphasize the power of privileged corporate groups like the East India Company, the Levant Company, and the London and Bristol Merchant Adventurers over traditional links with the Iberian Peninsula, the

---

[82] Thompson, *Divided*, Ch. 3; *Cambridge Cameos*, 1–5. See also Thompson, *Mobility and Migration*, chapters 1 and passim. Bristol, Dorset, see above, "Origins."

Mediterranean and the Far East. The enterprise of outsiders and newcomers was diverted to opening up fresh markets and commodities, especially in the North Atlantic and the Caribbean, not to mention interloping in forbidden areas and smuggling protected cargoes. As we shall see, several leading Charlestown citizens quickly exploited New England fisheries, the Maine fur trade, and the market in the Wine Islands and Spain for pipe staves, spars, and masts from northern forest sawmills. Significantly, many of these commercial outsiders were residential outsiders as well, coming from two predominantly commercial and industrial overspills, Stepney and Southwark. Here the influence and control of the great London merchants and financiers was much reduced.[83]

One other crucial business factor affected emigrants' motivations: their involvement in transatlantic family enterprises. Most Charlestown merchants and skippers had continuing old-country connections. Russell, for instance, kept up his ties with Bristol kinfolk and also with London investors and traders through his kinsman James Russell. Robert Sedgwick and Francis Norton, brother-in-law emigrants, were, as we have seen, in close business contact with their other brother-in-law Robert Houghton, back in Southwark, as well as Phillips kinsmen, haberdashers on London Bridge. Captains Graves, Coytmore, Trerice, Hawkins, and Hodges traversed the Atlantic frequently during the 1630s and 1640s. For businessmen and shipmasters such as these, emigration involved them as New England contacts and agents for international family firms. For them relations with the old world were not ruptured, and many of them returned to England on brief business visits, or, after the defeat of the monarchy, extended missions.[84]

It is surely no coincidence that the potential royal creditors, the Merchant Adventurers' Society of Bristol, received their new charter from Charles I enhancing their monopolistic privileges in 1639, during the royal Personal Rule. Since 1629 Parliament had not been summoned, and crown policies of increasing governmental centralization and uniformity on the French model were matched by the clampdown on any deviations within the English church by William Laud and his relentless henchmen. To the non-privileged as much as nonconformists, the decade after 1629 was both threatening and repellent. Many minds turned to thoughts of refuge from persecution and exclusion.[85]

---

[83] Brenner, *Merchants and Revolution*, xi–111; Sacks, *The Widening Gate*, passim.

[84] See above, "Origins," and below "Godly Merchants," and "Captain Norton's Estate."

[85] Bristol: see Sacks, "Bristol's Little Businesses," 79–85, and "Origins," above. Personal Rule: K.

Zachariah Symmes may not have had the pulling power of a Thomas Shepard or a John Cotton, but his devotees in Bedfordshire and Hertfordshire, perhaps as well as others from his earlier days in London, were confronted in 1634 with his probable silencing at Dunstable as the Puritan Feoffees for Impropriations were suppressed. Symmes's stipend had depended on their funds. Other Puritan emigrant source areas were similarly threatened. A shipmate of Symmes's was John Lathrop, whose Puritan cell had fled from Southwark to Stepney in the early 1630s. Their preacher had spent months in prison as a religious rebel. Every Puritan minister and lay group was under threat, especially after 1633 when Laud was elevated from the Bishopric of London to the Archbishopric of Canterbury. Cherished beliefs were thwarted by measures like the reissue of the *Book of Sports* in 1633, undermining the sanctity of the Lord's Day, or the requirement that the unpurified *Book of Common Prayer* be rigidly followed. Autocracy and Antichrist flaunted their triumph arm in arm. The Calvinist ideals espoused by Increase Nowell's uncle at St. Paul's, or Richard Sedgwick in Wapping, or Nicholas Morton and John Harvard at Southwark, or Thomas White at Dorchester, or Stephen Fosdick's minister James Hopkins at Great Wenham, or scores of other "godly ministers," were derided, demoted and dismissed by the Arminian dispensation. These preachers faced hostile interrogation, summary trial, dismissal, and imprisonment or exile; in Laud's words, he would "harry them out of the land."[86]

Old England was a toxic carcass to abandon; New England, increasingly familiar,[87] an unsullied opportunity to embrace. Charlestown offered the possibility of religious purity, a utopian fresh start. It also held out the prospect of free and ample land to the landless, to insecure tenants and stunted households. It was a West Atlantic base for the exploitation of rich natural resources by resident agents of family firms. Both a refuge and a springboard, the haven at the northern lip of the Charles River would weld together a remarkable and diverse collection of settlers into a biddable and cohesive town, at least for the first half-century of its existence.

Sharpe, *The Personal Rule of Charles I* (New Haven: Yale University Press, 1992); S. Pincus, *1688: the First Modern Revolution* (New Haven: Yale University Press, 2009), Ch. 2.

[86] Michael McGiffert, ed., *God's Plot: The Paradoxes of Puritan Piety; Being the Autobiography and Journal of Thomas Shepard* (Amherst: University of Massachusetts Press, 1972), 3–51.

[87] Familiar: see Emerson, *Letters,* passim; indicates how information about New England was communicated to potential emigrants back in England.

Part 2

Town

Charlestown Officeholders, 1634–92

The lists of Charlestown officeholders are mostly derived from the minutes of town and selectmen's meetings from 1634 to 1692. These records have never before been printed. The manuscripts are held in the Rare Book Department of the Boston Public Library, and microfilms are available in its Microtext Department. The roles of many of the officeholders are described in different sections below; here we can point to some general conclusions, analyze some more important posts and communal responsibilities, glance at precedents, and, in the next chapter, question where authority lay.[1]

DEPUTIES

1634: T. Beecher, W. Jennison, Ral Sprague
1635: E. Gibbons, A. Palmer, J. Woolrich
1636: T. Beecher (T. Lynde succeeds), E. Gibbons, R. Mousall;
      A. Palmer (Nov.)
1637: R. Sedgwick, T. Lynde, J. Mousall,
1638: R. Sedgwick, Ral Sprague, A. Palmer
1639: R. Sedgwick, Ral Sprague, T. Lynde
1642: F. Willoughby
1644: R. Sedgwick, Ral Sprague
1646: F. Willoughby
1647: F. Norton, J. Hill
1649: F. Willoughby, R. Sedgwick
1650: R. Sedgwick, F. Willoughby

---

[1] See Introduction.

1651: R. Russell, R. Mousall

1652: F. Norton, R. Russell

1653: R. Russell, F. Norton

1654: R. Russell, F. Norton

1655: R. Russell, F. Norton

1658: R. Russell, F. Norton

1660: F. Norton, Ric Sprague

1663: F. Norton, Ric Sprague

1664: F. Norton, Ric Sprague

1665: F. Norton, Ric Sprague

1666: F. Norton, Ric Sprague

1667: F. Norton, W. Stitson

1668: W. Stitson, J. Allen

1669: W. Stitson, J. Allen

1671: W. Stitson, J. Allen

1672: J. Allen, L. Hammond

1673: J. Allen, L. Hammond

1674: J. Allen, J. Lynde

1675: L. Hammond, T. Graves

1676: L. Hammond, T. Graves; Oct. session:[2] Jac. Green, J. Cutler

1677: T. Graves, Jac Green

1678: T. Graves, Jac Green

1680: J. Russell, J. Lynde

1681: L. Hammond, R. Sprague

1682: L. Hammond, R. Sprague (for 2 Nov. court)

1682: R. Sprague, J. Cutler

1689: R. Sprague

1690: J. Lynde, S. Hayman

1691: J. Lynde, S. Hayman

SELECTMEN

1634: I. Nowell, John Green, T. Beecher, J. Woolrych, Ral Sprague,
E. Hubbard, R. Cole, W. Brackenbury, E. Richardson, W. Palmer

1635: I. Nowell, T. Beecher, E. Richardson, W. Palmer, Ral Sprague, W.
Brackenbury, E. Convers, T. Lynde, A. Palmer, J. Mousall,
R. Moulton

---

[2]   Hammond and Graves had unusually been elected for the May session only. They had been chosen to attend a special session in August to discuss responses to a letter from Charles II about disputed boundaries. They may have sought substitutes for October, CTR 2:   189, 193.

1636: I. Nowell, T. Beecher, W. Baker, J. Mousall, E. Convers,
W. Learned, Ral Sprague, R. Hale, Ric Sprague

1637: I. Nowell, T. Beecher (W. Brackenbury succeeds), T. Lynde,
A. Palmer, J. Mousall, E. Convers, Ric Sprague, R. Hale, R. Long

1638: I. Nowell, E. Richardson, E. Mellows, Ral Sprague, A. Palmer,
W. Brackenbury, J. Mousall, Ric Sprague, W. Palmer, E. Convers,
R. Hale

1639: I. Nowell, Ral Sprague, E. Convers, J. Mousall, A. Palmer,
T. Lynde, R. Hale

1640: I. Nowell, Ral Sprague, E. Convers, A. Palmer, J. Mousall,
T. Lynde, R. Hale

1641: I. Nowell, F. Willoughby, R. Mousall, W. Brackenbury,
T. Coytmore, T. Pierce, E. Mellows

1642: I. Nowell, T. Lynde, R. Hale, R. Mousall, Ral Sprague, A. Palmer,
E. Mellows

1643: I. Nowell, R. Sedgwick, W. Stitson, W. Phillips, Ral Sprague,
E. Mellows, R. Russell

1644: I. Nowell, J. Hill, Ral Sprague, T. Lynde, W. Stitson, E. Mellows,
A. Palmer

1646: I. Nowell, J. Green, F. Willoughby, R. Mousall, R. Hale, T. Lynde,
W. Stitson.

1647: I. Nowell, J. Green, F. Willoughby, R. Russell, Ric Sprague,
F. Norton, R. Mousall.

1648: I. Nowell, J. Green, R. Russell, R. Mousall, T. Lynde, R. Hale,
W. Stitson.

1649: I. Nowell, J. Green, R. Mousall, F. Willoughby, R. Russell, R. Hale,
N. Davison.

1650: I. Nowell, J. Green, F. Willoughby, J. Allen, R. Mousall, R. Hale,
T. Lynde

1651: I. Nowell, F. Willoughby, J. Green, R. Russell, R. Mousall,
T. Lynde, R. Hale

1652: I. Nowell, J. Green, R. Russell, R. Mousall, F. Norton, T. Lynde,
W. Stitson

1653: R. Russell, R. Mousall, T. Lynde, W. Stitson, S. Adams, T. Gould,
R. Cutler

1654: I. Nowell, R. Russell, J. Allen, F. Norton, J. Green, Ric Sprague,
F. Rouse

1655: I. Nowell, R. Russell, R. Mousall, J. Green, T. Lynde, W. Stitson,
R. Nicholls

1656: R. Russell, R. Mousall, J. Green, T. Lynde, W. Stitson, Ric Sprague,
R. Nicholls

1657: R. Russell, J. Green, T. Brattle, R. Mousall, T. Lynde, W. Stitson,
R. Nicholls

1658: R. Russell, J. Green, J. Allen, F. Norton, T. Lynde, W. Stitson,
R. Nicholls

1659: R. Russell, F. Norton, T. Lynde, W. Stitson, Ric Sprague,
R. Nicholls, S. Adams

1660: R. Russell, F. Norton, Ric Sprague, S. Adams, R. Nicholls,
S. Phipps, J. Tidd

1661: R. Russell, F. Norton, N. Davison, Ric Sprague, T. Lynde,
R. Nicholls, S. Adams

1663: R. Russell, F. Willoughby, T. Gould, S. Phipps, R. Kettle, J. Carey,
J. Cutler

1664: F. Willoughby, R. Russell, T. Gould, S. Phipps, R. Kettle, J. Cutler,
J. Carey

1665: F. Willoughby, R. Russell, F. Norton, Ric Sprague, R. Nicholls,
T. Lynde, W. Stitson

1666: R. Russell, J. Chickering, S. Phipps, J. Cutler, W. Stitson,
R. Nicholls, J. Russell

1667: R. Russell, R. Nicholls, W. Stitson, J. Chickering, S. Phipps,
J. Cutler, T. Lynde

1668: R. Russell, Ric Sprague, R. Nicholls, W. Stitson, J. Tidd, S. Ward,
Jac Green

1669: R. Russell, W. Stitson, R. Nicholls, Jac Green, J. Cutler, S. Phipps,
J. Hayman

1670: R. Russell, W. Stitson, Jac Green, W. Dade, T. Rand, J. Cutler,
T. Lynde

1671: R. Russell, W. Stitson, L. Hammond, R. Nicholls, Jac Green,
J. Cutler, P. Tufts

1672: R. Russell, L. Hammond, W. Stitson, J. Long, J. Cutler, R. Nicholls,
Jac Green

1673: R. Russell, L. Hammond, W. Stitson, J. Cutler Jr., J. Lynde, P. Tufts,
J. Long

1674: R. Russell, L. Hammond, W. Stitson, R. Nicholls, J. Cutler,
J. Russell, J. Lynde

1675: L. Hammond, J. Cutler, J. Lynde, J. Tidd, R. Kettle, L. Dowse,
S. Pierce

1676: L. Hammond, J. Cutler, J. Lynde, T. Russell, J. Russell, L. Dowse, R. Kettle

1677: L. Hammond, J. Cutler, J. Russell, R. Kettle, H. Phillips, J. Lynde, S. Pierce

1678: L. Hammond, J. Cutler, T. Graves, R. Kettle, J. Lynde, L. Dowse

1679: L. Hammond, J. Russell, J. Lynde, R. Lowden, R. Kettle. R. Nicholls, R. Sprague

1680: L. Hammond, J. Russell, R. Sprague, J. Lynde, N. Rand, R. Nicholls

1681: J. Russell, L. Hammond, R. Sprague, N. Rand, J. Call, J. Newell, W. Clough

1682: J. Russell, L. Hammond, R. Sprague, J. Call, J. Phillips, N. Rand, J. Newell

1683: J. Russell, R. Sprague, J. Lynde, J. Phillebrown, J. Call, P. Fowle, N. Rand

1684: J. Russell, L. Hammond, R. Sprague, J. Call, J. Phillips, J. Lynde, T. Graves

1687: J. Phillips, R. Sprague, J. Call, J. Lynde, S. Phipps, J. Newell, S. Kettle

1688: R. Sprague, J. Phillips, J. Lynde, S. Hayman, Jac Green Sr., J. Fowle

1689: R. Sprague, Jac Green Sr., S. Hayman, A. Belcher, N. Rand, J. Fowle, J. Newell Sr.

1690: R. Sprague, P. Tufts, R. Lowden, N. Rand, P. Fowle, S. Hunting, J. Miller

1691: R. Sprague, R. Lowden, S. Hunting, P. Fowle, J. Miller, N. Rand, E. Wilson

1692: J. Call, S. Ballatt, T. White Sr, Jac Green Jr., E. Phillips, N. Carey

CONSTABLES

1635: E. Hubbard Sr.

1636: W. Palmer (half-year)

1637: W. Palmer, E. Mellows

1638: G. Bunker, T. Ewer

1639: W. Brackenbury, N. Stowers

1640: E. Johnson, S. Richardson

1641: T. Carter Sr., E. Jones

1642: W. Stitson, W. Phillips

1643: J. Penticost, F. Norton

1644: R. Cooke, E. Carrington

1645: ?E. Carrington, R. Cutler

1646: F. Rouse, T. Pierce, I. Wheeler.

1647: R. Woory, G. Bunker, T. Squire, ?J. Tidd

1648: S. Carter, S. Phipps, J. Waite.

1649: W. Dady, R. Chalkley, T. Lynde Jr.

1650: J. Swett, R. Lowden

1651: S. Adams, G. James

1652: T. Brigden, E. Drinker

1653: Jac Green, S. Switzer

1654: R. Rand, J. Fownell

1655: G. Hutchinson, J. Palmer

1656: L. Dowse (chief), T. Carter, J. Greenland (Mystic Side)

1657: J. Penticost, W. Johns, S. Blanchard

1658: J. Scott, J. Trumbull, J. Blanchard

1659: J. Tidd, E. Carr, S. Paine

1660: W. Allen, S. Carter (refused), R. Dexter, W. Dady

1661: F. Rouse, A. Ludkin, S. Ward

1662: A. Ludkin, Jac Green, R. Nicholls, J. Founell, T. Gould

1663: J. Cutler, J. Swett, R. Chalkley

1664: R. Lowden, T. Rand, E. Wilson

1665: S. Phipps, J. Smith, T. Hett

1666: J. Penticost, J. Lynde, J. Palmer (R. Lowden subs)

1667: E. Carrington, W. Johnson, J. Greenland (Mystic Side)

1668: J. Heyman, L. Hammond, J. Barrett (P. Tufts subs)

1669: J. Russell, J. Knight Jr, J. Lowden (R. Lowden subs)

1670: J. Tidd (refused), J. Wood, N. Dady (T. Lord subs)

1671: T. Chadwell, S. Phipps Jr., T. White

1672: R. Lowden, S. Kettle, N. Frothingham

1673: T. Russell, J. Larkin, N. Hutchinson

1674: J. Jones, D. Smith, J. Fowle

1675: S. Ballatt, H. Balcomb, P. Fowle

1676: G. Fifield, J. Fosdick, J. Cutler Jr., T. Mousall

1677: W. Clough, S. Dowse, Z. Johnson, R. Stowers

1678: J. Newell, J. Kettle, P. Frothingham, T. Welch

1679: S. Hunting, S. Waters, S. Frothingham, W. Symmes

1680: J. Phillips (refused), J. Ryall, J. Betts, W. Richeson, J. Mousall

1681: D. Edmunds, J. Fowle, J. Lowden, T. Crosswell

1682: E. Row (refused), J. Kettle, S. Lord, J. Miller Jr.

1683: Z. Long, J. Edes, J. Carey, P. Tufts

1684: N. Hayman (succeeded by E. Phillips), J. Hurd, J. Simpson, J. Whittemore

1687: T. Phillips, N. Adams, J. Chamberlain, T. Welch Jr.

1688: J. Rowe, J. Capon, C. Goodwin, W. Browne

1689: S. Phipps, W. Vine, J. Fowle, J. Turner, A. Stevenson

1690: W. Wellstead, N. Kettle, N. Davis, J. Frost

1691: S. Phipps (refused), H. Davis, J. Waters, T. Shepard, N. Carey (refused)

1692: J. Rand, J. Phipps, J. Whittemore, S. Stowers

Town Clerks

1635: I. Nowell

1638: A. Palmer (*Book of Possessions*)

1641: B. Hubbard (Clerk of Writs)

1645: John Green

1652: S. Adams

1656: J. Green

1659: S. Adams

1658–62: E. Burt (Recorder)

1662: N. Shapley (Clerk of Writs)

1662–72: J. Carey

1664: J. Green (transcribe town records)

1673–77: L. Hammond

1678: J. Russell

1679–86, 89–96: J. Newell

1688–89: S. Phipps

1690: L. Hammond (Clerk of Writs)

Hog Reeves

1646: A. Palmer, W. Stitson, J. Martin

1647: T. Wilder

1648: L. Dowse, T. Rand

1649: J. Penticost, W. Frothingham (E. Field); E. Drinker (High Field); T. Goble (Line Fd)

1650: T. Pierce, R. Mousall, J. Roper, W. Frothingham, R. Chalkley, W. Johnson, S. Phipps, J. Carter

1652: T. Pierce (West End); R. Mousall (High Fd); W. Johnson, T. Carter (Part East Fd); R. Harrington (remainder)

1654: S. Fosdick, T. Brigden, M. Gibbs, E. Drinker, T. Welch

1655: S. Fosdick, T. Brigden, J. Carter, E. Drinker, T. Pierce

1656: W. Dade, T. Rand, R. Pritchard, A. Ludkin, T. Phillebrown

1658: T. Pierce, R. Lowden

1664: J. Smith, J. March, T. Welch

1665: J. Miller, T. Adams, W. Bullard

1666: T. Carter, J. Wood

1667: A. Ludkin, N. Rand, W. Crouch

1669: T. Adams, W. Crouch, P. Wilson

1670: M. Wood, T. Barber, A. Smith, P. Wilson

1671: T. Carter, J. Fosdick, T. Hett

1672: T. Adams, T. Peachie, T. Smith

1673: P. Frothingham, D. Richeson

1674: J. Wood, N. Rand, J. Foskett, J. Lowden, S. Frothingham,
T. Crosswell

1675: S. Frothingham, W. Richeson, Z. Johnson, J. Whittemore,
J. Foskett, T. Adams

1676: T. Carter, T. Lord, J. Call, N. Hutchinson

1677: J. Foskett, P. Wilson, W. Brown Jr., Jac Cole, T. Barber

1679: J. Frost, T. Smith, W. Brown Jr., T. Barber

1680: T. Crosswell, T. White, S. Lord, S. Geary, J. Kettle

1681: A. Fowle, W. Brown Jr., A. Benjamin, J. Smith, J. Hurd

1682: N. Davis, J. Dowse, W. Wilson, S. Whittemore, S. Read

1683: T. Welch Jr., S. Griffin, H. Davis, J. Simpson, S. Leman

1684: J. Simpson, I. Johnson, S. Blunt, S. Whittemore, J. Pierce

Surveyors of Highways

1634: T. Lynde, E. Richardson, J. Mousall

1635: A. Mellows, Ric Sprague

1637: T. Ewer, W. Tuttle, S. Richardson

1638: T. Pierce, N. Stowers, Ric Sprague

1639: R. Long, E. Convers, J. Mousall

1640: J. Brown, J. Hall, T. Squire

1641: S. Fosdick, E. Carrington, W. Baker

1642: J. Penticost, J. Sibley, E. Carrington

1643: R. Morris, G. James, S. Carter, J. Hill (Mystic Side)

1644: T. Pierce, G. James, J. Burrage, Ric Sprague (Mystic Side)

1646: R. Chalkley, A. Hawkins, T. Goble, T. Call

1647: R. Chalkley, G. Hutchinson, N. Drinker, J. Greenland.

1648: R. Lowden, J. Palmer, T. Lynde Jr, (Mystic Side)

1649: T. Carter Jr., J. March, M. Sally, A. Hill

1650: R. Harrington, L. Dowse, R. Stowers, R. Cook (Mystic Side)

1651: L. Dowse, J. Penticost, E. Drinker, E. Carrington

1652: J. Scott, J. Carter, T. Wilder, P. Attwood

1653: R. Lowden, T. Rand, W. Johnson, L. Dowse, E. Carrington (Mystic Side)
1654: W. Dade, T. Welch, J. Hayden, J. Cutler, J. Barrett (Mystic Side)
1655: S. Fosdick, E. Burt, D. Edmunds, G. James, R. Dexter
1656: S. Phipps, J. Founell, R. Bullard, P. Attwood (Mystic Side)
1657: Jac Green, T. Pierce, I. Cole, J. Barrett (Mystic Side)
1658: R. Lowden, H. Harbord, E. Carrington, R. Stowers (Mystic Side)
1659: W. Bullard, R. Chalkley, J. Mousall, R. Dexter (Mystic Side)
1660: J. Penticost, A. Smith, S. Switzer, J. Smith (Mystic Side)
1661: E. Wilson, T. Welch, N. Hutchinson, S. Switzer
1663: J. Burridge, J. Founell, R. Lowden, S. Paine
1664: W. Dade, J. Penticost, T. Hett, D. Whittemore
1665: W. Johnson, J. Penticost, R. Lowden, R. Stowers
1666: R. Chalkley, B. Switzer, A. Ludkin, N. Whittemore
1667: R. Chalkley, J. Bunker, T. Carter, J. Scooly (Mystic Side)
1668: J. Wood, J. Smith, T. Welch, R. Stowers
1669: T. Rand, J. Palmer, P. Frothingham, S. Paine
1670: B. Davis, N. Hutchinson, R. Gardner, R. Stowers
1671: B. Switzer, J. Mousall, W. Dade, N. Whittemore
1672: L. Dowse, T. White, N. Rand, J. Barrett
1673: T. White, T. Crosswell, J. Bunker, R. Stowers
1674: L. Dowse, T. White, S. Pierce, J. Dexter
1675: W. Richeson, J. Fosdick, T. Mousall, R. Stowers
1676: R. Stowers, W. Richeson, N. Hutchinson, T. Carter
1677: J. Mousall, J. Trumbull, T. Welch, C. Cisc?
1678: J. Fowle, J. Foskett, J. Call, T. Carter, R. Stowers
1679: T. Crosswell, J. Lowden, T. White, N. Rand, J. Greenland
1680: T. Pierce, T. Lord, S. Phipps, Z. Johnson, J. Marable, J. Cutler Jr.
1681: J. Wood, E. Wilson, J. Whittemore, S. Frothingham, J. Marable, S. Waters
1682: N. Mead, J. Kettle, J. Frost, I. Johnson, B. Switzer, J. Betts
1683: J. Fosdick, J. Hurd, J. Kent, J. George, J. Pratt, N. Frothingham
1684: J. Miller Jr., T. Welch, J. Kent, A. Stimpson, T. Cutler, R. Stowers
1687: S. Lord, J. Mousall, P. Fowle, T. Shepard, J. Ryall, S. Payne

TREE WARDENS
1639: Ral Sprague, E. Richardson, J. Thomson
1642: R. Mousall, T. Pierce
1646: T. Wilder (and overall cattle control & trespassing)
1647: T. Wilder ("Town Officer")

1648: L. Dowse, T. Rand.

1661: W. Symmes, S. Phipps

1666: W. Stitson, R. Nicholls

1672: S. Pierce, J. Mousall

1673: J. Mousall, P. Tufts

1682: L. Dowse, T. White, J. Wood

Herdsmen

1634: N. Stowers

1646: W. Smith, T. Rand (milch), R. Layhorn (dry), M. Smith (calves)

1647: T. Rand, T. Osborne (milch)

1648: L. Dowse, T. Rand (milch)

1649: M. Smith Sr. & Jr. (milch)

1650: M. Smith Sr. & Jr. (milch)

1651: T. George, J. Geary, W. Mapes, vice T. Welch Jr (milch)

1652: M. Smith Sr. & Jr. (milch)

1654: M. Smith Sr. & Jr. (milch)

1655: M. Smith Sr. & Jr.

1656: W. Crouch

1657: W. Crouch (milch)

1662: T. Hale

1663: J. Miller

1664: T. Adams

1665: W. Crouch

1666: W. Crouch

1667: W. Crouch

1668: W. Crouch

1669: W. Crouch

1670: P. Wilson (milch)

1671: W. Crouch (milch)

1672: W. Crouch (milch)

1673: W. Crouch

1674: W. Crouch

1675: W. Crouch

1676: J. Crouch

1677: P. Wilson

1678: J. Mousall

1679: J. Mousall

1680: J. Miller

1681: J. Miller Sr.

1682: J. Miller

1683: P. Wilson

1684: P. Wilson

1687: J. Mousall

LAND ALLOTTERS

1634: T. Beecher, R. Moulton, J. Woolrich, Ral. Sprague, E. Hubbard, E. Richardson (and rate-makers)

1635: N. Stowers, E. Hubbard; I. Nowell, T. James, Z. Symmes, T. Beecher, R. Cole, W. Brackenbury, E. Richardson

1636: E. Richardson, W. Frothingham, T. Pierce, W. Baker, E. Hubbard Jr, T. Squire

1637: I. Nowell, A. Palmer, E. Convers, R. Hale, R. Long, T. Lynde

1638: R. Long, E. Convers, W. Brackenbury, R. Hale, G. Hutchinson, W. Palmer

1639: Ral Sprague, E. Richardson, A. Palmer, T. Lynde, J. Mousall, E. Convers, R. Long

1640: Ral Sprague, T. Lynde, A. Palmer

1641: T. Pierce, W. Baker, E. Mellows, T. Squire

1642: T. Lynde, R. Hale, Ral Sprague

1647: T. Pierce, W. Baker, R. Kettle

1647: J. Hill, R. Hale, E. Carrington

1647: Ric Sprague, A. Palmer, T. Danforth

1648: T. Lynde, W. Stitson, R. Hale

1648: R. Hale, T. Lynde (twice)

1649: R. Hale, W. Stitson

1650: H. Harbord, R. Temple, T. Pierce, W. Baker

1656: T. Lynde, W. Stitson

1657: T. Lynde, W. Stitson

1658: R. Hale

1662: T. Pierce, W. Dade, T. Gould, S. Phipps

1663: T. Lynde, W. Stitson, T. Gould, S. Phipps

1666: W. Stitson, S. Phipps

1668: W. Symmes

1669: W. Stitson, S. Phipps

1670: W. Stitson, J. Allen

1671: W. Stitson, R. Nicholls, P. Tufts

VIEWERS OF PIPESTAVES (INSPECTORS OF BARRELS)

1647: W. Cutter, R. Kettle

1655: T. Brigden

1656: T. Hett

1657: T. Hett

1658: Jac Green

1659: R. Kettle

1660: R. Kettle

1661: R. Kettle

1663: B. Lathrop

1665: T. Brigden, Jr.

1666: T. Brigden Jr.

1667: T. Hett

1668: T. Hett; after his death, B. Lathrop

1669: B. Lathrop

1670: B. Lathrop

1687: J. Kettle

FERRYMEN

1630: T. Harris

1634: W. Stitson

1640: P. Drinker (Neck)

1644: W. Bridge

1647: P. Tufts, W. Bridges.

1651: P. Knight (Penny)

1654: J. Harris (Penny)

1664: P. Wilson (Penny)

1669: R. Stowers (Penny)

1669: John Davis (Penny)

1669: J. Burridge

1685: N. Salisbury

BOUNDSMEN

1635: T. Beecher

1636: A. Palmer

1640: Ral Sprague, T. Lynde, A. Palmer

1641: Ral Sprague, W. Palmer, T. Lynde, A. Palmer, E. Hubbard (and four selectmen, view Chelsea line, then part of Boston)

1643: Ral Sprague, W. Stitson, E. Mellow, E. Hubbard, T. Lynde

1644: A. Palmer, W. Stitson, E. Mellows

1649: Selectmen agree bounds between Mystic Side and Malden.

1651: T. Lynde, R. Hale (with Malden)

1652: W. Stitson, R. Hale, L. Dowse (with Malden)

1656: R. Hale, R. Lowden, J. March

1657: R. Hale

1658: R. Hale

1666: W. Symmes, S. Phipps, J. Chickering, J. Cutler, J. Russell, W. Stitson, R. Nicholls, T. Pierce, P. Frothingham

1668: J. Greenland, J. Barrett

1669: J. Greenland, R. Stowers, D. & N. Whittemore, S. Pierce, T. Welch, W. Smith, S. Phipps, Jac Green, J. Hayman, J. Russell

1671: W. Stitson, Jac Green

1672: W. Symmes, Jac Green, N. Rand, T. Cutler, J. Dowse, T. Pierce, J. Frost, R. Lowden

1673: R. Stowers, J. Greenland

1675: T. Pierce, N. Rand, T. Mousall, S. Frothingham, T. Cutler, J. Mousall, R. Lowden

1678: R. Stowers, S. Phipps, J. Mousall, N. Kettle, N. Dowse

1681: T. Rand, S. Frothingham, J. Mousall, J. Call Jr., J. Dowse

1684: N. Rand, J. Mousall, T. Call, N. Dowse, J. Miller

CHIMNEY-SWEEPS

1649: N. Hadlock

1651: J. Geary

1658: T. Adams

1662: H. Salter

1671: T. Adams

TOWN CRIERS/MESSENGERS

1649–77: M. Smith

1677: J. Frost

1678: M. Smith

1679: T. Orton

1680: T. Lord (Messenger & Bellringer)

1681: J. Frost, T. Lord (Messenger & Bellringer)

1682: T. Lord

FENCE-VIEWERS

1649: T. Pierce, T. Goble, J. Sibley (West Fd.); T. Lynde, Ric Sprague, R. Hale, W. Frothingham (East Fd.)

1651: W. Frothingham, R. Hildrick (Cambridge), R. Lowden,
W. Johnson, W. Baker, F. Grissell, E. Carrington, R. Cook,
J. Barrett

1652: T. Pierce, T. Welch, W. Johnson, J. March, R. Hildrick, R. Lowden

1654: W. Dade, J. Penticost, G. James, J. Palmer, R. Temple, Bullard
(Cambridge), E. Carrington (Mystic Side)

1655: J. March, R. Lowden, J. Mousall, E. Drinker, T. Pierce, S. Phipps,
L. Dowse, G. Bunker, J. Burrage

1660: T. Rand, R. Lowden, G. Fowle, J. Palmer, T. Pierce, W. Bullard,
P. Frothingham

1661: T. Pierce, R. Lowden, T. Carter, J. Palmer, J. Greenland

1663: T. Pierce, W. Johnson, T. Welch, G. Fowle, J. Palmer, W. Dade

1664: S. Phipps, T. Gould, W. Johnson, J. Mousall, J. Call, J. Penticost,
R. Chalkley, P. Frothingham, R. Lowden, W. Dade

1665: T. Pierce, S. Ward, J. Cutler, G. Fowle, J. Palmer, W. Dade,
R. Lowden, E. Wilson, S. Paine; J. Smith, R. Stowers
(Stinted Common)

1666: T. Brigden, H. Harbord, A. Smith, G. Fowle, J. Mousall, T. Rand,
N. Hutchinson, T. Pierce, S. Ward (Stinted Common), J. Smith,
R. Stowers (Blanchards)

1667: R. Lowden, T. Carter, Ric Sprague, J. Palmer, W. Bullard, P. Mark,
W. Symmes, R. Gardner, J. Barrett, W. Seise; S. Ward, H. Harbord
(Stinted Common)

1668: N. Hutchinson, P. Frothingham, G. Fowle, J. Whittemore, A.
Smith, J. Kent, J. Bunker, T. Phillebrown, R. Stowers, S. Payne,
J. Smith, P. Fowle; S. Ward, H. Harbord (Stinted Common)

1669: T. Carter, T. White, J. Mousall, J. Palmer, S. Pierce, T. Welch,
T. Crosswell, P. Fowle, S. Paine, R. Stowers, R. Lowden, J. Fowle,
S. Ward, G. Fowle

1670: R. Kettle, W. Johnson, N. Rand, J. Whittemore, S. Pierce, J. Kent,
W. Symmes, R. Gardner, J. Barrett, S. Payne, J. Smith, J. Guppie,
R. Lowden, T. Welch

1671: T. Carter, P. Frothingham, G. Fowle, J. Palmer, A. Smith, T. Welch,
W. Symmes, R. Gardner, J. Greenland, J. Stowers, R. Stowers,
P. Fowle, S. Rand, R. Lowden

1672: T. Rand, N. Rand, P. Fowle, J. Whittemore, S. Pierce, J. Frost,
R. Gardner, T. Phillebrown, R. Stowers, S. Payne, P. Tufts,
N. Howard

1673: T. Rand, N. Rand, J. Palmer, T. Welch, J. Kent, W. Symmes,
R. Gardner, R. Stowers, J. Greenland, P. Tufts, J. Fowle

1675: T. Rand, N. Rand, T. Mousall, J. Fowle, T. Crosswell, A. Smith,
W. Symmes, R. Gardner, S. Payne, J. Dexter (sub S. Lee),
T. Shepard, S. Blanchard

1676: T. Rand, N. Rand, P. Fowle, J. Mousall, W. Symmes, R. Gardner, R.
Stowers, J. Greenland, T. Shepard, S. Blanchard, R. Lowden,
J. Penticost

1677: T. Rand, N. Rand, N. Hutchinson, J. Foskett, W. Symmes,
R. Gardner, S. Payne, T. Wheeler, T. Shepard, S. Blanchard,
S. Phipps, T. Lord, P. Mark, R. Lowden, L. Dowse

1678: W. Stitson, T. Lynde, T. Rand, N. Rand, N. Hutchinson,
T. Mousall, R. Stowers, J. Greenland, T. Shepard, S. Blanchard,
C. Brooks, W. Symmes, S. Payne, P. Mark, R. Lowden, L. Dowse

1679: J. Mousall, J. Whittemore, W. Symmes, T. Phillebrown,
R. Stowers, B. Switzer, T. Lord, Z. Johnson, T. Welch, J. Kent,
J. Fowle, T. Crosswell

1680: T. Carter, T. Rand, J. Foskett, J. Mousall, B. Switzer, S. Payne,
L. Dowse, S. Phipps, T. Welch, J. Kent, J. Fowle, T. Crosswell,
G. Blanchard, T. Shepard, W. Symmes, T. Phillebrown

1681: N. Rand, J. Wood, T. Welch, D. Read, R. Stowers, J. Pratt,
S. Blanchard, T. Shepard, T. Welch Sr., J. Miller, T. Phillebrown,
G. Swan

1682: T. White, N. Frothingham, J. Mousall, P. Fowle, S. Payne,
B. Switzer, S. Blanchard, J. Blanchard, L. Dowse, S. Phipps, J. Kent,
T. Crosswell, T. Welch, J. Miller, E. Prout, T. Phillebrown

1683: W. Richeson, J. Lowden, N. Hutchinson, J. Whittemore,
R. Stowers, S. Barrett, P. Tufts, T. Shepard, J. Foskett, T. Lord,
C. Carter, P. Mark, T. Welch, J. Kent, J. Miller, E. Prout,
T. Richeson, T. White, T. Phillebrown

1684: N. Rand, T. Rand, J. Mousall, A. Phillips, S. Payne, B. Switzer,
S. Waters, J. Phipps, T. Pierce, J. Frothingham, J. Miller,
T. Crosswell, E. Prout, T. Phillebrown, P. Frothingham,
N. Frothingham

Field Drivers

1637: W. Learned, W. Brackenbury, J. Mousall (Stinted Common)

1639: W. Palmer, E. Richardson (Stinted Common)

1645: T. Pierce (Stinted Common)

1649: T. Goble, T. Pierce (Fd to Cambridge), W. Johns, J. March
(Line Fd), W. Frothingham, R. Hildrick (Menotomy Fd), R. Stow,
J. Palmer (High Fd), W. Frothingham, J. Penticost (East Fd),
W. Johnson, R. Layhorn, M. Smith (Far Fd Mystic Side);
A. Ludkin, J. Carter (Lower Fd Mystic Side)

1650: T. Pierce, W. Baker, W. Johnson, J. Penticost, W. Frothingham, R.
Hildrick (Cambridge), R. Mousall, R. Leach, R. Chalkley,
T. Carter Jr

1651: T. Pierce, R. Mousall, W. Frothingham, R. Chalkley, W. Johnson,
S. Phipps, J. Carter, S. Fosdick

1652: T. Pierce, T. Welch (West End); W. Johnson, J. March (Home Fd);
R. Hildrick, R. Lowden (Menotomy)

1654: R. Lowden, P. Knight (Stinted Common)

1655: L. Dowse, T. Rand (Stinted Common)

1656: J. Fowle, R. Lowden, W. Bullard, E. Brazier, P. Frothingham,
W. Johnson; W. Dade, T. Rand (Stinted Common)

1658: H. Harbord, T. Rand (Stinted Common); J. Greenland, R. Dexter,
J. March, T. Carter, J. Mousall, J. Palmer, W. Johns, A. Smith,
T. Pierce, T. Welch, P. Frothingham

1659: H. Harbord, T. Rand (Stinted Common)

1663: T. Rand, J. Penticost (Stinted Common)

1664: J. Palmer, N. Dade, S. Phipps Jr. (Stinted Common)

1665: H. Harbord, R. Lowden, T. Crosswell (Stinted Common)

1667: H. Harbord, S. Carter, J. Palmer, J. Miller (Stinted Common)

1668: S. Ward, T. Crosswell, J. Fowle (Stinted Common)

1669: T. Crosswell, S. Phipps Jr, P. Fowle (Stinted Common)

1672: S. Pierce, J. Mousall (Stinted Common)

1673, 1674: R. Lowden, S. Pierce, J. Miller Jr., N. Howard, T. Crosswell,
G. Fowle (Stinted Common)

1675: R. Lowden, S. Pierce, T. Crosswell, W. Richeson, J. Foskett
(Stinted Common)

1676: R. Lowden, S. Pierce, T. Crosswell, W. Richeson, J. Foskett
(Stinted Common)

1677: S. Phipps, P. Fowle, T. Crosswell, J. Miller Jr., J. Foskett
(Stinted Common, and below)

1678: S. Phipps, J. Miller Jr., J. Lowden, P. Fowle

1679: P. Fowle, J. Lowden, W. Richeson, J. Miller Jr.

1680: J. Fowle, P. Fowle, N. Hutchinson, J. Miller Jr.

1681: S. Frothingham, N. Hutchinson, T. White, J. Wood,
T. Phillebrown
1682: S. Phipps, N. Hutchinson, T. White, S. Frothingham, J. Wood
1683: S. Phipps, T. White, N. Hutchinson, S. Frothingham, J. Wood
1684: J. Miller, W. Richeson, T. Lord, N. Hutchinson
1685: R. Lowden, J. Call, J. Miller, J. Fowle, J. Lowden (managers of
Stinted Common)

RATE COMMISSIONERS
1650: F. Norton
1651: T. Lynde
1655: R. Hale
1656: S. Adams
1657: T. Penticost
1662: J. Allen, Ric Sprague (value estates)
1665: J. Cutler
1666: W. Symmes
1667: Ric Sprague
1668: J. Allen
1669: T. Lynde; M. Smith, J. Carter (value estates)
1671: J. Lynde
1672: J. Tidd
1673: W. Symmes
1674: J. Lynde
1677: Jac Green
1680: J. Betts, J. Mousall (value estates)
1681: J. Lynde
1682: J. Lynde
1683: S. Ballatt, W. Clough (value estates)
1684: J. Cutler

SCHOOLMASTERS
1636: W. Witherall
1651: S. Stowe
1661: E. Cheever
1666: J. Mansfield (No license)
1671: B. Thompson
1674–84: Sam Phipps
1684: Sam Miles

GRAVEDIGGERS

1651: W. Johnson

16--: J. Miller

1670: M. Wood

1671: T. Hale

1676: T. Barber

CLERKS OF MARKET

1654: T. Brigden

1655: W. Dade

1656: J. Penticost

1657: T. Brigden

1658–61: J. Burridge

1663: J. Burridge, R. Kettle (Sealer Weights & Measures)

1664–72: J. Burridge

1673: T. Lord

1675: T. Lord, R. Austin

1676: W. Clough, S. Dowse

1680: S. Hunting

1684: W. Clough, R. Austin

1687: R. Austin, W. Jameson

SEALERS OF LEATHER

1654: S. Switzer, S. Carter

1655: R. Pritchard, M. Smith

1656: F. Rouse, S. Carter

1658: M. Smith, F. Rouse

1659: M. Smith, F. Rouse

1660: R. Pritchard, F. Rouse

1661: M. Smith, R. Pritchard

1663–69: R. Pritchard, M. Smith

1670: T. Lord

1675: T. Lord, S. Dowse

1679: N. Kettle, J. Baxter

1681: C. Carter

1682: T. Rand Jr.

1684: J. Damon

1687: T. Lord, C. Carter, S. Dowse

Packers of Flesh

1654: Jas Merrick
1656: R. Kettle
1657: R. Kettle
1661: R. Kettle
1663: B. Lathrop
1665–73: R. Kettle
1674: J. Kettle (and Fish)
1677: S. Hunting

Battery Gunners

1654: T. Brigden
1668: T. Brigden, Jr
1679: T. Brigden

Pound Keepers

1638: J. Mousall
1658: R. Lowden
1670: R. Lowden
1677: R. Lowden
1679: N. Hutchinson
1687: R. Austin

Fire Warden

1661: T. Brigden

Measurers of Boards

1659: R. Hale, T. Brigden Sr (Woodcorder—measurer of wood cords)
1660: S. Phipps, T. Brigden Sr (Woodcorder)
1661: S. Phipps, T. Brigden Sr (Woodcorder)
1663: S. Phipps
1664: S. Phipps, E Carrington (Woodcorder)
1665: E. Carrington (Woodcorder)
1666: S. Phipps, E. Carrington (Woodcorder)
1667: S. Phipps, T. Adams (Woodcorder)
1668: S. Phipps, T. Adams (Woodcorder)
1669: S. Phipps, T. Adams (Woodcorder)
1670: S. Phipps, E. Carrington (Woodcorder)
1679: T. Lord (Woodcorder)
1681: J. Hurd

1684: J. Damon

1687: J. Hurd, J. Damon (Woodcorder)

BELLRINGERS

1668: T. Lord

1669: T. Lord

1670: T. Lord

1671: T. Hale

1674: T. Orton

1675: T. Lord

1676: T. Lord, (Dec) Z. Sawtell

1679: T. Lord

1681: T. Lord, S. Geary (night watchman)

1682: J. Stride (night watchman)

VERGERS

1668: T. Brigden; June: M. Smith

1676: M. Smith

CULLERS OF DRIED FISH

1661: R. Kettle

1671: T. Shippie

1673: T. Brigden

1674: T. Brigden

1683: T. Shippie Sr.

1684: M. Long

1687: M. Long, S. Hunting

TREASURERS

1671–76: L. Dowse

1677: H. Phillips

1678: A. Ludkin

1681: T. Lynde

1684: T. Lynde

1686: S. Phipps

MEASURERS OF SALT

1676: T. Barber

1683: T. Shippie Sr. (and coal)

1684: J. Damon (and coal)

1687: M. Long (and coal)

Tithingmen

1678: J. Kent, J. Whittemore, S. Pierce, S. Phipps, J. Heyman, E. Wilson, R. Lowden, W. Clough, R. Taylor, J. Fosdick, A. Ludkin, L. Dowse, S. Dowse, J. Carey, J. Penticost, T. Lord, E. Row, W. Dade, E. Carrington W. Symmes, S. Payne, P. Tufts, J. Tidd

1682: J. Frothingham, J. Fowle, N. Hutchinson, T. Carter Sr., A. Benjamin, T. Chapman, E. Phillebrown, T. Cutler, S. Watts, J. Edes, S. Ballatt, T. Shepard, E. Prout, R. Stowers

1683: T. Welch, J. Lowden, P. Frothingham, I. Johnson, J. Waters, J. Kent, T. Rand Jr., C. Goodwin Jr., J. Hurd, J. Ryall, S. Blunt, G. Blanchard, J. Gould Sr., J. Pratt

Wheat Pricers

1683: R. Lowden, J. Fowle, J. Cutler
1684: R. Lowden, J. Fowle, J. Cutler
1687: R. Lowden, J. Fowle, J. Cutler Jr.

Cullers of Damnified Goods

1684: Z. Long, J. Phillips, R. Sprague
1687: J. Phillips, R. Sprague, J. Lynde

Cullers of Bricks

1687: C. Goodwin. J. Batchelor

Town Government

Running Charlestown was plainly a highly participatory business. Each year a large number of inhabitants were responsible for many aspects of the town's management. In 1638, when the town numbered about 110 families, 35 householders were elected or appointed to jobs. With some 200 households by 1658, 62 officeholders were named. 20 years later, 100 out of 256 families provided services to the town. Nor does the list here include all town contributions. Colonial and militia officers, church officials, nightly groups of watchmen, probate administrators, grand and petty jurors, bondsmen, arbitrators, committeemen, overseers of the boys in the meetinghouse—all these would have increased the annual proportion to well over fifty percent. Another major omission is women. They, as we shall see, performed many semi-official duties in town—as midwives and birth assistants, as nurses and foster mothers to orphans or children at risk. Widows were frequently named as executrices in wills. Women saints assumed responsibility for maintaining female discipline and good behavior. Charlestown was a community of involved and active residents.[3]

The multitude of offices points to a second conclusion. This was a highly regulated place. All the work activities of its residents were subject to inspection, control, and communal rules and standards. Farmers must have regulation fencing in place by a certain date, livestock promptly cleared from arable, hogs yoked and ringed, milch cows registered with the herdsman and awaiting him at certain places at certain times, dry cattle securely pastured. Artisans needed permission to cut timber on communal land, to excavate stone, to "burn" lime and bake bricks, to dig tanning pits, to extract clay and gravel. Their products were culled, measured, viewed, priced,

---

[3] The 1646–48 experiment of electing Thomas Wilder "Town Officer" to carry out many monitoring and regulatory functions in return for £20 a year was not continued. CTR, 1: 654.

inspected, and sealed by local experts. The market, local shops and stalls, traveling salesmen, and craftsmen were similarly subject to close scrutiny, as were licensees, brewers, millers, maltsters, and distillers. Much of the town business, from the early allotments of land, oversight of the weir, the tide-, wind-, and water-mills, and maintenance of the infrastructure, to the later regulation of the building of the dry dock and the privatizing of the stinted common, was designed to further Charlestown's political economy.[4]

Personal conduct was also regulated. The constables and the watch patrolled the town lanes and could be summoned when suspicions were aroused or violence loomed. The 9 p.m. curfew was strictly enforced. Rumor and gossip spread fast and could conjure up groups or crowds when town rules or mores were threatened. The behavior of youth, especially boys in the meetinghouse gallery, was closely monitored. Militiamen had to show proper deference and obedience to their officers and seniors. Shaming punishments were inflicted: both on parade, and in the congregation. The tightest town oversight was introduced after a clerical campaign for the reformation of manners and spiritual commitment after King Philip's War (1675–76), with the introduction of tithingmen in charge of ten neighbouring families. Charlestown lived in an interventionist culture of discipline.[5]

Within this largely self-governing community, there was a hierarchy of offices, mostly elected by the Town Meeting or appointed. At the top were the resident assistants or magistrates, elected on a colony-wide basis by freemen; they served as members of the upper house of the General Court and the Court of Assistants, the main appeal court of Massachusetts. Assistants sat on their County Court benches, and examined suspects. They often summarily disciplined minor offenders. Magistrates like Increase Nowell or Richard Russell had the power and influence to enforce good order in the town. The town's representatives to the General Court were elected by the town's freemen, who had been admitted to church membership and then to freemanship of the colony. The town's deputies were its ambassadors to the wider colonial world. Not only must they speak and vote there according to the town's wishes, but they must also report back on the ordinances, finances, and legal decisions of the General

---

4   B. Levy, *Town Born: The Political Economy of New England from its Founding to the Revolution* (Philadelphia: University of Pennsylvania Press, 2009), 1–153.

5   R. P. Gildrie, *The Profane, the Civil, and the Godly: Reformation of Manners in Orthodox New England, 1679–1749* (University Park: Pennsylvania State University Press, 1994), 23–44, 59–70, 91–127.

Court. With such responsibilities, the deputies had to be men of standing, education, and fluency. Often leading merchants, they were reelected year after year. Experience at the central legislature was invaluable.[6]

Initially, the Town Meeting of all "inhabitants"—normally house-holders—managed all the affairs of the struggling infant town. In January it elected all the important town officials. In the ten months from April 1634 to January 1635, it had to convene eight times. This proved too back-breaking for ordinary families facing a relentless and sometimes hopeless struggle for survival. On 10 February 1635, at their ninth meeting, the Town Meeting members resolved that, owing to

> the great trouble and charge of frequent meetings of the townsmen in general, and so many cannot easily come to a joint issue, therefore the eleven men [selectmen], with the advice of the pastor and teacher in cases of conscience, are to decide all business, save choice of officers; the inhabitants willingly submit to their decisions as their own proper act for the coming year.

By the 1640s the eleven men had been reduced to seven, and, though the 1635 submission was not repeated until 1662, the annually elected executive committee members, meeting monthly or more often if neces-sary, appear from their minutes to have handled most of the town's busi-ness, before taking needed refreshment at The Three Cranes.[7]

The selectmen's agenda was multifarious. In the first three decades their most important tasks were the screening of immigrants to Charlestown and the proportionate distribution of town lands. They also leased out some of the town real estate. They were responsible for creating the infrastruc-ture; for contracting with town employees like herdsmen, carpenters, or pound keepers; for detailed instructions for elected surveyors of highways,

---

[6] Freemen: see below, "Church: Introduction," and Thompson, *Cambridge Cameos*, 7–15; Char-lestown listed 76 freemen in 1677. CTR, 3: 201. Assistants: Later magistrates were Samuel Nowell, James Russell, and John Phillips.

[7] Householders: during the early 1640s, the town meeting consisted of "freemen" only; by 1646 the "*General* Town Meeting" was reinstated. CTR, 1A: 81, 99, 105, 116. January: in the 1630s, the town sometimes met in February; in 1680 the townsmen resolved to elect officers annually on the first Monday in March. CTR, 4: 20. 1634–35: CTR, 1A: 18–22; two meetings in April, one each in June, September, and October, two in November, and one in January. Seven: in 1641, the executive was referred to as "the Seven Men." CTR, 1A: 95. 1662: 21 February, "We commit the management of public affairs to the selectmen to prevent unnecessary charges coming on the town." CTR, 3: 28. More often: in 1637–38, the selectmen recorded 19 meetings, mainly between October and April; the following year they met 18 times. CTR, 1A: 61–73. From 1679, they met every first Monday of the month. CTR, 4: 10.

appointed fence-viewers, hog reeves and tree wardens. They punished infractions of regulations with fines. Sometimes the Seven took major decisions, like selling the old meetinghouse for £100 in 1639, or deeding the Indian lands of Squa Sachem to four town notables. Each year they set the town rate and supervised its collection. For most of our period, however, the town meeting approved most major policies, like building a schoolhouse and the master's pay; contributing a peck of wheat per household to support Harvard College; setting a maximum price for buying a town house; selling off town land; and passing the annual town accounts.[8]

After 1660, routine appointments and instructions continued annually, but other business supplanted land grants and basic infrastructure. Now time was increasingly taken up with maintaining the school, the meetinghouse, the town house, Mystic Bridge, and the valuable timber resources of the communal domain. Welfare for disabled, poor and elderly residents became more pressing, as did warning out (early notice to leave town in event of future penury) or taking bonds "to save the town harmless" of potentially needy incomers. Controlling unruly boys in the meetinghouse gallery involved up to 30 monitors each year, and the contentious issues surrounding meetinghouse seating occupied much committee time. Selectmen arranged annual salaries for ministers and in 1670 initiated the acquisition of a town manse for them. They warned drinkers to reform, masons to stop sabotaging each other at the quarry, "disliked" single women or absent seamen's wives taking French sailors as lodgers, and forced boundary contenders to submit to arbitration. They harried constables to deliver their accounts on time. They raised rates to improve defenses in the increasingly threatening era after 1675. The Neck was the town's natural fortifiable line; the battery and the watchtower (from which a warning flag could be flown to alert remote residents) needed frequent repair. Powder and shot were expensive. The "prudential men" certainly earned their refreshment at Long's.[9]

The Seven were the elite group of the town. Until his death in 1655, Increase Nowell, magistrate and leading colonial official, was chairman, succeeded by the equally influential Richard Russell during his lifetime.

[8] Land and infrastructure: see below, "Land." Instructions: CTR, 1: f. 659, 670, stinted common drivers, and hog reeves. Selling, deeding: CTR, 1A: 74, 81. Approved: CTR, 1: f. 671, 638, 639; 3: 61; 4: 5, 39.

[9] Maintain: see "Infrastructure" below. Welfare: CTR, 3: 53, 96, 99, 100, 124, 208, and passim. Warn out and bonds: CTR, 3; 25, 28, 50, 51, 60, 66, 77, 79, 165, and passim; school: CTR, 3: 84, 117, 167; 4: 5, 11, 21, 44; minister: CTR, 3: 110; 4: 51, and "Church: Introduction" below; control: CTR, 3: 62, 89; 4: 16, 26, 64 and passim; defense: CTR, 3: 203, 209, 220, 4: 90; CTrR, 1: f. 52v, 54, and "Mass Violence" below.

His son James was not elected to the executive until the year of his father's death. In 1681, after his promotion to the magistracy, he succeeded Captain Lawrence Hammond as chairman. Continuity and experience were the committee's strengths. Its members were mature, responsible, and proven neighbors, sometimes wealthy, but not necessarily so; they were reelected until old age, infirmity or death.

A similarly onerous office, as in English parishes, was that of constable. By the late 1640s, three were found necessary for the different clusters of settlement, and a generation later, four were customarily elected. Their multiple duties were spelled out by the General Court; the two most important and time-consuming were law enforcement and tax collection, for which they had to account to the townsmen and later the treasurer. The town meeting's choice came to fall on somewhat younger men. The average age in the 1650s was forty-two, with two in their late twenties and four in their thirties. By the 1670s it had fallen to thirty-eight and a half, again with two in their twenties, but nineteen in their thirties. The men in their thirties had been picked out as possible leaders of the next generation and given early responsibility. The constable had to carry his staff of office on duty, and could call the watch or neighbors to his aid. The office required authority, energy, sensitivity, patience, and persistence. It could be dangerous, as we shall see. Because of its relentless and testing demands, it was rare for a constable to serve more than one term.[10]

The town clerk obviously needed to be a good penman, methodical and attentive to detail. John Greene Jr. transcribed the earlier records of the town into a new book in 1664, and added some explorers' observations and early settlers' remembrances. The most businesslike was Lawrence Hammond, whose bureaucratic style and early copperplate script suggests scrivenal training. Edward Burt had an arabesque hand replete with curlicues and swagging. Sometimes the clerk combined the duties of Clerk of the Writs, concerned with legal documents; at other times these were separate appointments. The town clerk was paid £4 per year. He was the main provider of the town's memory, though, as we shall see, elderly men sometimes had to be summoned where the written record was wanting.[11]

Most of the artisanal and agricultural regulators were men with specialist skills or with interests in specific fields or fences. The town

---

[10] Duties: *GM Newsletter,* 12 (2003), 9–10; English: M. Goldie, "The Unacknowledged Republic," in T. Harris, ed., *Politics of the Excluded* (Basingstoke: Palgrave, 2001), 160. Dangerous: see "Ursula Cole" and "Dominion and Revolution" below.

[11] Elderly: see "Lowden's Wall" below.

herdsman was paid per head of cattle by individual owners. The pound-keeper received fines and daily rates from farmers whose cattle, horses, sheep, geese, or pigs had strayed or exceeded their owner's number of cow commons. The boundsmen who "beat the bounds" with colleagues from adjacent communities had to re-establish boundary markers if old ones, often trees, had disappeared. They also agreed onroutes of new roads with their neighbors. Usually the boundsmen were longtime residents; here, too, a long memory was an invaluable asset.[12]

All Charlestown residents had an obligation to keep alert for any hints of danger or misbehavior. The Middlesex County Court Records are full of depositions witnessing such close observation. Able-bodied males over sixteen had two other duties. All were required to serve in the Train Band[13] and attend town and county parades, firing practice, and maneuvers. They had to maintain muskets, ammunition, body armor, and in some cases, swords. Cavalrymen in the Middlesex Troop of Horse had to provide their own mounts, saddles, harness, and pistols. Militiamen had to be prepared to go to war, as many did in 1675–76, and again in 1690.[14]

The second communal male service involved workdays on the town's highways. Teams would be drafted by the annually elected Surveyors and would have to devote several days each year to the perennial tasks of fill-ing, draining, ditching, pounding and reinforcing after carts and cattle and weather had broken up unsurfaced trackways. Residents would be ex-pected to bring their own implements, handcarts or oxcarts, draft teams, and carpenters' tools for work on gates and bridges. Men and youths who failed to appear would be reported and fined. Training and working to-gether is a potent generator of community spirit.[15]

Finally, all householders had the citizen's obligation to support the gov-ernment through paying taxes. Three different rates were due: to the town, to "the country" and to the ministry. The 1658 Tax List, transcribed above, shows a total of £107-10-9d collected by three constables from 233 heads of households, an average of nine shillings and four pence a household. However, rates were levied proportionate to wealth. Captain Francis

---

[12] The following town officials were customarily appointed by the selectmen: boundsmen, sur-veyors of woodlots, herdsmen, drivers of commons, sealers of weights, fence-viewers, hog reeves.

[13] Each town had a militia company which formed part of the County Regiment.

[14] See "Mass Violence" below. Francis Norton was Captain of Horse after 1654. MxCC RB, 1: 58.

[15] CTR, 1: 655; boys of ten and over were also employed, CTR, 1: 639. On 27 August 1641 a spe-cial town meeting agreed that every male would contribute a day's labor to the task of broadening the dam on Twopenny Brook, preparatory to Thomas Coytmore's building a watermill, CTR, 1A: 92. Fines were often paid by days of labor.

Norton, a rich merchant, paid £2-10-0d whereas absentees with small parcels of land in town paid pennies, and paupers like Mr. Mansfield or Phineas Pratt paid nothing. Mr. Russell the magistrate and Mr. Symmes the minister were also exempt.[16]

The 1652 Constables' Accounts in the town's treasury records show the country rate to have been £37-17-11d, compared to a town rate of £141-18-6d. The constables' expenditures include £33 for buying a house for the town; repaying a £25 loan to the town by Captain Norton; sundry payments to fellow citizens for community work, like carpenter Solomon Phipps's £9- worth of repairs on the meetinghouse; £1-7-6d to the glazier for new panes for the building, and expenditures for all kinds of goods and services: deputies' diet at the quarterly General Courts, provision of a barrel of gunpowder for the militia and the battery, train oil for the gunner, schoolmaster's salary, welfare to poor families, coats as token rent to the Indians, and hiring fees for a bull for the propagation of the townspeople's herd. The manuscript account books are troves of information about town income and expenditures, including sections on poor relief, and about the fiscal effects of crises and war. Richard Russell, who served as Treasurer of Massachusetts, oversaw the town accounts. Lawrence Hammond, another efficient man of business, took over until an official town treasurer was elected after 1671. All in all, we are extremely fortunate to have such copious and revealing records for Charlestown. They enable us to build up a vivid and minutely detailed understanding of town government for the crucial founding generations.[17]

This sophisticated system of town administration was not invented from scratch by the newly arrived immigrants. In the outpouring of research in the last thirty years into early modern English local government, we can detect many precedents for New England practices. London parishes and manors, as well as provincial market towns and villages, were frequently run through popular participation. The "middling sort" of yeomen, craftsmen, merchants, and professionals, who predominated in emigration, manned a host of offices that regulated and monitored neighbourhood obligations and behavior. Order was an obsession; the Puritan cult of self-discipline and reconciliation bore down on vengefulness, violence and idleness. Each unit was a "little commonwealth;" in many, especially those of a "hot Protestant"

---

[16] "Country": due to the colony. List: see "Numbering" above. Norton: see "The Estate of Captain Francis Norton" below; Mansfield: see "Mary Mansfield and the Jarndyce Effect" below; Pratt: see "Incomer" above. Ministerial: see "Church: Introduction" below.

[17] 1652: CTrR, 1: 54v. Poor: CTrR, 4: 15v; war, 3: 60r; see "Mass Violence" and "Dominion and Revolution" below.

tendency, the *vita activa* of purposeful communal improvement pulsed. Here merit rather than blood were recommendations for office. A "moral economy" of "commonwealth rather than common misery" erected barriers against exploitation. These communities were hierarchical by wealth, education, age and gender. Leadership came from the top. However, all householders distinguished between the deserving and the undeserving poor, whom they strove to exclude or expel. They were hostile to "strangers" and suspicious of immigrants. Though many parishes were becoming increasingly oligarchic and unequal, there were still plenty of open vestries where most inhabitants regularly elected their officials.[18]

Old England differed from New England in many ways: its crush of people, its shortage of land and other resources, its wide range of "sorts" from hugely wealthy aristocrats and city merchants to desperate vagabonds and beggars. It had an interventionist monarchy and established church, and an increasingly centralized legal system. It had a traditional culture of merriment and indulgence. Nonetheless, at the local level, there were in its "parish states" many precursors of New England town governments.

---

[18] Excellent bibliographies and footnote leads can be found in J. Boulton, *Neighbourhood and Society* (Cambridge: Cambridge University Press [publisher of the next three studies], 1987); M. J. Braddick & J. Walter, eds., *Negotiating Power in Early Modern England* (2001); P. Withington, *Politics and Commonwealth: Citizens and Freemen in Early Modern England* (2005); P. Griffiths, *Lost Londons* (2008); J. Wilson, ed., "The Wymondham Town Book 1585-1620," *Norfolk Record Society*, 70 (2006) 1-177. Open vestries: B. Manning, *English People and the English Revolution* (London: Heinemann, 1976), 158-59; K. Lindley, *Popular Politics and Religion in Commonwealth London* (Aldershot: Scolar, 1997), 40, 57, 59, 62, 219. The Watertown and Cambridge town records have both been published: *Watertown Records, Books 1 & 2* (Watertown: Historical Society, 1894); Records of the Town of Cambridge 1630-1703 (Cambridge: City Council, 1901).

Who Rules?

The 1635 submission of Charlestown's inhabitants, in general meeting assembled, to be managed by their elected board of selectmen made perfect sense. Most townspeople had neither the time nor the energy to make all the decisions, regulations, and plans needed to render the local economy and community viable. They respected the sound judgment of these "prudential men" above their own often quarrelsome debates. They repeated their handover of responsibilities in the dark days of 1662, after the royal Restoration and the destruction of their "good old (Republican) cause." For much of our period, the town records give an impression of the ordinary citizens of Charlestown treating their "betters" with the deference due to education, experience, wealth, wisdom, and authority.

Even though they reserved the annual choice of the town's executive to their votes at the winter general meeting, the citizens of Charlestown nonetheless re-elected the same managers time after time. They trusted the board to take major decisions such as buying and selling town buildings, choosing schoolmasters, setting annual taxes, and negotiating the generous ministerial stipends that congregations would have to pay. When other important issues were put to the townsmen, we cannot tell if they were simply rubber-stamping measures already finalized by the executive. Given the power and authority of Mr. Increase Nowell or Mr. Richard Russell, might not the infrequent gatherings of their humbler neighbors have been inclined to do what they were told, to defer and obey?

This reading of the record may indeed be plausible for many decisions. However, some contrary attitudes, entries and exceptions raise doubts about the sheep-like conformism of the people of Charlestown.

The "rights of Englishmen" had made the crossing to New England. Three years after the townsmen's first submission in Charlestown, in May

1638, Thomas Hooker preached a justly famous sermon to delegates, recent immigrants from Massachusetts, who were gathered in Hartford to draw up a constitution for Connecticut. His central message was:

> The choice of public magistrates belongs unto the people… it is in their power, also, to set bounds and limitations of the power and place unto which they call them…because the foundation of authority is laid, firstly, in the free consent of the people.

Hooker may well have been reacting to events that had occurred in Massachusetts in 1634, when his friend Israel Stoughton had questioned the powers of the colonial executive. For his pains, he was furiously abused and spitefully punished. As we shall see, similar high-handed treatment was meted out in 1637 to twelve Charlestown men who dared to remonstrate against the draconian punishment of Rev. John Wheelwright. In 1628, just a year before the founding of the town, English precedents for resisting executive demands had been reaffirmed in the parliamentary Petition of Right. It was axiomatic that "free men should not be given up to the will of others." Charlestown-raised Samuel Nowell demonstrated that Hooker's ideals remained potent 40 years on:

> There is such a thing as Liberty and Property given to us both by the Laws of God and of Men; when these are invaded we may defend ourselves…God hath not given great ones in the world that absolute power over men to devour them at pleasure, as great fishes do the little ones; He hath set rulers their bounds and by His law hath determined people's liberties and property.

The concept of the householder's right to give or withhold his consent to the executive was deeply embedded in the minds of New Englanders.[19]

Various enactments of the Charlestown general meeting bear out this belief in the inalienable rights of Englishmen. The 1635 submission was only for one year, and specifically excepted the choice of officials. In 1646,

---

[19]   D. H. Stock, "'Thomas Hooker and the Democracy of Connecticut' Revisited: the Rights of Englishmen in the Creation of the Fundamental Orders of 1639," paper privately communicated; Stoughton: *ODNB*; T. H. Breen, *The Character of a Good Ruler* (New York: Norton, 1974), 66–67; Wheelwright: see "Charlestown and the Antinomian Crisis" below. When the minister in 1664 sought to hustle through the admonition of a Baptist, he was quickly reminded that the vote of the church was required, Frothingham, 167; similarly, a Charlestown constable intent on searching Jonathan Bunker's house was repelled when he was found not to have a warrant, MxCC D&O, 2: folio 51, 16 March 1669. Nowell: *Abraham in Arms*, 1678, quoted in Gildrie, *The Profane, the Civil, and the Godly*, 192; "free men": P. Withington, *Politics of Commonwealth*, 166, 231.

the January town meeting ordained that "the selectmen are not to dispose of any land upon any of the town's commons" without express permission from the inhabitants. In 1647, they laid down—perhaps to forewarn wealthy selectmen and neighbours against a disproportionate poll tax—that the country rate should be levied "by estates and not by heads." The executive's apparent imposition of a town rate on householders was mitigated after 1650 by the town's annual election of an independent rate commissioner, who oversaw on the householders' behalf the process of estimating the communal fiscal needs of the coming year. Alertness over town accounts is implied by the town's refusal to accept an auditor nominated by the selectmen in 1681. Such measures suggest legislative checks on the executive.[20]

That the townspeople meant what they said was demonstrated in the 1670s and 1680s. On 4 January 1675, the town meeting issued a series of "wholesome orders" to their newly elected seven men. They were to levy rates civil and ecclesiastical, and keep the meetinghouse, schoolhouse, town house, etc. in good repair; they were responsible for the care of the poor and sick, for the weal and common benefit of the town. They should fine transgressors of town regulations. Finally, the townsmen reiterated that land belonging to the inhabitants in general could not be sold or disposed of without the consent of the whole community or the major part thereof. I have not discovered what prompted this assertion of legislative sovereignty, but it provides the context for an unholy row in the next decade when the selectmen were inveigled into selling part of the stinted common to deputy governor Thomas Danforth of Cambridge. This led in turn to a battle royal over privatizing the common, as described below. Consensuality in town affairs had perished by 1686. Similarly, the breakup of elite concurrence had already begun.[21]

In 1679, Increase Mather preached a jeremiad titled "A Call from Heaven," in which he bemoaned "a great rudeness…a degeneracy from the good manners of the Christian world." Others criticized rising anti-authoritarianism and aggressive self-assertion. This would have rung true to Charlestown's doctor, Thomas Graves. His assertion of his Harvard-educated superiority of judgment led not to deference but to his dumping as the town's deputy. The extremely wealthy but autocratic Richard Sprague

---

[20]   1646: CTR, 1A: 117; this was enforced seven years later, CTR, 1: 639. 1647: CTR, 1: 659. 1681: CTR, 4: 28.

[21]   "Orders: CTR, 3: 168; row: see "Common Land" below; concurrence: see "Question of Succession" and "Dominion and Revolution."

had to wait 11 years after his father died in 1668 before he was elected to the town board, by which time he was almost 50.[22]

These shots across the bow of authority were as nothing compared to the defiance of senior royalist collaborators and Tory elitists after the Glorious Revolution. Rather than a newly minted piece of post-revolutionary bravado, however, the awareness of rights, embedded in townspeople's minds and in the records of their long-term resistance to their town board's tendency to overreach, argues for a less than deferential populace.[23]

---

[22] Mather: Gildrie, 105, 59–60. Graves: see "Question of Succession" below. He was only once subsequently elected to the town board. Sprague: see "People Trafficking" above.

[23] Tory: see "Dominion and Revolution" below.

Part 3

Land

Laying Out the Town

In the beginning, at least according to the white settlers, all the land in Charlestown was common to the town. By 1686, when the crown took over direct rule of Massachusetts, virtually no common land was left. The division of the town's surface area to individual proprietors involved the four types of land use necessary for sustainable mixed farming: arable (crop-growing), pasture (livestock grazing/manure), meadow/marsh (winter feed), and woodland (timber/firewood). Three large areas were conventionally named: "Within the Neck," the present-day Charlestown peninsula; "The Main[land]," or "Without- [or] Beyond the Neck," roughly modern Somerville; and "Mystic Side," the land between Medford and Malden (now the southwest portion of Everett) on the northeast bank of the Mystic River. In general, these districts divided up the farmers' needs.

The peninsula was the main area for habitation, homelots and arable land in the "East Field"—sometimes called "The Great Cornfield"—and the smaller "Northwest Field." (See Map 1.) The Main provided pasture in the huge (1,780 acres as late as the 1680s) "stinted [rationed] common" for grazing, and haylots for winter fodder. Mystic Side, south of the modern Stoneham line down to near the Medford Road (now mostly in Medford), was the site for woodlots. The Main also contained four large farms that had been awarded by the colony to leading founders. Around the edges of the Stinted Common, and beyond it, various fields had been enclosed: High, Line, Menotomy, West, The Field over the Creek. (See Map 2.) References are also made to Nearer and Further Fields on Mystic Side. Meadow lots—vital for the long winter forage for draught cattle, horses and the milch herd—were found along the banks of the Mystic, Menotomy, and Charles Rivers and other smaller tributary

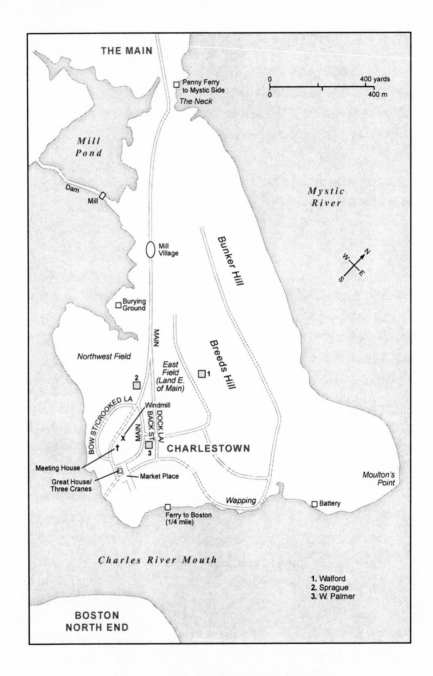

THE MAIN

Penny Ferry
to Mystic Side
The Neck

0   400 yards
0   400 m

Mill
Pond

Dam
Mill

Mystic
River

Mill
Village

Bunker Hill

Burying
Ground

Breeds Hill

Northwest Field

East
Field
(Land E.
of Main)

1

MAIN

2

Windmill

BOW ST/CROOKED LA

MAIN

BACK ST

DOCK LA

3

CHARLESTOWN

X

†

Meeting House

Great House/
Three Cranes

Market Place

Moulton's
Point

Wapping

Battery

Ferry to Boston
(1/4 mile)

Charles River Mouth

1. Walford
2. Sprague
3. W. Palmer

BOSTON
NORTH END

MAP 1. CHARLESTOWN PENINSULA

brooks. Meadow was the most valuable land in any town. In the absence of detailed and town-wide field maps, it is difficult to locate these fields and haylots.[1]

Charlestown was the smallest town by acreage in seventeenth-century Massachusetts. It was further truncated at its northwest end by the hiving off of Woburn in 1640 and of Malden, across the lower Mystic, in 1649. Although the remaining area of some 16,000 acres in Charlestown may still seem vast, its sustainable farming system could only support a limited number of households. The town's population of 45 families in 1630 had risen to about 120 by the start of the next decade, and to 256 by 1678. As early as 1637, when stinting or rationing of grazing was introduced, town meetings and selectmen's minutes were expressing concern about preserving resources, limiting "incomers," and preventing land sales to outsiders. By 1649 the stinted common was described as "overladen." As Charlestown's second generation came to adulthood with marriage and the creation of fresh households during the 1650s, the juggling act between different kinds of necessities became increasingly hectic. If more woodland or meadow was converted to grazing, or pasture was plowed under for additional grain crops, winter warmth or winter fodder or winter roasts would suffer. By the 1680s, the situation had reached a crisis point, and the town was riven with a third-generation rebellion.[2]

Charlestown's center was planned and laid out before the first settlers arrived. This was a task assigned to engineer Thomas Graves by the Massachusetts Bay Company in London in 1629. Graves sited the town nucleus

---

[1] Frothingham, 61–62; production: Brian Donahue, *The Great Meadow: Farmers and the Land in Colonial Concord* (New Haven: Yale University Press, 2004), passim; common, MxCC D&O, 4: Folio 100, 18 August 1682; farms: Ten Hills Farm (1,200 acres) to Governor John Winthrop, John Winthrop Jr.'s plat, *WP*, 4: 416, 2,500 acres in Medford to Matthew Craddock, first governor and heavy investor in the Massachusetts Bay Company, Rev. John Wilson's farm (200 acres) and a 500-acre spread to Charlestown's own Increase Nowell; Line Field Plat: George A. Gordon, "Ancient Line Field of Charlestown," *R*, 48 (1894), 56–59; hay: CTR, 3: 125 copies a 1637 town agreement with Winthrop to exchange town upland for his meadow between the Mystic and Menotomy Bridges.

[2] Acreage: computing from land grants, including the various farms (except Craddock's), I have reached a total of around 16,000 acres: stinted common 1,780; Mystic Side and Above the Ponds grants 1638, 6,565; Mystic side grants 1658, 4,716; Line Field 218; Farms 4,200; Mystic Side grants 1637, 405, Haygrounds 1635, 720; peninsular land 344, other Main fields and waste, perhaps 342; Watertown's acreage was 23,450. Woburn: in 1668 Charlestown petitioned the General Court for compensation "being straitened by parting with lands" to neighbors, *MR*, 4,2: 91, 579. Stinted common: Frothingham, 65;"overladen": CTR, 1: 675, 29 May 1649; juggling: cf. Donahue, Ch. 8. Population figures: Frothingham, 59, 83, 84–85, 182, and see above, "Numbers." During King Philip's War, 1675–76, Charlestown had to offer refuge to an additional forty-eight families from nine frontier towns, CTR, 3: 185–191.

on the southwest corner of the peninsula. At its center, in the lee of a hill and with access to the water, he built the "Great House," intended to house the founding leaders of the colony during the first months. Around the hill he plotted a circular road, Crooked/Bow-Main, with houselots, and another way from the landing place for a ferry across the Charles, over the hill and up the peninsula below Breed's Hill (Main Street). A marketplace opened out by the Great House, which initially doubled as a meetinghouse and then in 1637 became the Three Cranes Tavern. A second roadway, Dock Lane-Back Lane looped behind the start of Main, rejoining it at the foot of Breed's Hill. The long arc of Bow Street and Dock Lane gave access to the Charles River waterfront (see Map 1).[3]

After Graves's had laid out the town center, the 1629 migrant arrivals, the three Sprague brothers, Walter Palmer, five other families, and various company servants started raising shelters for themselves. As waves of settlers followed in the 1630s, they took up lots around the hill and along the lanes. Their holdings were recorded in a town Book of Possessions in 1638, and James Hunnewell has plotted the position and extent of their homelots. Many of the founding elite, such as Increase Nowell, Rev. Zachariah Symmes, Rev. Thomas Allen, Josiah Tidd, Joseph Hills, and Edward Johnson, occupied lots in the inner circle around the Hill, now Harvard Square. Homelots were most dense along the waterfront. Such was the value of riverside property that settlement spread east towards what was early known as Wapping Dock, and from there towards the northeast corner of the peninsula and the mouth of the Mystic, Moulton's Point. In all, Hunnewell's plan and description identifies 64 dwellings by 1638 (see Map 3).[4]

So far as farmland was concerned, the town made a series of grants outside the center, which are recorded in town records (as listed below). Once "improved," these grants became the freehold property of their owners, and could be bought and sold or rented out to tenants.

---

[3] The foundations of the Great House were uncovered in City Square during the "Big Dig." They are now displayed there in a historic park on the Freedom Trail.

[4] James F. Hunnewell, *A Century of Town Life: A History of Charlestown 1775–1887* (Boston: Little, Brown, 1888), 109–111. Settlement: Frothingham, 12–27, 41–43; Alexander Young, ed., *Chronicles of the First Planters of the Colony of Massachusetts Bay* (Boston: 1846, reprinted Baltimore: Genealogical Publishing, 1975), 371–87. Emerson, 38–40 has Graves's 1629 report to the company. Charlestown Book of Possessions was published in *Reports of Massachusetts Record Commissioners*, 3rd Report (Boston: 1883). The location of Moulton's Point (landlocked after extensive land reclamation) is indicated by a sign near the junction of First Avenue and 13th Street.

GENERAL TOWN GRANTS

1630:   Within the Neck: 2 acres per family for houselots. 2 acres for each male able to plant (East Field). By 1637, incoming artisans were granted a houselot and no more.

1635:   Scattered Hayground, 276 lots to 63 inhabitants, about 720 acres.

1637:   Mystic Side: 10 acres, soon reduced to 5, per inhabitant (i.e. household); 78 inhabitants, 405 acres.

1637:   The Main: 1780 acre Stinted Common rights to 113 inhabitants (proprietors). By 1657, 664 "cow commons."

By 1637:   Beyond Menotomy River (Alewife Brook): Line Field: 48 lots to 38 inhabitants, ranging from 1 to 18 acres, 214 acres in all, and a 10-acre lot of meadow.

1638:   Mystic Side: Further ("Above the Ponds") and Lower Fields: grants ranging from 10 to 260 acres; 108 lots, 4,010 acres "Above the Ponds," and 1,555 acres on Mystic Side, total 5,565 acres.

1658:   Mystic Side: Town allots 4,716 acres of woodland to 202 inhabitants, in parcels ranging from 4 to 89 acres.

1685:   Stinted Common: to be divided up proportionately to cow commons to the individual proprietors.[5]

All of these fields and the common were subject to minute regulation by the town meeting, the selectmen, and the proprietors of the stinted common. Each field had its annually appointed fence-viewers and field drivers, responsible for excluding any livestock during the growing season. Four overseers policed the common, ensuring that no one exceeded their stint and non-proprietors did not trespass. Illicit grazers would be driven to the town pen or pound; they would not be released until a fine was paid. Surrounding fences, gates, and watering places had to be maintained. Each year dates were announced for having sufficient fences in place, for fields to be cleared of stock, and for the milch cows to be herded out to the common. Hog reeves levied hefty fines if swine lacked nose rings and shoulder yokes. Starting in the 1670s, a shepherd was hired annually. Fencing responsibility was assigned proportionately to acreage in a field. Rights

---

[5]   1630: CTR, 1: 674 has a 30 February 1649 fencing agreement for East Field, and for 29 proprietors of West Field; 1635: CTR 1A: 31–33; 1637 Mystic Side: *Book of Possessions*, 73–74; 1637 Main: Frothingham, 66; 1658: ibid., 152–54. The average household used some 15 cords of wood every year, or 2000 cubic feet, N. Philbrick, *Mayflower*, 186; by 1637: Gordon, "Line Field," 56–59; 1638: CTR 1A: 63–65; 1685: CTR, 4: 68–74, and below, "Common Land."

of way had to be preserved, and resources, especially timber, protected. Winter town meetings and selectmen's regular meetings were dominated by such business for the coming growing season; dozens of inhabitants had responsibility for ensuring the rules were obeyed. As we have seen, this was a highly participatory little commonwealth.[6]

Another constant source of town business was the infrastructure. As well as field fences, gates, cattle pens, and watering places, the town needed a host of other facilities: highways and causeways, bridges and ferry landings, mills, public buildings, burial grounds, defenses, wharves, docks, and warehouses. We have already met surveyors of highways annually elected by the Town Meeting. Inhabitants' road service was proportionate to individual holdings of stock. In 1653, cash equivalents for service were introduced. Charlestown had three bridges and two ferries. Menotomy (now Alewife, Map 2) and Wapping Dock Bridges (Map 3) were glorified footbridges, but the maintenance of Mystic Bridge connecting northeastern towns to the center of the colony was a constant source of expense. In 1672 it needed a hundred cords of wood from John Winthrop's farm for major repairs. The huge £93 cost was shared between Charlestown and other users: Woburn, Malden, Reading, and Medford. When Massachusetts's first dry dock was built in Charlestown in 1678, Wapping Bridge had to be raised. Penny and Boston Ferries needed well-maintained landing places, just above the Neck (whose causeway needed frequent reinforcement), and below the marketplace, the commercial focus of the town.[7]

Winthrop noted in his journal in September 1636 that a windmill (possibly built by Robert Hawkins) had been raised at Charlestown, in time for grinding the grain harvest. Windmill Hill was on the north side of the marketplace. About 1642, however, a more ambitious tidal mill had been constructed on the west side of the Neck Creek, and this took over most of the flour production. Miller John Founall and his workers lived just below the Neck in an area that came to be known as Mill Village. Windmill Hill became the site of the first town-financed, purpose-built meetinghouse, of the Town House with its bell, sundial and watchtower, and after 1648, of the school. In that year appears the first reference to

---

[6] A typical example: CTR, 1: 659, 24 January 1648. For participants, see "Charlestown Office Holders."

[7] Pen: CTR 1: 678. Highways: CTR, 1: 655, highway orders; bridges: Menotomy, CTR, 3: 67, Wapping: ibid., 113, 207; Mystic: ibid., 90, 138. Middlesex grand juries frequently presented Charlestown for work needed on Mystic Bridge maintenance. Dry dock: CTR 3: 207, 4: 10, MR, 5: 180, MxCC D & O, 4: folio 83. Ferries: MR, 1: 205, CTR 4, 25.

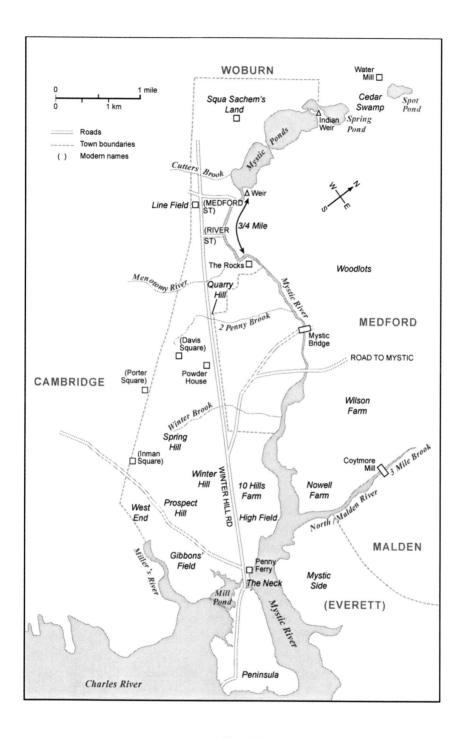

MAP 2. THE MAIN

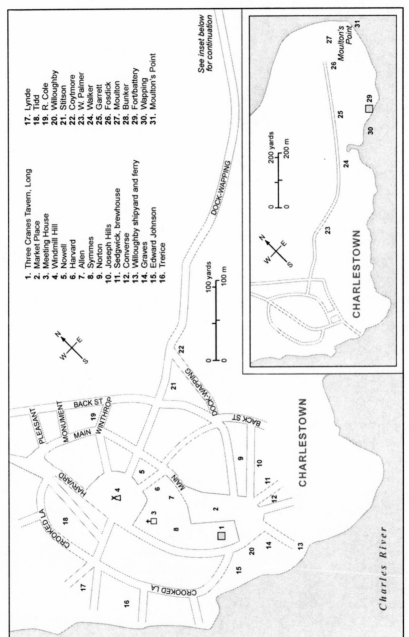

1. Three Cranes Tavern, Long
2. Market Place
3. Meeting House
4. Windmill Hill
5. Nowell
6. Harvard
7. Allen
8. Symmes
9. Norton
10. Joseph Hills
11. Sedgwick, brewhouse
12. Converse
13. Willoughby shipyard and ferry
14. Graves
15. Edward Johnson
16. Trerice
17. Lynde
18. Tidd
19. R. Cole
20. Willoughby
21. Stitson
22. Coytmore
23. W. Palmer
24. Walker
25. Garrett
26. Fosdick
27. Moulton
28. Bunker
29. Fort/battery
30. Wapping
31. Moulton's Point

See inset below
for continuation

MAP 3. TOWN CENTER CA. 1638

the town burying ground (on Phipps Street), west of modern Main Street about a quarter of a mile beyond Windmill Hill. Regular gravediggers were appointed by the selectmen, who stipulated their wages.[8]

Charlestown's domain had to be defended for its farmers, merchants, artisans, mariners, and womenfolk to go about their business. Attack from the sea by French, Dutch, or even Spanish forces was a serious threat, especially in the vulnerable early days and during international upheavals. A town fort and battery were established at Moulton's Point on the southeast corner of the peninsula. The Neck was the obvious defensive line against landward incursion. A watchhouse was strengthened during King Philip's War, and trenches in a "half moon" defensive work were constructed in the late 1670s against northern Indian forays. Maintenance of these facilities was a persistent charge on the time and money of the town.[9]

Without this infrastructure and these amenities, the inhabitants of Charlestown could hardly have survived, let alone prospered. They would have lacked all cohesion. Households, or groups of them, took responsibility for other parts of the infrastructure: wharves, docks, warehouses, tanning pits, lime, brick and pottery kilns, wells and pumps, a brewhouse, a distillery, forges, the fencing of gardens and homelots, barn building, and the transport of goods, wood and crops. All this activity in community, neighborhood, and household would render the town a center of sustainable agriculture, an exemplar of religious earnestness, and a hub of international trade.

Mixed farming in a close community like Charlestown depended on neighborly restraint, responsibility, and thoughtfulness. Despite the detailed regulations and the watchfulness of town officials, occasional conflicts erupted over land use, labor, boundaries, access, and the proportionate and just distribution of resources. Such cases spotlight the often unstated but deeply felt values that activated a seventeenth-century community.

---

[8] Windmill: Frothingham, 94, Dunn, 181; tidal mill: I. C. Hersey, "Charlestown's Mill Pond," *R*, 56 (1902), 235–39; the original shareholders were Thomas and Katherine Coytmore, Robert Sedgwick, William Stitson, Solomon Phipps, and John Allen. Meetinghouse: see below "Church: Introduction." Town House: CTR, 1 638, 647, 3: 48, 113, 4: 11. Schoolhouse: CTR, 1: 117, Frothingham, 97, 115. Burying ground, ibid., 94, CTR 3: 202.

[9] Fort: CTR 1, 639, 3: 55, 69, 88, 100; Neck: CTR 3: 209, Frothingham, 182.

Hay or Mills?
Symmes v. Collins and Broughton: Issues of Land Use, 1657

In our day, hardly a day passes without a story in the local or national press about conflict over land use: drilling for oil in an Arctic nature reserve, permitting tourists' snowmobiles in state parks, building houses, hospitals, roads or runways on land zoned for "green belt," damming Chinese rivers for irrigation and power while displacing large communities, or debating migrant encampments near expensive upmarket villages. The list is endless. Millions of man-hours are devoted to arguing and adjudicating land use issues, typically with powerful and passionate cases both for and against any given perspective.

Land issues can involve neighbors as well as nations. The most volatile condo meeting I have ever attended involved a tussle between sunbathers and enclosure-lovers over the felling of two small trees. My village took years to recover from sulphurous parish council sessions over whether a restricted lane should be opened to through traffic. A veteran of academic committees, I have nonetheless never witnessed such an ill-tempered and bitter confrontation. As we can see from the town records, such strong passions regarding land use and property rights would have been all too familiar to the early residents of Charlestown.

The fiercely fought 1657 civil action of Rev. Zachariah Symmes against Mr. Thomas Broughton and Mr. Edward Collins for committing nuisance to his property demonstrates that two sets of ambitions for future improvements (agricultural vs. industrial) have been colliding in Charlestown since the first generation of settlement. On 16 June 1657, the presence on the Middlesex bench in Charlestown of Governor John

Endicott and the visiting governor of Connecticut, John Winthrop, Jr., indicates the standing of the parties involved in this case, the importance of the issue, and the inter-town nature of the controversy. Symmes was first and foremost Charlestown's pastor, but he was also a landowner and he had to protect resources vital to his family's well-being. The damage to his property was in the "Great Meadow" on the south side of the Menotomy River (Alewife Brook). Symmes had acquired possession of some six and a half acres of meadow about fifteen years before from Edward Convers, who had begun channelling, draining and resowing the wetland near the junction of the Mystic and Menotomy Rivers before moving to Woburn about 1640. William Symmes (1627–91), a surveyor and already skilled farmer, was his father's tenant. By the early 1650s, after much expenditure, the meadow was well stabilized. Three of Symmes's farm workers testified that in summer "the meadows were never wet; they could cart off hay two days after rain," even from near the banks. The land produced "18 to 22 loads" of excellent fodder each year, on which Symmes claimed to be able to winter twenty head of cattle. After the mowing, his oxen fed on the rowen (second growth of grass) in the late summer and fall. To the pastor, and to the town, this improved meadow represented an invaluable asset.[10]

The two defendants had a different vision. Because of the collapse of Captain Cooke's mill at present-day Arlington, and Captain Coytmore's mill on Three-Mile Brook in Malden, they stressed the lack of milling facilities in the Medford-Upper Cambridge-Upper Charlestown region, and were eager to harness the waterpower of the Menotomy and Mystic Rivers. To build a water mill, they had first to dam the water to produce sufficient fall to turn the wheel. In 1655, their original partner, Rev. Henry Dunster, lately President of Harvard, impetuous entrepreneur and local landowner, supervised the erection of two dams: one near Mystic Weir just below the junction with the sluggish Menotomy, and a second above the Ponds. Deacon John Upham, 55, of Malden, reported witnessing a warning Zachariah Symmes had given his brother minister about the effect of blocking the flow, but Dunster characteristically persisted, promising compensation if necessary.[11]

---

[10] Documents in this case: MxCC D&O, 1: docs 1054–1067, 9–23 June 1657; MxCC RB, 1: 129. William: Doc 1511 records his surveying the bounds of Increase Nowell's land at the head of Mystic Ponds in 1650 or 1651. Testimony of Joseph Colls, 24, James Parker of Chelmsford, 37, Daniel Black and Josiah Convers, 40, both of Woburn. On 20 February 1650 Edward Convers had been sued by Robert Hale for damage caused by Convers's mill flooding Hale's meadow. Hale was awarded £7 in damages, *Book of Possessions*, 157–58.

[11] Cooke's Mill: *Cambridge Cameos*, 250; Coytmore's Mill: CTR 1A, 85; at a public meeting in Charlestown on 27 August 1641 it was agreed that the whole town would contribute one day's

Trouble rapidly ensued. On 12 December 1656, Dunster was sued by Widow Parnell Nowell and her son Samuel for "stopping the free flow of the waters in Mystic River and for flowing [flooding] their meadows above Mystic Pond." Symmes's action followed six months later, and initially targeted Dunster as well as his two "upcountry landowning" partners. Deacon Edward Collins of Cambridge had first leased and then bought Craddock's Farm in Medford from Matthew Craddock's widow. Broughton, a Boston merchant, was interested in diversifying into milling and frontier land. In 1656–57 he acquired the Nowell Farm. By the time Middlesex County Court heard the case, Dunster was dropped from the defendants. He may, by then, have gone into "exile" in Scituate.[12]

The Symmes side claimed that the weir dam had ruined their Menotomy haygrounds. William Johnson and William Locke, both 27, "having many years exercised by boats in the Ponds and the rivers," could certify that the permanent water level above the dams was "seven or eight inches higher than ordinary." Another expert witness put the rise at one foot. The effect on the vulnerable meadow was disastrous. The ground was "drowned" with stagnant water; "the bottom of the meadows became yearly rottener [producing] woods and rushes . . . a great deal of the best of the meadow ground was wholly killed . . . the very sward itself." Harvesting the paltry "eight jaggs [small cart-loads]" remnant proved perilous: "the mowers last year [had to labor] with exceeding toil and prejudice to their health . . . up to their knees in mire." When they tried to cart the hay away, the oxen sank up to their chests; the yield had to be carried out manually on poles. Even the highway to the barn was "bogged down." Symmes's stock could no longer fatten up for winter on the rowen. Not surprisingly, the present tenant, William Symmes, "was discouraged from continuing, and [the minister] had little hope of another tenant until the annoyance is removed."[13]

The view from the other side was truculently adverse. Collins and Broughton cast doubt on the meadow's purported yield supporting twenty

labor to "breadthen" the dam on Three-Mile Brook under Captain Coytmore's supervision, ibid., 94. Frothingham, 103. The site of Coytmore's Mill, later Tufts Mill, is shown on R. T. Ricker's "Plan of Malden" in R. K. Randall, *Malden* (Malden: Historical Society, 1975), 43. Dunster: *Cambridge Cameos*, 67–73.

[12]   Nowell v. Dunster, MxCC D&O, 1: doc 617, did not come to court; it may have been settled out of court, or Dunster may have left the colony. The Nowells claimed £50 worth of damage. Collins: Winifred L. Holman, "Edward Collins," *TAG*, 23 (1949), 149–51; his close relations with Cambridge ended in the early 1650s, when he sold his town lot to Daniel Gookin. Broughton: Bailyn, *Merchants*, 82, 101; he was an early developer of the New England fishery. Craddock Farm: MxD, 2: 302; Nowell Farm: MxD 1: 203.

[13]   Expert: James Parker; the remaining quotes are from Zachariah Symmes's statement and the three laborers' testimonies.

head of cattle over a winter. The pastor had had to buy winter forage before their dams had been built. The mirey condition of the meadows could well have been caused by trespassing cattle from nearby pasture because the tenant had neglected his fences. The standing water probably resulted from record rainfall in 1656 rather than the mill dam. They denied any decline in the quality of the grass.[14]

Before there was any question of a case in court, especially between the minister of one church and the deacon of another, the parties went to arbitration. They agreed to stand by the decision of four "indifferent men," including the meadow's former owner Edward Convers and his eldest son. The arbiters awarded fifteen loads of hay to the Symmeses by July, and payment for the transportation of three-quarters of it at four shillings a load. This was over and above the "free-will compensation" already paid. They also suggested that the mills and dams should be demolished.[15]

Collins and Broughton were outraged. In rejecting the award, they claimed that the arbiters had exceeded their instructions. If the pastor could not find a new tenant, they would. The idea of dismantling the mills and dams was particularly galling. It was like "throwing away a shilling in order to save threepence [a quarter of its value]." The mills (like our modern-day oil well, or tourists, or runway, or new hospital, or factory) were far more valuable to the region's economy. Their anger spilled over into personal slights. They "do not put [them]selves to be servants" in carting of forage. Broughton "aspersed [Symmes] for a causeless suit," and scorned his "'Vindication,' as he terms it." They had put a sluice and a lock gate in the dam, to prevent recurrence of problems. Any thought of demolition "would bring greater injury to the defendants."[16]

These "unjust" insults stung. Symmes's "name was more valuable to [him] than many farms." He cited two Old Testament texts to remind his despoilers to accept blame for their own negligence, and to justify his defense of his own land against incursions, like Naboth's defense of his vineyard against King Ahab. Perhaps these biblical precedents swayed the jury, along with the evidence of experts and the award of the arbiters. They found for the plaintiff, damages of 41 shillings and costs of £3-13-8. The Naboth of Charlestown triumphed over the mighty Ahabs of Boston and Medford.[17]

---

[14] "Answer of Edward Collins and Thomas Broughton," early June 1657, MxCC D&O, 1: doc. 1058.

[15] Doc. 1056, 10 June 1657; John Wyman and Samuel Richardson, also of Woburn, were the other two arbiters.

[16] Doc. 1058.

[17] Exodus 21: 33: "If a man dig a pit and not cover it, and an ox or an ass fall therein, the owner of the pit shall make it good and give money unto the owner of them." Naboth: 1 Kings 21: 1–3.

Naboth's reason for refusing Ahab's offer of payment or exchange for his vineyard was: "The Lord forbid it me, that I should give the inheritance of my fathers unto thee." For Symmes and many yeomen and husbandmen in England and New England, land was not just a commodity; it was a sacred family trust which must be maintained, ideally extended, and handed on intact and improved to the next generation. This thinking was at the heart of the ideal of sustainable and self-supporting farming, and it persisted in many agrarian families into the nineteenth century. Maps of Charlestown drawn then show the same families cultivating the same land as their ancestors two centuries earlier.[18]

By contrast, the large frontier holdings of Collins and Broughton involved a major element of speculation. Both men came from commercial backgrounds, were active in trade, and were oriented to markets. Both Craddock and Nowell heirs had been desperate to sell. Broughton soon sold Nowell's farm to Collins, who in turn sold it on to two Concord partners. He had already found another buyer for 1,600 acres of Craddock's farm in 1656. Merchants like these were rentiers rather than cultivators, land speculators rather than estate accumulators, entrepreneurs rather than agrarian traditionalists. They resembled the investors in the Connecticut Valley who caused Barnabas Davis such travails. Furthermore, millers were popularly regarded as not only lustful predators but also exploitative money-grubbers. The confrontation over the side effects of the two Mystic dams was thus a conflict between two diametrically opposed attitudes toward land and its use.[19]

---

[18] Cf. Thompson, *Divided,* 62–63, 101–102. Wyman includes Peter Tufts' 1818 field map of the Charlestown peninsula.

[19] Collins was the son and brother of London merchants; his eldest son became a merchant in North Germany and his youngest daughter married a merchant. He exported horses to Barbados and invested in potentially lucrative salt manufacture during the 1650s. MxCC D&O, 1: 655, 666, *MR*, 4-1: 224. For Broughton: see fn. 3. Their land deals: MxD, 2: 80, 302, 325; 3: 85. For comparable problems in Concord, see Donahue, *Great Meadow,* 184–90, and in Cambridge, see Thompson, *Cambridge Cameos,* 243–48. Millers: Bernard Capp, *When Gossips Meet* (London: Oxford University Press, 2003), 237, 256, 266; see below, "Ursula Cole."

Sharecropping Conflicts: Brackenbury v. Davis, 1660, and Gould v. Smith, 1676

By 1660 Charlestown was experiencing a "straitening" of land in addition to its perennial shortage of labor. The first generation, many born in the decades on either side of 1600, was aging. Those with generous grants or capital to buy additional lots could hand over sufficient acreages to their maturing offspring. For the less fortunate, however, prospects were bleaker. Newly independent sons might think about "going west," but frontier settlements would require considerable capital investment. Tenancy was a possibility, but with shortage of specie a system of "country pay" (payment in goods or services) developed. Between arable farmers, this exchange was most practical as sharecropping. An older landowner would contract with a "young beginner" to cultivate a specified area, and they would share the yield between them. Such deals, including specifics like responsibility for seed, draught animals, plowing, harvesting, gleaning, carting, and threshing, would be reached by word of mouth, and sealed with a handshake before witnesses. We only know about this mutually beneficial system, which was probably quite common, when something went awry.[20]

Alice Brackenbury had married Goodman William Brackenbury, a well-endowed and well-regarded yeoman, as his second wife in the mid-1640s. She was probably in her early forties, but her antecedents are unknown. In 1646 she had a son, Samuel. He joined her two stepdaughters, Anne (18) and Mary (12), and servants in the Brackenbury household

---

[20] See above, "Introduction."

in Charlestown. By the mid-1650s, when both daughters had married seafarers, the parents and young Samuel moved to neighboring Malden, joining other Charlestown families. However, they retained property in Charlestown, as well as a valuable one-eighth share in the Charlestown mill. In 1658 the Brackenburys contracted with Samuel Davis, aged 29, of Charlestown to "plow and plant arable fields" which may have been part of their Charlestown holdings. William seems to have been away during the spring and early summer of 1659. Alice, in his stead, became increasingly alarmed at Davis's headstrong self-assertiveness, and eventually refused to have any more to do with him. In April 1660, the Middlesex County Court heard a breach of contract case, which Davis won. In April 1661, however, William Brackenbury had the case reviewed.[21]

The contract between landlord and tenant was detailed. It specified the ten acres of fields to be tilled and the crops to be grown, except one acre which might either be pease or "what for my wife sees good." The Brackenburys would find the dung for manuring; Davis, recently married, with a premaritally conceived baby daughter, would provide two-thirds of the labor and one-half of the seed. He would also be responsible for "the looking to and tending of the crops until they should be ripe and inned [in the barn]." His reward would be half the yield. This appears to be a routine example of an early sharecropping deal. However, Alice Brackenbury came to regret that "her husband had made a very foolish bargain." Davis's exploitation of loopholes in the covenant and his disrespect for her led to increasing tension and eventual breakdown.[22]

At first all had gone well. Davis's sister Patience reported that Goodman Brackenbury came to her father's house, saying "he had a duty to bless god in that he had got such a good tenant to manure his land as my brother Samuel is . . . [who], said he, gave me and my wife good content." Paul Wilson had "heard Goody Brackenbury give Samuel Davis much praise and very good commendations." This contentment did not last. Alice became irritated by Davis's overuse of her draft animals. Her servant Francis Curry, 20, observed that Davis "worked my master's oxen almost all day, his own only one or two hours." The sharecropper informed Curry's dame that "he was

---

[21] William arrived in 1630 and was a frequent office holder, including Charlestown's Clerk of the Market in 1650, *GMB*, 199–202. Move: William was "late of Charlestown" in December 1650, and "of Malden" in 1656; Malden's town records have not survived from this period. The case and review are in MxCC RB, 1: 204, 231; D&O, 1: docs. 1495–1507, 1624, 1650–68; verdict: doc. 1497, 4 April 1660.

[22] Davis: MxCC D&O, 1: doc. 1076, 16 June 1657; see "Travels and Travails of Barnabas Davis" above; contract: D & O, 1: doc 1661, a copy from the review papers.

[hard] put to fodder his own cattle." When Alice Brackenbury had come "to the field she had brought hay for his oxen and her own vittals for his dinner. She and her maid helped clear the ground taking away sticks and stones to further the work."

Exploitation of oxen was a minor problem compared to Davis's inadequate workmanship. He only plowed the easy bits of the land, and then carried off the Brackenbury plow to do his own tilling elsewhere. When he was meant to sow pease, he "sent two or three times for more seed," according to Curry, even though he was contracted "to find half the seed in wheat and pease . . . My dame asked why he needed so many to the acre. He answered 'The sheep eat them,' but [in fact] he sowed ground [designated] for Indian [corn] which was more than the agreement with my master." When Curry expostulated that "My dame will be angry, he said he cared not. He would do what he would for all my dame. He would plow a part of [otherwise allocated land] for turnips."

Davis's high-handed contempt and his "deceiving me" outraged Alice Brackenbury. She took neighbors to corroborate her tenant's failure to honor his side of the bargain. They confirmed two and a half acres were untouched; Davis refused to hire help. He airily pronounced that Goody Brackenbury "should take no care so long as she could have hay and corn for money; her work would be done in season [when he felt like it]." When the weather "was good for planting, she did encourage him to go on according to the contract, but he said he would do it in his own time." This attitude convinced her that he was "a sorry, idle, fellow." She told his father that "my son should strike no stroke more, for he had overreached her husband in the bargain." When Samuel later sought a second chance, she told him "she would have no more to do with him . . . he would not follow his work when he had meat [feed] for his cattle, and now his meat was gone, he could not do it." "After many words passing, Sister Brackenbury said 'Here I leave it. I will go no further till I see the covenant.'" Rather than deal with Davis, she preferred to ask neighbors for help.[23]

On 27 March 1660, Samuel Davis sued William Brackenbury for £40 for breach of contract. What persuaded the jury to find for the sharecropper is unclear. The weight of surviving evidence suggests that the fault lay with the plaintiff, who broke his side of the bargain time and again. The

---

[23] Neighbors: Phillip Attwood, Thomas Pierce, and John Upham; doc. 1624, dated 4 April 1660, has testimonies from Attwood and Upham about eight acres out of the ten which Davis had plowed, of which three and a half had been sown with pease and wheat.

only doubt over Sister Brackenbury's motives was voiced by the less than reliable Paul Wilson. According to him, she came to realize the shortcomings of "the bargain, and she would endeavour to break it." In April 1660 Davis was awarded £4-10-0d damages and 1-15-5d costs.[24]

When he returned, William Brackenbury was flabbergasted. In March 1661 he brought an action to review the previous judgment, which was heard at the following June court. As well as copies of former depositions, he submitted a folio page in minuscule handwriting with point-by-point reassertion of the Brackenburys' case and rebuttal of Davis's complaints. He spent thirty-eight lines on the issue of breach of contract:

My wife did not have the power to end the contract. She spoke of the future . . . She did not mean she had finished with him, but that she would help him no more. No one molested or hindered him. He only offered to return after neighbors and others had given help . . . Samuel Davis said he would not give sixpence for what they had done after him. I said I would satisfy him for what he had done to the utmost. The reason he left was want of hay for his cattle and of residence and accommodation for himself. This is the truth; what is said concerning the covenant I desire to be proved by witnesses.[25]

The outcome of the case was ambiguous. The jury reversed the April 1660 judgment. They awarded Brackenbury damages of £6-0-5, with £1-1-6 costs. However, the bench "consented not." The arbitration of the Court of Assistants has not survived. Davis soon moved out to the new frontier settlement of Groton, but was driven back to Charlestown by King Philip's War, in which he served. In 1677 he was sued for the huge sum of £39 in unpaid taxes by Colony Treasurer James Russell, and charged with illegal grazing on the Stinted Common. Three years later his wife was accused of receiving stolen goods. All evidence points to the family's remaining poor.[26]

Meanwhile the Brackenburys burgeoned. Alice's son Samuel entered Harvard College in 1664, eventually practicing medicine in Boston. He married the daughter of Rev. Michael Wigglesworth, celebrated author of The Day of Doom. William Brackenbury died in August 1668; his estate was valued at £577, including £363 of real estate, £163-worth in Charlestown. Their house had nine rooms, and was valued at £70. His first bequest

---

[24] Docs. 1493, 1497, 1651, 1627; on Wilson, see "Common Rights" below.

[25] Doc. 1658.

[26] MxCC RB, 1: 231, 25 June 1661; D&O, 2: folio 43 has 2 January 1663 lease of Groton land; Mass Archives, 10 October 1667, "of Groton;" taxes: MxCC RB, 3: 203; illegal grazing: CTR, 3: 203, 2 July 1677; stolen goods: D&O, 4: folio 89, 5 April 1680.

was of £10 to his grandson Isaac Foster to buy books for his Harvard studies. Alice survived William for just over two years, dying on 28 December 1670, aged about seventy. She left £107 worth of real estate, twenty-five sheep, four cows, and sixty pounds of wool in a total inventory of £172. By the time of her death, her son and daughters had moved up the social scale: she remained Goody, my Dame or Sister, but they were addressed as Master or Mistress.[27]

Alice Brackenbury's role in the sharecropping fiasco with Samuel Davis proved ambiguous. As a "deputy husband," she assumed responsibility for monitoring, helping, warning, and finally terminating relations with the tenant. She was outspoken in her condemnation of his indolence, disobedience, deceit and selfishness. No one could be in any doubt about her disapproval. On the other hand, she was handicapped as a housekeeping wife in the husbanding world of arable farming. Part of Davis's arrogance arose from the fact that he was dealing with a woman. Brackenbury felt the need to summon male witnesses to give her account full credence. Without her sharecropper, she was dependent on neighbors for help on the land. Her returned husband had to rescue her from the lost lawsuit. To do so he had to put a patronizing gloss on her impetuosity: rephrasing what she really meant to say, making her appear muddle-headed and naive. It must have been profoundly galling for a woman of spirit and wealth to be put down by a young braggart, and then to need saving by a husband who had neglected to brief her properly on the all-important sharecropping agreement that caused all this trouble.[28]

Deputy husbands were not the only victims of this intergenerational conflict between the handless and the landless. Artisans were also vulnerable to sharecroppers' sharp practice. For instance, John Gould (1610–91), a town carpenter of modest means and a sullied reputation, made a "bargain" in 1675 with younger neighbor Nathaniel Smith, son of Michael Smith of Malden, to share a mixed crop of grain on part of Gould's "tenement." When the crop was harvested from the thirteen acres, however, Gould complained about short measure. When he attempted to "attach" three loads, he discovered that Nathaniel had already formally made them over to his brother. He had neglected several further obligations to Gould, who accused him of "juggling." Smith also threatened to burn down the

---

[27] Dr. Samuel Brackenbury died of smallpox in January 1678, Sibley. William's will and inventory: Rodgers, 2: 470–74; Alice's inventory: Rodgers, 3: 1–2; *GMB*, 199–202.

[28] Deputy husband: Laurel Thatcher Ulrich, *Good Wives* (New York: Oxford University Press, 1983) and *The Midwife's Tale* (New York: Vintage, 1991). See "Women: Conclusion."

barn where the disputed barley was stored "before [Gould] should have it." Again, the jury initially sided with the sharecropper, Smith; perhaps they were swayed by Gould's recent brush with Reading and Charlestown church authorities, or by his poverty. The verdict was similarly reversed at review.[29]

Like Samuel Davis, Nathaniel Smith was both irresponsible and slippery. Their swindles were ultimately recognized, but the trouble they caused was bound to deter other landlords. What seemed an ideal solution to land and labor "straitness" was not such a win-win situation after all.

---

[29]   MxCC D&O, 3: folios 72, 74; RB, 3: 135, 139; Hunnewell, v, reports Gould's admonition of 28 April 1667.

They Knew No Bounds:
The Blanchards

Every town in early New England had at least one problem family, whose name reappears in town, county, and colony records with wearisome monotony. At a safe remove three centuries later, we can chortle at the antics of some of these characters or admire their independence: the elderly William Knapp, for instance, offering to give a young woman a great "cleaving kiss" in comparison with the pathetic pecks of younger men, or the non-conformist Benanual Bowers's insubordinate verses ridiculing deputy governor Thomas Danforth, or cheeky glover Samuel Gibson appealing against mighty Harvard College's attempts to discipline him, and winning. Some recidivists were then and still seem tedious irritants: wasters of neighbors' time, property, and spirits, missing a social gene. Such were several of the Blanchards, and especially the eldest son of the clan, George (1622–1700).[30]

George was seventeen when he and his three brothers arrived in the Bay on the ship *Jonathan* in 1639. The father of the clan was Thomas Blanchard (ca. 1590–1654). It had been a traumatic voyage for him. Not only had his recently married second wife Agnes (Bent) (Barnes) and their baby died at sea, but Thomas had also nursed his mortally ill mother-in-law Agnes Bent, who died shortly after their arrival. Fellow passengers testified to his loving "care and pains for the old woman all the way . . . such that it was unseemly for a man to do, but no other" help was available. Blanchard became guardian of his stepson Richard Barnes.[31]

---

[30] Knapp: Thompson, *Sex,* 94, 101; Bowers: Thompson, *Cambridge Cameos,* 173–82; Gibson: ibid., 87–98, 289–94.

[31] Agnes Blanchard was the widow of John Barnes of Clanvill, near Andover, Hampshire. She had married Thomas Blanchard at nearby Penton Mewsey in May 1637, *R,* 68 (1914), 107; Black,

The Blanchards came from Clatford, near Andover, in the southern English county of Hampshire; the Bents had been a leading family in neighboring Weyhill and friends of the Noyes family. John Bent had come to New England the previous year (1638) from Southampton with his wife and five children, and sent home "for more of his family," his ailing mother Agnes and the Blanchard kin. Why the Blanchards stayed in Charlestown rather than joining the Bents in newly founded Sudbury is not known. They may have been too poor to move on. Peter Noyes had paid the fares of Agnes Bent, Agnes Blanchard, and Richard Barnes. Before the voyage, there had to be "a gathering [of money] among Christians in England to help [Blanchard] over." At sea, "he was conceived to be very poor and in great necessity by reason of his wife's and children's sickness, [so] that the passengers made a gathering for him in the ship to help put the child to nurse."

After seven years, Blanchard had recovered enough to move south to Braintree. By this time he had remarried a woman called Mary. The stay in Braintree only lasted four years; in 1650 or 1651 Thomas Blanchard bought a two-hundred-acre farm in Medford from Rev. John Wilson, the original grantee. There he specialized in raising cattle. He also helped raise Benjamin Thompson, the son of the depressive minister of Braintree. On 21 May 1654, the patriarch died at the age of about sixty-four. His dictated will both foreshadowed and caused the stream of problems that followed.[32]

After bequests of accommodation, cattle and corn to his widow Mary and son Samuel ("beside all former gifts now in his hands"), Thomas willed "all my farm, housing, and appurtenances" to George and Nathaniel, whom he appointed joint executors. However, possibly foreseeing trouble ahead, he also appointed his neighbor Mr. Edward Collins, purchaser of the Craddock estate in Medford, and Mr. Joseph Hills, a leading citizen of Malden, as overseers "to apportion the land and estate hereby disposed . . . and to settle all things as may be of doubtful understanding as to them shall seem just and equal for the establishment and preservation of peace, love and unity among all my relations." The house and ground

Goodman Ancestry, 82. On Blanchard's conflicts with the Bent, Noyes and Rutter kin concerning Richard Barnes's £20 legacy from his mother, see MxCC RB, 1: 38, 39; D&O, 1: docs. 163–192, 260–269, 5 October 1652; _Assistants_, 3: 19–21, 6 April 1653. Passengers: Thomas Call, doc. 183, Thomas Gould, doc. 192.

[32]   Fares and gatherings: _R_, 32 (1878) 409–411. Contrary to Savage, I have found no evidence of John Bent on the _Jonathan_. Farm: _Sfk Deeds_, 1: 223. Weyhill: S. C. Powell, _Puritan Village_ (New York: Doubleday, 1965), Ch. 1; Thompson, _Sex_, 56–59, 212–13. Cattle: Blanchard's 1654 probate inventory, in Rodgers 1: 159, listed 16 cows, 9 oxen and steers, 3 heifers, and 2 bullocks, all valued at £147-10-0. Thompson: Rodgers, 1: 157.

were valued at £300, out of a total estate of £642 on 25 May 1654. Thomas had certainly prospered in the New World.[33]

The following spring, at fencing and field-clearing time, the younger brother Nathaniel, who was only nineteen, requested the overseers to divide the farm's "meadow, planting ground, pasture, woodland, swamps, yards and orchards." Collins and Hills started at the front door post and plotted their lines to landmarks like "the great oak," "the landing place," "the highway," "Mr. Collins's line," and "the flax ground" for the two "dividends." Perhaps again predicting problems, they gave elder brother George (34) four days to make his choice in writing; otherwise Nathaniel should choose. Their last stipulation was that the fraternal division line in the corn ground and the pasture did not need to be fenced, but that external fences must be proportionately maintained. Sure enough, George failed to present his written choice, and Nathaniel took his pick on 10 March 1655.[34]

Seven years later, Hills and Collins fine-tuned the division, especially as to yards, highways and access. Another hand added an agreement about George Blanchard preparing "fencing stuff" and a new figure on the scene, Goodman Guppy, "setting up the fence on the new highway at the backside of the house." It is probable that the fine-tuning had been a response to questions raised by John Guppy in early 1661 at the time that he and Nathaniel Blanchard effected an exchange of land. Henceforward, Nathaniel moved to Guppy's spread at Weymouth (probable home of Nathaniel's wife Susan Bates and next door to Braintree) while Guppy took title to half the Blanchard Farm in Medford. Nathaniel may well have breathed a huge sigh of relief as he moved well away from his troublesome brother. Guppy was presumably unaware that he was about to take on the neighbor from hell.[35]

The character John Guppy was up against was scornfully described by George Blanchard's stepmother Mary, who had moved away from the Blanchard Farm to Noddle's Island by 1663. She told the Middlesex County Court on 16 June 1663 that executor George after nine years had still not paid his father's widow her legacy of £50. She described "sundry

---

[33]   Probate documents: Rodgers, 1: 156–66. Second son Thomas Blanchard Jr. had died at the age of 25 in 1650 at "Mystic" or Medford. His widow Hannah married Richard Gardiner the following year and moved to Woburn. Son Thomas left livestock valued at £105, but no real estate in his £240 inventory, Rodgers, 1: 45–47; he also left 38 debts totalling nearly £50. Thomas Sr. had acted as guardian for his two little grandchildren, Thomas Jr.'s daughters Mary and Sarah, and intervened with their new stepfather Gardiner to secure their legacies at the age of majority.

[34]   Rodgers, 1: 161–62.

[35]   Fine-tune: Rodgers, 1: 163–64; exchange: MxCC D&O, 3: folio 65, 25 March 1661. Susan Bates was probably a kinswoman of Edward Bates of Weymouth.

journeys, friendly demands, and proffers of arbitration . . . which [were only able] to extract deceitful promises from him which have issued to our great disappointment." She besought the court so to order things that the Blanchards would "not disturb or trouble the court or one another," but procure "the establishment of peace and quietness among us."[36]

George Blanchard's ability to disturb and trouble had already led his neighbor Mr. Edward Collins to sue him over faulty fences that let cattle wreak havoc on Collins's crops several times from 1655 to 1661. George was also reported for willfully destroying a section of fence in the winter of 1657. After Guppy's arrival, outbreaks escalated. On 17 June 1662, Guppy sued Blanchard for non-observation of their fencing agreement. Already in May a group of Charlestown selectmen had inspected the fence at issue. On 18 June, the Middlesex bench ordered Guppy and Blanchard to each post bond of £100 to accept arbitration. Thomas Danforth resurveyed and laid down a boundary line, and three experienced arbitrators issued detailed orders about fencing responsibilities, rights of way and payment of damages.

This disinterested ruling did not prevent George from (unsuccessfully) suing Guppy for mowing Blanchard grass on 16 June 1663, nor Guppy from counter-suing George for forcibly pulling up their dividing fence and allowing his "very unruly" oxen to trespass on Guppy's meadow. One of the oxen rooted out a post with his head and threw down the rails. Perhaps this was "Buck," named, along with "Spark," in Thomas Blanchard's will. Four oxen and other cattle had then strayed into brother Samuel's land, leaping over fencing, ravaging his corn and hayricks. In another confrontation, George had thrown down Guppy's fence across the divided farmyard and "pulled down Guppy's cow house in a rage." Constables, "artists," as surveyors were called, mowers, cattlemen, farm workers, and kinsfolk had all been sucked into this mini-cyclone.[37]

After a brief lull in 1664, when the Charlestown selectmen had stipulated the fencing proportions at "Wilson's Farm", Guppy and Blanchard renewed hostilities in 1665. On 17 July Guppy sued Blanchard for "striking him to the hazard of his life." Blanchard pled self-defense; his sister-in-law confirmed that Guppy had started the fight. The cause of the fisticuffs was predictably Blanchard's marauding oxen. Other neighbors also lost

---

[36]   Rodgers, 1: 167. She did not mention her legal action of 22 December 1656, and Samuel's of 18 April 1659, MxCC D&O, 1: docs. 619, 1161. Neither came to court, perhaps withdrawn thanks to "deceitful promises." The jury awarded Mary £42-15-0 damages and costs. In 1658, George was reported to be over £10 behind on his rates to the town, CTR, 1: 656, 28 August.

[37]   Collins: MxCC D&O, 1: docs 1590, 1596, 1621, 1710. "Buck": Rodgers, 1: 157. Guppy cases: MxCC D&O, 1: 2390–2411.

patience. Goodman Thomas Shepard won an arbitration award in 1665 about Blanchard's failed fencing obligations, and eventually Blanchard was forced to hand over some land in payment, which Shepard rapidly offloaded to ship's carpenter John Smith. Two years later, Smith sued Blanchard for £20 damages for mowing salt hay from Smith's marsh and for a debt; a leading witness was John Guppy. John Ball won another £6-9-0 in damages, a judgment Blanchard appealed. All round Blanchard's farm were neighbors aggrieved by his negligence, violence, trespassing, and shamelessness.[38]

Other Blanchard faults were presented to the County Court. In 1662 George Blanchard's wife had been persistently absent from church. She may have been drawn into Charlestown's Baptist cell by her sister-in-law Mary Sweetzer Blanchard, Samuel's wife, or she may have simply picked up her husband's slovenliness. In 1668 George neglected to pay his dues to the ministry. In 1671 he, too, was charged with absence from church, and then he missed his attendance at court. One of his children had been "put out" to the family of Samuel Sprague in 1665, but by 1672 Blanchard had not paid a penny of the £5 per year he owed. When dunned for the £25 debt, he promptly took the child away, even though he had been reported in 1671 for neglecting his children and their education. By the end of the 1660s, the Charlestown selectmen had resorted to seizing Blanchard's property, as the only way of making him pay.[39]

In addition to their perennial fencing strife, Guppy and Blanchard were also at odds about the precise bounds of twenty acres of meadow and marsh near the landing place. Guppy claimed four of these and took the valuable hay. Suit prompted counter-suit, new surveys had to check old, constables had to serve attachments and writs, one set of deeds had to be compared with another, and witnesses had to lose days of work tramping down to the court. A new player appeared in the fray: George's oldest son Joseph (1653–94). In October 1674 he was in the dock for having "molested" John Guppy, yanked out his fence posts, and scattered hay that he had just raked. He had to enter a £20 bond against further breaches of the

---

[38]   Guppy: MxCC D&O, 2: Folio 38; Shepard: CTR, 3: 181, MxD, 3: 170; Smith: MxCC D&O, 2: Folios 40, 41, 42, 43; Ball: ibid., Folio 43. Smith's account with George for his debt of £14 included money lent, several quantities of fish, items of clothing, sugar, cutting fencing stuff, rescuing an impounded ox, cutting firewood and board, helping with manuring, wages for his son's work, nursing a child, things borrowed from Goody Smith, and paying money owed to other people. The new neighbor seemed to have been conned into the role of supplier and benefactor to the whole Blanchard household, Folio 42.

[39]   Wife: MxCC D&O, 1: doc. 2101; dues: MxCC D&O, 2: folio 44; absent church & court, ibid., folio 55; Sprague: folio 59; child neglect: CTR, 3: 124; distraint, ibid., 92, 97, cf. folio 73.

peace. After eleven years of conflict, George Blanchard was arrested on 8 July 1674 as he ripped out of the ground a fifth surveyor's stakes "in a riotous manner," despite the presence and warnings of no less a figure of authority than the colony marshal. A few weeks later, Joseph was caught trying to pass counterfeit coins at pubs in Malden, Charlestown, and Boston. He too was arrested and remanded to prison.[40]

George Blanchard continued to irritate and infuriate fellow townspeople to the end of our period. Arbitrators were still working at the proportions of fencing on Blanchard Farm in 1683, more than twenty years after the first group was called in. Charlestown selectmen, exhausted by endless argument, appointed independent fence-viewers each year, and after 1674, they at least stilled the pugnacious John Guppy. Thereafter brother Samuel Blanchard bore the brunt of George's cussed indolence. George incurred a hefty fine in 1680 for failure to yoke, ring, and control his pigs. The next year seventeen-year-old Hannah Blanchard was part of the group of servants and adolescents involved with the unsavory Martin household. Two years later, her sister Bethia was presented for fornication. Parental neglect bequeathed a new generation of problems for the town.[41]

George Blanchard died in 1700 at the age of seventy-eight. He outlived his two eldest sons and two wives, but left a handsome £517 estate (£504 in real estate) to his eight surviving children, some of whom had married the children of neighbors who had earlier jousted with their father. Not atypically, his appraisers had great difficulty in tracing all his property, and his will when presented was disallowed by the probate court.[42]

Meanwhile, younger brother Samuel, who had suffered crop devastation from George's rambunctious cattle, gave the town the impression of greater responsibility. In 1657, at the age of twenty-seven, he was elected constable. However, he overreached himself with James Barrett. In his role as constable, he claimed that Barrett had stolen a horse and also had some of Blanchard's goods at his farm. Barrett sued for defamation and won damages of £3-5-6. Extracting his money proved to be a struggle. First Samuel tried to fob him off with a proposal to take the damages off Barrett's rates. After conceding payment in corn, he either missed appointments, brought

40   Meadow: MxCC RB, 3: 71, 78, 112; Joseph: ibid., 103; MxCC D&O, 2: folios 62, 63, 65, 66, 67; George's arrest: ibid., folio 67; counterfeit: folio 67, *Assistants*, 1: 22; Mass. Archives, 26 August 1674.

41   Arbitrators and Samuel: CTR, 3: 181, 191, 197; CTR, 4: 54, 56. Swine: CTR, 4: 26. Hannah: MxCC D&O, 4: folio 94; Bethia: D&O, 5: folio 105.

42   Marriage: Joseph married Hannah Shepard, and Hannah Blanchard married Shepard's brother Thomas Shepard Jr.; Rachel married John Smith, Jr. Wyman, 88–89. Probate: MxW 1870.

no "prizer" for valuing the corn, had no corn ready, demanded to have a legal bill, or refused to do business after sundown. One witness spoke of a "skirmish," of Barrett's band torn to pieces and "how blood did spring out of his face." It was nearly thirty years before Samuel was entrusted with serious responsibility again, as a trial juror in 1676 and 1677.[43]

As if Edward Collins's troubles with George's cattle were not enough, he had to impound five stray oxen and a steer of Samuel's in 1661. The defendant had to pay £3 damages and £1-2-4 costs. Samuel's fencing was judged deficient three more times in the next twenty-four years. He also refused or neglected to pay his assessment for the ministry, and by 1668 was £4 in arrears. He too may have been a Baptist sympathizer.[44]

The biggest test of his responsibility came with his appointment as executor of the estate of William Goodwin, a single man who sometimes worked for the Blanchards and was drowned at the age of seventy in 1666. Resident magistrates Willoughby and Russell were alarmed at the potential mismanagement and loss of property and papers in Samuel's custody, and appointed three leading townsmen as overseers. Goodwin's inventory was taken by these three; his assets were mainly loans totalling nearly £138, most of which was to go to the schooling of poor children of Malden and Charlestown. Samuel found himself trying to recover these debts from some very slippery Boston businessmen. This involved negotiation and arbitration in various Charlestown and Boston pubs. For instance, Blanchard had a bill for £10-6-4 which Goodwin had lent Thomas Hawkins in 1659. They met by appointment at Mrs. Long's "Three Cranes" and "exchanged a piece of money each to other" as an undertaking to stand by the arbitration or forfeit £20. Blanchard presented the bill, but the legalistic Hawkins pointed out that it was owed only to Goodwin because there was no mention of "heirs, assigns or attorneys," and was in any case invalid because it had no witnesses. Hawkins also produced his account book showing repayment of all but 17 shillings and three pence, and offered to attest to it. The arbitrators could not agree, and two more expensive meetings had to convene. In the end Samuel had to go to court, but the costs more than canceled out the amount recovered. Nonetheless, Samuel took his executorship seriously, and persisted in recovering what he could of the Goodwin estate. Thereby, he redeemed to some extent the Blanchard family reputation so besmirched by his elder brother.[45]

---

[43] Barrett: MxCC RB, 1: 132, 143; MxCC D&O, 1: docs. 945–50, 1022.

[44] Collins: MxCC RB, 1: 236, 238, 284. Fencing: CTR, 3: 181; CTR, 4: 54; MxCC D&O, 2: folio 60. Ministry: ibid., folio 44, CTR, 3: 94.

[45] Rodgers, 2: 312–15; MxCC D&O, 2: folio 43. Cf. Ralph Shepard debt, folio 40, Edward Page debt, folio 43.

Why did George Blanchard behave the way he did, with seemingly total disregard of his fellow townsmen, clashing not only with immediate neighbors great and small, but also marshals, selectmen, arbitrators, bondsmen, constables, surveyors, fence-viewers, church rate collectors, and field drivers? He certainly did not inherit his behaviour from his father, who was a highly responsible, trusted, and caring individual. Plainly George's personality (however formed or damaged) was the major reason—a poisonous mixture of idleness, carelessness, outrage, and insensitivity with a slithery instinct to evade, escape, and deny the effects of his actions, or more often his inactions. His classic pattern was to fall foul of a neighbor and resist (sometimes violently) demands for restitution, so that authority had to step in. He would agree to arbitration, enter bond to accept the award, and then, when it went against him, renege on the agreement, refuse to honor the bond, and resist by any and every means making restitution. Two town officials wrote that after one such bout with Blanchard, they would rather pay a part of what he owed than go through the experience again.[46]

In mitigation, he did own a large extent of land in a thinly populated area with long, uncertain boundaries to be maintained. He also had a considerable herd of cattle and other livestock to sustain and control. He lived on the edges of Charlestown and Medford, away from close neighborly contact in town and a sense of belonging. Although he left a small fortune, a most unusual proportion of it was in land. In 1666 two exhausted arbitrators referred to "defendant's condition" as their reason for reducing his obligation. The method of payment they stipulated was work and timber rather than the more usual cash, corn, or cloth. George may have been land-rich but cash-poor. He was certainly deeply reluctant to sell any land, and showed unwonted vigor in his fight to secure his twenty acres of marsh. In fact, his and his son's frequent uprooting of boundaries suggests that every inch of land was invaluable. Land to accumulate, to retain and to pass on to his numerous progeny: this seems to have been his main activating motive, perhaps his only one. It ultimately served him and his family well, though his consuming passion made his name a byword for trouble to the people of Charlestown.[47]

---

[46] Solomon Phipps and Randall Nicholls, 17 December 1666, MxCC D&O, 2: folio 41.

[47] Arbitrators: ibid.

Lowden's Wall, 1679

Among the busiest places in Charlestown were the various town landing places where the rivers met the land. Such were the perils of transport over land, along so-called "highways" which were in fact rutted, potholed, and often waterlogged cart tracks, that many townspeople preferred water-borne carriage of many goods, especially heavy or bulky loads like wood, timber or hay. As we have seen, waterfront property was essential for merchants, shipbuilders, and other artisans, and was rapidly taken up all along the southwestern peninsular shoreline. During the 1640s, land along the northeastern shore was also occupied (See Land, and Map 2).

One such occupier was Mr. George Bunker, who had a house, yard, and two-acre homelot "in East Field on the highway to Mystic River." On 9 January 1647 the selectmen agreed to grant him a piece of ground near the Landing Place at the Neck, provided "he leave sufficient highway." This was where the Penny Ferry crossed the Mystic to Charlestown's Mystic Side with its arable, haygrounds and woodlots, and routes to the northeast. On this land, Bunker built a barn with a yard. Part of the Symmes Company from Bedfordshire, he had arrived with his wife Judith and five children in 1634. He quickly became a town leader and a major landowner, especially in East Field, with lots running up and over the hill that bears his name in High Field, just beyond the Neck and on Mystic Side. He also had interests in Malden. Two more sons were born to Judith Bunker in Charlestown, the youngest, Jonathan, in 1638. Even after endowing his five eldest children, he still left £314 when he died in 1664. In his will, Bunker left Jonathan (whom he appointed executor) a "portion" of £75. The previous year, Jonathan (aged twenty-five) had married Mary Howard. They lived together for the next 15 years until Jonathan's death in 1678. He is not listed among the many smallpox victims of that terrible year, unlike his sister-in-law Sarah Howard. Although he was only forty when he died, Jonathan had amassed a small fortune of £606. His widow Mary was executrix of the estate. In 1679 she took a new husband, James Lowden (1647–1740), a wheelwright and son of shipwright and leading citizen Sergeant Richard Lowden (1613–1700).[48]

James Lowden took over running Jonathan Bunker's land, including the grant by the Neck Landing Place. Very shortly thereafter, trouble began. With the zest of a new landholder and the bumptiousness of a new husband, he decided to build a wall along his boundary with the access track to the landing place. His father and other kin and neighbors assured him that the proposed line of the wall was fine. It was on land "quietly possessed and improved by George then Jonathan Bunker before 1652 . . . there was sufficient [room] for three carts abreast on the way." The wall went up.[49]

Shortly after he had finished, James received a visit from Thomas Crosswell, 46, and Nathaniel Rand, 44, surveyors of highways, along with other experienced carriers. They told him that "they had been employed carting hay, wood and timber for 27 years. They had never been interrupted by any man from improving it as town land; where the stone wall stands was a choice place of carting up the beach." Others corroborated Lowden's encroachment. Carpenter Solomon Phipps (ca. 34) remembered Jonathan Bunker telling him shortly before he died that "he had no right to the [cartway] land, but he had to maintain a fence from the landing place to his yard." Young Thomas Welch Jr., 22, had "come to the landing place with a raft of timber. In carting it, I was straitened for room, and asked Jonathan Bunker if he might lay a few logs by his barn. He said that I had as much right to lay logs as he had; he had only five feet [from his barn]." This was completely at odds with the Lowdens' view. Richard, a resident for 40 years, asserted that "part of this land which [the authorities] brought testimony to prove the town's possession so long was part of Mr. Bunker's first purchased land; the town possessed it no other ways but upon sufferance and as trespassers."[50]

---

48 House: Hunnewell, 111; grant: MxCC D&O, 4: Folio 87, which has the documents in this case; land: *GM*, 1: 483–85; his 1635 grant of haylots (15 acres), his 1637 and 1638 cow commons (10, 15), and his 1638 Mystic Side lots (260 acres) were each the largest allotments, exceeding even magistrate Increase Nowell's. CTR 1A: 32, 58, 64. In his probate documents, *GM*, 1: 485, Bunker is described as "of Malden." Smallpox: Samuel A. Green, "Diary of Captain Lawrence Hammond," 2 *MHSP*, 7 (1892): 169, 22 January 1678. Fortune: MxCC D&O, 4: Folio 82. Jonathan, as we shall see, was associated with the Baptist cell in Charlestown. Lowdens: Wyman: 632–33.

49 Tests. Richard Lowden, 64, John Fowle, 40, and Nathaniel Howard, 38.

50 Richard Lowden test: Folio 86.

Soon the selectmen were drawn into the dispute. Accounts of a meeting at Richard Lowden's also differ. Michael Willis, 26, James's brother-in-law, recalled Lowden offering to remove his wall at his own expense, provided that the land remained Bunker property. The selectmen refused. Their minutes of the meeting read: "James Lowden's fence so straitens the place as to be wholly insufficient for the town's landing place. James Lowden refused to move the fence, and therefore the selectmen ordered the Surveyors of Highways to remove it." On 16 December 1679, James sued Crosswell and Rand for damages incurred by removal of "a parcel of stone wall."

The trial jury was nonplussed by such directly contradictory evidence. They therefore returned a special verdict: "If a man possessed [occupied] land before 1652 and since in his enclosed lines, does it give him legal title? If so, for the plaintiff; if not, for the defendants." The bench decided for the surveyors, awarding 19 shillings four pence costs. Richard Lowden was required to enter £10 surety on behalf of his son "that all fences from 1 May 1680 will be set as they were in Bunker's time." On 5 July 1680, when tempers had cooled, the selectmen and James Lowden agreed on the fence line at the Landing Place and the requisite orders were issued.[51]

Given the prevalence of intense territoriality to be encountered in the fracas, when Thomas Waffe started hacking away at Richard Martin's house which he deemed to have encroached on his family's land, this case of boundary creep had serious communal impact. The original grant seems never to have been surveyed or staked out. Rather, "sufficient highway" was the criterion for town access, and Lowden's and the surveyors' measure of sufficiency clearly differed. The bench doubted that Bunker had been granted the highway area, and, even if he had, that he had any title to it (and could thus fence it in). The word "possession" implies occupation and could be used of a tenant or a squatter; title gives ownership.[52]

Just as an aggrieved landowner like George Blanchard or anti-enclosure rioters in seventeenth-century England could throw down fences erected by authority, so, here, authority could throw down a wall that aggrieved town claims and interests. Young James Lowden may have landed himself a wealthy widow, but he had to learn the hard way that there was nothing so dangerous to meddle with as a traditional boundary line and right of way.[53]

---

[51] MxCC RB, 4: 298; CTR, 4: 25.

[52] See "Seadogs' Land War, 1676." Again, we see the crucial difference between Richard Lowden's recollection and the verified copy of the selectmen's minutes from the town records for 9 January 1647.

[53] See "They Knew No Bounds" and "Common Rights."

Common Rights, 1686

On 3 February 1686, a group of eleven townsmen marched out to the John Mousall lot on Twopenny Brook Plain (see Map 2), formerly part of the town grazing common, with axes, saws and sleds. Some began felling "a parcel of wood" including a valuable great white oak and another "great tree," while others logged the timber, loaded it on sleds and dragged it away. They made no attempt to hide what they were doing; indeed, their leader Samuel Whittemore had threatened to cut down twenty trees in the coming week. Rather, they were "tumultuous," almost riotous. One of them, Paul Wilson, was especially vocal: "Before he would lose his interest in the common, he would spend his house and land and tack his wife and children and show the townsmen (selectmen), and go to England to the king that now is and say 'Good King James, have mercy upon thy poor subjects that have been in exile with you, and if you will hang me I will die like a man rather than be gnawn to pieces by a crew of rats.'" He added several other unrecorded "threatening words." The wood belonging to John Cutler, Jr. was raided six weeks later on 16 March 1686. When he attempted to recover the "stolen" timber, he was forcibly prevented.[54]

As Cutler, Mousall's attorney, told the Court on 6 April 1686, these "high-handed" gestures were "not just about a tree." The very public defiance of the men charged with trespass, cutting, and carting was the culmination of months of rising tension in Charlestown about the division of the Stinted Common into individual holdings, and of decades of rivalry between proprietors and non-proprietors. This February incident did not

---

[54] Depositions in this case are in MxCC D&O, 5: Folio 122, and CTR, 4: 67–75; Wilson: test. Samuel Read, 29, 6 April 1686; prevented: MxCC RB, 4: 222. "Tack": Wilson, a herdsman, may have meant "put out" to the care of another family, *OED*. Exile: James had been abroad during the Civil War and Interregnum, ca. 1642–1660, and more recently in Scotland during the Exclusion Crisis, 1678–81.

just involve the Middlesex County Court. The axemen felt so powerfully about the justice of their cause that they had sought the intervention of the General Court. Their opponents had countered with a petition to the new royal council. Nor was Charlestown alone; neighboring Cambridge also experienced a similar outburst from inhabitants who thought themselves deprived of their rights. In broader terms, this conflict reflected a contest between communal and private property rights that had been slugged out since the later Middle Ages in countless English parishes and manors, equity and common law courts, populist and conservative manifestos, and radical, religious, and parliamentary debates. The laconic comment of Frothingham (a descendant of a Proprietorial Overseer of the Stinted Common) that "there was much controversy for a few years about the division of the Stinted Common" needs considerable elaboration.[55]

In 1637, Charlestown's grazing common, on the Mainland (roughly modern Somerville), was assigned by the town meeting to a hundred and thirteen inhabitants, known as the Proprietors. As was usual in England, the pasture was "stinted" or rationed to its proprietors, according to their number of "Cow Commons." A 1658 list of 192 families computed the total cow commons as 664, around three and a half per household on average, though some inhabitants owned considerably more, and many owned less. Cow commons were family property. They could be bought, sold, leased (to a fellow townsman), or passed to a member of the next generation. Nonproprietors who did not own cow commons were forbidden to graze any stock on the nearly two thousand acres. For much of our period the proprietors delegated the administration of the Stinted Common to the selectmen. Each year four or five overseers were appointed to maintain the outside fence and gates; to provide watering places for cattle; to impound any illegal grazers, and fine or prosecute their owners. In this responsibility they proved alert and aggressive; not even Deputy Governor Danforth escaped their vigilance. Proprietorial privilege was jealously guarded.[56]

A persistent problem involved the boundary between the Stinted Common and Ten Hills Farm, granted to Governor Winthrop in 1630 and leased to various tenants. Two arrangements were tried. The first was to graze "in common" with the farm, giving the owner a number of cow commons and

---

[55] General Court: *MR,* 5: 486, 4 June 1685; Cambridge: Thompson, *Cambridge Cameos,* 249–55; Frothingham, 185. Council: see below.

[56] Stinted Common regulations: e.g. CTR, 1: 658, 3: 65, 149, 150, and passim; Danforth: Thompson, *Cambridge Cameos,* 235–38. More: John Allen 17, Richard Russell 16, Francis Norton 15½, Nicholas Davison and Richard Sprague 15. Less: 38 young or poor men and widows only had one cow common each.

not bothering with fences. Given responsible tenants, this worked well, but renters like Benanuel Bowers, who insinuated an excessive two hundred sheep onto the common, destroyed the mutual trust. The alternative was for the proprietors to share fencing responsibilities with the Ten Hills tenant, which led to the usual recriminations. In 1662, Captain Richard Sprague undertook to fence and maintain the boundary for twenty-one years in return for twenty cow commons. Alas, he died six years later and his widow relinquished the responsibility and the cow commons in 1672. Every year, the protection and administration of the common pasture took up a considerable part of the selectmen's and overseers' time, but given the size and value of this resource, they must have felt it was time well spent. [57]

Charlestown's common was not just a grazing asset, however. The huge area contained other valuable necessities: timber, firewood, stone, sand, gravel, and clay. Ancient English custom decreed that these should be enjoyed by the community as common rights. Because of their value for building ships and houses, the town agreed that certain trees or types of timber could be reserved by the selectmen. At various times, tree wardens were appointed to mark special trees and to police illicit cutting. There was a major clamp-down against filchers of swamp cedar in 1673, for instance, when nineteen people were prosecuted and fined. Selectmen's meetings regularly issued tickets for specified felling, often to woodworking artisans. On 6 February 1682, the selectmen made custom explicit with an order allowing all unmarked wood to be cut on the Stinted Common. Occasionally non-townspeople were licensed to quarry stone at set prices. In 1681, three Charlestown masons had to be cautioned by the selectmen after pitching quarry spoil into each other's diggings by Twopenny Brook. Although the jealously guarded proprietorship must have caused resentment among the excluded, who would have had to rent common grazing or pasture their stock on their own enclosed land, the Stinted Common, privileging rationed grazing but allowing other common rights to all townspeople, appears to have operated pretty effectively until 1680. English people, after all, had generations of experience of the system. Then, starting on 14 February 1680, various decisions were reached which led to the tumult of 1686 and ongoing ructions.[58]

---

[57]   Ten Hills was inherited by John Winthrop Jr., and then by Waitstill and Fitzjohn, his sons; by the 1680s the owners were Elizabeth Lidgett Saffin and her son Charles Lidgett, Bowers's landlord, MxD, 6: 90, Winthrops to Lidgett, 1677, MxCC D&O 4: folio 100; Sprague: CTR, 3: 33, 129. Common grazing: e.g., CTR, 3: 135; 4: 47; fencing problems: e.g. MxCC RB, 1: 181; D&O, 1: doc. 1153; CTR, 1: 643; 4: 69.

[58]   On 3 January 1657 the town meeting agreed to apportion land on Mystic Side into woodlots; grants were proportional to cow commons held. However, the lots would remain "of commonage," or unfenced. Lots and trees there could not be sold to non-townspeople; the division

Under the heading "Doings of the Proprietors of the Stinted Pasture 1680–86" in the town's *Book of Possessions*, the first "doing" is recorded as done on 14 February 1680: a meeting of the proprietors "as to laying out part of it ... 1½ acres to a [cow] common ... in the near or hither part ... in fee simple [freehold]." On 2 January 1681, the proprietors' management committee registered 331 cow commons as belonging to 104 proprietors; most qualified for two to five acres. Nearly two years later, on 4 September 1682, the two overseers reported that Ensign Fiske the Lexington "artist" had surveyed the Stinted Common the previous year as containing 1780 acres, and that so far "not above 300 acres [of the hither part] had been taken up or fenced in." Nothing in court or town records indicates the reason behind this modest privatization, though trouble with Benanuel Bowers at Ten Hills Farm, abutting the near common, especially his invitation to Cambridge men to "hire commons of him ... and turn in their cattle on the common" is recorded in the County Court files under the same date as a copy of the 14 February 1680 privatization decision.[59]

The first major disagreement involved the selectmen's sale of five and a half acres of the Stinted Common on 29 February 1684 to Deputy Governor Thomas Danforth, whose large Cambridge farm abutted it. He had paid £21 in cash on 30 October 1682. The title was delivered to him on 3 April 1684 by four wealthy townsmen. This was not a popular move. Danforth had already provoked the overseers in 1681 with his straying horses. Now, on 24 June 1684, at the end of new instructions from the proprietors to its committee of management was the item that they should reconcile those proprietors unhappy with the sale of a town asset to a "foreigner," however grand. The provision that proprietorial voting was counted according to cow commons rather than heads may explain both the passage of the sale—rich favor the rich, even from Cambridge—and the opposition, by the less well endowed.[60]

Two weeks later, the "dissatisfied" had "much discourse" and made "sundry proposals," one of which was that Danforth's land and two cow

remained only a paper one until 1685. CTR, 1: 647. Tickets: e.g. CTR, 3: 37, 69; wardens: CTR, 3: 130; 4: 26, in both cases, John Mousall appointed. Stone: CTR, 3: 96, 112, 132, 134; quarry fight: CTR, 4: 27. Fines: cedar: CTR, 3: 142; other: CTR, 4: 4, 38, 42, 67. Non-townspeople: William Dixon of Cambridge was allowed to include his 12-acre pasture in the Stinted Common, with three cow commons, and allowed to take stones for his fencing, but he was specifically denied rights of commonage. CTR, 4: 45, 59.

[59]   *Book of Possessions*, 188–93, 195; MxCC D&O, 4: folio 100, 17 June 1682.

[60]   Sale: CTR, 4: 59, 60, 62; provoked: Thompson, *Cambridge Cameos*, 235–239; rich: James Russell, Richard Sprague, Joseph Lynde and John Cutler Jr.; named opponents: James Lowden, a wheelwright, Thomas Welch Jr., a stonecutter, and Samuel Read, a disabled war veteran, formerly of Mendon, who had bought land from John Mousall in 1680, and later married his daughter, *MR*, 5: 316, 454, 471, 485, 511, Mx D, 7: 361, Mx W: 15619.

commons should be bought back. If the majority of proprietors (voting by cow common) disagreed with this, then the dissatisfied should pay their own money proportional to their cow commons to recover the land. The last sentence of the minutes is full of foreboding: "Whenever the Common shall be divided, [the buyers back] shall have so much land laid out to them more than to others according to proportion of said land laid down in common." This is the first intimation that further division of the Stinted Common was an option.[61]

At this chronological point in the town minutes, the leaves of the original town record book became victims of "an audacious mutilation, or rather destruction. This escaped notice of officials until 1792." The intrepid editor, H. H. Edes, found eight missing leaves in the early 1870s "at the bottom of a barrel of miscellaneous materials" in the town clerk's office. They had been copied in a later hand. He reinserted them in the record book from which the originals had been torn. The date of and motives for their removal are unknown.[62]

The restored leaves record the momentous events of 1685. On the very first entry of the year, a young man recently arrived in Charlestown was caught "bringing away parcels of trees" from the common. The selectmen deemed his reaction contemptuous, and he was fined the considerable sum of £1. This was in spite of the fact that he had been "sore wounded in the Indian Wars." [63]

On 10 March 1685, at the time in the farming year when orders were issued about fences, grazing, oversight of livestock, and clearing arable fields, the Proprietors of the Stinted Common met and voted in principle to divide the whole remaining common into lots for individual proprietors. After a majority of cow commons agreed, a town meeting ensued at which the selectmen proposed that the woodlots on Mystic Side assigned on paper to families way back on 30 January 1657 should be laid out on the ground.[64]

Two and a half weeks later, on 27 March 1685, the Proprietors again met. They appointed a five-man committee charged with laying out the individual lots on the Stinted Common. Quite detailed instructions were included for the surveyor and the chain carrier about the area to be lotted

[61] CTR, 4: 62.

[62] Editorial comment after CTR, 4: 64. Edes: see "Introduction."

[63] CTR, 4: 67; he was Samuel Read (ca. 1656–95+), one of the three named objectors to the Danforth sale. The 1685–86 dispute about the Stinted Common is discussed in T. H. Breen, *Puritans and Adventurers* (New York: Oxford University Press, 1980), 90–92.

[64] CTR, 4: 68; *Book of Possessions*, 196.

out. Tree warden John Mousall was to warn proprietors the night before their proportional lots were due to be staked out, and was to accompany the surveyor. The expenses of this complex operation were to be met proportionately by the proprietors.[65]

Though news of these proprietorial votes must have fizzed around the town, the remaining inhabitants were not officially informed for another 19 days. On 15 April 1685, the selectmen put a legalistically worded series of proposals about common rights to the town meeting. They conceded that up to then all inhabitants had had a "general privilege on the Stinted Common or Pasture to cut wood, get stones, sand and clay." In order that "peace and love may be promoted and continued and all future troubles prevented," the selectmen specified certain common rights that would remain after the enclosure of the common: range and country highways through the common, two river landing places, ten acres at the stone quarry on Twopenny Brook, another ten at the Rocks by Patrick Mark's, the militia training ground, land dedicated to subsidizing the town school, clay pits, sand pits, and watering places. Any questions about claims to wood should be negotiated with the selectmen, who were empowered to sell wood on the privatized lots to the individual owners. The proposals concluded: "This shall be a final conclusion between us [the Proprietors] and them [other inhabitants]. Any further claims [rights] remain unto the Proprietors' good estate in fee simple [freehold] to them to use and improve as they shall see cause." The meeting was invited to vote on this and the inhabitants to "acquit [give up] any further claim in said Stinted Pasture to herbage, stone, clay, wood, sand or watering places." According to John Newell, the town clerk, "This voted by the inhabitants that were present."[66]

The Charlestown Town Record Book contains nothing more about the Stinted Common. However, two other sources fill the gap. The files of the Middlesex County Court have, on the same date as the town vote to accept the division, 15 April 1685, a document headed "Exception by the Inhabitants of Charlestown against the Proprietors of the Stinted Common, and Declaration." The 24 signatories assert that "neither they nor their heirs would directly or indirectly part with [any] privilege of wood, stone, clay or sand conveyed to them by their predecessors who did quietly enjoy it and they their successors for many years past." The copy forwarded to the General Court has appended: "20 persons more proffered to record their protests against the proprietors' proceedings in dividing the

---

[65]   *Book of Possessions*, 196; CTR, 4: 69.

[66]   CTR, 4: 72–75; *Book of Possessions*, 203.

common. The clerk could not attend [wait] to enter the other names." This was signed by Samuel Whittemore. Copies from Charlestown town records in the court files also show that as well as the objecting inhabitants, some proprietors had also opposed the division of the Stinted Common. Three holding small proportions objected at the Proprietors' meeting on 10 March 1685, and three more signed the Exception.[67]

The Stinted Common Proprietors' records, our second substitute source, reveal intense activity following the fateful 15 April 1685 Town Meeting. The very next day, the surveyor Fiske began the work of measuring and staking out the individual lots. The town and proprietors' Clerk John Newell listed the 1141 acres of grants to the 101 listed proprietors. Each cow common was worth three and a half acres, and though the average allocation was about eleven acres, or just over three cow commons, the grants ranged from one of fifty-seven acres down to the humble twenty who only received three and a half.[68]

On 27 May 1685, the scene shifted to the Massachusetts General Court. The "Inhabitants of Charlestown" presented a petition describing how they had been oppressed by their neighbors, the "so-called" Proprietors, who had already "fenced in hundreds of acres to particular lots and so have cut off all the rest of the inhabitants from all privileges they presently enjoyed." The original stinting had been the oligarchic proportioning by the elite, and some of the lesser sort, dissatisfied with their assigned shares, had sold up in an atmosphere of "great striving in those days . . . to get commons." The "deprived inhabitants judg[ing] ourselves to be the greatest part of the town and likewise suppos[ing] we do pay the greatest part of all rates and taxes," moved on to their requests. Since those in authority "should take care that things may be so ordered for the good of the whole family," and since the many poor already in Charlestown "are like to increase by these means," the signers ask the Court to "cause the Proprietors (as they call themselves) to return to us our rights and privileges to the Common." A barely veiled threat follows. If the General Court refuses to act, the petitioners will send an "address to the Supreme power," the King, to safeguard English privileges here, "namely free commons to poor as well as rich. If they in England

---

[67]   MxCC D&O, 5: Folio 122; Mass Archives, 15 April 1685; objectors, Thomas Welch Jr., 1⅜ cow commons, Caleb Carter, 1¼, and Josiah Wood Sr., 6; three signers of the Exception: Thomas Carter Sr., John Burrage, John Penticost. Five other notables, Captain John Phillips, Mr. Solomon Phipps, Josiah Wood, Mr. Jonathan Carey, and Samuel Kettle were subsequently named as dissatisfied proprietors, but this may have referred to their allotments, *Book of Possessions*, 204–5, 8 March 1686.

[68]   Ibid., 196–202, 204.

should go about to work as our proprietors have done and still do, they might ever so well hang up the poor [on the gallows] . . . as let them live amongst them to be starved." Kings and states, they assert, are especially responsible "for the livelihood of their poorest subjects." Denying that they ever agreed to the enclosure of the Stinted Common, the petitioners remind the Court that five of its members have personal interests in the divided common. The Court was not moved. A week later, they referred the petitioners "to common law," that is to the Middlesex County Court. On critical issues, individuals or groups regularly petitioned the General Court. Here the Court rejected the petition.[69]

From June 1685 to February 1686, I have found no record of further legal action. The petitioners had been rejected by the General Court. They did not expect anything but "trouble and molestation" from the County Court. Their legal impotence was emphasized when the Charlestown selectmen began on 15 January 1686 to sell off the common wood to individual lot owners. By 2 February 1686, four sales at knockdown prices had satisfied thirty-five owners. Seeing this wanton squandering of town assets, the protesters must have concluded that direct action was their only recourse. Thus the next day's laying of axes on John Mousall's trees, and later, on the younger John Cutler's. The threats against others followed, along with the "great disrespect and contempt to authority," an abortive attempt on 2 April 1686 by the Commissioners for Small Causes to deal with the protest, and the county court case of 6 and 15 April.[70]

For this legal confrontation, both sides worked busily to gather evidence. In all, thirty-four witnesses testified and thirty-three documents were copied to the record, out of fifty consulted from town, county, and colony records. The first plaintiff John Mousall appointed John Cutler Jr. as his attorney. Since there was little doubt about the offending act, much of Cutler's case was based on documentary evidence proving Mousall's ownership of the land and its wood, his cow commons inherited from his father Deacon Ralph, and on the selectmen's and proprietors' legal control over the Stinted Common, its timber, land grants and commonage. Ancient inhabitants like Edward Brasier, 86, William Stitson, 85, and John Penticost, 84, confirmed proprietorial control of the common ever since 1637. Cutler gave the lie to the petitioners' claim that they paid the majority of town rates by

---

[69]   Mass. Archives, 27 May 1685; *MR*, 5: 486, 4 June 1685. The petition had specifically asked that the Court should not refer the issue to the County Court. Five: Thomas Danforth, Samuel Nowell, James Russell, Richard Sprague, and John Phillips. On petitioning, see D. D. Hall, *A Reforming People* (New York: Knopf, 2011), 87–92.

[70]   *Book of Possessions*, 203.

listing the paltry sums levied in 1685 on some of the leading protesters. He also cited the fine levied on an opponent a decade earlier for illegal felling on the common. The plaintiff's declaration to the court radiated outrage: the defendants "combined together in a tumultuous manner little if at all differing from a riot, against all the rules of order, law and justice . . . high-handedly opposing themselves to the peaceful execution of town orders." The plaintiff sought to maintain "the King's peace and good government against disorder and confusion." The defendants' claims of title to timber on the common were, Cutler concluded, risible in the face of the documents he had submitted. Cutler's case was similar to what a modern attorney might argue, based on written records and town regulations. His self-satisfied tone and ponderous scorn would not be out of place in a court today. His approach completely ignored the principled arguments based on English custom advanced by the petitioners.[71]

The defendants' arguments centered on the town meeting of 15 April 1685, when the proposals to privatize the common were presented to non-proprietor townspeople. Five inhabitants deposed that they had not been legally notified of the meeting. Three senior inhabitants swore that most or all non-proprietors refused to accept the plan, and some proprietors also withdrew when it went to the vote. Another older resident described the non-commoners' refusal to part with their privileges on any account, and their being told by the moderator, Mr. Joseph Lynde, that "they should have nothing if they would not accept of these proposals." Another attender deposed that the protesters also refused to leave arrangements about wood on the common to the selectmen, and desired the town clerk to enter their protest. The enclosure of the town's Stinted Common had been rammed through a town meeting where major decisions were traditionally expected to be consensual.[72]

The statement of the defendants to the Commissioners for Small Causes on 2 April 1686 epitomizes their viewpoint. They asserted the "liberty that all Englishmen and His Majesty's subjects ought to have, but they had not": two weeks to answer properly drafted charges. They stoutly justified their actions: "What was done was not done feloniously, but openly, and that upon a claim of interest and property in the land on which the wood grew." Such behaviour should not be summarily judged by commis-

---

[71]   Fine: Josiah Wood, Sr. on 19 Jan 1674, CTR, 3: 156.

[72]   Five: Joseph Lamson, Steven Paine, John Pratt, Thomas Barber, Steven Barrett; three: Joseph Kettle, Nathaniel Frothingham Sr., Thomas White Sr.; another older: Patrick Mark; attender: Nathaniel Davis.

sioners, but was "triable before our peers, viz. twelve honest men of the vicinage . . . We desire the liberty of the law."[73]

The jury found for Mousall in a specimen case against Samuel Whittemore. The land and the wood, they were persuaded, belonged to the plaintiff; they awarded him five shillings damages and costs, which Cutler computed at the hefty sum of £4-19-10 (another modern touch!) Edward Wyer Jr. and John Bennett, who had cut and carried wood from Cutler's lot at Winter Hill, were also found guilty. This time they were also convicted of using threatening words against the constable. When told that the timber was Cutler's, they had replied "Prove it!" They were fined ten shillings each, as well as £1-11-0 costs and damages. The defendants promptly appealed to the Court of Assistants, but outside events overtook the Charlestown confrontation. On 17 September 1686, a new interim regime, the Royal Council for New England, issued a new kind of writ, a *scire facias*, for the appearance at a new court, the Court of Pleas at Cambridge, to Samuel Whittemore, Edward Wyer Jr., and John Bennett. On 1 October they were to "show cause why execution should not be granted forth" for payment of costs to Mousall and Cutler. On 8 December 1686, the Colony Treasurer and the Clerk of the Council were instructed to arbitrate court costs from an appeal court case brought by John Cutler and others of Charlestown. A week later, "several gentlemen of Charlestown petitioned concerning several persons trespassing on their proprieties." One of the Council's last acts before the arrival of royal governor Sir Edmund Andros was to appoint a committee to go to Charlestown and hear both sides. Thereafter the actions disappear from court records, but, as we shall see, the common became a focus of new political conflict.[74]

The "stolen" or "rightful" timber continued to cause trouble, however. Nestled among Mousall's and Cutler's civil actions for trespass was a criminal case brought by one of Charlestown's constables, John George, against John Bennett, for "rescuing a cart of green oak wood seized by warrant of Major Gookin." Mousall and Cutler were not only determined to assert their freehold property rights to the woodland on their new lots; they also wanted their wood back. Each got warrants from magistrate Gookin in Cambridge; Constable George went with Mousall and Cutler on the afternoon of 16 March 1686 to Benanuel Bowers's farm, where they formally

---

[73] Cf. Adam Fox, "Custom, Memory and the Authority of Writing," in Paul Griffiths, Adam Fox, & Steve Hindle, eds., *The Experience of Authority in Early Modern England* (Basingstoke: Palgrave, 1996), 88–102; Andy Wood, "Custom, Identity and Resistance," in ibid., 249–57.

[74] MxCC D&O, 5: folio 124; RB, 4: 219–220. Pleas: MxCC D&O, 5: folio 127. R. N. Toppan, ed., "Dudley Records," 2*PMHS*, 13 (1899), 282, 284. Conflict: see below, "Dominion and Revolution."

"seized" the timber and "delivered it to the hand of John Mousall to see it conveyed to John Cutler's house." George then gave Mousall his staff of office to legalize the transport. Mousall and Cutler inexplicably had no cart, so they commandeered a cart belonging to Patrick Mark, who was out; loaded it up; and ordered Mark's son Nathaniel to lead the cart to Cutler's. However, when they reached Taylor's Corner, they met Patrick Mark driving his cattle in the opposite direction to his farm at the Rocks, and were halted. Samuel Whittemore happened to be with Mark and testified: "Goodman Mark did request of Mr. Cutler and Goodman Mousall what power they had from authority to bring his cart from home from his work. If they had power and would show him power to press his cart, it should go where they pleased. If not, it should go no further." The meeting on the road quickly escalated into a shouting match that could be heard in nearby fields and houses. One of these houses was John Bennett's, where John Chamberlain was "at table at dinner." After repeated refusals to allow his cart to go further, Mark came into Bennett's asking for advice. Chamberlain suggested that Mark should "pull out the pin to swing out the wood, which he accordingly did, and left the wood in the street." Several witnesses corroborated Whittemore's statement that Bennett was not present at this point, between 5 and 6 p.m. This contradicted Mousall's evidence. Mark and his son drove their cart and cattle back out to the Rocks, and the pile of wood blocking the street was quickly transferred to Bennett's yard. The court merely admonished Bennett and ordered him to restore the timber to Cutler and Mousall. This mild sentence probably reflected the bench's suspicion about Mousall's evidence and the authoritarian seizure of Mark's property.[75]

Mousall v. Whittemore et al. and associated cases at the Middlesex County Court on 6 April 1686 raise many important and intriguing questions: about timing, about personnel, about socio-economic, legal, and constitutional principles, about contemporary readings of the past and visions of the future. The series of confrontations in Charlestown in the late winter and spring of 1686 brought to the fore, as Cutler saw, far more profound issues than a few loads of wood.

Why did a majority of the Proprietors of the Stinted Common decide

---

[75] MxCC RB, 4: 222; D&O, 5: folio 124. Bowers was Lidgett's tenant on Ten Hills Farm; Mark's challenge: test. Stephen Waters, 43, working at Mr. Harbord's between 5 and 6 p.m; other corroborators: Thomas Sheppie, 22, and John Mahoone, 20. The bench may also have wondered that two of the original fellers, Whittemore and Bennett, should have been in the vicinity of the confrontation with Mark, who had previously signed the Exception and given evidence supporting the protesters. Had Cutler and Mousall been somehow entrapped?

to divide it into private lots in the spring of 1685? Charlestown was unusual among Massachusetts founding towns in retaining a large common for so long. Almost all of Watertown's twenty-five-thousand-acre grant had been lotted out within twelve years of the town's founding, by 1642. Similarly, Cambridge had only a comparatively small cow common of 63 acres after the 1640s. Most of Concord's common land was privatized after 1653. Charlestown's retention of nearly two thousand acres of common was never explained. It may have resulted from the narrow shape of the town grant with its natural cinch at the Neck. The large number of merchants, artisans, and mariners in the population may have lessened pressure on tillage. Concentration on stock rearing for provisioning and for export could have been further factors.[76]

The reasons behind the 10 March 1685 division were also unrecorded. The effects of population pressure and frontier dangers on land values may have been on proprietors' minds. The town records after 1679 suggest that administering the Stinted Common was becoming more and more time-consuming and expensive. People had to be prevented from grazing geese; trees had to be marked and regularly inspected; complex felling arrangements had to be policed; fencing responsibilities were a struggle to enforce. Cambridge men were wont to trespass on one boundary; Charles Lidgett proved a very difficult neighbor at Ten Hills Farm, appealing cases up to the Court of Assistants. This may also have prompted the initial partial division of 1681. The overseers' accounts had to be audited and the proprietors dunned for dues. At the end of 1682, "nooks and corners" of the common were authorized to be sold to raise money—a possible rationale behind the cash sale to Danforth, though five and a half acres is hardly a nook.[77]

Surely, though, a major reason for enclosure in the spring of 1685 was the turning point in Anglo-colonial relations. On 23 October 1684, Massachusetts's 1629 Charter had been "vacated" in the Court of Chancery in London, after an eight-year struggle with royal authority. From being a virtually autonomous Puritan republic, the colony was brought under the direct rule of the crown. Among many other wrenching changes, the loss of the charter threw all land titles into doubt, and made any land not in private hands vulnerable to the depredations of land-hungry "courtiers" and speculators sympathetic to the crown. This fear was probably behind Cambridge's division of its "remote lands" in 1683–84, and Charlestown's

---

[76] Watertown: Thompson, *Divided We Stand*, 51; Cambridge: Thompson, *Cambridge Cameos*, 16; Concord: Donahue, *Great Meadow*, Ch. IV. Provisioning and export: see below, "The Sea."

[77] CTR, 4: 6, 38, 40, 47, 49, 52.

concurrent laying out of the woodlots on Mystic Side to their individual grantees. Paul Wilson's threat to go to England and appeal directly to "Good King James" thus had a topically chilling edge to it.[78]

Who were those townspeople who followed Samuel Whittemore, who "excepted," petitioned and finally invaded? Certainly the protesters liked to portray themselves as Charlestown's underdogs. They were by definition non-proprietors and non-beneficiaries of enclosure. They equated themselves with the poor in their petition: "deprived" of their liberties and privileges as Englishmen, "oppressed" ratepayers, "gnawn by a crew of rats." They knew their rights and were able to nonsuit summary judgement by the town Commission for Small Causes and later halt the illegal impressment of a cart. If their account of the tumultuous town meeting of 15 April 1685 is to be credited, they had forty to fifty inhabitants behind them. They believed fervently in the justice of their case; they followed legal procedures as far as they could. They were outraged at the slanting of precedents by their opponents, and contemptuous of the authority of town bigwigs intent on lining their own pockets.[79]

The ten defendants were a mixture of "young beginners" in their twenties and recently married; rather marginal recent arrivals; and suspect characters with sullied reputations. Two were Scots (inherently dubious in English eyes), two were tailors, and one was a shoemaker (among the poorest craftsmen). The shadowy William Richardson was involved in shepherding, and young Samuel Griffin had just begun a career as a housewright. Where probate inventories survive, their households were poor. Cutler's listing of sample rate assessments was derisively accurate. Two had been convicted of illegal cutting of cedar near Spot Pond in 1673. Scottish John Melvin had been drafted in King Philip's War in 1676; Hopewell Davis of the troublesome Davis clan fled from impressment in the Royal Army in 1686. Melvin and Whittemore were related by marriage. As members of "the lesser sort," the protesters had all the more reason to need common rights as a major source of independence and survival.[80]

---

[78] Thompson, *Cambridge Cameos*, 257–65, 279–80. In 1686 Connecticut distributed the bulk of its commons among individual proprietors in various towns. R. R. Johnson, *Adjustment to Empire* (Leicester: Leicester University Press, 1981), 80.

[79] For English similarities: Buchanan Sharp, *In Contempt of All Authority* (Berkeley: University of California Press, 1980); he argues from his study of anti-enclosure movements in the early Stuart West Country that "rioting was an extreme form of petitioning," 42.

[80] Edward Wyer, Jr., 24, Scot, tailor, father's assets £150; Andrew Phillips, ca. 26, married 1683; Samuel Griffin, 26, housewright; James Capon, had bought land from Joseph Lynde in 1678, MxD, 7: 62; first child born end of 1683; John Bennett, ca. 25, shoemaker; John Melvin, ca. 29,

Samuel Whittemore and Paul Wilson, the older ringleaders, both stood to suffer by the closure of the common: the former as a wheelwright needing special timber, the latter as a town herdsman who had spent several quite lucrative summers in the 1670s and 1680s superintending grazing. The Whittemore family had arrived in Charlestown about 1639 from Hitchin, Hertfordshire. With six other unwelcome families, they had been frozen out of the peninsula and forced to settle on Mystic Side. Among the "straitening" and "prejudicial" town orders against them, one involved exclusion from "common pasturage." Samuel (1647–1726) inherited a modest £10 from his father's £286 estate. Having fallen out with his brothers in 1670 over unpaid rent, he spent the first half of that decade in Dover, New Hampshire, where his first two children were born to his wife Hannah (Rice). He was back in Charlestown by 1678, and in 1684 had to pay £65 for Isaac Hill's house and one and half acres. His elder brother John only had one cow common, and though Samuel had bought a "nook" abutting his land the same year, no common proprietorship came with it. Samuel emerges from the court and land records as "downright quarrelsome" and "pugnacious." He was the only man of any substance among the protesters. Though he had endowed two children with portions, he still left £161 in 1726.[81]

Wilson's rascally life had included a period as a servant to John Mousall's brother Thomas in the early 1660s. Despite more than a quarter of a century in the relentless religiosity of Massachusetts, Wilson comes across as an unrepentant "merry Englander." In his wild youth, he led other kids in a noisy and destructive celebration of Guy Fawkes Night more usually celebrated by cavaliers. He orchestrated ribald demonstrations under the window of a newly married couple's bridal suite, to the outrage of the bride's deacon father. He haunted Charlestown alehouses, he fought, he roistered, and he wenched. He was one of a group of masterless men in 1668. He and his noisome friends would have been more at home in Restoration Wapping than in Puritan Charlestown. His celebration of good King James—to Puritans a Roman Catholic absolutist and enslaver of

---

Scot, tailor, war veteran; Hopewell Davis, ca. 39, married 1682, cedar filcher, sawyer brother fined for trespass 1677, see "Sharecropping Conflicts" above; William Richardson, helped hire town shepherd 1679, sold liquor to Indian tinker; all briefly noted by Wyman.

[81] B. A. & E. Whittemore, "The Whittemore Family in America," R, 106 (1952), 31–37, 94–97; ibid., 21 (1867) 169–72; W. M. Bollenbach, New England Ancestry of A. E. Johnson (Baltimore: Gateway, 2003), 382–86. Samuel was the seventh of nine brothers; his elder brother Daniel had been driven to suing him, and two other brothers gave evidence against him, MxCC D&O, 2: folio 52. By 1686, he and Hannah had five young children.

Massachusetts—was all of a piece. It comes as no surprise that Wilson's was the loudest voice in the demonstration.[82]

Allied with the demonstrators in their anger at the enclosure were the signers of the "Exception" against the town meeting's railroaded acceptance. They seem to have been driven by three motives. Some were liable to lose work or supplies through enclosure: Jacob Hurd, a joiner; Francis and John Shepherd, carpenters; Andrew Stimpson, a housewright; Zachery Long, a shipowner; Thomas Carter, Sr., a blacksmith; and David Crouch, a herds-man. A second overlapping group seem to have been motivated by loyalty to the traditional customs of the town and of the English countryside. Men like Long, Carter, Daniel Edmunds, John Burrage, John Penticost, and Rich-ard Austin were older, often wealthier, and respected as former officehold-ers. Finally, some excepters were members of a despised counterculture or people who had reasons to dislike the current elite. Some were hell-raising comrades of Wilson's, convicted of drunkenness and disturbance of the peace, like William Brown and Joseph Batchelor; others may well have been riled by heavy fines for unlicensed wood-cutting or other offences, like John Burrage, Daniel Edmunds, Richard Austin, and Patrick Mark. This mixed group had more weight in the town than the demonstrators, and could not be laughed off as a rascally mob. No doubt they discreetly applauded the flouting of a partisan and divisive decision.[83]

Why did the protesters target John Mousall and John Cutler Jr. in their gesture of assertion of their continued common rights? What made these two such symbols of rat-like gnawing and oppression of the poor? Both men came from Charlestown's ruling class. Both their fathers (and Cutler's grandfather) were deacons. Cutler (1650–1708) was already a reg-ular member of the town board, a militia officer, frequently performing executive functions for the town and consulted for his legal expertise. His grandfather was a wealthy blacksmith-cum-merchant and his father was allied by marriage to two leading business families. Mousall (1629–1703) was almost a generation older, but, despite his carpenter father's wealth and influence, had had a far more checkered career. Something about his character provoked hostility, even aggression. From the 1660s onwards, he and his family were regularly victims of defamation, battery, vandalism, and threats. One particular shadow haunted his reputation: the gossip that he was homosexual. He was not a major office holder in town, despite his

---

[82] Paul Wilson, 49, cedar filcher 1673, assets £58; see Thompson, *Sex in Middlesex*, 84–85, 89.

[83] See list of office holders; Wyman has entries for all the excepters. Batchelor and Austin had both bought land from John Cutler Jr. in 1684, MxD, 9: 155–56.

father's earlier importance. However, the Proprietors' Records reveal one reason for his targeting. He was the owner of the largest number of cow commons in the whole town, sixteen and one-eighth, more than grandees like Sprague, Russell or Lynde. He thus qualified for twenty-four acres of common in 1681, and a huge fifty-seven and a quarter acres in 1685. He also had far and away the most woodland on the Common. His relatively mundane office of tree warden obliged him to hunt down and report thieves of protected wood for expensive punishment. He had been appointed in 1673, and rewarded with regular grants of timber. Some of his commons may also have derived from the wardenship. He had, finally, assisted the surveyor in measuring and staking out the hated individual lots. This involvement, his unpopular office, and his unsavory reputation made him vulnerable in the febrile atmosphere of 1685–86.[84]

What more profound issues and attitudes divided these two groups, both of whom were convinced of the rightness of their actions? Plainly, a major divider was status or "sort" as they called it. The enclosers were led by "the better sort," many of them prospering through landholdings and trade; they saw enclosure, "particular lots," as the wave of the future where every household controlled its own resources and production to the family's benefit, "possessive individualism." Since allocation was proportional to cow commons, the division of the Stinted Common would make the rich, with the most commons, richer. By fencing off most resources, especially wood, it would deprive non-proprietors, almost always the "poorer sort," of their traditional "use-rights." Henceforth, "the rising generation" and artisans, so visible in the opposition, could look forward to harder times: "many poor . . . are to increase" They would have to either move out to the dangerous frontier or lapse into tenancy and dependency. The town would become increasingly polarized; individuals, especially "covetous freeholders," increasingly self-interested. This was a very far cry from Winthrop's "Model of Christian Charity," with its emphasis on community and "commonwealth." This neighborly ideal—"the good of the whole

---

84   Wyman; Robert Cutler, grandfather, left £602; Ralph Mousall £873. Business families: Nowell, Hilton. On aggression: see "Fosket Follies" below. John's younger brother Thomas Mousall left a fortune of nearly £1,000, MW, 15621. Homosexuality: *Sex in Middlesex*, 175. Tree warden: CTR, 3: 143, 146; 4: 24. Ironically John Mousall had been one of eight convicted of illegally taking cedar from near Spot Pond in 1673, CTR, 3: 142; almost immediately afterwards he was appointed tree warden. His probate inventory was only £86, but he had already endowed his "undutiful" son and two daughters with portions. MxW 15619. The three witnesses for the plaintiffs were all wealthy establishment figures: James Lowden, 38, had married the widow of Jonathan Bunker, who was worth £606; Joseph Lynde, 49, left more than £1,900; Nathaniel Hutchinson, 52, an overseer of the Stinted Common and pound keeper, left £632.

[town] family"—was the vision of past and future held by the opposition in Charlestown and in hundreds of English parishes and manors facing similar threats of enclosure. To the "improvers" on both sides of the Atlantic, "commoners," those people asserting their rights to firewood, dung, timber, stone, or sand were seen as idle freeloaders, an unreliable, improvident, tumultuous drag on the settlement's progress and prosperity. Such attitudes underlie Cutler's scornful tone and obsession about keeping order and avoiding a descent into chaos at all costs.[85]

Cutler's outrage signifies other cultural divisions. For instance, there is his emphasis, shared by many of the Proprietors, on the written record, copious documentation, and authorized memoranda. This is his conception of "proof." Such a mindset was completely at odds with the protesters' and petitioners' reliance on time-honored custom, popular memory, and entitlements to natural resources like timber "in the name of the commons of England, the righteous freedom [to use] the Creation." Several of the opposition were illiterate; they persisted in allegiance to an oral culture, reliant on inherited lore and wisdom. This wisdom included a rejection of the concept that any privileged group could lay claim to "proprietorship" of community property. To them, the very idea was a contradiction in terms.[86]

Some protesters, like Paul Wilson, seemed to embrace a counterculture in stark contrast to the exclusionary respectability and authoritarian discipline of the godly elite. Several had convictions for drunkenness or alcohol-fueled misdemeanors, suggesting a preference for the alehouse over the meetinghouse. None of the rioters, and few of the exceptioners,

---

[85] On English precedents and parallels which would have been familiar to many early settlers in Charlestown: Tim Harris, ed., *The Politics of the Excluded* (Basingstoke: Palgrave, 2001); Andy Wood, *Riot, Rebellion and Popular Politics in Early Modern England* (Basingstoke: Palgrave, 2005); Geoff Eley and William Hunt, eds., *Reviving the English Revolution* (London: Verso, 1985); Paul Griffiths, Adam Fox & Steve Hindle, eds., *The Experience of Authority in Early Modern England* (Basingstoke: Palgrave, 1996); Anthony Fletcher and John Stevenson, eds., *Order and Disorder in Early Modern England* (Cambridge: Cambridge University Press, 1987); D. Purkiss, *The English Civil War* (London: Harper, 2007) 103, 119, 131–2; M. Braddick & J. Walter, eds., *Negotiating Power in Early Modern English Society* (Cambridge: Cambridge University Press, 2001), especially "Introduction," 5, 6–10, 32–40, discussing J. C. Scott's *Weapons of the Weak*, S. Hindle "Exhortation and Entitlement," 102–22, and J. Walter, "Politics of Subsistence," 123–48; P. Withington, *Politics of the Commonwealth* (Cambridge: Cambridge University Press, 2005); A. Fox, "Popular Ridicule in Jacobean England," *Past and Present*, 145 (1994), 47–83, especially, 78. An analogous conflict between rich and poor broke out in Sudbury in the late 1650s over the division of the town's meadowlands, S. C. Powell, *Puritan Village* (Middletown, CT: Wesleyan University Press, 1963), 119–130.

[86] Quotation from an English Digger manifesto of 1649, in Wood, *Riot*, 155; written/oral: Thompson, *Cambridge Cameos*, 249–55.

were church members. Several seemed to the respectable sort to be idle, disorderly, improvident, and demanding—what Elizabethan Sir Thomas Smith dismissed as "the lowest and rascal sort of people." In contrast, the demonstrators saw their so-called "betters" as so many gnawing rats: voracious, self-interested, and repressive—"rich churls" as English "true commons" reviled them. Wilson and his mates chafed at the relentless joylessness of Charlestown. Like some visiting seamen and a furtive adolescent subculture, they wanted some old-fashioned merriment and spontaneity in their lives.[87]

Wilson's threat to appeal to "Good King James" echoed the less blatant blackmail of the petition to the General Court. It represented a touching myth among the oppressed that the monarch, be it Henry VIII, Elizabeth, Charles I, Charles II, James II, or George III, if only properly informed, would intervene to protect vulnerable subjects from their exploiters. The impending royal takeover seemed to offer escape from the local colonial oppression. This vision was at total variance with the hopes of the ruling elite, who treasured their self-governing independence. As the protesters knew by 1686, the days of Massachusetts's proud isolation were numbered. Soon their "oppressors" must bow the knee and doff the cap to royal officials. The beliefs of the disadvantaged in the benevolence of the crown would be put to the test and, as in the 1770s, found wanting.[88]

---

[87]   Drink: William Brown, Joseph Batchelor, John Burrage, William Richardson, Paul Wilson; quotations: Andy Wood, "Plebeian Language of Deference and Defiance," in Harris, ed., *Politics of the Excluded,* 73, 83; adolescent: Thompson, *Sex in Middlesex,* 83–108; seamen: ibid., 182–85, and below, "The Sea."

[88]   Royal benevolence: C. Holmes, "Drainers and Fenmen," in Fletcher & Stevenson, *Order and Disorder,* 180; Wood, *Riot,* 96; Sacks, *The Widening Gate,* Ch. 6; Roger Thompson, ed., *Samuel Pepys' Penny Merriments* (London: Constable, 1976), 24–32, 44–49; Colin Bonwick, *The American Revolution* (Basingstoke: Macmillan, 1991), 89. Wanting: see below, "Dominion and Revolution."

Conclusion: Sustainable Farming

Sustainable farming in seventeenth-century townships had to be mixed farming, and given the individual town boundaries, it could only serve a limited population. A nice balance had to be struck between the resources of a manageable area and the number of hands needed for the highest renewable output year after year. Because mixed farming was labor-intensive, the areas cultivated by each family unit would depend on the workers available, though forward-thinking patriarchs with capital to spare would try to acquire land for the next generation. Somehow the planters of Charlestown must gradually wring from their environment the necessities of life in "the wilderness." They must learn to live off the land without destroying it in the process.[89]

Properly treated, the sixteen thousand acres of "essential Charlestown" could meet most of the people's basic needs: fresh water, heat, staple foods, lighting, timber, leather, rope, brick, stone, pottery, beer, containers, draft animals, cartage, shipping, and homespun cloth. They would need to buy ironware, finer fabrics, and luxuries like sugar, wine or rum, and paper. All households would have a garden and a cow; most families, except essential artisans like carpenters, or the elderly and the poor, would have some arable land and a woodlot. Even ministers, like Symmes or Dunster, owned and managed farmland. Children started working at four or five; women, as we shall see, contributed to the family output through their farmyard and preservative enterprises. Goodwife Brackenbury was not above helping her young sharecropper by gathering sticks and stones off the land before he plowed. Only the very young and the very old were spared enlistment in the daily struggle for survival.[90]

---

[89] The major authority on this topic is Brian Donahue, author of the outstanding study, *The Great Meadow*; I am most grateful for his help, especially a guided tour of Concord in 2008.

[90] Essential: the land area less the daughter towns of Woburn and Malden.

Mixed farming presented a series of challenges. The first and most basic was the need for capital. Even if the starter-farmer rented land, he would need tools, draft animals, a cow, a cart or barrow, fencing timber, and payment for his rates and rent or mortgage. He would have tried to save as a servant or apprentice; he might have received help from parents or a dowry with his new wife. Nonetheless, he might well have to hire out his own labor for some days each week to make ends meet.

Every planter, however experienced, needed to strike a balance between the three elements of his business: crops, livestock, and wood. Land use had to be maximized: too many cattle would mean insufficient arable crops and winter hay, and too few would mean insufficient manure and declining crop yields. The canny farmer would use the stubble and rowen after harvest for late grazing (and early manuring), coppice his woodlot for steady growth, drain and replant his meadow, and drive his hogs out to the woods before planting season. He must assist the town officers—he might well be one— by ensuring clearly marked boundaries, preserving pasture against overgrazing, maintaining his proportion of fences and gates against straying stock, obeying and enforcing complex town regulations, and helping with work on the town infrastructure.

There were inevitable points of friction in this farming regime; some we have explored already. They might be inter-township conflicts, as with the Cambridge mill dam and the consequential flooding of a Charlestown meadow, or the straying or invading of Cambridge livestock onto the Stinted Common. Town bounds were "beaten" with neighbors every year, but individual negligence or envy sometimes flouted official agreements. Individual borders could also provoke fiery confrontations, as with the Blanchards on the old Wilson farm on Mystic Side and their abutters. Surveyors' lines sometimes had to use trees or rocks as markers; trees could die or be felled, and rocks could be moved. The last resort was often the recollections of ancient townspeople, as in the case of Lowden's wall, and elsewhere, as we shall discover. Cattle could stray *within* Charlestown, as did the Blanchards' and Bowers's. Almost invariably, a blame game ensued; was the damage the fault of insufficient fencing (usually the victim's, according to the stock-owner) or was it the inadequate yoking and ringing of hogs, hobbling of horses, or watching over cattle? States of undeclared war could seethe for months or years before bursting out into hostilities. Similarly, strife could follow intense competition for valuable resources such as wood. The final resort to violence on the Stinted Common arose from opposing lumber needs. How could the greedy need for firewood be reconciled with artisans' wood-working livelihoods, or farmers' fencing obligations, or infrastructure requirements, not to mention the necessity to conserve a precious commodity? Community life had plenty of chafing edges.

Another potential irritant was the differentiation in wealth and status of different farmers. It was, of course, imported from the highly stratified society of England, and manifested itself right at the start of settlement as the Sprague brothers cohabited with the Company servants the surveyor Graves had brought over. It continued throughout the Great Migration. In 1637, for instance, among other arrivals, came Mr. John Harvard, worth £1,600, and shoemaker Matthew Smith, whose probate inventory totalled £52.

These disparities were offset by several compensating factors. Wealth could not buy survival. Harvard died in little more than a year; Smith lived on in the town for forty-five years to the age of seventy-two. The early years were a time of mutual dependency, of all hands to the pump. When, for instance, Thomas Coytmore proposed widening a dam on Mystic Side to increase waterpower, the selectmen required all able-bodied men and youths to give a day's labor to the project, just as they must with highways. The first grants of land were egalitarian, two acres per hand, though the wealthier could more likely afford servants. Every household received the same amount of land in the first Mystic Side dividend of 1637. The rating system reflected landholdings; the more you had, the more you paid. Wealth, education, experience, and standing incurred the responsibility of time-consuming service to town, county, and colony. Like John Winthrop, Increase Nowell, first-generation boss of Charlestown, was so involved in official business that he died poor. The early leaders earned the deference they expected by their contributions to the town's administration and tax base. Other mollifiers of inequality were both religious and civic. Not only did the privileges of church membership cut across class and income, so that the poor saint was the brother or sister of the rich, but, as we have seen, the efficient running of the township required very broad participation; humble brother Matthew Smith served as long-term town crier, messenger, and verger, as well as occasional sealer of leather, trial juror, herdsman, appraiser, witness, census taker, and collector of fines—all this over and above his craft of shoemaking and his farming. Imported social and economic imbalances were reduced by all these counterweights.

During the second and third generations, however, the gulfs between the have-nots, the haves, and the have-mores widened. Disparities in land grants increased and went on increasing; the more you had, the more you got. As unassigned land dwindled and land prices rose—remember the small fortune of £65 the Whittemores had to pay for their dwelling and its grounds in 1684—more and more "young beginners" were forced into renting, or sharecropping (like Samuel Davis), or leaving town for less developed settlements, or lives of laboring and "making shift" after the pattern of Paul Wilson. In 1678, when Rev. Jeremiah Hobart preached that good Christians do not desire "lands and great farms," but only "the light and countenance of God's favour," Thomas Baker, in the congregation, found this so improbable that he burst out laughing.[91]

Another eroder of the gentle hills of social and economic harmony was the rise of large commercial fortunes. Import-export merchants like Francis Norton, Richard Russell, Nicholas Davison, Francis Willoughby, Ralph Sprague, and Thomas Lynde saw soaring profits from their investments in the fishing industry, the timber trade, shipping, shipbuilding, and West Indian, Mediterranean, and British trade. Like their counterparts in England, they invested this wealth in land. Russell bought the Craddock estate in Medford; Willoughby had £1,839-worth of real estate, including 2,500 acres of frontier land. Thomas Lynde, shareholder in various ships, had £1,218 of land out of £1,709 total estate. In some cases, this great wealth or association with it engendered a certain arrogance and sense of entitlement to control over town and church affairs. This, in turn, provoked resentment and feelings of grievance in those who felt excluded and patronized. Thomas Lynde's ultimatum at the 15 April 1685 town meeting that opposers of the Stinted Common privatization should take what was on offer or else get nothing was symptomatic of this elite swagger. The elites should have been less surprised at the direct action they incited. Land-use was only one of a series of confrontations from the late 1670s to the early 1690s in which overbearing and self-important notables were put in their places with blunt crossexaminations and disbelieving rejections. Mutuality had given way to distrust and dislike.

Compared to the section on the sea, topics and controversies relating to the land seem brief within the scope of the present book. Some other boundary and ownership disputes occur in other sections, notably that on

---

[91]   MxCC RB, 3: 198.

violence. However, we must not underplay the vital importance of land to Charlestown. The great majority of its inhabitants were committed to its cultivation. Only about eighty Charlestown men over three generations have been identified with seagoing or maritime connections. Without its farmers and its farmer-artisans, the town could hardly have survived, let alone thrived.

Part 4

Sea

Charlestown Maritime Inhabitants, 1630–86

SEA CAPTAINS

(Dates refer to active practice in Charlestown)

1630s: T. Beecher, 1630–1637; J. Hodges, 1633–1654; T. Hawkins, 1636–1643, to Boston; N. Trerice, 1636–1653; J. Garrett, 1637–1657; J. Allen, 1639–1675; E. Payne, 1638–1649; T. Coytmore, 1636–1644; A. Walker, 1638–1653; T. Graves, 1639–1653.

1650s: W. Foster, 1652–1698; M. King, 1654–1679; W. Hilton, 1655–1678; J. Trumbull, 1655–1686; J. Long, 1650s–1683; Z. Long, 1650s–1688.

1660s: W. Goose, ca. 1660–ca. 1678; T. Jenner, ca. 1660–1686; W. Walley, 1662–1671; R. Martin, 1660s–1694; J. Phillips, 1660s–1726; W. Hurry, 1660s–1689; E. Row, 1660s–1687; R. Sprague Jr., 1660s–1703; T. Tuck, 1660s–1687.

1670s: S. Hunting, ca. 1670–1701; W. Marshall, ca. 1670–1685; J. Blaney, 1672–1715; W. Wellstead, 1672–?; M. Soley, 1670s–1684; T. Waffe, 1670s–1685, to Boston.

1680s: T. Jones, ca. 1680–1686; J. Jones, c. 1680–1690.

SHIPBUILDERS AND CARPENTERS (C)

1630s: R. Moulton, 1630–1636; F. Willoughby, 1638–47, to England, 1661–1671; R. Lowden, 1638–1700; J. Martin, 1638–1664 (c).

1640s: W. Foster, 1640s–1652 (became sea captain in 1652)

1650s: E. Johnson, 1650s–ca. 1669; T. Orton, 1650s–1687 (c); J. Smith, 1650s–1673 (c).

1660s: S. Ballatt, 1664–1708; T. Chapman, 1669–1687 (c); C. Wadland, 1666–1668 (c); C. Wadland, Jr., 1665–1671 (c).

1670s: J. Edes, 1674–ca. 1693 (c); W. Vine, 1670s–1708 (c); S. Bissell, 77–82

1680s: J. Cutler, Jr., ca. 1680–1708, anchorsmith; J. Stacey, 1680s–1711, mastmaker; S. Geary, 1685 (c).

Merchants and Retailers (r)

1630s: A. Palmer, 1629–53; Ric Sprague, 1629–1668 (r); E. Gibbons, 1630–1639, to Boston; R. Sedgwick, 1635–1653, to Jamaica; R. Cutler, 1637–65, and blacksmith; F. Norton, 1637–1667; S. Carter, 1638–1681 (r); J. Hills, 1638–1646, to Malden; N. Davison, 1639–1661, to Pemaquid, Maine

1640s: R. Russell, 1640–1676; R. Woory, 1640–?, and leatherdresser; J. Carey, 1647–1681; T. Kemble, 1648–1689, and cooper; Mrs. Trerice, 1640s–1670s (r)

1650s: N. Shapley, 1652–1663; J. Tidd, 1656–1678 (r)

1660s: L. Hammond, ca. 1661–1699; J. Lynde, 1660s–1627; J. Russell, 1669–1680s (r)

Seamen and Fishermen (f)

1630s: T. Moulton, 1630–1645, to Malden (f); J. Hayden, 1635–1665; H. Lawrence, 1635–1646 (f); J. Burrage, 1637–1685; N. Hadlock, 1638–1653

1640s: T. Sheppie, 1644–1683 (f); A. Bell, 1647–1663; J. Lawrence, ca. 1640–1672

1650s: J. Ridgeway, 1650s–1675, to Pemaquid, Maine (f)

1660s: I. Potter, 1661; G. Fifield, 1661–1676; J. Poor, 1662–1686; S. Leman, 1660s–1699, lighterman; J. Nicholls, 1668

1670s: R. Manser, 1670s–1684+; H. Salter, 1674–1678; S. Blunt, 1670s–?; J. Goose, 1670s–1685; S. Johnson, 1679–?; W. Sheafe, 1672–1696, and ferryman; E. Moore, 1675–1686+

1680s: N. Hilton, 1683–1687; W. Marshall, Jr., 1683; J. Mitchell, 1681

Introduction:
The Challenging Sea

Samuel Eliot Morison, my favorite Massachusetts historian, is commemorated on Commonwealth Avenue in Boston with a statue depicting him as a sailor. Not only did he love to sail during Maine summers, but he also wrote the official World War II history of the Pacific sea war, in which thousands of men drowned, and others like future president John F. Kennedy barely survived. New Englanders breathing the salt air near the shore have always had a love-hate relationship with the sea. Whalers like Captain Ahab, fishermen like Disko Troop in *Captains Courageous,* China traders in their clippers, narrators of life afloat like R. H. Dana or Joshua Slocum, war heroes like Kennedy—all shared their appreciation of the ocean as a "way to wealth," an access route to a wider world, a means of importing an increasing variety of necessities and luxuries from abroad, and an insulation against foreign aggression. At the same time they were acutely, even superstitiously, aware of its perils, its unpredictability, its isolating loneliness. The sea was nature at its most unforgiving. The perfect storm might await them just over the horizon.

On 30 March 1643, Captain Thomas Coytmore returned to the Charles River on the *Tryal,* the first oceangoing ship built in Boston, from her maiden voyage to Faial in the Azores and St. Kitts in the Caribbean Leeward Islands. It had been a hugely successful venture, trading New England pipe staves and dried fish for wine in the Azores, and some of that wine for sugar, cotton, tobacco, and salvage from a wreck in the West Indies. Twenty-one months later Coytmore was dead, drowned off Cadiz in southern Spain on 27 December 1644. He was thirty-two. He had been the merchant on board the *Seafort* of Boston, a 400-tonner commanded

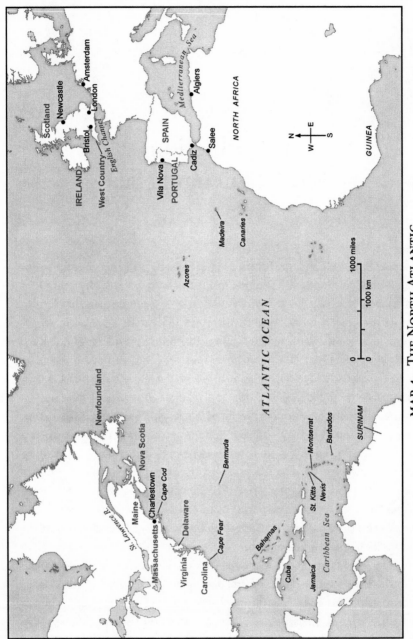

MAP 4. THE NORTH ATLANTIC

by Thomas Hawkins, when it was wrecked. The skipper survived, but the next year, leaving the Mediterranean on 2 February 1646, he was again wrecked off Gibraltar; again he was saved. He died at sea two years later, aged thirty-nine. Coytmore's kinsman Admiral Thomas Graves was killed at the Battle of Scheveningen in the First Anglo-Dutch War at the age of forty-eight on 31 July 1653. When Captain James Garrett's *New England Merchant* sank in the Atlantic in 1657, "the hope of the country," four recent Harvard graduates, traveling to England to gain pulpit experience, drowned with him and his company. Ships sailed out of Charlestown and would not be heard of for months. Sometimes they were never heard from again; like many others, Joseph Goose's ship was "supposed lost on voyage." However rewarding it might be, oceangoing sailing in the seventeenth century was a deadly dangerous game.[1]

Atlantic weather was not the only danger. Three years before he drowned, Garrett's ship, freighted with beaver, other furs, and masts, had been captured by the Dutch. The same fate befell Captain Nicholas Trerice in the fall of 1648, and a £2,000 ransom was demanded. In 1651, with his son-in-law Thomas Kemble as supercargo of a consignment of pipe staves from Charlestown to Madeira, Trerice's ship *Chapman* was again seized, this time by Portuguese port officials. The following year, the *Mayflower*, part-owned by Kemble, was returning from Virginia to Massachusetts with tobacco. Hurricane winds led to loss of provisions; after twenty days living on rawhide, the crew had to put in at San Domingo, where the Spanish continued to starve them in confinement. Captain William Foster was one of many seafarers captured in the western Atlantic by Barbary corsairs. Captain Thomas Waffe, hunting for Spanish wrecks and their treasure among the Bahama shoals, suffered from seeming friends:

> Two men came on board [his sloop *Swan*, anchored on the shoals on 5 April 1684] with twelve others. They pretended to be taking their leaves, having formerly sailed with him. After some time, they demanded provision of the sloop, which they pretended was theirs as former members of the sloop's company. They violently and forcibly opened the sloop's hatches and took from the hold one barrel of pork, half a barrel of flour on the deck. They threatened to bind this deponent hand and foot and in a hostile manner kept this deponent

[1] Coytmore: *R*, 7 (1854); Frothingham, 85; "Origins," above. Hawkins: Wyman, 482; Dunn, 599, 600; Coldham, 118. Graves: Wyman, 432–33; Frothingham, 139; *GMB*, 806; *WP*, 6: 346–47; Garrett: Wyman, 303; Savage; Coldham, 144. Harvard: Revs. Mayhew, Ince, Pelham and Davis. Goose: MxCC RB, 4: 190, 6 October 1685.

out of his cabin for some time, and more provision they said they would have, but this deponent and his company did so far defend themselves and what they had, that they took no more away.

Many mariners did not come off so lightly; they vanished without their stories being told.[2]

With water everywhere around their peninsula, Charlestown people did not have to go out to sea to encounter danger. In November 1641, Winthrop recorded how Thomas Knower, "coming down Mystic in a small boat laden with wood, was found dead in it: a good caveat for men not to go single in boats in such season of the year, for it was very stormy weather." The *Journal* and other diaries are full of accounts of people perishing on short coasting trips or crossing the Bay. Between 1666 and 1669 three Charlestown men are recorded in the court records as having drowned, including "a Negro fishing on Mystic." Captain Richard Martin's servant John Bennett was found dead in April 1674 between the ship *Blossom* and a lighter alongside. Coastal fishing, too, was extremely hazardous, as we shall soon discover. When few could swim, clothing was heavy, and safety devices rudimentary, drowning was a constant peril.[3]

Long voyages in packed, insanitary conditions, with poor diets and frequent drenchings, were similarly full of risk. We know of several masters and merchants who died at sea or in foreign ports: William Goose, 46, and young Francis Willoughby, both struck down by smallpox; others like Nathaniel Graves, 40, or Matthew Soley, 34, perished by unknown causes. Other officers just died at suspiciously early ages, like William Walley at thirty-four or Nowell Hilton, twenty-four. And how did Captain Thomas Jones grow blind and weak by the age of thirty-four? The names of a few seamen who died relatively young have survived, like Nathaniel Hadlock,

---

[2]   Garrett: Hull, Diary, 146, 179. Masts: timber was a major Maine export commodity: as sawn plank or clapboard, pipestaves for barrels (the main storage vessels), and ships' timbers of all kinds. The Piscataqua was an early lumber and processing center; Kittery had six of the basin's twenty-four sawmills by the 1690s. In 1671, 20,000 tons of deals and pipestaves and ten shiploads of masts were leaving Portsmouth every year. Both the West Indies and the Wine Islands were major markets. W. G. Saltonstall, *Ports of the Piscataqua* (Cambridge: Harvard University Press, 1941), 14; Bailyn, *Merchants*, 100–103; Clarke, *Eastern Frontier*, 55–56, 64–65. The authority on the early lumber trade is C. F. Carroll, *Timber Economy of Puritan New England* (Providence: Brown University Press, 1973). Trerice: *WP*, 5: 288; Kemble: Coldham, 128, 142; Hull lost a ship and cargo worth £640 to Dutch Capers in the winter of 1672–73, 161. Barbary: see below, "Ordeals of Foster;" cf. Richard Elson, 30 April 1679, MxCC D&O, 4: folio 91; see below, "Wealthy Women: Sarah Hayman."

[3]   Knower: *WJ*, 2: 44; accounts: e.g. Dunn, 42, 106, 151, 331, 384, 402; Hammond, Diary, 154; three: D&O, 2: folios, 40, William Goodwin, 47, Negro, 49, George Fen. Bennett: D&O, 3: 67.

under 40, or waterman Abraham Bell, drowned at 43, but many were too humble and transitory to be remembered.[4]

New England's weather proved unexpectedly fiercer than old England's. Especially scary were summer hurricanes. Winthrop left a vivid and amazed account of one that struck in 1635. It tossed a 400-ton ship on to the Charlestown shore; many fishing shallops were wrecked or sunk off the Isles of Shoals and Pemaquid. His *Journal* is replete with accounts of new arrivals to the colony receiving a savage baptism from storms along the Maine coast before reaching safety. John Hull recorded another hurricane on 5 June 1669. It struck about 10 a.m. with "many fishing boats in the bay, sundry were cast away." Not even havens were entirely free of risk. Seafaring was a career for the young. Any mariner or fisherman with sense would save up and acquire land. Many did not make it that far.[5]

Quite apart from such sensational perils of the deep and the not so deep, merchants and shipmasters faced other frustrations. For instance, John Trumbull, both merchant and master, who arrived in Charlestown from Wapping via Cambridge in the early 1650s, spent much time, money, and energy extracting freight payments from shippers. His battle with neighbor Joshua Tidd for a debt of £11 lasted nearly six years; in the end, after a series of settlement proposals had been rebuffed, the frustrated debtor dumped a load of casks on the refractory Trumbull's front step. Sailing in the busy fishing grounds could also prove hazardous and expensive. Early in 1662 when *Blossom* was returning from Barbados, Trumbull wished to speak to Francis Hooper's shallop, "at anchor about six or seven leagues in the sea at their calling of fishing." Unfortunately Trumbull ran the shallop down, and she sank. On 4 June, the owners Moses Maverick & Co. sued Trumbull for £92: loss of boat valued at £65, the three fishermen's gear

---

[4]   Goose: Hammond, Diary, 170; Willoughby, ibid., 171; Wyman reports Abraham Palmer dying on a Barbados voyage in 1653; Robert Sedgwick in Jamaica in 1656 (on military detachment); Augustine Walker in Bilbao in 1653; Elias Row's brother, at sea, in 1666; Matthew Soley in London in 1684; James Hayden in Barbados in 1665; Henry Lawrence, fisherman, in 1646; Mark King, aged 46, in 1679. Humble: see below, "Captain Jenner's Voyages," "Failure in *Success*." The only evidence of the existence of Robert Manser, of Charlestown, was his wife's getting into trouble while he was at sea. Thompson, *Sex*, 151.

[5]   1635: *WJ*, 1: 155–56; 1669: Hull, Diary, 229, cf. 142; weather: Karen O. Kupperman, "Climate and Mastery of the Wilderness," in D.D. Hall & D.G. Allen, eds., *17th-Century New England* (Boston: Colonial Society of Massachusetts, 1984), 3–38. Cf. the vivid account by Anthony Thatcher of shipwreck off the New England coast, in Increase Mather, *An Essay for Recording Illustrious Providences* (Boston: Green, 1684), ch. 1; see also Julie Sievers, "Drowned Pens and Shaking Hands: Sea Providence Narratives on seventeenth-Century New England," *WMQ*, 63 (2006), 742–76.

and their catch, plus an undetermined loss of wages. Despite Trumbull's claims that the shallop was "old and rotten and not fit to go to sea," and had caused the collision because she had "veered the road," arbitrators found for Maverick.

Shortly after this disaster, when Trumbull's hoy (small coasting vessel) *Hopewell* was wrecked at Point Jude, the crew illegally purloined some rescued cargo. He had to sue them to recover it. Members of his crews deserted; passengers failed to pay the balance of their fares. He had conflicts over the accuracy of accounts; one lasted twenty-two years! Goods he sent for sale up at the Piscataqua River in 1677 were temporarily mislaid and no one could be made to return them. Trumbull seems to have retired from seagoing and set up a shop during the 1660s, but he continued to hire sloops and ketches to distribute goods along the coast. His son John and son-in-law Richard Martin continued the ocean-going business. Trumbull lived to his late seventies, but at times during his long career his blood pressure must have been dangerously high.[6]

Frustration was not an elite monopoly. Life on the lower deck was always hard, sometimes unbearable. A volatile or ill-tempered skipper could drive men to mutiny. The whole seafaring life was so maddeningly unpredictable and uncontrollable. As well as the terrors and torments of wind (or lack thereof) and weather, there were potential problems and delays with the seaworthiness of the ship, with loading and unloading, and with the alacrity of local customers, consigners, shippers, officials, creditors, and agents. Seamen could spend months cooling their heels on half-pay in foreign ports. The transitory quality of their lives was suggested by how little impact they made on Charlestown records. Most of their historical footprints are so light as to be invisible from our range.[7]

Sailors compensated for this unseen impact with their range of travels and experience. By the early 1640s, Charlestown ships were beginning to sail all over the Atlantic. Already familiar with the waters of Maine, Nova

---

[6] Wapping: J.H. Lea, *R*, 49 (1895) 148–52, 322–32, 417–26. Tidd: MxCC RB, 1: 161, 1658–63; others: D&O, 1: doc. 656, E. Collins £29 for four horses to Barbados, 20 September 1656; doc. 924, P. Oliver 20 hogsheads of tobacco from Virginia, £17, 23 December 1657; doc. 1969: J. Allen, wages, £20, 7 August 1662; doc. 2228: Z. Thayer, fare, £2-10-0d, 27 July 1663; RB, 1: 129, W. Maston, freight and desertion at Manhattan, 16 June 1657. Maverick: *Essex CC*, 2: 390–91. *Hopewell*: D&O, 1: doc. 1950, 19 July 1662; desertion: N. Grey, D&O, 1: doc. 1208, £25, 7 August 1657; 22 years: A. Mason, Barbados, *Assistants*, 1: 97, debt from 1655, 4 September 1677; Piscataqua: D&O, 3: folio 81, J. Browne, yarn, candles, stockings, pattins, cod and mackerel hooks, 17 December 1678; shop: CTR, 3: 138, 158; in 1668 an exasperated Trumbull had to apologize for his reviling speeches against the magistrates, D & O, 2: folio 48.

[7] See below: "Caribbean Come to Charlestown," "Captain Martin," and "Failure in *Success*."

Scotia, and Newfoundland from long-term fishing expeditions, the town's seafarers were engaging in transatlantic voyages to England, Ireland, the Iberian Peninsula, the Mediterranean, and the Wine Islands (Madeira and the Canaries). They were also venturing southward beyond the Connecticut River ports to New Amsterdam, the Chesapeake, and the recently settled islands of the Caribbean. By the 1660s, certain well-plowed routes were established: with provisions, horses, and timber to the West Indies, then on to Europe with sugar, tobacco, cotton, and cacao, and then home with cloth and manufactured goods. Another favorite route was with pipestaves or dried fish to the Wine Islands or Spain, wine to London, and manufactures homeward. The outlooks of ships' crews that sailed these routes were inevitably broadened by their experiences in the tropics or European ports. This comparative perspective, along with a degree of freedom from grinding communal routine and blinkered thinking, helped to make Charlestown strikingly different from the inland towns of Middlesex County. Even if townspeople had not themselves traveled, they could not avoid foreign sailors or well-traveled neighbors. In the following studies, some of that difference will become more sharply focused.[8]

---

[8] Different: Thompson, *Sex*, 186–88.

Charlestown and the Atlantic World: Lady La Tour v. Captain John Bayley & Alderman William Berkeley, 1644–45

"Bizarre" is, for once, an apt adjective to describe a case involving Charlestown witnesses that began in Boston in the fall of 1644 and continued in London for much of the following year. The original plaintiff was a French noblewoman, the defendants London merchants and a French captain. The stakes ran to millions of dollars in modern equivalents. In broad perspective, the suit and counter-suit reveal how early New England ports were drawn into the complexities of international commerce and competition. On a local scale, they uncover the rivalry between the leading merchants of Charlestown and Boston.[9]

Though the founding Sprague family had been engaged in trade in the English West Country, it was the arrival of Increase Nowell and party from London in 1630 that set the mercantile tone of the first two decades of Charlestown. By 1640, firm relations had been established with major English transatlantic merchants and several enterprising Charlestown residents had become their agents or partners in New England. Leading town participants during the late 1630s and 1640s included Francis Norton, Robert Sedgwick, Nicholas Trerice, Nicholas Davison, Francis Willoughby, and Richard Russell. All of them had close connections with English merchants. Sedgwick and Norton were brothers-in-law of the Southwark,

---

[9] Winthrop has two versions of the case, *WJ*, 2: 199, 204, 205–7; 256.

London, brewer and fish trader Robert Houghton. Trerice had married into another Southwark trading family, the Hurlstons. Davison, who had a brother in the busy East Anglian port of King's Lynn, was initially the agent in Massachusetts of Matthew Craddock. Craddock was the first governor of the Massachusetts Bay Company and an extensive landowner on the border of Charlestown, as well as an influential London businessman and politician from the 1620s until his death in 1644. Davison soon traded extensively on his own account, and partnered Richard Russell in the Maine fishery. Russell had married into the famous Pitt family of Bristol, and was kinsman to the radical London Atlantic merchant James Russell. Such familial ties were considered the most trustworthy in the risky business of long-distance trade.[10]

Two surviving books of notarial records, covering the periods 1638 to 1641 and 1644 to 1651, illuminate the procedures of this new transatlantic commercial world. Though Massachusetts was deeply distrustful of professional lawyers—not without ample reason—merchants and shipmasters engaged in international business and finance needed legally binding documentation. Thomas Lechford and William Aspinwall provided it, and to cover themselves and their clients, they kept books of certified duplicates.[11]

The 800-odd pages of these books reveal the workings of the early fishing industry, of the trade to and from the Chesapeake and the Caribbean, and of agreements (and disagreements) with commercial partners in London, Bristol, Maine, Connecticut, Virginia, and Barbados. In this far-flung world, Charlestown merchants, skippers, and seamen were highly active participants. Richard Russell (1611–76), for instance, witnessed on 13 September 1645 a £500 bond whereby Boston fishery "shoreman" Thomas Fowle, in charge of groups of North Shore fishermen, undertook to pay Russell £172 worth of fish at Marblehead by 3 June 1646 on behalf of Hugh Brown of Bristol, England. Russell was fish-dealer Brown's agent in Massachusetts, and the dried catch may well have sailed on Brown's "sack ship" (nowadays, a factory ship) to a Spanish or Mediterranean port. Five weeks later, Russell was in partnership with Edward Gibbons to represent the London owners of the *Gilbert*, seized as a "malignant" or royalist vessel. On 21 November 1645, Russell had loaded goods at Charlestown on the

---

[10]   Bailyn, *Merchants,* 80; on family connections, see "Origins." On Sprague commercial interests in England and Massachusetts, see "People-Trafficking" and "The Ordeals of Captain Foster." On transatlantic contacts, see "Captain Francis Norton's Estate."

[11]   Lechford, Aspinwall.

Peter of Limehouse, London, bound for Barbados, the Canary Islands, and then home. Russell maintained close relations with Bristol merchants and represented them in New England. In December 1646, he was to be paid £80 owed to him for a 40-ton bark; the reimbursement was to be made in fish at Newfoundland. As well as fish, he dealt in hogsheads of muscovado sugar, dressed Spanish cloths, glass, provisions, wine, shipping, and real estate. Loans, bills of exchange, powers of attorney, mortgages, deeds of sale, double-entry account books, bonds, and the assigning of bills of credit were part and parcel of a busy merchant's transactions.[12]

Robert Sedgwick (1613–56) acted as "shoreman," the business intermediary between local fishermen and the English wholesale fishmongers. On 20 February 1646, his "brother" Robert Houghton of Southwark pledged to two leading London fish exporters that Sedgwick would load their ship *Mary* with 1,500 quintals (hundredweights) of dried and salted New England fish by a certain date; they would carry the cargo to Spain or the Wine Islands. Often in partnership with Valentine Hill, Sedgwick dealt in huge tonnages of dried fish, sometimes worth over £1,000. In 1649 he and Norton were owed £1,468 by London merchants. When Boston notary William Aspinwall called at Sedgwick's house in June of that year, "his sister Norton" reported that "he had gone eastward to the Isles of Shoals for fish" caught and prepared by the islanders. The collecting of the dried fish from the "stages" or "rooms" at fishing stations was one of Sedgwick's annual summer duties.

Sedgwick's commercial interests ranged wider than fish, the major "return of the country," or early New England export. He also imported manufactured goods, especially cloth and preservatives such as vinegar—£520-worth of freight in 1642 alone—which were desperately needed in the struggling new settlements. In 1644 he had been among the petitioners for a monopoly of the fur trade on the upper Delaware River, and bought pelts from French trappers down east. In the same year his name appears as a creditor of the new Saugus ironworks and he soon became a director of that complex manufactory. He invested in Charlestown's tidal mill and installed a horse-powered mill at his own house on the west side of Market Square. In 1637 Winthrop recorded his "setting up a brewhouse in Charlestown at great charge." Sedgwick, Russell, and Norton advanced £120 per year for four years to the Massachusetts Bay government in exchange for collecting the lucrative colonial custom on wine. From 1645, he was in time-consuming conflict with Boston merchant Thomas Fowle

---

12   Aspinwall, 8, 10, 11, 24, 27, 40, 67, 69, 76, 92, 127, 157, 170–71, 211, 216, 340; Coldham, 1: 150.

over bills of exchange, unpaid debts, and short-weight fish deliveries. All this commercial involvement went alongside multifarious civic and military responsibilities as a selectman, deputy to the General Court, committee man, commander of Charlestown and Middlesex militias, and supplier of arms, ammunition, and powder to the colony. This public spirit reflects the enormous energy typical of these first-generation entrepreneurs.[13]

The risk-laden career of sea captain Nicholas Trerice (ca. 1598–1653) was strikingly different from the two merchants mentioned above, in that he was frequently away from town on voyages of many months' duration. Already in his mid-thirties when he became associated with Massachusetts Bay, he crossed the Atlantic most years until his death. After the abortive 1633 command of the Massachusetts Bay Company's ship *Richard,* which quickly proved a leaky hulk, he became the master and part owner of the aptly named *Planter,* 350 tons, in 1634. His fellow owners were London merchants engaged in supplying New England with provisions, manufactured goods, and planters. Trerice was also closely associated with the dynamic Atlantic merchant Maurice Thompson, London ironmonger and leading investor in the Massachusetts ironworks Joshua Foote, and the Rich family, whose leader Robert, second Earl of Warwick, was hugely influential in Atlantic plantations, trade, and privateering.

Trerice became a Charlestown inhabitant in 3 January 1636. A highly resilient mariner, he survived potentially ruinous lawsuits and seizures of his ship *Chapman* in 1648 and 1650. Trerice was familiar with the Wine Islands, the Chesapeake, the West Indies, and the Maine coast. His outgoing cargoes from New England included dried fish, pipestaves, masts, beaver- and moose skins (not, as one transcription would have them, "mouseskins"!) From the Chesapeake he transported tobacco to London. Incoming freight comprised a vast range of supplies as well as passengers: 200,000 treenails (wooden pegs) for Massachusetts shipwrights, gold bars (seized by the customs searchers at Gravesend), cloth, ironware, cutlers' ware, "Crooked Lane ware," turners' ware, wine, and vinegar (lost on the *Richard*). This rough seadog and his crews were occasionally in trouble with authority for "miscarriage," for swearing and insubordination. Trerice's wife Rebecca had a small shop in Market Square. In the early 1650s

---

13   Important background material: *R*, 42 (1888) 64–69, 184–85, and *R*, 70 (1916) 366–67; H. D. Sedgwick, "Robert Sedgwick," *CSMP*, 3 (1901) 156–7. R. Gildrie, *ODNB*; Frothingham, passim. Lechford, 101, 263, 355; Aspinwall, 8, 17, 28, 29, 35, 46, 78, 122, 127, 183, 211, 214, 218, 222, 223, 224, 255, 257, 301, 356, 367. Robert Houghton's father and brother were both fishmongers. In 1635, Houghton and a partner shipped ten much-needed barrels of gunpowder to Captain Underhill as relations with the Indians deteriorated, Dunn, 748. "Returns of the country" was habitually used by merchant diarist John Hull to describe his outgoing cargoes.

she was reported for "living apart from her husband," and persisted in this separation despite court order. Nicholas's death in 1653 prevented a showdown, and Rebecca went on to marry the profoundly respectable community leader Thomas Lynde two years later. Trerice's inventory in Charlestown included a warehouse and wharf. His property there totalled only £146, but he had other estate in England. The seafaring life might introduce a skipper to leading figures in the Atlantic world, but dangers and setbacks prevented him from accumulating the kind of compensatory riches that some merchants amassed.[14]

This background to rapidly expanding North Atlantic trade was the setting for the Latour contretemps in which the three Charlestown men became involved. Charles de Saint-Étienne de La Tour was a French nobleman who had come to Acadia or Nova Scotia with his founding father about 1606. However, the French claim to the whole of Canada was strongly disputed by Scottish claimants and English merchants, and it was only in 1632 with the Treaty of Saint-Germain-en-Laye between England and France that the French claim was accepted. Thereafter La Tour, Jr., became governor of the part of Acadia east of the St. Croix River (the present border between Maine and New Brunswick), with headquarters at Port Royal on the Nova Scotia peninsula. The western territory conceded to the French, which was most of present-day upper Maine, was governed by Charles de Menou D'Aulnay, who eventually made his base at Penobscot. Though New Englanders first brushed with an aggressive La Tour in 1633 and 1635, his tune changed as he fell out with the more powerful D'Aulnay. From 1641, the Massachusetts government rashly allowed itself to be sucked into the rivalry between the two French officials. Winthrop's letters and journals are full of accounts of embassies, negotiations, expeditions, internal debates, and confrontations. To counterbalance D'Aulnay, La Tour held out the lucrative prospect of free trade—especially in fish and furs—between Acadia and Massachusetts. Boston merchants,

---

[14] Justin Winsser, "Nicholas Trerice," *R*, 143 (1989), 26–39; partners: George Foxcroft, a close neighbor of James Russell and an undertaker for the stock of the Massachusetts Bay Company (Savage, 2: 197), and Richard Hill, a pioneer of the Virginia tobacco, Newfoundland fish oil, West Indian sugar, and Guinea slave trades, Brenner, *Merchants and Revolution*, 165, 168. Inhabitant: CTR, 1A, 41; he may have moved briefly to newly founded Woburn in the 1640s, but was residing in Charlestown again after 1646. Seizures: see above, "Introduction: The Challenging Sea." Crooked Lane ware: "Crooked Lane, just north of London Bridge, was "long famous for its bird cage and fishing tackle shops." W. Thornbury, *London Recollected*, 1 (London: Cassell, 1872), 555. Separation: CTR, 1: 232, MxCC D&O, 1: doc. 361, 3 April 1653. Lynde: eldest son John Trerice had married Hannah Lynde in 1653; her father John (1594–1671) was a maltster, selectman, deputy, and church deacon. He left an estate of £1,709. Rebecca lived on to 1688, a widow for seventeen years. Nicholas's estate: Rodgers, 1: 112.

confronting the economic slump of the early 1640s resulting from the sudden stoppage of immigration, grasped at this opportunity. Their intervention was bound to upset the balance of power down east, and inevitably Massachusetts trading ships became involved in the Acadian civil war.[15]

In 1644, Lady La Tour, in Europe to raise supplies and support for her beleaguered husband, entered a "charter party" (contract) with the radical London politician and businessman Alderman William Berkeley, Captain John Bayley, and Isaac Berkeley, his brother's factor. Her understanding (and the contract's wording) was that the *Gillyflower* would take her directly to relieve her husband at Fort St. Jean, at the mouth of St. John's River, east of St. Croix. The Berkeleys and Bayley, however, had other plans, and claimed that the charter party was deliberately misleading in case of meeting royalist marauders. They proceeded to trade their cargo of goods and provisions down the French Canadian and Maine coasts, and finally dumped her outraged ladyship in Boston on 17 September 1644, seven months after embarkation. She had been injured when she was bundled into the hold as D'Aulnay hove into sight off Cape Sable (the southwest corner of the Acadian peninsula), and had incurred huge additional expenses. The relief of Fort St. Jean had been frustrated. Lady La Tour sued the Berkeleys and Bayley in Boston at a special court, but the case rapidly plunged into conflict and confusion. Awaiting the outcome of an appeal against the court's disputed award, she had to pledge a further £700 to Captain John Parris of Charlestown for three ships to sail her home to Fort St. Jean late in 1644.[16]

The dispute soon spread to London. On 1 March 1645, Stephen Winthrop, newly arrived there, reported to his elder brother John Jr. in Boston that Alderman Berkeley had "arrested all our goods and is at suit with some of us" Boston merchants involved in the case with assets in London. Berkeley's anger at the colony's perceived injustice to him in his confrontation with Lady La Tour had been fuelled by depositions from sympathizers in the Bay: "Major Sedgwick, Mr. Russell, Mr. Maverick and Trerice were they that did inform against the country under their hands."

---

[15]   The Winthrop involvement can be followed through the many index entries under La Tour in *WJ, WP*; similarly, La Tour index entries in *CSPCol*, 1, give important information from the English standpoint.

[16]   According to D'Aulnay, Lady La Tour was the cause of La Tour's "contempt and rebellion," *WJ*, 2: 201. She had fled from France despite a special restraining order from the King. Bayley was probably Jean de Bayley, a sea captain and merchant of La Rochelle, a Huguenot or Protestant enclave on the western French coast much involved in the Canada trade. La Tour had been driven out of Port Royal by D'Aulnay in 1639. In June 1643 La Tour had arrived in Boston en route to Acadia from La Rochelle with 140 settlers. *WJ*, 2: 105, 181.

They strongly opposed the colony's relationship with the French. Winthrop senior, whose impulsive partiality to La Tour had led to his loss of the governorship in 1644 and had plunged the General Court into crisis, bewailed that "this business . . . made some difference between the merchants of Charlestown (who took part with the merchants and master of the ship) and the merchants of Boston, who assisted the Lady (some of them deeply engaged for La Tour)." He claimed disingenuously that Berkeley's informants, "divers persons of good credit here . . . reported the truth for the most part yet not the whole truth being somewhat prejudiced in the case." This Charlestown support for the Berkeleys and Bayley against the La Tours infuriated the beleaguered Winthrop. Those whom he regarded as betrayers "were called into question about it after, for the offence was great and they had been [would have been] censured for it if proof could have been had for legal conviction." Antagonism between Charlestown and Boston simmered until 26 December 1644, when the Berkeleys' *Gillyflower* managed to slip out of Boston harbor and sailed to London with the incriminating depositions.[17]

What lay behind this face-off between Charlestown and Boston merchants? One probable reason was resentment against Bostonians Edward Gibbons and Captain Thomas Hawkins (until very recently Charlestown neighbors) and others for their mercenary support of La Tour in 1643 in his campaign to break D'Aulnay's blockade of the St. John River. During this unofficial expedition, the freebooters looted a D'Aulnay pinnace of its cargo of four hundred moose skins and four hundred beaver pelts. Gibbons had befriended and entertained La Tour and was known to have ambitions to control the commerce of Nova Scotia. This conflicted with the plans and interests of Charlestown's London allies. Winthrop himself expressed his displeasure at the volunteers' provocative depredations, which he described as "offensive and grievous to us."[18]

---

[17] *WP*, 5: 13; *WJ*, 2: 153, 206–7, 256. As well as Stephen Winthrop's assets, those of Captain Joseph Weld, a fellow passenger from Boston, were "arrested." Samuel Maverick (ca. 1602–69+), had been in New England since about 1624. The merchant son of a Devonshire minister, he lived on Noddle's Island in the Bay and was a frequent opponent of the Puritan authorities; he signed the Childe Petition against church-member-only franchise and served as a royal commissioner in 1665, seeking to curb New England independence. He was an elder brother of Charlestown resident Elias Maverick. Bailyn, *Merchants*, 83, 114–15; Aspinwall, 71–2, *GMB*.

[18] *WJ*, 2: 136; Dunn, 441. Charlestown was still smarting from Gibbons's refusal to hand over land that he had obtained from Squaw Sachem (the widow of the Pawtucket chief Nanepemashet; see below, Mass Violence) around Mystic Ponds in 1639. He had been acting as the town's representative in the negotiations, or so Charlestown thought. MxCC D&O, 1: doc. 1940. Edward Gibbons (ca. 1606–54) was an early Charlestown trader at Piscataqua, on the southern border of Maine, and in 1636 sent a bark to Bermuda. It returned, after brief seizure in Hispaniola, eight

Another ground for objection was that merchants like Sedgwick and Russell, with most of their assets invested in the fishing industry off the Maine coast, would oppose any Massachusetts adventures that would increase the prospect of reprisals against their unarmed fishermen. La Tour would reveal his perfidy late in 1646 when he suddenly turned on some English traders, seized their ship and £400 cargo off Cape Sable, and forced them ashore at gunpoint. They had local Indians to thank for survival in the middle of winter. Sedgwick may well have sympathized with D'Aulnay, whom he escorted from Boston as far as Castle Island on 28 September 1646 after a conciliatory meeting to settle his losses from the Gibbons-Hawkins raid.[19]

Lady La Tour's case arose when Massachusetts was experiencing a crisis of government. The assistants and the deputies in the General Court were engaged in a hostile standoff, which had already cost Winthrop his governorship. Sedgwick was a longstanding Charlestown representative, a leading voice among deputies outraged by the rash and arbitrary dealings of Winthrop and his Boston cronies with the wheedling La Tour. They were plainly unimpressed by the old governor's comparison of himself and the colony with the Good Samaritan, the Queen of Sheba, and other biblical exotics. Moreover, Sedgwick may still have been smarting from his stern 1639 admonition for overcharging and "oppression" in the fervid and bewildering price inflation that gripped Massachusetts in the late 1630s.[20]

The Charlestown merchants and the skipper Trerice sympathized with the new captain of the *Gillyflower* and his crew. The Massachusetts authorities seemed hopelessly mired in disagreement about the justice of the suit and countersuit. Since the main defendant in the case, Alderman Berkeley, was absent in London, and Captain Bayley had made his escape, the mariners stood to lose the huge sum of £2,000, and had already

---

months later in June 1637, escorting a captured prize for sale, with cargo of tallow, hides, and an alligator "which he gave to the governor." *WJ*, 1: 222.

[19] Dunn, 643; *WJ*, 2: 275. Ipswich, similarly concerned about its fishing and commercial interests down east, also protested against the La Tour imbroglio; ibid., 131, *WP*, 4: 401–10; cf. Endecott of Salem and Gorges of Piscataqua, ibid., 394–96. La Tour used the ship for piracy. As part of the reconciliation Winthrop was able to offload a Mexican sedan, a spoil of war which had recently been presented to him by the buccaneer Captain Thomas Cromwell, ibid, 273.

[20] In June and July 1644, D'Aulnay's Penobscot base had been attacked by an unofficial gang of Mainers and La Tour's men; they burned a farmhouse, killed cattle, and took two of D'Aulnay's men prisoner, *WJ*, 2: 170. D'Aulnay was away in France gathering further troops and official support. Winthrop's justification, ibid., 105–116; constitutional crisis, exacerbated by the "business" of Goody Sherman's sow: 127–28. "Oppression," Frothingham, 136; cf. Robert Keayne's undying sense of injustice: B. Bailyn, ed., *The Apologia of Robert Keayne* (New York: Harper, 1964).

had all their cargo offloaded and assets seized. Their wages, provisions, and paying passengers for the return voyage were all at risk. Not only did Sedgwick and Co. offer financial support and guarantees for the seamen, but they also raised the possibility of a review of the case in London. This set some Bostonian and provincial hackles rising; it seemed a dangerous challenge to the colony's virtual but vulnerable independence.[21]

What really clinched the Charlestown opposition to Boston was Charlestown's association with the Canadian commercial ambitions and political radicalism of the Berkeleys and their colleague James Russell. Berkeley and Russell were leading members of the "New Merchants" identified by Robert Brenner as a radical counterbalance to the traditionally dominant and royalist "Company Merchants." Excluded from the Mediterranean and the Indian Ocean by monopolist companies like the Levant, Turkey, East India, and Merchant Adventurers, these newcomers developed the transatlantic trade; after 1641 they seized power in London and orchestrated popular support for the parliamentary cause. Berkeley (d. 1653) was a member of the London Committee of Safety in 1641, an alderman and a parliamentary customs commissioner in 1643, and in 1649 a member of the Navy Regulating Commission and a judge of leading royalists. He and Russell had collaborated with Sedgwick's brother-in-law and partner Robert Houghton in the radicals' Additional Sea Fund to Ireland (private investment to put down the 1641 Irish Rebellion) in June 1642.[22]

James Russell (ca. 1610-55), an adopted Londoner from Hereford, was probably our Richard's elder brother or cousin. Like Richard, James was an apprentice of the Drapers' Company, but his master was also a Merchant

---

[21] WJ, 2: 205–9.

[22] William Berkeley's interest in "the Canada trade" had been sparked in the early 1620s, when James I granted the princes' Scottish tutor and court favorite Sir William Alexander (later Earl of Stirling) a patent for the eastern Canadian peninsula to be called Nova Scotia. Later in the decade, England and France went to war; Berkeley joined up with the Scots to take over the whole area south of the mouth of the St. Lawrence from the few French settlers, and exploit its teeming resources of fish and furs. They formed the Canada Company, removed or incorporated the French, and established a base at Port Royal. Their plans were derailed by royal negotiations in Europe. By the Peace of Saint-Germain-en-Laye in 1632, the Canada Company was forced to hand back its conquests to France; its rights, justifications, assets, expenditures, and losses were all disregarded. They did not rate against Charles I's urgent need to get his hands on the residue of Queen Henrietta Maria's dowry. However, as a result of approaches to the Secretary of State in 1636, the aggrieved parties were granted powers for three years "to surprise, to take, eject, enjoy and possess" French property in compensation for their extensive losses. The Bostonians' marauding not only endangered fishing and commerce, but also blatantly infringed the Canada Company's powers. *CSPCol,* I: 9, 114, 119, 128–29, 151, 240, 309–11, 313, 324, 432, 441, 444, 453, 471–72, 496. Royal licence: 219. Brenner, *Merchants and Revolutionaries,* 191, 123, fn. Coldham, 1: 31, 35; 3: 6. Brenner, 183, 322, 370, 397, 432, 484, 553, 548; Valerie Pearl, *London and the Outbreak of the Puritan Revolution* (Oxford: Oxford University Press, 1961), 313.

Adventurer and East India Company partner. By 1642, when he was elected to the populist Common Council of London, he had established a lucrative business with Spain and the New World, as well as interloping, like other New Merchants, into the East India Company's monopoly in the Indian Ocean. Thereafter he too was an important figure in London politics and parliamentary administration, especially the customs, the navy, and colonial affairs. He grew rich on episcopal and royalist lands. Russell lived in the notable Puritan parish of St. Stephen's Coleman Street, with its intimate New England connections.[23]

Despite the supporting depositions from Charlestown, the Berkeleys and Bayley were unable to obtain redress in the English Courts of Admiralty and Chancery or the House of Lords, and, as Winthrop wrote with relief and glee, "they lost all their charges." The deaths of D'Aulnay and Lady La Tour and the marriage of their relicts in 1650 brought unwonted unity to the Acadian settlements. In 1654, however, as Britain's first war against the Dutch was brought to a conciliatory end, Cromwellian relations with France deteriorated. Robert Sedgwick, by now a major-general and valued official of the Protectorate, who had been raising a force to attack New Amsterdam, switched his attentions to Acadia. His troops destroyed three French forts and he took the region back under British sovereignty as Nova Scotia. Though the French protested, Cromwell signalled his approval by naming a prize warship *Accadia*. This final justice and vindication must have given Sedgwick enormous satisfaction.[24]

Within little more than a decade of its foundation, Charlestown's mercantile leaders and seafarers had become deeply involved in the Maine and Newfoundland fisheries, the fur and timber export business, the carrying trade in tobacco and sugar, and the importation of a multiplicity of essential dry goods, notably cloth, ironware, and salt, as well as exotic produce like wine, dried fruit, spices, and oil. They were partners with English merchants and manufacturers, and their town was one of

---

[23] G. E. Aylmer, *The State's Servants* (London: Macmillan, 1973), 216; Brenner, 175–76, 193, 587; Pearl, 324. D.L. Kirby, "The Radicals of Coleman Street," *Guildhall Miscellany*, 3 (1970), 99–111. Many of the founders of New Haven, including Rev. John Davenport, had been members of the Coleman Street congregation.

[24] B. Capp, *Cromwell's Navy* (Oxford: Clarendon, 1989) 91; *ODNB*; Frothingham, 136–38; *WJ*, 2: 248, fn. The Council of State in London received a petition in May 1656 from Edward Gibbons's widow, who was in desperate circumstances because La Tour had failed to redeem a mortgage of £379 on Fort St. Jean advanced by her late husband. In all, he seems to have owed Gibbons over £2,000, *WP*, 5: 43–51. La Tour, under the Scoticized name of Sir Charles St. Stephen, baronet of Nova Scotia, was also required to pay £1,812 due to Sedgwick's occupying force in July 1656, *CSPCol*, 1: 444.

the terminals of the Atlantic trade network. They had kinsmen, agents, and attorneys at hubs around the ocean rim. They were in competition with other New England ports: most closely with Boston, which as the seat of colonial government seemed to be pulling ahead by the 1640s, but also with Salem, ideally situated for the fisheries. The removal of entrepreneurs like Gibbons and experienced navigators like Thomas Hawkins must have been galling. Nonetheless, throughout our period important merchants, skippers, and shipbuilders continued to live in Charlestown and gave it an outward-facing perspective very different from that of its upstream neighbors.

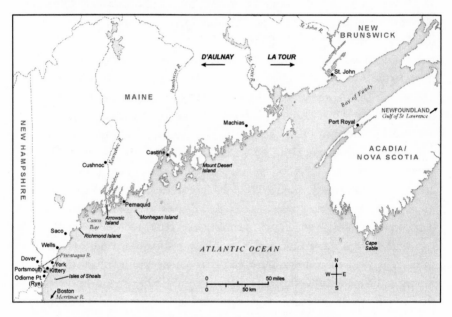

MAP 5. MAINE AND NOVA SCOTIA

The Caribbean
Comes to Charlestown:
Leverett, Norton, Clark,
Manning & Co. v.
Captain Augustine Walker, 1653,
and Walker v. Harrington, 1653

Charlestown harbor witnessed an act of piracy in June 1653, or so it must have seemed. A moored ship, jointly owned by some of the leading merchants of Charlestown, Cambridge and Boston, was boarded by Charlestown skipper Augustine Walker; its watchman was tied up, and it was "drawn up" to Walker's ship, where its guns were removed. When Charlestown merchant Nicholas Davison and others attempted "friendly persuasion to make peace" before the partners had to resort to a court order, "Walker said 'If the magistrates send anybody it [will] be upon their perils.' Whereupon Mr. Davison replied that, if the court ordered him, he would with four or six men demand the vessel, and if [Walker] did kill anybody he would be hanged for it, to which Walker replied, 'Then there will be an end to me.'" Another neighbor was similarly rebuffed. "If any vessel were to take again, he would take it. If I retrieved the vessel, he would cut off my head." This kind of talk smacked of the Spanish Main and the Jolly Roger, rather than the mouth of the Charles—less renowned for its "jollity."[25]

---

[25] Captains John Leverett and Thomas Clark of Boston, William Manning of Cambridge, and Francis Norton of Charlestown were wealthy and influential merchants and officials; see Bailyn, *Merchants,* "Captain Norton's Estate," below, and Savage. Nicholas Davison (1611–64),

When Walker was required to justify his seizure, he claimed "Mr. Welch had taken the ship in a piratical way from the French at Montserrat [West Indies]." Notarial records show that Walker was familiar with the island, but he offered no proof of his assertion, or any prior legal right he might have had to ownership. How Leverett and partners had acquired the ship is also undocumented, though a state of war existed in 1653, and purchases of captured or "prize" ships were not uncommon.[26]

Walker had arrived in Charlestown in 1638, and soon became a church member, as did his first wife Anna. According to family tradition, he was born in Berwick-Upon-Tweed, the fortified northeastern port on the lawless border between England and Scotland. He was a busy Atlantic sea captain, recorded at Faial in the Azores in March 1647 and again in January 1648; in Montserrat in the summer of 1648; Barbados, as master of the *John*, in the fall of 1649; and Bilbao, northern Spain, as master of the *Unity*, late in 1653, after the untoward events in Charlestown harbor. His reputation up to that point had been one of generosity and public service. He had helped Stephen Winthrop when the holed ship Winthrop was aboard limped into the Azores in the winter of 1647–48. He had expended his own money on behalf of Massachusetts in the early 1650s. At that time, he had also begun to import wine on his own account. His family was growing rapidly; by 1650 he had a daughter and three sons and was in the process of building a larger house on the waterfront.[27]

---

presumably another partner, had arrived in Charlestown in 1639 from London as agent of Matthew Craddock, first governor of The Massachusetts Bay Company. Davison soon began trading on his own account, especially in the Maine fisheries in partnership with Norton and others, and exported pipestaves to Madeira on behalf of Craddock's widow. He built a "great wharf" at Charlestown, and served twice as selectman. In London in 1647, he dealt in precious goods like watches, cut amethysts, plate, and silk.In 1653 he shared the purchase of fishing base Pemaquid, Maine, with Richard Russell, and two years later embarked on a commercial voyage to Barbados, England, and Ireland in the *Trade Increase*. He was by then also involved in cattle raising on 2,000 acres in the Connecticut Valley, and large Virginian tobacco shipments to London. His probate inventory totalled £1,896, of which £1,525 was land and livestock. He may have been a kinsman of Michael Davison, London clothworker and merchant, who was a close associate of Matthew Craddock and William Pennoyer and the son of Richard Davison, plumber and citizen of London. Nicholas was related by marriage to the Boston shipbuilder John Anderson. Wyman, 283–84; Rodgers, 2: 229–36; *Sfk Deeds*, 1: 4, 12, 29, 80, 81, 91, 110; 2: 68, 124, 126; 3: 46, 49, 50. Aspinwall, 43, 73, 75, 114–16, 142, 156, 232–39, 242–45, 290, 295, 330, 342–43; MxCC RB, 1: 130, 200, 255. Aspinwall, 1: 40–43 has, unusually, both court minutes and file documents. This suggests that the incident may have occurred while the court was sitting.

[26]   Welch: none of the New England Welches qualify; he was probably a Caribbean skipper. Notarial: see next footnote. Purchases: e.g. *Accadia* captured by Sedgwick in Nova Scotia, 1653, see "La Tour" above, note 18; cf. Capp, *Cromwell's Navy*, 4–5, 58, 232–34.

[27]   Berwick: Savage. Faial: Aspinwall, 109, *WP*, 5: 146 [Stephen Winthrop letter]; Montserrat: Aspinwall, 171; Barbados: ibid., 278; Bilbao: MxCC RB, 1: 77; money: *MR*, 3: 295, 23 October 1652, General Court reimburses. A letter from Samuel Winthrop on 7 August 1648 suggests that

Indeed, it may have been frustrating building problems as much as Walker's experience in various swashbuckling ports that brought his anger to boiling point and prompted his violent outburst against the authorities of the Bay. At the same June 1653 court session in which the seizure of the ship was first complained of, a thwarted Walker had sued the builder Richard Harrington for breach of covenant and damages in the large amount of £40.[28]

Walker's house was to be an imposing building by early Charlestown standards. It stood by the riverfront, three stories high, and made up most of his real estate inventory of £150. Walker also owned half a warehouse. It was for one or other of these buildings that he commissioned Harrington to construct a cellar on 4 June 1652. The specifications were quite detailed: thirty feet by twenty-six feet by five and a half feet deep, with walls "sufficient against water, rammed about with clay." This large cool store was to have a drain and pump, also rammed with clay. The work was to be completed within three months. Walker contracted to pay £40 in installments as the work went on, half the pay in goods and half in provisions. Harrington put his mark on a bond of £80 to fulfil his side of the covenant. Henry Ambrose, a carpenter recently arrived in Charlestown, witnessed the bond.[29]

The walls of the cellar seemed sound for most of the winter of 1652–53. Harrington called John Smith, 30, a ship's carpenter, to inspect his workmanship. Even "when the spring tides was about six feet above the foundations of the cellar . . . [Smith saw] no water to wash into the cellar through the walls." Yet water *was* coming in; three coopers "often at the cellar . . . found water in the cellar *before* the storms, and about 20 pipes of wine did swim about therein." Their explanation: "The pump and drain were insufficient." Michael Long, 30, son of Charlestown's tavern-keeper, and lighterman Abraham Bell, also 30, who both unloaded wine for Walker "at the cellar, found the water so deep that they could not go in but on

---

Walker had recently sailed from Rotterdam. On 17 November 1648, Aspinwall, 171, registered a protest on behalf of Roger Grice of Montserrat because Walker had sailed without waiting for Grice's cargo; the circumstances are unknown. Wine and house: see below.

[28] The documents in this case are: MxCC RB, 1: 38; D&O, 1: docs. 210–13, 225–240, 253–55, 277.

[29] Doc. 210; Harrington had arrived in Charlestown by 1643, when his wife became a church member. He was in considerable financial difficulties during the 1650s, and had to sell both his dwelling and his warehouse on Wapping Row in 1657. He died, worth only some £76, in 1659, two years after his wife. Wyman, 24, Rodgers, 1: 402. Ambrose had been itinerant since his arrival in Hampton in 1641; previous to Charlestown he had been in Boston. He died, quite wealthy, in Salisbury in 1658, Savage.

wooden skids. The pipes of wine were like to subside [cave in]. Long said one did subside." Even Smith had to admit that "one month [after his first visit] he saw water come through the cellar walls which he conceived was by the clay and gravel being washed away."[30]

Harrington was not without support. Stephen Fosdick, at age seventy one of the most experienced builders in Charlestown, had inspected the cellar with Captain Walker after the wine was stowed; neither found fault with the wall; "it was a sufficient wall." Richard Knight, 42, confirmed that "the wall was rammed with clay round about." James Barrett, another woodworker, corroborated that "the work was sufficient from beginning to end. The water arose out of the ground 18 inches within a week after the storms. He saw winds and storms were beat up against the wall and some over washed the clay from the wall." The contention of these witnesses for the defense was that the unusual spring storms must be blamed, rather than poor workmanship.

Walker was alarmed. He "entrusted [carpenter and witness] Henry Ambrose to go to Goodman Harrington to tell him that the wall was not good. He took part of it down and built it a second time and I [Ambrose] came to look at the summer beam; the wall shook and many stones fell out." In his barely legible hand, he added: "I was put to a great deal of trouble." Ambrose Leach, 37, observed "the carpenter at work to shore up the summer [beam], the wall not being able to bear them as did appear by being ready to fall in." At this point, Walker felt that the "great deal of trouble" and loss that he had suffered justified court action.[31]

Maddeningly for Walker, the jury were swayed by the experienced craftsmen who had declared the work to be "sufficient" and the flooding and collapse unpredictable and unpreventable. They found for Harrington, and even required Walker to pay his 10 shillings 4d costs. It is not hard to see this "outrageous" verdict as provocation to a blunt seadog; when a group of local notables appeared to have acquired a ship illicitly, he lunged into direct and vengeful action.

Walker soon came to his senses, thanks to the threat of imprisonment. He claimed he had been provoked into rash threats, but had quickly "given [orders to his crew] under his own hand that the magistrates should have

---

[30] Clay was commonly used for waterproof binding because no accessible source of lime for mortar had yet been found in New England; even the ironworks at Saugus had to use a substitute as a flux. E. N. Hartley, *The Ironworks on the Saugus* (Norman: University of Oklahoma Press, 1990), 149, 167. Coopers: James Mirick, 40, Thomas Brigden, Jr., 24, Benjamin Lathrop, 25. Pipe: cask holding some 105 gallons.

[31] Summer: main beam bearing the joists of a floor above.

the vessel, and that none should shoot a gun." At the second session of the court on 1 July 1653, Edward Collins, foreman of the jury, pronounced their verdict: "Captain Walker's offence had been heinous concerning his contempt for authority and sad issue that might a come [*sic*] of his riotous act . . . elsewhere the fine would have been greater, but here it should be £20 with costs and a bond in £100 to keep the peace for one year."[32]

Walker still smarted against the cellar verdict, and sought a review of the case in the fall of 1653. Though an attachment was served on Richard Harrington on 27 December 1653, the captain was unable to proceed. He died on board his ship *Unity* at Bilbao, Northern Spain, on 1 January 1654. He left behind him his second wife Mary and four children. His estate "was much indebted to several persons" both in New England and overseas. Edward Burt and George Bunker were deputed by the governor and magistrates on 27 July 1654 to discover the precise amount owed and administer the estate. Apart from real estate, the administrators found only £70-worth of personal assets, and for the rest of the 1650s wrestled to balance the books by selling property. Their main sales were the big house and the half-storehouse. Despite the probate valuation of £150, they could only coax £70 from Captain John Trumbull for both buildings. No doubt the buyer had heard about the cellar![33]

---

[32] MxCC RB, 1: 43. Walker's sureties for the peace were Richard Russell and Robert Long; his bondsman in £40 to pay his fine within three months was none other than Captain Francis Norton.

[33] Rodgers, 1: 178–82.

"Cutting One Another's Throats for Beaver": Tidd v. Collicutt, 1656–57

Visit any exhibition of Tudor or early Stuart portraits, and the importance of fur is immediately obvious. It served both as a practical comforter inside damp, chill, draughty buildings or similarly numbing conveyances, and as an item of conspicuous display. It covered winter bedding and softened stone or boarded floors; it lined gowns, warmed heads with beaver felt hats. Van Dyck's dazzling portrait of the great Puritan Earl of Warwick in pink and silver silk has him holding a broad-brimmed, black beaver hat—the only item of sobriety in his court costume. New England and Canada had long been known as sources of peltry from the casual trucking of European fishermen with Native American trappers near the coast. The fur trade was a major lure to investors in the Massachusetts Bay Company, and it is no coincidence that members of the London Company of Skinners (including furriers) were influential. When the Massachusetts Company and Charter migrated in 1630, the "Undertakers" who oversaw the company stock left in London were encouraged in an otherwise thankless operation by the offer of half the fur monopoly in the Bay. Among emigrants, many fantastic futures were conjured around the prospect of enormous riches from the frontier fur trade. With such expectations, "cutthroat competition" was almost inevitable.[34]

---

[34] Bailyn, *Merchants*, 23–29, 36; Francis X. Moloney, *The Fur Trade in New England* (Cambridge: Harvard University Press, 1931) remains the basic source. Matthew Craddock, first governor of the Massachusetts Bay Company, and investor Joseph Caron were both skinners. Frances Rose-Troup, *The Massachusetts Bay Company* (New York: Grafton, 1930), 19, 24, 147. Portrait: the ca. 1634 likeness, now at the Metropolitan Museum of Art in New York, is reproduced in the *ODNB* entry for Robert Rich, 2nd Earl of Warwick (1587–1658).

In May 1656 the bark *Swallow*, John King master, sailed into the mouth of the Kennebec River (Sagadahock) where the short-lived west-country Plymouth Company had briefly established their bridgehead fifty years before. Chartered by Joshua Tidd (1607–78) of Charlestown, the vessel carried "English provisions:" beer, liquor, sack (white wine), gunpowder, cloth, ironware, and trinkets, along with some newly traded beaver, otter, and moose skins. Vessel and cargo were worth £500. The local inhabitants, under their "captain," John Richards of Arrowsic Island in the estuary, "surprized" the crew, boarded the bark, and confiscated it and its cargo near Alexander Goyt's house. Their justification was that Tidd had traded contrary to their patent with the natives, and, they claimed, had trucked liquor for pelts with the local Abenakis on the Sabbath, thus committing two cardinal sins at once. George Munnings, a Boston shoemaker on board, asked the locals by what authority they acted. Was it Plymouth Plantation's down the coast? Richards answered that they had none. Munnings replied: "The magistrates of Massachusetts will not put up [with] this matter." Although one of the boarders admitted that he "would have given pounds not to have meddled in this matter or followed" his captain, nonetheless the rest "were resolved to take Tidd's estate from him." He begged them to "spare the moose and beaver, and rather take the English goods." Plainly, the furs were what he most valued.[35]

Richard Collicutt's role in this fracas was highly ambiguous. On the one hand, he was at Capanagassett, 20 miles away, when the bark was seized. He was consulted about Plymouth Plantation's patent and was urged by Tidd to arbitrate with the inhabitants. With Munnings's help, Collicutt persuaded John Richards to accept £50-worth of goods and leave the pelts and the bark to Tidd. He and Munnings went aboard and oversaw the handover to inhabitants' vessels of the "booty," which included two barrels of beer, one of sack, provisions, liquor, and powder. None went to Collicutt's boat. On the other hand, he was depicted by several of Tidd's company as the real perpetrator. John Richards was alleged to have said that he would have given £10 not to be involved, but "he was wished by Mr. Collicutt to go aboard." When Tidd sought to save his furs, the boarders were reported to have replied: "If Mr. Collicutt would be satisfied, it was all one to them." Mariner Matthew Clark was told by a local couple

---

[35] The case is in MxCC RB, 1: 132, and D&O, 1: docs. 987–1000. King may have come from Weymouth, Savage; Munnings was originally from Rattlesden, Suffolk. He lived in Watertown from 1634 to ca. 1645, before moving to Boston; he had lost an eye in the Block Island fight, 1637, and acted as Boston jailer. At this time, he was in his late 50s. Alexander Goyt may have been related to John Goyt of Essex County. *GMB,* 2: 801.

that "Mr. Collicutt had said he would weary the coasters out of the River; taking Joshua Tidd was a good deed." In these depositions, he seems to be the power behind the surprise attack.[36]

Tidd certainly thought so. It was Richard Collicutt he sued on 18 June 1657 "for taking away his estate to the value of £50 by joint consent with John Richards of Kennebec and associates." The jury were not persuaded. They found for the defendant, and awarded him £1–3–2 costs.

This case raises serious issues involving Charlestown's mercantile ambitions and the commercial environment of the third decade of settlement. What appears to be a blatant act of piracy or mob attack turns out to be far more complex once the characters and context are examined.

First, the characters: Joshua Tidd or Tead (1607–78), by now about fifty, had arrived in Charlestown in 1637 from Hertford, a renowned Puritan center twenty-five miles north of London, which gave its name to the capital of Connecticut. He became a church member in 1639. By trade he was a carpenter, a highly valued and well-paid profession. He served the town as constable, and Middlesex County as grand juryman, acting as foreman in 1655. In 1648 he built a shop and portal by the east door of the meetinghouse. In the 1660s and 1670s he was twice a selectman, as well as rate commissioner, ensign, and then lieutenant of the militia. In the year of the seizure, his eldest daughter Sarah married the successful sea captain Zechariah Long. During the 1650s, Tidd used Chelmsford fur trader John Cromwell as his agent in small transactions with Indian trappers. He also dealt with Captain John Trumbull for English goods, especially fabrics and haberdashery. His bruising experiences with both Trumbull and the Kennebec residents seem to have driven him back to woodworking. In 1668, he managed major renovations of the meetinghouse. Inside the building, he had been recruited as reliably orthodox by the three deacons in 1665 to help them contain and control the Baptist challenge. He refused an unusual third term in the responsible but time-consuming job of constable, and his reasons were eventually accepted. He lived a long and useful life in Charlestown, a reliable middle manager in the militia, church, and town government. The Kennebec imbroglio appears a rare external venture.[37]

---

[36] I have not been able to identify Capanagassett. Deponents: George Munnings and Johanna, his second wife, aged 45; Clark was a mariner aged 30, originally from Boston, but later of Marblehead, the major fishing port; John Lawrence, 35, Charlestown fisherman and son of Henry of Charlestown.

[37] Hertford: "John Dane's Relation," R, 8 (1854), 147–56; life: Wyman, Savage; Cromwell: Rodgers, 2: 60, and below, "Mass Violence." Trumbull and Tidd fell out in 1658 and again in 1663; Tidd won three cases of debt as defendant, MxCC RB, 1: 161, 278, 292; D&O, 1: docs. 758, 763, 2228, 2242, 2245, 2253; see above, "The Sea: Introduction." On 31 December 1671, he had bought £5

Richard Collicutt (ca. 1604–86), a near contemporary of Tidd's, was a very different character. Though a tailor by trade, he had come in 1632 from Barnstaple, Devonshire, with his young wife and child with the express intention of becoming a fur trader. Already in 1633 he was paying taxes in Dorchester (a West Country emigrants' settlement) on furs he had acquired. From the start he had quickly established relations with Narragansett Indian trappers to the south. From the late 1630s to the mid-1640s, Indian messengers regularly came to him and went to Rhode Island from his house in Dorchester. In 1641 he was licensed by the General Court as an authorized Indian trader and appointed to a standing committee to negotiate with the Indians about furs, wampum, and runaway English servants. John Winthrop recorded Collicutt sailing "eastward [towards Maine] about trading" in November 1648 and the divine providence of his open, storm-tossed, vessel being saved, after prayer, by a great wave lifting it to safety from certain destruction on rocks. This marks a change of his fur-trading focus from the south shore to the northeast. By October 1657 he owed north shore merchants £90 for cloth, a favorite trucking item with the Indians. At the time of his clash with Tidd, he enjoyed elite status in Massachusetts as a leading down-east merchant. It was probably his availability in the Bay that led the "frustrate" Charlestown entrepreneur to sue him at the Middlesex County Court rather than the immediate perpetrator of frustration, John Richards.[38]

Tidd's "surpriser," John Richards (1625–94), is in fact the biggest surprise of the three. From his behavior on the Kennebec in 1656, he sounds like a young piratical swashbuckler, more at home on the Caribbean Spanish Main than the chilly waters of Maine. Yet this John Richards was the same man who had just married into the Winthrop clan, whose in-laws were Bradfords and Hinckleys. He would become a major figure in New England from the early 1670s. By 1656, he was already an "old Maine hand." A decade earlier, his wealthy Weymouth merchant father had established

---

worth of carpenters' nails and steel imported from London. Hull, Letter Book, 46.

[38] *GMB*, 1: 439–46; Bailyn, *Merchants*, 27; he remained in Dorchester when his neighbors moved to Windsor, Connecticut; he was a regular representative and committeeman at the General Court in the 1630s and early 1640s, as well as a town selectman, rate assessor and militia sergeant. He traded with Virginia. *WP*, 3: 496–97; license: *MR*, 1: 322; Indians: *WP*, 4: 1, 26, 431; he had two Pequot servants: *WP*, 3: 435, 496. Collicutt briefly moved to Boston in 1658, before relocating in Maine in the 1660s. He may have returned to Boston before King Philip's War; D. Brenton Simons, *Witches, Rakes and Rogues* (Beverly: Commonwealth Editions, 2005), 210, reports him and Job Lane interviewing a woman suspected of adultery, in Boston in 1673. However, he regularly visited Maine; in 1675, John Hull appointed Collicutt his attorney to get five years' rent for Hog Island, Casco Bay, from Nathaniel Wallace; Letter Book, 261. His son was killed by Indians on Arrowsic Island in the Kennebec Estuary in 1676.

John on Arrowsic Island in the Kennebec Estuary for the fur and Indian trade. He married Elizabeth, daughter of Charlestown sea captain Thomas Hawkins and widow of Nathaniel Long and Adam Winthrop, in Boston on 3 May 1654, but was back east after pelts when Tidd arrived two years later. His membership in the mercantile elite suggests that his quasi-piratical behavior had a more responsible motivation.[39]

The great rivers of northern New England like the Merrimack, the Kennebec, and the Penobscot were the natural routes to penetrate the vast forests and reach the rendezvous where Native American trappers brought in their pelts and exchanged them for English trade goods. In 1603, Bristolian Martin Pring marveled at the range and availability of furs as he explored the lower Kennebec. Another reason for the 1607 Plymouth Company's choosing so northerly a site was that the Sagadahock (as the Lower Kennebec was called) promised furs as well as fish. Captain John Smith optimistically hoped to discover gold or copper in New England; if not, "fish and furs are then our refuge." In 1625, after a good Pilgrim harvest, Edward Winslow took a shallop laden with corn to the Kennebec; his return with 700 lb. of furs (worth roughly £700 in London) led to the establishment of the permanent Cushenoc trading post, forty miles up the Kennebec at the present-day site of Augusta. In 1630, the Council of New England granted Plymouth a patent to a thirty-mile-wide block of land on either side of the river around Cushenoc. Between 1631 and 1636, 12,530 pounds of beaver and thousands of pounds of otter skins were shipped from Plymouth Plantation to London, worth well over £10,000. William Bradford's probate inventory of 1657 listed £256-worth of "trucking stuff at Kennebec." The river was "the way to wealth."[40]

Like most El Dorados, the abundant peltry of the Sagdahock-Kennebec River system attracted the voracious attentions of fortune hunters. A

---

[39] Richards had arrived in Dorchester aged eight in 1633. The eldest son of Thomas and Welthian Richards, he had been baptized at Pitminster in Somerset. The family moved to Weymouth, Massachusetts in 1639. Thomas left a fortune of £1,300 in 1650. Richards returned to Boston in the 1660s; he was elected a deputy in 1671, and assistant in 1681. As well as rising to a senior rank in the militia, he was chosen as agent for Massachusetts to England in the fraught negotiations over the Charter from 1681 to 1683. He managed to fit the Treasurership of Harvard into his busy schedule. He was a member of Dudley's Council in 1686, but proved "a high friend of liberty" in 1689. He served as Councillor and Supreme Court Justice under the 1691 Charter. Richards was a member of the bench at the Salem witch trials. A ubiquitous presence in Sewall's *Diary* in the 1680s and 1690s, he was an enormously important member of the New England elite. *GMB*, 3: 1575–79; Sewall, *Diary*, 60–318, passim.

[40] Burrage, 27, 61, 71, 124, 185, 246; Bailyn, *Merchants*, 23–27; George F. Willison, *Saints and Strangers* (New York: Time, 1945), 309, 363. Charlestown-related fur trader John Cromwell worked in the Merrimack River system.

major problem for any group seeking to protect their patented monopoly of an envied area was the exclusion of interlopers. In 1625–26, the bane of the Pilgrims, Thomas Morton, of Merry-Mount fame, intruded his company up the river, sold forbidden guns, ammunition, powder and grog to the Indians, and consorted with their women. One of his men made £1,000 from furs in only a few years. In 1634, a swaggering gang from the Piscataqua under John Hocking insisted they were going to sail above Cushenoc and tap the headwaters of the Kennebec basin for furs. When their mooring was cut, Hocking killed a Plymouth man, only to be felled himself by return fire. This bloody incident prompted Winthrop's comment about throat-cutting over beaver.[41]

The correct procedure was for traders to obtain licenses from Plymouth and enter bond not to exceed a given quota or behave toward Indians with Mortonian abandon. For a small and weak plantation like Plymouth, however, enforcement was well-nigh impossible. The Plymouth authorities could not even prevent their own Isaac Allerton from insolently trucking on his own account along the Maine coast in 1630. They lost their more northeasterly trading post on the Penobscot (Castine) to the French in 1635; their attempts at recapture were farcical. The following year, Massachusetts merchants were surreptitiously sneaking up the Kennebec for clandestine dealings with the Abenakis. Though the Kennebec pelts had been heavily over-trapped by 1640, and Plymouth had farmed out its patent rights to a private consortium, enough profit persisted so that settled traders continued to resent unlicensed interlopers. Thus Collicutt's strategy to "weary the coasters out of the river" was the rationale for Richards's boarding and seizure. His father had paid a small fortune to set him up as a licensed trader on Arrowsic Island. Far from being a lawless buccaneer, Richards saw himself as a patent enforcement officer.[42]

Casco Bay was undergoing a major jurisdictional change in the mid 1650s. Despite the claims of Gorges heirs, Ligonia, and the Plymouth Plantation Kennebec patent, Massachusetts was inexorably expanding its authority to the northeast. Within two years of the seizure, the Kennebec Basin and the Sagadahock country would be incorporated into the new county of York. This was no doubt what lay behind George Munnings's warning to Richards that "the magistrates of Massachusetts will not put up

---

[41]   Willison, 299; Burrage, 246. Hocking's base on the Piscataqua was David Thompson's settlement at Odiorne's Point (now in Rye, New Hampshire). *WJ,* 1: 124. Morton: William Bradford, *Of Plimouth Plantation,* S. E. Morison, ed. (New York: Knoff, 1952) 204–10.

[42]   Allerton, Massachusetts: Willison, 316, 328; *WP,* 3: 418; Castine: Bailyn, *Merchants,* 23–24.

[with] this matter" of warrantless distraints of property. Soon Robin Hood Richards and his like would have to obey the sheriff of York. Significantly, the Kennebec Patent was bought out by four Boston merchants in 1661.[43]

Joshua Tidd, the Charlestown carpenter, seems to have been an opportunistic tiddler in shark-filled eastern waters. He may have been trying to profit from the overpowering of the French by his neighbor General Robert Sedgwick in 1654, which removed one menace to English trade in Upper Maine. He may have sought markets to offload overstock from the shop in Charlestown. Whatever his motives, he was quite out of his depth in the Wild East.

---

[43] See below, "Our Main End Was to Catch Fish," for this and the next paragraph. Patent: Willison, 508.

"Our Main End Was to Catch Fish": Ridgeway v. Jordan, 1653–56

When a preacher in a down-east coastal settlement assumed his hearers' consent or at least condescension to his claim that "the main end of planting this wilderness" was to extend the kingdom of God on earth, he was in for a shock. "Sir, you are mistaken, you think you are preaching to the people of the Bay," he was informed by one of his hearers. "Our main end was to catch fish." Fish had been what first attracted adventurers to New England. Since the late fifteenth century, enterprising merchants from western European ports, notably English West Country centers like Bristol, Plymouth, Weymouth, or Dartmouth, had sent out ships to harvest and cure the teeming inshore banks from Cape Cod to Newfoundland. By 1622, between three hundred and four hundred vessels a year were fishing from their shallops off the Maine coast. These expeditions were usually seasonal affairs with a temporary shore camp where a few of the company could process the daily catches and prepare them for the lucrative Spanish, Portuguese, and Mediterranean markets. Hands would be hired for each voyage, and would be paid an agreed wage and a small share of the catch.[44]

The early seventeenth-century impulse towards permanent settlement on the North American mainland started with an ambitious but abortive bridgehead at Sagadahock, Maine, in 1607, financed by the Devonshire-based Plymouth Company. Fish lured them freezingly north. The Dorchester Company's similarly short-lived Cape Anne plantation

---

[44] Quote: C. Mather, *Magnalia,* 15; Stephen Hornsby, *British Atlantic, American Frontier* (Lebanon, NH: University Press of New England, 2005); Charles E. Clark, *The Eastern Frontier* (Hanover, NH: University Press of New England, 1983), 13–35; M. Kurlansky, *Cod* (New York: Penguin, 1997), 18–90. 1622: N. Philbrick, *Mayflower* (New York: Viking, 2006), 13; W. J. Bolster, "Putting the Ocean in Atlantic History," *American Historical Review,* 113 (2008), 19–47.

near Gloucester, Massachusetts (1624–26) was also intended as a fishing station. Within two decades of Charlestown's establishment, a necklace of fishing bases had been strung along the northeast coast from Marblehead through Gloucester, Ipswich, and Newbury to the Isles of Shoals, Richmond Island, Pemaquid Peninsula, Damariscove Island, Monhegan Island and beyond. Many of these centers where fishermen began overwintering or settling were bywords for brawling, drunkenness, and masculine mayhem. Such were the lurid lives of the 1,500 fishermen at the eight barren Isles of Shoals off the mouth of the Piscataqua River during the early winter and summer fishing seasons. Even Marblehead, which was a precinct of godly Salem, was a law unto itself: a necessary evil shunted out to its peninsula of misrule.[45]

Fishing by line from open shallops was a hazardous and exhausting job, especially in wintertime when feeding cod were plentiful, but fogs, sudden raging storms, snow, and especially ice, which could capsize open boats laden with catch, caused many losses. It was a young man's game, a way of making some money to buy a farm and settle down. That was the dream. Too many succumbed to the water, or to the strong waters which traders or grog huts temptingly proffered, or to the septicemia from filthy fish hooks impaling frozen fingers, or to extended exposure to damp subzero conditions. The shore stations where they "pewed [forked] out" their catches on to the stages were cramped for space for "flakes" [racks] to dry the fish. Fights flared over incursions into other crews' "rooms," broken bounds or disputed moorings. Two centuries before the Wild West, this fishing frontier was the Wild East.[46]

Where was the sheriff? Officially, north of the Merrimack, the vast stretches of forest bisected by great rivers like the Piscataqua, Kennebec, and Penobscot came under the jurisdiction of the Council of New England in London, the successor of the Plymouth Company. However, despite grandiose plans in England, the few early Maine settlements like the Isles of Shoals, Kittery, Pemaquid, York, Casco, Wells, or Saco went their own ways, either with the credulous followers of unorthodox or womanizing ministers on the run from Massachusetts, or roistering, lawless collections of hard-drinking, fistfighting fishermen.[47]

---

[45]   Clark, 3–12; C. L. Heyrmann, *Commerce and Culture* (New York: Norton, 1984), 209–230; H. S. Burrage, *The Beginnings of Colonial Maine, 1602–1658* (Portland: State of Maine, 1914), passim; W. G. Saltonstall, *Ports of the Piscataqua* (Cambridge: Harvard University Press, 1941), 14.

[46]   Hornsby, 14–15, 25, 32–35, 75–85.

[47]   In 1630, the Council had assigned the area between the Kennebunk and Kennebec Rivers to "The Company of Husbandmen," who never developed the territory. By the 1640s, it had been

One less anarchic fishing station was on Richmond Island, just off Cape Elizabeth in what is now part of Scarborough, at the western end of Casco Bay. This excellent haven for oceangoing ships was acquired in 1631 by a young Plymouth merchant, Robert Trelawney (1598–1643), and manned by as many as sixty West Country fishermen under the command of John Winter. For the next decade it proved highly profitable, but war, deaths, desertions, and depression brought reverses. In 1648 it was owned and run by the late John Winter's son-in-law, Rev. Robert Jordan.[48]

Robert Jordan (1612–79), the son of a Worcester bookseller, went up to Balliol College, Oxford, in 1632. Through his mother he was related to the mercantile Broughton family of Boston and the Purchases of Brunswick, Maine. He had arrived at Richmond as Anglican chaplain in 1641, provoking Puritan outrage. To a neighbor, he was "a minister of Antichrist . . . blasphemous against the Churches of Christ (congregational) in this land." Evidence that "greed was his mastering passion" includes Jordan's monetary feuds with locals, his elbowing out of other Winter and Trelawney heirs, and "his notorious intrigues to elicit personal legacies from his parishioners." His dismissal of a rival as "well nigh able to deceive the wisest brain" is seen as "the judgement of an expert" in such deceptions. Anyone doing business with Robert Jordan needed an extra pair of eyes.[49]

The Trelawney papers include a set of accounts between Robert Jordan and John Ridgeway of Charlestown for a fishing voyage in 1651. Jordan's outlay of £99 included £24 for salt, and the same amount for the

---

sold to Colonel Alexander Rigby, a leading Lancashire parliamentarian, and was known as Lygonia. The Council had earlier granted what is now New Hampshire to John Mason, recently governor of Newfoundland and a dedicated colonizer who died in 1636, and Maine to Sir Ferdinando Gorges, of Plymouth and Bristol. Gorges, an Elizabethan throwback, had aristocratic fantasies about a vast feudal domain, "Gorgeana," with subsidiary vassalages between the Piscataqua and the Kennebec. His elaborate plans for his fiefdom went down to the level of bailiwicks, hundreds, and parishes with municipal officers and law enforcers. None of this ever got far beyond paper projections. Burrage, 156–356; Clark, 16–20, 47–51. Mason, Gorges, and Rigby: *ODNB*. Mason: see "Captain Norton's Estate" below. Ministers: e.g. Rev. Stephen Bachiller or Richard Gibson, at Strawberry Bank (Portsmouth, NH).

[48] J. P. Baxter, ed., *The Trelawney Papers* (Portland: Hoyt, Fogg and Donham, 1884); Clark, 21–26; "Focus on Richmond Island," *Great Migration Newsletter,* 8 (1997), 31–32; Burrage, 301, has an account of Trelawney employees absconding from Richmond Island for the Piscataqua to "fish for themselves." Trelawney died in 1643, Winter in 1645: *GMB*, 3: 2036–38, Burrage, 342. The crisis in the Maine fishing industry was widespread in the late 1640s and English fish merchants complained about variable quality, "cheating" New Englanders and shortfalls in catches, G. F. Steckley, ed., "Letters of John Paige, London merchant, 1648–58," *London Record Society,* 21 (1984) 9–10.

[49] *GDMNH*, 390–91; *GMB*, 3: 1529–35 has a sketch on Thomas Purchase which omits any mention of Jordan. Neighbor: *WP*, 4: 434. Territorially, Richmond Island was claimed by Lygonia, by Gorgeana and by Massachusetts.

hire of two boats. Ridgeway claimed £70 spent on salt, £88 on men's wages, £26 for himself, and £22 for diet, expenses and work, with other expenditures coming to £332 in all. Though no contract survives, presumably Jordan had gone into partnership with Ridgeway, who would oversee catching and curing while Jordan would arrange delivery of the cargo to an English or Bay exporter. The accounts are not signed off.[50]

We know little about John Ridgeway before 1648. He had been born in 1623 and was a witness to a Boston letter of credit in cash or fish dated 23 December 1648. About 1651 or 1652, he married Mary Brackenbury, and their son John was born in 1653. He appears in the early Middlesex County Court Records in cases involving mariners, fishermen, shipmasters and merchants. He comes across as a very active and ambitious young skipper, but short of capital at this early stage of his career. The partnership with Jordan should have provided a handy profit; instead, it plunged him into a sea of troubles.[51]

The first dousing came in the late fall of 1652. In the words of Ridgeway's undated "Declaration" for the Middlesex County Court, describing his next expeditions in 1652:

> I had [laid] out on fishing, desiring for the good of myself and this country, £700 to £800. My dealings in that design are not unknown. 5,000 to 6,000 pounds were fished and weighed out to me at Monhegan [Island]. I then bought a bark of Mr. [William] Brown of Salem and William Lillaby [whose] receipt is with Mr. Danforth. Having great occasion to send my bark eastward, I sent her with my servants and hired a master and fishermen, salt and provisions, and so to bring her laden with fish back again. As they were bound along the shore they put in at Richmond Island and landed to an anchor the east side thereof. The next morning Mr. Jordan came aboard with servants and other men and carried away my bark and caused her to be hauled up, and nobody to look after her, and my goods spoilt, and cask he keepeth to this day there . . . This caused great loss to me; I paid £200 for the freight of my goods since, besides the loss of my fishing.

Ridgeway had three witnesses to these events, including Thomas

50 Baxter, 488–90.

51 MxCC RB, 1: 49, 3 Jan 1654, v. Mr John Phillips; D&O, 1: doc. 304, 18 Nov 1653, v. William Waters; doc. 324, 10 Oct 1654, John Long v.; doc. 328, 5 Dec 54, John Tomlins v.; doc. 379, 16 Sep 1654, v. John Culliver. All of these cases probably arose from his expensive and distracting conflict with Jordan.

Sheppie, probably the hired master of the seized bark.[52]

This opportunistic confiscation was authorized by a local attachment issued in support of Jordan's suit for the amount he claimed Ridgeway owed him from their 1651 partnership. A major problem in interpreting this conflict is that little on Jordan's side of the argument has survived. Ridgeway's riposte was to seek arbitration. He traveled up to Richmond Island in March 1653, where Henry Fordlyn and Ambrose Bowden (probably kinsman to Winter's wife Joan) agreed to act as referees. However, when Ridgeway was required "to give in security to stand to the award, he refused, and the business fell." Nonetheless, he indicated that he was prepared to make major concessions to recover his bark: £50 plus one hogshead of train oil, another of "custe," and the remains of the fishing craft [shallops?]. Ridgeway had a writ of replevin to recover his bark, but had insufficient caution money to deposit as a guarantee that he would bring his action to a Maine court. Then, probably fearing local prejudice, "abruptly he went his way without doing anything therein."[53]

For the next three years, an impoverished Ridgeway suffered a Kafka-esque ordeal against a devious and rapacious opponent. His attempts to regain his property were frustrated by jurisdictional disputes, false or inaccurate accounts, vexatious counter-suits and petitions, whereby Jordan "added affliction to affliction and oppression to oppression." By May 1656, Ridgeway, "lying under loads of oppression," petitioned the Massachusetts General Court. In three foolscap pages he poured out his outrage at the "many insupportable burdens" he had endured over the last three and a half years: his original catch lost, his bark and its cables rotting, his £18 per month to hire a replacement, his seamen needing pay, his time wasted waiting at court when he might have been organizing fishing expeditions. The committee perusing petitions remarked on its "voluminous" nature, and thought its "reproaches upon lower and higher courts merited rebuke." Nonetheless, they concluded that Ridgeway had had a raw deal, that Jordan should therefore forfeit a £300 bond, and that if indeed the accounts erred, a special court and jurors should be recalled. If mistakes were found, Ridgeway should be relieved and Jordan should pay costs:

---

[52] Documents covering this case are at MxCC RB, 1: 60, 64, 67, 69, 80, 87; D&O, 1: docs. 516–523. Sheppie was a Charlestown fisherman, to be encountered in "Water Everywhere" below. William Brown was a leading wholesale fish merchant. Monhegan Island, a major fisheries rendezvous 10 miles off Pemaquid Point, was at this time mortgaged to Richard Russell of Charlestown, Burrage, 307.

[53] Doc. 520; I have been unable to identify Fordlyn. OED has no suitable entry for "custe." Replevin, or recovery of goods or stock impounded, usually entailed the recoverer subsequently having to pay compensation.

by this time estimated at £50, an enormous sum. The General Court approved the committee's report.[54]

This is the last we hear of Mr. John Ridgeway in either Charlestown or Middlesex. He may have been in Pemaquid in 1675, but that could have been his son. Jordan, however, continued very much in evidence. He was appointed a magistrate of the Massachusetts county of York in July 1658 in a territorial settlement. He even appears in the English colonial records. Driven out of Casco Bay during King Philip's War, 1675–76, he died at Newcastle on the Piscataqua Estuary in 1679 leaving an estimated 4,000 acres of land, as well as Richmond Island and Cape Elizabeth, to his widow and six sons.[55]

While the main end of those in northern New England waters was, indeed, to catch fish, the fate of John Ridgeway shows that there were other hazards than the anti-social and the environmental. It is ironic that his nemesis in his calling was a minister, though the motives of Robert Jordan were a great deal less pure than those of the preacher in Cotton Mather's anecdote.

---

[54] Mass Archives, May 1656.

[55] *GDMNH*, 391; *CSPCol, America and West Indies*, 2: docs. 200, 220, 255, 302, 317, 320, 774, 1010, 1024, 1220, 1300.

Water Everywhere:
Cole v. Sheppie, 1655–57

You could not go far in seventeenth-century Charlestown without reaching water's edge. To get to Boston or Mystic Side or Malden, the only practical means was by ferry. Heavy goods were best transported by water. The wharves and docks of the town were often laden with sea- or river-borne goods. The mariners, merchants, and fisherman of the town spent much of their lives on or by water. For local trips, two kinds of vessel were popular. The canoe was light, maneuverable and capable of carrying modest cargoes, while the shallop was heavier-built, rowed or sailed: the workhorse of inshore fishermen, lightermen, and movers of heavy loads like firewood, timber, loaded barrels, hay bales, or bricks. The contretemps between John Cole, a seaman, and Thomas Sheppie, a fisherman, beginning in the fall of 1655 illustrates the importance and use of these vessels and of waterborne transport.[56]

Sheppie (ca. 1620–83) had been in Charlestown since at least 1637, and usually appeared in colonial records in company with other mariners. By the 1650s, he was fishing for mackerel, which were seasonally abundant in Massachusetts waters, and had leased from Charlestown Lovells Island at the mouth of Boston Harbor, halfway between Deer Island to the north and Hull and Nantasket to the south. He may have intended to use part of the island as a fishing station, but by the fall of 1654, he was also planning to overwinter cattle, cut firewood, and raise some revenue from his lease. On 23 September 1655, he renewed "a bargain" before two witnesses with John Cole, aged about 32, a recently married seaman, to rent

---

[56] Vickers, *Young Men and the Sea,* 14–15, 29–30; W. A. Baker, "Vessel Types in Colonial Massachusetts," P. C. F. Smith, ed., *Seafaring in Colonial Massachusetts* (Boston: Colonial Society of Massachusetts, 1980), Ch. 1.

one-third of the island and a dwelling with some milch cows until 29 September 1656. The contract was specific about how the rent should be paid. The land was leased for 33 shillings a year, the house for 30 shillings, the cows for £1 each, and a heifer for 30 shillings. The cattle were to be paid for in butter and cheese every quarter, and the real estate in cordwood valued at 3/4d per cord and delivered at the island's waterside for collection. If any cattle died, Sheppie would replace them, but if Cole failed to pay his quarterly rent, he must pay double. This agreement appeared mutually advantageous. Sheppie got his firewood cut and his butter and cheese made, thus providing more seagoing time and perhaps some additional income. Cole got a house and land to support his young family, and the wherewithal to produce his rent. Working men in their early thirties had to watch every penny.[57]

Alas, the agreement soon turned sour. One source of trouble may have been payments or collections of rents. Much of the evidence offered by Cole involves corroboration that he had honored his side of the bargain. Thus on 3 November 1655 a witness confirmed that "twelve months agone, Goodman Sheppie fetched John Cole's wood what I saw." Another deposed that "living at Lovells Island in the summer a year ago, John Cole paid Thomas Sheppie 25 cords of wood in three payments, and so his butter and cheese to his content last at Michaelmas [September 29]. Goodman Sheppie promised Cole's wife to give her an acquittance [receipt]." The Coles could produce a receipt dated 29 December 1655 for £2 rent for the first quarter.[58]

However, the first official sign of trouble involved not rent, but a canoe. Conflict began in the fall of 1654. Faith Patterson, 23, reported seeing John Cole on shore at the island while Thomas Sheppie was collecting some wood corded for him by his tenant. Cole "took up a canoe adrift on the Lord's Day and [emptied] the water out of her and launched her and fetched Goodman Sheppie and myself ashore. We went to Nantasket to meeting and on the Monday we rowed the canoe home to Charlestown," presumably along with Sheppie's wood-laden boat. Cole had saved Sheppie having to haul all his cargo down to meeting. Two

---

[57] Fishing: see above, "Our Main End was to Catch Fish." Bargain: MxCC D&O, 1: doc. 1104. Lovells Island had been granted to Charlestown in 1633. In April 1634 the Town Meeting agreed on annual rent of £20, CTR, 1A: 18. On 1 May 1650 the rent was appropriated towards the schoolmaster's salary, CTR, 1: 677A. In 1670 Richard Russell leased the island for a mere £5 per year, CTR, 3: 90.

[58] The documents in the Cole and Sheppie cases are in MxCC RB, 1: 86, 145, and D&O, 1: docs. 488–494, 1093–1104.

other deponents "heard Thomas Sheppie resign up the canoe to John Cole for his use."[59]

Sheppie soon regretted his generosity. At a subsequent meeting with his tenant, a bystander, Margaret Albone, 24,

> heard John Cole ask Thomas Sheppie whether he intended to carry away the canoe or no. Sheppie said he would but Cole told him he would not. Cole boarded the canoe and was about to untie the rope when Sheppie said he would knock him down, and took up a paddle and stood upon the cuddy of the shallop and struck Cole several blows, the last two upon his neck, at which Cole fell down. My husband thought he had been dead for they could not see his [breathing] for about half an hour. I called Goodman Sheppie to carry Cole to town to bury him, but he answered that he must stay until he died.

In the event, Cole survived. Thomas Starr, Charlestown's physician, recounted treating him "for a contusion in two places about his shoulder . . . About twelve or fourteen days after, Cole complained about inability of action." Starr treated the bruising with "a new application," but Cole continued "disabled from his present employments" for a considerable time. On 26 December 1655 a jury at Charlestown awarded Cole damages of £2-6-0d against Sheppie "for using violence to him and striking him." Cole's attempt to recover the canoe was "cast out" because it was worth less than £2, and thus beneath the dignity of the County Court. However, Sheppie was persuaded to discount Cole's rent by five shillings "about the canoe" on 29 December 1655.[60]

We do not know why Sheppie lashed out. He may have been taking the canoe in lieu of rent unpaid or as a surety for future payments. He had betrayed a violent streak after drinking in the past. As a fisherman, he would be inured to physical conflict. Whatever his reasons, relations with Cole continued to rankle. In December 1657, two years after the assault case, he sued Cole for non-performance of covenant, namely failure to

---

[59] Patterson's testimony of 3 November 1655, doc. 488, refers to events a year before; she was the heavily pregnant wife of carpenter Edward Patterson of Hingham, near Nantasket, and bore another Faith in mid-January 1656. The other two witnesses were Cole's respectable brother-in-law Richard Lowden, 40, and church member George Hepburn, 63.

[60] Cuddy: cabin, *OED*. Margaret Albone's account was corroborated by Daniel King, 30, doc. 494. Her husband may have been related either to Elizabeth Albone or Olbon the wife of Winthrop's fraudster agent at Ten Hills Farm, bigamist James Luxford, L. R. Paige, *History of Cambridge* (Boston: Houghton, 1877), 257, or to a "Sister Olbon, lately Cole" mentioned in the Cambridge Church Records in 1658, *GM*, 1: 14. Starr, son of Dr. Comfort Starr, had recently arrived in Charlestown, and in 1654 had been appointed the town's Clerk of the Writs. He died in 1658.

pay two years' rent, amounting to £15. Despite Cole's calling five mariners who had sailed or rowed out on various occasions to Lovells Island or had met Cole canoeing in the bay, and who swore to loading or seeing cords of wood at the waterside, rent ready for collection, and butter and cheese duly weighed by the Charlestown Clerk of the Market, and despite receipts and a favourable acquittance from Hingham Commissioners for Small Causes, the jury nonetheless found for Sheppie. They awarded damages of £3-12-10, much less than Sheppie claimed, but more than Cole thought he owed. Their reason was "that the butter and cheese pleaded by the defendant to have been paid was not allowed because there was no evidence of weight and value" produced. This verdict sounds nit-pickingly legalistic and the damages suspiciously close to Cole's award two years earlier. However, he and especially his wife Ursula suffered from tainted reputations, as did some of their witnesses. The jury may have sympathized with Sheppie's struggle to make ends meet as a fisherman with a wife and two young children. After his involvement with Ridgeway's disastrous Maine venture, he had only recently been sued for withholding a hogshead of mackerel and impressing a four-ton fishing shallop in a catch-sharing deal with another boat owner. As a boy, he had saved a nine-year-old girl from rape by a seaman, and would appear as a witness for prosecutions in future years. His wife, later a church member, seems to have had several miscarriages during the 1650s, and the Sheppies had just lost an infant son. His probate inventory was only £127 when he died in 1683.[61]

Apart from the clash of interests and personalities, the Sheppie and Cole cases illustrate the watery nature of life, transport, and communication in 17th-century Charlestown. No one nowadays would dream of rowing from Charlestown to Nantasket on the far side of Boston Harbor to attend a church service; they would hop in their cars and steam down the interstate. Admittedly, some of these events took place on an island, but seven witnesses earned substantial parts of their income by carrying goods like wood on lighters and shallops, and passengers on journeys of up to ten miles in canoes and rowing boats. Water transport was so normal that it only merited mention if some incident or accident occurred. In

---

[61] Mariners: Michael Long, 40, John Burridge, 40, Thomas Grant, 28, Abraham Bell, 40, and Daniel King, 30. Weight: Thomas Grant, 28, deposed that in the Spring of 1656 Thomas Sheppie had received "a pot of butter and a parcel of cheese from Goodwife Cole, but since the cheese was not yet dry, they had not weighed it but took it by the lump." Grant was probably a Scottish seaman from Rehoboth, recently arrived in May 1652 as a prisoner of war captured after the Battle of Worcester in England. Taint: Thompson, *Sex*, 26, 44, 106, and below "Church," and "Women." Sheppie: see "Our Main End Was to Catch Fish" above. Sued: Swoetman v Sheppie, 5 October 1653, MxCC RB, 1: 30. Rape: *MR*, 1: 155. Probate: Wyman, 863.

December 1630, for instance, Winthrop described three servants bound for Boston from Ten Hills who were caught in a "tempest . . . coming in a shallop from Mystic [and] driven by the wind to Noddles Island and forced to stay there all night without fire or food." We have already met Thomas Knower, who perished while bringing a load of wood down the Mystic in November 1641. We will encounter several ferry-goers: young men crossing to the pubs in Boston, women groped by John Harris on the Penny Ferry. Ferryman James Hayden was accused of abusing two passengers and hazarding their lives in 1653. We read in the town records of lighters overladen with stones that "bulged" blocking the town landing places, so frequently used that Lowden was forced to dismantle his impeding wall. The early equivalent of trucks, buses, delivery vans, and courier bikes all floated. When water was a stone's throw from many townspeople's homes, taking to it came naturally. Logistically, early Charlestown's nearest modern equivalent is Venice.[62]

---

[62] *WJ*, 1: 55; Knower; see above, "Introduction"; ferrygoers: see "Adolescent Port Life" and "Young Women Abused," below; Hayden: MxCC RB, 1: 52; his accusers were Zechariah Symmes and Francis Norton. Lighters: CTR, 1: 649; see above, "Lowden's Wall."

Captain Francis Norton's Estate, 1667

In mid-June 1667, Francis Norton was "visited with the hand of god with some bodily weakness." Six weeks later, on 27 July 1667, he died. The next day, the Lord's Day (Sunday), he was interred in the Charlestown burying ground. He left behind not only grieving family and friends but also a business inundated by debt, neglect, and confusion. His widow was still mopping up eleven years later. However, the putting in order of Norton's affairs by her, the four probate overseers, and four commissioners specially appointed by the Middlesex County Court in December 1667 provides a revealing window on the commercial relations of one of Charlestown's leading first-generation merchants.[63]

Francis Norton immigrated to Charlestown in 1637 with his wife Mary and daughters Abigail and Mary. On 2 February 1649, Boston notary William Aspinwall drafted a bond in favour of "Francis Norton, haberdasher," and my first English sighting of him was in the records of the Haberdashers' Company of London. On 3 September 1619, Francis Norton, son of John Norton lately of Markyate Street, Hertfordshire, husbandman, was apprenticed to William Patsill, citizen and haberdasher of London, for seven years. His birthplace is a village on Watling Street, four miles southeast of Dunstable on the London side. In the seventeenth century, Markyate was part of the Bedfordshire parish of Caddington. Its parish register records that "Francis son of John Norton" was baptized on 29 September 1602. The Dunstable parish register records the marriage of John Norton and Alice Bicknald on 23 December 1585 and her death on

---

[63] Norton's will and probate administration papers are in Rodgers, 2: 392–400, and MxCC D&O, 2: folio 50. A fuller version of the genealogical material in this chapter is in *R*, 165 (Oct. 2011).

22 May 1621. In 1628 Francis was admitted to freemanship of the Haberdashers' Company and of the City of London.[64]

We know from a pedigree in the Herald's Visitation of London in 1633 that Francis Norton, haberdasher, was married to Mary, the sister of Robert Houghton of London, brewer. A letter of 6 February 1651 from Robert Houghton mentions her. Mary was the daughter of Nicholas and Elinor (Newman) Houghton of London and Woburn, Bedfordshire. In 1653, she was the beneficiary of the London will signed on Christmas Day by Robert Houghton. He was a wealthy brewer and merchant of St. Olave's, Southwark, and left "my dearly loving and pious sister Mary Norton, wife of Francis Norton of Charlestown in New England, the sum of £20." However, the 2 March 1629 Bishop of London's Marriage License Allegations record Francis Norton, of St. Olaves, Southwark, haberdasher, aged about 27, alleging that he intends to marry Mary Phillips, widow, of the Diocese of London, 29 years old. Whether this Mary had been born a Houghton is not yet known; nor is the identity of her first husband. A 23 June 1640 letter from John Evance of New Haven refers to Norton as "brother" and Mary as "sister."[65]

On the eve of Norton's emigration to Charlestown, another Norton family resided in Markyate. In 1634 Sir Richard St. George of the College of Arms conducted a Visitation of Hertfordshire to record armigerous

---

[64]   Aspinwall, 191; J. J. Howard & J. L. Chester, eds., "Visitation of London, AD 1633, 34 & 35," *Harleian Society Publications,* 15: 369; Guildhall Library, London: MSS Haberdashers' Company Records: List of Apprentices, folio 138; Apprenticeship Bindings, 1611–30, folio 138 v; Register of Freedom Admissions, folio 206.

[65]   According to the International Genealogical Index, a Francis Norton and Mary Houghton were married in 1625 at Woburn, Bedfordshire, just off Watling Street, ten miles northwest of Dunstable. IGI source: 1553835. There is no such entry in the Woburn Parish Registers. Will: *R,* 42 (1888), 66. London Metropolitan Archives: Allegation Books, 1, vol. 13, 112. The Widow Phillips may have been related to a well-known family of haberdashers, who had premises in 1649 at the "Sign of the Anchor" on London Bridge, and later "under London Bridge," and supplied our Norton in Charlestown. Henry Phillips's tradesman's token stamped "Henry Phillips at Bridgefoot, Southwark," and with initials H-P-S, where the S stands for his wife, are illustrated in Gordon Home, *Old London Bridge* (London: John Lane, Bodley Head, 1931), 246, 329. Many haberdashers lived on and near the Bridge. Phillips forebears had been members of the Haberdashers' Company since 1529. Phillips: Apprenticeship Bindings, folios 38, 153; Henry, son of John of Narbott, Pembrokeshire, yeoman, was bound in 1620; John, son of John of London, citizen and clothworker, in 1614. James and Richard Sedgwick, kinsmen of Robert, were also members of the company (ibid., folios 218v, 287). The parish registers of St. Olave's have not survived between 1628 and 1639. A John Phillips was buried there on 2 November 1628. On St. Olave's, see above "Origins: Southwark." Evance: *R,* 41 (1887), 363. According to Boyd's Marriage Index, Evance had married Anne Young at St Stephen's Coleman Street, London, in 1624. Though Francis had moved to London after 1619, Markyate, 27 miles to the northwest, was accessible enough for regular visits, *Handbook of Hertfordshire. . .* (London: Murray, 1895), 90.

families. The right to a coat of arms was symbolic of gentry status. One of the families listed was that of "Norton of Marketcell." Markyate Cell was (and is) a country house set on the far slope of Cell Park on the northern edge of Markyate. Its name originated in the medieval cell that had housed the famous reclusive mystic Christina of Markyate. The 1634 resident was Robert Norton, Esq. A later owner, Mr. Thomas Coppin of Markyate, was the son-in-law of Luke Norton, Esq. of neighboring Great Offley. Though I have found marginal evidence of a relationship with Francis, his arms on the seal on his will are quite different from those of the Hertfordshire family.[66]

The indirect Norton connection derives from records not of Hertfordshire or Bedfordshire, but of New Hampshire. On 6 May 1638, Anne (Greene) Mason, the widow of Captain John Mason, first proprietor of New Hampshire, sent instructions from East Greenwich, Kent, to Ambrose Gibbons, her steward at Piscataqua, to "deliver her swine speedily to the bearer hereof, Francis Norton, whom I have made my general attorney for all my estate in your part." Norton was later alleged to have made off with Mason's valuable great cattle as well.[67]

Why did Mrs. Mason choose Francis Norton? In 1634, when the bounds of Mason's patent were to be set out, the local advice of Captain Norton was recommended. This was Walter Norton, one of the leading patentees of Agamenticus (York, Maine), 12,000 acres just up the coast from the manor of Mason Hall (Rye, New Hampshire). Other, non-emigrant, Agamenticus patentees included Thomas Coppin, Robert Norton, and Richard Norton with Markyate connections, and George Norton of

---

[66] W. C. Metcalfe, ed., "Visitation of Hertfordshire, 1634," *Harleian Society Publications,* 22 (1886), 80–81, 78, 46, 28, 88, 152. Arms illustrated on page 80; Francis Norton's arms were a chevron between three tuns, Emmerton & Waters, 95. The Nortons leased the house from Sir John Ferrers; Coppin bought it in 1657. *The Book of Markyate* (Tiverton: Halsgrove, 2002), 25–27; *Markyate Past,* 10 (2006) 1–7.

[67] Nathaniel Bouton, ed., *Documents and Records of the Province of New Hampshire,* 1 (Concord, NH: Jenks, 1867), 99, 45–47, depositions of Francis Small (8 September 1685), Nathaniel Boulter and John Redmayne (6 November 1685), and George Walton (18 December 1685). Isaac W. Hammond, ed., *Provincial Records of the Province of New Hampshire,* 17 (Manchester: State of New Hampshire, 1889), Miscellaneous Provincial Papers 1629–1725 [from the Public Record Office in London], 517, 522, includes the Mason heir's 1674 account of Norton's "unfaithfully exercising his office," and the deposition of William Seavey of Portsmouth, 3 September 1676 about Norton's "fetching away of the cattle." Nathaniel Adams, *Annals of Portsmouth* (Hampton: Randall, 1971 [first published 1825]), 18, and *R,* 2 (1848) 39, list Francis Norton as one of Captain Mason's "stewards", but I have found no further evidence of this. On Piscataqua, *Great Migration Newsletter,* 2 (1991), 27–29. In 1644, Norton bought land in Great Bay, Piscataqua; his brother-in-law Houghton had a five-year lease on land there in 1639, *GDMNH,* 514; Norton was acting as the Masons' attorney on 7 January 1650 when he gave Sampson Lane legal permission to cut timber on Mrs. Mason's Great House patent. Aspinwall, 251.

Sharpenhoe, Bedfordshire. Walter Norton, a professional soldier, was the uncle of both Coppin and George Norton; unbeknown to Mason, he had already been killed by Pequot tribesmen in 1633. It seems plausible that Francis Norton may have been suggested to Mrs. Mason by one of this Norton-Coppin clan, and that they shared either undiscovered kinship or undoubted neighborliness.[68]

Why did the Nortons choose Charlestown when they emigrated? The proximity of Markyate to Zechariah Symmes's parish of Dunstable may have been one reason. Another incentive would have been kinship with the Sedgwicks, already ensconced in Charlestown. Robert Houghton's wife was Robert Sedgwick's sister; notary William Aspinwall described Mrs. Norton as Sedgwick's "sister" in a 1649 affidavit. Houghton addressed Francis as "Loving Brother." These patterns of affinity and regional origin were common in the Great Migration. Eldest daughter Abigail Norton married John Long, whose parents lived in Dunstable prior to emigration in 1635. Her sister Elizabeth married Timothy Symmes in 1671.[69]

Norton quickly impressed his new neighbors. Edward Johnson described him as "one of a bold and cheerful spirit and full of love to the truth." Francis and Mary were admitted as church members, and he became a freeman in 1642. They had three more daughters, one disabled. Charlestown regularly elected Francis to important offices. Twice a selectman in 1647 and 1648, he then served as the town's representative to the General Court ten times. As "a well-disciplined and able man," he was nominated lieutenant in 1646 and promoted captain of the Middlesex Troop in 1654. In the General Court he served on many committees. He was one of the "Farmers of Wines" whose profits paid for the colony's gunpowder, and in partnership with Sedgwick and Richard Russell a "Farmer of Customs" in 1648. The town nominated him one of its three commissioners for small causes in 1658. When the selectmen decided to petition the General Court for five hundred acres of land in compensation for losses to other towns, Francis and his regular business partner Nicholas Davison were the successful town spokesmen. Norton's many services to Charlestown were recognized by a grant of five hundred acres of town land.

---

[68]   Bounds: Boulton, 1: 88; Walter Norton:*GMB*,1341; Agamenticus: C. E. Banks, *History of York, Maine* (Boston: privately printed, 1931), 85–87; Mason Hall, 4000 acres at Odiorne's Point, by Little Harbor, at the southern mouth of the Piscataqua River, now in Rye, Clarke, *Eastern Frontier*, 53. Clarke alleges that Norton sold the 100 head of great Danish cattle in Boston at £20 per head and pocketed the money; apart from the partisan and much later depositions, I have found no Massachusetts support for this contention. Sharpenhoe in nine miles north of Markyate, and four miles north of Dunstable.

[69]   Aspinwall, 390; Wyman, 710; *R*, 42 (1888), 66. Thompson, *Mobility and Migration*, Ch. 8.

His business skills led to frequent appointment as administrator of estates, auditor of accounts, and attorney in complex commercial suits. He was the natural choice for commissary in charge of supplies for Massachusetts's military expedition in 1645. Francis Norton proved a devoted public servant for over 20 years.[70]

It was as an entrepreneur, however, that Norton's career was most impressive. By the 1640s he was heavily involved in the fur and fishing trades. In 1644 he was one of the partners in the bid to break into the hugely profitable Delaware fur trade, which had brought such wealth to the Dutch West India Company. Norton was still investing in the pelt business in the 1660s. He was owed £14 by Merrimack trader John Cromwell in 1662, and exported £32 worth of moose skins to London in the middle of the decade. In 1649, in partnership with Sedgwick and two others he undertook to deliver three hundred quintals (hundredweights) of dried cod to Europe. In the following year, he and two partners would send £547 worth of cod to Bilbao in northern Spain. When Aspinwall tried to serve a legal document on Norton in 1651, Mary told him "he was at eastward," probably the Isles of Shoals gathering from fishermen another 308 quintals of fish for export. His partner in London was "brother" Robert Houghton. Other agents and partners there were James Russell at the Golden Fleece, London Maurice Thompson, William Pennoyer (all leading London Parliamentarian merchants), and Henry Phillips, haberdasher. As the 1650 agreement shows, very large sums of money were involved. In 1649 Norton and Sedgwick jointly were owed bills of exchange worth £1,468 by London merchants. Norton was also due £200 from Boston merchants, to be deposited with Henry Phillips in London on Norton's account. The transatlantic fishing industry was very big business.[71]

Nor did Norton neglect his haberdashery business. The Phillipses were his main suppliers. In 1657, he entered bond to pay London drapers for imported goods within a year. Three years later, in partnership with his son-in-law Joseph Noyes, he brought over goods worth £147, probably mostly cloth.

---

[70]   Johnson, *Wonderworking Providence*, 143, 230; Wyman, 710; Frothingham, 112, 116, 156. *MR*, 3, 4,1 & 4, 2: see index. CTR, 1: 628, 640; *GMB*, 1311, 1379, 1855; Mass Archives, 16 October 1645; Aspinwall, 88. Farmers: individuals or groups who pay a lump sum to authorities to collect taxes, and then keep any excess as profit; common procedure in seventeenth-century England and Europe.

[71]   Delaware: Bailyn, *New England Merchants*, 51; Russell Shorto, *The Island at the Center of the World* (New York: Vintage, 2005), 194. The New England "Company of Adventurers" proved unable to break the Dutch monopoly. Cromwell: Rodgers, 2: 61; moose: ibid 396. Fish: Aspinwall, 249, 295, 308; London partners: ibid, 191, 218, 255, 390; Brenner, *Merchants and Revolutionaries*, passim. Due: Aspinwall, 255, 191. See above, "Our Main End Was to Catch Fish."

Norton had a shop in Charlestown's Market Square, in which he stocked thread, yarn, "haberdashery ware," hats, ribbons, knitwear, canvas, fabrics, ginger and sugar. The tropical ginger and sugar came from the West Indies. In 1664 he imported 3,400 pounds of "merchantable muscovado Surinam sugar." The next year he sent six horses to Barbados; the £84 he earned was part repayment to the Phillipses. At his death Norton owed £30 to Joachim Hames of Jamaica.[72]

Norton's business interests were widely diversified. In 1645, his "brother Houghton" was a leading investor in the Massachusetts ironworks. The following year Norton was in London; no doubt the vulnerable enterprise was high on their agenda. In 1660, Norton agreed to supply bar iron to Charlestown blacksmith John Johnson. He was joint owner of various ships, such as the *Chapman* captured by the Portuguese in 1657, his son-in-law John Long's ketch, and the ship seized by Augustine Walker in 1653. He belonged to partnerships exporting pipestaves to Madeira and importing wine from London. All of this mercantile activity went hustling along at the same time as his multifarious administrative and service obligations, for example "supplying a sufficient bull" for the town in 1662.[73]

After Norton's death on 27 July 1667, three appraisers set about the simple part of estate administration: assessing the worth of his real and material property. On 2 August 1667, they moved through the seven rooms of the house, shop, brewhouse, stable, and warehouse evaluating their contents. They valued the shop's stock at £57. Then they turned to the real estate—"house, orchard, stable, cellar" and six cow commons— appraised at £276. Finally they listed the livestock: six horses and colts, a heifer, and swine; and Norton's servant, "A Negar Man," £26. The total inventory came to £629–12–7, and Mary Norton attested to its accuracy before Francis's old partner Deputy Governor Francis Willoughby and Recorder Thomas Danforth on 26 September 1667.[74]

There had been previous warning signs that Norton could be dilatory and that his business was in difficulty. From 1651 to 1659, he had failed to pay the £57 he owed the estate of Thomas Accres or Akers, who had died

---

[72] MxCC D&O, 2: folio 50. Rodgers, 2: 396–97, 399.

[73] Ironworks: Hartley, *Ironworks,* 71; Johnson: Rodgers, 2: 396. Ships: Coldham, 1: 125; "Caribbean comes to Charlestown," above. Pipestaves: Coldham, 1: 128; wine: Rodgers, 2: 396. Bull: CTR, 3: 31.

[74] Rodgers, 2: 393–94. This was very much a merchant's inventory, with comparatively little real estate —no farmland, nor the 500 acres of wilderness land previously granted by the town. However, Norton owned well over £100 in bedding, linen, and clothes, and £38 worth of plate, pewter, and money.

at sea in 1651. Norton's delays led to an accumulation of interest at 8% per annum, so that when he finally settled on 27 December 1659, he owed nearly twice the original sum. On 5 March 1655, the attorney of John Hart of London, late of Bilbao, Spain, bewailed Norton's repeated failures to provide £390 worth of cod pledged way back in June 1650. Much more worrying was the letter of 22 February 1666 from two London suppliers. They complained that Norton's answer to their demands for the £100 he owed them was "in no manner answerable to our expectations." Debts in Barbados were met only by "delays and excuses." Another London creditor expressed "very much wonder that you should deal so with me all this time not to have repaid me" and issued an ultimatum on 20 April 1664: Norton must send payment "by the first ship that I may not be forced to do that which I am very unwilling to do." In the last decade of his life, Norton was a merchant whose estate, like that of Shakespeare's Antonio, was "very low." [75]

The full depths were only plumbed when Norton's various account books were opened on 29 September 1667. He owed his creditors a total of £1,368-2-5. Within New England, his debts totalled £399: this included £318 to nine Boston merchants, and £44 to Charlestown neighbors (including £30 to butcher William Dady). John Richards had supplied Norton and his son-in-law John Long with £20 worth of pork, not yet paid for. Norton also owed Rev. Thomas Allen back in England £35 in rent for the Charlestown brewhouse. [76]

These sums, however, pale into insignificance when transatlantic debts are examined. The largest was £422 owed to Henry and John Phillips, haberdashers. Norton's actual obligation was £298, but he had entered bond of £598 to settle on 17 July 1663. He had only managed £176, including £84 repayment through the sale of horses in the West Indies. Other merchants familiar with New England like John Childe, James Burton or Burkin, John Harbin, and Robert Thomson were each owed £100 or more. The four overseers appointed in Norton's will to assist Mary, the executor,

---

[75]   Akers: MxCC RB, 1: 46, 97, 102, 185, 197; D & O, 1: docs. 1137, 1163–1166; Hart: *Sfk Deeds,* 2: 124–26; letters: Rodgers, 2: 397, D & O, 2: folio 50, from James Burton and John Harbin, Mr. Parke of Barbados, George Waterman. *Merchant of Venice,* 3:2.

[76]   Rodgers, 2: 396; D & O, 2: folio 50. Books: there is a reference to "Shop Book No. 2." Boston: the largest creditor was Thomas Dean (£97), who was a recently arrived royalist and factor for London exporters. He often partnered another royalist, Peter Lidgett, owed £21. Bailyn, *New England Merchants,* 122–23. The second largest debt was owed to Thomas Savage (£66). He was principal collector for the Ironworks, Hartley, *Saugus Ironworks,* 225–51, 260–67. Large purchases of meat suggest that Norton and Long had gone into the provisioning business, either of ships or of military forces. Norton also owed the children of Mr. Sherman of Watertown £35.

must have blanched when they read through the accounts. All but one, a creditor, resigned. On 17 December 1667, the Middlesex County Court appointed four commissioners, "that so the payment of each creditor may be in proportion to their debts" owed them by the estate. One of these proportioners was William Stitson, who would marry the widow Mary Norton in 1670; another was James Russell, whose namesake uncle "of the Golden Fleece" had done business with Norton in the 1650s. In one case, the claim of £64 by London vintner Daniel Butler could be legitimately reduced, by evidence of receipts, to a mere £11. Otherwise, most debts were formally "owned by Mrs. Norton," or accepted as valid by the commissioners in their 4 February 1668 report. The following year Mary sold the Norton "Mansion Place with garden & backside appertaining" on the north side of Charlestown's Market Square. The buyer was sea captain William Foster. His £200 may have gone to estate creditors, or it may have been part of a marriage settlement with William Stitson. If the former, and if Norton's will that "my debts being first paid" was obeyed, his creditors might have received between forty and fifty percent of their money. In the real world, however, they would have been lucky to get half of that. In 1670, the General Court did grant 250 acres to Mrs. Norton for her late husband's "charge and pains." Compared to the obligations she had "owned," this was very modest recompense. [77]

How had this once "bold and adventurous" entrepreneur plunged into "the stairless pit of debt?" Age—Norton was about sixty-five when he died in 1667—may have blunted his vigor and his commercial edge. It may too have exacerbated a dilatoriness evident even two decades before his death. A lack of adult sons to support him or even to take over the family firm was a serious disadvantage; son-in-law Joseph Noyes, a partner in 1660, died prematurely months later. A disabled daughter would take much of his wife's and daughters' time and energy. International commerce depended on trust, and trust was most likely among family members. By the mid-1650s, two of Norton's most trusted kinsmen and partners were dead: Robert Houghton at the end of 1653 and Robert Sedgwick in Jamaica in 1655. Frequent collaborator and neighbor Nicholas Davison was in England from 1655 to 1656, and then moved north to Pemaquid in 1658. The

---

[77] English creditors: see Appendix of Norton's creditors. MxCC D & O, 2: folio 50 also contains a bill of account for Captain Francis Norton between 1656 and 1663 from an unnamed English merchant for "wares" totaling £538; see Appendix. Overseers: Francis Willoughby, Thomas Clarke, Thomas Lake, and John Richards. Commissioners: the chairman was Boston merchant and creditor Thomas Clarke; the fourth man was Edward Tyng. Mansion House: Rodgers, 2: 399. *GMB*, 3: 1764 includes deeds of sale by the Stitsons of haylots, cow commons, and arable, 1671–76. Proportions: total inventory of Norton's estate was just under £630. Grant: CTR, 3: 107.

Phillipses remained "under London Bridge" and advanced Norton large amounts of goods, but his other English suppliers and customers were kinsmen of other New Englanders, like Richard Russell or Ephraim Child, or else strangers.

For all transatlantic businessmen, the 1650s proved a depressed decade. Royalist privateering and the First Dutch War paralyzed trade between 1649 and 1654. Confrontations with Spain in European and Caribbean waters followed. On 9 May 1657, Norton's neighbor Robert Long complained, "trading now is so dead . . . for want of shipping [and] scarcity of money which is the life of trade." No amount of boldness and adventurousness could overcome such conditions.[78]

The merchants of the Bay were changing in the 1660s. Two of Norton's Boston creditors, Thomas Dean and Peter Lidgett, were new men—the breed identified by Bernard Bailyn: royalists and imperialists with influential partners in London and the West Indies, disdainful of provincial Puritanism, and ruthless in exploiting the resources of "the wilderness." These resources were changing too. Lidgett's fortune would be based on masts for the Royal Navy and the English merchant marine. The furs of Norton's early career had been effectively hunted out by Bay exporters. Fishing had been disrupted in the 1650s and 1660s by wars against the French, Spanish, and Dutch, and anyway, the down-east assembling of cargoes for London fishmongers was work for young men. It is no surprise that "new interests were taking over Maine fishing in the 1660s." The disastrous Second Dutch War (1664–67) severely interrupted all Atlantic trade and added to the gloom already cast over Puritan New England by the Restoration backlash, imperial control of trade and navigation, and the arrogant interference of the King's Commissioners (1664–66). The Half-Way Covenant of 1662 sowed dissension among and within the churches. For the haberdasher from Markyate Street who had risen so high in early New England, the 1660s must have been a desperately depressing time in many ways. The ending of his "frail life" may well have come as a relief.[79]

---

[78] Stairless: Graham Robb, *The Discovery of France* (London: Picador, 2007), 84. Dilatoriness: Aspinwall, 306. Kin: Norton's son-in-law, mariner John Long, partnered Norton in pork purchases in 1666, but he had had to take over The Three Cranes two years before when his father Robert Long died. Trust: Roger Thompson, "Reflections on Early-Modern Extended Families," in U. J. Hebel & K. Ortseifen, eds., *Transatlantic Encounters* (Trier: Wissenschaftlicher Verlag, 1995), 62–78; Bailyn, *Merchants*, 135–37. Deaths: *R*, 42 (1888), 66. Davison: Wyman, 283–84; Burrage, *Early Maine*, 307; Long: Mass Archives.

[79] New men: Bailyn, *Merchants*, 112–42; Lidgett, ibid., 133; furs: see above, "Caribbean Comes to Charlestown," and "Cutting One Another's Throats for Beaver"; fishing: Bailyn, 125; war: ibid., 131. "Frail life": Rodgers, 2: 392.

APPENDIX: NORTON'S CREDITORS, 1668

New England

4 February 1668

From 30 April 1667: 7 barrels of gunpowder. No value. [Say £18-0-0]
[This was a debt due to the colony; it may have been connected with his farming of the import duties on wines. Norton also supplied gunpowder to Charlestown. MR, 4,1: 423; CTrR, 1: 84r.]

From 12 March 1667: owes John Richards £20-0-0.
[Norton's account with Richards is for pork delivered to Norton and son-in-law John Long of The Three Cranes; Norton had reduced the original debt to £20 by paying £4-10.]

From 1 November 1664: bond to supply Thomas Savage with 3,400 lbs of Muscovado sugar, and accounts of debts for bar iron and impost collector's salary. £66-17-0.
[Savage was a Boston merchant and collector of Ironworks debts totaling some £3,500. The bar iron was owed to John Johnson, Charlestown blacksmith. The unpaid wine impost collector was Lt. Howes. These debts had probably been assigned to Savage. Gunpowder delivered to one of the Massachusetts surveyors is itemized.]

From February 1660: for broadcloth supplied by William Bartholomew, £3–11–0, but offset by custom owed by Bartholomew on two pipes of Canary wine. £1–1–0.
[Bartholomew was a Boston innkeeper, brewer, and merchant who had recently moved from Ipswich. GM, 1: 180–86.]

29 September 1668

From 10 March 1667: owed to Hezekiah Usher, by book, £20–11–11.
[Usher was a Boston merchant; his second wife was Elizabeth, daughter of Rev. Zechariah Symmes. He imported goods and books from London. Bailyn, Merchants, 128, 135, 137.]

Due to children of Mr. Sherman of Watertown, £37–0–0.
[This may refer to the 19 March 1657 bequest of £5 each to the seven children of Rev. John Sherman of Watertown by his neighbor Hannah, widow of Thomas Hammond. Norton's role in this is unclear. Rodgers, 1: 258.]

Due to Thomas Dean of Boston, £97–0–0.
[See above, fn. 16.]

From 6 June 1658: due to Peter Lidgett of Boston £53–13–6, of which £33 has been paid, £ 20–13–6.
[Ibid.]

From 20 October 1656 to the present: due to Thomas Clarke, Boston, £21–14–2.
[Clarke was a Boston merchant, official and military officer; at this time he was Speaker of the Massachusetts House of Deputies. *Savage.* He had been a partner with Norton in the Delaware fur venture in 1644; he was also involved in the Ironworks. Like some other merchants, he was a strong opponent of religious persecution.]

One other Bostonian whose name has become illegible, £6–0–0.

Due to [illegible]les, £64–2–0.

Charlestown creditors: William Dady [butcher], £30–0–0.

Thomas Rand [shoemaker], £3–2–0

Deacon Thomas Lynd [maltster], £7–0–0

John Knight [cooper], £0–15–0.

John Smith [ships' carpenter], £1–4–0.

John Taylor [joiner, of Cambridge], £2–0–0.

Total New England debts: £399–0–7.

Overseas

4 February 1667

From 5 June 1657: bond of Norton's to pay £50 owed to Matthew Tindal, draper, Edward Story, ironmonger, William Beale, merchant, all of London, and James Russell, gentleman of Westminster, witnessed by Thomas Turner and William Pitt, and presented by attorney Richard Russell of Charlestown, £50–0–0.
[Tindal was a bound apprentice in the Drapers' Company in 1622; he died in 1676. P. Boyd, *Roll of the Drapers' Company of London* (Croydon: Andress, 1934), 183. Story was a Presbyterian merchant active in London after the Civil War as Common Councilman, Warden of the Ironmongers

Company, and major in the city's regiment of horse; he died in November 1660. J. R. Woodhead, *Rulers of London 1660–80* (London: London & Middlesex Archaeological Society, 1965), Brenner, *Merchants and Revolutionaries*, 5, 92, 482; no connection seen with Saugus Ironworks. In March 1661, Beale was one of seventeen merchants trading with Barbados who petitioned the crown for assistance in recovering debts there. CSP Col, 2: doc. 40. On James Russell, freeman of the London Drapers' Company by gift or purchase in 1634, Boyd; see "La Tour," and on William Pitt, probably nephew of Richard Russell, see "Origins."]

From 12 June 1657: bond to secure payment of debt of £60 due in 1658 to Daniel Butler, vintner of Candlewick St, St. Swithin's, London, but £49 repaid, £11–0–0.
[Butler had been apprenticed in 1618, about the same time as Norton. Norton's repayments were in moose skins and fish.]

From 26 February 1665: letter of Elizabeth Lacock, executrix of husband, owed £12–18–5.

From 22 February 1665: impatient letter from James Burton/Burkin and John Harbin about long overdue debt owed to Mr. Gilpin, their debtor, £100–2–9.
[James Burkin, born in Colchester in 1622, was a London citizen and clothworker, master of the Clothworkers' Company in 1673. He was elected common councilman for Tower Ward, having been fined for refusing the office of alderman for Bread Street Ward in 1672; he and his wife Jane were married in 1649 and lived in Mincing Lane. As holder of £1,000 stock he was a grantee of the New Africa Company Charter on 27 September 1672, along with Waterman and Harbin. CSPCol, 3: doc 934; Woodhead. The Harbin family, originating in Somerset, lived in the parish of St. Helen, Bishopsgate, London. 2,500 lbs of sugar should have been paid to Mr. Parke of Barbados. Burkin and Harbin's attorney was Joshua Atwater of Boston, a former London merchant.]

From 20 April 1664: threatening letter from George Waterman, London, £12–14–5.
[Waterman was a skinner, living at the "sign of the Helmet" on Thames Street in Bridge Ward Within; he had been Sheriff of London 1664–65, knighted 1665, and would be Lord Mayor in 1671–72. He was a £500 stockholder of the slave-trading New Africa Company in 1672, CSP Col, 3: doc. 934; he had been a supporter of the Republic, but switched to

royalism after 1660; Pepys often mentions him as a leading merchant. *Diary,* 6: 78–79, and passim; Woodhead.]

29 September 1668.

Sgt. William Peat's money owed by Norton to be paid in England, £66–17–8.

[Peat may have been a Serjeant at Law, but is not listed in J. H. Baker, ed., *The Order of Serjeants at Law* (London: Selden Society, 1984); however, there are gaps in the records of the 1650s and 1660s. William Pead, fourth son of Thomas, gent., of Bury St. Edmunds, was admitted to Gray's Inn on 10 October 1627; Joseph Foster, ed., *Register of Admissions to Gray's Inn, 1521–1849* (London: privately printed, 1889). A William Pate was a plaintiff three times in the Court of Chancery during the 1660s and 1670s. E. A. Fryer, ed., *Index of Chancery Proceedings 1649–1714,* London: British Record Society, 1904).]

Mr. Joakim Hames of Jamaica is owed, £30–0–0.

[Hames had risen to notice in Jamaican records and in the State Papers by the 1670s. His marriage to Angelina Fant in St. Catherine's Parish was confirmed on 16 May 1670; by the 1680s, the Hameses owned 750 acres of land in two other parishes. V. L. Oliver, *Caribbeana* 1 (London: Mitchell, Hughes & Clarke, 1910), 13, 104, 105, 149, 151. Hames served as deputy secretary of the colony in 1670, and as an assemblyman in 1672, and 1675, CSP Col, 3:222, 736; 4: 536.]

From 1 May 1660: John Childs of London sent goods worth £147–11–2 to Joseph Noyes [Norton's son-in-law, who died 1660/61]. On 19 September 1662, Norton paid £43–4–0 in cloth, leaving due, £104–7–2.

[Child, Common Councilman for Bridge Ward Within, 1657–60, lived in the Third Precinct of London Bridge, in the parish of St. Magnus. He may have been a relative of the great Restoration merchant banker Sir Josiah Child, who was involved in the mast business.]

From 16 July 1663: Simon Lynde, Boston, attorney for Henry and John Phillips, haberdashers, London, presents bond of £598–14–0 to repay by 1 April 1664 £298–7–0 owed. Norton repaid £84 from selling horses and mares in Barbados, and some undisclosed contribution, leaving £422–7–0.

[According to Savage, Lynde had been "bred to trade in Holland," probably at Middleburg in Zealand, and arrived in Boston from London in 1650 at the age of twenty-six; he later returned to London, but appears to have been back in Boston by 1664. MxCC D&O, 2: folio 50. On the Phillipses, who lived at the southern end of London Bridge, see note 2 above. Bonds were customarily for double the value of a debt.]

From 29 September 1666: due to Rev. Thomas Allen in rent for Charlestown brewhouse, £35–0–0.

[The brewhouse had been built by Robert Sedgwick; Allen, former Charlestown minister, had returned to Norwich, England, in 1651 and married the widow Joanna Sedgwick in England after 1655. He had sold all his own town land. He had been ejected from his pulpit in St. George's Norwich in 1662 as a nonconformist, and was probably in need of money.]

From 24 September 1668: Francis Willoughby as joint renter with Norton of Major Robert Thomson's old meetinghouse grounds is owed half the outstanding rent, £125–0–0.

[Rent of £26 per year had been due since the leasing covenant of August 1648. Norton's half share, £260, had been partially paid. The original meetinghouse grounds had been bought by William Rainborough and later acquired by Thomson, a transitory Massachusetts resident in 1639. Norton had sold his share in John Long's ketch to contribute to rent payments. Thomson (1622–94) of Stoke Newington, north London, had paid £160. He was the brother of Maurice and George Thomson, who were so influential in transatlantic commerce. Robert was said to have nearly married Cromwell's daughter. In 1656, he was a fellow Navy Commissioner with Willoughby. During the Restoration period, he was a proponent of England's trade in the Far East and of liberty of conscience at home. *ODNB*; Brenner, *Merchants and Revolutionaries*, 176, 522, and passim; Savage; CSPCol, 1: 447; 2: doc 289.]

Total Overseas Debt: £970–7–5.

An addendum lists £1–5–7 credited to Norton's account.

All debts: £1368–2–5.

Folio 50 also contains a "Bill of Account for Francis Norton reckoning interest in several parcels of ware after twelve months delivery" between 1656 and April 1663, when his overall debt stood at £538, including £107 interest. Norton's repayments include assigning £36 owed him by John Leverett and received on 5 September 1658, and £53 worth of sugar, a total of £89.

Another 1657 document records a debt of £150. The £50 interest has been forborne, and £50 has been repaid; no creditor is named.

Adolescent Port Life:
Russell v. Harris, 1669, and
John Hayden's Libel, 1671

When Mr. James Russell went to his shop on a Tuesday morning in early April 1669, he found that it had been "broken up [into]." Inside, he discovered his counter also broken up and about £5 in small change and some cloth missing. On closer investigation, he detected hair clinging to the rough wood of the bottom shelf, under which the burglar had "crept in." His apprentice Ephraim Angier, 17, corroborated this account and put forward a possible culprit. About three weeks before, "Joseph Harris came into my master's shop and looked up and down and came to the counter and knocked upon it and said 'Will the money jink?' or 'Doth it jink?' He [Harris] said that he had frequently come to the shop and once or twice had been in the inner room." Harris, 20, admitted the March visit, but denied any reference to money jinking in the counter drawer.[80]

Money jinking in unexpected pockets might bolster suspicions, and Russell and Angier gathered incriminating evidence from two young men about happenings elsewhere on that Tuesday morning. Joshua Benjamin, 27, described how he had met Harris and Sylvester Hayes on the ferry between 8 and 9 a.m. He asked what took them to Boston, and Harris replied: "To

---

[80] Documents in this case are in MxCC D&O, folio 52. Russell (1640–1709) was the eldest son of assistant and colony treasurer Richard Russell, the wealthiest merchant and landowner of his generation in Charlestown. James would follow in his father's footsteps as a merchant and major officeholder. Angier (1652–79) came from a famous Cambridge family, where his father was a wealthy merchant and innkeeper who left the fortune of £651. By the time Ephraim died in the smallpox epidemic, he was already a prominent merchant. He owned a ketch and two black servants, and traded to Jamaica, importing such luxury items as Spanish snuff. His inventory, which totaled £367 and included the large amount of £46 in cash, credit of £78, is analyzed in Thompson, *Cambridge Cameos*, 34–35.

see whether Boston beer [is] better than Charlestown's." Harris pulled out his spending money, much of it in pennies. Their tasting trials began at John Vyall's tavern, the Noah's Ark, near Boston's North Battery, where Benjamin left them. He was later accosted by Harris and Hayes from William Wardwell's chamber, and they went on with several others to William Pollard's. At this point Harris disappeared for an hour, but on his return "the company" went on to Captain William Hudson's. Harris "called for a quart of wine, and at the reckoning proffered a shilling, but the company would let him pay but six-pence." After going on another errand, Benjamin bumped into the group "re-turning to Vyall's, where Hayes fell to quarrelling. Harris pulled out a shilling and said he would lay ten to one that Sylvester would beat the other man."[81]

The second witness, William Gerrish, 21, met up with Harris and Hayes at Hudson's. They asked him "What's the best news?" He answered "He heard but little." Gerrish described how Harris, with Boston friend John Corbin, was drinking beer more thirstily than the others. He also expanded on the details of the wager. Harris put his first bet of a shilling "into the barkeeper's hand and afterwards made it up to two shillings." However, when the barkeeper "understood what the wager was about, he gave [Harris] his money back again and said they should not fight."[82]

This circumstantial evidence gave a strong impression that Harris had money to burn. Drinking, gambling, and perhaps, during his hour's absence, wild women were, even in certain circles in seventeenth-century Boston, a conventional way of squandering ill-gotten gains. The examining magistrates of Middlesex County, Thomas Danforth and Richard Russell (James's father) would need some convincing to acquit Harris when he appeared before them on 9 April 1669. His story was that he had gone to bed at 10 p.m. on Mon-day and slept the night through. His visit to Boston concerned "some wheat

---

[81] Harris claimed that he had asked Benjamin to accompany him to help bring back some wheat from Boston. Benjamin (1642–84) may, as the youngest son, have been living with his widowed mother in Watertown. He would not marry until he was nearly forty, and then his brief mar-riage was childless. The North Battery and Hudson's Point by the ferry to Charlestown are both marked on Bonner's famous 1722 map of Boston. Vyall had been licensed since about 1662; his tavern was on North or Ship Street in the North End. Wardwell had originally sold wine in Wells, Maine. William Pollard, innholder of the Horseshoe on the corner of School Street in the South End, was in Boston from 1644 to 1686; his wife Ann claimed to have been the first to step ashore at Boston in 1630. Savage, 3: 419. Hudson, owner of the Marlborough Arms just east of the Town House, near the corner of Kilby and State Streets, was a survivor both of the English Civil War and of his wife's "adulterous carriages" with a young neighbor during his absence, Dunn, 609–11; D. Brenton Simons, *Witches, Rakes and Rogues* (Beverly, MA: Commonwealth Editions, 2005), 179–81; *GMB*, 2: 1035–37. Locations: Annie Thwing, *The Crooked and Narrow Streets of Boston* (Boston: Marshall Jones, 1920), 38, 137, 152.

[82] Corbin was a marginal Boston character who was drafted for King Philip's War in 1675; Savage.

he had there." He had four or five shillings on him, and spent a shilling at Pollard's, ninepence at Vyall's, another shilling at Hudson's and something at Carmes. He had wagered two shillings at Vyall's. During his hour's absence, he had gone walking on the Common and discoursing with Joseph Baker and Mr. Samuel Danforth. "He came in no house [of ill fame?]." Before returning to Charlestown about dark, he had his hair cut, for sixpence. And the source of all that money? Two shillings from Goodman Allen of Boston, two more from a stranger for a pair of gloves, two shillings and sixpence from his father, and a shilling from his mother on the Tuesday morning. And his declared reason for the trip, the wheat? "He had done nothing about it."[83]

Due to the lost Court Record Book for sessions from 1663 to 1670, we do not have a verdict for this case. However, we can add one other ingredient that would have swayed examiners, bench, or jury: reputation. There are two possibilities about Joseph Harris's connections. He may have been kin to John Harris (ca. 1630–82+), who was Charlestown's Penny Ferryman across the Mystic River near the Neck and sold beer and bread there to travellers, at first illicitly. In 1669 John Harris had had a bad fall that left him unable to work; a majority of selectmen grudgingly voted to give him a license as an alternative source of income. His house soon became a hangout for thieves, absconding servants, Indians, and heavy drinkers. Harris was exposed as a sexual predator and pedophile, and his son, another Joseph (1665–1732), tried to rape a serving maid. The whole Harris gang eventually moved to North Yarmouth, Maine, in 1682, to the undoubted relief of Charlestown's moral guardians. If our Joseph was connected to this crew, then his conviction was virtually guaranteed.[84]

Another possibility: Joseph may have been related to Charlestown's first Boston ferryman, Thomas Harris, who had died in the early 1630s, leaving a daughter and five sons. A Mary Harris, wife of Joseph, had a child in 1672, the first of six in Charlestown. This man's meager record is pretty clean, making him a less likely candidate.[85]

---

[83] It is suggestive of Harris's low status that Russell saw no need to recuse himself. Carmes: unidentified. Baker was a Boston tailor; Rev. Samuel Danforth (1626–74) was a minister at Roxbury and the brother of examining magistrate Thomas of Cambridge. House: in 1672, Alice Thomas was convicted of keeping a brothel in Boston. Simons, *Witches, Rakes and Rogues,* 99. The "goodman" was possibly William Allen, who was related to Joshua Benjamin's mother, Savage.

[84] Beer: CTR, 3: 106; D&O, 2: folios 44, 48, 51, 53; 3: folio 74; 4: folios 89, 94; RB, 3: 155, 215; hangout: folios 56, 74, 78; RB, 3: 232; see below, "Young Women Abused;" pedophile: D&O, 3 folio 78, RB, 4: 12; abuse: CTR, 4: 37, RB, 4: 13, 14; D&O, 4: folios 93, 94; Thompson, *Sex in Middlesex,* 129; Maine: Noyes, Libby & Davis, 312; Savage: Joseph Harris, Casco.

[85] Thomas: *GMB,* 2: 864–66; Joseph, Charlestown: Savage. Record: CTR, 3: 164, 13 October 1674, has Charlestown selectmen admonishing Joseph for taking a Boston man as a servant; he quickly sent him back.

His companion on the Boston pub crawl was a very different matter. The sonorous name of Sylvester Hayes was synonymous with sexual misdeeds, petty crime, violence, negligence, and dumb insolence. In 1668, the previous year, he had been fined for missing his statutory work on the town's highways and then arrested for failing to pay the fine. He had been caught by the constable and the watch drinking after hours and partying with other ne'er-do-wells at a house where Deborah Hadlock was the serving maid. He was one of the riotous group of young militiamen who had caroused and groped at Ursula Cole's, and he was missing from the magistrates' subsequent examination. That was just one year's mayhem. In the next decade he was prosecuted for "riding [presumably menacingly] about Widow Hill's house at night" and engaging in wanton dalliances; he was warned by the Charlestown selectmen and placed with one of them for a year's service. He proved incorrigible. In the 1680s he was whipped and imprisoned for abusing the constable, back inside for "breaking open" a vacant house belonging to Captain Lawrence Hammond and camping out there, and charged with setting fire to another widow's shop. Throughout these decades Hayes remained among the poorest townspeople: his rates abated, a recipient of doles and small wages. Anyone who chose Sylvester Hayes as a drinking partner would condemn himself by association.[86]

Compared to Hayes and Harris, the three deponents came from a different world. Gerrish would later become Charlestown's doctor, and a hero for treating the poor during the terrifying smallpox epidemic of 1677–78. The Benjamins were a large and respected Watertown family; John, the patriarch, addressed as Mister, was a well-educated church member and was early elected constable. Angier, as we have seen, was already on the road to increasing the affluence in which he had been raised. A jury would not have had much doubt about which witnesses to believe.[87]

What is particularly revealing about this minor incident is the picture it conveys of adolescent port life. Here we have two young, working-class lads heading off to test the beer of Boston exhaustively on a *Tuesday morning*. They went from pub to pub, swaggering with their money, shouting from windows and knocking back wine, provoking a fight and placing bets. Only

---

[86]   1668: CTR, 3: 92; D&O, 2: folios 43, 45, 48; 1670s: RB, 3: 12; D&O, 3: folios 56, 57; CTR, 3: 124; 1680s: RB, 4: 177; D&O, 5: folio 116; poor: CTrR, 4: 38 r, B (18)r, B (38) r, B 43, v. Thompson, *Sex* , 86, 146, 162.

[87]   Gerrish: Wyman, 405; he was the son of Captain William of Newbury and Joanna , the widow of John Oliver. The Gerrishes and Olivers were both Bristol families, as were the Russells. William Jr. may have been staying with them in Charlestown, where he moved about 1675. Benjamin: *GMB*, 1: 160–64. Note, however, that Gerrish and Benjamin were not above drinking and keeping company with Harris and Hayes.

in the relative anonymity of port towns could this happen in broad daylight. In a tightly interwoven, inward-looking agricultural community like Watertown or Cambridge, there would be little space for two young men on the loose. Hayes and Harris behaved like the "masterless men" against whom the General Court had passed draconian (but apparently ineffective) legislation only the previous year. They were plainly not inhibited by any religious brakes on their behavior. They were equally unimpressed by a culture of delayed gratification. Harris had money in his purse, and all he could think of was "spend, spend, spend," as conspicuously as possible. There were others like them along the wharves of Boston: the marginal John Corbin is named as their drinking companion, but "the company," or "several," or "persons unacquainted" to Benjamin are also mentioned. By 1669, Charlestown and Boston were habituated to groups of sailors, casual laborers, fishermen, merchants' assistants, and small traders, many with time on their hands and some with pay in their pockets. A significant number of responsible family men would be absent on long or short sea voyages or overland journeys. Their households could become resorts for male loiterers up to no good, as were the noisy inns and alehouses near the water, like John Harris's. Joseph and Sylvester and their boozy day out in Boston are examples of an alternative culture, especially appealing to adolescents and the poor, but not limited to them. In little more than a decade, Charlestown would witness similarly un-Puritanical behavior among far higher classes and age groups.[88]

Meanwhile, misfiled fragments in the Middlesex County Court Records dated less than two years after Harris's spree expose an arrested adolescent spreading smutty verses that would be more at home in London's disreputable East End. Indeed, the title of the "libel" put up by John Hayden, 31, was "The Maids of Wapping Head Bay." Quoted in the 21-year-old Jehosaphat Starr's 4 February 1671 deposition were the lines: "The Maids of Wapping Head Bay go very fine/They sing to one another/ 'My thing is wider than thine' . . . " The chorus seems to have involved named young women boasting of their genitalia. Those appraised by Hayden were Hannah and Elizabeth Sheppie, Rebecca Allen, Sarah Hose, Elizabeth Peachie, Hannah Sowers, and Sarah Kempthorn. The only other witness's statement to survive is that of the less mealy-mouthed Sarah Convers, aged 21. She repeated the following lines: "They sing one to another/'My cunt is [illegible]'/They are gone very well-haired/Good swiving girls . . . " This

---

[88] See Thompson, *Sex*, 83–109, 149–54, 186–87. On Boston: Simons, *Witches, Rakes and Rogues*, 39–91.

lack of inhibition may have prompted Starr's addendum: "Hayden also said in the libel that all the maids had good fat cunts." [89]

Several bawdy English ballads about the notorious "maids" and wives of Wapping, their eagerness to console recently landed seamen, and their infidelity to seaborne husbands and sweethearts are listed in catalogues and collections of seventeenth-century printed material. Their mimicking at new Wapping in Puritan Charlestown is another example of wharfside fantasizing and countercultural ridiculing of authority. It could be compared to modern graffiti on the stall walls of men's rooms. Most of those involved or named came from seafaring families. The well-endowed maids were in their late teens or early 20s, and would soon marry.[90]

Other libels occur in the Middlesex Records. Like Hayden's, they were sexually explicit. Their intended audience seems to have been adolescent males, and their dirty-minded content helps explain why the colonial and the town authorities were so intent on watching over and controlling boys and young men, the group most likely to subvert godly discipline.[91]

---

[89]   John Hayden, son of mariner James who had died in Barbados in 1665, had married sixteen-year-old Hannah Maynard in 1669, probably against her father's wishes; she is not mentioned in his will of 1672, *GM*, 3: 277–80, Rodgers, 3: 190–92. Ferryman James Hayden had been accused of abusing two passengers on the Boston ferry "to the hazard of their lives," MxCC RB, 1: 52, 4 April 1654. Jehosaphat Starr was the son of Thomas Starr, who moved to Charlestown in 1654, served as Clerk of the Writs and died in 1658, when Jehosaphat was only eight; though Thomas's brother, Comfort Starr, was a minister, Thomas was punished for "scoffing" at religion and was never a church member. Jehosaphat was a kinsman of Hannah Maynard Hayden. Maids: Rebecca Allen, 17, daughter of Captain John Allen, merchant and ship captain, married in 1676; Sarah Kempthorne, 15, daughter of the late mariner Simon and Mary (Long), would die in October 1671; Elizabeth Sheppie, 23, eldest daughter of fisherman, Thomas, would soon marry; Hannah may have been her younger sister, aged about 20; Sarah Hose, was probably Sarah House, 30, daughter of Samuel, a Scituate shipwright with Cambridge connections; Elizabeth Peachie may have been a younger sister or daughter by a previous marriage of tailor Thomas Peachie, see below, "Young Women Abused;" Hannah Sowers was presumably Hannah Stowers, daughter of Richard of Charlestown; she had married Abraham Hills in 1666. Sarah Convers was the daughter of James and Ann (Long) of Woburn, formerly of Charlestown. Swiving: copulating.

[90]   See Donald Wing & John Morrison, eds., *Short-title Catalogue of Books Printed in England, Scotland, Ireland, Wales, and British America, and of English Books Printed in Other Countries, 1641–1700* (New York: Modern Language Association, 1988); C. Hindley, ed., *Roxburgh Ballads* (London: Reeves & Turner, 1873–74), 2: 175, 295, 493; Hyder Rollins, ed. *Ballad-Entries. . . Stationers' Company, 1557–1709* (Hatboro, PA: Tradition Press, 1967); Hyder Rollins, ed., *A Pepysian Garland* (Cambridge: Cambridge University Press, 1922).

[91]   Libels: Thompson, *Sex*, 180–82, 185–86; cf. A. Fox, "Popular Ridicule in Jacobean England," *Past & Present*, 94 (2001), 47–83, esp. 56–64. Charlestown selectmen had various schemes to supervise the young men in the meetinghouse gallery, Frothingham, 157, 178; CTR, 3: 68, 100, 152; 4: 44, 59. The County Court regularly appointed guardians for minors: e.g. MxCC D&O, 3: folio 87; publicans risked losing their licences if they entertained servants or youth, ibid., folios 58, 74, RB, 1: 197. In 1668 the General Court clamped down on unmarried young men "living from under family government," D & O, 2: folio 49; Thompson, *Sex*, 83, 89, 91, 146. *MR*, 5: 59–63 has consolidated legislation, passed November 1675.

Long Houses: The Three Cranes, 1635–1712, and Keeping Up with the Spragues, 1675

Compared with other early Massachusetts towns, present-day Charlestown suffers by its lack of surviving seventeenth-century buildings: no Fairbanks house, no Brown, or Whipple, or Cooper-Frost-Austin. Most of these "antiquities" have very little of the original materials; they have been patched, renovated, made over. They have also been enlarged, added to, heightened, or underpinned, thus reducing their seventeenth-century appearance and authenticity. Despite heritage sites like Plimoth Plantation, imagining the domestic space of early New England life remains a major challenge.[92]

Houseless Charlestown has two alternatives to offer. The first, discovered in the 1980s excavations in City Square for Boston's "Big Dig," is the foundation pattern of the first public building in the town, the "Great House," erected in 1629 on the orders of the Massachusetts Bay Company by the engineer Thomas Graves, who also laid out the original town plan. The stone footings, some original, which replaced Graves's post-holes are set out on their 1629 site in the historic park in City Square. The two-story Graves structure measures thirty-two feet by sixteen feet. It was probably "fortified" like the later garrison houses in frontier towns during King Philip's War. Such refuge would no doubt reassure town founders like the three Sprague brothers or the Palmers, who were also constructing shelters the same year.[93]

---

[92]   The authority on early housing is Abbot Lowell Cummings, *The Framed Houses of Massachusetts Bay, 1625–1725* (Cambridge: Harvard University Press, 1979). Old Charlestown was destroyed in the Battle of Bunker Hill in 1775. Frothingham, 4.

[93]   Graves, not to be confused with the mariner Thomas Graves, had been propounded to the Company in London on 5 March 1628 as "experienced in iron works, salt works, in measuring

After Governor Winthrop moved down from sickly Salem to the Charlestown peninsula in his search for a suitable central site, he and other patentees lived in the Great House along with their families. It must have been extremely cramped with just two rooms on each floor, a fireplace, and front and rear entries. The House was the Bay Colony's first meeting-house and seat of government, until the governor, concerned about the water supply, moved across the Charles River to the facing Boston peninsula in October 1630.[94]

The town bought the Great House from the Company in 1633 as a temporary meetinghouse and town hall. Then in 1635, it was sold to the newly arrived Mr. Robert Long (1590–1664) and soon turned into The Three Cranes Tavern. It remained in the Long family until Samuel Long sold it to Ebenezer Breed in 1712. The Longs were a large clan: by 1642 Robert and his second wife Elizabeth (1605–87) had thirteen children, five boys and eight girls, ranging from twenty-seven-year-old Michael, through twelve-year-old Zachary, to newborn Deborah. At first, this crowd had to live in the south end of the house because the rest was needed for worship and administration. The Long family were part of the "company" that followed Rev. Zechariah Symmes, rector of Dunstable, Bedfordshire to Charlestown in the *Defence* in 1635. Their new home was next door to the minister's; the marketplace was on the other side. It was thus ideally sited for merchants or farmers to do business and for visitors to take refreshment.[95]

In 1663 the tavern was renovated and extended; the addition measured fifteen feet by sixteen feet, thus making the building forty-eight feet long, still quite small considering its business. The following year Robert Long died, aged seventy-three, and his sea captain son John took over the license under the aegis of the Widow Long. By this stage the Three Cranes had a wine cellar, double fireplace, and stone foundations. A drain and

and surveying land, and in fortifications, in lead, copper and alum mines, etc." His contract was signed on 10 March 1628. *MR*, 1: 30, 32–33, 390–91. He arrived in Charlestown on 24 June 1629 and returned to England in 1633, *GMB*, 2: 805–7. A map of the archaeological finds is displayed in City Square. Founders: Frothingham, 20–22.

[94] Frothingham, 41.

[95] Wyman, 625–7; *GM*, 4: 316–20. Long was licensed in 1638, and took over from Thomas Lynde. Frothingham, 84. The name may derive from a famous wharf with three cranes on the north bank of the Thames, about 500 yards above London Bridge. As early as 29 September 1638, visitor John Josselyn recorded a meeting at "one Long's ordinary [public house]" with Captain William Jackson, privateer and commissioner for the Providence Company, and others. *John Josselyn, Colonial Traveller: A Critical edition of Two Voyages to New England*, Paul J. Lindholdt, ed., (Hanover: University Press of New England, 1988), 23. Josselyn also recorded seeing a rattlesnake consume a live chicken "walking on the back side" of the ordinary.

"round house" were added. We have no description of the tavern's appearance at this period, but given the constricted public space and the large number of clay pipe shards recovered by the archaeologists, we can imagine a congested, ill-lit, smoky, and noisy atmosphere, especially on court and market days, lecture days, and when ships arrived in port.[96]

For one skipper, the Three Cranes would be a homecoming. Captain Zechary Long (1630–85) was involved in trade from 1655 onwards. He owned a one-eighth share in the *John and Sarah*, which he commanded on a 1663 voyage to Surinam. The ship was sold in London a few years later, and Zechary had his share in cash. His wife, Sarah (Tidd) died on 3 July 1674, and he was soon remarried, to Mary (ca. 1640–81), the daughter of Rev. Jonathan Burr (1605–41) of Dorchester and stepdaughter of the affluent Richard Dummer of Newbury. By the mid-1670s, Captain Long was rich enough to contemplate building himself a new house, and on 8 September 1674, he signed a contract with carpenter Stephen Bissell. This edifice was intended to display Long's success and to cost the enormous sum of £200.[97]

The contract was very detailed and is a second pointer to the town's appearance. The house was to have a full cellar six feet deep with a drain and a partitioned chamber sealed with lime, and a closet. The ground dimensions were thirty-four feet by twenty-five feet, and the wall height sixteen and a half feet. The two chimneystacks would vent four fireplaces: two on the ground floor, and two on the second. They were to be built of cement-bonded brick. The upper floor would jut out. The shingled garret roof would be pointed with lime and sealed throughout. Each floor was to be ceiled underneath, and the spaces between the upright wooden studs would be filled with bricks on the first floor and roughcast above. The rooms were to be whitewashed throughout. The four sets of windows, two on the south side and two on the east, must each have "four lights [panes] more than Captain Sprague's windows have." The most unusual feature was to be a "widow's walk," a twenty-foot-wide platform on the roof with rails and turned banisters, entered from one gable end. The house walls must be raised by 1 May 1675, when Long would pay Bissell £100. Construction must be completed by 30 August 1675, when the remaining £100 and 50

---

96   Extension corners are marked on the lawn of City Square Park. Drain, cellar, and fireplace are marked on the site archaeological map. Mr. Long's round house was mentioned as the place of servant Mary Stanwood's impregnation by Zechary Crisp, MxCC D&O, 3: folio 62, 8 October 1673.

97   In 1655, Edward Burt owed Zechary £28-19-0 by bill, MxCC D&O, 1: doc 421. Ship: D&O, 2: folio 54, 20 December 1670. Dummer: *GMB*, 1: 588–95. "Even a modest house needed at least 12 tons of timber." Philbrick, *Mayflower,* 186. I have found nothing about Stephen Bissell's background; a Bissell family lived in the Windsor, Connecticut area.

shillings worth of goods would follow. In August Bissell handed the key of the new house to its owner before three witnesses. If there were any teething troubles, "he would not stand for two or three days [extra] work for peace and quietness sake."[98]

Alas, peace and quietness did not ensue. Captain Long was not happy with Bissell's craftsmanship. On 27 August, each agreed to appoint an arbiter to inquire "Is the work workmanlike?" If they could not agree, a third "indifferent workman" would decide. The two referees, masons Christopher Goodwin and Samuel Bickner, reported in the fall, using inspired spelling: "The staircase, chimneys, plastering and sealing is so-fish-ent [sufficient]." However, they judged the east and north cellar walls too thin and the back of the house "not workmanlike." Perhaps because he found this verdict "in-so-fish-ent," Long launched a suit against Bissell. Other experts went to "view Mr. Long's house," including shipwrights John Smith and Edward Johnson and Woburn carpenter Matthew Johnson. They found several leaks: around the windows, down the support for the widow's walk, or "battlement" as they called it, and at the gable. Botched plastering round the chimney was one cause, an ill-fitting door to the battlement another. Bissell had mis-sited the chamber staircase and failed to carve the chimneypieces as agreed. The inspectors estimated the cost of making good at a modest £3, which the Middlesex County Court jury duly awarded to Zechary Long on 21 December 1675.[99]

We must hope that the Captain's assertively grandiose mansion became weatherproof and comfortable for his new wife. The specificity of the contract gives us a rather clearer sense of its appearance than the archaeological traces of The Three Cranes. The widow's walk which caused the housewright so much trouble would have given the place an unusual, innovative feature. The extra panes (always a sign of affluence) would make the interior less gloomy than most dwellings, and also demonstrate that Long's house could outdo fellow mariner Sprague's. Though the instructions to the builder might have been purely descriptive, it is far more likely that window space was a symbol of commercial and social rivalry. Despite ministerial pleas to focus on higher things (especially when Indian attacks indicated the Lord's anger with His chosen people), the merchants of Charlestown seemed intent on flaunting their wealth through conspicuous consumption.[100]

---

98   The contract and subsequent reports are in MxCC D&O, 3: folio 69, MxCC RB, 3: 133, 21 December 1675. The selectmen voted to mend the "platform" on the meetinghouse roof of 18 July 1690; this was a lookout during times of threat, CTR, 4: 101.

99   Joseph Frost and Joseph Parker of Chelmsford were the other two experts.

100   "Captain Sprague" was probably the Richard Sprague (ca. 1630–1703, son of Lieutenant

Captain Jenner's Journeys,
1674–78

From November 1674 to November 1678, the ship *John and Thomas* sailed on five voyages comprising about 22,500 rhumb miles. The ship was owned by three men: Thomas Colleton had a seven-sixteenths share, as did John Strode. The master, Thomas Jenner of Charlestown, owned the remaining two sixteenths. During these five journeys, the skipper expended £1790-18-4½d, out of which pay for himself and the ship's company of eleven cost £648-0-4d, or more than a third. Sailors' wages were paid for twenty-eight and three-quarters months out of the forty-eight covered by Jenner's records, though thirteen of these months fall in the blank period of May 1675 to June 1676. The earnings on these voyages totalled £3541-16-7d, almost twice the expenditure. The main cargo was valuable brazilletto wood; slaves were also carried. Hefty freight charges added to the partners' income.[101]

Ralph Sprague) who helped to found both Charlestown and Malden, and left £742 in 1650. This Richard, the same age as Long, had married in 1673 and became a leading citizen of Charlestown. His uncle was another Captain Richard, a childless merchant and ship owner, whose probate inventory in 1668 totalled the huge sum of £2,398. See "People Trafficking" above and "The Ordeals of Captain Foster" below. On new materialist values: Bailyn, *Merchants*, 134–42.

[101]   Rhumb: as the crow flies. Transatlantic skippers had by this time become so knowledgeable about using prevailing winds that they probably did not usually sail more than ten percent extra sea miles on their voyages. I am most grateful to Richard Crockatt and Clive Wilkinson for their help to an ignorant landlubber. Blank: it is possible that the ship may have sailed a sixth voyage to Boston and back during this period. The records (folio 17) include the item: "By 4 month's hire of the ship from London to New England. . . £280." Jenner served on Court of Assistants' grand juries in Boston in September 1675, and September 1677. How he returned to Boston in the summer of 1675 is unknown.

The five voyages were as follows:

1. 20 September 1674 to 6 May 1675: Boston, New Providence (Bahamas), Barbados, Faial (Azores), London. About 7,130 miles.

2. 20 June 1676 to 26 December 1676: London, Vila Nova de Gaia (Portugal), London. About 1,560 miles.

3. Spring 1677 to 11 July 1677: London, Boston. About 3,300 miles.

4. 20 October 1677 to 4 July 1678: Boston, New Providence (Bahamas), London. About 5,700 miles.

5. Late summer 1678 to November 1678: London to Barbados. About 4,800 miles.

The source for this information and much more about the workings of Atlantic commerce is twenty-four foolscap folios of accounts kept by Jenner and signed off by him in Barbados on 1 November 1678. Though highly illuminating in their detail, they have a frustrating shortcoming: a dire shortage of dates. The account folios only have the year at the heading; very occasionally, the margin will include the precise day certain expenditures were made or income received. The heading years are sometimes unreliable. From these meager and slippery clues, the periods of the five voyages have had to be deduced.[102]

The accounts are most revealing about the first and fourth voyages. The first entry for the first voyage, headed "Boston in New England A.D. 1674, Accounts of Disbursements at Boston," records for 20 September: "Lighterage of 47 tons of brazilletto wood . . . £3-17-6d," followed by porterage, housing, and rental of warehouse space, £7, and customs, £1-10-0. Brazilletto wood grew in the Bahamas, and is an orange-red dyewood that had already been well known for two decades in London. On folio 2 is a reference to a previous voyage to [New] Providence, one of the two main islands in the Bahamas (now Nassau). Other goods laded at Boston included "One barrel of Oysters for Barbados . . . 14 shillings," six barrels of mackerel worth £5-8-0d, and forty-one hundredweight of deal (pine) at £9-4-6d. [103]

---

[102]   The accounts are in Mass Archives, 9 November 1674. Headings: the income from hiring out the *John and Thomas* is entered under 1678 Credits, but there is no period within that year when the ship would have been available for a transatlantic round trip.

[103]   Lighterage is the payment for carrying of cargo from shore in a lighter, a small cargo vessel, to the oceangoing ship at anchor. The OED has London references to brazilletto from 1656 and 1662; the Dutch in New Amsterdam imported the dyewood from Curaçao as early as 1647. R. Shorto, *The Island at the Center of the World* (New York: Vintage, 2008), 179. Brazilwood, which was thought superior to brazilletto, had originally come from the Far East. It had been known in

The export of fish and timber from New England to the West Indies was well established by the 1670s, but mystery surrounds the main cargo, the brazilletto. Were it not the first item on the list to which "at Boston" has been purposefully interlined, we would assume that the dyewood had been taken aboard at the Bahamas. Why that large amount was in store in Boston is unexplained. The account entry is the Western Atlantic equivalent of taking coals to Newcastle, though income folios 17 and 19 have entries showing that the wood was taken on to London. It was valued at £5 per ton; a possible interpretation for its roundabout journey will be offered below. The *John and Thomas,* which was probably two-masted and about 120 feet long, sailed in the last weeks of 1674, with "a new suit of colours," a great gun, and a longboat costing £12.[104]

The next glimpse of the *John and Thomas* comes in a marginal entry for 28 March 1675. She had been caught in a late winter Atlantic storm heading towards London from Barbados and had to limp into Faial in the Azores. Here, with help from the consul, Jenner had to have his damaged rudder jury-rigged, and because of the delay, he had to revictual with two hundredweight of bread, beef, pease, fish, beer, wine, and brandy. The crew eased the ship up to the English Channel. At Cowes on the Isle of Wight, Jenner got "my rudder shipped and hung," some leaks tarred, a new anchor, and a case of wine. At Deal, a pilot came aboard and took the ship up the Thames Estuary as far as Gravesend; from there the master was rowed upstream and on 6 May 1675 he entered the ship at the Customs House, just above the Tower of London. In the nearly eight months since the first Boston outlays, Jenner had spent £388-7-9d, including wages.[105]

Before the Vila Nova voyage, the *John and Thomas* had a major overhaul: graving, caulking, re-rigging by "ye boatswain for 17 days," new cordage and sails, repainting. All this work required taking on extra seamen, three boys, and specialist craftsmen, as well as boat hire to and from the shore. The ropemaker's bill was almost £35, the carpenter's £15. The chandlers required more than £12 for gunpowder, candles, and a host of "other necessaries."[106]

England since at least Chaucer's time; *OED.* "Its red is a fiery, quick-fading scarlet," H. Mantel, *Wolf Hall* (London: Fourth Estate, 2009), 269. Hull's Letter Book often refers to brazilletto at New Providence after 1672; he recorded cargoes to London by Jenner on 8 April 1678, 388, and 7 June 1680, 413; five other references to shipment by other ships, 413, 455, 463, 509, 518.

[104]   Folios 1, 3, 10.

[105]   Folios 1–3.

[106]   Graving: cleaning a ship's bottom by burning off accretions, and paying it over with tar, etc.. while aground on a beach, *OED,* v. 2. A preferable improvement was the dry dock, of which

Vila Nova de Gaia is a town on a steep hill overlooking the Douro River and, on the opposite (northern) bank, the sweet wine center of Oporto. At Vila Nova, merchants had their "lodges" or warehouses where the port wine was matured and stored. Since the Anglo-Portuguese treaty of 1661, English merchants had been able to trade on preferential terms in both Portugal and its seaborne empire. The town was in the process of becoming a major entrepôt for English port wine importers. Though no details of cargoes are given in the accounts, bringing home port wine was presumably the main purpose of this voyage; the outgoing cargo may have been cloth or dried fish, along with 25 tons of ballast.

There, between September and November 1676, the *John and Thomas* revictualled, including some fresh vegetables such as cabbages. They called in at the Isle of Wight and Deal again on their way back to London; at one anchorage, the ship broke loose and local boatmen had to be paid to tow her back. Someone, probably Jenner, hired a horse to ride to London and back; there were frequent ship-to-shore-to-ship boat trips. Jenner had to employ a wherry (sailing barge) to tow the *John and Thomas* to the Key (probably Bear Key in the Pool of London, near the Customs House and just below old London Bridge). Most of the Vila Nova round-trip crew were new, including the mate and the carpenter. Only three of the original Charlestown men were on a pay roll totalling £107 for five months. Total disbursements on the Vila Nova voyage were £173.[107]

The 1677 voyage from London to Boston required another partial refit: new yards from the mastmaker, new scuppers, £27-worth of carpentry work, £20-worth of new sails, £16-worth of new ropes, £9 to the smith. Jenner bought a carpet for his cabin, a new compass, and £500-worth of insurance coverage costing £25. The galley furnace had a new cover and chimney, built by the "bricla [bricklayer]." The carver made several brackets for shelves; the pumps' leather was renewed, and painters freshened up and resealed surfaces. The ship's company even had new wooden bowls and platters from the turner. We can imagine the *John and Thomas* swarming with artisans, porters loading provisions—£23 worth of meat, £10 of beer, two lots of fish costing £26-10-0d —and customs officers checking for infractions of the Laws of Trade. As the

---

Charlestown had the first in Massachusetts by 1679, MxCC D&O, 4: folio 83; Frothingham, 181–82, says work began in 1677. Caulking: ramming oakum between the ship's outer boards to make it watertight. Folio 4.

[107] English importers: firms like Crofts, Warres, Taylors, and Sandemans developed lodges at Vila Nova. Anglo-Portuguese: Ronald Hutton, *Restoration* (Oxford: Oxford University Press, 1985), 188–89. Cabbages: fresh fruit and vegetables were crucial antidotes to scurvy on long voyages. Folios, 5–7.

ship dropped down the English Channel, she picked up fresh supplies: beef, beer, and water at Deal, and more of the same at Falmouth, Devonshire, in preparation for the perilous haul across the North Atlantic.[108]

Already, sickness had broken out and £1 was spent on "Physic for sick men at Falmouth." The nature of the disease revealed itself during the crossing. By the *John and Thomas*'s arrival at Boston Harbor in early July, smallpox had taken several lives, including that of Francis, son of the recently deceased Deputy Governor Francis Willoughby of Charlestown, buried at sea on 15 June. Despite quarantining the ship at Pillager Island because one person was still sick, some passengers smuggled themselves ashore by night; soon Boston and Charlestown were swept by an epidemic.[109]

Though the *John and Thomas* had had a "salvatory box" on board since 1674, the experience of the smallpox was probably behind the acquisition of a larger medicine chest for the long Boston–Bahamas–London voyage of 1677–78. Once again, the preparations were elaborate. The ship's bottom had another graving; topmasts and a boom were replaced. A cooper trimmed barrels and casks; a gunner cleaned and mended the ship's ordnance, and powder was purchased, along with sixty-six yards of canvas, locks, and three yards of baize for the ship's lanterns. Two or three cords of wood were loaded for the furnace, and over and above the usual pease, bread, dried fish, and beef, a much more varied selection of fresh food was listed: neats' (beef) tongues, flour, fowls, corn, turnips, cabbages, oysters, eggs, butter, spice, cranberries, and cider. Among those preparing the ship were a "stavender" [stevedore?], and several laborers including a Negro. The *John and Thomas* cleared Boston on 20 October 1677; she had her old mate, Samuel Lynde, and six of the previous company, including Thomas Jenner, Jr. Total expenditure on this voyage was £271-6-8d, including £127 wages for twelve crew for twenty-two weeks.[110]

Nothing in the expenditure accounts indicates cargo stowed either at Boston or at New Providence. However, later folios with details of earnings

---

[108] Insurance: this policy was arranged by London merchant Hugh Strode; a decade later, marine insurance gravitated to Edward Lloyd's coffee house in Tower Street, London. For earlier examples of insurance, see I. Origo, *The Merchant of Prato* (London: Cape, 1965), 137; *R*, 49 (1895) 252, and Hull Letter Book, 160; H. E. Raynes, *History of the London Insurance Industry* (London: Longman, 1948). Laws of Trade: the first Act of Trade and Navigation of 1651 was confirmed and extended by others in the early 1660s. Parliament had passed the Staple Act in 1673. These laws were designed to protect English imperial shipping and commerce, and especially to exclude Dutch merchants from the lucrative carrying trade. Bailyn, *Merchants*, 127–30, and index s.v. Navigation Acts. Folios 8–9.

[109] Hull, Diary, 243; Sewall, Diary, 44, 11 July 1677; Lawrence Hammond's diary has a list of Boston and Charlestown fatalities, 2 PMHS , 8 (1892), 144–72; supplemented by entries in Charlestown VR, total recorded 1677–78 epidemic deaths are 130.

[110] Folios 10–12.

suggest that Jenner carried forty-one hundredweight of deal and six barrels of mackerel from Boston to New Providence, where he then made rendezvous with two other skippers from Barbados and Bermuda bringing in about forty-four tons of brazilletto, to add to sixty-two already in the Bahamas for transport to London. The sixty-two tons were bought for £964 by the Bohemia Company in July 1678. The remainder was left unsold in London with Mr. Hugh Strode. By July 1679, Jenner had disposed of the forty-four tons for £385-17-0d.[111]

The final voyage in this saga was from London to Barbados. Before departure the ship was yet again graved, which required removing the stone ballast, remooring her inshore at high tide, "two men to heave the fire irons," and a ship's carpenter to inspect the keel. All laborers involved expected drink; the ship's watchmen had to be fed as well. Then the ballast was heaved back in, along with twenty-one cauldrons of coal, for which Jenner had to pay customs plus an additional levy to the Lord Mayor of London. The biggest bills came from the carpenter, £29; the sailmaker, £29; the baker, £19; butchers, £16; the ropemaker, £13; and the fishmonger, £12. Four barrels of gunpowder cost £11, three chandlers charged over £18, and the brewer charged £6. Compared to these large maintenance and victualing outlays, four gallons of vinegar, four bushels of salt, luxuries like a case of brandy, a dozen bottles of wine, firkins (small casks) of butter and cheese, sugar, spice, and fruit, all totalling less than £6, seem relatively cheap. The full expense of getting the ship seaworthy and supplied came to £220. She probably got under way in the late summer of 1678.[112]

The route of the *John and Thomas* on this last voyage is not known. However, among the credits in New Providence in 1678 were eleven Negroes: five men, including Dick and Barron, and six women, including an older and a younger Sarah. One woman was "Sir Peter's"; this refers to Thomas Colleton's elder brother and the clan patriarch who had 180 slaves on his St. John Parish plantation in Barbados, but spent most of his time in London. Dick was valued at £30, the older Sarah at £27-10-0d; even "one sick Negro" was priced at £20, but "a lame Negro sold for £15." These eleven people were together worth £259-10-0d. They are listed along

---

[111] Folios 23–24. The other two skippers were Captain Matthew Norwood from Bermuda in the *John*, and Captain John Salmon from Barbados in the *Bonaventure*.

[112] Folios 13–15. The last London date on the accounts was 8 August 1678; Jenner signed off on the accounts on 1 November 1678 in Barbados. He sailed *John and Thomas* to New Providence from Barbados in May 1679, James Brandon, *Omitted Chapters from Hotten* (Baltimore: Genealogical Publishing, 1982), 368, 404: "Barbados Tickets of Leave."

with 460 gallons of rum, a pipe of wine, four barrels of sugar, and bolts of fabrics. We cannot know from the accounts where these slaves embarked, but after the huge quantity of rum, they were far and away the most valuable part of the "cargo."[113]

Apart from the expenses of maintaining and refitting the ship, paying and feeding the crew, and loading and unloading her cargoes, a major outlay of Jenner's accounts was for various bureaucratic and fiscal fees and levies. The heaviest charge came from the customs; the dyewood, for instance, was taxed at about £1 per ton. In the 1678 entries at London, Jenner itemized a total of £104 in duties. Strode paid another £47 on 28 June 1678. Before such charges were levied, various customs officials had to assess the amount due. Many items on one folio refer to money spent on "waiters." These men were responsible for weighing cargoes, and the master had to pay not only their fees, but also their transport, the moving of their tackle and weights, feeding them while they worked, and wining them after they had finished. Customs searchers' and surveyors' bills also had to be paid at Gravesend and Falmouth en route down the Channel, and at Boston and Barbados. When the ship arrived or sailed, it had to make formal "port entry" or "clearance," costing up to £1-15-0d. At Boston, Jenner had to get a certificate from the governor before sailing, and the colony secretary added a charge of 17s. 6d for a fair copy. Contracts or "charter parties" with merchants freighting goods had to be legally watertight and covered by bonds. When one party went to court, proceedings were sometimes costly. Short of suing, a skipper, merchant or owner could issue a formal "protest" specifying how the contract had been broken. The other party was required to answer by a certain date. Jenner employed this shot across the bows against his employers in Boston in 1677. During the four years, Jenner's legal bills for charter parties, protests, arrests, petitions, bonds, certificates, and customs seals were almost £10.[114]

Along with profits from the sale of their wood, slaves, fish, and food items like the barrel of cranberries, the other major source of income for Colleton, Strode, and Jenner was freight payments. Going through the credit folios at the end of the accounts, freight income for the five voyages totals £980. If we add Hugh Strode's wood account of 1679, this increases to £1,056. As well as wood, three entries refer to freight of "old iron"—

---

[113] Folios 19, 24. One of the brazilletto buyers in London was John Barron; the slave's name may be connected to him, or it may be coincidence.

[114] Expenses described in this paragraph are entered on folios 2, 3, 6, 7, 10, 11, 12, 13, 22–24; these include port fees charged at Faial and Vila Nova. Duties of £104 represented 25 percent of the wood's value.

some £192 at a rate of 10 shillings per ton. In what was still predominantly an age of wood, iron was a precious commodity, used sparingly and then recycled. Only two fare-paying passengers are recorded, providing a modest £13 including their luggage. Masters could by tradition charge "primage," a small fee like sixpence on the pound or two and a half percent, for looking after the goods in their custody. "Primage for wood" is occasionally debited.[115]

So much for the information that can be gleaned from the accounts. We must now uncover from other sources more about the crew, the three owners, and the nature of their business ventures.

Thomas Jenner (1627–86) was an experienced and trusted mariner. We shall meet him again in an earlier context, sailing from Jamaica to Virginia in 1667. Son of a minister and son-in-law of a transatlantic skipper, he had already been employed once by Thomas Colleton and John Strode in December 1670 as commander of the *John and Thomas* to convey Barbadian emigrants and supplies to the infant settlement at Ashley River, Carolina, and to return to the island with pine wood. His mate, Samuel Lynde (1644–80), was also his son-in-law, recently married to the eldest Jenner daughter, Rebecca (born 1656). This 1673 union linked the Jenners to one of the most influential mercantile families in Charlestown. Also, on two voyages out of Boston, sailed Thomas Jenner Jr. (born 1658). He would literally be "learning the ropes." To have two close family members on board would be a huge reassurance to a skipper.[116]

Jenner would have needed such support, given what little we know about the other crewmembers. Henry Salter of Charlestown came from a persistently troublesome family, and was himself often before the town selectmen or the county bench for cursing, carousing, fighting, profligacy, and subversion of authority. If the John Johnstone on the crew list was the

---

[115] Freight earnings: folios 17, 21, 23, 24. Passengers: folio 17; on the 1678 London to Boston "smallpox" voyage, Sewall gives the impression that there were a number of quarantined passengers; maybe Jenner had private arrangements with them. *Diary*, 44.

[116] "Earlier context," see below, "Katherina Kidnapped." Carolina: *CSPCol*, 3: docs. 364, 430, 433; Jenner left Carolina for Barbados in early March 1671. On 1662–63 New England attempts to settle the [New] Charles River at Cape Fear, North Carolina, see Louise Hall, "New Englanders at Sea," *R*, 124 (1970), 88–108. Several Charlestown men were involved in the 1662 exploratory voyage and the aborted February to April 1663 emigration: Captain Nicholas Shapleigh, Captain William Hilton, John Greene, William Hurry, Captain John Long, and Captain Elias Rowe. Hilton also brought the first Barbadians to Cape Fear in the fall of 1663. Lynde: Samuel's father was Deacon Thomas, a maltster worth £1,709 at his death; the deacon's third wife in 1665 was Jenner's mother-in-law, the widow Rebecca Trerice. Samuel's elder brother, Joseph (1636–1727), was a leading New England merchant. His sister Hannah had married John Trerice in 1663. Jenner was extremely well connected.

fourteen-year-old son of Charlestown shipwright Edward, he too would soon be punished for "contumacious behavior in the meetinghouse" and "evil practices" involving his brother's prenuptial fornication. Thomas Brigden (ca. 1629–83), the Charlestown cooper and town gunner, who signed on at London in 1677 for the voyage to Boston, was a far more respectable and responsible individual, though he had been recently convicted of buying stolen goods from an Indian. His skills would be invaluable both for safeguarding cargo and for helping defend the *John and Thomas* from marauding pirates in the western approaches of the English Channel. John Stride, on the same journey, may have been a relative of John Strode, the joint owner. Charles Chapman, another regular crewmember, had risen to the rank of first mate of wealthy merchant Samuel Lillie's vessel *Samuel* by 1706. When the owner replaced the skipper for the voyage to London laden with logwood, furs, and sugar, Chapman led a strike of the twenty-two mariners in the crew; the ship was unable to sail, and the cargo had to be unloaded. Others like Aaron Townsend, who was a regular crewmember from Boston 1675 to Boston 1678, have left no further mark on the record.[117]

The major shareholders of the *John and Thomas* were Barbadians: Thomas Colleton was an island grandee, and John Strode was a successful Bridgetown merchant. Both came from prominent West Country mercantile families: Colletons from Exeter in East Devon, Strodes from Plympton at the western end of the county. Both were products of royalist family branches. After military and monetary loss in the Civil War, John Colleton sought refuge and financial recovery in the Caribbean. In the 1650s, Barbados was converting from small-scale tobacco and cotton production to great sugar plantations and slave workforces. At the Restoration, Colleton hastened back to England, where Charles II rewarded him lavishly for his loyalty. He was soon at the heart of the Whitehall colonial establishment. Until his death in 1667, Sir John oversaw the English end of the family Atlantic business, while his three sons managed the Barbados plantation, the new Carolina settlements, and local and island politics.[118]

---

[117] Salter: Thompson, *Sex*, 118; Johnstone/Johnson: MxCC RB , 4: 24, 17 May 1680; MxCC D&O,4: folio 102, 1682. Brigden: MxCC RB, 3: 121, 6 April 1675; D&O, 3: folio 70; *GM*, 1: 397–400; Chapman: Coldham, 2: 134. Others who signed on at Boston: Job Martin, Thomas Towman (may have been Tolman, whose family provided jurors for the Court of Assistants from 1674 to 1682).

[118] Mark Stoyle, *From Deliverance to Destruction* (Exeter: University of Exeter Press, 1996); Colleton claimed to have spent £4,000 on the king's cause: *CSPD, Charles II, 1660–61*: 322, ca. October 1660. Ibid., *1650*: 553, 2 August 1650 records passes issued to John Colleton by the Commonwealth Council of State to travel to Holland, and to son Peter to "pass beyond the seas." R. S.

His eldest son Sir Peter took his father's place in London, and proved to be a chip off the old block. As a well-connected member of the "[Absentee] Gentlemen Planters of Barbados in London," he was a leading lobbyist in parliament, court and city for Barbados, Carolina, and the Colleton family. His brother Thomas, our joint ship-owner, took over the family plantation, rich cane-growing land in the central plateau of Barbados north of St. George's Valley, called "Top of the Cliff." He also had to supervise and replenish the small army of 150 to 200 slaves, oversee clan interests in Carolina, finally flourishing after teetering early years, and in the Bahamas (New Providence). In the 1670s and 1680s, he was active in colonial and local politics and business, before retiring to England in 1691. Thomas and his younger brother James had reputations as arrogant and swaggering cavaliers. Thomas killed a fellow planter in a duel in 1668; James murdered a constable in a drunken night brawl in 1675. Such loud, loutish excess by privileged grandees would soon sully the prim streets of Charlestown and Boston. [119]

Much less is known about the background of Mr. John Strode, merchant. The Strodes were notorious for their opposition to the monarchical pretensions of Elizabeth and the early Stuarts, but one branch had moved to London in James I's reign, made money, and supported the royal cause. John and Hugh Strode may have sprung from this source. John first appears at Bridgetown in 1670, when he was an enthusiastic promoter of settlement and investor in Carolina. He acquired large spreads of land. He was still in Barbados in 1688, and is regularly seen in the Colonial State Papers for the West Indies. Hugh Strode managed the family business in London, had shares in three ships, exported Newfoundland fish to Lisbon, and traded regularly with Bilbao. He

---

Dunn, *Sugar and Slaves* (Chapel Hill: University of North Carolina Press, 1972), 20–79. Colleton's meteoric rise can be followed in the Restoration *CSPD* collections, 1660–1666. As well as his baronetcy and lucrative wine-licensing monopoly, he became a member of the Council for Plantations and the Royal African Company, and a Lord Proprietor of Carolina. He was a valued client of the Dukes of York and Albemarle, and a colleague of the Earl of Shaftesbury and his secretary John Locke. J. M. Sosin, *English America and the Restoration Monarchy of Charles II* (Lincoln, Nebraska: University of Nebraska Press, 1980), 37, 63, 77, 126–29, 343; L. Gragg, *Englishmen Transplanted* (London: Oxford University Press, 1987) 66–68.

[119] Lobbying: Gentlemen: *CSPCol*, 2: doc. 1804, 22 July 1668; Westminster and King: ibid, 3: 134, 17 February 1671, doc. 782, 11 March 1672. Hilary Beckles, *History of Barbados* (Cambridge: Cambridge University Press, 1990), 24, 44. Barbados: *CSPCol*, 3: doc. 1064, 5 April 1673, doc. 1104, 28 May 1673; Carolina: ibid., 3: docs. 89, 91, 454, 665, 721, 746, 1388; Bahamas, ibid., docs. 153, 338, 916, 1015. Duel: ibid., 3: doc. 26, 338, *CSPD, Charles II, 1668–69*: 126, 5 December 1668. Clan estates and offices: Dunn, *Sugar and Slaves*, 112, 114–15. James: *CSPCol*, 4: 616, July 1675; other evidence: ibid., 407, 421, 486, 526. Cavalier: J. H. Wilson, *Court Satires of the Restoration* (Columbus: Ohio State University Press, 1976), xi–xxiii, 227–95; Roger Thompson, *Unfit for Modest Ears* (London: Macmillan, 1979), 117–32.

was also a regular lobbyist in the clan interest at court. [120]

The vital importance of family connections in international trade could not be better demonstrated. Jenner had his kinsmen among the ship's company, Colleton and Strode had father or brothers strategically placed on the opposite Atlantic shore. In London, they organized the marketing and sale of tropical produce, supply of manufactured exports, provisions, and a workforce of servants and African slaves; they also lobbied ministers and committees on family or colonial concerns. Meanwhile, kinsmen in Charlestown, Barbados, or Carolina managed shipping, plantations, land transactions, new settlements, and the acquisition and transportation of valuable tropical raw materials like brazilletto. Clan or kinship was the vital cement of long-range commerce in these dangerous and volatile times and places. [121]

Mention of slaves and brazilletto prompts the last probe behind the opacity of Jenner's accounts. Why was he carrying brazilletto to the brazilletto-supplying island of New Providence en route to London, and why was the complement of slaves so mysteriously listed? Where and when were they acquired? Why is the last voyage from London to Barbados so sketchily recorded?

In both cases, the answer is that brazilletto and slave cargoes were illegal. In the case of New Providence, the new plantation regulations forbade the cutting of brazilletto and other valuable timber, except on personal property. All the rest of the dyewood and logwood was reserved to "The Company of Adventurers for New Providence," chaired by no less an English grandee than the Earl of Shaftesbury. The Bahamian governor was more than once commanded from London "to prevent underhand dealing to deceive the Adventurers and prejudice their trade." In 1674, his Lordship made the shipping of further supplies from England contingent upon enforcement of the investors' monopoly on cutting and shipping the wood. The following year he singled out "Mr. [Thomas] Colleton" as having seduced the governor to his "interest." Colleton "did not walk by the rules of honour . . . but sought to overthrow the design." If the governor

---

[120] Sir Richard Strode had been a leading investor in the Dorchester Company's settlement at Cape Ann, Massachusetts in 1624–26, Thistlethwaite, *Dorset Pilgrims*, 52; on Strode family, see *ODNB*. Another cluster was centered in western Dorset, e.g., *CSPD, 1660*: 231; *1661*: 149. John: *CSPCol, 1670* et seq. In 1688, he and Thomas Colleton, merchants of Barbados, sued Rebecca, widow of Thomas Jenner for debts owed by her husband's estate. Mass Archives, 20 April 1688. Hugh: *CSPD, 1671–72*: 37, 20 December 1671; *1673–75*: 272, 3 June 1674; ships: *Golden Peacock, Pelican, Hopewell*.

[121] Roger Thompson, "Reflections on the Early-Modern Extended Family in Old England and New England," in Udo J. Hebel & Karl Ortseifen, eds., *Transatlantic Encounters* (Trier: Wissenschaftlicher Verlag Trier, 1995), 62–78; Bailyn, *Merchants*, 135–38.

wished to keep his job, "he must break off all correspondency" with Colleton. The spiriting of the brazilletto to Boston was thus either a paper expedient, a deceit in the accounts, or a physical means of throwing the Adventurers off the scent.[122]

The slave trade was similarly regulated. The 1663 charter of the Royal African Company conferred a monopoly on purchases and shipments from West Africa to British American colonies. By law, the company had a stranglehold on a desperately needed labor supply. This monopoly was hugely unpopular among excluded slave traders, ship captains, and plantation owners. Typically, on 26 October 1676, the Barbados Assembly complained about the scanty supply and excessive prices of Negro servants. At other times, the Africans arrived more dead than alive, or injured, and were unemployable. The company's seizure of illicit slave ships and sale of their cargoes led to frequent outrage and countersuits. Few organizations were so hated by so many transatlantic planters as the Royal African Company.[123]

What Captain Thomas Jenner was engaged in was smuggling, or, as smugglers preferred to call it, interloping. Under the orders of the Shaftesbury suspect, Mr. Colleton, and his co-conspirator Mr. Strode the merchant, and with the enthusiastic support of Barbadian and Bahamian planters, the *John and Thomas* was running dyewood and slaves past the threats and patrols of privileged English companies, thumbing a highly profitable nose at organizations popularly regarded as price-gouging monopolists. Interloping had a long and daring history among English, and especially Devonian, seadogs like John Hawkins, Humphrey Gilbert, Walter Raleigh, and Francis Drake. It was a speciality of the pre-Civil War "new merchants" against established city monopolies like the Levant Company and the East India Company. The essentially furtive illicitness of such activity may explain the frustrating lacunae in certain aspects of Thomas Jenner's otherwise fascinatingly detailed accounts.[124]

---

[122]   Shaftesbury: *CSPCol,* 4: doc. 567, 17 May 1675, 3: doc. 986, 12 December 1672, doc. 1262, 10 May 1674.

[123]   Charter: *CSPCol,* 2: docs. 121, 408: On 10 January 1663, Sir John Colleton had been a founding member of the company, but this did not allow the Colletons to carry on their own slave voyages; in fact, it should have obliged them to safeguard their company's monopoly. Assembly: ibid., 4: doc. 911; cf. 2: doc. 693, 31 March 1664, Dunn, 157; seizures: doc. 1055, 17, 24 June 1665.

[124]   J. A. Williamson, *The Age of Drake* (London: Black, 1960); Brenner, *Merchants and Revolution,* 168–81.

Whose Coat?
Knight v. Robb, 1679

The mystery surrounding a thief's coat in the case of Knight v. Robb illustrates some of the problems raised by the presence of foreign seamen in port. What should have been an open-and-shut case collapsed into a confusion of cross-accusations and murky motivations, leaving magistrates and jurymen at a loss to know whom to believe. Given the fact that many of the witnesses came from Britain's Celtic fringe, they may have had great difficulty even understanding what was being said.[125]

The generally accepted part of the story concerned events between 3 and 4 a.m. on the night of 14 April 1679. John Knight (1633–1714), a much-married Charlestown cooper, grand juryman, and pillar of respectability, was awakened by noises in his house. Having no light to hand, he twice called out "Who's there?" before discovering that his back door was wide open. Creeping along in the dark with his hands held out in front of him, he suddenly touched and grabbed a coat. The wearer of the coat managed to wriggle out of it and bolt. When Knight was able to light a candle, he found out that the coat was white. More upsetting, he discovered that nine shillings in money were missing from his purse. Also gone was a tobacco box worth two shillings; a box lock and a pair of scissors had been broken, another two shillings worth of damage. His newly married fourth wife Mary (Clements), aged thirty-two, and his fifteen-year-old daughter Abigail corroborated his evidence, adding that household items had been "tossed about" by the burglar. They must have been heartened by the thought that they had caught the thief, if not red-handed, at

---

[125] The case is in MxCC RB, 3: 278, 17 June 1679, 291, 7 October 1679, and D&O, 4: folio 85, April to October 1679.

least white-coated. Furthermore, the garment was quite distinctive. It was "a stuff coat lined with shalloon, with a piece of a different colour stitched in at the lower end."[126]

News of the night crime at Knight's soon spread, and eventually reached the foreign visitors in the port. Four days later, a party arrived at Knight's door. A Mr. William Browne, an Irishman aged twenty-five, who was lodging at the Three Cranes Tavern next door, introduced himself. With him were Charlestown tailor Thomas Peachey and local sea captain Matthew Soley (ca. 1650–84). Brown said that his coat had been stolen before the break-in. At first he identified the white coat as his, but then, on closer inspection, decided "it was none of his." Ten days later, however, he "did own it . . . to be my coat, which I brought with me from Virginia, sent to me from Curratuck," and described the patch in it. He may have been persuaded to "own" the coat by three factors. Peachey the tailor deposed that Brown had asked him to replace the discordant patch with a matching white one. Three other witnesses swore that they "saw the coat in controversy on William Brown's back . . . before Mr. Long's brewhouse door." Finally, two other witnesses attested to having heard Three Cranes landlord, John Long, say "that it could not be Mr. Brown who broke open John Knight's house for Mr. Brown was drunk in bed" at the time. This alibi, and evidence of his ownership, encouraged him to reclaim the coat.[127]

By this time, ownership of the coat was "in controversy"; a second candidate may have sealed Browne's decision. This was James Robb, mate of the ketch *Mary and Elizabeth*, which had recently arrived in Charlestown. The master had been Nathaniel Graves (1639–79), the third son of the famous Admiral Thomas Graves of Charlestown's founding East London company. Graves had signed on his crew, including Robb, in Scotland, but had tragically died at sea. Robb would have assumed command.

---

[126] Knight had been a church member since 1668, constable in 1669, petty juryman in 1674 and 1677, and was a grand juryman at the time of the robbery, Wyman. Abigail was the daughter of Knight's second wife Abigail (Stowers)." Stuff: a woven, woollen, worsted material; shalloon: closely woven woollen material used for lining, *OED*.

[127] Coldham, 2: 52, has a record of a William Browne, merchant of St. Benet in the Exchequer, on 21 January 1693, who had been resident in London for three years. He had been born in Carrickfergus, Ireland, and had engaged in trade with Virginia. However, his age is given as thirty-two, so he may not have been the same man. Peachey was poor and had a suspect reputation as a sexual predator, see below, "Young Women Abused." Three: Alexander Lochan, 25, a Scottish seaman, Timothy Pratt Jr., a barber in Boston, and his intended, Grace Sheppey, 20. They married on 19 November 1679. Two: Zechery Johnson, 33, a brick maker and brother-in-law of Knight; his brother Nathaniel was married to Long's sister. Nathaniel was a mariner, as was second witness, Captain Samuel Hunting, 35. Curratuck: a town on Curratuck Sound, a northerly extension of Albemarle Sound on the northernmost coast of North Carolina, just south of Norfolk, Virginia.

Shortly after the burglary, a whispering campaign began, alleging that the coat was Robb's and that he was therefore the escaped criminal.[128]

The Middlesex authorities decided that they must investigate these claims. On 18 April 1679, magistrate Thomas Danforth examined Robb under oath. He declared himself "not guilty and denied ownership of the coat John Knight had in his custody." The sources of the rumours were then examined. One of his seamen, Charles Sturges, 22, gave evidence that Robb had "a stuff coat which he sometimes wore on the ship and [Sturges] was present in the cookroom when the coat was brought in to dry, and then burnt a pretty big hole in the side, the buttons on the piece sewn in by James Haxton, a Scottish boy. The coat in John Knight's custody is verily the coat James Robb wore." Two other crew members, William Hardee, 17, and George Wilson, 13, corroborated the mate's ownership. Danforth concluded that there were "sufficient grounds to suspect Robb guilty of the fact," and took bond for his appearance at the next (June) court. Robb's surety in £10 was James Russell, the Widow Graves's brother.[129]

At the June court, Robb asked for a jury trial, and the case was adjourned to the October court, eight months since the *Mary and Elizabeth* had arrived in Charlestown. Robb was represented by an attorney, Captain Floyd, and they mounted a highly effective defense. It emerged from witnesses that on the voyage from Scotland, a feud had developed between Robb and a passenger, John Somerset. Robb "did divers times chide Somerset with frequent lying." In response, Somerset vowed "he would pistol or shoot Robb to be revenged of him." This confrontation polarized passengers and crew. To confound the rumormongers, Floyd assembled Robb's supporters. John Pattison, 20, a passenger, swore "the coat was none of James Robb's. He never wore it on the ketch nor at Mr. Shrimpton's Island when at the house of Elizabeth Croad, but wore a coat made at Charlestown." "Kibing [cabin] boy" Samuel Wilson, 17, "did often order the clothes of Mr. Robb both in his chest and his cabin; he never saw a coat like this one." Three Charlestown women came forward with evidence concerning Somerset's behavior ashore. They all deposed that, under examination by Mr. Joseph Lynde, commissioner for small causes, he refused to "take his oath that it was James Robb's coat." Indeed, he had gone so far as to swear that it was not. Finally, seaman James Allen gave

---

128 Graves: see "Origins." Nathaniel had married Elizabeth, the daughter of Mr. Richard Russell.

129 Sturges: there was a Sturges family in Yarmouth on the Cape, but I have found no Charles among them. Samuel Hunting claimed that he had heard Peachey and Pratt both say that the coat was Robb's, in complete contradiction to what they had said about Browne.

Robb an alibi for the night of the burglary. "Mr. Robb was writing at his cabinet table after the bell was rung at Boston for 9 o'clock [night curfew]. I also see him between 4 and 5 o'clock of the next morning when he called people belonging to the ketch to go to work." The presumption was that Robb betrayed no involvement in recent events at Knight's. That at least was how the jury read the evidence. They acquitted Robb on 7 October 1679.[130]

No one was ever convicted of the burglary. John Knight never recovered his losses, and presumably had to return the coat to William Browne. Much official and witness time had been spent, to no avail. The crew of the *Mary and Elizabeth* had had to cool their heels in port (unless they had managed to go coasting between June and October), and Robb's reputation had been sullied. Had the principals and witnesses in this case been locals rather than visitors from far-flung places, the whole affair would have been settled within hours. Examiners would have known whose words were to be trusted, and whose not. As it was, the Charlestown court found itself sucked into a seaboard vendetta most of whose participants would rapidly (and thankfully) disappear. We are now committed to disinterested juries, arriving at verdicts on the basis of evidence presented. This was not the seventeenth-century convention. Then, local reputation was all-important and judgement depended on it.

---

[130] It was unusual, but not unprecedented, to ask for a jury trial; Thompson, *Sex*, 7. Robb, Somerset, Allen, Wilson: I have found nothing about them beyond this case. Floyd: probably John, of Boston in 1679, formerly of Romney Marsh [Chelsea]. Pattison: he may have been related to the James Patterson, Scottish prisoner, who arrived in 1651, and later settled in Billerica, though Pattison was a common Scottish name. Three: Elizabeth Banfield, 28; Dorothy Bell, 19, daughter of Katherine Bell; and Somerset's landlady, Elizabeth Robinson, who was also Widow Bell's daughter and the sister of sea captain Thomas Waffe. Croad: widow of John of Salem, died 1670; Shrimpton: may have been Noddle's Island.. See Savage, s.n. Henry Shrimpton.

Captain Martin's Day in Court: 7 October 1679

At the Cambridge session of the Middlesex County Court on 7 October 1679, three of Richard Martin's chickens came home to roost. He lost the review of a case with shipbuilder Samuel Ballatt; members of the crew of his ship *Blossom* succeeded in their suit for unpaid wages; and Jacob Hill's grey mare was ordered returned from Martin's illegal custody. It was not the Captain's finest hour.[131]

Richard Martin (1632–94) is recorded as master of a ship called *Blossom* bound for the West Indian island of Nevis in 1665. In December 1669, when Martin was at sea, his wife, Elizabeth (Trumbull), was sued by shipwright John Smith for £28 owed for work on the vessel. About this time, Martin decided to replace his ship. He contracted with ship's carpenter Samuel Ballatt (1637–1708) to build a vessel of 182 tons, 23 feet in the beam. Ballatt would charge £3-18-0 per ton, or £713, with an additional £30 for fixing the mast and yards. The new ship was also named *Blossom*, and sailed until 1690.[132]

Ballatt's accounts showed that by 29 November 1675, Martin had paid him £618 (including an inflated one-sixteenth share in the vessel). By 16 December Martin had reduced his debt to £61, and that day entered a £100 bond to pay it off by April 1677. However, nothing was forthcoming by December 1677, and Ballatt went to court. The jury awarded him

---

[131] MxCC RB, 3: 285, 287; D&O, 4: folio 86. This Richard Martin must be distinguished from a different Richard Martin of Piscataqua, who became a leading figure in early Maine.

[132] Wyman, 658; *Blossom*: this earlier vessel may have belonged to Martin's father-in-law, Captain John Trumbull; see above, "Introduction: The Challenging Sea." Smith: D&O, 2: folio 51, outcome unknown. On 8 December 1677, Ballatt referred to a bond for payment 8 years previous. Length of the ship in the contract is unclear.

£61 and costs, and on 4 April 1678 a court warrant to execute the award was issued. At the same December court, Ballatt sued Martin for the £100 promised a year before by bond in event of nonpayment.[133]

Martin's finances were in serious trouble, and it was decided to call in an accountant. The man chosen to sort out the confusion was Mr. Benjamin Thompson (1642–1714), son of Rev. William Thompson of Braintree, and a Harvard graduate in the class of 1662. His testimony later in 1679 was that "he never heard Samuel Ballatt demand anything further of Richard Martin, but did look at the £61 as the issue of all accounts and transactions concerning the ship." Ballatt's accounts showed that he had only received £43-15-0d; the marshall's deputy had distrained five parcels of kersey and three of pennistone worth £23-16-8d. This more than covered the £61 debt, plus eight percent interest and costs.[134]

So far as we can tell from the records, Samuel Ballatt, probably exhausted after years of slow extraction, seems to have decided to rest satisfied and not pursue the issue of the £100 bond. Martin, however, begrudged the final seizures and sued for review of the judgement, on the grounds of Ballatt's inaccurate accounts. This was the first case to be heard on 7 October 1679. The jury were not impressed and found for Ballatt, with costs.[135]

Events on the Ballatt-built *Blossom* in mid-Atlantic on 15 June 1678 form the background to the next case, and give grim insight into Captain Martin's style and personality. The ship had sailed from Newcastle, England, bound for Barbados. Local crew had been "shipped" in February 1678 on that understanding, which Martin conceded. The *Blossom* would return to London from Barbados, perhaps via Boston. One or two seamen, "hearing what our master was [like]," jumped ship, and once "at sea, he [Martin] sold their clothes [by auction] before the mast." Other aggrieved crew members described what the two had escaped:

> Our master's carriage was such as harried most of his men
> by smiting us with his cane and kicking us with his foot ordi-
> narily, beside the wicked language we had from him, but for

---

133 MxCC RB, 3: 202, 208; D&O, 3: folio 76.

134 Benjamin had taught at the Boston Latin School, and replaced Ezekiel Cheever as schoolmaster in Charlestown in 1670. After resigning on 7 November 1674, he may have tried his hand as town physician. In January 1679, he was looking for a new job, and accountancy was a fill-in before he moved back to Braintree as schoolmaster. Thompson had two daughters born in Charlestown in 1673 and 1677, and a third born in November 1679 in Braintree. Wyman; MxCC RB, 3: 199, 8 December 1677. Kersey and pennistone are both types of fabric, probably imported from England.

135 MxCC RB, 3: 285.

anything that was good we never heard it any. Nothing of the mention of the name of God unless it was in cursing and banning. For the Sabbath we knew nothing of it, but as we kept account [of the days]. It was God's great mercy that we came safe to land . . . [136]

This brutal godlessness did not go unchallenged. According to boatswain Thomas Allen, 26, who had been on the bridge on 15 June 1678, he "heard a quarrelling, and the captain came out [of his cabin], his face all bloody. The captain and the carpenter had fallen out." According to the ship's surgeon, John Wyllie, 25, Martin "received a blow on his face, [which] had taken the skin off his nose, and off his hand in two places." The cause of this outbreak was contested. According to some, discipline had broken down, not because Martin was a martinet, but because of the sinister influence of Stephen Drayson, the mate. He had "so insinuated himself with the men, that they could bear no command," said Allen. Rather than preventing the carpenter's attack on the skipper, "the mate stood by." When the bloodied Martin commanded his second-in-command to discipline the carpenter with the lash, Drayson had told "the master before most of the ship's company he could not answer it to strike any man aboard . . . if that were the trade he would carry the ship to a port." In other words, Drayson threatened to seize command.

Whether it was the cause of the mutiny, or a result of it, Martin decided in 15 June to alter course. The *Blossom* would head not for Barbados, as agreed, but for Boston. Eleven days later, at latitude 43° 40', the vessel ran into a storm; the mast was severely damaged. Boston was now the port of refuge.[137]

Once there, the shipboard hostilities escalated to the issue of pay. John Briggs and Benjamin Martin (no known relation to the captain) had been taken on at Newcastle at 30 shillings and 28 shillings per month, respectively. Martin had "no punctual [explicit] bargain" but had assumed the rate. Once ashore, Captain Martin began disputing the sailors' worth. A shipmate reported him to "say to John Briggs: 'Was he

---

[136] Testimony of Stephen Drayson, John Hilton, Denis Goble, Samuel Brown, John Briggs. According to Martin's 7 October 1679 testimony, Briggs and the other seamen had been shipped on May 9, 1678, folio 88. On godly seamen and the ideal of "the floating commonwealth," see Capp, *Cromwell's Navy*, 214–18, 323–26. Other godly Newcastle seamen are described in John Trumbull's confession, G. Selement & B. Woolly, eds., *Thomas Shepard's Confessions* (Boston: Colonial Society of Massachusetts, 1981), 107. On Puritan revulsion against "cursing and banning," John Spurr, "A Profane History of Early Modern Oaths," *Transactions of the Royal Historical Society*, 6th Series, 11 (2001) 49–54.

[137] The latitude of southern Maine.

a man for 30 shillings a month? He did not deserve three pence.'" The bosun agreed that "John Briggs was no able seaman." As five complainants described this development:

> He denied not our labour till upon complaint to the governor [who] advised him to give us money and he shortened us and denied us our wages and had provisioned us this [?] 5 weeks and for our wages and clothes essigns [makes excuses] to deprive us of them . . . [138]

After a long and unexplained delay, John Briggs and Benjamin Martin sued Richard Martin for "detaining wages and clothes." The marshall caught up with Captain Martin at Salem in September 1679. The critical and humiliating details were attested to in his second court appearance of 7 October 1679. The jury found for the two sailors, and Richard Martin had to pay costs as well.[139]

In the case involving the white-coated burglar, the court and jury had been blindsided by their lack of familiarity with the Scottish crew and the Irish visitor. They did not know whom to believe. In this case, however, the disadvantages of the visitors were emphasized; they pleaded, "Being strangers in this land of justice, we hope the court and jury will consider [our handicaps]." This may have swayed the jurymen, as may have the information that the governor had shown them sympathy.[140]

However, Middlesex justice was not finished with Martin yet. A third case on 7 October 1679 was a complaint by young Jacob Hill (1657–89) that Martin had Hill's grey mare with a wall eye and a blackish tail and mane, and refused to return it. Since Hill had sold the mare at Marblehead for £3-5-0, it was crucial for him to recover her. Hearing various testimonies that the mare was indeed Hill's, the jury found against Martin for the third time, with 24/3d more in costs.[141]

---

[138]   Shortened: by dating crews' "shipping" from 9 May, rather than 12 February 1678; "able seaman" may refer to the rank above ordinary seaman. I have found no evidence to connect this John Briggs with several contemporaries of that name in New England. 15 members of the crew are named, but all of them seem to have come from Newcastle.

[139]   John Trumbull, Martin's father-in-law, stood surety in £30 for his appearance. The Charlestown Commissioners for Small Causes heard on 16 December 1679 that Briggs had been shipped by Mr. Ward. They ordered Richard Martin to pay Ward what Briggs was "worth [owed] upon his return to England," folio 88. Martin's location at Salem and later Marblehead suggests that he may have been engaged in the fishery business since his return from Newcastle.

[140]   See "Whose Coat."

[141]   Jacob was the youngest son of Abraham Hill, of Charlestown and Malden.

The Martin family was deeply suspect in Charlestown as irreligious and licentious. The revelations of these cases would hardly have gilded the reputation of their often absent patriarch. His complete neglect of religious observance on a Charlestown ship, as well as his financial untrustworthiness, would have shocked his God-fearing neighbors. Even allowing for the seamen's partiality, the court and jury believed the basis of their version, and Martin never brought any charges of mutiny or disobedience against any of them, even his mate. The captain emerges from the copious testimony here as choleric, cantankerous, and confrontational; a flogger, a kicker and a curser. Though this may sound unexceptional in a seventeenth-century seadog, it was certainly outrageous to the Newcastle crew, and to the Middlesex jury. Martin seemed to carry a permanent chip on his shoulder; he could never accept that he might be in the wrong. He was a habitual appellant, and never persuasive.[142]

The last voyage of the *Blossom* was a spectacular disaster, even by her master's standards. She left Boston on 10 February 1690 with the prosecution witnesses against hated Dominion of New England officials, and a cargo including sugar and 917 hides. The vessel reached Bristol on 31 March 1690; the five witnesses went on to London by road. In late summer Martin proceeded up the English Channel "coasting round to[wards] London." However, according to three experienced seamen, "a storm arose when we were at anchor between St. Margaret's and the North Foreland [East Kent coast]." Despite their entreaties, Martin refused to lower his heavy sheet anchor, or to cut loose the impeding bower anchor line, or to allow any but "the boy" at the helm. Though they might safely have "weathered the Foreland," the skipper "cund [directed] her right on shore . . . upon the Foreness [corner of northeast Kent and southeast Thames Estuary] about three of the clock in the morning of August 31 1690." Having earlier rejected the services of a Dover pilot, he now rebuffed local seamen's offers to refloat the lightly damaged *Blossom*. Instead, he "made her a wreck and sold her . . . He had insured his ship, yet keeps out of sight . . . so much of his business is known that he will hardly get his money from the insurers." About 800 hides were saved and sent for sale in London. Whether he acted "carelessly or wilfully" is debatable; he indisputably displayed the

---

142   Reputation: see below, "Seadogs' Land War." His 2 March 1680 appeal against the Middlesex review of Ballatt v. Martin ended yet again in defeat, *Assistants*, 1: 152–53. Newcastle: the great coal port on the Tyne in Northeast England had a strong Puritan tradition; both Thomas Shepard and Thomas Jenner, Sr., had preached there. Martin's father-in-law had Newcastle connections; several Cambridge families emigrated from there. Thompson, *Cambridge Cameos*, 3–5, 324.

same dictatorial arrogance and recalcitrance of his earlier career. His reputation had become international.[143]

Martin died of a fever on 2 November 1694. Having sailed all over the Atlantic for three decades, he was quite unusual as a skipper to die in his bed. He left the comfortable estate of £561. He was evidently a representative of an alternative culture to that of most of his neighbors in Charlestown, but, by the time he died, they had begun to get used to more of his type in their midst.[144]

---

[143] The voyage and wreck are vividly described in depositions by Jonas Richards, James Farewell, and Daniel Mahon, Mass Archives, 25 October 1690, 2 January 1691. "Made a wreck" means that Martin had *Blossom* officially declared a wreck. Elisha Cooke, a former passenger let down by Martin, sent an account to Governor Bradstreet from London, adding "Your £50 bill will fail being paid by him [but] may be recovered at home." R. E. Moody & R. C. Simmons, eds., *Glorious Revolution in Massachusetts* (Boston: CSMP, 1988), 451, 465. Hides: according to an Edward Randolph letter of 29 May 1689, 4,000 hides looted by pirates from a Spanish ship were to be sold in Boston. Ibid., 246.

[144] Wyman, 658.

Coasting: Fleg v. Bissell, 1681

Much of the maritime trade we have discussed was far-flung: Thomas Jenner sailing from Boston to Jamaica and Virginia in 1667; or to Barbados, the Bahamas, London, Portugal, and probably West Africa from 1674–78; or Richard Martin's planned trip from Newcastle to Barbados, Boston and London; or Nathaniel Graves arriving in Charlestown from Scotland, as familiar with the Atlantic as his father, the Admiral, or as Jenner's father-in-law, Nicholas Trerice. Yet the sloop and the shallop for inshore fishing or local coasting were far more typical of Charlestown's ships and sailings.[145]

The problems of Gershom Fleg of Woburn with Stephen Bissell, housewright of Charlestown, arose from this more modest seagoing enterprise. The chain of events began in July 1680. John Knight, 47, who had grabbed the thief's white coat the year before, asked Gershom Fleg for the money Fleg owed him. Gershom had bought seven new barrels from Knight. Fleg replied that he had used the barrels "to venture nine barrels of cider with Mr. Bissell, and as soon as Bissell came home he expects effects [results] for his cider and then he would clear" with Knight. Two Woburn carters deposed that they had delivered the nine barrels of cider to Bissell. Fleg had a 24 September 1680 receipt from Bissell for the cider

---

[145]   Cf. Augustine Walker's journeys, 1647–53, above, and other first generation skippers mentioned in "Origins" and the introduction to this section. Sloop: We have very detailed specifications for a sloop built in 1683 by Edward Johnson, Jr. for Captain Stephen Codman and five other owners: 37 feet long with a ten foot rake (i.e. keel length of 27 feet) by 13½ feet beam, by 6½ feet deep, with a cabin and cooking galley. The frame was to be of sound black and white oak, and the outside planks 2½ inches thick. Johnson would caulk and tar the sloop and fit masts, etc. He had nine months to complete the job. The sloop weighed just over 34 tons, and at £2–6–6d per ton, cost £73–8–9d. MxCC D&O, 4: folio 111. Cf. W. A. Baker, "Vessel Types in Colonial Massachusetts," in P. C. F. Smith, ed., *Seafaring in Colonial Massachusetts* (Boston: CSMP, 1980), 18, and illustrations.

"delivered on the sloop *Expedition* according to bargain for £4-10-0d in silver." Bissell had paid Fleg £2 down, and owed him £2-10-0d.[146]

Despite Bissell's promises, the £2-10-0d was not forthcoming, so a year after the barrels had been loaded on the sloop (and no doubt after several Knight reminders) Fleg formally complained against Bissell, and on 3 September 1681 an attachment of £9 in silver was issued against Bissell to answer Fleg's complaint for non-payment. Stephen Bissell on 28 September appointed John Betts, boatman of Charlestown, his attorney, and Betts immediately set about defusing the situation. That same morning, he "made approaches to Gershom Fleg; if Stephen Bissell owed him any money, [Betts] would pay him forthwith upon sight of Bissell's contract, before [he] put authority to any trouble." This intervention seemed to have worked. The case did not trouble authority to the extent of cluttering the Middlesex County Court Record Book in October 1681.[147]

The *dramatis personae* of this mild ripple on Charlestown waters had connections with Charlestown's daughter town of Woburn. John Knight's parents John and Mary had spent the latter part of their peripatetic lives in Woburn. Knight's sister was married to Robert Pierce of that town. Gershom Fleg (1641–90) was the son of the tailor Thomas Fleg of Watertown and his wife Mary, married for 58 years when the patriarch died. The eldest of seven surviving brothers and four sisters of a humble family, Gershom moved to more promising prospects in Woburn, after marriage to a townswoman there, Hannah Leffingwell, in 1668. He went on to found Woburn's first tannery in what would later become "Tan City."[148]

Little is known of the backgrounds of Bissell and Betts. A Bissell family had settled by the Connecticut River at Windsor. Stephen had been employed by Captain Zechary Long in 1675 to build his showy house in Charlestown, and had not given complete satisfaction. Nonetheless, two years later he was contracted by Samuel Ballatt to build the first dry dock in Massachusetts, with white oak gates, apron, and wharf, and black oak and walnut side walls. Various Charlestown craftsmen described Bissell "hewing knees and other mouldings" as well as heating timber to bend it to shape. Problems arose about the wood used, and in April 1679 Ballatt sued Bissell for taking timber from his shipyard without payment. The

---

[146] MxCC D&O, 4: folio 93.

[147] Fleg seemed to be claiming the whole £4-10-0d for nine barrels from Bissell, even though Bissell had given him £2 already. The carters said that Bissell had told them that he would pay for the barrels; these may have been what increased the original valuation. One of the carters was Fleg's brother-in-law. No entry in RB, 4: 17.

[148] Thompson, *Divided*, 229; Wyman, 591.

contract stipulated that Bissell should be paid 15/6d per ton for the wood he used on the assumption that he would have to buy it; taking it smacked of sharp practice. When Bissell the housewright took to coasting is not known. He may have opened up trade with Windsor, Connecticut, which did have regular commercial links with Charlestown.[149]

John Betts was in Charlestown from 1678 until his death in 1684. He was respected enough by his new neighbors to be elected both constable and town valuer in 1680. He had given evidence in favour of Bissell in the dry dock case. Had he not died aged forty-one only three years after the Fleg complaint, he might have gone on to higher office.[150]

Fleg v. Bissell in 1681 was a minor contretemps compared to other storms darkening the New England skies, but it does highlight several important developments. Gershom Fleg was a relatively humble townsman, farmer, and tanner in an inland town, yet he "ventured some cider" up or down the coast. As a tanner, he probably dealt with neighboring towns, buying skins and selling hides and leather. Here, though, he showed both enterprise in producing and disposing of his very considerable cider surplus, and also a canny market knowledge that it was worth his while to ship it a considerable distance to thirsty mouths.[151]

We also see here a simple example of a pervasive and often highly complex chain of indebtedness. Fleg had to get his money from Bissell so that he could settle with Knight for his seven new barrels. As well as merchants, skippers and town officials kept books with accounts of debtors and creditors. Many artisans also had financial records. In the vast number of cases, we only discover this web of financial relations when someone died and their probate inventory shows money owing and owed; sometimes debts owed to an estate are described as "desperate." These tangled obligations could take years or even decades to settle. So much in borrowing and lending depended on trust and reputation. In this case, the

---

[149]   Long: "Long Houses," above. Dry dock: MxCC RB, 3: 262, 1 April 1679, and D&O, 3: folio 83. Ballatt alleged that £11-worth of wood had been taken. Bissell appealed on the grounds that he had been singled out and not jointly accused with other contractors. On 2 September 1679 his damages to Ballatt were significantly reduced, *Assistants*, 1: 140–41. Windsor: see D&O, 4: folio 111, Codman v Johnson. Partner Mr. James Russell complained that because Edward Johnson did not honour his contract to have the sloop finished by 15 March 1684, she could not sail up the Connecticut River to Windsor fully freighted before the spring floods. Cider: this strong alcoholic drink might also have proved highly profitable down east, at the Isles of Shoals or other thirsty fishing havens along the Maine coast.

[150]   CTR, 4: 25; D&O, 4: folios 82, 83, 91, 99, 102.

[151]   Storms: e.g. the crisis with the crown, the effects of King Philip's War, and the smallpox epidemic.

situation was not helped by the parties' coming from different communities. Furthermore, Bissell's record did not inspire confidence. Thankfully, the responsible attorney could cut through distrust and delay.[152]

Bissell's change of calling from builder to sloop skipper may have been inspired by his work on the dry dock, where he had to adopt new construction techniques. Whether he built or bought his boat, its name confirmed one and contradicted another of its owner's characteristics. *Expedition* can mean a voyage of discovery, and Bissell's readiness to try new things is striking, whether fashioning a widow's walk or a dry dock or sailing a coaster. On the other hand, the name of the sloop can imply speed, and in regard to honoring contracts or repaying debts, expedition was not his watchword.

---

[152] Probate inventories: see Rodgers, 1, 2 and 3, passim; cf. Elson estate: D&O, 4: folio 91, Willoughby estate: folio 110, both discussed below, "Wealthy Women"; books: Thompson, *Divided*, 100–01.

The Ordeals of
Captain William Foster, 1658–85

All contracts involving voyages included the stock phrase "Dangers of the seas excepted." As we have seen, potential menaces confronting skippers were many and various: contagious disease on long voyages as well as the chronic threat of scurvy, storms and the resulting damage to ship and cargo, attack and seizure during times of war (almost endemic in the seventeenth-century Atlantic) or at any time by buccaneers, pirates or corsairs, and, ironically, conflicts with owners, shippers, customers and merchants over contraventions of these very contracts (charter parties) or alleged negligence and carelessness therein. During a long and honorable career at sea, Captain William Foster (1618–94) endured most of these dangers.[153]

He had arrived in Boston in 1644, but fairly soon moved to Charlestown where he married Anne, the eldest daughter of William and Anne Brackenbury, influential town and church founders. Foster and his wife were both admitted to membership in the Charlestown church in 1652. By then he was established as a ship's carpenter, with business contacts at Pemaquid, Maine, and among leading Massachusetts merchants and skippers. He seems to have risen from ship's carpenter to higher rank during the late 1650s. In 1660, the Fosters bought "a parcel of riverfront" in the town, expensive but invaluable for a seafarer. In 1661, "Master Foster" brought news from London about Venner's abortive Fifth Monarchy Men's uprising against the restored Stuart monarchy. As a transatlantic skipper, Foster had become one of the elite of the seafaring community.[154]

---

[153] "Introduction: The Challenging Sea."

[154] Wyman, 362; Pemaquid: Aspinwall, 230; merchants: ibid., 267; waterfront: *Book of Posses-*

The first "ordeal" involved his initial business as a ship's carpenter. On 2 March 1659, John Lawrence (1620–72), a mariner who had lived in Charlestown for 24 years, told a neighbor how, the previous year, "Mr. Foster did hear a noise in the night and a rumbling in his woodpile, and looking out of his window saw a man taking a piece of wood on his back, at which he followed him to his house, and it proved to be John Smith." Smith (ca. 1623–73) was another ship's carpenter, who would amass a fortune of £616 by his death. Later witnesses swore that "Sister Foster" had started the story. Two decades later, she would be bitterly accused of malicious gossiping by the family of Captain Richard Martin. Smith probably contemplated suing the Fosters as originators of the slander, but they both quickly denied uttering any such accusations. This appalled Goody Stitson (another rumormonger): "Believe me, I am horribly troubled in my spirit to hear Sister Foster denying what she had said, and it made me tremble to hear her say she never spoke or thought such a thing . . . She did speak those words." Mr. Foster's categorical handwritten denial of defamatory words, "I never spoke them," may have carried more weight, and redirected Smith's attention to the secondary spreader of the slander, John Lawrence.[155]

Foster's first two maritime tests of endurance were alarming, but not uncommon. "Pestilence" broke out during a homeward voyage in the early fall of 1665. On 16 October, his newly arrived ship was boarded by the Massachusetts marshal, and, in accordance with a General Court order, placed in quarantine. No goods, passengers, crew, or livestock could come off the vessel until further orders. After a long voyage, run down by poor diet, fear, boredom, lack of exercise, and seasickness, passengers would be at their wits' ends to escape onto dry land; instead, they and the crew were cooped up with contagious and dying sufferers. The cargo was at risk of decay, spoiling by vermin or water, contamination, and loss of value; arrangements for unloading and distribution were put at risk. It was the last thing a young skipper needed.[156]

By 1669 and the next ordeal, the Fosters had eight children, the eldest of whom was at Harvard. Foster, just past fifty, was in command of

sions, 152–53; Venner, Hull, Diary, 200.

[155] Lawrence: Wyman, 606, *GM*, 4: 244–46; Smith: Wyman, 872. Depositions: MxCC D&O, 1: docs. 1527, 1534, 1538, 1541, 1542. 1681 Martin case: Thompson, *Sex*, 184; Goody Martin described "the [church] members" as "a crew of Devils. . . sister Foster, sister Taylor and your sister Smith [possibly John's wife, but there are four other candidates!] that gather together under pretence to pray, but it is to kill and slay [reputations] and do all the mischief they can." Stitson: see below, "Young Women Abused."

[156] Mass. Archives, 16 October 1665.

the *Dolphin,* a vessel of about 150 tons, valued at £640. His ship was in Ipswich Bay on 19 May 1669 when a sudden spring storm blew up; her topmast sail and rigging were destroyed, heavy costs incurred, and the voyage delayed. This was a fairly commonplace danger of the sea, but no less frightening for that, even near land.[157]

One of the most terrifying dangers that transatlantic ship masters faced in the seventeenth and eighteenth centuries was the possibility of capture in East Atlantic waters by North African pirates from "Barbary," "Sallee," or Algiers. In 1626, for instance, some 3,000 English seamen were held in Sallee (Salé in present-day Morocco) alone; in the first half of the seventeenth century, 20,000 English captives were dragged into Algiers. In 1637, Captain William Rainborough, the father of emigrants Martha and William, led an English naval expedition to rescue 350 hostages from Sallee and blockade the corsairs. Relief was only temporary. By 1671, 140 mariners from twenty-two ships from Rainborough's own East London parish of Stepney were prisoners in North Africa. Two Dutch passengers returning on a Boston ship to England in 1680 learned from her skipper that he would be sailing around the north of Ireland because "there were many English vessels taken daily, and we ran some danger of being plundered, fighting with them, and perhaps being carried into Barbary." The account book of Cambridge Church has frequent entries in the 1680s of large contributions towards freeing "Captives in Turkia slavery." North African pirates were active between the late fifteenth century and 1830 (when the French conquered Algeria), but their depredations were at their worst in the seventeenth century. By this time, they had converted from galleys to sailing warships, and in the anarchic climate of the Barbary coast and its fiefdoms ruled by various independent Beys, Deys, and Pashas, the corsairs could make a fortune by selling captives into slavery, auctioning their cargoes, and demanding huge ransoms for their wealthier hostages.[158]

---

[157] *MR,* 4, 2: 425. £640: in 1668, three-sixteenths of the ship was valued at £120, Rodgers, 2: 526; tonnage: see "Fleg v. Bissell," above.

[158] Stephen T. Riley, "Abraham Brown's Captivity by Barbary Pirates, 1655," in P. C. F. Smith, ed., *Seafaring in Colonial Massachusetts* (Boston: CSMP, 1980), 31–33; Linda Colley, *Captives: Britain, Empire, and the World, 1600–1850* (London: Pimlico, 2004), Part 1, esp. 48–64, Ch. 3; Hester Blum, "Pirated Tars. . . in Barbary," *Early American Studies,* 1 (2003) 133–58, esp. 137. Rainborough: see "Origins" above, and *ODNB.* Dutch: H. C. Murphy, ed., "Journal of a Voyage to New York," *Memorials of the Long Island Historical Society,* 1 (1867), 381. Cambridge: I am editing the manuscript account book at Houghton Library, Harvard; see, for instance £16 on 25 July 1680, folio 22, left; captives named: Samuel Gould, Joseph Guanes, Moses Eyres, Thomas Gould, Thomas Thatcher.

In the early summer of 1671, Foster sailed with his newly graduated eldest son Isaac, bound for Bilbao in Northern Spain. The next that was heard of them and the crew was news of the ship's capture, which reached Charlestown on 21 October 1671. Cotton Mather, eight years old in 1671, later described the Fosters' ordeal:

> There was a godly gentleman of Charlestown, one Mr. Foster, who with his son was taken captive by Turkish enemies. Much prayer was employed, both privately and publicly, by the good people here, for the redemption of that gentleman; but we were at last informed that the bloody prince in whose dominions he was now a slave, was resolved that in his life time no prisoner should be released; and so the distressed friends of this prisoner now concluded "our hope is lost!" [159]

What happened to Foster and his crew when they were taken into the corsair port was probably similar to Abraham Brown's account of his sufferings at Sallee in June 1655. He and fellow captives had been herded into a dungeon below the main market. Above was a "sale room" where the Christian "dogs" would be put on show during the daytime. On the following Sunday, the prisoners would be taken two or three at a time outside to the marketplace, to confront a great concourse, endure a brutal physical examination, and parade up and down for an hour and a half. Then followed an auction, at which ordinary seamen would fetch £35, boys £40, and people of higher status like Brown, £75 and more. Brown was lucky to be bought by "the best master to captives in the place," but still had to work under a black foreman who "refused to drink from the same bucket" as the despised slave. After three months, Brown had been ransomed by an English merchant for £125, along with forty other captives.[160]

The Fosters were also fortunate. Charlestown's hopelessness reached the ears of the Apostle to the Indians.

> Well, upon this, Mr. [John] Eliot, in some of his next prayers, before a very solemn congregation, very broadly begged, "Heavenly Father, work for the redemption of thy poor servant Foster; and if the prince which detains him will not, as they say, dismiss him as long as himself lives, Lord, we pray thee to kill that cruel prince; kill him, and glorify thy self upon

---

[159] Hull, Diary, 232; *Magnalia*, 544–45.

[160] Riley, "Abraham Brown's Captivity," 39–41.

him!" And now, behold the answer: the poor captived gentleman quickly returns to us that had been mourning for him as a lost man, and brings us news that the prince which had hitherto held him, was come to an *untimely death* by which means he was now set at liberty.

In November 1673, John Hull recorded the Fosters' return to Charlestown in a small boat laden with fish.[161]

Compared with his North African "captivation" (as the seventeenth century called it), Foster's ordeals a decade later at the Leeward Island of Nevis, and subsequently at the Middlesex County Court in April 1685, were relatively painless. By now, he commanded the pink *Return*. Among the cargo from Charlestown were horses, probably for use in driving the island's sugar mills. One of these horses was shipped by Mr. Samuel Sprague of neighboring Malden.[162]

During the voyage, the horse was "bruised," but concern arose when *Return* anchored in Nevis Road and lighters came out from the island to unload her. John Foster, 19, "saw the horse of Samuel Sprague hoisted into the boat at Nevis to carry ashore, but he would not stand, though the men used means with him to make him." Richard Foster, 24, his father's mate, took up the account: "The horse lay down in the boat . . . going to the shore, the surf of the sea overcame the boat . . . using my best endeavours I grasped his halter, but it tangled and unfastened, so I held his head above the water on my shoulder, but he died on the beach." The crew's "best endeavours" were corroborated by another skipper on the scene, Captain Nathaniel Norden of Marblehead.[163]

Captain Foster sent a letter posthaste informing Samuel Sprague of the horse's death, and visited Richard Sprague in Charlestown on his return from the islands in May 1684. On 14 May 1684, negotiations between Foster and Samuel Sprague were held at his brother Richard's house. No permanent settlement was reached, because a year later, on 7 April 1685, the court heard the suit of Samuel Sprague against William Foster for £20 damages for "carelessly drowning a horse in good state."[164]

---

[161] Mather, *Magnalia*, 545; Hull, *Diary*, 232. On 29 April 1674 Foster commanded the *Swan* sailing to Barbados and England; Hull was a joint owner, Letter Book, 167. In January 1675 Hull reported that Foster had not yet arrived back from London; he feared storms off the Caribbean coasts. ibid., 235. Foster was entered in Barbados Tickets of Leave on 18 June 1679 as commander of *Concord* bound for London. J. Brandon, *Omitted Chapters from Hotten*, 390.

[162] Pink: two- or three-masted cargo ship of considerable size and narrow stern, *OED*. On Nevis as a sugar-growing colony, Dunn, 122–28.

[163] MxCC D&O, 5: folio 114, 4–7, April 1685.

[164] MxCC RB, 4: 149, 7 April 1685.

The plaintiff's witnesses attested that William Foster had admitted that "the horse was lost through the men's negligence and they should pay and he had told them so." Richard Sprague had advised the master to stop the men's wages to ensure compensation to his brother. Mary Edmunds, 50, added that "the horse had drowned through the men's leaping into the boat." The defense stressed the care taken by the crew, and cast doubt on the Spragues' valuation of their horse. Mate Richard Foster testified that "prizers of the horses had come aboard the ship" before unloading, and had appraised Sprague's horse at £3-5-0d. Eleazer Phillips, 30, opined that "the horse was not worth more than £3; he had bought better for less." The jury were sympathetic. They thought William Foster had been justified in refusing to make satisfaction. The accident arose from "a danger of the sea" rather than human negligence. They found for the defendant with costs.

In their verdict, the jury supported an underdog family against Charlestown and Malden grandees. The Spragues were people to emulate, to "keep up with," as Captain Zechary Long had specified a decade before in his grandiose house plan. The three founding Sprague brothers had separated during Charlestown's early years. William (ca. 1611–75) moved in 1636 to his new wife's home in Hingham. Eldest brother Ralph (ca. 1595–1650) had been a founder of Malden during the 1640s, while Richard (1605–68) remained in Charlestown. Though he made a huge fortune as a merchant and landowner, Captain Richard had no heirs, and so left most of his wealth to Ralph's second surviving son, Richard (ca. 1630–1703). A mariner, young Richard moved back to Charlestown; he is the Richard Sprague in this case and elder brother of Samuel of Malden. His attitude towards William Foster comes across as rather threatening, and foreshadows the browbeating of pregnant Elizabeth Mellins in 1698 by Samuel, the horse owner, and his son Samuel Jr., the father of the illegitimate child. The Spragues were members of a group of wealthy mercantile families in Charlestown who were prepared to collaborate with the royal government of Massachusetts in 1686, and were objects of popular outrage after the Glorious Revolution of 1689. Their cooperation with royal agent Edward Randolph in the early 1680s and their disdain for popular provincial resistance may have swayed the jury's minds.[165]

The Spragues and the Fosters went back a long way. Old Captain Richard had been a shareholder in Foster's *Dolphin* during the 1660s.

---

[165] Long: see "Keeping up with the Spragues" above; Spragues: see "People Trafficking," above, Wyman, *GMB*, 3: 1728–39. Mellins: Thompson, *Sex*, 23. Group: see "Dominion and Revolution" below.

The Spragues had sent horses to Nevis on previous Foster voyages. Young Richard Sprague shared seafaring experience with William Foster and his sons. Yet in this encounter, the two families were ranged against each other. William Foster's refusal was buttressed by two of his sons and by his Boston brother-in-law Eleazer Phillips, who scathingly diminished the Spragues' equine valuation. Samuel Sprague had not only brother Richard and nephew Jonathan as witnesses, but also sister Mary Edmunds, with her hearsay story of negligence. In this family feud, the hugely inflated monetary demands and the insistence that humble crew members, rather than one of the richest families in Middlesex County, should bear the loss of one clapped-out nag probably also affected the verdict.[166]

The court's evaluation of the Foster family and its reputation was critical, however. Cotton Mather's tone in the captivity account indicates that Foster was a very different kind of skipper than the likes of Augustine Walker or Richard Martin. His early church membership and his eldest son's ordination indicated the family's religious commitment. The contrast was emphasized when Mrs. Elizabeth Martin alleged in 1683 that "[Church-]Sister Foster" was one of the members behind the gossip that young Margaret Martin was pregnant and the Martin ménage was little better than a brothel. During the 1680s, the Fosters saw their son Reverend Isaac marry into the distinguished Russell family and be chosen as pastor of Hartford, Connecticut, one of the leading New England congregations. Younger sons Richard and John were beginning seafaring careers that would take them both to masterships. In 1694, Charlestown church nominated their 76-year-old father to be one of its deacons, but the ancient mariner declined on the grounds of age. Four years later he was dead. For a seafarer to have endured what he had, to reach the age of eighty, and to die in his own bed was no mean feat, given the dangers of the seas.[167]

---

[166] Share: Rodgers, 2: 516; before: test. Jonathan Sprague, 28, 4 April 1685. Mary Sprague (1634–1717) married Daniel Edmunds of Charlestown before 1664.

[167] Sister: MxCC D&O, 4: folio 105; Thompson, Sex, 184; deacon: Hunnewell, xi. Cf. "Captain Martin's Day in Court" above.

Failure in *Success*:
Captain Marshall's Long Voyage,
1683–85

Captain William Marshall (ca. 1640–88) first appeared in Charlestown in 1666 when he married Mary Hilton (1645–78). He thereby allied himself with two of the town's most distinguished families: Mary was the daughter of Captain William Hilton (1617–75), mariner, navigator and cartographer, who had been in New England since 1623, and stepdaughter of Mehetabel (Nowell) Hilton, the Captain's second wife since 1659. The Marshalls produced three future mariners and two daughters over the ensuing twelve years, but Mary the mother was a victim of the smallpox epidemic in 1678. William was probably at sea when she died; that year he captained the *Relief* carrying horses, a hogshead of stockings, and bundles of shingles to Nevis, and returning with sugar. William's second wife in 1681 was Lydia (Maynard) Hale, the well-endowed widow of mariner Captain Samuel Hale. In 1683, Marshall was again in the West Indies, this time with horses and other cargo for Barbados. After both Caribbean voyages, he had to go to law to extract payment from shippers. Apart from this, his growing experience as an oceangoing master betrayed no signs of other problems, such as the personnel management of his crews.[168]

This early promise, alas, would not continue in succeeding years. The transatlantic voyage of the inappropriately named *Success* proved a disaster

---

[168] Wyman, 657; Hilton: *GMB*, 953; *Piscataqua Pioneers*, 232–3; *R*, 124 (1970), 90–98. Marshall's estate included maps, probably inherited from Hilton, MW, 14729. Consigners: MxCC D&O, 3: folio 81: Marshall, aged 38, against Boston carpenter and dealer Benjamin Thwing for £6-18-0d unpaid freight of 1150 lbs. of sugar, 18 December 1678; RB, 4: 84: Marshall against Henry Sanford, Charlestown, £15 owed for freight of two horses to Barbados, 15 December 1683.

for the skipper, the owners, and the crew. The accounts of what went wrong and why are sharply divided, and those competing interpretations produced a series of court cases embroiling all three parties.

Success was owned by ambitious Boston merchants Richard Wharton and Daniel Allen. She had a crew of twelve; in December 1683 they sailed from Boston to Surinam on the northeast coast of South America, to purchase sugar and lime juice. This cargo was to be carried to Amsterdam and sold. The vessel would then return to Boston. Marshall assured the ship's company that the whole voyage would take from nine to eleven months. Thanks to various reverses, however, it was twenty-three months before they returned.[169]

The first reverse occurred in Surinam. According to Marshall's badly stained and damaged account, no sugar or lime juice was to be had on the coast, and so they headed up the Surinam River in search of these goods. The tropical climate and marshy terrain brought on sickness among the crew; by the time *Success* had its cargo, several months had passed, and discipline had broken down. In describing this point in the voyage, the accounts sharply diverge. According to identical sworn statements from three junior members of the crew, on the eve of departure from Surinam, "the master came on board at night, and struck the bosun; he went to his cabin, fetched his rapier, and so terrified the bosun that he was forced [to climb] to the tops." The skipper then, in a crazed fury, chased the crew around the ship with his drawn rapier. "The bosun was turned out of his place" before they sailed.[170]

Marshall's slant gives some justification for his behavior:

> When the ship was near leaving, the crew were merry with drink, and quarrelling, one says, "A company of mealy-mouthed fools, I'll no more to do with your plot." I could not understand what they were about. Going ashore, I could not

---

[169] Wharton, see Bailyn, *Merchants,* 173–74; Allen often appears in Sewall's *Diary.* He was a cousin of John Hull, and spent several years during the 1670s in London, Letter Book, 3, 46, 89, 129, 139, 241. He is not to be confused with Dr. Daniel Allen, of Boston. Portledge, or signing-on money, was paid on 25 October 1683, and left with the owners. The monthly wage bill was £22-10-0. The agreement was for two months' pay at Amsterdam and the remaining balance on return to Boston, MxCC D&O, 5: folio 118, which contains all the documents for this account.

[170] Surinam, east of Guyana, had been founded about 1650 by English settlers from Barbados; at the 1667 Peace of Breda that ended the Second Anglo-Dutch War, it was exchanged with the Dutch for New Netherland, renamed New York (which then included New Jersey, Pennsylvania, and Delaware). In 1700, Surinam produced about 4,000 tons of sugar a year. Dunn, *Sugar and Slaves,* 20, 23, 62n, 111, 205, 314. The bosun, properly boatswain, was the expert sailing officer on board, responsible for sails, rigging, cordage, anchors, masts, spars, and boats. He transmitted orders to the crew with his pipe or whistle.

find the bosun, but, after, found him in a hammock with a Spanish woman, which is a Miss to a Jew. On our return to the ship in the boat, the bosun sheared the boat causing damage. I went to strike the bosun, but the mate grabbed me from behind and tore my clothes.

Earlier, mariner Nowell Hilton, 27, had heard the master warn the bosun "to take more account of the goods" being loaded.[171]

On the transatlantic voyage, a mood of sullen suspicion settled on *Success*. "At sea," recalled Marshall, "the mate [Enoch Moore] sends down a boy to tell [me] to beware of [my] pocket-book, for the crew had a plot to remove it." This warning was repeated when they reached Amsterdam.[172]

The arrival at Amsterdam, by then many months overdue, triggered outbursts of pent-up emotion. Again, accounts conflict. The lower-deck view was that their master was obsessed by suspicions of cargo-theft and pilferage. When a lighter came alongside,

> The mate offered to take account of the goods going over the side, but the master refused and said, 'Mind your own business!' . . . He would be hanged but he would take account of the goods himself . . . The master said that only he, not the mate nor any man should stay on board. If anything was lost on the vessel, he would lay it to our charge. We were forced to stay on shore to our great [financial] damage.[173]

Marshall's account explains his misgivings. With the lighter alongside, he had "told the [replacement] bosun to open the hatches, break bulk, and take account of the goods. He refused. I said, if he would not, he should have no more wages than a foremastman. He cared not. Therefore I took the account." The banishment of the crew could be justified by suspicions of theft and talk of a "plot;" that of the mate, by Moore's threat to sue the master, who replied "Why should I keep him who is going to law with me?"[174]

Further trouble ensued. Ten hogsheads of sugar and three of lime juice, marked "YA" and consigned to an Amsterdam Jew, seemed to be

---

[171] "Ashore": probably Paramaribo, 14 miles upstream from the coast.

[172] Pocket-book: this was a new term, *OED* has a 1685 usage: a small, book-like, leather case with compartments for paper, notes, bills &c. The (first) mate was the second-in-command of a ship.

[173] Tests. John Mitchell, 21, Gershom Marble, 23, and James Rutherford, 19, 19 November 1685.

[174] Break bulk: open the hold and start to unload the cargo, *OED*, "break," 43. Presumably, the bosun refused because he did not consider it his job. Keep: here meaning pay his board and lodging on the ship. Moore was angry at the excessive time the voyage was taking.

missing. The Jew threatened to sue Marshall. Yet again, accounts differ. Twenty-one-year-old apprentice seaman John Mitchell attested that "after a rummage in the [Jew's] storehouse, the hogsheads were found . . . Mr. Moore asked the master about the missing barrels, and the master replied 'The lost sheep is found and brought home.'" Mitchell added that Marshall alleged that the Jew had taken one of the [lime juice?] hogsheads out of his warehouse and had burnt it to prevent discovery. Back in Charlestown months later, however, Marshall swore that "he knew not what became of the ten hogsheads of sugar and two of lime juice wanting in the cargo, and how they were lost or dispossessed either directly or indirectly." Given the skipper's threat to the crew that the value of any lost goods would be docked from their pay, and that the sugar and lime juice were worth £62, the question of loss or recovery was crucial.[175]

Forced ashore, fearing loss of pay and a highly volatile master, and many months behind schedule, the senior crew members, mate, bosun, carpenter, and cook decided they must formally sue the master for their full wages, which he interpreted as desertion. Marshall's brother-in-law Nowell Hilton, after having to pay his own way for two weeks in an expensive port, "was seduced to do the same." The bosun made application to the Lords of Amsterdam "to see justice done." According to the mate, "One day the bosun came and told me to come before the Lords; the master and Captain Cotton were drinking," and when invited to put his side to the court, Marshall said, "Go and be poxed and be damned with the rest of the rogues." The plaintiffs could get no satisfaction from the Lords.[176]

Success was a ship without a crew. Marshall had to hire other labor to "careen, grave, and fit" the ship before her return to Boston. She had been in the water for well over a year, and "lay at the pales at Amsterdam four months and two days." Despite the possibility of finding alternative seamen, Marshall took on the old crew again, though without any financial agreement. Although he felt "much wronged by the [ship's] company," yet "he could no means [*sic*] leave them there in Holland." Meanwhile, the owners had had to foot the bill for the twelve lost hogsheads.[177]

The third act in this three-port drama was set in Charlestown, and the bitter end-of-voyage argument was about pay. There were quarrels about

---

[175] Remembering the previous bosun's careless accounting, it was possible that the missing barrels had never been loaded at Surinam.

[176] Cotton: unidentified.

[177] Careen: turn ship on side; grave, burn off accretions to hull. Pales: may be mooring stakes, *OED*. A Mr. Robb volunteered to sail *Success* home in return for his passage; he may have been the James Robb falsely suspected of stealing William Brown's white coat. See above, "Whose Coat?"

whether the two months' wages had been paid in Amsterdam, as per sign-ing-on contract. Marshall insisted that the money had gone to those who had not deserted, at the rate of ten Dutch stivers to the New England shil-ling. However, the "desertion" was disputed by the crew; they contended they had been "banished." Neither Marshall nor the owners were particu-larly eager to shell out twenty-three months' worth of pay: £517-10-0d for the whole ship's company, nearly three times the original estimate.[178]

From December 1685 until the onset of royal government in May 1686, Middlesex County Court and the Assistants Court heard contradic-tory claims, counterclaims, and appeals from crew members, the skipper and the owners, said to have been "damnified" to the tune of £200. In most cases, William Marshall was the loser. Only the termination of the First Charter regime terminated this tragicomedy of errors.[179]

The central cause of this series of misadventures was the increasingly distrustful relations between the master and the ship's company. Marshall did have some allies on board: his eldest son William, aged 14 in 1683, who probably matured fast in this climate, and a Henry Marshall, aged 16, who corroborated the skipper's account of their arrival in Amsterdam. Nowell Hilton, the master's brother-in-law, was an experienced mariner of 27. Most of his two testimonies were supportive of the skipper, espe-cially against the first bosun, but he contradicted Marshall by claiming to have found the missing barrels in Amsterdam, and allowed himself to be "seduced" into "desertion" there. He could hardly be relied upon by his embattled kinsman.[180]

Though many ordinary seamen appeared only on the portledge bill when signing on, they nonetheless became increasingly restive and threat-ening. The leader of the opposition in Marshall's eyes, was Enoch Moore, the mate, who finally led the walk-out down the gangplank and sought jus-tice from the Amsterdam authorities. Moore was of similar age to Marshall, and had been in Charlestown since 1675. He had married into the wealthy and distinguished Converse and Long families. He had warned Marshall of the crew's plotting and had offered to take over accounting for the cargo be-ing unloaded in Amsterdam. He had rented accommodation for his family

---

[178] Pay: Marshall's share, at £5 per month, would be £115.

[179] MxCC RB, 4: 199, 201, 205; *Assistants*, 1: 289; Mass Archives, March 1686. Wharton and Al-len: their 26 March 1686 suit is recorded in *Assistants*, 1: 297, but lacks a verdict; they sought the return of three months' wages overpaid. Marshall was able to recover three years' Charlestown rent from Enoch Moore and £3 lent to Moore's wife.

[180] William Jr. went on to become a mariner, and died in England. Hilton died in London in 1687, a year before Marshall. Wyman. 504–5.

from the master more than a year before the voyage. However, he was also related by marriage to Henry Sanford, Marshall's 1683 antagonist in court. His manhandling of the master just before sailing from Surinam may have soured their relations. Sheer frustration seems to be the most likely reason for his final breach. The two mystery members of the opposition were the two bosuns, neither of whom is ever named. The first was jettisoned for incompetence and indiscipline in Surinam; the second refused to obey the master's orders to break bulk in Amsterdam, and despite warning, "he cared not." He initiated proceedings in the Amsterdam City Court. It is likely that he did not sail with *Success* back to Boston; otherwise, it would be incredible that his name remains unknown.[181]

William Marshall's behavior seems to fit the Martin/Walker model of hard-drinking, foul-mouthed, sword-wielding seadoggery. Marshall's anti-Semitism was nothing unusual in the seventeenth century, and he did have to face considerable frustration and provocation in both Surinam and Amsterdam. It is possible that the spirit of populism already encountered in the Stinted Common conflict may have motivated lower-deck resistance. Nonetheless, the desertion of his brother-in-law and the decisions of two juries against him in several cases are damning commentaries on his alienation of his crew. It is telling that the foreman of one of those juries was a representative of an alternative type of sea captain, the godly and uncomplaining William Foster.[182]

---

[181] Moore: his wife, Rebecca (Converse) of Woburn, was daughter of the former Ann Long; he was related to Sanford through the Longs. Moore had been a Court of Assistants' juryman on 28 August 1680, *Assistants*, 1: 160.

[182] Cf. "Succession Crisis" and "Dominion and Revolution" below.

Conclusion:
A Violent and Unpredictable
Commercial Culture

The introduction to this section stressed the risks merchants and mariners ran as they went about their business. One notable feature of the challenges faced in the preceding studies is the prevalence of violence. It might be the armed seizure of one's ship or its cargo or provisions, as happened to the Davison Company, Joshua Tidd, John Ridgeway, William Foster, or Thomas Waffe. It might be the mutinous attack of seamen, as with Captain Richard Martin, or the terrifying, sword-clashing rampage of the outraged Captain William Marshall. John Cole was severely bludgeoned by his fisherman landlord Thomas Sheppie over ownership of a canoe, no doubt a pretty commonplace method of asserting property rights among the fishing stations Sheppie visited down east. A drink in a Boston pub could suddenly explode into a challenge to a fistfight, with money wagered on the winner. Competition for furs could pitch even Plymouth Pilgrims into murderous gunfights. These explosions occurred even between fellow Englishmen, fellow colonists. The blast was magnified when foreign rivals were engaged: the French in Acadia, for instance, or Dutch or Spanish in the Caribbean, or Barbary corsairs in the Eastern Atlantic.[183]

Some of the reasons behind these instances of violence can never be recovered, but two general causes can be stressed: commercial control, and the culture of shipboard and port. Several attacks were intended to defend hard-won rights. Collicut and Richards, for instance, were seeing off a coaster encroaching on their patent, as were Pilgrim fur traders at

---

[183] See below, "Violence."

Cushenoc. John Ridgeway's ship was seized at Richmond Island to protect the independence of Ligonia, the Trelawney fishing patent, and Robert Jordan's rights as a creditor. Even Captain Augustine Walker's seizure of the ship in Charlestown harbor had the alleged intention of protecting the original owners, victims of piracy in Montserrat, against receivers of stolen goods (who happened to be some of the town's leading merchants!) On a wider scale, both Thomas Jenner and William Marshall were in breach of English trade or monopoly laws aimed at protecting imperial interests. Marshall's frustrated employers complained that *Success* was further delayed in English ports because they had broken the Staple Act. Had Jenner been caught with his illegal cargoes of brazilletto or slaves, he would have lost everything. Governments and large-scale investors sought to protect and control trade and navigation. The original "New Merchants" who first opened up Atlantic trade, colonials, and smaller fry, all had strong incentives to interlope and undermine established monopolies. The clash of interests was bound to lead to violence.[184]

The many shipmasters we have met fall into two broad groups. The "godly" captains like first-generation Thomas Beecher, Thomas Graves, or Thomas Coytmore, and their successors Thomas Jenner and William Foster, were Charlestown church members who took their faith on board with them and tried to recruit companies of similar religious dedication. All seafarers were deeply superstitious, but the godly captains regularly worshipped at sea and put their trust in the Lord. Among the mariner confraternity, they were outnumbered by the seadogs: skippers like John Hodges, Nicholas Trerice, Thomas Sheppie, Elias Row, Thomas Waffe, William Marshall, or Richard Martin. Their rambunctious shipboard arrogance got them into trouble both at sea and when they brought their loutish values ashore with them. A few masters like Walker or Trumbull were church members who would normally resort to arbitration or law rather than violence; however, under provocation, their sabres would start to rattle. They lapsed from one moral level to a lower.

Seadogs set a tone on their vessels that influenced their crews, and, when they were ashore, their families too. They fuelled an irreligious, strident, anti-Puritanical counterculture which caused considerable unease, even alarm, among the devout and the authorities. They gave Charlestown a reputation for edgy raciness, in contrast with other more biddable Middlesex towns. Add to this a sex ratio with a frequent majority of female residents onshore, since so many husbands or male partners would

---

[184]   New Merchants: Brenner, *Merchants and Revolution,* passim.

be away at sea. However, foreign seamen like James Robb and his fellow Scots, the Newcastle crew on *Blossom*, and visitors to the port like the boozy Irishman from Virginia, William Browne, redressed the balance. Sometimes they sought to replace absent husbands temporarily; sometimes they were enthusiastically welcomed. If, in the 1630s, the godly inhabitants of the moral maelstrom of Wapping sought religious refuge in Charlestown, by the 1680s, their faithful offspring must have feared that Wapping vice and misrule were catching up with them.[185]

Seadogs met the frightful unpredictability of the cruel sea with swagger; godly captains with prayer. Both relied for mundane assistance on family connections, as did their merchant neighbors and their plantation shippers. Merchants needed relations on both sides of the Atlantic to safeguard their interests and act as trustworthy trading partners. Dealing with strangers was a last resort. Merchant families married their children into other merchant clans; seafarers wed seafarers' daughters and produced seafarer sons who learned their trades on their fathers' ships. Moreover, a skipper benefited from the reassurance of kinsmen in his ship's company. The commercial world was a network of intermarried groupings, an exclusive world where blood was a great deal thicker than water.

Despite the reassurances of clan trust, skippers also had to deal with the sorts of people that their neighbors in Charlestown, let alone inland towns, rarely encountered. These commercial acquaintances often held values very different from those in the Bay. They might for instance be swaggering Anglican monarchists, like the Barbadian Colletons and Strodes who shared ship-ownership with Thomas Jenner, as well as employing him in their nefarious activities. John Ridgeway's tussles with Rev. Robert Jordan were exacerbated by hostile beliefs and evaluations, which also probably contributed to Elias Row's falling out with Jamaican victualler Joseph Deacon. Charlestown seamen would be familiar with cavalier planters and their armies of terrorized slaves in the West Indies, the hordes of desperate indentured servants in the Chesapeake and Carolina; their eyes would have boggled at the dramatic differences in culture created by such planters and workforces mass-producing tobacco or sugar. International skippers like Jenner, Marshall, Martin, Walker, or Foster would have to conduct business with foreigners: the Dutch in Amsterdam and Surinam, for instance; the Portuguese in the Wine Islands and the mainland ports; the Spanish in Bilbao, Cadiz, and the Caribbean; and the French in Acadia and eastern Maine. They dealt even with Barbary

---

[185] Thompson, *Sex*, 149–52.

pirates; with pragmatists, Catholics or Muslims. The tight parochialism of the villager was bound to be stretched at sea. [186]

With energy, luck, daring and industry, these family firms could reap high rewards. The wealthy grandees of Charlestown were all merchants: in the first generation, Ralph Sprague, Richard Russell, Francis Willoughby, Francis Norton, Thomas Lynde; in the second: nephew Richard Sprague, sons James Russell, Thomas Graves and Joseph Lynde, and Willoughby cousin, Lawrence Hammond. All were blessed with family connections and started their enterprises with sufficient capital and credit. Their energetic spirit was contagious. We find quite small producers shipping out their surpluses, like Gershom Fleg with his cider, or Peter Bulkeley with a load of onions, or whoever supplied a barrel of oysters and one of cranberries on Jenner's voyages to the West Indies. Joshua Tidd and John Trumbull were both in a small way of business in their Maine dealings, but hoped for a tidy profit nonetheless. In the rivalry with Boston, the town might be lagging, but there was still plenty of money in Charlestown. With money and control of credit came presumptions of control over policy and appointments.[187]

Those who prospered began, even in the 1650s, to build themselves ample accommodation, though this often included storage facilities like Captain Walker's ill-fated wine cellar. By the 1670s, competitive display drove the new generation, like the younger Richard Sprague and Zechary Long. A widening gap between the elite and humbler inhabitants produced social and economic ructions over the Stinted Common. It would also create far more wounding splits in the town as the old colonial charter was lost and royal government took over.[188]

Charlestown's commercial culture and the international horizons of its merchants, skippers, and seamen were bound to divide the town's elite and undermine deference. As we shall soon see, residents like Richard Russell, Francis Willoughby, John Trumbull, Mary Newell, and even Pastor Morton had been battered by Stuart autocracy or enlightened by Dutch or Cromwellian tolerance. They could not stomach the rigid uniformity demanded by more parochial leaders. Cultural clashes opened opportunities for defiance of dictatorial conformism.

---

[186] Row: see below, "Katherina Kidnapped." Even the relatively sophisticated John Winthrop quickly lost his bearings when negotiating with La Tour and his wife.

[187] Some Charlestown men followed the early lead of Edward Gibbons and Thomas Hawkins and moved across the Charles: Robert Sedgwick, Jr., Captain Thomas Waffe, and Thomas Kemble. Presumptions: see below, "Succession Crisis," and "Dominion and Revolution."

[188] On personal display, see Thompson, *Cambridge Cameos,* 34, 36. See below, "Dominion and Revolution."

As the Restoration royal government sought to encase colonial trade in its protectionist, monopolistic, and exploitative envelope, the colonial governors and governed found themselves evading and defying the laws of trade. Godly Captain Jenner was an unabashed smuggler. Royal enforcer Edward Randolph was confronted by Massachusetts juries who cynically disregarded the most convincing evidence of imperial law-breaking. Elite colonial defiance was hardly the best example to sustain popular deference. Such developments as these were bound to encourage a new spirit of questioning, not only of unreasonable captains, but also more broadly of the social, economic, and religious status quo.

Part 5

Church

Introduction

Merchant and sea captain John Trumbull made his public church confession about 1638. He had grown up in a town "without means," that is, without godly ministers or a nurturing group of "saints," without challenging catechisms or inspiring sermons, without close pastoral care or bracing discipline. He received no "contradiction [when] not only abusing God but [also] His people... regarding [thinking about] nothing but back and belly and fulfilling my own lusts." Having chosen the sea as a livelihood, Trumbull "came to London [and] I heard Mr Sedgwick" preaching about "repentance." His conversion was under way. Trumbull's experience has three applications in this section: it was typical of many Puritan autobiographies about how the authors began to cleave to godliness. It was also specifically the soul-baring of a member of the merchant class, whose commercial interests and mindset have often been depicted as antagonistic or self-serving towards religion. Third, it emphasizes the centers of "hot godliness" in Old England in stimulating the Great Migration of the 1630s. Rev. Richard Sedgwick was the famous radical preacher and lecturer in Wapping, an influential source for the first-generation merchants and church members of Charlestown.[1]

This section will cover the provision of "means" by a succession of ministers or "elders" from 1632, when Charlestown separated from Boston and founded its own church, to 1698, when the sixth minister, Rev. Charles Morton, died. A group study, linking up with the personnel in "Sea," will explore "godly merchants," and whether they could satisfactorily reconcile profits with the prophets. Charlestown was notorious in the seventeenth century for two major dissident groups. In the 1630s, the town divided over the issue of "free grace," or antinomianism. This crisis

---

[1] Thomas Shepard's *Confessions*, 106–9. See "Origin" and "The Challenging Sea."

had a serious impact on the membership of the church, and rumbled on into the 1640s and 1650s. In the late 1650s another opposition cell began to split away: the Baptists, who—despite persuasion, threats, ostracism and increasingly brutal punishment—persisted in their convictions, established their own church, and eventually decamped in the 1670s to Boston. The confrontation of orthodoxy and heterodoxy is vividly documented, and throws light on both doctrine and attitudes, including those of ordinary people like John Trumbull.

The fragility of religious consensus in Charlestown, even after the Baptists had moved across the Charles, comes through in the bitter struggle over the appointment of a new minister in 1678. The two sides prefigure divisions during the political crises of the 1680s: the conflicting responses to both the royal takeover of Massachusetts and the "Glorious Revolution" of 1689. The section's conclusion highlights the changes in church life from Pastors James and Symmes to Morton, in ministerial styles as well as developments in church rituals and popular religiosity, as measured by Mary Ramsbottom from Charlestown's outstanding church records. Did godly fervor decline, or did its emanations subtly change over three generations?[2]

Before embarking on these detailed revelations of godly life in an important outpost of the Atlantic economy, this introduction will examine how "means" were provided to the hungry and not-so-hungry souls of the town: financing the ministry and the meeting house, organizing the regular religious rituals of life and their settings, the level of popular devotion, the disciplining of backsliding and dissent, and the relationship between church and town authorities, the sacred and the secular.

The prime "means," as in Trumbull's conversion narrative, were the clergy themselves. The following university graduates were ordained as Charlestown pastors or teachers, or combined both posts, in our period:

1632–37: Rev. Thomas James (1595–1683), pastor

1634–72: Rev. Zechariah Symmes (1599–1672), teacher/pastor

1637?–38: Rev John Harvard (1607–38), teacher

1639–51: Rev. Thomas Allen (1608–73), teacher

1659–77: Rev. Thomas Shepard Jr. (1635–77), teacher/pastor

---

[2] See "Dominion and Revolution" below. Mary Macmanus Ramsbottom, "Religious Society and the Family in Charlestown, Massachusetts, 1630–1740," PhD dissertation, Yale University, 1987.

1678–79: Rev. Daniel Russell (1646–79),
          died of smallpox before ordination

1680–85: Rev. Thomas Shepard III (1658–85), pastor/teacher

1686–98: Rev. Charles Morton (1627–98), pastor/teacher

Of these, the three eminences were Symmes, the elder Shepard, and Morton; much more will be said about them below. James, from Lincolnshire, was a paranoid depressive who was effectively dismissed from the post. After brief appointments in Providence, New Haven, and Virginia, he returned to England in 1649. He died in Needham Market, Suffolk. Allen, from Norwich, became increasingly disillusioned with the colony's ecclesiastical establishment and returned to his birthplace in 1650 or 1651. The third Shepard and Russell both died young, without fulfilling their promise (if any, in Russell's case!) Similarly thwarted was John Harvard, probably ordained in late 1637 in Charlestown, who died barely a year after his arrival in 1638; his widow married Thomas Allen. In the intervals between permanent ministers, "locum" (substitute) preachers would be paid ten shillings per sermon; this was often an opportunity to try out potential candidates for permanent appointment.[3]

The leading lay official of the church was the ruling elder. He was the manager of the church's spiritual affairs, its disciplinarian, mediator, moderator, and facilitator. Increase Nowell was Charlestown's first ruling elder, but resigned because his spiritual office was deemed incompatible with his many lay duties in town and colony. He was succeeded by John Greene, who held the office until his death in 1658; he was not replaced.[4]

The deacons dealt with the church's financial affairs. They received church rates collected by the town from *all* inhabitants, whether members or not. They paid ministers, ruling elders, vergers, and welfare recipients, as well as craftsmen who maintained the meetinghouse and those who supplied bread and wine for the sacrament or other goods

---

[3] James: *GMB*, 2: 1072–76. Allen: Wyman, 16–17; Frothingham, 131–33; Ramsbottom, 100–3, analyzes a letter from Allen to John Cotton dated 21 November 1642 in the Mass. Archives, spelling out questionings and criticisms of the New England Way. He was particularly unhappy about the discrepant practice in different churches, the non-biblical requirement of public confession before admission to church membership, the resulting harmful exclusiveness, and the unwarranted equation of "Christians" with covenanted membership. Such cliquishness led to outsiders' grumbling that the Puritan authorities "come to make Heathens, rather than convert Heathens to Christians." Harvard: Samuel Eliot Morison, *The Founding of Harvard College* (Cambridge: Harvard University Press, 1936), 372; *ODNB*. Locums: e.g. CTR, 3:158, 208; 4: 23.

[4] On duties: Richard D. Pierce, ed., "Records of the First Church of Boston 1630–1868," *CSMP*, 39 (1961), xxii. Appointment and resignation: *WJ*, 1: 37, 97; Roger Williams approved his "surrender up [of] one sword," *WP*, 3: 86.

and services. Their accounts survive only from 1671, but the ledgers of neighboring Cambridge give a clear idea of both church and welfare outlays; much of the latter went to aged widows in the form of firewood, bushels of corn, joints of meat, and doctor's payments. As time went by, the church benefited from legacies; it also had grants of land, which produced rental income.[5]

The center of town life, the meetinghouse, was sited on the southern flank of Windmill Hill, close to the houses of the clergy. Its construction and major repairs or replacement were the responsibility of the town. After much patching and mending, the early meetinghouse was replaced in 1672 by a larger and sturdier building, and the town records have entries of specifications, craftsmen's contracts, and payments for laying ground sills, carpentry, glazing, and shingling. Three years later, three galleries were added. In one of these, seats were allocated to black male servants. Other back benches were occupied by white youths, and keeping them in order took up much time and energy. The town records contain annual rotas of meetinghouse monitors, and detailed regulations for boys' behavior. Misdeeds were reported to the selectmen, and punished with admonitions or, on one occasion, a public flogging. In 1677 a cage was approved for profaners of the Sabbath and other offenders. Adult congregation members were seated according to town rank in separate male and female blocks. A town committee was responsible for this most touchy of tasks. By the late 1670s, the elite of Charlestown had bought the right to their own designated seats.[6]

The meetinghouse accommodated the rituals of church and community life: the two Sabbath services obligatory to all, the weekly Friday

---

[5] The following served as deacons: Ralph Mousall, before 1652 to 1657; Robert Hale, no date of appointment, but died 1659; Thomas Lynde, 1652–71; Robert Cutler, 1659–65; William Stitson, 1659–91; John Cutler, Sr., 1672–94; Aaron Ludkin, 1672–94; John Kettle, John Call, Samuel Kettle, all appointed in 1694. Duties: Pierce, xxii. Hunnewell, 167, transcribed items from the Deacons' Accounts. The elder Shepard was paid £140 per year in the 1670s; his son and Morton received £100 each a year. Cambridge: I have edited a transcription and description of the Cambridge Deacons' Account Books, forthcoming in *Harvard Library Bulletin*. Legacies: e.g., £50 from Richard and Mary Sprague in 1674, CTR, 3: 158; or £100 from their nephew Richard in 1705. See "People Trafficking." Land: e.g. 40 cow commons on Mystic Side, CTR, 1: 647, 30 January 1657.

[6] Build or repair: e.g., CTR, 1: 638, 19 March 1650, £52 for major repairs; 1: 677, portal for doorway, 5 January 1652; 3: 79, 29 January 1667, 16,000 shingles for new roof; Frothingham, 187: replace meetinghouse and new galleries; seats for black males: CTR, 3: 208; regulations for boys: CTR, 3: 68, 1 January 1666; admonitions: CTR, 3: 114, 9 November 1670; flogging: CTR, 4: 24, 17 May 1680; seating: CTR, 3: 109, 123, 203, 213, 216–19, 4: 3, 23, 54. On 2 May 1670, the Town Meeting agreed to build "a ministerial house" which would continue to belong to the town, CTR, 3: 110.

lecture, the monthly sacrament of the Lord's Supper for church members, special days of thanksgiving and humiliation responding to the merciful or wrathful providences of God, baptisms for members' children (or grandchildren, after 1662), covenant renewals, admissions to full or halfway membership, ordinations of new ministers followed by lavish banquets, and the occasional solemn gatherings of members to discipline miscreant or divergent fellow members with admonitions or even excommunications.[7]

The spiritual life of many ordinary residents of Charlestown was, as we shall see, central to their world. Midwives asked single mothers in labor for the fathers' true identities "as in the presence of God," where some, at least, feared they might soon be. A serving maid being threatened by a predatory male explained later that she did not summon her master, "he being at prayer." She was believed. The only reading matter recorded in most people's inventories was the Bible. The major public events most weeks were the two Sabbath sermons and Friday's religious lecture. The triggers of unexpected events were believed to be the workings of divine will.[8]

Some few scoffed: mostly unawakened youths, visiting sailors, or town ne'er-do-wells. In 1671, servants were reported for clandestine drinking in public houses on the Lord's Day. In 1684, one serving man was charged with boasting that he "worshipped in the church of the pint pot." Raucous Ursula Cole declared that she "had rather hear a cat mew" than the sermons of Mr. Symmes and Mr. Shepard. Such derision was uncommon, and deeply offensive to most. Townspeople were alert to ungodliness and made sure that it was punished by authority. Several victims complained about the intrusiveness of church members. Anyone missing services without good reason would be reprimanded. "Live and let live" was an alien philosophy in 17th-century Charlestown.[9]

Wild outbursts or indolent negligence were irritants to the spiritual life of the town, but they were confined to the least regarded residents.

---

[7] Hunnewell, ii–xi. Funerals were not marked by formal services or prayers; the coffined body was taken in a procession from home to the burying ground. There would be a gathering with food and drink afterwards. In 1679 the selectmen allocated £10 towards the funeral of Richard Russell, CTR, 4: 3. Similarly, marriages, regarded as civil contracts, were performed by magistrates, Frothingham, 202.

[8] Thompson, *Sex,* 188–89, 196–97; single mothers: e.g., Sarah Poor, MxCC D & O, 5: folio 113; serving maid: 2: folio 48.

[9] 1671: MxCC D&O, 2: folio 56; 1684: 4: folio 197; Cole: 1: doc. 2261, 8 August 1663; intrusiveness: e.g., 4: folio 105. Elizabeth Martin grumbled about church sisters' gossip and nosiness: see Roger Thompson, "'Holy Watchfulness' and Community Conformism," *NEQ,* 56 (1983) 500–21.

Far more worrisome were the principled demonstrations and rebuttals by committed dissidents. These were people who could not be cuffed back into line. Often inhabitants of some wealth, learning, and authority, they advocated alternative theologies or philosophies. They would create long-term disunities, eventually overturning the Massachusetts culture of uniformity. Their resistance would also excite the sympathies of influential townspeople, including some of Charlestown's godly merchants.

Godly Merchants:
Sedgwick, Willoughby, and Russell

The famous merchant of Prato Francesco di Marco Datini (1335–1410) inscribed on the front page of his ledgers, "In the name of God and Profit." This formula was copied by the Medici financiers of neighboring Florence, who also entered their charitable donations in a section headed "God's Account." Although these merchants of the Italian Renaissance saw their wealth as a tool of godly service, some seventeenth-century commentators scorned the idea of the godly merchant as an oxymoron, a contradiction in terms. They would have approved of the statement: "The grand object of English navigators . . . is money, money, money," or the stereotype of the cheating dealer as "the chattering and changing merchant with his counterfeit balances and his untrue weights," or the metaphor of fraudulent selling: "The harlot is one that herself in both merchant and merchandise." Early seventeenth-century England seemed to fall prey to these disreputable commercial characteristics with its plague of monopolists, engrossers, rackrenters, regrators, usurers, enclosers, foreclosers, and forestallers: all obsessed with profit at any price. They were seen as pitiless exploiters, flouters of the Sermon on the Mount or the model of Christian charity. The exploitive financing of Plymouth Plantation by London merchants in the 1620s seemed to typify such slippery commercial trickery. Winthrop, in his reasons for emigrating, bemoaned that "all arts and trades are carried in that deceitful and unrighteous course as it is almost impossible for a good and upright man to maintain his charge and live comfortably in any of them."[10]

---

[10] Datini: I. Origo, *The Merchant of Prato* (London: Cape, 1957), 13, 136. Medici: T. Parks, *Medici Money* (London: Profile, 2006), 108, 242. Commentators: Thomas Carew, *Four Godly and Profitable Sermons* (London: Phipps, 1605), Francis Bacon, "Of Riches," and "Of Usury" in *Essays,* ed. John Pitcher (Harmondsworth: Penguin, 1985), 165–68, 183–86, and sources cited below, in

As too much money brought in by 1630s immigrants to Massachusetts desperate for supplies and services started chasing too few goods, the profit motive and harsh market values seemed to have traveled there too. By 1634, prices were rocketing out of control, closely followed by the inflated wages of scarce craftsmen. The price of a cow quadrupled to £20. Attempts at government regulation proved fruitless. Gestures against price gouging, like the huge £200 fine in November 1639 and church reprimand against Robert Keayne for his hundred-percent markup on a bag of nails, created commercial uncertainty and long-lasting grievances without touching the underlying problem. Economic crises encourage the search for scapegoats. In Massachusetts as in England, merchants were fair game for blame. They were depicted as putting their personal fortunes above the good of the community, private wealth above commonwealth. By so doing they exalted individual greed over Christian charity, or in the clichéd puns of the time, gold over God, the world over the Word, profits before the prophets.[11]

Despite these deep-seated suspicions, the popularity of Calvinism in commercial centers of Europe suggests that merchants believed that their calling was conformable with godliness. Success in trade did not require double-dealing. "The good merchant fears to do any wrong, so that if a poor child or a silly woman should lay him down a groat or tester more than his commodity is worth, he dares not take it, but gives it back again."[12] John Cotton's congregation at St. Botolph's, Boston, Lincolnshire, had plenty of devout businessmen; several emigrated to Boston, Massachusetts. Their preacher told them that they could maintain a God-centered outlook. "Though a godly man is busy in his calling from the sun rising to the sun setting and may by God's providence fill both his hand and head with business, yet a living Christian when he lives a most busy life in this world, yet he lives not a worldly life."[13] Merchants' conversion narratives

exploiters; money: Ignatius Sanchez, London freedman, 1778; cheater, harlot: quoted in Andrew Delbanco, *The Puritan Ordeal* (Cambridge: Harvard University Press, 1989), 69, 13; Plymouth: Bailyn, *Merchants,* 24–25; exploiters: C. G. A. Clay, *Economic Expansion and Social Change in England 1500–1700* (Cambridge: Cambridge University Press, 1984), I: 69–71, 183 (usury), 230 (price controls), II, 204 (monopolies); Richard Grassby, *The Business Community of Seventeenth-Century England* (Cambridge: Cambridge University Press, 1995), 272–302 (religion and ethics); Louise A. Breen, *Transgressing the Bounds* (New York: Oxford University Press, 2001), 51–55; Winthrop: *WP* 2: 111–15, 122–24.

[11]   Bailyn, *Merchants,* 32–41.

[12]   T. Hooker, *Soul's Vocation,* in A. Delbanco, *The Puritan Ordeal* (Cambridge: Harvard University Press, 1989), 173.

[13]   J. Cotton, *Way of Life,* in Delbanco, *The Puritan Ordeal,* 33.

stress that their sin had not been engagement in trade, but allowing their minds to promote their worldly hopes over their otherworldly fate. They must trust in the providence of God; reverses were God-given messages just as much as successes. Their ventures, their voyages, their stock, their wealth, their contracts, their financial instruments, their account books must all be construed as part of a divine plan which mere men could never hope to plumb. A merchant must get his priorities right: always God first, then his community and its welfare, and last his own business. If he stuck to these values, living as a "the godly merchant" was an achievable objective rather than an insuperable clash.[14]

The problem for us is to burrow into the minds of businesspeople three and a half centuries ago. While plenty of accounts, contracts, bonds, stock inventories, and depositions about commercial disputes have survived, relatively few personal memoirs, letters, or spiritual autobiographies of people engaged in commerce have come down to us. However, a few such documents of Charlestown merchants are extant, and through them we can explore whether the ideal of the godly merchant was attainable there.

In 1639, at the height of the Massachusetts inflation, merchant Robert Sedgwick (1613–56), a Charlestown church member for two years, was admonished by the General Court "for selling goods too high and for oppression." He escaped with a far more lenient reprimand than his fellow import merchant and officer in the newly founded Artillery Company, Robert Keayne. Sedgwick's reaction is not recorded, but Keayne's outrage festered until his death, and burst forth in his last will and testament. His comments make it clear that the pressure to impose such draconian punishment came from consumers who felt that traders were profiteering from shortages.[15]

This shot across Sedgwick's bows did not seriously deflect his course. He continued to serve as a deputy for Charlestown through 1644, and again from 1649 to 1650. In 1641 the General Court appointed him auditor of the

---

[14] Conversion: e.g. William Manning, G. Selement, and B. Woolley, eds., *Thomas Shepard's Confessions* (Boston: *CSMP,* 1981), 96, William Andrews, 112–13; Winthrop's "Model of Christian Charity" and Cotton's "Moses His Judicials" propounded specific rules for the godly merchant to follow, such as the just price, and 6 percent or 8 percent interest charges, Bailyn, *Merchants,* 21–22. Providence: see below, John Hull, *Diary,* and *Letters.*

[15] Admonition: *MR,* 1: 251, 13 March 1639; Keayne was fined in the following November. Frothingham 102, 136. On Sedgwick, see above, "Charlestown and the Atlantic World." Keayne's will, begun 1 August 1653, is published in Bernard Bailyn, ed., *The Apologia of Robert Keayne* (New York: Harper, 1965); see especially 45–61. On the Artillery Company and merchants, see L. A. Breen, *Transgressing the Bounds* (New York: Oxford University Press), 3–6.

Treasurer's Accounts and named him to several important committees. He was not cowed from voicing dissent. In 1645 he was a signatory to a petition for tolerance toward Anabaptists and for repeal or amendment of the prohibition of alien visitors beyond three weeks. He was shocked in 1646 at the vicious treatment of Dr. Robert Childe and his fellow petitioners by the General Court, and suspicious of the authoritarian Cambridge Platform of Congregational orthodoxy in 1649.[16]

His military career prospered; "Nursed up in London's Artillery Garden . . . stout and active in all feats of war," according to neighbor Captain Edward Johnson, Sedgwick was elected captain of the Charlestown Train Band (militia company) within a year of his 1635 arrival. On 29 May 1644 he was promoted to major in command of the Middlesex Regiment, and major general and commander-in-chief of the Massachusetts military in 1652. Like other leading merchants and military officers in the colony, Sedgwick was drawn to the England of Oliver Cromwell. In 1653 he traveled to England, now at war with the Netherlands. From Cromwell he received a commission to lead a force of about 900 troops in four ships against the New Netherlands; the expedition was forestalled by news of the peace, and, instead, Sedgwick sailed east with his brother-in-law John Leverett to French Nova Scotia (Acadia) and captured three main bases there. Sedgwick's letter to Cromwell's intelligence chief, John Thurloe, about his providentially slow voyage from England is our first evidence of his theocentric outlook:

> When I considered the various and strange turns in God's workings and dealings within our voyage, it makes me now believe and apprehend that He stood in our way . . . causing our voyage to be longer than is usual at that season of the year, and bringing in that ship that brought news of peace with a short and prosperous voyage.[17]

Sedgwick's triumph in Acadia led to Cromwell's choosing him to help lead the "Western Design," an ambitious Caribbean expedition to capture Hispaniola (present-day Haiti and the Dominican Republic) and wrest control of the West Indies from the Papist Spaniards. Although he and

---

[16] *MR*, 1: 288, 294, 341; Breen, 5–6; he was also elected selectman in 1643. Petition: *WJ*, 1: 220; David D. Hall, ed., *The Antinomian Controversy* (Durham: Duke University Press, 1990), 252, footnote.

[17] H. D. Sedgwick, "Robert Sedgwick," *CSMP*, 3 (1895), 156–73; the letter to Thurloe is dated 1 July 1654. Other re-migrants: Daniel Gookin, Francis Willoughby, Edward Gibbons, John Leverett, Thomas Graves, and Nehemiah Bourne, as well as Charlestown ministers Thomas Allen and Thomas James. Commission: See "Charlestown and the Atlantic World" above.

Gookin had little success in recruiting New England soldiers, Sedgwick embarked "in some singleness of heart and eying God and His glory in this venture." Alas, by the time he arrived, the Design was reeling towards disaster. Repelled at Hispaniola, the Cromwellian army had captured Jamaica in May 1655, but there yellow fever, dysentery, malaria, and hunger were scything through the ill-led and chronically indisciplined expeditionary force at a rate of 150 deaths a week. By November 1655, the original 8,200 men were down to 3,700. Sedgwick was faced with a hugely daunting task as commander-in-chief.[18]

His reactions to the chaos, and how he confronted the challenge, are revealed in four letters to England in 1655 and early 1656, and in the observations of colleagues. He had a premonition that he would not survive long: "I am sometimes sick and think I may fall away among the rest of my countrymen . . . Another place will be my portion before I hear again from your highness." He asked the Lord Protector to remember his "dear and religious wife who through grace has much of the fear and knowledge of God in her . . . and five children, to me dear and precious." He was appalled by the quality of the troops: "The army is worse than would have been thought possible for Puritan and English soldiers . . . people so basely unworthy, lazy and idle . . . those in command are nearly as bad as the men." Yet, "when I consider the thousands laid in the dust in such a way as God hath visited, my heart mourns." He was equally upset that "your highness's fleet should follow this old trade of West India cruisers and privateers to ruin and plunder poor towns and so leave them." Some twenty thousand cattle had been killed, fruits and provisions destroyed, leaving "nothing but ruin . . . We are not able to possess any place we may attack, and so cannot dispense any knowledge of the true God in Jesus Christ to the inhabitants." He thought of the "Western Design" as a mission, in more ways than one.[19]

The whole tone of Sedgwick's comments is shot through with piety. Whether he succumbs to "dumpishness and confusion" or steels himself "to encourage and strengthen the [men's] hearts and hands," he confesses that in such "revolutions and turnings of heart . . . I have been willing to go to heaven, to the God of counsel, what advice and which way to act." His determination did have some impact: the death rate fell to about fifty a week; a fort, palisado, and magazine were slowly rising; and the 2,500

---

[18]   Sedgwick, 166–68. On the Western Design, see R. S. Dunn, *Sugar and Slaves*, 152–53, and sources cited there.

[19]   Sedgwick, 164–66; letter of 12 March 1656.

survivors were "in better condition" by 1656. This, to Sedgwick, is "a marvellous great mercy" of God. He feels himself to be part of a heavenly plan. To Cromwell, he writes: "Let the Lord send by whom he pleases, we believe you have an interest in Heaven, and hope we are the subjects of your prayers . . . If Christ own us, we continue and conquer." In his despondent moods, he attributed reverses to divine punishment: "The truth is, God is angry and the plague is begun . . . My heart and soul grieveth when I think of the Hispaniola business, one or two Negroes to make 500 Englishmen fling down their arms and run away. Oh, tell it not in Gath, nor publish it in Askelon, lest the uncircumcized rejoice . . . [This broken expedition is] a senseless hearted people, not affected with His dealing with us." He worried about the Spaniards, mulattos and runaway black maroons lurking in the hills: "What God will do with them or with us by them, I know not." As his secretary, Aylesbury, wrote the day after Sedgwick's sudden 24 May 1656 death, the commander's heart broken by his impossible responsibilities, "He was a truly religious man, and of the most innocent conversation I ever accompanied." Another colleague, on the same day, called Sedgwick "a person, I have cause to believe, [who] truly feared God."[20]

This is the same man previously accused of market oppression, who was one of Massachusetts's major fish exporters, partner in trade and enterprise with the commercial elite of New England, agent of London merchants. He had earlier advocated greater toleration in crimping Massachusetts. He had been a trusted representative of Charlestown for many years. His life and his death demonstrate that the term "godly merchant" was a realizable ideal. When an individual felt so flimsy and impotent in a capricious and terrifying watery world, to deny devotion to the Almighty was akin to suicide.

Francis Willoughby (1615–71) was about four years younger than his friend and neighbor Robert Sedgwick, and arrived in Charlestown three years later in 1638. He was a Wapping shipwright by training and inheritance and married a shipwright's daughter, but also became involved in trade in New England. His house was at the Ferry Way, by the Charlestown area called Wapping; here he constructed wharves and a yard where he built one of the earliest ships in the town in 1641. Shipbuilding was the most technically advanced woodworking skill, and brought employment and profit to the town. Like Sedgwick, Willoughby was opposed to the persecution of Anabaptists, but his relations with Dr. Robert Childe were less sympathetic. Although in 1645 Willoughby delivered seeds from

---

[20] Sedgwick, 169–73; Gath was the birthplace of the enemy giant Goliath, 2 Samuel, 1: 20.

English gardeners on behalf of Childe in Gravesend to John Winthrop Jr. in New England, Winthrop's father reported a vicious confrontation three years later in London.

> The Doctor, meeting with Mr. Willoughby upon the Exchange, (this Mr. Willoughby dwelt at Charlestown, but his father was a colonel of the city,) and falling in talk about New England, the Doctor railed against the people, saying they were a company of rogues and knaves; Mr. Willoughby answered, that he who spake so, etc., was a knave, whereupon the Doctor gave him a box on the ear. Mr. Willoughby was ready to have closed with him, etc., but being upon the Exchange, he was stayed, and presently arrested him. And when the Doctor saw the danger he was in, he employed some friends to make his peace, who ordered him to give five pounds to the poor of New England (for Mr. Willoughby would have nothing of him,) and to give Mr. Willoughby open satisfaction in the full Exchange, and to give it under his hand, never to speak evil of New England men after, nor to occasion any trouble in the country, or to any of the people, all which he gladly performed.

Back in Charlestown in 1650, after partnering Sedgwick as town deputy in the General Court, Willoughby was elected an assistant. However, the following year, having built the great ship *Adventure*, he sailed in December for London, under the command of Thomas Graves, with a crew of forty and eighty other passengers. It seems likely that this return was due to his father's death in July 1651. [21]

Willoughby's shipwright father, William, a senior officer in the London militia during the Civil War, had been appointed as one of sixteen "Regulators" of the Navy by Parliament two weeks before Charles I's execution on 30 January 1649. From February 1649 until his death two and a half years later, he had served as resident commissioner of the Commonwealth Navy at the great English Channel base of Portsmouth. On 28 September 1652, Francis Willoughby was appointed to his father's old post. There he showed firmness along with sensitivity in securing for mutinous seamen their long overdue pay, and in conciliating striking Portsmouth

---

[21] Wyman, 1036–37; I. J. Greenwood, "Willoughby Family," *R*, 30 (1876), 67–78; his father-in-law John Taylor was a partner of Francis's father William Willoughby in a project to raise a sunken ship in the Thames Estuary in 1637. Trade: he dealt in tobacco, and laded ships in Boston, Lechford, 267–68, Aspinwall, 7, 12–13. Yard: Frothingham, 141, CTR, 1A: 93, CTR, 1: 173. Childe: *WP*, 5: 11; *WJ*, 2: 340. *Adventure*: Coldham, 1: 141.

landladies demanding rents from sailor lodgers. He was less successful in his handling of a suspected royalist plot involving Admiral John Lawson; the Admiralty blamed him for not informing them in time. In 1655 and 1656 he was an enthusiastic supporter of Cromwell's policy of readmitting Jews to England. Briefly member of Parliament for Portsmouth in 1659, he travelled with Samuel Pepys on the *Naseby* towards Dunkirk in April 1660, as the restoration of the exiled Charles II was being orchestrated. Three months later, Pepys, as Clerk of the Acts with the Royal Navy Board, took over Willoughby's quarters in Seething Lane near the Tower. By May 1662 Willoughby was back in Charlestown.[22]

In 1665, Francis Willoughby was elected deputy governor of Massachusetts. With his wealthy second wife Margaret, he began a new family: stepsiblings to his previous five surviving children. His life was filled with public service, for which he received a thousand acres of frontier land in 1669. He donated considerable sums to Harvard College, where he was a leading fundraiser and managed various college accounts. He also gave an endowment to the Charlestown school. Deeply distrustful of arbitrary royal power, he was a leading opponent of the King's Commissioners from 1664 to 1666. In 1666 he was charged with strengthening the fortifications of Portsmouth—but this was Portsmouth, New Hampshire. In May 1670, he was excused from traveling out to Marlborough to reconcile warring factions, on the grounds of infirmity. He died, aged 56, on 4 April 1671. John Hull, co-owner of ships with Willoughby, attended his funeral. He had specified a shallow grave covered only with turf. The procession included eleven foot companies, who marched "to the doleful noise of trump and drum in their mourning posture . . . Three thunderous volleys of shot were discharged, answered with loud roaring of the great guns, rending the heavens with noise at the loss of so great a man." His estate was valued at the huge sum of £4,762. His widow married his cousin and executor, Captain Lawrence Hammond of Charlestown.[23]

---

[22]   On Colonel William Willoughby's career, see Greenwood, *R*, 30 (1876), 67–71; Bernard Capp, *Cromwell's Navy* (Oxford: Oxford University Press, 1989), 48–9, 144, 280–81, 290–91, 301; N. A. M. Rodger, *The Command of the Ocean* (New York: Norton, 2006), 34–44, describes the returned New Englanders involvement in the Commonwealth Navy; *Pepys Diary*, 1: 105, 197, 208; Claire Tomalin, *Samuel Pepys, the Unequalled Self* (London: Viking, 2002), 111. *CSP Col*, 2: 289, April 1662: license to Willoughby family to return to Massachusetts in *Society*.

[23]   Margaret: see "Wealthy Women" below. Public service: see *MR*, 4-2, passim; Harvard: his eldest son Jonathan, born in England in 1636, attended the college in 1651, but did not graduate. In his will Willoughby left only £10 to Jonathan, a prodigal who had already cost his father hundreds of pounds. Rodgers, 3: 11–12; he also gave no more to Harvard, in protest at the failure of his contemporaries to follow his earlier philanthropic example. The estate inventory included real estate, part ownership of four ships, fishing boats and gear, salt, provisions, liquor, fabrics,

As well as this fortune, derived from commerce and industry, Willoughby left three invaluable documents manifesting his feelings and beliefs. Two were prompted by political crises. In 1666 after the critical reports of the royal commissioners, Charles II sent an order to the Massachusetts governor to dispatch agents to London in orderto answer complaints against the colony. Whereas assistant Simon Bradstreet (later a collaborator with the imposed royal Dominion government) counselled obedience to the royal prerogative in the debate about the colony's response, Willoughby, with two years' personal experience of the restored royal regime, adamantly opposed bowing to dictatorial commands:

> [We chartered colonists] have not been governed by commission, and if this be allowed, how easily may the king in one year undo all that he hath done [in guaranteeing colonial rights]; and we must as well consider God's displeasure as the king's, the interest of ourselves and God's things, as his majesty's prerogative; for our liberties are of concernment, and to be regarded as to the preservation; for if the king may send for me now, and another tomorrow, we are a miserable people.

Feeling summoned by the Almighty to counter Bradstreet's buckling, Willoughby depicted Massachusetts as a chosen outpost of God, a refuge from the licentious and cavalier world of Whitehall. Kowtowing would not only jeopardize the colonists' closely guarded freedoms; it would also offend the king of kings. Such persuasive anti-authoritarian advocacy coincided with his sympathies for persecuted Baptists, expelled Jews, and unpaid seamen who had served their nation. [24]

The second personal testament is a letter, dated 28 May 1670, which the ailing deputy governor wrote to the bitterly divided General Court. It opens: "The all-wise God seeing fit to lay me under" house-bound illness, and aware that the two houses are "solicitous to know the cause of God's displeasure," bewails that "their courses . . . beget animosities and distances of spirit one part of the court against the other." "Misrepresentation" and "prejudice" have arisen "since we all being but men and capable of acting but as men, and so subject to fail and miscarry in everything we do." His concern is not only about the paralyzing political confrontation between the two houses, nor only the reputation of "this poor wilderness" in the Atlantic world whose "eyes are in great measure upon us," but most

---

shipbuilding timber, money and plate, sugar, and Barbados goods. Probate records: Rodgers, 3: 11–21. Hull, Diary, 231.

[24] Frothingham, 143; "Danforth Papers," 2 *MHSC,* 8 (1826) 99, 14 September 1666.

of all about provoking "God to a further degree of displeasure," and about "the name of God eminently professed, most dear and precious to us" suffering from General Court jealousies. He "beseeches" his colleagues that " all things should be done in Love [with] affection and tenderness to the name of God and one another." His tone, throughout the long letter, is diffident, earnest and prayerful, rather than hectoring and dogmatic. Had he been able to be present, the crisis might have been averted. Certainly, his pleas were God-centered and shot through with piety.[25]

The third intimate document giving insight into Willoughby's feelings is a manuscript diary which has survived as a fragment of a larger spiritual record. Significantly, its 78 folios (156 sides) contain both monetary accounts and spiritual records, arguments, and self-examinations. Forty-four folios—over half the diary—are taken up by carefully copied 1644 sermons by Thomas Allen and Thomas Shepard Sr. Two folios list arguments and biblical grounds for baptizing the children of believers—a burning question in Massachusetts from the mid-1640s onwards. Folios 50 to 76 contain Willoughby's "daily observations" from 20 November 1650 to 28 December 1651, on the eve of his departure for England. The first entry typifies the pervasive tone of "obsessive spiritual auto flagellation":[26] "My heart & spirit hath not been right with God . . . but much deadness & vanity & folly of spirit . . . regardless of Him . . . a spirit of contentedness [self-satisfaction] . . . great loneliness of soul . . . carnality of my soul . . . " and so on for a page and a half, a stream of consciousness without punctuation or pause. His reaction to his house being spared in the great Charlestown fire the very next day, 21 November 1650, was: "The Lord leave me not to slight & to neglect such a dispensation, [otherwise] my house may be the next thro' some wise judgment." A dominant theme is the tug-of-war between "labouring after further supply of mercy" from the Lord so that He "may pity me and heal me and come in graciously upon me," and the perpetual contrary heave towards "my many occasions [business interests] that take up much of my time [and induce] wandering and erring, carnality, and vanity . . . " He found a similar "snare" between his mercantile career and the calls of public service, exaggerating his unfitness for religious debate and civil administration and his "call to England

---

[25]   Mass. Archives, 28 May 1670. The impasse had been created by disagreements about the splitting away of Third from First Church in Boston over the issue of the Half-Way Covenant, and about the intrusions of the clergy in secular business; see Stephen Foster, *The Long Argument* (Chapel Hill: University of North Carolina Press, 1991), 195–221.

[26]   Francis Sypher, "'The Dayly Observations' of an Impassioned Puritan: A 17th-century Shorthand Diary. . . ," *Proceedings of the American Antiquarian Society*, 91 (1982), Introduction.

the latter end of the year [1651] if God spare my life." Death was always at the back of his mind, "may the Lord . . . fit me for my change, not knowing how soon it may be." Such apprehensions concentrated the busy mind wonderfully.[27]

Willoughby's angst emphasizes the spiritual stresses of a merchant leader in a godly society. Always his "occasions" must be offset, even trumped, by prayer, bible reading, meditation on sermons, and personal conduct. Public service and philanthropy were signs of godly works, but without grace they were of little worth. Divine grace must infuse all the dealings of the godly merchant. It was a challenge that Francis Willoughby, like Robert Sedgwick, relentlessly struggled to meet.[28]

Our third exemplar of the godly merchant, Richard Russell (1611–76), was a leading member of the Bristol contingent. He had close kinship connections with London and with his birthplace, Hereford. He arrived in Charlestown in 1640 with his bride Maud, who was the daughter of the great Bristol merchant William Pitt. They were both quickly admitted as church members, and Russell soon became a leading citizen: twenty-six times a selectman, eleven times a deputy, and five times speaker of the lower house. He was treasurer of the colony for 20 years and assistant from 1659 to 1676. He was active in trade, partnering with Sedgwick, Willoughby, Francis Norton, and Nicholas Davison in domestic and overseas voyages, financial schemes, fishing ventures, and frontier land speculation. A member of the Artillery Company, he agreed with many fellow officers in opposing the huge fines imposed on Dr. Robert Childe and his co-remonstrants who demanded an extension of the franchise in 1646. He also criticized the handling of the Charlestown Baptist cell in the 1660s. His immediate estate in the 1676 inventory totalled £3,505, but final reckonings of debts and credits rose to £9,194 (including his treasurer's accounts and his personal

---

[27] Sypher, "'The Dayly Observations' of an Impassioned Puritan," *Proceedings of the American Antiquarian Society,* 91 (1982), 91–107. I have authenticated Willoughby's authorship by comparing his handwriting in the longhand sections of the Diary with his examination of two cattle thieves in MxCC D&O, 2: folio 47, 17 September 1668. The ms. contains about 43,000 words. Death: cf. the preamble to his will, Rodgers, 3: 11.

[28] On the many surviving conversion narratives and spiritual self-examinations, see Patricia Caldwell, *The Puritan Conversion Narrative* (Cambridge: Cambridge University Press, 1983), and footnote 3 above. Especially valuable are the writings of John Hull, (1624–83), merchant of Boston; "Some Passages of God's Providence about myself," *Archeologia Americana,* 10 (1857), 141–66. For instance, 146: "The loss of my estate will be nothing if the Lord please to join my soul nearer to himself and loose it more from creature comforts; my loss will be repaired." Or 161: "The Lord give me spiritual and heavenly treasure, when he taketh from me earthly! And that will be a good exchange." His manuscript letters at the American Antiquarian Society, Worcester, Mass. are also very revealing, e.g. 105: "In my whole life, I have dealt in the fear of God."

loans to the colony). His public service was wide-ranging and extremely time-consuming; it can be followed on many pages of town, county and colony records.[29]

I have not found any spiritual autobiography or conversion narrative left by Richard Russell. We must make do with his last will and testament, which he wrote two years before he died. Its preamble rings more heartfelt than the often formulaic openings of many wills:

> It being according to the mind of God, that man who is appointed to die should seasonably set his house in order, for the preventing of trouble and discord among surviving relations after his decease, I do therefore ordain and declare my last will and testament in manner and form following: Imprimis: I do through the grace and strength of Christ Jesus resign my immortal soul into the everlasting arms of God, father, Son and Holy ghost, trusting that through his grace I may say, whose I am, and desire to serve, and being persuaded that Jesus Christ is made of God a complete object of faith fully to rest and rely upon for Justification to life eternal, into whose bosom and bowel mercies I desire to roll and cast myself.

After generous bequests to his wife, her children, his children, and other kin and friends, he made many philanthropic legacies. He left the income from £100 for the upkeep of two poor students at Harvard. "To the Church of Christ in Charlestown with whom I have been in sweet Christian fellowship for many years, I do give and bequeath £100 . . . Also towards the building a house to remain in the use of the ministry in that place . . . £50." To the poor of the town, he left capital of £200 to provide an annual towards their assistance. Eleven local ministers benefited from his largesse, with Thomas Shepard of Charlestown receiving £40, and most others £10, out of total clerical bequests of £190. These were huge sums of money. At the end of the document he reiterated his providential assumptions: "If the Lord shall in his infinite wisdom see meet to exercise me with losses either by sea or by land as that my estate will not hold out to pay each legatee . . . each one shall be abated proportionable to his legacy." Though we know much less about the inner workings of Russell's spiritual life, his testamentary values, like those of his commercial friends and

---

[29] See "Origins" above; Russell's business dealings can be followed in Aspinwall: 8, 10, 24, 27, 40, 67, 69, 76, 92, 127, 157, 211, 216, 340, 430, 445, 451. Land: R. R. Johnson, *Adjustment to Empire* (Leicester: Leicester University Press, 1981), 20; *MR*, 4-1: 398, 1,600 acres beyond the Merrimack, 12 November 1659; Frothingham, 144–46, Pemaquid Patent. Inventory: Rodgers, 3: 387–400, over £1,000 in stock goods, real estate £1,078; shipping £722; the colony owed him £477.

partners, argue for his being both (in John Hull's words) "a godly man" and a God-fearing merchant. [30]

The godly merchants of Charlestown trod a fine line. They were, on the one hand, exposed to the multiple risks and losses inherent in seventeenth-century commerce: shipwrecks, pirates, untrustworthy debtors, demanding creditors, inflation, deflation, endemic war, glut, shortage, bartering, peculation, and corruption. The overseas business world was described as "carnivorous." Without careful precautions against these dangers, they would soon find themselves on the town welfare rolls. Their faith in divine protection and acceptance of God-given reverses needed to be frequently boosted to overcome natural fears, distractions and despair. Their preachers, on the other hand, condemned the profit motive, the very life-blood of business. "In our callings, we must be diligent," taught John Cotton, "but we are never to desire more than we may have good use of." What was his solution to surplus? "Should a man offer his house full of treasure for Christ, it would be despised . . . And yet . . . many times without laying out of money, He cannot be had . . . the holding fast a man's money lets go the Lord Jesus Christ . . . so that though Christ cannot be had for money, yet sometimes without expense of money he cannot be had." Sedgwick, Willoughby, and Russell were devout—as their surviving words confirm. Yet their arduous public service, their philanthropy, and their time-consuming communal efforts to defend, to reconcile, and to pacify all represent a pious "expense" whereby Christ could "be had." [31]

The mindset of merchants is not the only element of the early modern world that is hard to plumb. The insecurities, risks, reverses, and terrors of their environment are also barely imaginable. Compared to our contemporary developed world, with its sophisticated and wide-ranging infrastructure with instant communications; its copious artificial energy supplies; its predictive, preventive, and curative skills; its pooling and reduction of risk; and other barely recognized advantages, the apparent capriciousness of nature on which early settlers were completely reliant was blood-chilling. They were dwarfed in confrontation with the heartless unexpectedness of their daily lives and the gigantic potency of their natural challenges: climate, disease, dearth, destruction, death. When hurricanes, or contrary winds, or pillaging plagues of pigeons and locusts, or disappearances of loved ones, or great fires, or smallpox epidemics, or harvest

---

[30]   Rodgers, 3: 387–90. Hull, Diary, 242. Walter K. Watkins, "Russell Family," mss. 5528, 5529, NEHGS.

[31]   Delbanco, *Puritan Ordeal*, 121, 126, 144, 161.

failures, or a hundred other troubles struck, it was some kind of explanation to cite the providences or the warnings, angry or merciful, of an all-knowing, unknowable God.[32]

Merchants faced more risk than most, and their successes or reversals were explained not as results of their business acumen or blunders, but as the workings-out of the divine plan. However, the cliché that wealth derived from God's approval and that therefore Puritan predestinarianism encouraged capitalistic enterprise omits the crucial element: the saint's sense of impotence and insignificance. Two of our godly merchants died wealthy men, but plenty of others were not so successful. Edward Gibbons lost his fortune through the double dealing of La Tour, John Winthrop through his steward's. Daniel Gookin and Increase Nowell spent so much time and energy on public service that they died poor. Richard Russell inherited only £30 in 1614 because his young father Paul died suddenly. Captain Francis Norton's estate was mired in debt. The grim reaper stalks the lines of many spiritual autobiographies and conversion relations. If you believed supernatural forces were lying in wait for self-congratulation, pride came before a fall, and hubris prompted nemesis, you would be wise to abase yourself and your ambitions, and to seek the mercy of the Lord.[33]

[32] On the uncertainties of the early modern world, see the classic opening chapter of Keith Thomas, *Religion and the Decline of Magic* (Harmondsworth: Penguin, 1973).

[33] Gibbons: see above, "Charlestown and the Atlantic World"; Winthrop: *WJ*, 1: 325; 2: 3–4; Gookin: Thompson, *Cambridge Cameos*, 153–54; Nowell: *MR*, 4: 181–82; Russell: *R*, 43 (1889), 426; Norton: see above, "Captain Norton's Estate." The conversion experience of women during pregnancy was very common; see below, "Women."

Charlestown and the Antinomian Crisis, 1637–38

The winter of 1636–37 was a grim season for Massachusetts. To the west and south, the powerful Pequot Indians were preparing to attack new white settlements in the Connecticut Valley and along Long Island Sound. Many of Charlestown's recent neighbors, Thomas Hooker's Newtown congregation now in Hartford, were in danger of annihilation. To the east and north, trouble was brewing with the French along the Maine coast, and anarchic fishermen were proving impervious to the Puritan culture of discipline. The news brought by the flood tide of hungry and dependent refugees from England was of a bubonic plague epidemic, on top of the persecution of the saints and the silencing of their ministers by the all-powerful Laudian church hierarchy. The Arminian Counter-reformation seemed to many New Englanders a precursor to the return of Roman Catholicism, which was again resurgent in Germany after the death of the Protestant champion Gustavus Adolphus at Lutzen in November 1632. Laud was already casting his baleful eye upon the shocking nonconformity of New England with a view to forcing New Englanders back into line. The apparently unstoppable spread of the forces of the Antichrist would have been enough to cast gloom over the chilly settlers, but even worse threats were right on their icy doorsteps. Massachusetts Puritanism was threatened by division. Its most distinguished minister and a charismatic young colleague, its governor, and its highest-born and wealthiest woman had mounted a fervent challenge to its newly minted orthodoxy. Facing the prospect of civil as well as religious strife, the obvious response was to try to discover the causes of God's anger and to seek His merciful forgiveness. 20 January 1637 was therefore appointed a solemn fast day.[34]

In the Boston meetinghouse that day, Rev. John Cotton, renowned preacher and subtle theologian, invited that young charismatic member of the congregation, Rev. John Wheelwright, to "exercise as a private brother." Wheelwright's address, rather than fostering conciliation (as had been the aim of the authorities), was a challenge to theological combat. He made a sharp distinction between the covenant of works and the covenant of grace, as had his sister-in-law, Mistress Anne Hutchinson, and their more emollient mentor, John Cotton. Most ministers, and most of their congregations, declared Wheelwright, labored under the delusion that human effort (works) could prepare the soul for infusions of divine grace, and must be constantly exerted in order to keep the heart pure and undistracted. Francis Willoughby's "Dayly Observations" and dozens of other self-punishing soul-searchings were account books of *sanctification*, that inner sense of "godliness that elect saints manifest after being *justified*," or saved, by "the imputation of Christ's righteousness to the sinner." Like "Papists" and "Pharisees," Wheelwright continued, believers in works "are given much to fasting and punishing themselves with whips [humiliation]." There was always for them that nagging doubt that they had *imagined* slow and painful justification, that they were really hypocrites, publicly obeying the law, but in the eyes of God, rotten-hearted do-gooders. Anyway, they were on the wrong track. The harder they tried "with their burthen and travaile," Wheelwright told the Bostonians, the more "they make the Lord absent Himself from them." The very reason that "here now [are] divers evils" was God's anger at the preponderance of "those under a covenant of works."[35]

Wheelwright's fast day exercise was a call to arms on behalf of the covenant of grace. This freely God-given gift removed the need for human effort from the conversion experience and from living the saintly life. Such anxious striving they derided as a covenant of works, with its Roman Catholic associations. All depended on the Lord:

> We are not able to do any work of sanctification, further than
> we are acted [upon] by the Lord Jesus Christ that must apply

---

[34] *WJ*, 1: 208–9; see above, "Charlestown and the Atlantic World" and "Our Main End Was to Catch Fish."

[35] David D. Hall, ed., *The Antinomian Controversy* (Durham, N.C.: Duke University Press, 1990), 155–72, esp. 164–67; Charles Francis Adams, *Three Episodes in Massachusetts History* (Boston: Houghton Mifflin, 1892), 444.

Himself and His righteousness to us; and we are not able to redeem ourselves from the least evil, but He is our redemption; when Christ is thus holden forth to be all in all, all in the root, all in the branch, all in all, this is the Gospel . . .

Wheelwright, Anne Hutchinson, and many Bostonians believed passionately in this doctrine of free grace, or antinomianism (literally "against the law"), as a joy-filled present of heaven-bound certainty, a release from the grinding, despairing anxiety of the majority in neighboring towns. Wheelwright's address reiterated the words "fight," "battle," and "fire." He admitted that "this will cause a combustion in the Church and Commonwealth." He seemed to equate his opponents with Philistines, King Herod, Pontius Pilate, the Whore of Rome, and the Antichrist. A champion wrestler at Cromwell's old Cambridge college, Wheelwright gloried in "combats and fightings," strife and contention, "violence and power." His rabble-rousing had all the marks of a revivalist crescendo, and, indeed, Boston had been spiritually astir ever since John Cotton's arrival in late summer 1633. Wheelwright was preaching to the converted, for most of Cotton's congregation had already embraced the free grace cause.[36]

Two notable exceptions to the "spiritist" frenzy gripping Boston were its founder-minister John Wilson, recently returned from England, and John Winthrop, the deputy governor. On 9 March 1637, at the next meeting of the General Court, Winthrop led a colony-wide counterattack against saber-rattling antinomianism. Wheelwright was charged with sedition and contempt, and found guilty by the majority of the Court. However, hoping that time would cool heads and heal the breach, his sentence was deferred. The Court's actions seemed to some both disproportionate and inappropriate. A majority of the Boston church presented a

---

[36] The antinomian rebellion against orthodox Puritan teachings had already developed in England during the 1620s. Thomas Shepard, by the 1630s the champion of orthodoxy in Massachusetts, had been briefly attracted. Martha Collins's conversion narrative in Cambridge credited a London antinomian preacher with rousing her spirit. Giles Randall, a curate at Wapping in 1628, subsequently embraced the doctrine of free grace. Like Arminianism on the opposite wing of Protestantism, antinomianism was an expression of deep dissatisfaction with the crimping uniformity of Calvinism. It echoed Luther's cry "Let God be God," and lifted the responsibility for conversion from frail human shoulders. Its belief that the saved saint's actions were motivated by God-given grace rather than mere obedience to legal conditions and duties alarmed authorities with its inherent threat of anarchy. Its basic ideology encouraged the growth of various sects such as the Fifth Monarchy Men, Muggletonians, Quakers, and other "Ranters," who helped turn the English religious world upside down in the 1640s and 1650s. Three outstanding recent studies: T. D. Bozeman, *The Precisianist Strain* (Chapel Hill: University of North Carolina Press, 2004); D. R. Como, *Blown by the Spirit* (Palo Alto: Stanford University Press, 2004); and M. P. Winship, *Making Heretics* (Princeton: Princeton University Press, 2002). See also Sargent Bush Jr., "John Wheelwright's Forgotten *Apologia*," *NEQ*, 64 (1991), 22–45.

petition through Governor Vane, and the notary William Aspinwall drew up a remonstrance, which more than 60 people signed in March 1637. This document was written in a truculent tone: denying sedition since Wheelwright used "expressions of the Holy Ghost"; brusquely demanding explanation or acquittal; comparing the preacher with Amos, Elijah, St. Peter, and Christ; accusing the Court of meddling against the prophets of God and offending the Lord of Hosts. "If we receive repulse from you, with the Lord we will find grace." Winthrop described the remonstrance as "a reproach and a slander."[37]

Twelve of the signatories of the remonstrance lived in Charlestown: William Learned, Edward Carrington, Richard Sprague, Ralph Mousall, Ezekiel Richardson, William Baker, George Bunker, James Brown, Thomas Ewar, Benjamin Hubbard, William Frothingham, and Edward Mellows. They included some of the elite of the town. In 1636 and 1651, for instance, Ralph Mousall was elected Charlestown representative at the General Court, and served regularly from the 1640s as a town selectman. Before 1652 he assumed the elected office of Deacon. Mr. Edward Mellows was a gentleman, a pensioner of Emmanuel College, Cambridge in the late 1620s, whose father Abraham had invested £50 in the Massachusetts Bay Company. He came from Cotton's old town of Boston, Lincolnshire, as did many leading antinomians. He too served on the Town Board between 1638 and 1644, and was sergeant of the militia after 1641. Richard Sprague was one of the town founders in 1629, and served as a selectman in 1636 with his brother Ralph, and often thereafter. Both Learned and Baker were on the town board in 1636. Benjamin Hubbard served as town surveyor and clerk of the writs from 1641. Ezekiel Richardson was elected to the first town board in 1634, and again in 1635 and 1638. Many of these men served as land allotters and surveyors of highways, as did William Frothingham. Mr. George Bunker, who was very active in the Middlesex land market, Richardson, Ewar, and Mellows, were all constables in the 1630s. The remonstrants took leading roles in the running of the infant township.[38]

Many of the Wheelwright sympathizers left considerable estates. Captain Richard Sprague was hugely wealthy, as we have seen, amassing £2398 by his death in 1668. Samuel Richardson and Ralph Mousall left fortunes of £869 and £822 respectively. William Frothingham had an ample estate of

---

[37]   Verdict: *MR*, 1: 189; Wheelwright was finally sentenced to be banished in November 1637. The remonstrance is included in "A Short Story," in Hall, ed., *Antinomian Controversy*, 249–50; Winthrop's comment: 251. Bostonian spiritists were noisily anti-clerical, and aggressively cross-examined other ministers after their sermons. Ibid., 208. Vane: Winship, *Making Heretics*, 127.

[38]   See "Office Holders." Most of the Remonstrants are detailed in *GMB*, or *GM*.

£308 in 1651, even in his mid-forties. George Bunker had already handed on most of his property (in 1638 he had had 22 parcels of land) when his inventory was appraised at £314; likewise, Edward Carrington (£102) in portions to his two married daughters. Ezekiel Richardson had £190 in personal property alone apart from land and housing, which were usually the lion's share of any estate. Most of the surviving inventories of the remonstrants also list Bibles and other books. Mellows had a most impressive catalogue of classics and theology; he also had English works by Camden, Bacon, and Quarles. Hubbard was a considerable inventor who went to London in 1644 to "demonstrate his longitude machine." In London, he was welcomed at Gresham College and met leading Congregational ministers. These remonstrants, far from being a bunch of lower-class agitators, were an influential, educated, and independent element of the Charlestown establishment.[39]

Charlestown remonstrants were often linked in various ways. Learned, from the South Bank of the Thames in London, was Ewar's father-in-law, and in January 1637 he was involved in land exchanges with fellow remonstrants Baker and Ezekiel Richardson. Mellows, in addition to his ties with Lincolnshire remonstrants in Boston (including his brother Oliver), was brother-in-law to Charlestown's minister Thomas James, and through his mother, a Bulkeley, was linked to the Bunkers, who had been neighbors of the Bulkeleys at Odell in Bedfordshire. Mellows had been baptized at Odell in 1609; his daughter married one of Bunker's sons in 1655. Two of Mousall's sons married two of Samuel Richardson's daughters, perhaps an indication of long-term parental closeness. Ralph Mousall's elder brother John was overseer of Ezekiel Richardson's will and a witness to younger brother Samuel's, to whom he was a close neighbor. Frothingham was next-door neighbor to the Bunkers in Charlestown; several other remonstrants were abuttors on Bunker land. Richard Sprague appraised Ralph Mousall's estate, and his nephew married one of Edward Carrington's daughters. A somewhat disreputable incident may link Brown and Hubbard. Three months after the remonstrance, on 6 June 1637, a James Brown was censured by the General Court for drunkenness and sentenced to be set for two hours in the bilboes on market day in Boston; he was also fined forty shillings for selling strong waters to the Indians without a license. Hubbard was "solemnly admonished for his failing, for being in company with Brown and the rest, and often drinking of the strong water bottle with them, and not reproving them."[40]

---

[39] For estates, see Wyman and the invaluable three volumes of Rodgers.

[40] Learned: *WP*, 3: 513; Mellows: *GMB*, 1249; Bunker, see "Origins," and Wyman, 151; Mousall, Richardsons, Carrington, Sprague, ibid., and Rodgers. Brown, *MR*, 1: 199. Though another

A fourth common characteristic of the Charlestown remonstrants was that they often migrated from the town. In 1640, Woburn was granted four miles square on the northern boundary of Charlestown to form a new township. The Richardson brothers both moved there, as did Learned and Ralph Mousall's brother John. They were all pillars of the new church at its anti-authoritarian foundation. Frothingham had a lot there as well. During the 1640s, parts of Charlestown's domain on Mystic Side seceded to form another new town, Malden. Carrington, Bunker, and Richard Sprague's brother Ralph joined that exodus. They were soon in further conflict with the General Court over their ordination of their first minister, Rev. Marmaduke Matthews. He had already been detected in "errors and weak expressions" while serving at Hull, on the South Shore; in fact, he had antinomian tendencies, and Malden was censured and disciplined for his unmonitored appointment. Carrington was one of those nominated to collect the hefty fine. Hubbard seriously considered migrating to Providence, Rhode Island, to join the banished Roger Williams along with Charlestown's dismissed minister, Thomas James. Instead, he returned to England in 1644. Baker, who sold his house in 1637 but seems to have remained a member of the Charlestown church, later joined Billerica (in 1655), and Brown, even later, relocated to Newbury (1662) and then Salem (1668). None of the leavers gave reasons for departing, but involvement in the protest probably would have been an important element for several.[41]

The Charlestown Twelve (as they would no doubt be called nowadays) differed from the much larger Boston antinomian contingent in two ways. There was far less correlation between commerce and "familism" (as detractors called antinomianism) in Charlestown than Boston. Only one signer was a merchant: Richard Sprague. Edward Mellows's wife Hannah

James Brown lived in Boston, the presence of Hubbard suggests the Charlestown resident, *GMB*, 249–54.

[41] Woburn: Unusually, Charlestown church appointed Woburn's first board of seven selectmen; they were adjured to "exclude the exorbitant or turbulent," i.e., antinomians. Johnson, 212–18, is the classic account of Woburn's foundation. Winthrop, *WJ*, 2: 83, was alarmed at the "disorderly" ordination of Thomas Carter as the town's first minister on 22 November 1642: "Some preferred the elders of other churches to have performed it [ordination] but others supposing it might have been an occasion of introducing a dependency of churches etc., and so a presbytery, would not allow it. So it was performed by one of their own members, but not so well or orderly as it ought." He presumably received a highly critical report of proceedings from Symmes and Nowell, who were present. S. Sewall, *History of Woburn* (Boston: Wiggins & Lunt, 1868), 20–21. Malden: Frothingham, 133–39; Deloraine P. Corey, *History of Malden* (Malden: privately printed, 1899), 136–64; Hubbard: *WP*, 3: 509; Baker: CTR, 1A: 70, house sale; *GMB*, 80–83; Browne, ibid., 249–54.

had a brother, Nathaniel Smith, who was a merchant in England. Otherwise, the remonstrants were either artisans, like Carrington, a turner, or Brown, a glazier; professionals, like Mr. Hubbard, a surveyor, and Mr. Mellows, a scholar; or else landowners. Four became successful livestock farmers: Bunker, Samuel Richardson, Frothingham, and Mousall. Furthermore, the Twelve did not share the Bostonian core group's fervent commitment. None emigrated to Rhode Island or New Hampshire with the banished leaders, Anne Hutchinson and John Wheelwright. In fact, we only know their names because in November 1637, after Wheelwright had been banished, ten asked the General Court to allow their names to be excised from the Remonstance. Two "refuseniks," Brown and Bunker, were sentenced to be disarmed on 20 November, about two days later. Brown soon signed an acknowledgment written in Winthrop's hand: "I never saw the said Petition, and I do disallow of it as evil and unwarrantable."[42]

Indeed, none of the Charlestown remonstrants ever explained why they had signed Aspinwall's protest. They may have been genuinely convinced by Wheelwright's address, and remonstrated with the Court as antinomians. The fact that Joan Sprague, Jane Learned, and Elizabeth Carrington were among the first signatories of a 28 October 1651 Malden women's petition on behalf of the unorthodox Marmaduke Matthews might support this view. So might William Baker's subsequent interest in Quakerism and membership in an Anabaptist cell, along with Bunker's son Jonathan. The assertive independence of both the Woburn and Malden churches, and Thomas Ewar's statement reported on 3 October 1637 that "if the King did send any authority hither against our Patent, he would be the first to resist," might suggest a vein of opposition to the heavy handed exertion of centralized power in favor of the rights of Englishmen and Congregationalists. The browbeating interrogation of the silent champion of the covenant of grace was reminiscent of Laud's Court of High Commission, from which ministers like Shepard, Symmes and Cotton had fled. Some remonstrants may have agreed that sedition was a wholly inappropriate charge, especially against religious beliefs espoused by Vane, Cotton, and many of the richest residents of the colony.[43]

---

[42]   Commerce: Emory Battis, *Saints and Sectaries* (Chapel Hill: University of North Carolina Press, 1962), 262–64; Breen, *Transgressing*, 3–13. Cattle: Bunker had given his second wife £56 worth of cattle, Rodgers, 1: 443; Richardson had £192 worth of cattle and sheep, ibid., 312–14; Mousall: £142 worth of cattle and sheep, ibid, 284–87; Frothingham: £82 worth, ibid., 72–74. Excision: *MR*, 1: 209; Brown: *WP*, 3: 515.

[43]   Malden women: Frothingham, 126; Ewar: *WJ*, 1: 228; he was elected Constable of Charlestown in 1638, and approved by the General Court on 6 March 1638, *MR*, 1: 220. Interrogation: Winship, 121.

By the time of the remonstrants' 15 and 16 November 1637 recantations, much had changed. Vane and his followers had been driven from political office on 17 May 1637. On 2 November 1637, an unrepentant Wheelwright had been sentenced to banishment in the spring; his sister-in-law, Anne Hutchinson, was then examined and also exiled. Their staunch supporters had been disfranchised and fined. A Boston deputy, Mr. John Coggeshall, was summarily dismissed from the General Court for asserting that "John Wheelwright was innocent . . . he was persecuted for the truth." In the spring, Mrs. Hutchinson would be tried by the Boston Church and excommunicated. The remonstrants could see that the tide had turned decisively against advocates of "a fair and easy way to heaven." Short of going into exile, they had little option but to concede.[44]

In these traumatic and sometimes tumultuous events, three Charlestown leaders played important roles. Rev. Zechariah Symmes (already familiar with Mrs. Hutchinson) was one of the elders at her examination in early November 1637. His prepared remarks were as follows:

> For my acquaintance with this person, I had none in our native country, only I had occasion to be in her company once or twice before I came [prior to embarking on *The Griffin*] where I did perceive that she did slight the ministers of the word of God. But I came along with her in the ship, and it so fell out that we were in the great cabin together and therein did agree with the labours [sermons, &c.] of Mr. Lathrop and myself, only there was a secret opposition to things delivered. The main thing that was then in hand was about the evidencing of a good [spiritual] estate, and among the rest about that place in John concerning the love of the brethren [1 John 3:14]. That which I took notice of was the corruptness and narrowness of her opinions, which I doubt not but I may call them so, but she said, when she came to Boston there would be something more seen than I said, for such speeches were cast about and abused as that of our saviour, I have many things to say but you cannot bear them now. And being come and she desiring to be admitted as a member, I was desired to be there, and then Mr. Cotton did give me full satisfaction in the things then in question. And for things which have been here spoken, as far as I can remember they are the truth, and when I asked her what she thought of me, she said alas you know my mind long ago, yet I do not think myself disparaged

---

[44] Winship, 166–86. "Fair and easy": Winthrop's dismissive description.

by her testimony and I would not trouble the court, only this one thing I shall put in, that Mr. Dudley and Mr. Haines were not wanting in the cause after I had given notice of her.

Symmes's statement was powerful evidence of Hutchinson's arrogance and her upper-class disdain for ministers. He later recounted reproving her for foretelling the date of their arrival from a revelation, and for her high-handedness toward her husband. His *coup de grace* was yet to come, however.[45]

Increase Nowell was not called upon to make a detailed deposition, but his remarks show that he was plainly hostile to Mrs. Hutchinson. He once caught her in a lie. He cut off Cotton's attempts to excuse her rashness as a delusion: "I think," said Nowell, "it is a devilish delusion!" Most importantly, however, he asked the crucial question that caused her to incriminate herself. She had been describing to the court certain revelations she had had on a day of solemn humiliation. They had "let me see which was the clear ministry and [which] the wrong," which clergymen echoed the voice of "my beloved" Christ, and which mimicked the Antichrist.

Mr. Nowell. How do you know that that was the spirit?
Mrs. H. How did Abraham know that it was God that bid him offer his son, being a breach of the sixth commandment?
Dep. Gov. By an immediate voice.
Mrs. H. So to me by an immediate revelation.
Dep. Gov. How! An immediate revelation.[46]

This equating herself with Abraham and asserting a special relationship with the Almighty effectively sealed her fate. It is no surprise to find both Symmes and Nowell monitoring the founding of Woburn Church when the authorities were still so jittery about continuing heresy. They had shown themselves to be sharp-eyed watchdogs of orthodoxy.[47]

The third Charlestown leader, soon to move to Boston, was noted merchant Lieutenant Edward Gibbons, who spoke at Anne Hutchinson's church trial in March 1638.

---

[45] Hall, *Antinomian Controversy*, 322–23, 336. Thomas Dudley had been governor 1634–35, John Haines 1635–36. Upper-class: on her mother's side, Anne Marbury Hutchinson was a Dryden, one of the most distinguished Lincolnshire county families.

[46] Ibid., 337.

[47] Johnson, 215; Symmes preached and prayed at Woburn for four to five hours! Nowell would later prove the most persistent critic of Marmaduke Matthews, writing letters and advising against his ordination. Corey, *Malden,* 139, 142, 147, 149, 150. Thomas Lynde was another hostile reporter of Malden church rashness, ibid., 152–54.

I desire leave of the church for one word: not that I would
open my mouth in the least kind to hinder the Church's proceeding in any way of God. *For I look at our sister as a lost
woman* and I bless God to see the pains that is taken to reduce
her: but I would humbly propose this to the church's consideration seeing *Admonition is one of the greatest censures* that
the church can pronounce against any offender and one of the
last next to excommunication and to be used against impenitent offenders, but seeing God hath turned her heart already
to see her error or *Mistake as she calls it* in some of the points.
Whether the church had not better wait a little longer to see
if God will not help her to see the rest and to acknowledge
them, then the church may have no occasion to come to this
censure.

This plea for more time drew from Pastor Symmes (already witnessing against Hutchinson's "mortalism," the denial of the resurrection of the
same body that dies) a powerful and effective rebuke:

I am much grieved to hear that so many in this congregation
should stand up and declare themselves unwilling that Mrs.
Hutchinson should be proceeded against for such dangerous
errors. I fear that if by any means this should be carried over
into England, that in New England and in such a congregation there was so much spoken and so many questions made
about so plain an article of our faith as the resurrection is,
it will be one of the greatest dishonours to Jesus Christ and
of reproach to these churches that hath been done since we
came hither.

In early 1639, Gibbons was sent with two other senior Bostonians to
check on the "wandering sheep" in exile in Rhode Island. Though they
found some impenitent, others were less obstinate. This time, the church
did decide, against Winthrop's advice, to give the disgraced exiles (still officially church members) more time to repent. By this time Gibbons had
moved across the Charles to Boston. Within a few years, as we have seen,
he would make himself deeply unpopular with his former neighbors by
his buccaneering involvement in Maine.[48]

So ended Charlestown's involvement in the first major strife in Massachusetts religious history. For the next decade, the forces of orthodoxy rep-

---

[48] Hall, *Antinomian Controversy*, 366–67, 390–95. See above, "Charlestown and the Atlantic
World."

resented in Charlestown preeminently by Pastor Symmes and Magistrate Nowell would clamp down on any whispers of disagreement or questioning. Unlike mid-century England, Massachusetts would not contemplate toleration. Those who doubted, like Rev Thomas James or Rev. Thomas Allen, returned to England. So, as we have seen, did several of Charlestown's uncomfortable godly merchants and skippers. However, uniformity was an impossible goal. During the 1650s another alternative cell arose which all the potency of town, church, county, and colony would prove unable to crush.[49]

---

[49] Breen, 37, 100; Bozeman 326–29; Winship, 211–38.

Thomas Gould and
the Baptist Debates,
1655–68

Breathe the word "Anabaptist" to a Puritan migrant to New England, and another would come instantly to mind: "Münster." In this north German city during the 1530s, the radical Protestant John (Bockholdt, a tailor) of Leiden established a utopian religious community that rapidly became a byword for "extravagance, lawlessness . . . fanaticism and madness, credulity and imposture . . . unbridled profligacy." Its beliefs emphasized personal faith and biblical literalism; its zealots practiced polygamy, social egalitarianism, and reliance on divine revelation, all of which were pilloried by its critics. Overwhelmed by its "rightful" ruler—the bishop—and his army in 1535, it became a byword for religious mania, similarly to modern Jonestown or Waco, Texas. Orthodox Protestants and Puritans, like the Massachusetts General Court and clergy, habitually used "Anabaptist" (literally, "those who re-baptize") as a smear: a forerunner of the McCarthyite "Red," the neoconservative "Liberal," or the Tea Party "Socialist."[50]

The "Particular" or Calvinist Antipedobaptist (shortened to "Baptist") cells and churches which emerged in England in the late 1630s, and soon

---

[50] Anabaptist: W. G. McLoughlin, *New England Dissent 1630–1833* (Cambridge: Harvard University Press, 1971), 3–7. General Court: Order against Anabaptists, 1644: "Incendiaries of the Commonwealth from 100 years ago," quoted in W. G. McLoughlin and M. W. Davison, "Baptist Debate 14 to 15 April 1668," *MHSP*, 76 (1964) 93, 98. See Rev. John Allen, moderator of the 1668 Debate: "Creditable histories do declare strange things of it. Such as came in sheeps' clothing, they appeared quickly to be devouring wolves: allowing polygamy and running out into many false prophecies. . . " Ibid., 108. In September 1643, Oliver Cromwell described his troop as "a lovely company. . . they are no Anabaptists, they are sober Godfearing Christians." D. Purkiss, *English Civil War* (London: Harper, 2006), 325.

after in New England, distanced themselves from the excesses of Münster. Their major difference with Massachusetts orthodoxy was their opposition to infant baptism as unscriptural. In the young colony still licking wounds inflicted in the Antinomian Crisis, the myth of liberty of conscience had been early defined as the liberty (and space) to keep away. Early Baptist preachers, such as Rev. Hanserd Knollys or the mature Roger Williams, were removed along with their followers. This happened to the small cell of Baptists in Watertown in the 1640s. Those who could not afford to leave were silenced, as the Cambridge Platform of 1648 spelled out the clerically imposed orthodoxy.[51]

The doubts the Baptists raised about biblically licensed infant sprinkling, and about clerical dominance over individual conscientious judgment, would not go away. In Cambridge in late 1653, such qualms were voiced from the meetinghouse pulpit. The preacher was not some inexperienced graduate student, but the long-serving president of Harvard College, Rev. Henry Dunster. Then, on 30 July 1654, Dunster interrupted a baptism in the meetinghouse and tried to prevent what he now believed was an unwarranted sin.[52]

It was at this time that a neighbor in Charlestown, Thomas Gould, was similarly wracked by misgivings:

> It having been a long time a scruple to me about infant baptism, God was pleased at last to make it clear to me by the rule of the gospel, that children were not capable nor fit subjects for such an ordinance, because Christ gave this commission to his apostles, first to preach to make them disciples, and then to baptize them, which infants were not capable of; so that I durst not bring forth my child to be partaker of it; so looking that my child had no right to it, which was in the year 1655, when the Lord was pleased to give me a child; I staid some space of time and said nothing to see what the church would do with me.[53]

---

[51] England: McLoughlin, *Dissent*, 4–6; S. Wright, *Early English Baptists, 1603–1649* (Woodbridge: Boydell & Brewer, 2006); B. R. White, *The English Baptists of the Seventeenth Century* (London: Baptist Historical Society, 1983), 20–23, 58–92. Watertown: Thompson, *Divided*, 70–72; Cambridge Platform: Hall, *Faithful Shepherd*, 115–20.

[52] Thompson, *Cambridge Cameos*, 68. Cf. Dunster's nephew-in-law, Benanuel Bowers, ibid., 173–82; by the early 1660s, Bowers had embraced Quakerism, but after 1666 worshiped with the Baptists.

[53] Isaac Backus, *History of the Baptists in New England* (Newton: Backus Historical Society, 1871), 290.

So, two decades after the Antinomian Crisis, began the second, and far more drawn-out, intrachurch conflict in the town. Eventually, it spread to neighboring churches, and, unlike the antinomian heresy, it proved resilient. The 176-foot stone tower of the First Baptist Church founded in 1665, with its trump-blowing angels the corner of Commonwealth Avenue and Clarendon Street in Boston proudly proclaims its endurance. For the next fourteen years, until he moved to Noddle's Island in Boston Harbor, Thomas Gould and his associates were in a state of confrontation with the church of Charlestown, of which several of them were full members.[54]

Twice these disagreements flared up from the relentless secular routine of grand-jury presentments for absence from services, court appearances, fines and prison terms, and concurrent church disciplinary appearances with arguments, admonitions, and eventual excommunications. On 6 June 1658, and on 14 and 15 April 1668, Baptists were able to dispute with ministers and lay leaders about the legitimacy of their differences. Two accounts of the first meeting survive; the record of the second, much more elaborate, debate, mainly in shorthand, is also extant. These little-known contemporary documents give a vivid picture of the issues and individuals involved.[55]

We have already met one of the principals of the first debate, Rev. Zechariah Symmes, Charlestown's minister from 1634 to 1672, as an early and persistent harrier of antinomians. His major opponent twenty years later was a parishioner and church member since 1640, Thomas Gould (1607–75). Gould, a wheelwright and wagon-maker by training, arrived in New England in 1639 with his first wife Hannah (Miller), who died in 1647. By then, Gould was leasing John Winthrop's Ten Hills Farm on the border of Charlestown and Medford. There he raised and fattened his own herd and other people's cattle. He was regularly nominated for grand juries and trial juries from 1650, served as a town selectman in 1653, 1663 and 1664, and was twice a land allotter in 1662 and 1663. By 1654, he had married the well-connected widow Mary Harwood. In the 1658 tax list

---

[54] Neighboring: Woburn, Boston, Billerica; tower: E. M. Bacon, *Boston, A Guide Book* (Boston: Ginn, 1903), 170. Associates: see below. William Baker (ca. 1600–58), husbandman of Charlestown and Billerica, was presented on 29 December 1657 for absence from baptism and possession of Quaker books; he claimed in court to have burned the books and promised to attend baptisms in future. However, he was again in court on 7 April 1658 for "anabaptism." His family was associated with Gould's and John Russell's. MxCC RB, 1: 145; D&O, 1: doc. 839; *GMB*, 80; Rodgers, 1: 374–80.

[55] First debate: Nathan E. Wood, *History of the First Baptist Church of Boston* (Philadelphia: American Baptist Publishing Co., 1899), 39–51, 305–7; second debate: McLoughlin and Davison, "Baptist Debate," 91–133.

he was among the dozen wealthiest men in the town. Over the course of his life Gould had amassed a fortune of £782. Despite the hundreds of man-hours he had exacted from clergy and officials, he was described by Rev. William Hubbard in his *History of New England* as "a man of a grave and serious spirit and of sober conversation." Gould's second wife proved a persuasive advocate, and left a lively, well-argued account of the injustices meted out to her imprisoned husband and his colleagues, refuting the charges against them.[56]

During the second debate, toward the end of the first day's disputing, Thomas Shepard, teacher of Charlestown church, was called upon to give "an account of the casting out of Gould" from the church records. This will provide a context for the issues in the first debate.

> 1655: The 1 occasion was the not bringing of his child to baptism: to which he answered he saw no warrant in the word of God.
>
> He was thought fit by many brethren for the highest censure not for casting off the ordinance of infant baptism: but for reproaching and casting dirt upon it. Upon motion of admonition to be given to him: it was propounded that he should withdraw from the sacrament of the Lord's Supper . . .
>
> 6:6:58: He was called forth for withdrawing from the ordinances on the Lord's day. He answered he had not turned from any ordinance of God: but attended the word in other places.
>
> He was admonished for . . . schism.
>
> Novem. 18: 63 . . . Gould denied himself to be related to the church when he was called to give an account for his withdrawing from public ordinances. When a copy of the 2: admonition to Gould was read: he stiffly denied that he had been twice admonished.
>
> Reasons why he lay so long unexcommunicated.
>
> Some . . . moved that the utmost censure might be forborne: hoping that he would not press to the sacrament of the supper until that he had given satisfaction. To this day he never sought to be reconciled to the church in any meet way... Gould declared to be under the great offence of the church and rebuked for this great sin of his.
>
> Feb 28: 64: Gould again admonished

---

[56] Wyman, 428; *R*, 42 (1888), 64–66; *GMB*, 2: 873–74. Ten Hills: *WP*, 5: 162; 6: 99. Well-connected: Mary Gould was related to Shapleighs, Harwoods, and Bunkers; see below, "Women and the Churches." 1658: McLoughlin, *Dissent*, 51; advocate: Backus, 305–7.

June 9: 65: Information being given that Gould, Osborne and others had embodied themselves in a church way [formed their own church]: were again sent for by the deacons: a negative answer returned to the church: and denied himself to be a member of our church . . . and saith plainly that he will not come: And they proceeding thus incorrigibly: it did further increase the offence of the church against them. Not one brother objected against their excommunication. With the consent of the brethren in the name of the Lord Jesus Christ they are delivered up to Satan for their schismatical withdrawing themselves from the churches of Christ.[57]

Most of this record had in fact been written by Symmes, since ruling elder John Greene had died on 22 April 1658. Gould contested its accuracy. His own account of events of the first confrontation in 1655 paints a grimmer picture of the minister:

On a First-day [Sunday] . . . Master Sims told the church, that this brother did withhold his child from baptism, and that they had sent unto him to come down on such a day to speak with them, and if he could not come on that day to set a day when he could come, and they be at home, but he refusing to come would appoint no time, when we writ to him to take his own time and send us word.

I [Gould] replied that there was no such word in the letter. Mr. Sims stood up and told me, *I did lie* . . . They bid me let them see the letter, or they would proceed against me for a lie. Brother Thomas Wilder, sitting before me, stood up and told them, that it was so in the letter as I said, for he read it when it came to me . . . He said, I think I can produce the letter, and forthwith took it out of his pocket, which I wondered at; and I desired him to give it to Mr. [Richard] Russell to read, and so he did, and he read it very faithfully, and it was just as I had said . . . so that their mouths were stopped, and Master Sims put it off, and said he was mistaken . . .

Observe the providence of God in the carriage of this letter. Brother Wilder was with us when their letter came to my house, and after Mr. Dunster had read it, he gave it to Brother Wilder and he put it into his pocket, and it lay there eight or nine weeks, till, that day I was called forth, going a good space from his house, finding it too cold to go in the clothes he had

---

57   McLoughlin & Davison, 120–21.

on, [he] returned again and put on another pair of breeches which were warmer, and when he had so done, put his hand into his pocket to see if he had any paper to write with [to take notes on the sermon], and there found that letter, and put it in again and went to meeting, yet not knowing what would be done that day concerning me. God had so appointed it, to stop their fierce proceedings against me for a lie . . .

Being met [a week later] at Mr. Russell's house, Mr. Sims took a writing out his pocket wherein he had drawn up many arguments for infants' baptism, which I suppose he had drawn from some author; and told me I must keep to those arguments. My answer was, I thought the church had met together to answer my scruples . . . So we spent four or five hours speaking to many things to and again; but so hot, both sides, that we quickly forgot and went from the arguments that were written. At last one of the company stood up and said, I will give you one plain place of Scripture where children were baptized. I told him that would put an end to the controversy. That place in the second of the Acts, 39th, 40th verses. *The promise is to you and your children, and to all that are afar off*; and he said no more, to which I replied, *Even so many as the Lord our God shall call.* Mr. Sims replied, that I spoke blasphemously in adding to the Scriptures. I said, pray do not condemn me, for if I am deceived, my eyes deceive me. He replied again, I added to the Scripture which was blasphemy. I, looking in my Bible, read the words again, and said it was so. He replied the same words the third time before the church. Mr. Russell stood up and told him it was so as I had read it. Ay, it may be so in your Bible, saith Mr. Sims. Mr. Russell answered, Yea, in yours too if you will look into it. Then he said he was mistaken, for, he thought on another place; so after many other words we broke up for that time.

At another meeting the church required me to bring out my child to baptism. I told them I durst not do it, for I did not see any rule for it in the word of God. Afterwards, I went out at the sprinkling of children, which was a great trouble to some honest hearts and they told me of it . . . They told me . . . I might stay, for they knew I did not join with them. So I stayed and sat down in my seat . . . Then they dealt with me for my unrevent carriage . . . One stood up and accused me, that I stopped my ears; but I denied it.

At another meeting they asked me if I would suffer the church to fetch my child and baptize it? I answered, If they would fetch my child and do it as their own act they might do it . . . A brother stood up and said, Brother Gould, you were once for children's baptism, why are you fallen from it? I answered, It is true, and I suppose you were once for crossing in baptism, why are you fallen from that? The man was silent. But Mr. Sims stood up in a great heat, and desired the church to take notice of it, that I compared the ordinance of Christ to the cross in baptism!

[In 1664/65] Mr. Sims told the church that I was ripe for excommunication, and [he] was very earnest for it; but the church would not consent . . . Then said Mr. Russell, We have not gone the right way to gain this our brother, for we have dealt too harshly with him. But still Master Sims pressed the church to excommunicate me. Mr. Russell said, There were greater errors in the church in the apostles' time, and yet they did not so deal with them . . . Mr. Sims was earnest for another admonition. Then stood up Solomon Phipps and said, You may clap one admonition on him upon another, but to what end, for he was admonished about seven years ago! Mr. Sims said, Brother! Do you make such a light matter of admonition, to say, Clap them one upon another? It was not seven years since I was admonished, and that was for schism. Mr. Sims then pulled a bit of paper out of his pocket and said, This is that he was admonished for, and that was but three years since. Brother Phipps asked him when that paper was writ, for he never heard of that admonition before? He answered, he set it down for his memory; then he read it, that it was for schism, and rending the church . . . Then there was much agitation when the admonition was given, and what it was for? . . . After many words we broke up, which was the last time we met together. Now let any man judge of the church records that were drawn up against me, and read at the dispute at Boston [Second Debate] which contained three or four sheets of paper; read by Mr. Shepard, and drawn up by him a little while before the dispute, who was not an eye nor ear witness to the church's actings not above half the time.[58]

---

58 Wood, 43–50. Thomas Wilder (1619–67), a church member since 1640, had been appointed by the Town Meeting in 1646 to oversee all commons, fences, trees and cattle in the town and deal with issues of trespass and neglect, at a salary of £20 per year. Solomon Phipps (1619–71), a carpenter, and a church member since 1642, was a leading citizen, selectman regularly from 1663, grand juror and trial juror, and town builder. On Richard Russell, see "Godly Merchants"

This account, severely abbreviated here, is an extraordinarily skillful piece of narrative. It is not only vivid, with dialogue, incident and a sense of drama, but it also manages to locate Gould as a victim of exclusion and relentless punishment. "I did not rend from the church, but the church put me away." From this, all other alleged misdemeanors follow. Moreover, he establishes the inaccuracy of the church's record of events, and the deep misgivings of many senior members about the handling of a delicate issue of conscience. The narrator emerges as humble, concessive, and reasonable in the face of intimidating bluster.

Of course, Gould was hardly an objective observer of these nine years of controversy. He could, no doubt, be infuriatingly closed-minded to arguments in favor of infant baptism. Nonetheless, baptism in the New Testament, including Christ's, was performed by immersion on *adults*. Arguing from "the seed of Abraham" or from the Jewish precedent of circumcision, or from the text presented from Acts 2:39, 40—"the promise is to you and your children"—might satisfy the vast majority of orthodox Puritans, many of whom voted in the 1662 Half-Way Covenant to extend baptism to the grandchildren of members. The more general justification for infant baptism, advanced during the 1640s by ministers such as Thomas Shepard, claimed that christening brought children of saints "under the wings of Christ" so that "God is beforehand with [them] that whenever [they] shall return to Him He will undoubtedly receive [them] and this is a high and happy privilege . . . for the sons [and daughters] of God by promise." Shepard besought "those brethren that do scruple" to embrace "the comfortable hope of their children's salvation because they be within the pale of the visible church." The legacy of baptism was "a symbol and instrument of continuity within families"; this initial church affiliation represented, to pedobaptists, "all hopes of posterity for all time to come."[59]

To biblical literalists like Thomas Gould and his cell, none of this persuasiveness was enough. Their consciences rebelled. In 1662 or 1663, mason Christopher Goodwin was provoked into "throwing down the basin of water in the [Charlestown] meeting house and striking the constable in the meeting house and kicking him on the Lord's Day and expressing

---

above. Lie, blasphemy: as breaches of the Ten Commandments, these were were viewed as the most heinous sins. Note-taking: this was a common practice among congregations, and often a sole surviving source of sermon topics.

[59] These arguments were all rehearsed in the Second Debate. I am most grateful to David Hall for help with Shepard's role; A. S. Brown & D. D. Hall, "Family Strategies and Religious Practice: Baptism and the Lord's Supper in Early New England," in D. D. Hall, ed. *Lived Religion in America: Towards a History of Practice* (Princeton: Princeton University Press, 1997), 41–68.

himself in court with high contempt of the holy ordinance [of baptism]." This from a mature, law-abiding craftsman, who ironically would later be employed by the town to build a tomb for Zechariah Symmes.[60]

On 28 May 1665, after "God sent out of Old England some who were Baptists," nine people gathered themselves into a new Baptist congregation in Charlestown. This prompted a summons to Charlestown church next Lord's Day. Gould demurred, because

> We were to break bread next Lord's Day . . . [but] three loving friends [came] to me and [said]: Brother Gould, though you look upon it as unjust for them to cast you out, yet there be many that are godly among them, that will act with them through ignorance, which will be a sin of them . . . [and] it is your duty to prevent anyone from any sinful act . . . I promised them that if I was alive and well, I would come the next [but one] Lord's day if the Lord permit . . . The word was carried to the elder [Symmes], yet they were so hot upon it that they would not stay, but Master Sims when he was laying out the sins of these men, before he had propounded it to the church, to know their mind, the church having no liberty to speak, he wound it up in his discourse, and delivered them up to Satan, to the amazement of the people, that ever such an ordinance of Christ should be so abused.[61]

Zechariah Symmes's performance in this first drawn-out church debate is deeply disturbing. He emerges from the Goulds' accounts as arrogant, hasty, and intemperate. He talked to Gould, other Baptists like Thomas Osborne, and respected members of the church such as magistrate Richard Russell, Mr. Thomas Wilder, and selectman Solomon Phipps as though they were naughty schoolboys. He was all too ready to twist the truth and fabricate a false record. He flew at Gould with accusations that "You lie," and "You blaspheme," wrongly in both instances. He treated Gould as someone to be lectured, even hectored, rather than persuaded. He was typical of that "humane learning" which condescended to the spiritual scripturalism of non-intellectuals. He would not let other church members try to help Gould with his doubts; he said that "he was able to deal with [Gould] himself, and [Gould] knew it." Rushing through the final awesome excommunication without discussion caused

---

[60] Goodwin: MxCC RB, 1: 287; CTrR, 3: 54v, 1673. It is possible that this outburst resulted from his church member wife's attempt to have their youngest son Timothy baptized, Wyman, 414–15.

[61] Wood, 50–51; Backus, 306; the section from "the word" is taken from Sister Gould's account.

popular consternation. In the Gould account, Symmes was a tragicomic petty tyrant.[62]

The Charlestown church was divided. Some wanted quick solutions. Even before the first admonition in 1658, at one of their interminable meetings, William Dady, town butcher and frequent juror, stood up and said, "Put him in the Court! Put him in the Court!" Indeed, Gould, along with his "company," often appeared in court for absence from church or refusing to pay the church rate. Another church member was outraged that Gould allegedly stopped his ears during the rite of infant baptism. Most, however, were either ignorant of the issues or sympathetic with Gould's scruples of conscience. The most authoritative voice among these was Russell's. He was publicly critical of Symmes and favoured a less confrontational approach. Phipps and Wilder both corroborated Gould's version of events. The three "loving friends" were eager that Gould should defend himself. At least twice, the church declined to enact admonitions, and would not initially consent to excommunication, despite their pastor's zeal. Most remarkably, in the midst of these troubles, Charlestown Town Meeting twice elected Gould as one of their seven selectmen. The final rift only came after nine years of lay stalling, when Gould and company set up their own church in 1665. It is surely significant that in the far wider-ranging Second Debate, Pastor Symmes was virtually silent, probably purposely silenced.[63]

Two of the members of the Baptist church founded on 28 May 1665 were Charlestown church members: Gould and Thomas Osborne, who had transferred from Malden church in 1662. Edward Drinker was the son of a full church member, and thus eligible for half-way membership. John George had never been admitted to church fellowship. This Charlestown core was joined by three men and two women "who had walked in that order in old England" but fled from Restoration persecution. Four had settled in Boston: mariner Richard Goodall and his wife Mary, William Turner, and Robert Lambert. The fifth was Charlestown saint Mary Newell. Mistress Newell was from a most distinguished Bristol merchant family, and more to the point in Massachusetts, she was Richard Russell's sister-in-law. These nine were quickly joined by eight others, including Benjamin Sweetzer (son of Charlestown church members) and his wife Abigail, who was the sister of Rev. Michael Wigglesworth of Malden; a group from Woburn; and more Bostonians. In September 1665, the

---

[62]   Wood, 41, 45.

[63]   Court: MxCC RB, 1: 117, 133, 184; D & O, 2: folios 40, 43, 44, 45, 47, 49, 51, 52, 53, 57.

church drew up its simple Confession of Faith, in most cases similar to the doctrine of New England Congregationalism, but including implied adult baptism and the stipulation that "when the church is met together they may all prophesy [expound scripture] one by one that all may learn and all may be comforted."[64]

Once the Baptists had set up a church without government permission, they were breaking the civil law. Gould and the Osbornes had already been presented by the Middlesex Grand Jury for withholding children from baptism, absence from church services, and refusing to pay church rates levied on all by the town towards the minister's salary—they disapproved of "hirelings" and tithe-like levies. Before his excommunication Gould spoke of eight court appearances; because of their obstinacy and refusal to pay fines, Gould and the other Baptists were referred to the Court of Assistants. Gould escaped some penalties by attending the Cambridge church for a while, but once the Baptist church began, escape became impossible. On 11 October 1665, the General Court disfranchised Baptist freemen, and threatened Gould, Osborne, Drinker, Turner, and George with prison if they persisted. On 17 April 1666, before the Middlesex County Court, Gould, Osborne, and George were fined for absence from Charlestown meetings; refusing to pay or to be bound, they were imprisoned. Five months later, the assistants ordered their release on 11 September 1666, provided that they pay. When they were actually let out is not recorded. Throughout 1667, they were back and forth to the County Court for the usual offenses. Their insistence that they were a proper church seems to have elicited some sympathy. On 7 March 1668, the governor and council of magistrates, in order to "endeavour the reducing

---

[64] Osborne: both Thomas and Sarah became Charlestown church members in 1644; they lived on Mystic Side, and she was as zealous as her husband; she was warned for attending meetings with Quakers. RB 1: 297, 6 October 1663. Even as late as 1676, they were presented for absence from meeting, D&O, 3: folios 69, 73. George had been in town since 1650, and died in 1666, leaving only £41. Drinker, see below. On English persecution by parliament, magistrates, courts, and mobs, see White, *English Baptists*, 93–138, C. E. Whiting, *Studies in Puritanism 1660–1688* (London: Cass, 1968), 82–132. Turner and Lambert were said to have recently arrived from Dartmouth, Devonshire, where they had been members of "Mr. Stead's" persecuted Baptist cell, Backus, 288, Frothingham, 166. The Goodalls were from William Kiffin's church in London, ibid. Mary Newell (1607–84), widow of Andrew, merchant of Bristol and of Lyme Regis in Dorset (home of a Baptist cell), was sister of Maud (Pitt) Russell and daughter of William, sheriff of Bristol, and of Mary, who disapproved of the younger Mary's marriage; her son John Newell was a Charlestown cooper and town clerk. A Jonathan Newell was later a member of the Baptist church. Wood, 90, H. Black, *Ancestry of Frances Maria Goodman* (Boston: Newbury Street Press, 2001), 345–47; see below, "Women and the Churches." Sweetzer and Woburn, see below. Bostonians: the most prestigious recruit was John Farnum, founding member and deacon of the Old North Church; see Pestana, *Quakers and Baptists*, 52–54. Confession: Wood, 65–66; the members were also rebaptized by immersion.

of the [Baptists] from the error of their way and their return to the Lord and the communion of His people from whence they are fallen, do judge meet to grant [them] a full and free debate [with six leading ministers] with the Governor and magistrates upon the 14th day of [April] in the meeting-house at Boston, at nine in the morning." This was the invitation to the Second Debate, before "a great concourse of people," whose exchanges were recorded verbatim in shorthand by Thomas Danforth.[65]

Such was the invitation, but as the meeting opened, the "reducing" rather than "full and free debate" dominated moderator John Allen's mind, as he delivered a long assault against the sin and error of Anabaptism with all the clichéd canards against polygamy, false prophesies, devouring wolves in sheep's clothing, disgracers of the faithful ministers of Christ, and betrayers of the reforms of Luther and Calvin. Such prosecutorial belligerence, so reminiscent of Symmes in the First Debate, led Gould to ask Governor Bellingham whether this was a debate or a court. The tone of several ministers continued to be sharp, notably that of the ultrafrosty Cobbett, but also Mitchell and Higginson. The magistrates, especially Russell and Daniel Gookin, were far less confrontational.[66]

If the six ministers expected the Baptists to be pushovers, they were in for a shock. From the first moments, when Gould asked why his company could not have a voice in the choice of moderators, the Baptists treated their opponents as equals, and misguided equals at that. While the clergy were circling round, pontificating about peripheral issues, William Turner quickly came to the nub of their differences: "3: things I separate from you for. 1: Baptizing infants. 2: Denying prophecy to the brethren. 3: A spirit of persecution of those that differ from you. These are the reason why I differ from you." When ministers emphasized the need for obedience and the force of custom, Gould responded: "Many answers are given, but no Scripture given . . . Holding up the Bible in his hand, he said: We have nothing to judge [by] but this." In a long argument about separation and schism, Shepard cited texts for church authority, only to be trumped by

---

[65]   Backus, 300–2; the ministers were John Allen, Thomas Cobbett, John Higginson, Samuel Danforth, Jonathan Mitchell, and Thomas Shepard. Frothingham, 165–68, on court appearances and imprisonments; Wood, 68–69.

[66]   Cobbett: e.g., McLoughlin and Davison, 110: "You come not on equal terms but as delinquents to answer for what you have done. . . The Council declares that you have done thus and thus: You must not put us to prove it." Cobbett, minister of Lynn, had published *A Just Vindication. . . of [Infant]Baptism* in London in 1648, after conflicts with Baptists in his congregation. McLoughlin, *Dissent,* 27. Cf. K. E. Durso, *No Armor for the Back* (Macon, GA: Mercer University Press, 2007), 210–19. Russell supported Gould's version of certain crucial points in the First Debate with Symmes, which had been inaccurately reported to this meeting, ibid., 121.

Gould's citation that a church's judgement must be "according to the rule of Christ," and Paul's command "Anything that is unclean [like Charlestown church] I am to withdraw from."[67]

One of Mitchell's persistent pests in Cambridge, Benanuel Bowers, who lived within the Charlestown line, insisted that "the spirit of God in every Christian tells them whether the other be right [in their heart] or in form only." This was just the kind of "inspired" subjectivity that made ministerial flesh creep. In the ebb and flow of textual, procedural, and analogical dispute, the Baptists did not give an inch. They pointed out that the New England had Puritans provided them with a precedent by seceding from the Church of England. When, in a scriptural dispute, Mitchell incredulously asked if they were comparing the Congregational churches to "obstinate, blasphemous Jews" from whom Jesus separated, the answer shot back: "You have put the words into our mouth."[68]

Turner and Gould were spokesmen for most of the opening session, but gradually other believers and sympathizers joined in. One of the most insistent was Master John Trumbull, the sea captain. Initially he was upset by ministerial browbeating: "six or more persons to speak to one poor man before he hath done, not permitting him to speak." Soon, however, he was criticizing the unscriptural basis of infant baptism, the church's exclusion of non-members' children. He criticized the church's inclusion of grandchildren of members in the rite, while they simultaneously condemned Baptist practice. He demanded that the new church be allowed the same liberty of conscience Congregational ministers had sought at the Presbyterian-dominated Westminster Assembly of Divines on 4 December 1645. He cross-questioned a clearly rattled Higginson (who had recently described the Baptist church as a "synagogue of Satan") about the Puritan flight from the Church of England. Later, he spoke approvingly of governmental maintenance of toleration in Holland. "If you counsel one thing, and we another, bear one with another." To the orthodox, this was anathema—toleration was the gateway to perdition. Trumbull was plainly well-read, well-traveled and quick-thinking. He referred to the Cambridge Platform (more then once); to the Abrahamic sin of Aspurgama (possibly, sprinkling), to Apollo's convincing the Jews by scripture; to Diotrephes, the rival of St. John; and to the absence of a public assembly for the persecuted Hebrews. He was so confident of one point that "I will forfeit all the estate I have that Master [Samuel] Danforth hath abused the Scriptures." In one session, he took on five minis-

---

67 Ibid., 112–16; Paul: 2 Corinthians 6.

68 Ibid., 114; on Bowers, see Thompson, *Cambridge Cameos*, 173–82.

ters at once. He took a dig at their hard-nosed negotiation with towns about their salaries before they would agree to preach—this was the "hireling" criticism yet again. Though never formally listed as a Baptist, Trumbull was clearly deeply unhappy about clerical closed-mindedness and the lack of a climate of toleration in Restoration New England.[69]

Another emergent voice in the debate was that of Edward Drinker. He spoke movingly, as a believer who had nonetheless never been admitted to membership in Charlestown church. He pointed out the illogicality of charging people like him with separation. He used a nice turn of phrase: something they had forgotten "had eloped out of our memories." Drinker had lived in Charlestown since the age of 14, and had followed his father as the town potter. On 6 April 1669, he petitioned from prison for two days' furlough, since he did not want "a great parcel of [earthen]ware ready for burning" to be ruined; it would harm many of his customers. He later wrote a letter full of news to Dr. John Clarke's Baptist church at Newport, Rhode Island.[70]

John Johnson of Woburn explained why he had joined the Baptists: adult rather than infant baptism, and "that [Baptists] give liberty for prophesying and edifying of one another which you deny." Mitchell replied that the Protestant churches had practiced infant baptism for 130 years; Johnson shot back, "I cannot remember what was done 130 years ago," highlighting the contrary perspectives of the book-learned and the oral traditions. The two traded texts for a good five minutes, Johnson asserting the biblical precedents for immersion over the Congregationalists' sprinkling. His wish for all members of a church to be able to speak about their spiritual revelations reflected a common lay disquiet at the clerical monopolization of holy discourse.[71]

Throughout this lively and sometimes heated to-and-fro of debating points, Charlestown's teacher strove to convince those present via formal argumentation learned at Harvard. Shepard (1635–77) had been ordained as a colleague to Symmes in 1659. Three years earlier, he had married the heiress Anne Tyng. His style was that of an eager-beaver graduate student: "I shall propose an argument to prove the negative to the question." A little later,

---

[69] McLoughlin and Davison, 114, 116–17, 130, 132. Holland: toleration, even of Quakers, had spread to New Netherland by the early 1660s, Kenneth T. Jackson, "A Colony with a Conscience," *International Herald Tribune*, 4 January 2008. On Trumbull, see above, "The Sea: Conclusion."

[70] D&O 2: folio 51; Wood, 92–95.

[71] Johnson was a son of the ultra-orthodox Captain Edward Johnson, author of *The Wonderworking Providence of Sion's Saviour*. Pestana, 45, 88–90. His brother, Edward Jr., continued to live in Charlestown.

having made no headway: "I shall propound another argument . . . I shall prove both these ways . . . I shall propound [yet] another argument . . . I shall prove the excommunication of these persons is by the rule of Christ . . . I will prove that it doth so . . . You have broken down this hedge I shall thus prove . . . " Talking later to Samuel Sewall, Shepard, discoursing of "reformation, especially the disorderly meetings of Quakers and Anabaptists," showed his true persecuting bent: "if all did agree, i.e. Magistrates and Ministers, the former might easily be suppressed, and that then, the Magistrates would see reason to handle the latter." "Handle" here surely meant more suppression. His 1672 election sermon, *Eye Salve, or a Watch-word from Our Lord . . . to take heed of Apostacy,* bemoaned both the insubordination of the laity and the weak will of magistrates who, instead of being "determined steersmen," had declined into "man-pleasing, temporizing, humourizing [gluttons for] popularity." He was specifically outraged that dissenters could simply ignore court orders and colony decrees. Shepard was enthusiastic for the Half-Way Covenant; indeed he told Sewall that he would like to see *all the children* in the country baptized. This placed him out on the opposite extreme to those who were unconvinced by his proofs.[72]

To a considerable extent, the Second Debate of 14 and 15 April 1668 proved a dialogue of the deaf. Clergy attempted to dominate proceedings by their social grandeur, scholastic skill, and disputational finesse, but the Baptists were deeply learned in the Scriptures, quick-witted in debate, gifted in the use of transatlantic comparisons, and utterly underwhelmed by their learned opponents' arguments. The Baptists, led throughout by an implacable Gould, behaved as equals; indeed, at times, as superiors, gifted by God with a spiritual assurance that swatted away the "humane learning" of the ministers. Some in the listening concourse found this self-confidence shocking: "Cobbler stick to your last!" called out one to Woburn shoemaker John Russell Jr., "You're [just] a wedder-dopped [sheep-dipped] shoemaker." Another critic shouted "If you [Gould] are fit for a minister we have but fooled ourselves in building colleges." Conformist John Hull described the Baptists as behaving "obstinately, absurdly and ignorantly." The shorthand record stops suddenly; significantly, the Baptist spokesman William Turner, elaborating on Acts 17, has the last word.[73]

The rest of the story can be quickly told. After the Second Debate,

---

[72] *Eye Salve* is excerpted in A. Heimert & A. Delbanco, eds. *The Puritans in America* (Cambridge: Harvard University Press, 1985), 247–60. Shepard's estate at his early death from smallpox in 1677 at the age of 42 was an enormous £2,386, Sibley, 1: 327–35. Foster, *Long Argument*, 198–99.

[73] Barracking: Frothingham, 169, quoting Samuel Willard, *Ne Sutor ultra Crepidam;* Hull: Diary, 226. Wedder: F. H. Russell, "A Cobbler at his Bench," *R,* 133 (1979), 133, fn. 37.

the unbowed Baptists were sentenced on 7 May 1668 to banishment by 20 July. They stayed. On 30 July 1668, they were jailed. In October, a petition was presented to the next session of the General Court from over 60 "sober and serious Christians" for the release of Gould, Turner, and Farnham, and for a modest measure of toleration. It was signed by some of the leading merchants of Boston and several important Charlestown officials, including selectmen Randall Nicholls and Solomon Phipps, constable John Hayman, and sergeant Edward Wilson. The General Court was not amused. Their investigations discovered that Benjamin Sweetzer, a Charlestown Baptist, and Joshua Atwater, "a busy trader" of Boston, had collected signatures from door to door; they were heavily fined and other signers forced to apologize. On 13 March 1669, thirteen English Independent [Congregationalist] ministers, including giants Thomas Goodwin, John Owen, and Phillip Nye, wrote urging freedom for the Baptists. Two weeks before, perhaps during Gould's furlough from jail, Charlestown constables raided Gould's house on the Sabbath, 7 March 1669. There they found nine neighbors, seven Bostonians and two Woburn men, one of whom was exhorting the group. A week later, Gould had disappeared. He later surfaced on Noddle's Island (then owned by members of a petitioning family, the Shrimptons). Thereafter Baptist meetings took place on the island, uninterrupted by authority.[74]

Thomas Gould died on 27 October 1675, leaving a fortune of £782. A year earlier, still unwelcome in Shepardian Charlestown, the Baptists had begun meeting in a rented house in Boston. During King Philip's War, after first being rebuffed, they formed a company under Captain William Turner and Lieutenant Edward Drinker and fought with great bravery. Turner was killed on 19 May 1676 on the Upper Connecticut, in the place soon called Turners Falls. The Baptists' meetinghouse in

---

[74] On 1 May 1668, the trial jury of the Court of Assistants surprised the bench by special verdict with the choice of acquittal of Gould for absence from church; their legal nicety was overruled by the magistrates, Backus, 300. Petitioners: Thomas Temple, Peter Lidget, Thomas Clarke, Samuel Shrimpton, John Usher, Jonathan Shrimpton, Jeremy Fitch, Benjamin Negus, Thomas Buttolph, Richard Collicut, Timothy Prout and John Fayerweather. Henry Shrimpton left the Baptists £10 in his will, Frothingham, 173. John Gould of Charlestown also signed; he had earlier had trouble with the church at Reading and had refused to pay his church rate in Charlestown; however, he had made his peace with Charlestown church on 28 April 1667; his relationship to Thomas Gould is unclear, Wyman. The petition is in Mass. Archives, October 1668. Sweetzer (1633–1718), a lastmaker, was son of 1637 immigrants Seth and Bethia, from Tring, Hertfordshire, both of whom had been church members since 1639. It may be that his £10 fine led to his throwing in his lot with the Baptists, MR, 4, 2: 413. Independents: McLoughlin and Davison, 96, Backus, 319–20; raid: Wood, 90. Prison: On 27 October 1670, William Turner petitioned the General Court for release from Boston Prison, having already spent seven months through the preceding winter there, Wood, 95.

Boston's North End was opened on 15 February 1679. Drinker and others were summoned to court on 5 March 1680. They informed the assistants that Charles II had commanded that "we should enjoy liberty of our meetings." The official response was to lock the gate and nail up the meetinghouse door. Though the indomitable Baptists built a replacement shed, they returned to find governmental locks and nails removed. On 19 May 1680, a face-saving truce was patched together, and a blind eye was thereafter turned upon their activities. This official climbdown marked the muted triumph of "the sin of Jeroboam, who made priests of men so obscure and inconsiderable." It also signalled the onset of the "loathsome" principle of toleration, which would be incorporated in the new charter of the colony in 1691.[75]

The checkered career of the early Charlestown Baptists can only be fully understood in the context of transatlantic imperatives and of wider Massachusetts conflicts. For instance, it was surely no coincidence that Gould and his company set up their own church during the time that the Commissioners of the tolerationist King Charles II were intrusively investigating Massachusetts's illicit extensions of its charter. We have just seen that the Baptists' temerity in opening their own meetinghouse in Boston was supported by Charles II's letter commanding freedom of conscience. Gould had already cited the king's wishes in 1665 as justification for establishing the Baptist church. After 1676, the colony was again under serious threat of royal interference, in the person of implacable royal agent Edward Randolph. In 1684, he would engineer the loss of the beloved 1629 charter. Several signers of the 1668 petition would later collaborate with the new royal government of the colony. The Independent ministers in London had been eager for Charles II to issue a "Declaration of Indulgence" for nonconformists to counteract the punitive Anglican Clarendon Code (1661–65); the non-indulgence of nonconformists by their Massachusetts co-religionists was an embarrassment. Whereas toleration had sprouted during the English Interregnum (1649–1660), and the concept of nonconformity had been recognized after the 1660 Restoration, Massachusetts still maintained its uniformist policy of allowing liberty of conscience only to those who stayed outside its jurisdiction. As a result, in the case of the Baptists, as one of the 1669 English letter-writers had opined: "Fetters put on the feet of errors and

---

[75] Gould: MA: *Sfk Probate Record,* 7: 362. Shepardian: Symmes had died in 1672; Trumbull and Osborne were both fined £1 at June 1673 Middlesex County Court; both appealed to the assistants, Backus, 326; Boston: Backus, 392. War: Savage; Turner had been a sergeant in Cromwell's army, McLoughlin, *Dissent,* 74; see "Mass Violence" below.

heresies . . . have proved wings whereby they raise themselves higher in the thoughts and minds of men."[76]

Conflict within the colony also determined attitudes and policy towards the Baptists. The Half-Way Covenant of 1662 would prove a long-running sore in civil and ecclesiastical politics. While most clergy favored baptismal eligibility of church members' infant grandchildren whose parents were not members, many saints were opposed, as were some vocal ministers such as Increase Mather of the North Church and John Davenport of the First Church, Boston. The situation became critical when in April and May 1669, a group of wealthy merchants and other Half-Way supporters finally broke away from the conservative First Church of Boston and set up the Third Church or Old South Church, which immediately adopted the Half-Way Covenant. There was extreme hostility between these two churches, which spilled out into colony politics. The majority of the Upper House of Assistants were sympathetic to the seceeders, while most deputies were antagonistic both to the new church and to the political influence of the ministerial "interest group." For months in 1670 no colonial business could be done, because each house vetoed the proposals of the other.[77]

The Baptists benefited from this standoff. Those notables opposed to the Half-Way Covenant tended to be sympathetic to the Baptists because they, at least, honored the importance and exclusiveness of baptism. In this camp were Rev. John Oxenbridge, minister of First Church after 1670; Governor Richard Bellingham, and his successor from 1673 to 1679, John Leverett. The move of the Charlestown/Noddle's Island cell to Boston in 1674 assumed Leverett's tacit acquiescence. Other magistrates like lieutenant governor Francis Willoughby and Richard Russell favored the Half-Way Covenant, but also espoused toleration. John Hull grumbled to his diary: "Some of the Magistrates will not permit any punishment to be inflicted on heretics as such." Like Willoughby and his brother-in-law Robert Sedgwick, Leverett had been in republican England and had seen toleration at work. Russell had a Baptist sister-in-law. "The English contagion" had infected the upper reaches of Massachusetts government.[78]

---

[76] Commissioners: see Jack M. Sosin, *English America and the Restoration Monarchy of Charles II* (Lincoln: University of Nebraska Press, 1980), 100–5, 124; *MR*, 4, 2: passim. 1665: McLoughlin, *Dissent*, 59. Randolph: Thompson, *Cambridge Cameos*, 258–65. Collaborators: Lidget, Shrimpton, Usher, Temple. "Fetters": Hull, Diary, 227, quoting Goodwin.

[77] Foster, *Long Argument*, 194, 206–13.

[78] Ibid., 205, 356–57; Hull, Diary, 238.

A "vociferous, bold," convinced, and determined group of "plough-men and tailors" refused to "stoop and bow to everyone." They defied their "betters" with their scriptural certainties. Fortuitous political and international circumstances helped them, but their resistance to ridicule, imprisonment, and threats of banishment was the vital factor in their survival. Over the generations, they grew and prospered, as their Boston church tower demonstrates. In present-day America they are the largest Protestant denomination,[79] dwarfing their erstwhile persecutors.[80]

---

[79]   T. H. Johnson, ed., *Oxford Companion to American History* (New York: OUP, 2006), 62.

[80]   "Vociferous:" Pestana, 57; "ploughmen," Backus, 306; "stoop," Foster, 194.

Succession Crisis, 1678

The Baptists may not have thought much of Rev. Thomas Shepard Jr., Charlestown's teacher since 1659, but he earned a more enviable reputation among the orthodox in both town and colony. In 1672, he was chosen to deliver the prestigious annual election sermon to the General Court, which was published under the title of *Eye Salve*. Still smarting from his rebuff in the 1668 debate, alarmed by calls for toleration and attacks on the clergy in the General Court, he warned that allowing the New England Way to be breached or diluted would surely call down divine wrath on Massachusetts. "Take heed of apostacy" was his watchword. The magistrates should suppress Quakers and Baptists, and encourage higher education to maintain the supply of orthodox ministers.[81]

By 1677, given Governor Leverett's leniency towards the Baptists after 1673, Shepard's providential prediction seemed all too true. Not only had the Almighty inflicted King Philip and King Charles on the colony, but, in 1677, a ship from England brought a smallpox epidemic. "It raged with great malignity at Charlestown."[82] Captain Lawrence Hammond recorded the almost daily deaths in his diary. In December, "one of Mr. Shepard's flock sick with it desired a visit from him. He thought it his duty to comply with his request, caught the disease, and died, aged 43." Shepards did not make old bones. His eulogy by his friend and colleague, Rev. Urian Oakes of Cambridge, described him as "A man of love and peace: wise . . . grave . . . steady . . . serious . . . without enemies . . . active . . . thoughtful . . . modest" and civic-minded. These he chose in preference to "wily . . . morose . . . stiff . . . sour . . . ambitious," which may have been how his opponents depicted him. More simply, Hammond, his parishioner, recorded "22 December

---

81   David D. Hall, *The Faithful Shepherd* (New York: Norton, 1974), 231; Sewall, *Diary*, 30.

82   Hammond, Diary, 168.

1677. Mr. Thomas Shepard, the Reverend and Super-Eminent teacher of this Church, died of smallpox."[83]

In the year of his election sermon, 1672, Thomas Shepard's namesake son entered Harvard at the age of fourteen. A letter with the father's advice to his son has survived. As well as warning him against "youthful lusts, speculative wantonness and secret filthiness, which God sees in the dark and for which God hardens and blinds young men's hearts," he emphasized the cultivation of personal piety. This counsel proved effective. Cotton Mather later celebrated the young Thomas Shepard as a species of elderly teenager showing "maturity, gravity, authority and affection."[84]

His father's health seems to have been delicate for some time. In 1670, the Charlestown selectmen voted £10 "to defray the stipends of assistants in the ministry on the occasion of Mr. Shepard's weakness." After Symmes's death in 1672, various young graduates helped out in preaching and catechising. Between 1674 and 1676, Mr. Joseph Brown, son of the merchant William Brown of Salem, had accommodation rented for him by the town. Another assistant was Mr. Daniel Russell, who had graduated from Harvard in 1669 and preached for a time at New London, the home of John Winthrop Jr. [85]

Cotton Mather's long-winded funeral eulogy of his "dear friend" Thomas Shepard III acknowledged that Charlestown's "very considerable church, under this bereavement [of the sudden death of Thomas Shepard Jr] had now prospect of supply from several quarters." They had already sounded out Joseph Brown as a possible colleague for Thomas Shepard Jr., and after a meeting at Captain Lawrence Hammond's, a committee agreed to renew the church's call to him. However, Brown had already agreed to go to Boston. The committee then invited "Sir Shepard" (a graduate student at the time) to preach to the congregation. Some members felt that at nineteen and without an M.A. he was not ready, and, meeting at Deacon Joseph Lynde's house, proposed consulting neighboring ministers. Isaac Foster (1652–82), the eldest son of Captain William Foster and member of the Harvard class of 1671, was another possible homegrown candidate,

---

[83]   King Philip's War raged from summer 1675 to 1676. See below, "Mass Violence"; Edward Randolph, the royal investigator, arrived on his first visit in 1676. Epidemic: see "Ordeals of Captain Foster," above. Hunnewell, 166; Hall, *Faithful Shepherd*, 263. Old bones: Thomas Shepard Sr. had died aged 45 in 1649 when Thomas Jr. was 14; his uncle Rev. Samuel Shepard of Rowley died at the age of 26. Hammond, Diary, 168–71.

[84]   Mather, *Magnalia*, 2: 142–53. At this time, Harvard was entering its period of near-extinction under the presidency of Leonard Hoare. Morison, *Harvard College in the Seventeenth Century*, 390–409. Thomas Shepard Jr. resigned his college fellowship in protest in 1673.

[85]   Hunnewell, 167; CTR, 3: 110; CTrR, 3: 59A; Savage.

but he was appointed a fellow of Harvard in 1678. The search committee must have suspected further providential interference.[86]

In the spring of 1678, a meeting of the church members was convened. As is typical of such gatherings, a large number of candidates was proposed: another approach to Joseph Brown, or Gershom Hobart (1645–1707, HC 1667), or four local possibilities: Samuel Nowell (1634–88, HC 1653); who had published *Abraham in Arms* in 1678 asserting liberty of property; Zechariah Symmes Jr. (1638–1708, HC 1657), preacher at Bradford, Mass.; Daniel Russell; or Thomas Shepard III.[87]

On 19 May 1678, Shepard, by now a "little more than 20 years of age . . . with a very charming, solid and serious gravity" preached his invited sermon "on Exodus, xv, 2: 'He is my father's God, and I will exalt Him.' Upon this," continues Mather, "his father's flock were at no rest until they had obtained his establishment" as their choice. Here, the normally wordy eulogist ruthlessly telescopes a long confrontation and skates over powerful opposition to his friend.[88]

At this point the doubts were voiced by Mr. Thomas Graves. He was a leading citizen and church member of Charlestown as well as a former Harvard tutor, and objections from him about Shepard's inexperience and immaturity would be taken seriously. At a church meeting on 9 June, when the committee canvassed proposals, Mr. Elias Maverick nominated erstwhile ministerial assistant Daniel Russell. Many members present voiced their approval, and in the absence of other nominations, a majority of the church and some committee members voted for Russell. Captain Lawrence Hammond, chairman of the committee and of the Charlestown board of selectmen, complained that this decision-making was "too sudden, it was imposing of [on] them"; he asked for a delay. After much haggling, a postponement of sixteen days was agreed upon.[89]

---

[86] Committee: Lawrence Hammond, Thomas Graves, William Stitson, John Cutler, Aaron Ludkin, Jacob Green, John Hayman, Joseph Lynde, and James Russell. "Charlestown Church Affairs," 3*CMHS*, 1 (1825), 248–64, here 254; Brown: Hammond, Diary, 170; Brown died in May 1678, having been ill for some time. Foster: shortly after graduating, he had been captured by "Turks" along with his father; see "Ordeals of Captain Foster" above. He eventually settled as minister at Hartford, Connecticut.

[87] Hobart: son of Rev. Peter, minister of Hingham, ordained at refounded Groton after King Philip's War in 1679, but dismissed in 1685. Nowell: he had occasionally preached, but never held a settled ministerial post; in 1680 he was elected an assistant, and was very active in defense of the old charter. Symmes: he would preach for 14 years at frontier Bradford on the Merrimack before being ordained there in 1682; he was married to Susannah, the sister of Mr. Thomas Graves.

[88] *Magnalia*, 146.

[89] On the names in this paragraph, see below. Graves was a brother-in-law of Russell, through his brother's marriage to Russell's sister, but he was far from ardent in Russell's favor, as will be

One of the committee members, Deacon John Cutler, had the arduous task of moderating the full church meeting of 25 June, six months after Thomas Shepard Jr's death. "Spirits [and probably voices too] were raised." The first proposal was to call Thomas Shepard III. This immediately provoked the Daniel Russell camp, who contrasted their man's experience and maturity. The majority agreed, but Hammond argued that they would lose the incomparable Shepard, whose sermon had made such an impression only seven Sabbaths before. Some suggested that the easy way out of this impasse was to call both men, but Hammond, Graves, and Deacon Ludkin, significantly town treasurer in the aftermath of the financially ruinous Indian War, dismissed this expensive solution as "irregular, unreasonable and out of the way of God." After "much talk to little purpose," the ill-tempered meeting closed without decision.[90]

The church was not unanimous for either candidate, the normal requirement for important decisions, and the committee had also become irreconcilably divided. Hammond, Graves, Ludkin and Jacob Green (merchant son of late Elder John Green) resisted the compromise of a joint call, but as a minority "would be passive." At yet another church meeting on 7 July, however, they reiterated their objections, and despairing of unanimity, the church agreed to seek outside advice. But where? Some committee members wanted to consult Boston's ministers, but (perhaps because of bitter divisions among the Boston churches) Deacon Joseph Lynde and Mr. James Russell proposed Rev. Urian Oakes of Cambridge and Rev. John Sherman of Watertown. Without a unanimous call, neither would come!

At the fifth church meeting in two months, the search committee, with four favoring a joint call and five against, threw in the towel. The aged Deacon William Stitson (1602–91) took over the chairmanship of the 22 July meeting. His ancient authority seems to have restored order. A joint approach to both Shepard and Russell was "passed generally," and Daniel Russell agreed to supply "present help." A new committee under Stitson's chairmanship was elected. Former members Cutler, Lynde, and James Russell remained; Elias Maverick, Richard Kettle, and John Phillips were new. The committee quickly went to work. A week later they could report that Thomas Shepard would "in time come to help us." On 15 September, with Russell's formal letter of acceptance, Deacon Stitson, seeking unanimity, asked if there were any objections. Suddenly, the unwonted calm of the previous two (harvesting) months was shattered. Thomas

<hr />

seen. On Russell, HC 69, twice chosen a Fellow, or Tutor, of Harvard, see Sibley, 2: 284–87.

[90] "Charlestown Church Affairs," 254.

Graves and Lawrence Hammond both opposed. At last the real reason clattered out. "Mr. Daniel Russell is not a fit man," said Graves. Nonetheless, the church proceeded to vote for Russell "generally." Then Hammond was on his feet. Mr. Shepard had not been asked "if he could close with Mr. Russell." The church's actions had been "very rash and unreasonable." In the no doubt shocked aftermath of this personal vilification, some understandably confused member asked whether the church should renew its call to Thomas Shepard. Graves lashed out: "It was unreasonable and unseasonable!" When asked "a reason, he said he would give none, and so departed the house." A conciliatory voice suggested calling a council of neighboring churches. This took the sting out of the local, festering dispute. On 20 October formal letters went out from the committee to Boston, Cambridge, and Watertown.[91]

The Special Council for Ministerial Appointment that met at Charlestown on 5 November 1678 was extremely high-powered. Its moderator was Rev. John Sherman, long-serving minister of Watertown; its scribe was John Richards, rising figure in colonial politics and inveterate opponent of the Half-Way Covenant at the North Church in Boston. His minister Increase Mather was present, along with other Boston clergy, Samuel Willard of the Third Church (Old South), and James Allen of First Church. The Magistrates were led by Governor Leverett and assistants Thomas Danforth and Edward Tyng, with colony secretary Edward Rawson. The elders and deacons of the three towns made up a total of twenty-three councillors.[92]

---

[91]   Stitson had been an inhabitant since 1632, a church member, with his wife, since 1633, and a deacon since 1659; he had been a selectman 19 times and deputy five; a brewer by trade, he left estate of £503, of which nearly £400 was real estate. Cutler (1628–94) was also a deacon, and Lynde (1636–1727) the son of a deacon; both were rising men in the town where they had lived since childhood. On James Russell, see below. Mr. Elias Maverick (1604–84) was a somewhat shadowy figure. He had come in the *Mary and John* with his father Rev. John in 1630. He had married Anna Harris, daughter of Charlestown's first ferryman, about 1634, a year after becoming a church member. Fellow Devonian William Stitson was his stepfather-in-law, having become Anna's mother's second husband in the mid-1630s. Maverick's elder brother Samuel, in New England since 1624, proved a thorn in Massachusetts's side, especially as one of Charles II's commissioners 1664–66. Elias lived on Mystic Side and owned land on Hog Island, but by the 1660s was ensign of Boston's North Company. Richard Kettle (ca. 1614–80), a cooper, seven times selectman, and church member since 1633, was sergeant in the militia and very active in town business. Captain John Phillips (1633–1726) was a master mariner and merchant who had been a church member since only 1676, though his wife had been admitted in 1660; however, he already had a seat in the meeting house next to Mr. James Russell's and would soon become a leading figure in Massachusetts; see below "Dominion and Revolution." The first record I have found of him in connection with Charlestown is in 1654, MxCC RB, 1: 47.

[92]   Full list: "Charlestown Church Affairs," 254. Sherman: Thompson, *Divided*, 74–80. On Richards, see above, "Cutting One Another's Throats." Allen and Mather had both opposed the Half-Way Covenant, which Willard favoured. Urian Oakes of Cambridge (president pro tempore of Harvard) was a notable absentee, for reasons unknown.

The first document they considered was a dissent against the call to Daniel Russell by Lawrence Hammond, Thomas Graves, John Hayman, Aaron Ludkin, all of the first committee, and Mr. Samuel Ward (1593–1682), a wealthy Charlestown cooper and cattleman. The call had been "too undeliberate and over hasty . . . Brethren had slighted the advice of neighbouring reverend elders . . . but had concentred on Mr. Russell to give an immediate call . . . They were troubled at us because we demurred at the sudden vote . . . [Their response to counsel from the pulpit to] take advice was to proceed to a vote the very next day." This rush to Russell had been deeply unjust to Thomas Shepard III, another near-unanimous choice. He had not been consulted about Russell, and the dissenters had "grounds to fear that Mr. Russell and Mr. Shepard could not agree." They thought this far more worrying for the future than concerns that Shepard would effectively take the choice of a colleague away from the church if given a veto. Finally, apologizing for their "bluntness," they opined, "Mr. Russell is not meet for this place."[93]

The unsigned answer to these charges claimed, "We have proceeded according to the law . . . Mr. Russell is a well-known member of our church, a preacher able and orthodox and held in high account among our people." Nothing explicit was said about Shepard, his youth, his lack of an M.A., or his inexperience as preacher or pastor.[94]

Events, or divine providence, again intervened. Before the Council had time to come to a conclusion, Daniel Russell died on 4 January 1679, at the age of 32. Two days later, the Town Meeting approved spending £10 from Richard Russell's bequest towards his son's funeral and the costs of the Council. On 1 September 1679, Thomas Shepard III was voted £100 per annum as town minister. He was ordained on 5 May 1680. Five years later, Cotton Mather recorded in his diary: "7d. 4m [June 1685]. My dear Friend, Mr. Shepard of Charlestown, being taken suddenly ill, I preached for him in the forenoon . . . At night, unto the consternation of me, and

---

[93] "Church Affairs," 248–53. On Hammond and Graves, see below. Deacon Aaron Ludkin (ca. 1618–1694), a glover probably from Norwich, had settled in Charlestown ca. 1651 after marrying Anna, daughter of glover George Hepburne and widow of Manus Sally. He had previously lived in Hingham, 1635–ca. 47, and Braintree, *GM*, 4: 358–59; Wyman, 635. Hayman (ca. 1611–86), a ropemaker, had arrived in Charlestown in 1663. He was constable in 1668, selectman in 1669, frequent member of town committees, and foreman of the Court of Assistants jury in 1673. He had three black servants, and a son-in-law merchant-skipper who died in Algerian captivity in 1678. With James Russell, John Phillips, and others, he was an investor in the Charlestown Dry Dock in the late 1670s. A church member with his wife in 1668, he occupied a front seat in the meetinghouse by 1678. Wyman 489, MxCC RB, 3: 121, 237, D & O, 3: folio 70, Mass Archives 12 June 1679, Hull, Diary, 163, CTR, 3: 216; see below, "Wealthy Women: Sarah Hayman Elson." Ward: Wyman, 993, *R*, 143 (1989), 346–49).

[94] "Church Affairs," 253.

all his friends, he died." Like his uncle Samuel, he had failed to reach his twenty-seventh birthday.[95]

This yearlong hiatus in a settled ministry for Charlestown exposed disturbing divisions within the church. It pitted some leading men of the second generation against the majority of members. It is time to examine the two most vociferous of these notables. Lawrence Hammond (ca. 1638–99), a first cousin of deputy governor Francis Willoughby, had arrived in Charlestown (possibly from Virginia) in 1661. The next year he became a church member and rose rapidly in military and civil rank. Captain of the militia company in 1669, he was elected selectman twelve times, and deputy six; he proved a highly efficient town clerk and man of business, but failed in his candidacy for assistant in 1677 and 1685. His mercantile wealth increased through his four marriages; his well-endowed brides included the widows of Francis Willoughby and Dr. William Gerrish. He was much in demand as an accountant and auditor. As holder of a foreseat in the meeting house and as chairman of the church's search committee, he was not afraid of voicing his opinion and expected to be heard with respect.[96]

His collaborator and almost exact contemporary, Thomas Graves (1638–97), was the son of the famous "Admiral" who had so distinguished himself in the Cromwellian service. A Harvard graduate in the class of 1656, a tutor there, a doctor and husband of two doctors' widows, he too occupied a meetinghouse foreseat and was selectman, deputy, and commissioner for small causes in this contentious year. His former pupil Samuel Sewall described Graves as "obstinate" and somewhat eclectic in his church attendance: "He kept to the church of Charlestown as to his most constant attendance, especially on the Lord's Day." Together, or with their well-heeled allies, they plainly resented being swept along by the unreasoning enthusiasms of the "generality." Their education, wealth, offices and prestige should have bestowed special privilege. However, Hammond, Graves, Ludkin, Hayman, and Ward had all arrived late in Charlestown: Ward and Ludkin in the late 1650s, Hammond and Hayman in the 1660s,

---

[95] CTR, 4: 3, 15. In 1680, Russell's widow Mehitabel (Wyllys) married Rev. Isaac Foster, and returned to Hartford. Shepard: Magnalia, 2: 151.

[96] Wyman, 461–62; CTR, 2-4: passim. MR, 4.2, 5: passim. Willoughby's mother had a sister Jane Hammond in Virginia in 1662; I have been unable to locate her or Lawrence in Virginia records, or to find any links with the famous Captain Thomas Willoughby of Lower Norfolk County, Virginia. Mercantile: "Extracts from the Gerrish Papers," R, 36 (1882) 396, has a somewhat waspish 15 December 1685 Hammond letter to "Dr Br," Captain John Gerrish, and accounts of Hammond's supplies of rum, molasses, fabrics and shoes sent north to Dover in part payment for 23,500 feet of boards from the Piscataqua sawmills.

and Graves possibly not permanently until the 1670s. In an age that treasured longevity, continuity and tradition, this lack of founding experience could have reduced their authority.[97]

Although Graves and Hammond seem to have differed in their opinions of Shepard's readiness to lead so important a church as Charlestown, they both agreed that Russell was a second-rater. It is difficult to tell how justified this judgment was. Russell (1646–79) came from the leading family, and the richest family, in the town. He graduated from Harvard at the elderly age of twenty-three, and had he survived, Charlestown would have been his first settled ministry, at the age of thirty-three. His father's 1674 will had no specific legacies for Daniel, as it did for his elder brother James or his two sisters, though he did inherit a residual third of the estate, £500, and was a witness to the document. At about age thirty, he married the sixteen-year-old Mehitabel Wyllys, daughter of a leading assistant of Connecticut and niece of James's wife. Other than the majority's declared confidence in him, little is known about his ministerial qualities.[98]

Another mystery surrounds the attitude of Daniel's elder brother, Mr. James Russell (1640–1709). He had assumed his father's mantle in Charlestown after 1674. He was administrator of his large and highly complex estate for ten years, ran the family fishery and trading business, invested in the Atherton Associates' Rhode Island land speculations, and was deeply engaged in town, county, and colony affairs. Though James Russell was a member of both search committees, we never learn his opinion of any of the candidates. His remaining on the second committee even when other notables such as Hammond, Graves, Hayman, Ludkin and Green had resigned hints at his unobtrusive support for his brother after Elias Maverick had nominated him on 7 June 1678. It is also feasible that he had doubts about Shepardian attitudes to toleration. He may have foreseen difficulties with fellow officers and business partners that could arise if he were too aggressive an advocate.[99]

---

[97] Graves: CTR, 3: 203; Sewall, *Diary*, 374; Wyman, 432–33; wives: Elizabeth Chickering and Sarah Alcock. Though born in Charlestown, it is not clear whether Thomas accompanied his father back to England in the late 1640s; from 1652 he lived in neighboring Cambridge.

[98] Richard Russell's will is in Rodgers, 3: 390–98. On the testator, see above "Godly Merchants," and "Thomas Gould."

[99] Business: see above "Adolescent Port Life," and MxCC D&O, 4: folios 82 (fishery), 83 (timber from New Hampshire), 111 (trade with Connecticut). *Book of Possessions*, 168–69, partner in Charlestown Dry Dock (with Hayman, and Phillips); Atherton Associates: Johnson, *Adjustment to Empire*, 20; offices: *MR*, 5: passim; deputy 1679, assistant 1680–86, colony treasurer 1680–86, 91 seq. Town: constable 1669, selectman 1674–84; town clerk 1677–78. He had married Mehitabel Haynes, the aunt of Mehitabel Wyllys, Daniel's wife, in 1664.

The alleged incompatibility of Russell and Shepard may have been purely personal. There could have been some envy by the older Russell of Shepard's "star quality," though Russell left his "rival" a bequest in his will. The prospect of a Shepardian "apostolic succession" excluding other ministerial candidates may have grated. However, theological differences may have divided them as well. Shepard's father had been a powerful advocate of the Half-Way Covenant and of Massachusetts uniformity. His role as fierce, if ultimately ineffective, harrier of Baptists was part and parcel of the non-tolerating Half-Way attitude. Richard Russell, on the other hand, had favored toleration. The North Church in Boston, which Maverick probably attended, was similarly critical of the Half-Way compromise, and was where the Baptists eventually set up their church. The pastorate of Thomas Shepard III would certainly show a marked rise in those "Children of the Covenant," grandchildren of full members, taking the Half-Way Covenant, though 1681 also saw a large number of new full members, and even more baptisms. Shepard may have been implementing his father's stated wish that *all* children should be eligible for baptism. Exclusivity seemed to be ebbing.[100]

The conflict over who should succeed Thomas Shepard Jr. in 1678 pitted a small group of Charlestown notables led by Captain Lawrence Hammond and Dr. Thomas Graves against the "rash, sudden . . . unreasonable and unseasonable" whims and fancies (as the notables saw them) of the great majority of church members. The authority of these recently established second-generation leaders was being challenged. As we have seen and shall see again, this was not the last time in the tumultuous 1680s that they would experience discomfiture. The previously biddable followers had begun to exert agency. Church membership—brotherhood and sisterhood—conferred not just spiritual privilege but also the potential for shaping events and decision-making. No wonder the grandees were rattled.[101]

---

[100] Thomas Shepard III had been the verbatim shorthand recorder of the confrontation between Benanuel Bowers, Baptist/Quaker, and the fiercely intolerant Middlesex magistrate Thomas Danforth in the summer of 1677, Thompson, *Cambridge Cameos,* 173–82. See above, "Thomas Gould and the Baptist Debates," and Ramsbottom, 177–78, 184–85.

[101] See above, "The Stinted Common," "Thomas Gould," and below, "Dominion and Revolution." At the Reform Synod of 1679, where the "pride" of servants and the poorer sort was a major issue, Thomas Danforth and Rev. Solomon Stoddart expressed indignation when Ralph Wheelock of Medfield described as a "provoking evil" the fact that ministers and magistrates were not taxed proportionately. Their sense of social hierarchy was outraged at such egalitarian urges. R. P. Gildrie, *The Profane, the Civil, and the Godly* (University Park: Pennsylvania State University Press, 1994), 33–44, 59, 105. Sewall, *Diary,* 326, 16 January 1695, hints that Graves was again resisting the appointment of "another minister" at Charlestown to help Rev. Charles Morton, despite the recommendations of a committee chaired by the Massachusetts lieutenant governor. Agency: Diane Purkiss, *The English Civil War: A People's History* (London: Harper Collins, 2007), 453.

Conclusion:
From Symmes to Morton

Between its foundation in 1632 and the death in 1698 of its sixth minister, Charles Morton, the Charlestown church underwent considerable change. Its 1690s services, sermons, shared attitudes, membership, and facilities would have been recognizable to its early members but nonetheless subtly or strikingly, even sometimes worryingly, different. Some developments, like the Half-Way Covenant, resulted from internal pressures or needs. Others were externally induced: by different English regimes and policies, or by the growth of the Atlantic economy. We will examine these transitions in two ways, comparative and developmental. This section will contrast the era of the first settled minister, Zechariah Symmes, with Morton's ministry; then explore the gradual evolution of the church as revealed by its surviving records.[102]

Symmes's and Morton's lives all but spanned the 17th century: the one born in 1599, the other dying in 1698. If we think of the differences in English society, and its economic and international standing in the dying years of Queen Elizabeth's reign and those of King William III, the contrast is breathtaking. While distance might insulate Massachusetts from some of the more revolutionary twists and turns of Stuart history, that cushioning was decreasing (as we shall see) as the century progressed. The ministries of Symmes and Morton reflected both the English experience and its heightened impact.[103]

---

[102] Here we ignore the troubled ministries of Revs. Thomas James and James Allen, neither of whom were in sympathy with the spiritual or communal "personality" of the church. Both eventually returned to England; see the Introduction to this section.

[103] Barry Coward, *The Stuart Age* (London: Longman, 1989), 409–60.

Symmes was thirty-five when he was ordained at Charlestown in 1634; he ministered to the church and people there for the next thirty-seven years. He never explained why he came with his family to Massachusetts, but the date of his embarkation suggests that he was driven to emigrate by the promotion of William Laud to the Archbishopric of Canterbury in 1633. This gave nationwide thrust to the campaign of anti-Puritan persecution, announced by its opening salvo, the 1633 reissue of James I's *Book of Sports*, which outraged godly sabbatarians.[104]

Symmes was a rising young Puritan star. Son of a famous Kentish minister, he had been one of the elite preachers at St. Antholin's in London, and then was selected by a wealthy Puritan pressure group for funding at the important parish of Dunstable. Several leading families followed him from this district to Charlestown, where he was quickly welcomed and ordained.[105]

In education Symmes was typical of the founding generation of New England ministers. He had studied at Emmanuel College, Cambridge, under its iconic founding master Laurence Chaderton, graduating in 1621. His preparatory schooling at Canterbury, a notorious Puritan hotspot, would have been fiercely disciplined, with repetition, rote learning, drilling of academic boys in Latin, and frequent resort to the birch or cane. At Cambridge, Latin would continue to be the language of instruction and response; the method of logical argumentation would be the syllogism; and the dominant theological approach would be Ramist, a combination of the Aristotelian and Calvinist methods. The usual effect of such an regimented and closed educational system was that clergy and pious lay graduates would speak in a similar arcane way using a similar arcane language, but as we have seen with Thomas Shepard Jr., they might find it impossible to argue effectively with scriptural literalists like Thomas Gould or graduates of "the university of life" like Captain John Trumbull. Few of Symmes's peers displayed an adventurous, secular curiosity.[106]

---

[104] The *Book of Sports* listed games and exercises permitted on Sundays. Thompson, *Divided,* 29–31; Thompson, *Mobility and Migration,* 19, 23, 53.

[105] Edward Johnson, long familiar with the Symmes family, mentions Zechariah's father William in *WWPSS,* 101. See above, "Origins."

[106] Chaderton was Master of the Puritan hotbed from 1584 to 1622. Schooling: Keith Thomas, "Rule and Misrule in the Schools of Early Modern England," Stenton Lecture, 9 (1975), University of Reading. Thomas Shepard's "Autobiography," in Michael McGiffert, *God's Plot* (Amherst: University of Massachusetts Press, 1972), 39–46 is one of many accounts of Cambridge life at this time. On Cambridge syllabus and intellectual atmosphere: S. E. Morison, *The Founding of Harvard College* (Cambridge: Harvard University Press, 1936), chs. 1–6. On Ramus: Perry Miller, *The New England Mind: The Seventeenth Century* (Boston: Beacon, 1965), passim, esp. 493–501.

Captain Edward Johnson was born in the same year and in the same Canterbury parish as Symmes. His brother had married a Dunstable parishioner, and he himself spent his first New England years in Charlestown. He thus wrote with considerable authority about Symmes. The identifying personal quality he emphasizes is "zeal," being "valiant in faith," a "Champion in Prayer." As an excoriator of antinomianism, Johnson bid "Zachary" to deploy his religious devotion in the battle for conformity against "sin, Satan, and all the enemies of Christ's kingdom." He should make war against "all crooked ways that Christ true worship miss." He "wilt not suffer wolves thy flock to rout [with false doctrine], though close they creep with sheep skins on their back." Symmes did not need any additional coaxing. As we have seen, throughout his long ministry he was a zealot against any dissent from the New England Way. Almost his first action after disembarking from *The Griffin* was to report the unorthodox opinions of his shipmate Anne Hutchinson to Governor Dudley. His hot-tempered hostility toward Thomas Gould and the Baptists was recorded in revealing detail by his victim. In October 1659, he was one of the ministers who went to the prison where once-banished Quaker missionaries awaited execution. He "reviled them," and doubtless applauded the subsequent hanging of two leading Friends. In May 1662, Symmes was one of four spokesmen of the synod who commended the Half-Way Covenant to the General Court. The Covenant was intended to be a modest expansion of associate church membership which would also ensure that "the rising generation" would be subject to church discipline. It was an anti-tolerationist assertion of continued uniformity, at a time when even vengeful recrudescent English cavaliers recognized that enforced conformity was no longer feasible.[107]

Though Charlestown, along with its neighbors, represented a utopian experiment in a remote "wilderness," a project to establish a model scriptural church by God-chosen groups, its whole mindset was traditionalist and providential. In its founders' eyes harked back to the primitive churches established by the first Christians before the corrupt sediment of human inventions coated their original purity. Its belief system was rooted in the theocentric universe, where all events and all fates resulted from divine intention. The saint's life work should be to discover God's will and unquestioningly obey it. Ideal believers should be essentially passive in relation to the Almighty. Their early modern world was dangerous, unpredictable and

---

[107] See above, "Origins," "Antinomian Crisis," and "Thomas Gould." Robert G. Pope, *The Half-Way Covenant,* (Princeton, NJ: Princeton University Press, 1969), 7, 53. *WWPSS*, 101.

uncontrollable. Without divine help, they were doomed. These were the apprehensions, the attitudes, and the ambitions that Zechariah Symmes and his generation brought to the New World.[108]

Charles Morton (1627–98) was born in Symmes's second year at Dunstable and would have been seven years old when his forerunner emigrated. Morton was baptized in Cornwall and his mother was Cornish, but when he was three his father, Rev. Nicholas Morton, an Emmanuel graduate, was translated from his remote West Country parish to be preacher and chaplain at the hectic South Bank London church of St. Saviour's, Southwark. Here he would have been a neighbor of John Harvard and several other emigrants to Charlestown, as well as their business partners who remained behind. Nicholas died in 1640, when Charles was thirteen. At the end of the Civil War, he went up to Queens' College, Cambridge, but after royalists were expelled from Oxford, he transferred there, and took his B.A. as a member of Wadham College in 1649.[109]

Morton might have said, like Dean Acheson, that he was "present at the creation." Wadham College, Oxford, under its new warden John Wilkins, was the center of mathematical and scientific research and thinking that would lead to the creation of the Royal Society in 1660 and to the British Scientific Revolution, a major engine of the eighteenth-century Enlightenment. Morton was a brilliant young mathematician whose genius was encouraged in Wilkins's circle, which included later emigrant Samuel Lee. Here he developed scientific problem-solving through close observation and experiment along Baconian principles. These methods and approaches towards the natural world would continue to affect the rest of his long career.[110]

In 1653 Morton left Oxford, and after a brief ministry at Takeley, Essex, he returned to Cornwall, where he married Joan (_____), and became minister at Blisland on the northwest edge of Bodmin Moor.

---

[108] T. D. Bozeman, *To Live Ancient Lives* (Chapel Hill: University of North Carolina Press, 1988); Keith Thomas, *Religion and the Decline of Magic* (Harmondsworth: Penguin, 1974), 3–24.

[109] There is an outstanding sketch of Morton's life in *ODNB* by Dewey D. Wallace, Jr.

[110] A. R. Hall, "The Royal Society," in Robert Latham, ed. and comp., *Companion to the Diary of Samuel Pepys* (London: Bell & Hyman, 1983), 10: 361–68. The most famous members of Wilkins's circle were Robert Boyle, William Petty, and Christopher Wren; others are described in S. E. Morison, "Introduction," Charles Morton, *Compendium Physicae* (Boston: Colonial Society of Massachusetts, 1940), xii–xiii. The group was called "Oxonian Sparkles" in the history of the Royal Society, *ODNB*, s. n. Wilkins. Recent studies of the "new science" include Harold Cook, *Matters of Exchange: Medicine and Science in the Dutch Golden Age* (New Haven: Yale University Press, 2007); S. Shapin, *Leviathan and the Air Pump* (Princeton: Princeton University Press, 1994); and S. Shapin, *The Scientific Revolution* (Chicago: University of Chicago Press, 1996).

Here he established an association of ministers, who met regularly, like a Presbyterian "classis" (group). He was ejected as a nonconformist at the Restoration. He returned to London in 1666, having lost property in the Great Fire. In 1672, after Charles II's Declaration of Indulgence to dissenters, Morton started his "Dissenting Academy" at Kennington, beyond Southwark, moving north across the river to Newington Green in 1675. He continued teaching until the accession of James II in 1685, when he was forced to close his academy after harassment and arrest. In his sixtieth year, he sailed for New England with fellow Cornishman and former pupil Samuel Penhallow, arriving in Charlestown in June 1686.[111]

Morton was a great catch for Massachusetts. He arrived with a dazzling reputation among Puritans as a thinker and an educator. His academy had helped to revolutionize teaching and learning. His paternal approach to teaching was to "awaken and excite" the interest and enthusiasm of his fifty-odd students. He encouraged curiosity, experiment, and observation; his own study of the migration of birds was published by the Royal Society in 1676. The usual dominance of classics was leavened by scientific, philosophical and mathematical inquiry. Instruction was in English. Morton had had philosophical training at Oxford, where Ramus's system of logic, so pervasive in Cambridge, was not popular. He was attracted to the ideas of the French Jansenists who sought to explore and explain the interaction between faith and reason. For them, "reasonableness," or "rational living," was the great virtue. Morton defined the purpose of logic as fulfilling "the need of some methodical frame to hold things together." Newton's *Principia* and Locke's *Second Treatise of Civil Government* aimed to meet just such needs. Morton produced manuscript textbooks such as *A Logick System, Pneumaticks,* and *Compendium Physicae* that referred not only to Galileo, Copernicus, and Descartes, but also to contemporary giants like Robert Boyle and William Petty. Morton's pupils in England included Daniel Defoe, Samuel Wesley, and many who later became Puritan ministers. The curriculum and teaching at his school and other dissenting academies were far superior to what Oxbridge offered. Morton hoped to become president of Harvard, but his arrival during the threatening Dominion period ruled out his appointment as provocatively "offensive" and "obnoxious."[112]

---

[111] Classis: see Thompson, *Divided,* 26; Penhallow (1665–1726) became a great man in New Hampshire and a historian of later Indian wars. Samuel Lee, an Oxonian colleague at Newington, arrived in August 1686 and became minister at Bristol. Samuel Sewall described meeting a former pupil of Morton's at Deal in Kent in 1689, *Diary,* 236.

[112] *ODNB;* Morison, *Harvard in the Seventeenth Century,* 236–51; J. W. Ashley-Smith, *The Birth*

"America's first professional philosopher," as Morton has been called, was a breath of fresh air both to Harvard College and to Charlestown church. Though deprived of the presidency of the college, his books and ideas led to major curricular reform there during the 1690s. He was influential for young academics like Thomas and William Brattle and John Leverett. Jonathan Edwards inherited Mortonian methods and ideas through his father Timothy (who graduated in the Harvard class of 1691). Morton's scribal textbooks were adopted for students. Captain Lawrence Hammond described in his diary an experiment conducted by Morton about the sense of hearing:

> We pricked a knife's point into the belly of a harpsichord, causing [a deaf and dumb man] to hold the haft in his teeth; then two of us severally played in his sight, the one harmonically some tunes, the other clashing many of the keys at once; the poor man expressed wonderful joy at the harmony, and embraced him that played it; but withal showed as much displeasure and contempt of him that had troubled him with the discord. Then, blindfold, we set him in the former posture; and he that before had clashed, now played regularly, and the other that before had made music, now jumbled with the keys; this we did several times, shifting hands as we thought fit, and between every time unbound his eyes. The man still after a musical playing showed his kindness and affection to him whom he had seen play when at first it pleased him, and so on the contrary. By which it appeared plainly that, though he mistook the persons, yet he very well perceived the sound and its affections, and distinguished between the harmony and the discord, with an answerable satisfaction or regret. Mr. Morton gave this instance to note a probability that the mouth is not devoid of a power of perceiving sound, and that by the tender nerves of the teeth etc.

This kind of experiment was typical of the new scientific method. Morton briefly ran an informal academy in his house at Charlestown, but closed it when Harvard expressed disquiet at such competition. In 1692 he was appointed a fellow of Harvard, and held the honorific post of Vice-President. Eighteenth-century Harvard would be a radically renewed center of

of Modern Education (London: Macmillan, 1954), 55–61; F. A. Turk, "Charles Morton and the Development of British Science in the 17th Century," *Journal of the Royal Institute of Cornwall*, New Series, 4 (1961–64), 353–63. *Compendium Physicae*, with an introduction by S. E. Morison, was reissued in *CSMP,* 33 (1940).

learning after decades in the doldrums, thanks in considerable part to his impetus.[113]

Such was Morton's reputation when he arrived in Charlestown, such was his unfamiliarity with the New England Way, and such the political situation, that he had the opportunity to dispense with religious practices he disagreed with. Since he was more of a Presbyterian (as he described himself on his teaching license in 1672), these changes were several. When he assumed his office on 5 November 1686, for instance, he insisted on installation, or self-seating, rather than ordination with chosen ministers' "laying on of hands." Unconventionally, he himself gave the address, drawing attention to the date, the eighty-first anniversary of the popish Gunpowder Plot against James I and his parliament. The current presence of a popish James on the English throne would not have been missed by his hearers. Traditionalists like Cotton Mather found these variations deeply offensive, but Morton had the authority to insist. On 30 January 1690 Morton joined in marriage Luke Greenough and Abigail Hammond, the daughter of Captain Lawrence Hammond. This office had previously been performed by magistrates, but political uncertainties cast doubt on magistrates' legitimacy. The Cambridge association of ministers, which Morton founded, was based on a Presbyterian model he had encountered in Cornwall. He revived the idea of spreading the gospel to the Native Americans, less than popular since King Philip's War and frontier fighting in Maine. Despite these innovations, he was quickly welcomed into Massachusetts society, and Sewall records not only hearing his sermons and lectures in Charlestown and Boston, but also attending a group fishing trip, making a visit to Morton's farm in Mystic, and walking with him on the frozen surface of the Charles.[114]

The church at Charlestown was treated to important innovations in membership policy soon after Morton's installation. In 1687, he performed eighty baptisms, compared to six in 1686—reflecting "a far more comprehensive [and Presbyterian] view of church membership." He also encouraged greater flexibility in admission to the Half-Way Covenant, and presided over a church renewal campaign that resulted in twenty-one new full members. In the absence of town meetings (banned by the Dominion), the church was the only community center, and Morton's practice of

---

[113]   Edwards: Perry Miller, *Jonathan Edwards* (New York: Sloan, 1949). Edwards, at the age of eleven or twelve, wrote a natural history essay on balloon spiders, based on careful observation. Hammond, Diary, 148–49.

[114]   Sewall, 122–25, 118, 119, 132, 143, 177, 345; Hammond, Diary, 151; *ODNB*.

baptizing "professing" (as opposed to covenanting) adolescents and young adults strengthened communal solidarity in the face of serious threats to the town's rights and property. Morton became something of a hero to the "popular" party in September 1687 when his sermon on persecution was deemed seditious by the royal authorities. He was eventually acquitted. By the end of his pastorate, Charlestown had more of the sense of an inclusive parish than an exclusive, members-only church.[115]

In the late summer of 1688, four children of John Goodwin, a stone-mason in Boston but still a member of Charlestown church, were afflicted with horrific pains in various parts of their bodies. Along with four Boston ministers, Morton took his turn in praying with the children for an hour. The eventual diagnosis was of "possession" [more accurately "bewitchment"] by a neighboring Irish washerwoman, Mary Glover, who was hanged after trial on 16 November 1688. Four years later, the even more hair-raising witch craze erupted at Salem. Morton was one of the signatories to Increase Mather's *Cases of Conscience*, which condemned the use of unsupported spectral evidence and effectively snuffed out the hysteria. This was the last such witch-hunting outbreak in Massachusetts, and the consequent decline in superstition among the educated classes can be seen as a mirror of rising scientific and philosophical skepticism.[116]

On 1 June 1697, Charlestown grandee Thomas Graves was buried. Sewall was there. "Mr. Morton is very short-breath, sat upon a tomb in the burying place, and said, for ought he knew he should be next." In the harsh January weather of 1698, this proponent of "cheerful Christianity" and "warm-hearted practical piety rather than concern with theological orthodoxy" was taken sick. Sewall paid his last visit to him on 8 April 1698, and Morton died three days later. In response to Sewall's suggestion that since speaking was so difficult, he should rather converse silently with God, Morton's last feverish words were "Excellent things. If I could receive them and live up to them." The preacher at his funeral "insisted pretty much . . . that the life of persecutors was as vapour." How, one wonders, would zealous Zechariah, with his passion for enforced conformity, have reacted to that?[117]

---

[115] ODNB, 155; see "Dominion and Revolution," below.

[116] John was the son of the Charlestown mason, Christopher, who violently objected to baptisms in the church; see "Thomas Gould," above. Glover case: David D. Hall, ed., *Witch-Hunting in Seventeenth-Century New England* (Boston: Northeastern University Press, 1991), 265–79, where "possession" is used.

[117] Death: Sewall, *Diary*, 374; sermon: the text was *James*, 4: 14, ibid, 392; *ODNB*.

Contrasting the Symmes and Morton regimes gives a dramatic sense of change, but it also runs the risk of oversimplifying their personalities and their approaches. Symmes was far more than a conformist zealot. He hosted the dismissed minister Thomas Gilbert and his wife at his Charlestown house for many months, until Gilbert's death. Three leading town families named sons after him. He was asked to help arbitrate the dangerous feud between Richard Temple and Thomas Goble. The General Court sought his advice on issues of witchcraft, ecclesiastical questions from Connecticut, and the state of Harvard's finances. They rewarded his service to Massachusetts with large land grants. Charlestown was similarly appreciative, and his neighbors supported his stand against outsiders flooding meadowland with their milldams. Despite his troubles with dissenters, with the paranoia of Thomas James, and the ecclesiastical doubts of his colleague Thomas Allen, Symmes's 37-year tenure was reasonably equable, and gave much-needed stability to church and town.[118]

Charles Morton was fortunate in the timing of his arrival. The colony was still reeling from the loss of its independence. The town was likewise shell-shocked by the sudden death of the young Thomas Shepard III, who had planted some of the promising seeds that Morton would harvest. Though he was committed to the new attitudes towards the natural world, we should not exaggerate Morton's modernity. He was still a believer in witchcraft, and endorsed Cotton Mather's superstitious *Memorable Providences*. Though he advocated the reconciliation of faith and reason, he was first and foremost a minister. At the crunch-point, faith would take precedence.[119]

The "before and after" comparison also omits the causation, the process, and the pace of change. It focuses on the roles of two admittedly influential individuals, but misses important contextual pressures on godly decisions and developments. It also underplays the contributions of those who collaborated with or served between the second and the sixth ministers. To fill these gaps, we are fortunate to have the valuable account of Charlestown church history in the seventeenth century by Mary Macmanus Ramsbottom, "Religious Society and Family in Charlestown 1630–1740."[120]

---

[118]   See above, "Origins," "Communal Conciliation," and "Hay or Mills." Gilbert: a Scot who arrived in 1661 and was ordained in Topsfield; there, "his imprudence and intemperance required his dismissal." He died after Symmes in 1673. Savage; MxCC D&O, 5: folio 115. Land: CTR, 1A: 94; 1: 6; J. B. Threlfall, *Ancestry of M. B. Threlfall* (privately printed, 1985), 3: 1118. Witchcraft: *WP*, 6: 362–64. Connecticut: *MR*, 3: 419. Harvard: *MR*, 4,2: 92.

[119]   Morison, *Harvard in the Seventeenth Century*, 248.

[120]   PhD dissertation, Yale University, 1987. I am most grateful to David Hall for drawing this

From its separation from Boston in 1632, the records of church membership and baptisms for First Church down to the present day have survived. Ramsbottom has subjected those from the seventeenth century to rigorous decade-by-decade analysis, with especial interest in the different membership criteria, gender balance, demographic cycles, ministerial changes, and external stimuli. Her findings put flesh on the comparative skeleton.

Four sets of criteria governed admission to church membership at different times: conduct, confession, profession, and inclusion. At the start, the only test was good behavior; more than two out of three settlers quickly became members, usually husbands and wives at the same time—"co-covenanting." Many non-applicants seem to have been merely perching in the town before moving on to permanent planting elsewhere. After the Antinomian Crisis of the mid-1630s, however, applicants were required to relate to the church the workings of grace in their souls—"confession"— and admission took longer to achieve. "Full membership" was highly personal and "intense"; the church became far less inclusive. Elite arrivals, like the Russells or the Willoughbys, acquired sainthood faster than humbler planters, probably reflecting their value to the town. Between 1645 and 1658 the number of confessing members declined sharply: only one-third of the number of members admitted in the period 1632–44. In 1658, only about half the households were affiliated with the church. In 1662, in response to this general shortfall, the Synod introduced the Half-Way Covenant— the third criterion. Children of church members, formally pledging to follow church rules ("professing" or "owning the covenant"), but unready to relate the work of grace within them (confessing), were granted "associate membership." They were allowed to bring their children to baptism, but associates could not participate in the Lord's Supper (communion). Though three quarters of the church favoured the Half-Way Covenant, it was not commonly used until 1677. In that year, as many "children of the church" were granted half-way membership as in the whole preceding fourteen years. In the 1677 "revival," twice as many people achieved full membership as half-way. By the end of 1677, two out of every three families had church affiliation. Finally in the 1680s and 1690s, the criteria for baptism and the half-way covenant were relaxed, and people from non-church families became eligible. In the 1690s, the number of associate members was almost twice that of full members, and baptism was available virtually on request. Young adults' "renewing the

---

dissertation to my attention, and allowing me to borrow his copy.

covenant" [initially entered at baptism] or "professing" had become a key rite of passage in family life. Group renewals produced a heightening of the religious temperature and individual enthusiasm. Ramsbottom doubts the argument that changing criteria meant "declension." They were more likely the result of evangelistic outreach, which in turn may have been spurred by fears of toleration. It was preferable to include as many families as possible rather than to bar the over-scrupulous, the faint-hearted, the questioning, or the unready.[121]

This recital of different criteria and changing rates of membership masks two important variations. The first involves gender. In the 1630s, the sex ratio of saints was pretty well equal. After the demand for a confessional "relation" raised the bar, women tended to precede their husbands as members. The men usually joined eventually, and two out of every three church families included both spouses as saints. By the 1650s, however, half the admissions were of women only, and by 1677 half of all church families relied on the wife for their affiliation. Membership also tended to be matrilineal, with young married or marriageable daughters following their mothers into sainthood. In the 1690s, three out of every four new associate members were single women.[122]

Until the final Mortonian decade, a major compulsion for young wives to confess, or at least profess, was the imminence of childbearing and the urge to have their children eligible for baptism. When infant deaths were so common, this wish was even more powerful. Other causes (discussed below) may have played a part in creating this preponderantly female church membership and matrilineal pattern. What is most mystifying is why young men and husbands were not similarly moved. Ramsbottom can find no convincing explanation.[123]

A second reason for the ebb and flow of new saints is demographic. After the cessation of mass immigration in the early 1640s, the number of applicants depended on the availability of homegrown young adults. For instance, in the later 1640s and the 1650s, there were many more baptisms in the records than admissions. The generational cycle meant that young first-generation immigrant families were busy producing children, but these offspring had yet to reach adulthood and the concurrent onset of spiritual stirrings. The large number of baptisms in the late 1680s may also

---

[121] Ramsbotton, 32,53–55, 66, 89, 109, 131, 159, 177, 192–98. On inclusion as opposed to toleration; see above, "Thomas Gould."

[122] Ramsbottom, 42, 67–68, 88, 105, 111, 119, 136, 154, 168, 178, 192, 198.

[123] Ibid., 270.

have arisen in part from a similar generational wave. Ramsbottom links highs and lows of admissions across several generations to such rhythmic patterns.[124]

During the troubled solo ministry of Thomas James (1632–34), very few new applicants came forward to join Charlestown church; indeed, some members under the leadership of Increase Nowell debated leaving it and rejoining Boston. There, under the vibrant leadership of John Cotton, a revivalist fervor gripped the town between September 1633 and February 1634, and a large number of the awakened became members. However, in 1635, Charlestown enrolled twenty-five new members. This undoubtedly resulted largely from the arrival of Zechariah Symmes as teacher. Even after public confessions were instituted about 1636, a steady line of applicants presented themselves in the succeeding years, only to shorten in response to the end of mass immigration in the early 1640s.[125]

We have seen similar upsurges in religious enthusiasm producing increases in membership with the ordination of Thomas Shepard Jr. in 1659, his son in 1680, and the installation of Charles Morton in 1686. 1660 saw the first of a series of family covenantal affirmations channeling the enthusiasm triggered by the arrival of a fresh young face with a celebrated name in the pulpit. Another church covenant renewal occurred in 1671, when Shepard effectively took over ministerial control as Symmes sank into old age. The third Thomas Shepard presided over a "revival year" in 1681. Many inhabitants without kin connections to the faithful entered into covenant, broadening the half-way compromise and creating a more "embracive" church. "Ministerial renewals" responded to the powerful charge that a chosen new and lively minister imparted.[126]

We have often alluded to the unpredictable dangers of early New England life. Fear would be frequent. These alarms could be either external or internal to the town. Outside threats could arise from international wars, Indian attacks, piracy, shipwrecks, economic chills, or imperial interference. Internally, disease, bad harvests, violent weather, political or religious divisions, and serious accidents, like the Charlestown fire of 1651, could all create frightening problems. These reversals were not seen as

---

[124] Ibid., 187–91, 194; see above, "Numbers."

[125] Ramsbottom, 21–32.

[126] See above, "Succession Crisis." Ramsbottom, 190, 175–86. The 1680 revival, which also coincided with the results of the 1679–80 Reform Synod, netted 24 new full members, 17 associates and 60 baptisms.

capricious events, but as divine signals. The godly must heed them and reform or face worse. Thus, the Reform Synod met in 1679, after the series of blows from King Philip, King Charles, and smallpox.[127]

Several of the changes we have been charting in Charlestown church membership and development coincide with communal or colonial traumas. The tightening and loosening of criteria for affiliation, for instance, partly derived from internal crises: the confessional requirement from the antinomian heresy, and the Half-Way Covenant from the rise of the Baptists. The revivals of 1677 and 1681 reflected both intense relief at victory in King Philip's War, and the perceived need for spiritual renewal. Externally, the Second Anglo-Dutch War (1664–67) had a particularly devastating effect on Charlestown's commerce, and the covenant renewal of 1668 would have mirrored gratitude for the return of peace. As we saw, the welcome to Morton gathered warmth in reaction to the menacing Dominion experiment of 1686–89. The church's role as sole center of communal resistance and the need for town unity justified his inclusive "parochial" vision. However much ministers might demand constancy in devotion, intensity of religious zeal was inevitably affected by the sighting of threatening storm clouds.[128]

The changes in church membership and family affiliation that Ramsbottom charts so painstakingly between the pastorates of Symmes and Morton were unsurprising in a gradually maturing community over a period of three generations. Apart from the individual impacts of a series of impressive ministers and the capricious but potent workings of divine providence, there were two striking developments. The first was the gradual "parochialization" of a formerly exclusive and inward-looking clique of godly residents. By 1699, "church" and "town" approximately corresponded as communal groupings, as in the very early days. However, "church" now included three rings of worshippers: the outer comprised those baptized; next, associate members; and at the center full communicants. Absence from one of these categories represented an act of willful demurral rather than exclusion. The second development, the increased feminization of church affiliation, we will discuss below.[129]

---

[127]   Foster, *Long Argument*, 217–30.

[128]   David D. Hall, *Worlds of Wonder, Days of Judgement* (New York: Knopf, 1989), Ch. 4; Ramsbottom, 52–55, 127–36; see above, "The Sea: Introduction," and "Ordeals of Captain Foster." The success of resistance to the intrusive King's Commissioners by 1667 may also have prompted thanksgiving; see Jack M. Sosin, *English America and the Restoration Monarchy of Charles II* (Lincoln: University of Nebraska Press, 1980), 100–14, 124.

[129]   Ramsbottom, 203. Town: Throughout this period, *all* households, members and non-mem-

We have focused on change in this conclusion, but we should not underestimate the extent of continuity both in the religious institutions and in the public and private devotions they fostered. If we compare the changes in belief and practice over the last three generations nowadays, the retention rate in the seventeenth century is in fact remarkable. Sermon styles, structure, and concerns were recognizably similar, for instance; likewise, forms of service. Family prayers, lay discussion and devotional meetings, the roles of ministers and church officers persisted. Well-laid foundations endured.[130]

---

bers, were required to pay church rates towards the minister's salary—£100 per annum after 1660—(e.g. CTR, 3: 161, 4: 15, 51); for upkeep of the meetinghouse (CTR, 1: 638, 677, 3: 79, 94); wages for verger and bellman (CTR, 4: 56); and building a parsonage (CTR, 3: 110). The select-men oversaw discipline in the meetinghouse, especially among the boys (CTR, 3: 68), and the sensitive allocation of seating (CTR, 3: 86). In 1672 the town paid for a new meetinghouse; three years later three galleries had to be added, Frothingham, 160, 187. The church had endowments from legacies and town grants, like the forty cow commons on Mystic Common in 1657, CTR, 1: 647, cf. CTR, 3: 128, 134, Rodgers, 3: 389. Feminization: see below, "Women and the Churches."

[130] Ramsbottom, 270.

Part 6

Women

Introduction

One of the most popular and persistent depictions of woman in early New England is Hester Prynne in Nathaniel Hawthorne's *The Scarlet Letter*. Hawthorne's romantic heroine who had the courage to follow her heart is ostracized, hounded, and expelled by bigoted church and lay authorities and by her self-righteous, puritanical neighbors. Her sinister husband hovers menacingly in the background. Her lover dies of shame. An equally influential literary depiction is Arthur Miller's *The Crucible*, in which good women like Elizabeth Procter are accused by a murderous mob and harried by popular hysteria to a death sentence from prejudiced magistrates. No wonder many modern women shudder at the thought of their forebears' sufferings.

However exaggerated and unhistorical these dramatic literary works may be, they have fixed in the popular imagination a belief that Prynne and Procter typified the down-trodden, persecuted "second sex." Women are seen as victims in a narrow, superstitious, punitive society that is obsessed with female chastity and fidelity. Their lives were stunted by patriarchal clans, whose reputation or "fame" was essential to family honor. Any besmirching, especially by its womenfolk, represented social and psychic disgrace. Only ruthless cleansing could restore the kin's good name. Such purification was a male duty.[1]

The rationale for this unbending discipline is seen as scriptural. The Levitical decrees are the word of God; any society or family that ignored them could expect the fate of Sodom and Gomorrah. The sermons of

---

[1]   On the influence and inaccuracies of *The Scarlet Letter,* see D. D. Hall, *A Reforming People* (New York: Knopf, 2011), 84–86; on *The Crucible,* Roger Thompson, *Witchcraft at Salem* (London: Folio Society, 1974), Introduction.

published ministers and the stern pronouncements of certain magistrates help support such an analysis.[2]

The critical portrait of Puritan persecution of "the weaker sex" may well have been reinforced in the last decade by intense publicity of the maltreatment of women in modern fundamentalist societies. News stories, novels, movies, analyses, and memoirs highlight female suppression, segregation, and suffering. Male betrayal and husbandly violence, enforced yoking of young women to elderly mates, double standards of morality, rigid clothing requirements, and vicious, humiliating state punishments are all described in horrifying detail. In the closed worlds of Taliban-controlled Afghanistan or Madrist Teheran, honor "is vested in the woman, but is the property of the man It is what women must keep intact and men must defend fiercely." Observers report women murdered by their families when they try to escape arranged marriages and assert their own choices. Homicidal revenge attacks go unpunished by collusive authorities. Caste and class lines are rigidly drawn. Widows are segregated and pauperized. Rapes are justified on the grounds of female provocation. Women are deprived of education, of political and religious voices, of any sense of marital equality or mutuality. Their fate is to be treated as commodities, drudges, or inferior forms of humanity. Passivity, obedience, and forbearance are their recommended qualities. Such is the fate of women in modern-day fundamentalist societies.[3]

---

[2] The classic assertion of female victimization is L. Koehler, *A Search for Power* (Urbana: University of Illinois Press, 1980); for correctives, see Hall, *A Reforming People*, 216.

[3] News: Tariq Ali,"Diary," *London Review of Books,* 18 December 2008. In the summer of 2010, for instance, a *Time* cover showed a beautiful young Afghan woman who had fled her in-laws' abuse, only to be tracked down and have her nose and ears cut off (an alternative to acid attacks on women with exposed faces). A few days later, the *New York Times* (17 July) reported the suspected murder of a young Indian woman graduate by her Brahmin mother; the daughter was pregnant by a lower-caste boyfriend. Five thousand cases of honor killings every year were reported by the United Nations Human Rughts Commission. According to M. El-Naggar in the *International Herald Tribune* (8 September 2010: 2), one in three Afghan women were estimated to be victims of violence. BBC Radio 4's 6 p.m. News on 17 December 2009 reported Criminal Prosecution Service estimates of an annual average of a dozen honor killings in the U.K.; hundreds of women forced to flee abroad to escape killings or punishments; and thousands harmed domestically. Jonathan D. Spence, *The Death of Woman Wong* (Harmondsworth: Penguin, 1979), is a classic account of women's servility in seventeenth-century China. Memoirs: Azar Nafisi's *Reading Lolita in Tehran* depicts secret domestic liberation among a small group of university women intellectuals. On the bookseller of Kabul's successful Norwegian lawsuit against Asne Sierestad, author of *The Bookseller of Kabul,* see the *Guardian,* 7 July 2009, 20 July 2010, 27 July 2010. Novels: Arundhati Roy, *The God of Small Things*; Khaled Hosseini, *A Thousand Splendid Suns.* Movies: Mohsen Makhmalbaf, *Kandahar*; Deepa Mehta, *Water.* Analyses: Cf. N. Kristof and S. Wu Dunn, *Half the Sky* (New York: Vintage, 2010), 81–83, 149–59, chapter 9. See also "A Piece of White Silk," by Jacqueline Rose, *London Review of Books,* 5 November 2009, 5–8, 48–51, the brilliant review of Rana Husseini, *Murder in the*

The Massachusetts Puritans were fundamentalists. Their God was great, indeed literally Almighty; they interpreted all events as His providences, and they policed their society according to His scripturally revealed word. Their preachers and teachers, highly trained interpreters, exerted immense authority; the punishments meted out to transgressors were frequently humiliating, sometimes terrifying. Widespread popular consensus and the power of gossip enforced acceptable behavior at an informal level. Flouting public opinion led to ostracism; excommunication meant what it said. This section examines the domestic and economic roles as well as the religious involvement. of a very varied group of twenty women in Charlestown from 1630 to the 1680s. How did they experience their pervasively theocentric community and deal with the demands and challenges it presented?

Name of Honor, Unai Wikan, *In Honor of Fadime: Murder and Shame,* and Ayse Onal, *Honor Killing: Stories of Men Who Killed..*

Arrald Cole's Letters
to Her Children,
1655, 1661

Surviving personal letters between ordinary people in the seventeenth century are extremely rare. Two dictated letters from the widow Arrald Cole probably survived because her daughter-in-law in England kept them in the hope of claims to future legacies. I reprint the first letter in full as a remarkable insight into the mind of a Charlestown matriarch. The abstract of the second letter reveals a different side of her character: a tactful but tough businesswoman fully apprised of her legal rights.

> Son and daughter James Ruth Cole,
>
> My unfained love unto you both. I have received a letter from you both and therefore I write unto you both by this return, which being suddenly upon the receipt of yours, forces me to brevity. I find son by your writing that which I often spoke to you about is by the holy Providence of the Lord come to pass: that is that you are married, and I hope your choice has been in and for the Lord, and though your wife be unknown to me yet now I perceive that she is a gift of the Lord unto you for he that findeth a wife findeth a good thing and obtaineth favour of God, which I trust shall be so to you, wherefore I beseech the Lord to give your wife a heart so to know you and herself in your places [roles] as she may show the Lord has brought you together in Love and mercy. And I exhort you in your place to walk [behave] towards your wife as a man of knowledge [experience, understanding] and so in love to demean yourself towards her she may have cause to bless the

Lord for you, and my daughter, let me advise and counsel you in your walking towards your husband so to consider of his spirit and temper[ament] as to win him by your modest and virtuous behaviour to be not only in love and affection with the person but with your virtues and graces so as he may bless the Lord that brought you together: And I shall pray the Lord to help you both so as that we may kneel all together in the presence of God never to part from him nor one another. I desire you if the Lord please to give opportunity to let me see you here . . . for I have a great desire to see your wife as well as yourself, the Lord do his holy will. Daughter, whereas your husband writeth to me of his going to the Canaries [Canary Islands] and of his likelihood to come in New England, if it be so I shall be glad but I desire you however to write to me and your brethren and sisters who all remember their love kindly unto you wishing you blessing and prosperity in your body and soul. I shall in my daily prayers be mindful of you, and I desire the like of you. I am old and daily expect my change [death], yet I have no greater joy as that my children walk in the truth, and still desire you all may grow in grace and godliness till you attain eternal salvation, oh my daughter mind and think of such things. Again I desire you to write to me and write large [at length] that I may have something of you to delight myself in in your absence, yet with honest desires of your presence here if it may come to pass. Here is a letter enclosed to your husband; I desire you to reserve it for him if he be not with you (till he come home) if he come hither my purpose is to write again to you, this enclosed directed to you is from your sister Lowden which accept of, and send an answer upon opportunity. So in some haste I cease to write, but not to love and pray for you to the Lord to whom I recommend you abiding your loving mother to my power till death

Charlestown, New England   Arrald Cole
The 20th of August 1655

Your brother and sister John Cole and his wife

Your brother and sister Thomas Peirce and his wife They all remember their love Your brother and sister Richard Lowden and his wife   unto you

Sergeant Hale and his wife. And Elder Greene and his wife remember their loves unto you and your wife though unknown.[4]

---

[4]   MxCC D&O,1: doc. 2063, in the hand of John Green Jr, who would transcribe the early Town

Ruth Mudd and Loving daughter. I received your letter of 1 May 1661 per our friend and loving neighbour John Smith . . . [You] desire me to deliver into [your] hands what did really belong to my son James your [late] husband which I am very willing to do were there anything due . . . I have sent you the abstract of his father's will which we have already shown to neighbour Smith . . . There is nothing due to your [late] husband but a heifer (which he hath already converted to his own use) until my decease . . . Your thirds you cannot be deprived of . . . When the Lord shall carry me away that which belongs to you will be delivered into the hands of any whom you shall appoint . . .

Charlestown, 27 September 1661 Your loving mother in law, Arrald Cole[5]

7 August 1662. Henry Mudd of Stebenheath or Stepney, Middlesex, mariner and Ruth, his wife, the relict of James Cole, mariner, make John Smith of Charlestown their attorney. Thomas Burgis attests to Mr. Russell [Charlestown magistrate] that he was present when Ruth Mudd signed the deed.[6]

Thanks to her unusual first name and the intrepid researches of Leslie Mahler, we know a considerable amount about the background of Arrald (sometimes Harrald) Cole or Coles. She was born in 1587 in the parish of Great Bowden, close to Market Harborough, Leicestershire, and twelve miles southeast of Leicester, where the emigrant minister Francis Higginson later preached. Her parents were Edward Dunnington and Margaret (Cox), who had married in 1579. Her father died in 1588 when she was still a baby, and her mother was remarried in 1589 to Miles Poole. In 1612, Arrald Dunnington was married at Great Bowden to Rice (Rees?) Cole, who came from outside the district. They had five surviving children: Robert, Elizabeth, Mary, John and James. Since none of their baptismal

---

Records in 1664. Cf. Rodgers, 2: 56–57. Like many women of her generation, Arrald Cole could probably read, but not write fluently. The two skills were taught serially. Scriveners such as Green, John Mansfield, Edward Burt, or James Carey were employed not only in letter writing, but also in composing petitions, wills and depositions. Experienced writers like Thomas Danforth, Francis Willoughby and Edward Rawson used early systems of shorthand, as did sermon annotators; see above "Godly Merchants," and "Thomas Gould." Correspondents often excuse the brevity and lack of polish of their mail by reference to the imminent departure of a ship. They might have to wait weeks for the next sailing.

5   Doc. 2019. This long letter is transcribed in full, with another, in Rodgers, 2: 57–58. Smith (ca. 1623–73) was a successful ship's carpenter.

6   Doc. 2062.

records have been found, it is probable that Arrald went to live in Rice's so far unidentified parish.[7]

The seven Coles joined the Winthrop Fleet to Massachusetts Bay in 1630, and settled in Charlestown. Both parents were admitted as church members, he in 1631, she in 1632, and Rice became a freeman in 1633. The two eldest children, Robert and Elizabeth, both teenagers, were employed as servants by Samuel Fuller of Plymouth, who remembered them in his will of 30 July 1633. Rice died at the age of fifty-six on 15 May 1646, leaving all his estate to Arrald during her life. By this time, their two daughters were married: Elizabeth to Thomas Pierce of Woburn and Mary to Richard Lowden, a Charlestown shipwright. Robert, John, and James all became mariners. Robert died in 1654; his widow Philippa was remarried the following year to William Morris and died within the next decade. John married the spirited Ursula, of whom much more will be heard. In 1646 a James Cole served with Captain Thomas Cromwell, the parliamentarian privateer, in the West Indies. He was said to have earned £200 in prize money. James was in Middlesex, England, in December 1654, when his brother John, as attorney, and his mother sued Alexander Brinsley for withholding a fur coat that James had given Arrald. The news of James's marriage in England reached Charlestown by the last week of August 1655. The identity of his wife is not known; she may have come from the parish of Stepney, Middlesex, just east of London and a source of many settlers in Charlestown.[8]

Arrald seems to have been a formidable woman. In 1649 she was engaged in a bitter dispute with Ralph Hall about payment of £3-10-0 in English goods which he owed her. She went to Captain Savage's newly arrived ship, but, despite many attempts at persuasion, was adamant that she would only accept woollen cloth, which Savage did not have. When Hall finally sued her, she called a witness who confirmed that the agreement stipulated that she be paid "to her content." Hall lost. When he tried again, he lost again. Her firm rebuttal of her former daughter-in-law's impetuous claim seems very much in character.[9]

---

[7] *TAG*, 78 (2003), 181–84. Higginson sailed to Massachusetts in 1629, and soon sent three letters to his friends in Leicester, painting a generally very rosy picture of New England, Emerson, 11–38. John Hull, famous Boston merchant and diarist, was born in Market Harborough in 1624. Savage.

[8] *GMB*, 426–29; Cromwell: WJ, 2: 272–74, *WP*, 5: 81; Brinsley was the son of William, noticed by Savage in Charlestown from 1650–54. A Peter Mudd acted as a surety to Thomas Sheppie, a Charlestown fisherman and frustrated landlord of John Cole, in 1652, MxCC D&O, 1: doc. 98.

[9] MxCC RB, 1: 3, 4, 30 October 1649; MxCC D&O, 1: docs. 2, 66, 237.

Another side of her character emerges from her letter to her new-lywed youngest son and his wife. Though she had often urged James to marry, she seems to have been content to leave the choice of bride to him. Her tone is matriarchal and authoritative. She proffers a loving welcome to the family for Ruth, a few words of motherly wisdom, and the desire to meet Ruth as soon as possible. Until then, she is hungry for letters, to which, as here, she will no doubt quickly reply. All this is framed by Arrald's encircling sense of a God-driven universe. The union results from "the holy providence of the Lord." She hopes James's "choice has been in and for the Lord," rather than a result primarily of personal attraction or financial calculation. The biblical maxim "he that findeth a wife findeth a good thing" divinely affirms James's betrothal. Hopes will only be fulfilled "if the Lord please." Daily prayers to the Almighty for growth in grace and godliness and for eventual salvation were central rituals of life and a form of supernatural transatlantic linkage. The Widow Cole had been a church member for a quarter of a century, but her zeal seems undimmed. The first item of her will reads: "I give my soul to god that gave it me and to the Lord Jesus Christ that redeemed it." Her first earthly bequest was "A bible that was my husband's." [10]

Arrald Cole died in December 1661. Her estate was valued at £93. Her sons-in-law and Ruth Mudd soon sought court involvement to ad-judicate its distribution according to Rice Cole's will of 1646. The suit of Ruth Mudd against the executors was finally heard on 16 December 1662; the bench concluded that the Cole land grant on Mystic Side had indeed been bequeathed to James, and that Ruth was his rightful heir. The Lord had provided! [11]

---

[10] The research on popular religion in this period is reviewed and greatly enhanced in David D. Hall, *Worlds of Wonder, Days of Judgment* (New York: Knopf, 1989). Arrald Cole's will: Rodgers, 2: 52.

[11] Rodgers, 2: 58. Rice Cole's will is at ibid., 55; inventory: 53–54. On 26 March 1670, however, Henry Mudd had to sue Richard Lowden for unforwarded rent for the late James Cole's Mystic Side inheritance.

Women and the Churches

In a seminal article comparing the roles of godly New England women in orthodox and radical groupings, Mary Maples Dunn argued that as the numbers of women church members outpaced men in the congregational churches of New England, so the role of the laity declined, and that of ministers and officials increased. The feminization of the godly was not a sign of rising feminism. This passivity stood in striking contrast with the passionate activism of unorthodox cells, notably the Quakers.[12]

Certainly in Charlestown, even by the late 1630s, wives often entered full communion before their husbands. Their minds seem to have been jolted by the prospect of childbirth, presenting both the risk of mortality and the desire for vulnerable newborns to be eligible for baptism. By the 1650s, church admission was becoming "a female affair" with over fifty percent of godly families represented by wives only, who would henceforth become "the agents of church status in their households." The second-generation mother was frequently "the bearer of covenant legacy." Mary Ramsbottom discusses whether the preponderance of women saints after the 1662 adoption of the Half-Way Covenant led to conflict within families, or whether mothers assumed roles as religious educators of children. By the 1690s, when Charles Morton's inclusive membership policy was well-established, three out of every four Half-Way Covenanters were young single women. Though there is evidence of waves of male zeal during the seventeenth century, this enthusiasm was not translated into numbers of married men entering into full communion. Despite this, however,

---

[12] "Saints and Sisters: Congregational and Quaker Women in the Early Colonial Period," *American Quarterly*, 30 (1978) 582–601.

there is little written evidence of women saints playing an active official role in church affairs.[13]

In less formal ways, however, "sisters" could be highly influential. They were the role models and the trainers of their daughters and maidservants. In various ways, they were censors and inspectors who monitored reputations in the town and enforced social norms. The notorious Margaret Martin saucily retorted to the chastisements of her equally notorious mother

> Why mother you were talked of as bad before we were born and will be when you are dead. Goody Martin said 'These [gossiping Longs] are the people of God . . . the [church] members a crew of Devils of them . . . sister Foster, sister Taylor and your sister Smith that gather together under pretence to pray, but it is to kill and slay [reputations] and do all the mischief they can.

The women saints showed themselves in this case and others to be well informed about intended secrets, and highly skeptical about cover stories. Even when miscreants trysted during services or fasts, sharp, saintly eyes and ears caught the sinners red-handed.[14]

Women's "truth-telling" about immoral or unacceptable behavior sometimes triggered ill-judged defamation suits (as with the Martins). These could provoke a further chorus of accusations and allegations, some carefully nurtured over years or even decades. Masters or their sons attracted to resident serving maids, unfulfilled wives to young bucks or visiting seamen, would be given pause by the probability of exposure and social shaming. Should they nonetheless succumb to temptation, resultant pregnancies would give town matrons more formal jurisdiction. It was their task to adjudicate on extramarital or suspiciously early postnuptial births and to discover during the agonies of labor the father's identity and the circumstances of conception. They would report their findings to the court, where their evidence had the authority of expert witnesses. The unofficial matriarchy of Charlestown exerted powerful pressures on both women and men in the town; the good opinion of "sisters" was highly valued.[15]

---

[13] Mary Ramsbottom, "Religion, Society and Family in Charlestown," Yale Ph. D. 1987, 38, 42, 68, 70, 86, 88, 105, 107, 119, 136, 168, 198. Zeal: regular covenant renewals and affirmations from 1660 onwards involved men in full and half-way covenant. In 1703, Charlestown's Young Men's Association, modelled on those in Boston, began redressing the gender imbalance, 191–94, 270.

[14] Thompson, *Sex*, 184; miscreants: 147.

[15] Ibid., 149–54, 171, 173, 174–89; cf. Laurel Thatcher Ulrich, *Good Wives* (New York: Oxford University Press, 1983), 55–57, 96. For English examples, see Bernard Capp, *When Gossips Meet* (London: Oxford University Press, 2003) 185–87, 212–14, 224; Laura Gowing, *Domestic Dangers*

On one occasion, a large group of first-generation women, many originally Charlestown church members but recently transferred to the new Malden congregation, did plunge into public life with a petition to the General Court on 28 October 1651. The twenty-eight former Charlestown sisters included some elite names: Sarah Sargent, Joanna Sprague, Widow Jane Learned, Mary Wayte, Sarah Hills, Rebecca Hills, and Elizabeth Carrington. Their plea was in favor of the suspected antinomian minister of the town, Reverend Marmaduke Matthews. He had been called and ordained despite high-level doubts and neighborly disapproval. His female defenders stressed their pastor's "pious life and labours [which produced] many saving convictions, directions and consolations" for them. They asked the Court "to pass by some [of Matthews's] personal and particular failings." Why were Malden's church sisters rather than church brethren taking this lead? Given that the Malden church was soon to be fined £50 for its provoking obstinacy, it is possible that the female saints were a front for shared feelings. However, it is just as likely that these petitioners acted on their own initiative. After Anne Hutchinson, they knew that women could play leading roles in devotional disputes. They must also have been aware that they were laying themselves open to serious repercussions. A major cause of Malden's contumely was its church's assertion of group independence from central direction. It is no coincidence, as we shall see, that one of the signatories was Sarah Osborne.[16]

Before examining the exploits of courageous nonconformists like Sarah Osborne, we first celebrate the life of Charlestown's highly orthodox and emblematic Sarah Symmes (1604–76), wife of pastor Zechariah. She was the daughter of the wealthy Humphrey and Alice (Hickman) Baker, and married Symmes when he was Lecturer at St. Antholin's in the City of London. The wedding took place on the south side of London Bridge at the great Puritan church of St. Saviour's, Southwark, on 13 February 1622. Twelve years later, Sarah left Dunstable with six children under the age of ten, and traveled on the *Griffin* with the Hutchinson clan. Despite bearing five more children in the next nine years, she found time for active philanthropy. "Mrs. Sarah Symmes" is twice recorded in the Cambridge Deacons' Book as a contributor to their welfare funds. Edward Johnson, born in Canterbury in the same year as Zechariah Symmes and a fellow

(Oxford: Clarendon, 1996), and *Common Bodies* (New Haven: Yale University Press, 2003).

16 Frothingham, 126; Deloraine P. Corey, *History of Malden* (privately printed, 1899), 131–64. See above, "Antinomian Controversy."

church member at Charlestown, singled Sarah out as a model for church-women everywhere:

> The virtuous woman, indued by Christ with graces fit for a wilderness condition, her courage exceeding her stature, with much cheerfulness did undergo all the difficulties of these times of straights, her God through faith in Christ supplying all her wants with great industry, nurturing up her young children in the fear of the lord, their number being ten both sons and daughters, a certain sign of the lord's intent to people this vast wilderness . . . these poor people [in Charlestown] welcomed with great joy their new come guests.

After the tetchy Scot Rev. Thomas Gilbert, was voted out of Topsfield by his congregation in 1666, Sarah characteristically took in his family in Charlestown for a period of many months.[17]

Most illustrative of Sarah Symmes's quiet authority is her husband's will, originally written in 1664, and later clarified. His "dear and faithful . . . and dearly beloved wife" emerges as the business manager of the family. She keeps the accounts and is "privy to . . . any household or personal debts." She has "set by a portion for Ruth," their twenty-nine-year-old unmarried daughter. The patriarch records that "far most of our first estate came by her" dowry when explaining to his other heirs why their mother should have "the use of benefit of all my temporal estate," totalling £681. He specifically gives her "the large English bible," as well as volumes of Sibbes's and Preston's sermons and all his own published and handwritten sermons and sermon notes. His token bequest to his brother William in England has her approval. The codicil of 19 December 1667 reveals that Sarah is overseeing the building of a shop on ground she has bought. The elderly husband gives her greater than usual authority over the whole estate, and "frees her from all entanglements" as a widow.[18]

Mistress Symmes was a matriarch who combined financial and entrepreneurial ability with spiritual and intellectual qualities to make her an example of "the good wife" for her fellow sisters and for townswomen generally. She was a discreet but effective power behind the pulpit who raised a large and talented family.[19]

---

[17] Wyman; Roger Thompson, ed., "Cambridge Deacons' Books," forthcoming: 7 February 1639, 10 shillings; 1640, £2. Johnson, *Wonderworking Providence*, 101. Gilbert: MxCC D&O, 5: folio 115; *MR*, 4,2: 307.

[18] Rodgers, 3: 3–6.

[19] Zechariah Jr. became a minister; daughter Sarah married first one minister, then a second;

In the long struggle to establish Charlestown's first Baptist church from the mid-1650s to the mid-1670s, three socially prominent townswomen, all church members, played courageous roles: Sarah Osborne, Mary Harwood Gould, and Mary Pitt Newell. Goody Osborne had arrived in Charlestown with her husband Thomas in 1644. As latecomers, they settled on Mystic Side, where Sarah had six children between 1647 and 1660, three of whom survived. Both parents became church members. As well as signing the Malden/Mystic Side petition in favor of Marmaduke Matthews, Sarah also showed interest in Quakerism during the 1660s, and was a close friend of the Bowers family. From 1663 onwards, she received a series of warnings for absence from church meetings, but she was just as obdurate as her husband, on the grounds that infant baptism "was against her conscience," and she wished to be dismissed. When admonition was about to be pronounced on her, she left the meetinghouse, and "went home from the Assembly." With "nothing of repentance manifested," she was finally excommunicated on 30 July 1665. After April 1666, Sarah had to manage the Osborne farm and family on her own, because Thomas had been sent to jail for refusing to pay accumulated fines. The date of his release is not recorded, but he was still imprisoned in September. He had missed one whole growing season. [20]

When the Baptist Church was formally instituted on 28 May 1665, neither Sarah Osborne nor Mary Gould were named as founder members. However, there is little doubt that both attended. As late as 1676, Osborne's persistent absence from Charlestown Congregational Church was reported to the Middlesex County Court. It required great personal strength and spiritual commitment for a woman saint to face down the indignation and ostracism of her fellow members, her minister and her deacons, the displeasure of magistrates and selectmen, as well as the prospect of fending for herself and her family when her husband was imprisoned indefinitely.[21]

William, a surveyor and militia captain, was a leading figure in both Charlestown and Woburn; Mary, Rebecca, Ruth, and Deborah all married merchants. Youngest son Timothy, duly set up in the 1667 codicil, was a tailor. Wyman, 927–51.

[20] Absences: MxCC D&O, 1: doc. 2288, 28 August 1663; doc. 2498, 7 June 1664; RB, 1: 297, 6 October 1663; D&O, 2: folio 39, 7 June 1665; folio 40, 21 March 1666; folio 44, 11 February 1667, 5 June 1667; folio 49, 13 November 1668; Hunnewell, ii, 18 November 1663; Nathan E. Wood, *History of the First Baptist Church of Boston* (Philadelphia: American Baptist Publishing Co., 1899), 40–41.

[21] MxCC D&O, 3: folios 69, 73. The Osbornes may have moved temporarily to join other Baptists in Woburn. McLoughlin and Davison, "Baptist Debate," 107. A Thomas Osborne family was warned out of Billerica in 1676, folio 73.

Mary Harwood Gould was also lauded as "one of the unsung heroines of American history, whose fortitude gave courage to dissent." The Harwoods were important London Puritan merchants, though I have been unable to discover who Mary's Harwood husband was, or when she arrived in Charlestown. She had by her first marriage a son Nathaniel; a daughter Mary, who married into the nonconformist Bunker family; and a daughter Abiah or Abiel whose husband was Charlestown mariner Joseph Shapleigh. Another son or stepson, John Harwood, had remained in London. Thomas Gould, already a Winthrop tenant at Ten Hills Farm beyond Charlestown Neck, married Mary as his second wife before 1654, possibly in the late 1640s. In September 1655 the Goulds invited Henry Dunster, president of Harvard until he insisted on his repudiation of infant baptism, and other likeminded objectors, to a thanksgiving at Ten Hills for the birth of a child and for God's mercy shown to Mary.[22]

Our first glimpse of her in religious affairs is on 6 June 1658, when Zechariah Symmes confronted her husband because "he should forbear or stay away [from meeting] when he could not but know that his pastor [would be] speaking largely to that subject [infant baptism]." Gould "confessed his wife told him of it." By 8 November 1663, she was the target of "vigorous, hostile action from the General Court." Her most glorious moment came in late 1668. Her husband and others had been imprisoned for refusal to pay fines. She masterminded appeals for support from England and wrote a long account defending the Baptists in general and her husband in particular. The group "desired to live quietly and peaceably . . . to obey God rather than man." Thomas Gould had been summarily excommunicated without a chance of explaining himself. Mary derided the conformist fear "that eight or nine poor Anabaptists should be the destruction of their [Congregational] churches." She cited the call for toleration from "the 65 hands to the petition that was put into the General Court." This

---

[22] Quote: McLoughlin, *New England Dissent*, 51. Gould's first wife Hannah (Miller) had died at Ten Hills in 1647. WP, 5: 162. George Harwood, haberdasher of London, was Treasurer of the Massachusetts Bay Company in 1629, as well as a Feoffee for Impropriations, responsible for Symmes's funding at Dunstable; see "Origins." A Henry Harwood and wife Elizabeth came to Charlestown with Winthrop in 1630, *GMB*, 873–74; he died in 1637, *MR*, 1: 218; *Stepney Marriage Registers*, 1: 225; G. B. Roberts, ed., *English Origins of New England Families*, 6 volumes in 2 series (Baltimore: Genealogical Publishing, 1984), 2, 2: 270, has research by Elizabeth French on a John Harwood, in Massachusetts from 1645 to 1657, than back in London. Waters's "Gleanings" on Harwoods are in *R*, 42 (1888), 64–65. Nathaniel settled in Concord, and on 1 June 1682 was appointed attorney by his brother John Harwood, merchant of London, MxCC D&O, 4: folio 103; RB, 4: 68. The younger Mary's husband was probably Jonathan Bunker (1638–78) who married Mary "Howard" in 1663, *GM*, 1: 486. Child: probably Elizabeth, Wood, 43.

was a popular protest against the official policy of harassment, imprisonment, and banishment. How much of this was Mary Gould's composition it is impossible to say, but the circulation of her answer to the authorities kept the persecution of the Baptists in the limelight. When Thomas Gould was given a three-day release from prison in March 1669, a last meeting at the Goulds' was attended by eighteen worshippers, including Mary's daughter Abiah Shapleigh. Then, according to a prearranged plan between Mary Gould and the Shrimpton family, the Goulds were spirited to Noddle's Island in Boston Harbor. There, Thomas and Mary were beyond the interference of the authorities, and they and their fellow Baptists met regularly until the group moved to Boston in 1675. Our last sighting of Mary Gould is in a petition to the General Court of 24 January 1677, asking that Benanuel Bowers be released from prison for two days to help her with the administration of the late Thomas Gould's very considerable estate.[23]

One of the eighteen attending the last Baptist meeting in Charlestown in March 1669 was Jonathan or John Newell (1634–1704). He was the cooper son of the third remarkable Baptist sister, and he later went on to a valuable career as town clerk. His mother, Mary (1607–1684), was well connected. She was a daughter of William Pitt, wealthy merchant and sheriff of Bristol. Her sister Maud had married up-and-coming merchant-draper Richard Russell and emigrated with him to Charlestown in 1640. Mary's marriage had been less prudent. Andrew Newell was a mere mariner, from the once thriving Dorset port of Lyme Regis on the English Channel. Mary's mother bitterly disapproved of the match, and insisted in her 1634 will that her son-in-law should be totally excluded from the £120 legacy to Mary. Though Mary seems to have become a Charlestown church member in 1647, her next appearance in the records is in Lyme Regis, in a deed dated 22 January 1664. She is by then a widow, and would have been in her late fifties. Her son John is described in the document as "late of Lyme Regis, and now of Charlestown in New England." For £155, they sell a long lease of property in Lyme to kinsman Edward Edwardes, merchant of the port. John had been in Charlestown on 16 September 1661, but had returned to England and then sailed back to Boston on the *Defence* from London. Shortly after

---

[23]   Wood, 39, 55, 90; Backus, *History of the Baptists in New England*, 304–7; petition: Mass Archives; fellow Charlestown Baptist Edward Drinker volunteered to serve as Bowers's surety; estate: MA, Suffolk Probates, 7: 362; the £782 inventory included 80 sheep and wool worth £80, a ketch, £250 of real estate, including frontier lands on Merrimack River, and debts owed to Gould totaling £131.

his return to Massachusetts, on 15 February 1665, he married Hannah Larkin of Charlestown.[24]

His mother may have accompanied him on the return to Boston, because the name of Mistress Mary Newell occurs in the first entry of the First Baptist Church records in Charlestown. Wood has a facsimile of the minutes of the 28 May 1665 inaugural meeting. Four local leaders "were baptized: Thomas Gould, Thomas Osborne, Edward Drinker and John George And joined with [five] who had walked in that order in old England." The fifth name was "Mary Newell."[25]

Lyme Regis is known to have had a Baptist congregation during the 1650s, and two other English arrivals had been members of a West Country cell in Dartmouth, down the coast in neighboring Devon. At least two Baptist churches had been established in Bristol, but there is no sign of Mary's name in the surviving Broadmead records. Thanks to persecution after the 1660 Restoration, secrecy was a necessity; potentially incriminating documents would therefore be destroyed or concealed. As a result, tracing nonconformist names and places is a hit-or-miss business.[26]

As Mr. Richard Russell's sister-in-law, Mrs. Newell was treated with kid gloves by the authorities. Nonetheless, her absence from church ser-

---

[24] In the time of James I (1603–25), "the merchants of Lyme being engaged in trade to Newfoundland, acquired large fortunes and raised the town considerably." The 1630s saw a decline. Thistlethwaite, *Dorset Pilgrims,* 34. Lyme Regis town records have references to Newells from 1554 into the 18th century. In 1575, a leet-court roll lists Roger Newell as "mariner." In 1599, three Newells lived on the Combe or Street in town. In 1629 and 1640, John Newell, merchant, was mayor; in 1653 Mr. William Newell was churchwarden and foreman of the grand jury; three years before he had been grand jury foreman in the court-baron. The only notice of Andrew Newell is in a list of about 150 "residents within the precincts" who failed to attend the 6 May 1650 court-baron. A Mary Newell, widow, was buried on 4 or 9 May 1672, but no late husband's name is given. Dorset History Centre, Dorchester, DC/LR N/6, N/7, A7/1, A4/2, 3, B2/10a, F2. The early parish registers are incomplete: Mic/R/584. John: MxCC D&O, 1: doca. 1ca. 1763, 16 September 1661. The Charlestown Newells do not seem to have been related to either the Roxbury Newells or the New(h)alls of Lynn. See above, "Godly Merchants;" deed and kinship: *R,* 49 (1895) 256, reprinted in H. Black, *Ancestry of Frances Maria Goodman* (Boston: Newbury Street Press, 2001) 343–45.

[25] Wood, *First Church,* 56–57.

[26] B. R. White, *The English Baptists of the Seventeenth Century* (London: Baptist History Society, 1983), 7, 9, 83; B. R. White, ed., *Associated Records of Particular Baptists to 1660,* 3 vols (Baptist History Society, 1971–77), 3: 133; A. C. Underwood, *History of the English Baptists* (London: Kingsgate, 1961), 81. The most recent authority is Stephen Wright, *Early English Baptists* (Woodbridge: Boydell & Brewer, 2006). Broadmead: R. Hayden, ed., "Broadmead Records," *Bristol Record Society,* 27 (1974). In October 1662, Quakers and Baptists in Dorset and further west rose in rebellion because of broken royal promises of toleration. Some two hundred, mainly Quakers, were imprisoned in Dorset; about fifty Baptists were arrested in Plymouth. After the insurrection was crushed, the authorities instituted a savage crackdown. Thomas Goodwin, "Dorset Quaker Rebellion, 1662," *Somerset & Dorset Notes & Queries,* 34 (1998), 189–94.

vices could not be ignored. On 21 March 1666, Middlesex County Court warned her to appear to answer the grand jury's presentment. On 17 June 1667, she was reported for refusing to pay accumulated fines of £3 to Charlestown's constable. She was again before the bench in 1668, and the constables listed her among the eighteen Baptists at Gould's house on 7 March 1669. There is no evidence that she ever paid her fines; however, unlike male leaders, or Quaker women missionaries, she was not imprisoned. She died on 26 September 1684 in her seventy-eighth year, in Charlestown—just before the loss of the First Charter, the death knell of New England uniformity. Her gravestone described her as relict of Andrew Newell of Bristol, merchant, and daughter of William Pitt, sheriff of Bristol.[27]

In the debates at Charlestown about how the church should deal with its recusant Baptist brethren, Richard Russell was, as we have seen, outspokenly critical of Zechariah Symmes and other hardliners for their intolerance. Russell read out evidence "very faithfully" in support of Thomas Gould; he hosted meetings to seek reconciliation, and publicly corrected his impetuous pastor on biblical texts. It is probable that he was the powerful influence against repeated admonitions of the first dissenters, and in 1665 he managed to delay excommunication as punishing "too harshly." Like his friend and neighbor, deputy governor Francis Willoughby, Russell was familiar with the advantages of toleration of minor differences among "hot Protestants" as practiced in Interregnum England. It seems inconceivable that he would not also have been affected by his sister-in-law, a refugee from renewed persecution in Restoration England. Lyme Regis's Baptist preacher, Sampson Larke, was imprisoned for ten years from 1661; Willoughby had seen the beginnings of this surge in royalist vindictiveness before he fled England. The irony of 1630s religious victims' victimizing the next generation was not lost on many in Charlestown, who signed petitions and resisted their minister's wrath.[28]

Three of these Charlestown sisters came from wealthy commercial backgrounds in large and developed cities. Yet other less exalted women also defied authority and conformist pressure, leaving their congregations and joining the Baptists. Mary Goodall of Boston (a Baptist from England); Sister Barney, wife of Jacob of Boston; Sarah Champney Rus-

---

[27]   Wyman, 698. MxCC D&O, 2: folios 40, 43, 47, 52. The inscription about Andrew is not supported by any Bristol records. Knowledgeable kinfolk like Maud and Richard Russell were long dead by then.

[28]   Wood, 44–51; see above, "Godly Merchants." Larke: White, ed., *Associated Records,* 3: 133.

sell of Woburn; Abigail Sweetzer, a Wigglesworth by birth; Sister Brooks of Woburn and Sister Watts: all these names appeared in the early pages of the Baptist Church record book. At a later raid, on 7 March 1669, the constables listed "Goode Gockeling," who was probably Mary Goodwin; Sarah Howard, sister of Rev. Samuel Willard of Old South Church, Boston (the scourge of non-graduate ministers); and Mary Gould's daughter "Joseph Shapleigh's wife," along with her mother. True, most of these women were married to Baptist saints, but their defiance of community and ecclesiastical pressure is nonetheless impressive. Just as much as the indomitable Mary Gould, they too should count as "unsung heroines of American history." While conformist sisters informally circumvented the pattern described by Mary Maples Dunn of passivity in the face of clerical and decanal authority, these more radical dissenters exemplify her depiction of open religious activity.[29]

---

[29] Wood, 57, 90; Willard: on his *Ne Sutor Ultra Crepidam* [Cobbler (John Russell, Jr.) stick to your last], see F. H. Russell, "A Cobbler at his Bench," *R*, 133 (1979), 125–33. In Tewkesbury, England, in 1663, the Baptist conventicle had eighty-six women members and forty-three men. Capp, *Gossips*, 358.

Ursula Cole (1632–78):
Unorthodox Alewife

No letters from Arrald Cole to another daughter-in-law, Ursula, have survived. Any communication between the two women would likely have been pretty tart. In lapses both of modesty and of piety, Ursula would have horrified her godly mother-in-law. Fortunately (and maybe not coincidentally), her worst brushes with authority took place after Arrald's death in December 1661, though she did not wait long.[30]

Ursula (of unknown origin) had married waterman and fisherman John Cole by 1655. They started their married life as tenants on part of Lovells Island in Boston Harbor, where Ursula helped provide the rent by making cheese and butter for their landlord Thomas Sheppie, who also rented them the cows. They had three children during the 1650s, and by the early 1660s had moved back to Charlestown. Their penury was somewhat relieved by John's inheritance of one-third of his mother's estate of £92 in her 1661 will. She also passed on to him his father's Bible, and forbade him to dispose of the iron pot she had bequeathed his son John Jr.[31]

Ursula Cole's name had appeared in the 1655 suit her husband brought against Sheppie. She was soon back in the records because of her Quaker sympathies. In June 1662 and again in October 1663, she was warned to answer in court "for entertaining . . . abetting and encouraging vagabond Quakers" in Charlestown. Her co-defendants included the endlessly subversive Benanuel Bowers and later Baptist heroine Sarah Osborne.

---

[30] See above, "Arrald Cole's Letters."

[31] See above, "Water Everywhere." Arrald's will and inventory, Rodgers, 2: 52–58; John's two brothers Robert and James had both predeceased their mother, without issue. John shared the modest estate with his two sisters: Elizabeth Pierce of Woburn and Mary Lowden of Charlestown.

Quakers excited outrage in orthodox Massachusetts. Two had been executed when they persisted in returning from banishment to preach their
noxious "heresies." They specialized in egalitarian insults, and sensational
interruptions of sermons. Ursula was therefore very much in role when,
visiting Robert Chalkley's house, she opined of the sermons of Zechariah
Symmes and Thomas Shepard Jr. that "she had as lief hear a cat mew as
their preaching." [32]

   Less typical was her abject apology, induced by a heavy £5 fine.
Though she claimed not to recall uttering such "vile expressions," she was
full of "sorrow for it" and "would pray that it would be a warning to her . . .
she would never [again] say the like, with the help of the Lord." She ended
by "humbly entreating the honored court to pass by this offence." She acknowledged this confession with a mark. There is no record of her fine's
being reduced, but she was not again associated with religious dissent. [33]

   While her husband was often away during the 1660s, fishing, cutting
and shipping firewood and timber for building, Ursula diversified from
cheese and butter-making into selling beer and baked goods, to help pay
debts and increase the family's inadequate income. She also had some expertise as a nurse. These enterprises got her into further trouble. [34]

   The first incident, in May 1667, ostensibly arose from her nursing
skills, but probably began with some drinking at Ursula's house. At about
10 p.m., the Charlestown watch encountered Ursula, her elder daughter,
and a couple of visiting seamen standing against a neighbor's door. The
four watchmen "bid them stand. They hoped they would not be offensive to the watch." Goody Cole replied that "they took some fresh air and
would go home presently [immediately]." Half an hour later, the watchmen on their rounds heard a disturbance from upstairs at the house of
Henry and Hannah Salter. Finding the Cole women and the two seamen
there, they told them, "This is a time for honest folks to be at home at their
lodgings." When they returned soon thereafter, Ursula greeted them with,
"What fellows are here? They are rogues and jackanapes and fools that say
I am dishonest [immoral]. I am as honest as any of their mothers." When
one of the watchmen "took the maid [Mary Cole] by the arm and asked

---

[32] MxCC D&O, 1: docs. 1970, 2243; Bowers and Osborne: "A Thirty Years War," in Thompson,
   Cambridge Cameos, 173–82, and "Thomas Gould and the Baptist Debate," above. "Mew:" doc.
   2261, 8 August 1663. On Chalkley, another dissenter, see below, "A Damned Whore."

[33] Doc. 2278, 15 December 1663.

[34] Debt: the Coles owed John Smith, shipwright, £8 for a debt he had taken over from Boston
   merchant John Woodmancey that went back to 1661. D&O, 2: folio 38, 11 October 1665.
   Thomas Sheppie claimed the Coles owed him £15 in 1657; see above, "Water Everywhere."

whether she was Goody Cole's daughter," Ursula snapped, "What's that to you? She is not bound to answer." With that volley, the Cole women returned home. Later, Constable Carrington found the two seamen lurking in a back lane, and asked them where they lodged. When one answered "At Goody Cole's," Carrington declared, "He should not lodge there, and he would get another place, and so he did." When reporting on 20 May to Mr. Russell, the constable said that Ursula had claimed her midnight presence at the Salters' was because Henry had summoned her to see his sick wife. However, the Salters adamantly denied this. In most cases, this would have sufficed to convict Ursula, but the Salters' reputations, especially Henry's, were as jaded as hers.[35]

A second incident at Ursula Cole's followed six weeks later on 4 July 1667. According to the overworked Constable Edward Carrington, he had entered Cole's house at about 11 p.m.—two hours after curfew—and found there two Cambridge men: unsavory printer Marmaduke Robinson, and tailor William Barrett, who claimed he was there about a hat that he had already bargained for. Goody Cole had been out when they arrived, but her daughter, who was there with a young man who referred to Ursula as "mother," let them in and provided two pots of beer. They had smoked a pipe or two of tobacco, and "time run on." They reported that Ursula came home past ten o'clock with her thirsty, unruly nephew, John Lowden. She told John there was no more drink in the house, but he produced a shilling and she discovered a bottle of strong waters. After "he had drunk his part," Lowden mounted his horse and his aunt climbed on as pillion. It was at this point that Carrington arrived. He told the Cambridge men it was "time to be home," and they promised to leave. Ursula demanded, "What is it to you if the two men should lie here this night?" Lowden was equally truculent. He replied to the constable's question about "what he did abroad at that time" with, "What had I to do to summon him?" As the watch had now appeared, Cole sought to justify the hubbub by saying "she was going to her cousin [Sarah] Lowden because she was sick and had sent for her." Later, however, her two daughters, Mary, 17, and Elizabeth, 15, deposed that their cousin John Lowden "earnestly desired our mother to lie at his house; then she should be ready to go to the mill at break of day." Whatever the excuse, the law enforcers were unconvinced. They followed up to Lowden's house at the Neck. Sure enough, they heard another racket.

---

[35] Thomas Danforth's examination of witnesses was dated 20 May 1667. Henry Salter was a seaman and seems to have been an alcoholic; liquor made him belligerent. The Salters were prosecuted for illegal beer sales and carousing on 5 June 1667, and again on 29 April 1668, and yet again on 4 June 1670. D&O, 2: folios 44, 49, 51, 53, 62.

Carrington and his watchmen found three men there as well as Lowden and his aunt. Barrett persisted in his claim that he was merely seeking his hat. When asked if anyone else was present, Lowden answered "No more than he would own." He first threatened, then struck, one of the watch. Carrington commanded him "to keep the peace and took him by the left arm, and he with his right took me by the throat. The watch were fain to put him off, and I caused them to get him out of the house."[36]

Ursula's explanation for her outing to the Neck was blown by five witnesses. Two swore that Goodwife Lowden had not sent for her. Two more recounted her coming to the mill the next morning: "She called to the miller, saying 'George, I made account to lie with thee last night, but the watch hindered me, but if I come thou must provide clean sheets." This was corroborated by miller George Stedman, 19, himself. John Lawrence, who happened to be standing by the mill while Ursula was stipulating her bedding requirements, said ironically, "They must be new ones, must they not?" She replied, "I care not whether they be new, if they be sweet and clean." Later, at Goody March's, she burst out, "there was not but rogues and rascals and rogues and whores that meddle with or busy themselves with her."[37]

Lowden presented two cringing petitions to the court, as well as giving £1 to the constable and ten shillings to the watch. His aunt compounded her problems by failing to appear at her examination before deputy governor Francis Willoughby and Mr. Richard Russell on 23 July 1667. Registrar Mr. Danforth issued an arrest warrant on 30 July. Her surety William Dady stood to lose his £20 bond for her appearance. Fortunately for him, Dr. John Chickering could vouch for Ursula's "dejection and great head and heart passion, difficulty in breathing or speaking . . . her pulse in great measure failing . . . not judging her able to go abroad . . . on the day she should have appeared before the magistrates." She too groveled, "requesting tenderness . . . [to] pass it by, a warning to me as long as I live . . . [to] repent of time passed amiss from God and reform for the future."

Various depositions about these two late-night confrontations emphasize that Ursula Cole had a waspish tongue that stung authority

---

[36] Carrington's report on events "last night" was dated 5 July 1667, D&O, 2: folio 43. Barrett had provided a room for Johnson's illicit and passionate courtship of Samuel Green's daughter, *Cambridge Cameos*, 64. Lowden may have been a hatter; in folio 66, a 6 December 1674 document mentions that he had "hats boiling." The young man may have been John Cole, Jr.

[37] Witnesses: John Cutler, Jehosephat Starr, Henry Swayre, George Stedman, and John Lawrence (another mariner). Some accounts have the incidents at the Salters' and at the mill on succeeding days.

figures like constables or members of the town watch. These loud-mouthed insults and rebuffs might be regretted in the cold and sober light of following days, but in the moment, Goody Cole resented being told what to do. Another element of her lifestyle emerging from witnesses' statements is her free and easy attitude towards young males, which might be interpreted as sexual availability. "Lying with" nineteen-year-old George Stedman at the mill might just be sleeping there in order to make an early start next day, but witnesses seem to imply that it might involve more. Similarly, having seamen sleeping at her house in her husband's absence was suspiciously indiscreet. Unattached and unaccompanied males seemed to gravitate towards the thirty-five-year-old Goodwife Cole and her nubile daughters. Her dejection and "heart passion" may point to her feeling a sense of victimization, of being an object of gossip and smirking innuendo, of having no husband present to safeguard her reputation. However, in the protection of her good name, she proved through her impetuosity and disrespect her own worst enemy.

All this would help explain another fracas at her house on 27 July 1667, a militia training day. Because of rain, the exercises ended early. As the officers went off to dine at Goodman Kettle's, a bunch of young militiamen, several of them wild and disreputable, including John Lowden's younger brother James, descended on Cole's house "to drink some beer . . . spending six pence a piece . . . they being merry, the daughter of the goodwife left the room and shut to the door in with the men. [Ursula] was very merry, and sat among the men drinking with them. Thomas Geere, lying on the bed, she was thrown on the bed to him, where he kissed her she making no resistance and she was kissed by most in the room." Two deponents "left the house before sunset, leaving several there."[38]

The Cole women told a very different story. Danforth added to the self-serving soldiers' account: "To this she answered. She was thrown on the bed . . . but when they were so uncivil, she sent for the constable and they went aways. Three or four strove to cast her on the bed." Seventeen-year-old Mary added further details. The soldiers had already been drinking when they arrived. Her mother had told them she had no beer to sell them. They had replied that they would draw it themselves. She and Ursula had both left

---

[38] Test. John Goodwin, Thomas Geere, folio 48. Wild: Paul Wilson and Thomas Jones, sexual predators, were soon convicted of "living from under family government." Michael Tandy was a suspect in the Largin and Crouch fornication cases; Sylvester Hayes was a notorious lawbreaker; Samuel Frothingham was charged with fighting. See Thompson, *Sex,* index entries, "Adolescent Port Life" above, and "A Damned Whore" below. On the drinking and rowdyism common after training, see *Sex,* 94–95.

the room, "about our business." The intruders had locked the door and were themselves "busy" about something. Eventually mother and two daughters broke the door open, "they huddling about my mother, dragging her to the bedside, throwing a curtain over her head. My mother sent my sister Elizabeth to fetch Constable Johnson; she would have her house cleared of all such base fellows; one came up from the cellar with a drink drawn in his hand. Though the constable was not at home, my mother told them 'Begone! You have stolen my drink and I will make you pay for it.' They said they had had but three pots and offered to pay, but my mother refused." Whatever the truth, the swarming of this gang of ne'er-do-wells to Cole's seems to have had more than a skinful of beer as its motivation.[39]

Ursula Cole survived for another eventful decade. On 6 June 1669, she was a witness in the lurid Sarah Crouch/Christopher Grant/Thomas Jones fornication case. On 9 March 1671, she owned to selling mince pies, bread and sausages to two thieves. Though she self-righteously made no charge for their beer, "it being the Sabbath," she was nonetheless a receiver of stolen money. Two *agents provocateurs* went to her (unlicensed) house on 18 February 1672 and asked if they could buy some beer or ale. She willingly, and incriminatingly, obliged. She was sentenced to a £5 fine on 18 June 1672 for disorders at her house, and sent to prison until she paid. Twice in 1673, Charlestown selectmen fined her a total of £3 for entertaining a man at her house without permission. He had been a lodger for over a month. On 15 December 1674 her daughter Elizabeth, aged about twenty-one, was convicted of fornication with the disreputable John Largin, and sentenced to 15 stripes the following April. Both were warned out of Charlestown, as were her brother John and his wife of both refugees from endangered Groton in 1675. Elizabeth was in Boston by 1674, when she became pregnant by Samuel Eaton, who had promised to marry her. Paul Wilson entered £20 bond for her court appearance (as did parents John and Ursula), but he became so concerned that she might bolt that he requested Middlesex magistrates to lock her up in Cambridge prison.[40]

Meanwhile, when not away on fishing, coasting, or timber trips, Ursula's husband John had a combative record in town. He was in conflict with relatives who tried to dispose of his property in his absence, and

---

[39]   D&O, 2: folio 47.

[40]   Crouch: D&O, 2: folio 52; thieves: Thomas Slade and Nathaniel King, D&O, 3: folio 74; *agents*: D&O, 2: folio 61; disorders: RB, 3: 33; entertaining: CTR, 3: 145, 153; Largin: RB, 3: 114, 120; Eaton: D&O, 3: folio 70; Wilson may have married Mary Cole; Cole Jr: folio 70; they needed fifteen shillings relief as war refugees in 1676, and four years later, as a destitute displaced family, the younger Coles had rate relief, CTrR, 57Ar, B (7) r.

violence flared with neighbors over boundaries and ownership of crops. Money was always desperately short. In 1667, John and Ursula had to sell a cow common for £7. Then the orchard had to go. In 1674 they forfeited land because they could not keep up with the mortgage payments. John Hull, the stoic Boston merchant, finally had to sue for a debt of £3-10-0 in cash, long overdue. In 1678, John was a member of a crew in court to recover unpaid wages. Later that year, he died at sea; his executor Paul Wilson told the court that Ursula had also died. Their estate inventories do not appear in the probate records; we can assume they were meager.[41]

Ursula Cole and her family were an endemic threat to the peace, good order and prevailing morality of Charlestown. Her boozing, merriment, sexual tolerance, contempt for authority, and late-night hijinks represented a counter-culture which Puritans had left corrupt old England to escape. Sometimes the Coles might be more sinned against than sinning, but their suspect reputations deprived them of much official or neighborly sympathy. Ursula fought off poverty with spirit and enterprise: baking, brewing, nursing and renting rooms. Without a license, her beer had to be sold illicitly; without a husband present, her lodgers similarly broke the law. Charlestown, as a port, had a larger than usual surreptitious underground. By 1678, the town had managed to purge one leading family of this alternative world. It is unlikely that anyone in authority shed many tears about the departed Coles (except for the ghost of Arrald).[42]

---

[41] Relatives: Robert Cole, D&O, 2: folio 51; neighbors: D&O, 3: folio 76; sales: *Possessions*, 162, 167; mortgage: RB, 3: 111; Hull, Diary, 116; wages: *Assistants*, I: 128; Wilson: RB, 3: 230.

[42] On "alehouse" culture in England: Thompson, *Divided*, 28–31. Port: Thompson, *Sex*, 14, 187–89.

Mary Mansfield (1610–82)
and the Jarndyce Effect

In my early book *Women in Stuart England and America*, comparing women in seventeenth-century England and America, I suggested that many women stood to benefit by emigrating. Certainly women who settled in Charlestown often came to enjoy a comfortable standard of living as well as social and religious esteem in a supportive, purposeful, and relatively stable environment. Maud Pitt, for instance, shared in the remarkable rise of her young husband, Richard Russell, instead of enduring the horrors of Bristol during the Civil War. Even a scapegrace ex-servant like Sarah Largin Streeter could eventually find prosperity in a frontier community. In the teeming streets of London or Bristol, "Go west, young woman" would not have been bad advice. Yet, in their still-patriarchal new world, that sentiment would need to be allied to tips about finding a mate likely to thrive and survive.[43]

In 1648, Mr. John Mansfield (1601–74) should have been quite a catch for the thirty-eight-year-old widow Mary Gove. True, he was still a bachelor at the age of 47, but he was nonetheless a trained goldsmith after an eleven-year apprenticeship, a freeman of the City of London, a fine scrivener, and extremely well connected. His namesake father, a Yorkshire gentleman (1558–1601), trained as a lawyer at the Inner Temple in London, had represented the Lord President of the Council of the North there. By 1588, he had moved to Huttons Ambo near York. In 1593 he was a member of Parliament for Beverley, Yorkshire. He left a great estate when he died prematurely in 1601. Our John's two elder sisters had married

---

[43]   Thompson, *Women in Stuart England and America* (London: Routledge, 1974). Bristol: Purkiss, *English Civil War*, 252, 285. Streeter: see below, "A Damned Whore."

leading founders of Massachusetts Bay: Elizabeth (1592–ca. 1658) was the wife of Boston's first minister, Rev. John Wilson; Anne (1596–1667) had married the London Cornhill merchant tailor Robert Keayne on 17 April 1617. Sadly, John's father had died in the year of his birth, but he was said to have bequeathed one-third of his estate to his infant son, which should have provided an income of nearly £2,000 a year. Mansfield had lived in London with his mother at the Keaynes' until she died in 1633. Two years later, he crossed to Boston on the *Susan and Ellen* and worked for Keayne "to try mines" (seek and assay mineral lodes) until 1638, when he was granted a house-lot in Boston and land in Braintree.[44]

Mary Gove was the daughter of Humphrey Shard, clothier of St. Nicholas, Cole Abbey, London. On 6 March 1631 she had married John Gove, a brazier of St. Giles Cripplegate, London. In the early 1640s the family had emigrated to New England. They had perched in Hampton, New Hampshire, before moving with their two young sons, Edward and John, and daughter Mary, to Charlestown, where John began a career as a merchant in 1647. On 29 September of that year, Edward Larkin sold the Goves a dwelling and grounds in the town for £10. Tragically, John Gove's time there was cut short. He died a few days after making his will on 22 January 1648. His estate, at this early time of his new career, was worth only £9. He left his daughter Mary to be raised by Ralph Mousall, deacon of Charlestown church. The widow Mary was no wealthy heiress when she married John Mansfield later that year, yet his "kindred wished him to his loving wife," as he later recalled. As Mary would discover, for all his background and affiliations, her new husband turned out to be an appalling liability to her, to his clan (so eager to ship him off across the Charles), to Charlestown, and to Massachusetts in general. His grandiose expectations, sense of entitlement, and self-pitying personality guaranteed nearly three decades of deprivation and deep unpopularity in their unwelcoming adopted town.[45]

Mary soon had twins, John and Elizabeth; the household had four children (including the two from her previous marriage) within a year of marriage. By October 1649, the parents had their first brushes with authority. Their immediate neighbor in Charlestown was Major Robert Sedgwick, leading citizen, merchant, and soldier. On 9 October 1649,

---

[44]   R. C. Anderson et al., "Mansfield Ancestry," *R*, 155 (2001), 3–35; R. C. Anderson, *GM*, 5: 14–17; Brian Dietz, "John Mansfield," P. W. Hasler, ed., *House of Commons 1558–1603* (London: Her Majesty's Stationery Office, 1981), 3: 13. Rodgers, 1: 238; MxCC D&O, 1: doc. 1664. Widow Anne Mansfield Keayne married Samuel Cole, a Boston innkeeper, in 1660.

[45]   *Possessions*, 106. *New Hampshire Genealogical Register*, 11 (1994), 174–79.

Mansfield, after confrontations over bounds and fences, agreed to arbitration by Rev. Thomas Allen. As a result, John "acquitted Major Sedgwick of all matters controversial between us, and will never again open his mouth to complain." This promise seems to have expired five years later. Four witnesses described how Mansfield, set in the town stocks, "abused Major Sedgwick with reviling speeches calling him a cheating cozening man, his soul would fry in hell. This [session in the stocks] was his chance for an hour together to [tell] everyone that passed by, and this he [Sedgwick] had done [to him] for sundering the major's fence within these few days." In December 1655 the Middlesex County Court ordered Charlestown constables to "take special inspection into the manners of Mansfield and his wife . . . of such misdemeanours . . . in their words and actions." John had been accused of "misgovernment of self and wife."[46]

On 28 December 1659, Mistress Mansfield was in the County Court for an outburst against another Charlestown grandee, Mr. Richard Russell. Eight or ten days earlier, a witness had heard

> Mistress Mansfield say to Mistress Russell that they had sworn her husband [Mansfield] out of twenty pounds and that they would all go to the devil, and be damned, further she said some women would play the whore for maintenance before Mr. Russell should have the children, or the disposing of them, for he was her enemy, and worse than a Jew. This speech was with many other unseemly words and gestures of clapping her hands in a disdainful manner.

The £20 may have referred to the negative response to the Mansfields' 21 June petition, in which Mary had sought work as a spinner of flax and a linen seamstress. She would again petition for "tailorly work, sewing, making stockings, sail shirts" two years later. Her sister-in-law Widow Anne Keayne refused to pay them their rightful legacies. Her husband John had a hernia and a lame leg from working for his old master, the late Robert Keayne. He had been rebuffed in 1654 when he asked to join John Hull and Robert Sanderson at the Massachusetts mint, despite his qualifications as a goldsmith. In 1656 Mary had seen her twins ("the greatest comfort in the world . . . who learn their books and letters with us, so loving to us and we to them") taken into care at the age of eight: John to his

---

[46] MxCC D&O, 1: doc. 332; Rodgers, 1: 235. The deposition about the stocks is undated, but occurs among other 1654 papers. It could however be misfiled, as other testimonies are, and may refer to events of 1649. Rodgers's dating of a similar statement to October 1659 would place it three years after Sedgwick's death. Ibid., 235–36.

Aunt Keayne and Elizabeth to Rev. John Whiting, Jr. of Lynn. Such "disposing" threatened to make her "run quite mad." This bitter blow, brought on by poverty, town ultimatums, and family instability, contrasted with the immoral single mothers to whom Russell's court awarded maintenance to keep their illegitimate offspring. No wonder Mary was "troubled in her mind at such wrongs." All this perceived injustice, victimization, and deprivation spewed forth at the sight of the wealthy, well-regarded Mrs. Russell. The defamation earned Mary ten stripes on her bare back.[47]

The kind of mayhem from which the twins (and probably the young Gove boys) were being protected was reported in April 1662 by two Charlestown brothers-in-law who happened to be passing the Mansfields' house between 8 and 9 p.m. They "heard a great prating . . . and heard Mrs. Mansfield cried [sic] . . . both went in at the door and met Master Mansfield, he taking an axe in his hand. We both prevented him striking this Richard Cooper and so we parted them. Robert Wyeth and Mrs. Mansfield was a-sitting with this Richard Cooper, and so we parted them and bid them be silent, with which we sent for the constable." [48]

Silence did not suit the Mansfields. A frequent, more pacific, form of signaling their sufferings was their petitioning to town, to County Court, and to the General Court, usually in John's neat, well-formed hand. Seven petitions have survived, covering nearly twenty years. All tell of grinding poverty, a tumbledown house, chronic illness, lack of suitable employment and wrongs "both in our estates and our good name." Mary was the initiator in the fall of 1650: "She desires her husband may have liberty to sue certain debtors *in forma pauperis* [a special action for a poor man]." The General Court allowed her request. Why she petitioned on his behalf is not known. The debtors may have owed money to the Gove estate.[49]

On 31 May 1660, exasperated by the Mansfields' obsessive claims against Robert Keayne's fortune, the General Court acidly informed John: "He hath so many answers thereto that he hath nothing given to him, with which he ought to rest satisfied; & if ever he trouble this court with such needless and frivolous requests [again], he must expect some sharp

---

[47] Rodgers, 1: 236, MxCC D&O, 1: doc. 1308; 21 June: ibid, doc. 1145; 18 December 1661 petition, doc. 1721. The disposing of the twins is covered in Rodgers, 1: 235–240. Sentence: MxCC RB, 1: 196.

[48] MxCC D&O, 1: docs. 2182, 2183; Barnabas Davis, Jr. aged 24 and William Ridland, 29, husband of Patience Davis. Wyeth and Cooper families lived in neighboring Cambridge, but I have been unable to identify these two. They may have been servants in Charlestown.

[49] *GM,* 5: 15.

reproof from the court, that judgeth it not convenient to be so abused by him as to spend any more precious times thereabouts."[50]

A clutch of Middlesex County Court papers around 25 April 1661 provides a mass of hearsay evidence from fifteen people who had heard about legacies due to Mansfield, ranging from £100 to £2,000 to "a great deal." The Mansfields were insistent that the newly married "Sister Cole," formerly Keayne, should be made to divulge on oath what they should inherit out of their mother's plate, rings, jewels, gold and land. They had never been allowed to see documentation. One of Mansfield's less turgid efforts was that of 2 June 1663 to the Middlesex County Court, written in doggerel.[51]

This relentless repetition of requests did have some effect. Since the Mansfield dwelling was rapidly decaying by the late 1650s, it was becoming a threat not only to its residents but also to its neighbors, as both a firetrap and a rickety hazard. In December 1661, Middlesex County Court ordered Charlestown selectmen to provide materials to repair the house and to support Mary's needlework. The town was reluctant to spend a penny more than the minimum, so the demands and plaints continued. By the end of the 1660s, the town board had been persuaded to build a new house on the understanding that it would revert to public use after the occupants died. On 21 December 1668 they agreed to use slate and timber from the old meetinghouse. When Samuel Hayward had finished the new house, the Mansfields could not decide whether to move out of their familiar hovel with winter approaching. This suggests that the jerry-built alternative was less than draft- and waterproof. [52]

The unemployed, unendowed, and unpopular Mansfields were dependent on charity for their maintenance. They were given £5 a year by "Brother Wilson and Sister Cole," which was passed on to the Charlestown selectmen. As early as 1652, only three years after their marriage, the town accounts record doles of £3 to the family. These continued up to John's death in 1674, with the County Court setting the annual sum at £4. Mansfield picked up a little money writing petitions for others, but when he tried to teach a few pupils in 1666, schoolmaster Ezekiel Cheever complained to the selectmen. Mansfield was stopped. In 1671, Mary and John were ordered by the court to pick oakum: a painful and demeaning job,

---

[50] *GM*, 4: 133.

[51] Rodgers, 1: 237–40; MxCC D&O, 1: docs. 1664, 1721, 2378, 2496. Cf. Mass Archives, 1654, 15 May 1672, MxCC RB, 3: 15, 130.

[52] MxCC D&O, 1: docs. 1721, 2372; CTrR, 2: 29.

quite unsuitable for the hands of a scrivener and a seamstress. Mr. Hayman was to supply a hundredweight "of old junk" from his ropewalk. The following year, the penny-pinching Middlesex magistrate Thomas Danforth answered yet another Mansfield petition for assistance by telling him to sell their old Gove house. People indebted to the town were sometimes told to supply the Mansfields. So in February 1674, Timothy Cutler delivered them a load of wood to help pay his town rent. [53]

John Mansfield died on 26 June 1674 leaving £8-10-6, slightly less than Mary's first husband John Gove in 1648. Charlestown could not wait to escape further responsibility for her. On 13 July 1674, her son Edward Gove of Hampton, New Hampshire, entered bond clearing the town of "all charges for his mother Widow Mary Mansfield." She was ushered northwards and died at Edward's on 4 March 1682. She thus missed "Gove's Rebellion," in which Edward, a New Hampshire militia officer, selectman and assemblyman, unsuccessfully tried to topple the arrogant English fortune hunter Edward Cranfield, recently appointed royal governor. Gove, unkindly described by James Savage as "being either drunk or insane, perhaps both," but in fact a garrulous advocate of English liberties, was lucky to escape his sentence of being hanged, drawn, and quartered. Shipped to the Tower of London, he was eventually pardoned and returned to New Hampshire. His poor mother was well spared this tragicomic, if prophetic, attempt to challenge royal prerogative.[54]

Mary Gove Mansfield deserved this final break. After the sudden early death of her first husband, with a son of only seven years old, she had quickly married the deceptively attractive John Mansfield, who moved into the Gove house in Charlestown. Robert Charles Anderson claims that her new husband "demonstrated serious mental imbalance throughout his adult life." Her brother-in-law, Captain Robert Keayne, left them no legacy (except two cows for the twins), but a scathing report of Mansfield in his 1653 will:

---

[53]   CTrR, 1: 44A, 51 r, and passim; petitions: MxCC D&O, 2: folio 49 has two petitions for Ursula Cole in Mansfield's hand. School: CTR, 3: 76. Oakum, a loose fiber obtained by picking old rope to pieces to be used for caulking: CTR, 3: 126. Danforth: CTR, 3: 130. Cutler: CTR, 3: 157; cf. William Crouch to deliver parts of two dry trees, CTR, 3: 84.

[54]   Estate: Rodgers, 3: 262–63. Bond: CTR, 3: 163. Rebellion: W. H. Gove, *The Gove Book* (Salem: Perley, 1922), 13–49; D. S. Lovejoy, *The Glorious Revolution in America* (New York: Harper, 1974), 151; Charles E. Clarke, *The Eastern Frontier* (Hanover: University Press of New England, 1983), 61; Savage, 2: 288; T. B. Lewis, "Royal Government in New Hampshire 1679–83," *Historical New Hampshire*, 25 (1970), 2–45, esp. 28–36; Jeremy Belknap, *History of New Hampshire* (Bowie, MD: Heritage, 1992), 99, 477–87; Nathaniel Bouton, ed., *Province Papers of New Hampshire* (Concord, NH: Jenks, 1867), 1: 458–63, 490–97.

who hath proved an unworthy & unthankful brother to me, though I have done very much for him, in England diverse times, in releasing him out of prisons, in paying his debts for him, furnishing him with a stock to set up his trade, when he had spent all his own in taking up many quarrelsome businesses, which he in his distempered fits had plunged himself into of dangerous consequence; yet I compounded them for him & at his sister's my wife's entreaty with some other friends of hers I sent him over into New England, when his life was in some hazard, I paid his passage & some of his debts for him in England & lent him money to furnish himself with clothes and other necessaries for his voyage, for many years I found him diet and clothes gratis, till for his distempered carriages & unworthy behaviour, I was fain to put him out of my house. All the work that ever he did for me, not being worth his clothes, yet was he never quiet in disturbing my whole family & pursuing me with continued complaints to our Elders & others seeking to pull a maintenance out of my estate while himself lived idly and spent what he got in drink & company keeping.[55]

Keayne was an angry and vinegary man in later life, but we can recognize the "distempered fits" and the idleness he criticizes.

It may be more charitable to think of Mansfield as someone who should never have been sent to a frontier enterprise. He had none of the essential qualities of the pioneer. He might conceivably have supported himself in an English provincial town as a goldsmith or a scrivener or a schoolmaster, but not in early Massachusetts. The Mansfields also suffered from what might be called "the Jarndyce effect," after the disastrous impact of a large but ambiguously bequeathed fortune upon expectant legatees in Charles Dickens's *Bleak House*. John and Mary shared similarly tantalizing dreams, repeatedly dashed by counterclaims and institutional indifference.

The extent to which John Mansfield relied on Mary and identified with her is touchingly shown in what is, in effect, their joint will of 21 August 1665. It included, of course, one-third of £5,600 a year in lands in Yorkshire in old England as well as a less grandiose estate in New England. Bequests were "to whom we will and we make use of while we live." Mary put her mark on the document beside her husband's signature. Despite her many

---

[55]   Gove's death occurred at the most vulnerable time for his young family. *GM*, 5: 14–17, reproduces the passage from Keayne's will.

misfortunes and sufferings, she showed extraordinary spirit and loyalty, supporting and steadying a wayward but affectionate yokefellow.[56]

Mary Mansfield's heartfelt outburst against the Russells in 1659 represents her sense of lost opportunity and hopelessness. As daughter of a London clothier, born in a wealthy parish just south of St. Paul's, she could have expected a privileged future. Marrying a brazier with mercantile ambitions should have promised a comfortable life, like that of Boston brazier's wife Elinor Shrimpton. This was the same kind of world that Maud Pitt enjoyed. Yet Mary Mansfield had to live in a hovel, had her children forcibly removed into foster care, her pleas for needlework answered by an order to pick oakum like a common vagabond, her back stripped bare and lashed like a lippy whore. When John died, she was hustled out of town with brutal dispatch. All the time, exacerbating the bitterness, but exciting glimmers of hope, was that vast inheritance, an entitlement withheld. Here was an unfortunate emigrant, who would have done better to stay east.[57]

---

[56] Rodgers, 3: 262.

[57] Shrimpton: Bailyn, *Merchants,* 35.

"A Damned Whore":
Sarah Largin Streeter of
Charlestown and Whorekill,
1668–1709

One of the most extraordinary and unexpected success stories of Charlestown-raised women began at the lowest rung of the social and economic ladder. In her youth,

Sarah Largin (ca. 1650–ca. 1709) posed an altogether more serious threat to the peace and respectability of the town than the loud-mouthed Ursula Cole. Some twenty years younger, Sarah was a representative of a third-generation rebellious adolescent sub-culture that rejected the celibate morality demanded of the unmarried. As well as talking about sex, Sarah brazenly indulged in it. In an international port, with foreign seamen idling on the wharves, with local masters and men away at sea, the potential for breaches of the rigid rules of behavior was widespread. Sarah Largin was one of several young women who were drawn into this exciting but dangerous alternative world.[58]

Information about Sarah's background is, significantly, sparse. She came from an obscure and challenged family. Her father Henry had married a widow, Alice Moore, in the late 1640s or early 1650s. Alice already had three children, and the administrators of the estate of the late Jeremiah Moore seemed distrustful of Largin as a stepfather. They made Boston innholder William Courser and his wife trustees of the £40 left as portions for the young Moores. Sarah Largin was born in a rented house in

---

[58] See Thompson, *Sex*, 83–109, 149–53, 182–87. On casual attitudes to extramarital sex in Wapping, origin of many mariner families in Charlestown, see Capp, *When Gossips Meet*, 38.

Boston, but when she was between six and eight she and her brother John were both fostered out to the childless Chalkley household in Charlestown in 1658. Robert Chalkley (1608–72) was a wheelwright. In 1647 he was admitted a church member; two years later he was elected constable of Charlestown. His wife Elizabeth, also entering her fifties, would have been responsible for Sarah's domestic training.[59]

Sarah's contempt for Goody Chalkley's instructions first came to public notice in 1668, when Sarah was in her late teens. On 6 October the Middlesex County Court heard testimony about "the wanton carriages" of Sarah Crouch, and, as the evidence spilled out, of her friend Sarah Largin. Indeed, Largin seems to have outdone Crouch in wantonness. One witness was William Morgan, a seaman from the visiting *Ambrose*. He recorded that he had spent a good part of a day in Largin's company. They had been at Chalkley's, and the wheelwright later confessed that even though he knew that Morgan and another man were in his house, he had nonetheless "gone off to his work and left them there." Sarah had crossed to Boston in the afternoon to buy some yarn. At some point, Morgan and his ship's cooper had had "a tumble [with Largin] in the hay behind Goodman [Solomon] Phipps's barn." Then in the evening she and Morgan had gone off to the house of Sarah Crouch's master John Knight. She stayed until "two or three in the morning," when she was stopped on her way home by the watch.[60]

This was not an isolated infraction. Knight, a widower, deposed that in the middle of another night, he was awakened and found the two Sarahs "both undressed . . . Sarah Largin ran off still undressed shedding clothes . . . I asked [Crouch] what men were these. At length she said Peter Briggs. I asked if the other were Thomas Jones but she gave me no answer. I warned her that I would turn her out of doors [if it happened again]."[61]

Gossip about such outrages as this flushed out other stories. Goodwife Carrington remembered seeing "Sarah Largin with four or five men, and coming from the Neck of Land saw a fellow kissing Sarah Largin several times in Goodman Chalkley's porch. When I reproached her, she denied it not." Sarah herself admitted that it was "a common thing for her to go out anights, sometimes with young men and sometimes alone. She had not carried

---

59   Largin: Wyman, 599; Courser: *GM*, 2: 219–220; Chalkley: Wyman, 197, Rodgers, 3: 175–77. Chalkley was later tarnished with a reputation for religious dissent. Ursula Cole disparaged ministerial preaching in his house. In 1668 he referred to the meeting house as "the pewhouse", a favorite Quaker put-down. CTR, 3: 89. On 12 February 1671 Charlestown church formally admonished him for reviling authority. He repented on 1 September 1672. Hunnewell, viii.

60   MxCC D&O, 2: folio 47.

61   Thompson, *Sex*, 43. On Knight's thievish servant Nathaniel King, see below.

herself with that modesty that became her but hath had wanton carriages." One man testified that he had found "Sarah Largin asleep on top of hay bales in a barn. He often saw young men in her company, in the mill yard [a common meeting point] and other places." While one young man diffidently voiced the opinion of his age group that "Sarah Largin was said to be a very whore," Thomas Jones, one of Sarah Crouch's suitors, was more brutally blunt: "Sarah Largin is a damned whore." He spoke with authority.[62]

Sarah's fate in this October 1668 case is unknown because of the loss of the second Court Record Book. It is likely that she would have been sentenced to ten lashes, as a refractory servant and wickedly behaved adolescent. She surfaced in court the following year on 6 June 1669, in the notorious Crouch-Jones-Grant fornication scandal. Her companion in wantonness Sarah Crouch had given birth to a bastard on 3 January 1669. In the torment of labor, she had named Christopher Grant, Jr. of Cambridge as the father, but he was certain that "dirt-dauber" Thomas Jones was the begetter who should pay weekly maintenance. Sarah Largin (along with Ursula Cole) was one of eleven witnesses. She betrayed her erstwhile friend by testifying that Crouch had on 1 April 1669 pleaded with her not to give evidence incriminating Jones, but "to abide in Boston" outside the Middlesex County Court territory.[63]

Fourteen months later, on 4 June 1670, both Sarahs, Crouch and Largin, were presented by the grand jury for fornication. Largin had given birth to a boy, though no father was prosecuted. Given her previous associates, he may well have been a foreign seaman long since departed. An undated petition probably relates to her failure to appear in court, and her punishment. Sarah ritually rehearsed her sense of shame and guilt. She explained that she had "been tarrying in Boston when the court sat, but was unable to appear because of sickness . . . Now in prison with her child," she begged to be released on bail, "because she did not wish to expose the child to hazard in winter." On 6 January 1671 Henry Largin placed his mark and Robert Chalkley his signature on a £5 bond undertaking that "Sarah Largin now in the House of Correction would attend the next court." Out on bail, she received wine, cakes, and tobacco from servant Nathaniel King. He had bought these treats with money he had stolen on 9 March 1671 from Sarah Crouch's old master John Knight. Again, no record of Sarah's punishment for fornication has survived. Her reputation

---

[62]   D&O, 2: folio 47, tests. Thomas Grover, Ambrose Spencer.

[63]   RB, 2, covering 1663 to 1671, was destroyed by fire. Crouch-Jones-Grant: *Sex*, 41–44; witness: D&O, 2: folio 53.

did survive, however. In 1676 the predatory Charlestown miller Robert Montgomery "attempted lewdness with her." She was one of several women who testified at his trial.[64]

By 27 August 1672, when seventy-year-old Robert Chalkley made his will, Sarah had married Henry Streeter or Stretcher (1637–1704). After Widow Elizabeth Chalkley's death (in 1678), they would inherit the Chalkley barn and surrounding land in Charlestown. An intriguing clause covers the "care of the child Bennoni now in the family, and my will is that my wife expend £10 on that child's education." A Bennoni "son of Sarah Streeter" (but not of Henry) is entered in the Charlestown town records on 6 January 1679 as being bound out as an apprentice to childless wheelwright Jonathan Cane of Cambridge for 13 years; he died in 1690. It is virtually certain that this was the illegitimate child born in 1670. [65]

Equally little is known of Henry Streeter's background; like married like. He earned his meager living as a woodworker. On 9 February 1674, his kleptomaniac brother-in-law John Largin was charged with breaking into a Charlestown shop. When questioned by Mr. Russell about the instrument he had used, John replied "an adze from my brother Stretcher's." Sarah and Henry were desperately poor. By 1673 they had two children, and the town had to abate their already modest rates by eleven shillings. More children followed: John 1673, Robert 1674 and Edward ca. 1677. Charlestown selectmen "bound out" the three eldest to respectable families. In 1678, the year of Elizabeth Chalkley's legacy, the town clerk described Sarah Largin as "late of this town." That phrase must have been music to the selectmen's ears.[66]

---

[64] Grand jury and bond: folio 53; petition and theft: folio 56; Montgomery: folio 73.

[65] Will: Rodgers, 3: 175–77; Bennoni: CTR, 4: 4; Cane: Thompson, *Cambridge Cameos*, 47, 326. The Streeters' Letter of Attorney of 16 June 1702 (see below) complains that the £10 left to "our son" Bennoni had never been "expended." Mx D, 13: 549.

[66] Streeter: Wyman, 197. Rodgers, 1: 91–92 has the 10 June 1652 will of shoemaker Stephen Streeter of Charlestown, but among the three sons and three daughters, no Henry is mentioned. On 18 January 1672 Henry Streeter served on a coroner's jury inquiring into the death of Joseph Indian, D&O, 2: folio 59. John Largin: he had already been arrested in 1671 and sent to the House of Correction for encouraging two servants to run away; during their absence they had visited Sarah Largin in Cambridge, RB, 3: 26; D&O, 3: folio 61. On 24 January 1671, "His master complained that he lay from home several nights that week without leave. He was so idle he could get him to do nothing, or spoilt [it] if he did ought. He confessed he absented himself from meeting. Though his dame turned him out of the house, he secretly returned in again." D&O, 3: folio 74. Russell discovered that Largin had stolen £4-4-0 worth of fabric, 302 nutmegs, cinnamon, and combs valued at £1-15-7. Three great tankards, three gallons of brandy, ribbons, and a hat brought the total to a very considerable £7-18-7. On 7 April 1674, Largin was sentenced to be branded with "B" for burglar on his forehead. RB, 3: 90. On 5 October 1674 John was fined ten shillings for climbing into Goodman Bullard's orchard at 10 p.m. in early August and shaking down pears. He had first lied, then refused to answer when caught.

A 1702 letter of attorney empowering sale of the Chalkley bequest is a vital clue to the Streeters' subsequent adventures on a new frontier. Their address in that year was "Lewes alias Whorekill in Sussex County annexed to the Province of Pennsylvania." Whorekill, a creek named after the Dutch town of Hoorn, was also a county name and port town on the western side of the huge estuary of the Delaware River, the Delaware Bay. It had originally been settled by Swedes and Finns in 1638, but Dutch influence in the Lower Delaware Valley gradually throttled the colony, and in 1655 it was absorbed into New Netherland. In turn, the Dutch had been overcome by the English sent by the Duke of York in 1664. The duke's proprietary colony was grandiosely described as stretching from the west bank of the Connecticut River to the east bank of the Delaware. His claim was challenged not only by Connecticut in the north, but also by Lord Baltimore, expansionist proprietor of Maryland, in the south.[67]

After York's representative took over the Lower Delaware in 1664, the new rulers felt an urgent need to recruit English settlers to leaven the population lump of assorted Finns, Swedes, and Dutch and see off the Marylanders. The land was rated "the best and most fertile . . . the like is nowhere to be found." It proved ideal for tobacco and grains. The climate was "good and healthy." The Whorekill "wanteth nothing but people." New York was not finally confirmed to England until the end of the Third Dutch War in 1674. Thereafter, promotion accelerated with offers of fifty-acre headrights for every British immigrant, peppercorn quitrents, and extra land grants from the governor for favored planters. By the 1680s, more than half the settlers in what had been renamed Kent and Sussex

---

D&O, 3: folio 67. At the end of 1674 this "servant of Robert Chalkley" was warned out of Charlestown. RB, 3: 114. During King Philip's War, Largin was accused of killing friendly Indians, but was acquitted; in April 1676, however, he was referred to the Middlesex County Court on a lesser charge of wounding. *Assistants*, 1: 57, 21 September 1675; see "Mass Violence" below. Bound out: Bennoni to Cane, CTR, 4: 4, 6 January 1679, John to Richard Stowers, ibid, 22, 8 March 1680, and Henry Jr. to Matthew Bridge of Cambridge, RB, 4: 107, 1676. He was listed in Watertown in 1687. Selectmen: From 1676, the town was crammed with western refugees from King Philip's War. The New England frontier could no longer act as a "safety valve."

[67] Letter: Mx D, 13: 549. Whorekill (the anglicized name) County was 30 miles long, and 12–14 miles wide, C. H. Turner, *Some Records of Sussex County, Delaware* (Philadelphia: Allen, Lane & Scott, 1909), 20. The early history of the region is explored in B. Fernow, comp., *Documents Concerning the History of Dutch and Swedish Settlements on the Delaware River, Documentary History of the Colony of New York*, Vol. 12 (Albany: Argus, 1877); C. T. Gehring, ed., *Delaware Papers (English Period) New York Historical Manuscripts, Dutch* (Baltimore: Genealogical Publishing, 1977), 20–21, 203, 227–28; W.K. Kavanagh, ed., *Foundations of Colonial America*, Vol. 2 (New York: Chelsea House, 1973) 827–29; John A. Munroe, *Colonial Delaware* (Millwood, NY: KTO Press, 1978); R. C. Ritchie, *The Duke's Province* (Chapel Hill: University of North Carolina Press, 1977). W. J. Cohen, *Swanendael in New Netherland* (Lewes, DE: Historical Society, 2003) has an excellent map of early Whorekill County.

Counties owned more than 500 acres of land. By 1693, one in ten Sussex householders owned property worth more than £200. This was a proprietary land boom.[68]

The Streeters were attracted to this land grab in 1676. On 24 July, Henry Streeter/Stretcher was granted 600 acres in Whorekill County, among a group that received a total of 5,261 acres from New York's Governor Andros. On 17 October 1677, Henry was listed as one "of the company at Delaware." In 1678 he was measured a further 400 acres by the surveyor of the three "Lower Counties." Another 800 were granted by the County Court in 1682. At its height, the family real estate amounted to 1,800 acres, including 500 acres in Broadkill Hundred called "Stretcher Hall." The Streeters were active in the Whorekill land market, buying town land and selling to incomers tracts of upland and islands. The despised paupers of Charlestown had enjoyed an unimaginable transformation.[69]

Whorekill in the 1670s had something of a frontier atmosphere. As a petition as late as 20 February 1683 put it: "Much of this county is in its infontse [infancy]." On 30 June 1679, senior residents sent outraged complaints to Andros about the abusive behavior of county magistrates who behaved more like buccaneers and outlaws than upholders of the law. One was involved in piracy in the Indian Ocean and coerced the crew of a Lewes vessel to join him. As late as 1698, about 50 French pirates came ashore at Lewes and plundered almost every house in the town.[70]

---

[68] 1674: New York had been briefly recaptured by the Dutch in 1673, but was permanently restored by the Treaty of Westminster in 1674. Whorekill/Sussex County: Munroe, 33–34, 74–78, 94, 95; Turner, 1, 3, 6; Ritchie, 110, 191; Fernow, 498. *CSP Col*, 3: 1167: a letter from York's secretary to a New York official: "Give all encouragement to any inhabitants that will come with their goods and families from other plantations," 30 November 1676. Cf. 436, a query of 13 February 1675 about the "likelihood of drawing more English to inhabit there." Marylanders: after the Lower Delaware was confirmed to the English, Baltimore initiated a land-bidding war against New York, offering as much as 1,000 acres per family in the Whorekill. C. A. Weslager, *Englishmen on the Delaware, 1610–85* (New Brunswick, N.J.: Rutgers University Press, 1967), 219.

[69] I have not discovered how the Streeters heard about the Whorekill or moved there. The only Bostonian I have identified there is Nathaniel Walker, but he had moved first to the Virginian Eastern Shore. R. S. Dunn and M. M. Dunn, eds., *Papers of William Penn*, 2 (Philadelphia: University of Pennsylvania Press, 1982), 313. Turner, 3; Gehring, 108, 109, 136, 203, 208–9; Fernow, 544, 586; 1682: Craig W. Horle, ed., *Records of the Court of Sussex County, Delaware 1677–1710* (Philadelphia: University of Pennsylvania Press, 1991), 81, 153, 154, 368, 387, 428, 686–87, 921, 972; W. G. Egle, *Early Pennsylvania Land Records* (Baltimore: Genealogical Publishing, 1976), 490; E. J. Sellers, *Allied Families of Delaware* (Philadelphia: privately printed, 1901), 5–9.

[70] Petition: Dunns, *Penn Papers*, 2: 623. Turner, 41; Munroe, 108; Fernow, comp., *Calendar of New York Council Minutes 1669–1783* (Harrison, N.Y.: Harbor Hill, 1987), 133; Fernow, *Documents*, 12: 603, 624–25 prints two communications: magistrate Edward Southrin's of 1678 graphically describes the court behavior of erstwhile pirate John Avery and Henry Smith. The former pub-

Between 1682 and 1701, Whorekill became part of Pennsylvania. Its county name was changed to Sussex, more seemly to Anglophone ears. The town was rechristened Lewes (after the county town of Sussex, England). The western shore of the bay and the valley of the southern stretch of the river were called the Three Lower Counties, as distinct from the three Quaker Upper Counties. In the first decade of the eighteenth century the Lower Counties seceded and, with their own assembly after 1704, they effectively became a separate, unchartered colony.[71]

Henry Streeter became a prominent figure in Sussex County affairs. In 1684, 1686 and 1687, he was elected a representative to the Pennsylvania General Assembly. He was a Lewes "innholder" by 1688; the County Court met at his tavern. He continued his career as a woodworker, contracted to build stocks and a whipping post in 1680, helped to repair a sloop, and participated in unspecified town "improvements." In 1683 he was one of a party who rescued a stranded boat and its passengers from the bay. He was perennially involved in the County Court: as juryman and foreman, estate appraiser and administrator, as arbitrator and as plaintiff or defendant. Most of the 117 civil cases in which Streeter or Sarah were parties concerned debts, and most of them were withdrawn, suggesting that the threat of a suit usually pried out the sum owed. The majority were small, but Streeter's debt of £55 to New York merchant Thomas Phillips led to the participation of the deputy secretary of Pennsylvania and the seizure and sale of Streeter land to satisfy Phillips's long-suffering widow. As an innkeeper and artisan, Streeter would be expected to give customers credit; he would likewise defer reckoning on what he owed for liquid and solid supplies until the last possible moment.[72]

---

licly called a fellow magistrate "rogue & beggarly rogue . . . Sirrah, you pitiful lousy rascal," and threatened violence when a licensee refused to "draw him a bottle of rum for an Indian he had hired on the Sabbath Day." Smith would not execute any warrants issued against his friends or family. Captain Avery was the target of magistrate Luke Watson's denunciation on 30 June 1679. When crossed, "he have in a great rage and fury went [sic] out of court cursing and swearing, calling the rest of the court fools, knaves and rogues, wishing that if ever he sat amongst us again, that the devil might come and fetch him away . . . and did strike one of the magistrates with his cane, and had he not been prevented by the spectators might have done much damage that way." He had performed marriages without banns, one for a woman already engaged to another, whose fiancé died of shock, and a second for a man who already had a wife living in England. He had freed a female thief. He boasted that he was not "accountable to any court . . . and [was] above any power here." In short, he was "an encourager and upholder of drunkenness, theft, cursing, swearing and fighting to the affrighting, amazing and terrifying of his Majesty's quiet and peaceable subjects . . . [a man] of gross wickedness and unhuman conversation."

[71]   Horle, 9, 11; Munroe, 114.

[72]   Horle, 53, 110, 235, 244, 317, 357, 384, 387, 447, 465, 499, 837, 1070, 1103; the Streeters were

Far from Streeter children being fostered out, Henry and Sarah became responsible parent figures, with poor or fatherless children in their care. They also had servants in their household. Former hellion Sarah now experienced the type of underling behavior that had so outraged her old mistress, Elizabeth Chalkley. One of the Streeters' more fortunate hirings was Nehemiah Field, an indentured servant with legal and drafting experience, who represented them in court.[73]

Not all the Streeters' appearances in court concerned mundane issues like credit and debt. The newfound veneer of respectability was scratched by contemptuous or forbidden activities, like smoking in court, swearing "By God," and illicit card-playing, and more deeply scarred by a series of cases in the late 1680s which confirmed that old habits died hard.[74]

From 4 to 6 October 1687, the Sussex County Court heard a defamation suit brought by General Assembly representative Streeter against boat builder Adam Johnson, who had claimed that Sarah Streeter "had had a bastard child by a Negro, and he would prove it." One of five witnesses for the defense, present at the birth, deposed: "The child born of the body of Sarah Streeter looked swarthy like a black bastard at birth but thereafter grew whiter and whiter." The jury found for Streeter, and ordered her slanderer either to ask forgiveness in open court, or pay the modest damages of £5. Johnson, however, appealed to Philadelphia.[75]

Six months later, on 7 February 1688, Henry was a defendant in two slander suits that may have erupted from the "black bastard" allegations. In the first, the plaintiff was William Clarke, the president of the court. He alleged that on 10 January 1688 Streeter had called him "a perjured rogue and said that he could prove it, and testified to it with many gross and barbarous oaths and curses and said the he had often times told him [Clarke] so much to his face." Henry rebuffed suggestions that he had had too much to drink when he offended. "No! It was not the drink, for he would say the same now." The defendant's sobered and "pensive acknowledgment" imploring "your worship's pardon" seems to have extricated him.[76]

The second case on the same day further exposed Streeter's crudity and coarseness. According to plaintiffs Samuel and Susannah Gray, "Hen-

---

plaintiffs in 65 actions, defendants in 52. See index s.n. "Stretcher" for 248 entries.

[73] Ibid., 317, 667, 1159.

[74] Ibid., 249, 419, 522.

[75] Ibid., 481; the outcome of the appeal is not known.

[76] Ibid., 533. Already in 1684, Clarke had been "charged with telling several lies and untruths reflecting upon Lord Baltimore." He wrote a long rebuttal to William Penn, *Penn Papers,* 2: 551.

ry Stretcher, rude of behaviour and corrupt of life, maliciously intending and designing to destroy and take away the[ir] repute and good name" at the previous October Court, "in the hearing of many . . . did utter, publish and declare in wicked and depraved manner several scandalous, injurious and abusive words against . . . Susannah Gray. [He] falsely, scurrilously and brutishly in clamorous and barbarous sort charged and affirmed that [she] was forsworn (a liar) and further he would prove her forsworn." Henry's attorney offered no defense; the slanderer was sentenced to pay a £5 fine (offsetting damages in October) and costs. Two years later, his loud mouth incriminated him yet again. On 4 February 1690, he had to apologize "for several foolish words" uttered when a woman made her escape from the sheriff's custody. 1687 was Henry's last year as a county representative in Philadelphia.[77]

Two more cases, a decade and more later, confirmed that gentility eluded the Streeters. The first suggested that their inn served as a wenching house; the second that its owners were receivers of stolen goods. On 9 June 1698 Peter Cartwright, a local merchant, was charged with "filthily and abominably making use of the body of [his servant] Rachel Jones in the house of Henry Streeter." Sarah's deposition on 1 March had put it more bluntly: Cartwright had boasted that "he had fuckt his maid thirty times." Sarah and son Edward, now "20 and upwards," had both seen the pair "abed together; [but they] went for man and wife." The court accepted Rachel's solemn oath that "she was his wife before God," but the louche atmosphere of the inn recalls Sarah's own adolescent easy virtue.[78]

On 12 April 1700, Henry was one of a party of five Lewes men who "had gone on board Captain Kidd the privateer (who in July last lay some days before Cape Henlopen [just below Lewes]) and had corresponded with him and received from him and his crew some muslins, calicoes, moneys and other goods which were East Indian and prohibited goods, and that they had brought them on shore, hid, sold and given away most of them without acquainting the king's collector [of customs] . . . if not piracy, at least [this amounted to] confederating with them, accessories to promiscuous and illegal trade." There is no record of the Pennsylvania Colony Council's reaction to these breaches of the Navigation Acts and profiteering from piracy. No doubt the Streeters' inn did a roaring trade in contraband.[79]

---

[77] Horle, 536–37, 692.

[78] Ibid., 1050.

[79] Turner, 42.

Though the Streeters' large landholdings, communal prominence and Henry's offices were a world away from their obscurity and low esteem in Charlestown, some of their behavior over the following twenty-five years accords with their New England reputations. Sarah's wild adolescence (like that of her brother) resulted from a fractured and poverty-stricken upbringing and the lascivious opportunities offered by the port life of Charlestown. The Chalkleys had been too elderly and ineffectual as foster parents to curb her recklessness. At least their legacy helped their ward's search for a better life.

Though King Philip's War (1675–76) had set back frontier opportunities in New England, the English acquisitions after the Third Dutch War had created exciting alternatives on the Delaware. The Streeters capitalized on this new frontier. When Sarah and Henry finally sold their small parcel of Massachusetts land in 1704, their tenuous connection to Charlestown ended. That year Henry died, shortly followed by Sarah. Their son Edward took over much of their land, and married Margaret, daughter of the Upland County magnate and Quaker founder of New Salem in New Jersey, Major Thomas Fenwick. The Streeters would be gentry by the mid-eighteenth century. Such was the meteoric rise of the progeny of that damned whore of Charlestown and Whorekill.[80]

---

[80] Horle, 1252, 1289, 1292; L. de Valinger, *Calendar of Sussex County, Delaware Probate Records, 1680–1800* (Dover: Delaware Public Archives Commission, 1964), 40, 57, 77; Fenwick: Munroe, 78. In 1674 Fenwick and partner had bought the whole of West New Jersey for £1,000; he settled Salem in 1675 and proceeded to sell 148,000 acres. Weslager, *Englishmen on the Delaware*, 232.

Katherina Kidnapped:
Deacon v. Jenner, 1670

In 1667, Captain Thomas Jenner's ketch was preparing to sail, outside the Keys of Jamaica Road, when a wherry (a type of rowing boat) came alongside. On board were the wife of Jamaican victualler Joseph Deacon of Port Royal and a black woman named Katherina. Mrs. Deacon requested Jenner to take Katherina on board "until some difference between Mr. [Elias] Row and her husband was issued." After an hour or two, Jenner sent to Row's ship to have Katherina taken ashore, but Deacon "pretended sickness" and excused himself. "A day or so later [Deacon] said he would fetch her, but then parted from us." Jenner seems to have been bound for Barbados, but contrary winds blew him to Virginia, with Katherina still on board. She protested that she had been "trepanned [kidnapped] from Jamaica. She was a free woman and had a writing from the Governor of Jamaica . . . She was no man's servant. He could not sell her [as a slave] but [only] for four year's time . . . which did but pay for her passage," as though she were an indentured servant working off her fare. Under these conditions, and "according to the customs of the country," Jenner sold her services to Captain William Moseley in Virginia for two thousand pounds of tobacco, and then sailed back south to Barbados. On 20 December 1670, Deacon sued Jenner for £30 for not paying "the produce" of Katherina's sale, or redelivering her to him.[81]

---

81   Documents in MxCC D&O, 2: folio 54. Deacon, who died in late October 1671, had well-established commercial connections with Boston; his partner there was Arthur Mason. His widow Rachel married William Shute and continued to live in Jamaica, *Sfk CCR,* 45, 65. Port Royal was the main port of Jamaica until the 7 June 1692 earthquake; it had a very seamy reputation. L. Colley, *The Ordeal of Elizabeth Marsh* (New York: Harper, 2007), 3. On the "minuscule number" of free blacks in Jamaica, see Dunn, *Sugar and Slaves,* 255. Elias Row (1629–87), a Charlestown shipmaster and merchant, had married into the Long family and lived next

Both Jenner and Deacon were represented in the Middlesex County Court by attorneys: Humphrey Hodges appeared for Jenner, and Peter Golding for Deacon. Witnesses included Elias Row, 40, who had seen the woman on Jenner's ketch, as well as Jenner's crew members Daniel Remington, 27, and Peter Codner, 30, who attested to their skipper's attempts to return Katherina to Deacon in Jamaica. A crucial issue was whether or not Katherina was indeed free, as she asserted. If she was, then Jenner owed Deacon nothing, and had every right to the tobacco in return for her passage and "her keeping five or six weeks in Virginia." On this issue, the most extraordinary witness had to have an interpreter. He was a black servant called John Sims; by 1670 he belonged to Mr. Peter Lidget, a merchant who had arrived in Boston from Barbados and was amassing a fortune in the lucrative mast trade. Lidget's son Charles would use some of his inheritance to acquire the Winthrop Ten Hills estate in Charlestown. John Sims deposed:

> He lived in Jamaica four or five years employed to keep cattle in the country. His master came and told him and wife Katherina to take their clothes to go to another plantation. He and Katherina divided the clothes. They were on separate boats, he and the man that sold him there, Mr Deacon, aboard Mr. Row's. Mr. Deacon's wife returned to shore. Katherina is a free Negro from Cuba. He never heard she was a slave to any. She was married to him two years before they left Jamaica. She always bore him company and dressed his victuals. His master asked Katherina if she would go with [Sims] and she answered, 'Yes.'[82]

door to their Three Cranes tavern, CTR, 4: 44. Row had immigrated from Devon, and his son John had a black servant called "Devonshire." Elias emerged as an untrustworthy and ruthless man when his son was accused of raping his maidservant. Thompson, *Sex,* 61–64. These qualities may have fueled his row with Deacon. In 1687 his personal estate was valued at the huge sum of £764; he also owned extensive real estate, Wyman, 825. Wind: Jenner may have been caught in the hurricane season. Sailing west from Jamaica to Barbados was anyway problematic because of the prevailing northeast trade winds, CSPCol, 2: 158. £30: this represented her value as a slave. Moseley (ca. 1634–71) was the second generation of his family in Lower Norfolk County, on the coast south of the mouth of the Chesapeake Bay. About 1660 he married Mary Gookin, the niece of Daniel Gookin of Cambridge, Massachusetts, formerly of Virginia, L. E. D'Amtolo, et al., *Descendants of William Moseley* (privately printed), 7–9.

[82] Hodges, of Boston, later became a Quaker and was whipped in 1677; I have found no connection with the Captain John Hodges family of Charlestown. Peter Golding (ca. 1635–1703) was also a Bostonian. Daniel Remington may have been kin to John Remington of Haverhill, who named his eldest son Daniel in 1661. Codner was a Boston mariner; a large branch of the family were fishermen in Marblehead. Interpreter: Freegrace Bendall (1635–76), Clerk of the Superior Court in 1670, Savage, *GMB,* 1: 151–56. Lidget: Bailyn, *Merchants,* 133–38. His 1676 will makes no mention of Sims, MA, Suffolk Probates, 6: 160–63, will 777. No inventory

This remarkable account of Katherina's background and freedom, along with the evidence of Jenner's mariners, no doubt swayed the jury in the defendant's favor. So, too, would their awareness of Jenner's career. He was the son of Rev. Thomas Jenner, who had twice stayed in Charlestown in the late 1630s and 1640s before returning to England in 1650. In 1655, the younger Thomas had married Rebecca, daughter of Captain Nicholas Trerice, Charlestown's famous transatlantic shipmaster. The following year he petitioned Lord Protector Cromwell protesting that his vessel and goods worth £349 had been taken from him at Boston by impressment power derived from Major-General Robert Sedgwick. A report by New England arbitrators was forwarded to the Privy Council in London, and, on 10 July 1656, an order was issued for restoration of ship and goods. Jenner was about forty years old when the events surrounding Katherina took place, and already an experienced sea captain. He was familiar with Caribbean waters, and during the 1670s and 1680s, as we have seen, frequently crossed the Atlantic, often entrusted with important and confidential business. In 1680 he bought and conveyed a new bell for Charlestown, probably from Whitechapel, by Wapping. Jenner was plainly a man of integrity, and, to the jurymen, he was one of their own. They found for the defense.[83]

I have not been able to discover what happened to Katherina and John Sims. However, Katherina's outraged reaction to her "trepanning" and her assertion of her rights as a free black woman, backed by a governor's certificate, were highly effective in convincing Captain Jenner that he could only recover her passage money and board; she was not "freight" to be sold in perpetuity. Sims's testimony emphasized her willingly accompanying him to another plantation. It is revealing of the flexible and individualized racial attitudes of early generations in Massachusetts that Sims was encouraged to testify, and that his evidence was accorded equal weight to that of white witnesses. We can only hope that his spirited, free-born wife was reunited with him.[84]

---

survives. Sims describes Deacon as "the man that sold him there," presumably on board Row's ship. Row may have been acting as Lidget's agent.

[83] Jenner: *GM*, 4: 46–50; *MR*, 3: 393; 5: 271, 465; MxCC RB, I: 139, 236; Mass Archives, 20 September & 9 November 1674; CTR, 3, 134; 4: 30, 24; C Tr R, 4: 19 r. Impressment: *CSPCol*, 1: 444. See above, "Captain Jenner's Journeys, 1674–78."

[84] Cf. Thompson, *Cambridge Cameos*, 271–75, 286. M. L. Sanborn, "Angola and Elizabeth, an African Family in Massachusetts," *NEQ*, 52 (1999) 119–29 analyzes twenty documents concerning these black servants in Boston, who married in 1654 and had their first child in 1661. Angola died in 1675 and left an estate of £44. "Negars" were bought and sold in Charlestown, e.g. Mx CC D&O, 1: docs. 1566–76, 2 October 1660, where £28 was promised for a black male before three witnesses at The Three Cranes.

A Wild Ward:
Mary Robinson, 1676

On 25 December 1676, an arrest warrant was issued to the constables of Boston or Charlestown to "apprehend John Walley and bring him to Governor Leverett or another magistrate at 9 or 10 in the morning to answer the complaint of Mr. Joseph Rock [guardian] on behalf of his niece Mary Robinson for pulling down from the post at Charlestown Meetinghouse the publication of marriage [banns] betwixt Mary Robinson and Mr. Jacob Green Jr." Bond of £100 for court appearance was taken of Walley; one of his £50 sureties was Robert Sedgwick (1651–ca. 1683), son of one of Charlestown's leading merchants, Major-General Robert Sedgwick.[85]

The statements that were taken after Walley's arrest gave two diametrically opposed accounts of his relationship with Mary. In his favor were witnesses from the Sedgwick household, most notably Thomas Mander, aged 25, who lodged there. He attested that "Mr. Walley had an affection for Mary Robinson. She often came to the house. I asked her if she had any love for Mr. Walley, and she said she loved him above any man and would never marry any other, often asking for Mr. Walley and expressing as much love as any maid could honestly [within the bounds of modesty] and invited me to her wedding which should be speedily [accomplished]. Afterwards at Mr. Rock's, discoursing about the matter, Mr. Rock said 'Let her go; she'll never be in our house more.'" Mary's passion was corroborated by Mrs. Mary Willoughby, 40, and by her own sister-in-law Sarah Robinson, 19: "Several times before and since [she] moved from Uncle Rock's to Mr Hammond's to dwell, I have heard her promise to marry Mr.

---

85   MxCC D&O, 3: Folio 74 has all the court papers in this case. Sedgwick: see above, "Godly Merchants."

Walley; she should have him, and before Mrs. Sedgwick and myself [she did] consent that she might be published with him in order to marry . . . " Sarah Sedgwick, 21, deposed that "being at Mr. Rock's, John Walley asked Mr. Rock if he could entreat Mary Robinson to marry. Mr. Rock said if he can tame a wild colt he should have his consent and god bless him." Nor would he "take any advantage of the law against him." Two weeks later Mrs. Sedgwick heard that the young couple had agreed about publishing the banns and had seen a certificate to that effect. Robert Williams, the Boston verger, certified to the court that Walley and Robinson had been published there three times without any opposition observed by him. Robert Sedgwick added to his wife's account that Joseph Rock and his wife had said they would neither hinder nor further John Walley's suit.

The Rocks utterly rejected this version. They produced four mature witnesses who agreed that Rock had "discharged [forbidden] Mr Walley at his shop from making any suit to Mary Robinson." One described Mrs. Rock ordering the ardent suitor to "begone from our house." Rock was so outraged at the defence's evidence that he could not refrain from "declaring Robert Sedgwick and his wife at the County Court in Charlestown in open court to have taken a false oath." He was promptly sued for defamation, and given the choice of paying the Sedgwicks £100 in money, or "acknowledging in open court false accusations of perjury within 24 hours when the court is full."[86]

The impasse was broken from the obvious but, in the seventeenth century the least expected, source: the "untamed colt" Mary Robinson. Her "Short Reply to the Allegement of John Walley" rebutted four of his claims. First, "she did not break her promises, saying she would have him and then she would not . . . she had never promised [him anything] against her friends' [family's] consent." Second, "his great importunity, and his brother's and sister's, and his so basely abusing himself with drink made her utterly averse to any engagement." Third, the "Publishment from the Sexton of Boston [was] so far from being done with her consent as done without her knowledge." Fourth, when she asked him if he had her uncle and aunt's consent, "he replied he had not, nor never would go to them for it though he never had her."[87]

The 19 December 1676 session of the Middlesex County Court heard Rock's complaint against Walley for publishing himself in marriage to Mary

---

[86] *Sfk CCR*, 770–71, 30 January 1677.

[87] On early modern conventions about courtship and parental authority, see Thompson, *Sex*, 34–36, and *Divided*, 127–28.

Robinson, and for pulling down the Green-Robinson banns at Charlestown. The court heard the contradictory evidence, and sentenced Walley to the relatively mild penalty of admonition. He had to pay 23 shillings in costs.[88]

Behind this case lurk much misery and two mysteries. The misery derives from Robinson family tragedies. Mary was the only daughter and fourth child of Thomas Robinson and his second wife Mary (Coggan). She had been born in 1657, but her first blow was the death of her mother when she was only four. Her father soon married Widow Elizabeth Sherman, but this relationship produced husbandly unhappiness. "My wife has not carried herself as a wife should towards me . . . having withdrawn herself from living with me." On 23 March 1666, Mary's abandoned father died. He left £271 to Mary and her three brothers. He appointed his brother-in-law, man of business Joseph Rock, estate executor, and Mary went to live as a ward in her aunt Rock's household in Boston. Mr. Rock was distracted by his responsibility for the complicated Coggan estate, so that his relationship with the guardians of the other Robinson heirs became increasingly ill-tempered during the 1670s, culminating in time-consuming court cases. The fraught atmosphere in the Rock household may have contributed to Mary's wildness and her removal to the family of Captain Lawrence Hammond in Charlestown.[89]

Joseph Rock, Mary's guardian, had been fortunate to marry a wealthy Coggan heiress. His wife Elizabeth bore ten children between 1652 and 1667, but only six survived, five younger than Mary Robinson. Both Joseph and Elizabeth were church members, and in the late 1660s Joseph was a leading proponent of the bitter breakaway of merchant Half-Way Covenanters from Boston's First Church and the founding of Third, or Old South, Church. He seems to have been frantically busy; infuriated at being harried by business and probate colleagues, he blurted out angry ripostes about wild colts and false oaths, which came back to haunt him. Elizabeth Rock comes across from court testimony as imperious and chilly. Neither was a suitable guardian for a deprived and willful teenager.[90]

Mary Robinson's engagement to Jacob Green Jr. (born 1654) of Charlestown was probably arranged through the mediation of Hammond, a leading town figure. Young Jacob was three years older than her, the

---

[88] MxCC RB, 3: 161.

[89] Robinson will, and quote: MA, Suffolk Probates, 1: 402, 462, 463. Court Cases: *Sfk CCR*, 78, 109, 155, 217, 334, 369–72; Mary Coggan Robinson and Elizabeth Coggan Rock were sisters. On the wealthy merchant John Coggan, their father, see *GMB*, 401–5, and below, "Wealthy Women: Martha Rainborough."

[90] Rock: Savage; Half-Way: see above "Thomas Gould and the Baptist Debate, 1655–68."

eldest son in a distinguished town family, grandson of ruling elder John Green (1593–1658). His father Jacob (ca. 1623–1701) was a merchant involved in the fishing industry, with a wharf in Charlestown and considerable real estate both in the town and in surrounding towns and counties. He served Charlestown as constable in 1653, selectman from 1668 to 1672, and deputy to the General Court from 1676 to 1678. He was elected rate commissioner in the daunting aftermath of King Philip's War (1675–76). At his death, Jacob Green Sr. left a fortune of £1,038. His son was thus a very good financial match for a young woman who had inherited about £75. What a pity that Mary had not herself chosen him.[91]

The first mystery is John Walley. Even the indefatigable James Savage conceded, "After many hours devoted at various times to this name, I acknowledge little confidence and less satisfaction." There were at least two John Walleys in Boston in the 1670s. The first was a mariner whose transatlantic voyages are often recorded in Hull's letters. He had married Elizabeth Wing (1644–73) in 1661, and had five children. He would have been aged somewhere between thirty-six and forty in 1676, twice Mary Robinson's age, and his eldest child was only five years her junior. He married, second, Sarah—but no child is recorded before 1683. Furthermore, he sailed for London on 16 July 1676 and would have been unusually speedy to have been back in New England within five months.[92]

The other candidate is John Walley, the merchant. Joseph Rock testified to visiting the ardent suitor "in his shop," and Mary Robinson mentions a "brother and sister" importuning her; the merchant had seven adult siblings. However, this thirty-two-year-old son of a minister, who was soon to become a senior military officer, and eventually a colony councilor and judge, had already married and was a father. He cannot have been eligible either. Perhaps there was yet another John Walley, a friend of the Sedgwicks, a shopkeeper in his early twenties: young, unattached, ardent, and a trifle reckless. If so, I have been unable to find him in the records.[93]

The second mystery is how we can reconcile the diametrically opposed accounts of Mary Robinson's reaction. The Sedgwicks' successful defamation suit against the impetuous Rock suggests that they were confident

---

[91]   Green: Wyman, 435; *GMB*, 811–13; Frothingham, 81, 223–24. Real: *Essex CC*, 8: 122, 398; fishing: ibid, 2: 401–02, *Assistants*, 1: 174. Fortune: MW, 9744, 9 April 1703, real estate, £771.

[92]   Savage; Hull, "Letter Book," 314; speedy: see above, "Captain Jenner's Voyages."

[93]   F. H. L. Barclay, "Blossom-Davis-Walley," *TAG*, 64 (1989), 117–18; Rev Thomas Walley was minister of Barnstable, in Plymouth Plantation, ca. 1663–1678. The merchant died in 1712, very wealthy. Savage. The mariner had a son John, born on 27 August 1662, and therefore too young for candidacy.

of their account, and those of their friends and household. On the other hand, Mary's item-by-item reply represents a complete rebuttal. However, if we place the Walley-Robinson relationship on an attraction-revulsion continuum, we may see the changing dynamic. Mary Robinson is known to be a headstrong young woman with a profoundly unhappy background. She has lost her mother as a small child. She has been imposed upon and then abandoned by a disillusioned stepmother. Her tetchy and distracted guardian regards her as feral, and ships her across the Charles to the snobbish Hammonds. There she is matched with a young Charlestown male, almost like a financial commodity. Then a lover appears and sweeps her off her feet. She is enraptured by his proposal. He moves into action, publishing new banns in Boston, hoping his furtive speed and resolution will outwit the Rocks. However, Mary soon had second thoughts as Walley rushed ahead and wiser heads urged caution. She saw his other side: he drank to excess and was importunately harrying her with his plans. Perhaps the wealthy, young Jacob Green suddenly appeared a happier choice. Or perhaps Green threatened to renounce his offer. In summer 1677 Joseph Rock sued him, but then withdrew the action. Yet again, finance may have intruded. In the end, it was Jacob she married, and their first surviving child was baptized in 1683. Six more followed, up to 1699. The "wild colt," so far as the records go, seems to have been tamed by motherhood, maturity, and responsibility. [94]

Courtship among young people from wealthy families was considered by parents or guardians to be far too important to be left to the ill-considered lusts and whims of the courters. While physical and emotional empathy were taken into consideration, the ethos of the corporate merger was often dominant. This no doubt dictated the Green-Robinson alliance. The hair-tearing passion of the Walley-Robinson romance was deemed a recipe for disaster. Only Mary's fostered background and non-familial residence in Charlestown during a period of war-torn turmoil gave her a brief freedom that was rapidly curtailed. A tug on the bit of convention curbed the wild colt.

---

[94]   1677: *Sfk CCR*, 817, 31 July 1677. Torrey.

Whose Herbs?
Wadland and Geary, 1682

Around the year 1670, the women of the Wadland family, which had only arrived in Charlestown in 1666, suffered a series of grievous blows. First, the matriarch, Agnes (1612–83), lost her husband on 20 April 1668. Crispin Wadland (ca. 1608–68) was a mariner and ship's carpenter. His estate was very modest: £88, including a house worth £45 and £12 in money. About the same time, the Wadlands' only daughter, also Agnes (born 1644), was widowed by the death of her husband of only four years, William Gillingham. In 1670 she married Joseph Batchelor (born 1644), who had run with a roistering crew during the 1660s, attracted the displeasure of the selectmen, and been fined £2 for "misdemeanours at night" by the County Court. The third victim was Elizabeth, wife of eldest son Crispin Jr., like his father a ship's carpenter. He died in 1671, leaving an estate of £122. His widow was remarried in 1672 to Daniel Smith (ca. 1641–1707), a gunsmith, who had only lived in Charlestown for three years. Another son, Amos Wadland, seems to have already left Charlestown. So within a few years of arrival, the Wadland family had been totally transformed and the prospects for the widowed matriarch with a meager inheritance must have appeared bleak.[95]

By 1682, it appears that Agnes Wadland, now seventy, had had to either sell or rent out the house and ground which was the main family asset, retaining a room and a patch of garden for herself. The buyer or tenant was yet another fairly recent arrival in Charlestown, Stephen Geary (born 1651), who was first recorded in the town as an indentured servant on 15

---

[95] Crispin, Sr.: Rodgers, 2: 463–64; Batchelor: MxCC D&O, 2: Folios 48, 49, 51, 52; CTR, 3: 92; Smith: CTR, 3: 102: 19 July 1669 selectmen admit to town provided he lives under family government.

September 1668. On 2 May 1681 he was paid £9-10-0 wages for ringing the town bell, acting as town crier and messenger. By 14 December 1685 he was being described as a ship's carpenter, like the two Crispin Wadlands. Early in 1682 he had been in trouble with Deputy Governor Danforth; he was ordered to attend at 4 p.m. on 4 March to answer "reports of evil practices."[96]

It was shortly after his confrontation with authority that Geary had another, equally alarming, confrontation with the Widow Wadland. "About sunset" on 15 May 1682, the elderly matriarch went down "to the end of the garden to gather herbs." When she came back to the house, Geary stormed up to her "demanding . . . what [she] did there." He "was troubled at her [and said] 'You do not well without my leave. Pray make bold with your own, but not with mine.'" She shot back: "You young saucy rogue, I will black your eye!" She claimed to have said: "I thought I might gather a little herbs, I setting of them there." Geary remembered saying "'If it must be common, I will take down the fence,' and a maule standing by, I took it up." At which, he continued, "She cried out 'Murder!' and presently [instantly] went away." This was not how Agnes Wadland recalled events. She attested that Geary pushed her down on her face and side next to the stairs, which much bruised her, as did his kicking her when she was down. Unable to help herself as formerly, the "very ancient" lady was "full of pain."[97]

"Mother Wadland's" cry of "Murder!" alerted her son-in-law Daniel Smith, who sent his wife over to her mother's and soon followed. They ensconced themselves upstairs in her chamber, and "among other discourse, mother did ask me [Daniel] to read a letter from her son Amos." The discourse (according to Geary, downstairs) included Smith saying "Young sassy fellow! He hath nothing to do [with?] the garden. We shall have contention with him." Geary admitted to being "moved," and called up "Come down out of my house, or I'll fetch you down. I will not be hectored in my own house." No one, he added, had any right to be there in the chamber except the widow. When Smith shouted down "Be quiet, I do not know

---

96   Buyer or tenant: I have found no deeds in the Middlesex Register of Deeds. Arrival: Rodgers, 2: 517, 526: Geary was servant to Capt. Richard Sprague, merchant and shipowner; in 1668 he had two and a half more years of his indenture to run. On 24 March 1669, he was a probate witness along with three Lowdens; Richard Lowden was a shipwright, ibid, 541. He was a witness to the presence of two men at Samuel Ballatt's shipyard on 1 April 1679, aged 28, MxCC D&O, 4: Folio 83. Bellman: CTR, 4: 35. Danforth: D&O, 5: Folio 102. Ship's carpenter: MxD, 9: 529.

97   MxCC D&O, 4: Folio 99 has the relevant documents. Maule: mallet. According to his own "Declaration," Geary's tone sounds almost courtly. However, Hannah Salter, 41, corroborated that Widow Wadland came to her "full of pain and hurt, and she saw two or three bruises very blue."

[accept that] I'm in your house," Geary rushed up "very furiously, and broke open the locked door." He advanced on Smith, demanding "had I nothing to do there what I had spent so much money for?" In the ensuing melee, "the old woman called me several times dog and damned dog, struck me on the shoulder and chest, with much bad language." Fortunately, at this point, two tithingmen appeared. Before they could find out what had happened, Agnes's daughter Batchelor charged in: "Where is that rogue? There is a jade in piss for him! Had I been there, I would have pulled out the rogue's hair off his head!"[98]

The poor tithingmen tried to calm this hornets' nest, but Geary was furious with Smith, and "the old woman was worst by far," screaming "cursed dog and wretch and the like." When they asked Geary the reason for "this strife . . . the widow did furiously interrupt . . . and struck him on the chest with something she had in her hand." The officials persuaded Geary to go downstairs and "to let it alone for the present while this was in cold blood."[99]

At the Middlesex County Court at Charlestown on 30 June 1682, both Agnes Wadland and Stephen Geary were admonished for "sundry abusive carriages and speeches" and had to stand bound to good behavior. What must have been tense relations between the two floors came to an end the following year when Agnes Wadland died. Stephen Geary seems to have left Charlestown about 1685.[100]

Why this fury? The widow's palpable anger must have derived to some extent from her straitened circumstances and sense of powerlessness. It must have been deeply galling to the old lady to be forced to retreat to an upstairs chamber and to be supplanted in the house by a man half her age whom she despised. In her mind, the land was still *her* garden; had she not planted the herbs that were now claimed by Geary? She was unable to read, so any written document might increase her sense of victimization. To make up for her humiliation and fear, she shouted the loudest and was physically aggressive. At least she had what remained of her family nearby, though both her son-in-law and daughter seemed intent on fanning the flames.

---

[98] Tithingmen were responsible for ten families in their neighborhood.

[99] Test. Samuel Ballatt, 44, and William Vine, 31. Geary's "Declaration," probably written by Ballatt, depicted his own behavior as more restrained despite intense provocation. Ballatt and Vine also described Geary as less culpable than the widow, and dismissed the statement of a neighbor as hearsay. In 1685 Ballatt, a shipbuilder, stood £10 surety for Geary. It is possible that Geary worked in his yard.

[100] Died: MxCC RB, 4: 88, 18 December 1683; left: MxD, 9: 529.

What did they have against Geary? Old Mother Wadland considered him "a dog, a wretch and the like" and her daughter called him a "rogue." She also gave the clue to explain his doggish, roguish wretchedness: "there is a jade in piss for him," which in modern parlance means "he has gotten a young slut pregnant." We may presume that these were the same "evil practices" reported to Danforth the previous March. The woman in question was the teenage daughter of mariner John Poor, Sarah, who had given birth to a bastard in 1682. At the same court that heard the evidence about the Wadland-Geary fracas, Sarah accused Stephen of being the father of her child. She was sentenced on 19 December 1682, after a non-appearance in October, but there is no record of Geary's being punished or being required to maintain the child. He may have denied paternity to Danforth and Sarah may have refused to swear to her accusation. This evasion of public responsibility was growing more common during the 1680s, and would have been particularly galling to poor ratepayers like the Wadlands, the Smiths, and the Batchelors, as well as to the older generation who expected fathers of bastards to own up to their misdeeds.[101]

Three years later, Sarah Poor again bore a bastard. This time, in the agony of labor, she adamantly refused to name the father. She told the midwife that "the father's name would not pardon her sin." On 17 July 1685, the bench—mindful of the expense to ratepayers of "another bastard on the town"—sentenced Sarah to a severe twenty-stroke whipping, one year's hard labor, and a further flogging each month until she divulged the father's name. On 14 August 1685, she accused Stephen Geary. Though he denied paternity, Sarah repeated her accusation on oath and Geary was required on 16 October 1685 to enter bond to maintain the children in the custody of the Charlestown selectmen. Sarah seems to have thought of herself as "bound" to Geary, and resisted the eagerness of another man "to have been naught with her." She may well have been living in Geary's house, even using his herbs.[102]

---

[101]   Wyman gives Sarah's date of birth as 1671, but that would make her only 11. MxCC RB, 4: 44, 47, 57. Thompson, *Sex*, 193. "Rogue" had strong sexual connotations in the seventeenth century, *OED*.

[102]   Midwife: test. Anna Ballatt, 35, 16 June 1685; case: MxCC RB, 4: 177, 179, 192; children: the magistrates plainly decided that Geary was father of the first bastard, now three; bound: Thompson, *Sex*, 138; on 14 December 1685 Geary had pledged his dwelling house and land as security for weekly payments of two shillings to Sarah Poor for a year, and "at the end of the year take such care of the child as the town shall not be chargeable." Mx D, 9: 529. At Geary's: midwife Martha Collins, 75, believed the father of the second child was "the man of the house where she then was." Sarah did not deny it. She died in 1687 in Cambridge jail.

Sarah Poor and Agnes Wadland represent two of the most vulnerable groups in early Charlestown: virtual orphans and aged widows. Sarah's mother, also Sarah, had died in the smallpox epidemic in 1677, when the girl was probably only about ten. Her father remarried another mariner's widow in 1680, but he was presumably often away for long spells. She would have been eager for affection and would, having "lost her reputation," and being regarded by some men as easy game, have had to take Geary on his own terms. Her vow of silence to this self-deluding, violent, and suspect man is particularly pitiful, given his denial. Elderly widows suffered from dependency on their offspring, and a sense that they were depriving the rising generation of scarce resources. Being beaten up for nicking a few herbs symbolized an old woman's pathetic marginality.[103]

---

[103] Cf. Thompson, *Divided*, 134–36, 189–90.

Two Widows:
Alice Rand (1594–1691)
and Mary Nash (ca. 1605–74)

If a woman's husband died, her usual strategy would be to remarry, often within a year or so. If she had young children, she would feel greater urgency. Even for mature women (and men), however, the married state was the norm. Nonetheless, most towns had a group of widows. Many were elderly and frail, needing doles from the selectmen if they lacked family support. A few seem to have remained unwed and to have pursued independent lives that included service to the town.[104]

Robert Rand (ca. 1590–ca. 1639) was in his mid-forties when he arrived in Charlestown in 1635, with his two sons and two daughters and his pregnant wife Alice. He was "allowed to set down [in the town] provided there was no justified ground for exception." Despite this tepid welcome, the family did stay, and Alice gave birth to another son and two daughters. By the time the last daughter arrived, Robert was dead.[105]

---

[104] Men: the most famous example of eagerness to find a new wife is that of Samuel Sewall, *Diary*, 882, seq. Welfare: see, e.g., CTR, 4: 54, Widow Cole, 56, Widows Pratt, Dady. Long widowhoods: cf. Elizabeth Green of Cambridge, Thompson, *Cambridge Cameos*, 123–28. On some notable English Puritan widows: S. Mendelson and P. Crawford, *Women in Early Modern England, 1550–1720* (Oxford: Clarendon, 1998), 180–81, 312, 334. On remarriage: L. Gowing, *Domestic Dangers*, 26: 42 percent of women marrying in early seventeenth-century London were widows; B. J. Todd, "The Remarrying Widow: A Stereotype Reconsidered," in M. Prior, ed., *Women in English Society 1500–1800* (London: Routledge, 1991), 54–91. Todd reports some widows rejecting remarriage because of continuing "intense love for their late husbands," 79. Ex-Bristolians in Charlestown would have been aware of Dorothy Kelly, later Hazzard: a High Street grocer's widow, a radical separatist, and a founder of the Broadmead Church of Christ in the late 1630s, P. Crawford and L. Gowing, *Women's Worlds in Seventeenth-Century England* (London: Routledge, 2000), 60.

[105] According to a 1651 will, Rand may have come from Barham, Suffolk, though this origin required that the Suffolk family would not have heard of the emigrant's death for 12 years, *R*,

Though Alice may have been supported by her brother-in-law, the childless Captain Richard Sprague, she still had four children under the age of seven, and her eldest were only teenagers. Rapid remarriage would have appeared crucial. Yet Alice remained a single widow for the next half century, managing family and personal affairs with aplomb. All seven of her children survived to adulthood. Two of her sons became artisans: Thomas (1627–83) a cordwainer or shoemaker, and Nathaniel (1636–96) a woodworker. Both became sergeants in the militia and fought in King Philip's War. Eldest daughter Margery (ca. 1624–1714) copied her mother's long life and was married to Lawrence Dowse for over fifty years (ca. 1645–98). Her younger sisters married away from Charlestown, Alice Jr. to Ipswich, and Susanna and Elizabeth to Roxbury. Matriarch Alice had fifty-six grandchildren, including three sets of twins.[106]

In both town and county records, Alice Rand's service and business career can be glimpsed. In 1649, "Sister Rand" was paid for unspecified work by Charlestown's constable, and was owed the considerable sum of £10-8-0 when Malden separated. This may have been for fostering orphan children. In 1657, she was one of the jury of experienced midwives and matrons who were deputed by the Court of Assistants to examine Seaborn Batchelor. Alice agreed with their verdict that her unmarried neighbor was probably pregnant, but that "bodily correction at present may prove dangerous and hurtful to her." The court overrode this counsel. A chastened Seaborn was shortly after married to Indian trader John Cromwell. Twelve years later, Widow Rand reported to the Middlesex County Court as town midwife. She had supervised the delivery of the illegitimate child of the Tufts' saucy maidservant Elizabeth Wells. She deposed that Elizabeth, in the agony of labor, being solemnly warned that she might soon meet her maker, stuck to her story that the child's father was the affluent James Tufts rather than impoverished fellow servant Andrew Robinson. In these circumstances, the role of midwife, always vital, was awesomely inquisitorial. During her mature years, she must have attended dozens of childbirths less sensational than this scandal.[107]

---

37 (1883), 239; furthermore, the son would by then have been aged 61, making his testator father unusually elderly. There were alternative Rands in Stepney, including ship master William Rand, Coldham1: 45, 175, T. Colyer-Fergusson, ed., *Marriage Records of St. Dunstans, Stepney,* 1 (Canterbury: privately printed, 1898), 243, 261.

[106] *GMB,* 1736, has the 1668 will of Richard Sprague, and his widow Mary's of ca. 1674. The two sisters may have been surnamed Sharpe. On Alice's two sons: see "Dominion and Revolution." There is debate about whether Robert Rand of Lynn was the eldest son. Not all of Alice's grandchildren survived beyond infancy, Savage.

[107] Payments: CTrR, 1, 43; Frothingham, 148. Batchelor: Mass Archives, 13 May 1657; Thompson,

Alongside these community activities, Alice kept a close eye on the family real estate. In the town *Book of Possessions* we can follow her land dealings. Sometimes her transactions involved small parcels; in 1650, however, in partnership with her son-in-law Lawrence Dowse, she bought the Manus Sally dwelling and land on Mystic Side for a considerable £27-10-0. Five years later she exchanged marsh and hay land with John Hodges. The probate inventory of her property taken on 11 August 1691 listed £206 worth of holdings: valuable meadow, three cow commons on the Stinted Common, enclosed land near the town, woodlots and arable on Mystic Side. All this she managed and bequeathed in her 1683 will to her daughters and grandchildren.[108]

A second long-lasting Charlestown widow, Mary Wightman Nash (ca. 1605–74) was a distant relative by marriage of Alice Rand. Mary had been married to William Nash in Maidstone, Kent, in 1628, and emigrated with their two children in 1634. Both Nashes quickly became church members, and William received grants of eight parcels of land, house lot, garden, arable, meadow, marsh, and woodland. Even more quickly than Robert Rand, William died, within four years of arrival. In the Charlestown *Book of Possessions* the 1638 family holdings were listed to "Mary Nash, widow, late wife of William Nash." She remained a widow for 36 years.[109]

Mary had much less capital than Alice Rand, so managing the Nash resources must have been a constant struggle. Her son Peter took over farming in the 1650s, and in 1662 sold off both of their Mystic Side woodlots to John Mansfield and William Frothingham. Mary helped set Peter up with some sheep, and maintained "house, barn, orchard, garden and yard" adding a "new end" to the house, so that it was worth £50 at her death. Mary may have overextended herself on this construction, because on 20 November 1671, she was forced to borrow 5/- from each selectman for six months. In fact she had repaid the whole 35/- by 21 February 1672.[110]

Sex, 220, fn. 23; Widow Seaborn Cromwell repeated her fornication with Robert Parris five years later and received 15 more lashes, ibid., 101. Wells: ibid., 45–47, 50–53.

[108] *Possessions*, 113–16, 135. Though Nathaniel was still alive, he had probably already been provided for. MPR, 7: 192, 326–28. Personalty amounted to £24, making a total estate of £230.

[109] Mary's sister Elizabeth Wightman had married Edmund Eddenden in 1632, and had a daughter Hannah, who was named in her Aunt Mary's will, Rodgers, 3: 265. Alice Rand's son Thomas married Sarah, daughter of Edmund Eddenden of Boston in 1656. Given the unusual Kentish name, it seems almost certain that Hannah and Sarah were sisters, Savage; GM, 5: 229–31. *Possessions*, 60–61.

[110] Resources: ibid., 159; GM, 5: 250; Rodgers, 3: 265. Loan: CTR, 3: 127, 131. She may have been helped in repaying by a £1 legacy from Deputy Governor Willoughby in 1671, Rodgers, 3: 14.

Almost all of Mary's £73 estate was left to her daughter Mary Hale and her Hale grandchildren. Daughter Mary had not married until she reached 30, and then had become the second wife of an impecunious stranger, Thomas Hale, from Norwalk, Connecticut. She helped raise her stepson Thomas, but did not have children of her own until the sixth year of marriage, when John was born. Her daughter Mary was also a late marrier.[111]

Mary Nash's family was unusual. Her son Peter never married, dying in 1693 "a single man aged 63." We cannot help wondering why daughter Mary's marriage was so long delayed and so unenviable. After the Widow Nash's death in 1674, son-in-law Hale moved back to Norwalk, though it is not clear whether Mary went with him. His Connecticut probate inventory of 1679 referred to "an estate . . . in the custody of his relict in Charlestown." That year, she needed relief from the Charlestown selectmen. The following year, a Widow Mary Hale was accused of bewitching a child called Michael Smith who died. She was acquitted by the Court of Assistants, and either she or her daughter Mary became a Charlestown church member in 1687. It is impossible to tell what troubled Mary Nash's children to produce such largely unattached adult lives. Perhaps lack of money or lack of a father figure played a role. Mother Mary's standing in the town is reflected by the fact that the town board of selectmen would unprecedentedly dig into their own pockets to lend her money, and that she counted such worthies as Deacons Aaron Ludkin and Edward Wilson as her "loving friends."[112]

Alice Rand and Mary Nash lived long and useful lives in early Charlestown running farms, managing finances, raising families, and contributing to community life. Within their financial limits, they demonstrated an independence, an economic breadth, and an enterprise then more usually associated with the male gender. They provided their daughters and the rising generation of women with impressive role models. They were invaluable and sometimes powerful matriarchs in a very masculine port culture.[113]

---

[111] *GMB*, 2: 838–40. Just before his marriage to Mary, Hale had been sued for debt in Connecticut.

[112] Ibid.; *Assistants*, 1: 189; a Michael Smith was living on Mystic Side in the 1660s, Savage. Deacons: Rodgers, 3: 265.

[113] On misogynistic attitudes to widows as "unheaded women" who had "cast their riders," see M. P. Tilley, ed., *Dictionary of the Proverbs of England in the Sixteenth and Seventeenth Centuries* (Ann Arbor: University of Michigan Press, 1950), H 372, M 18, 700, W335–42; Todd, 75, 79–82.

Young Women Abused

In a previous book, *Sex in Middlesex,* I have already described several Charlestown cases of townsmen abusing young women. Elizabeth Dickerman, for instance, was the servant of Penny Ferry publican John Harris. During 1681, when the saintly Goodwife Harris stayed at the meetinghouse for the sacrament, Elizabeth's master "laid her upon the bed" and proceeded to grope under her clothes. His son called her urgently to the cellar, where he displayed his erect penis and enticed her to hold it. Or there was Martha Beale, raped by her master's son, John Row, in 1686, and then deprived of marital or monetary recompense by her wealthy merchant employer. Most horrific was the abuse in 1689 of eighteen-year-old Mary Phipps, daughter of town leader Solomon Phipps. Her exploiter was thirty-one years older, the twice-married John Walker, a sexual scavenger, who fathered a child on Mary. Poor Mary was "void of common reason . . . next to a mere natural in her intellectuals . . . uncapable of resisting a rape hav[ing] one side palsied." Sometimes abuse might involve brutal corporal punishment, as in the case of Rebecca Lee who died at the hands of her employers, the Crosswells, who regarded her as "a nasty slut" and a petty thief, and beat her mercilessly. Consider Sampson was sadistically battered with a club by her employer Andrew Mitchell in 1690. When she reported him, he broke a stick across her back, already black and blue. Maidservants, especially from poor homes or other towns, were vulnerable to sexual advances or physical violence, but all young women needed to be sharp-eyed and resolute.[114]

---

[114] Harris: see "Adolescent Port Life," above, and this chapter; *Sex,* 129, 139, 230; Row: ibid., 61–64; Walker: ibid., 137–38; four other maids reported his sexual assaults; Crosswell, 1691: ibid., 159–62, and this chapter; Sampson: ibid, 159. On English examples of male sexual boasting, expectations, and seduction, see L. Gowing, *Domestic Dangers* (Oxford: Clarendon, 1996), 1–13; and "Ordering the Body," in Braddick & Walter, eds., *Negotiating Power,* 43–62, esp.

Several other young Charlestown women suffered abuse. How these incidents came under official cognizance (as opposed to unofficial rumor, or "fame") is often the result of subsequent quarrels. The charges spill out in the course of seemingly irrelevant confrontations.

Take the early case of Goodwife Jane Moulton, recorded only in the notarial records of Thomas Lechford. Twenty-year-old Jane had travelled in the 1630 Winthrop Fleet with her new husband, farmer-fisherman Thomas Moulton (ca. 1609–57), probably from the emigrant village of Ormesby, Norfolk. In 1631 she alleged she was

> assaulted by John Treble who feloniously did endeavour to ravish her when she was alone in a house in the fields where- upon she cried out & ran away from him to another house a good way off and afterwards prosecuted against him so that he fled out of this jurisdiction unto Piscataqua and thence into England.

Nine years later, fellow church member Elizabeth Stitson (ca. 1590– 1670) started spreading rumours that Jane had accused Treble because she "did owe unto said Treble beaver or money . . . and when he came to ask [for payment] she put this Trick upon him, meaning the said accusation of rape and said she would have him before the Governor for it." This smear not only caused "great hurt to the good name of the said Jane," but also "much disquiet and contention" between her and Thomas.[115]

The Moultons' 1640 complaint graphically described a street confron- tation six months before between the two women in the presence of three neighbors. When challenged, Goodwife Stitson recounted the 1631 story, adding that her son-in-law, Elias Maverick, had the paper proving Jane's debt to Treble. When asked why she had kept mum, Elizabeth said that Sister Moulton would be believed against non-saint Maverick. The next

---

46, and A. Fletcher, *Gender, Sex and Subordination in England, 1500–1800* (New Haven: Yale University Press, 1995), 88, 93, 160, in which Sir Ralph Verney's uncle Dr. Denton sends him a teenage serving maid "who will match your cock," 277. On child victims: Martin Ingram, "Child Sexual Abuse in Early Modern England," in Braddick and Walter, 63–84.

[115] Moulton: *GM*, 1305; Barbara MacAllen, "More Thoughts on the Moulton Family," *R*, 147 (1993). The Moultons were Mystic Siders who later joined Malden. He was chastised in the winter of 1630 for abandoning a gentleman in Plymouth without a pilot, *MR*, 1: 82. The Moultons had seven children in ten years. Thomas left £113 in 1657, a modest estate. Treble: Lechford, 259. Stitson: *GM*, 1306–09, 1763–77; Elizabeth had been the wife of Thomas Harris of Winnisimmet (Chelsea), who began the ferry to Charlestown. After his death, she mar- ried William Stitson who took over the ferry. William was at least ten years her junior. As she was past child-bearing age, this marriage was childless. They moved from Winnisimmet to Charlestown in 1637. Stitson was later selectman, sergeant and deacon. He left an estate of £503 in 1691.

question, "how comes it to pass that it is *now* spoken of?" was met with the gossip's shrug: "It is nothing to me."[116]

She lied. Lechford's next document is a notarized copy of a Moulton petition. "Divers times," they have been "put off by the Worshipful Mr. Nowell," when seeking a warrant against the Stitsons, who "had trespassed in [our] meadow ground near 100 pole [550 years] long." Outraged at this preferential treatment, Moulton had exploded "at a neighbor's house with some misbeseeming words of injustice against Mr. Nowell." Fearing that he might be whipped for insulting authority, he begged forgiveness. Perhaps, implicitly, he also sought justice.

Subsequent events suggest that Jane Moulton had "differences" with other neighbors, as did her husband, though the causes of these controversies are unknown. Elizabeth Stitson in this fracas had the ulterior motive of averting a trespass warrant. She would later point the finger at a neighbor, who she claimed was lying about stolen goods. She emerges from the court and notarial records as a self-righteous and self-serving gossip. The Stitsons seem to have exploited their status and wealth at their poorer neighbors' expense. Increase Nowell hardly covered himself in even-handed glory either. Jane Moulton's original plight had been lost in a welter of innuendo.

Eighteen-year-old Mary Bell's ordeal only emerged through her being falsely accused by her master, Captain John Jones (ca. 1642–90). As she and her widowed mother were coming ashore from the Boston–Charlestown ferry in early October 1671, "Master Jones [was standing] on the new wharf thereby. Widow Bell said she had brought her daughter; he told her her daughter was a thief . . . You are both thieves." A bystander recalled remarking that "these were hard words." Only at this point did the purpose of the Bells' arrival become clear. Mary had left the Joneses, "because she did not like her master's carriage towards her. When she went down to the cellar, he followed her and would have kissed her and put his hand under her apron." A witness deposed that "Mary Bell said about six months since that her master Jones followed her up and down . . . she could never be quiet for him." These equally "hard words" were common knowledge among the young wives of Charlestown. Two were sworn as defense witnesses when Jones sued Mary Bell for £50 damages for defamation. He had corroboration from his heavily pregnant wife, Rebecca (Sally), 25. The maid "never said any such thing, nor never had any such reason to say so."

---

116 Maverick was the husband of Anna Harris, Elizabeth's daughter; he had become a church member in 1633, *GM*, 1241–43.

Two other older women backed her detailed denial. Nonetheless, Jones was "cast." The jury found for Widow Bell and her daughter. Jones was to publicly acknowledge before Widow Bell that he had done her wrong, or else pay her £10 damages. By the time the case came to court in December 1671, Captain Jones was at sea; but this verdict would await his return. Once again, it was Jones's initial accusation of thieving that prompted the counter-charge of sexual abuse, though rumour of Mary's complaints had been in the air for some time.[117]

As a port, Charlestown had to endure sex-starved foreign seamen as an additional hazard for unaccompanied young women. The terror of Edward Winn's maid is palpable in her 6 October 1668 examination. She had gone

> to [Charles]town about business, and a man dogged her from Joseph Kettle's to Goodwife March's. She went to William Johnson to desire Zechariah Johnson to go home [to Woburn] with her. At Solomon Phipps Jr's house the man overtook them. He called himself Peter Grant. He would have led her, but she refused it thrice. At Winn's he would have kissed her but she refused it. Her master being at prayer, [Grant] dragged her between Winn's and William Frothingham's house, flung her down in the shoot and got atop of her. Zechariah called upon the fellow to be civil and not abuse her. Mr. Winn ran out, got hold of Grant demanding what did he do to his maid. Grant asked whether she was Winn's wife, for he did nothing to his wife. Grant swore that he would be the death of Winn. He would bring ten men to pulverize his house, and so ran away. They followed as far as Phipps's where they met John Terry and George Chin with clubs. Zechariah went to Constable Hayman. Mr Winn went home [where he found] Grant in the shoot but he departed. The maid [he added] cried out several times.

---

[117] MxCC D&O, 2: folio 57; folio 62 has the 8 November 1671 attachment against Mary Bell for defaming John Jones, and illegible testimony by Thomas Larkin. John Jones, his brothers Thomas and Isaac, the sons of Kathleen Jones, were all mariners. John had married the daughter of the late Manus and Sarah Sally in 1666. At his death, he left a considerable estate of £351, £290 of which was real estate, including a farm beyond the Neck, a dwelling, land, wharf and warehouse in town, and land at Casco Bay, Maine. His ship the *John and Kathleen* was in Barbados in 1688. Mary Bell was the daughter of Abraham (1620–62), a waterman, and Katherine (1623–92), who was the widow of John Waffe. Abraham was drowned on 31 December 1662. Mary's stepbrother Thomas Waffe Jr. became a sea captain; see "Seadogs' Land War." Mary eventually married John Hands in Boston. Two young wives: Elizabeth Sheppie, 23, and Joanna Johnson, 25. Older: Mary Kempthorne, 43, and Hannah Perkins, 34. At sea: jury verdict: damages to be paid by attorney or "when Captain Jones comes home."

Andrew Grover (abed at Mr. Winn's) and Robert Chalkley added more of Grant's braggadocio: "He swore by his Maker to be the death of him [Chalkley]. Asking [Grant] what countryman he was, he answered he was a Spaniard. He swore many times, he would stab him 50 times after he was dead. He would know what a seaman was."[118]

This was no isolated incident. Deborah Hadlock, who had recently been fined £1 for involvement in a late night party at Salter's, had also suffered. She had "met Peter Grant at Goodman Pritchard's and he dogged her to her master's, and threw her down and lay upon her, but had not the use of her body. He swore several oaths that he would lie with her and get her with child before he got home." Grant's contradictory plea was first a complete denial, and then the classic excuse that he was "drunk and knew not what he did." What became of him is not recorded.[119]

The most astonishing feature of the first "dogging" and attempted rape is that we never learn the victim's name. The fright, despite young Johnson's presence, was prolonged: all the way from Charlestown to Woburn, a good eight miles. Her master's prayers preventing immediate retribution and safety have already been noted as an example of lay piety. Grant's threats of violence and bloody murder were unusual in restrained and generally law-abiding Middlesex County, and would be that much more horrific.[120]

A similar anonymity clouds the identity of a new serving maid apparently raped by her master. The deposition, sworn on 15 May 1675 by Susan Bacon, 25, wife of Daniel Jr., gives a vivid and disturbing picture:

> On Election Day, being 12 May, around 8 of the evening, I saw Thomas Peachey of Charlestown going to his new shop, and he carried a maid or young woman with him against her will. She prayed him to let her go, but he would not and locked the door [behind him]. Presently I heard a tumbling or a scraping things on the shop boards. I went home for half an hour, then I came to my door and heard groaning or crying in the shop. I went nearer and heard her say 'Oh pray no!' and 'Pray I am so sick I am ready to die!' and she spoke very faintly like a woman that was spent. I went back in again and called my husband, 'There is a poor creature in distress,' but he going to

---

[118] MxCC D&O, 2: folio 48. Edward Winn, briefly in Charlestown, was one of the founders of Woburn in 1641. William Johnson (1608–77), probably brother of Captain Edward, was Charlestown's brickmaker and a trusted neighbor. In 1667 he was one of the town's constables. His son Zechariah was aged 22 and a mariner.

[119] Hadlock: see "Ursula Cole," and MxCC D&O, 2: folio 49, 16 June 1668.

[120] Piety: see "Religion: Introduction."

bed, said 'Go tell his wife.' I desired Samuel Jewell [Peachey's servant] to go, and she went to the shop and called to her husband. It was noised about the town that he had a woman in his shop near upon an hour. [Some said] 'Come out or the shop will be broke open.' There was no answer. This was about 9 o'clock or later.[121]

Peachey (died 1683) had only arrived in Charlestown in 1664, and had been granted residency "provided he behave orderly." A tailor by trade, he had married 34-year-old shopkeeper Mary Robinson (1631–90) in 1665. By 1677 she had had six children, including twins; only two offspring survived. Peachey was poor, and, unusually, had received violent abuse three times while serving as a watchman. He was fined five shillings by the selectmen for missing highway repair duty. His suit about an apprentice who had withdrawn from his indentures showed him to be self-willed and hasty. He had reneged on an undertaking to accept arbitration in another dispute. Just before the rape, he had been convicted of receiving stolen cloth worth 35 shillings from an Indian. We begin to understand the selectmen's reservations about his settling in the town.[122]

The reaction of Susan and Daniel Bacon seems inexcusable. Why did Susan wait half an hour before summoning help? Why was Daniel so callous? Were the two of them embarrassed? Or scared? Or turning blind eyes on master-servant relations? Or just ignoring a servant's rights? Finally it was Mary Peachey who summoned her husband, while a crowd gathered as the assault was "noised about town." By this time, Peachey seems to have made his escape. The aftermath is similarly mystifying. Peachey failed to appear at the Middlesex County Court for trial a month later on 15 June 1675 and forfeited his bond. Perhaps he had fled temporarily. He was back as an expert witness on 18 April 1679. His name next appears in the records in Widow Peachey's attestation of the late Thomas's tiny £36 probate inventory on 19 June 1683.[123]

By 1681, when John Harris groped his servant Elizabeth Dickerman, he was already known as a notorious lecher among the women of Charlestown,

---

[121] MxCC D&O, 3: folio 69.

[122] Wyman, 733. Violence: from John Lowden, 1667, MxCC D&O, 2: folio 43 (see "Ursula Cole"); from Henry Salter, 1669, folio 49; and from a drunken servant, D&O, 3: folio 62. Apprentice: Peachey v. Luke Perkins, 1 April 1673, MxCC RB, 3: 54, D&O, 3: folio 64. Stolen goods: folio 70, 13 May 1675.

[123] Absent: MxCC RB, 3: 129; fled: Wyman describes him as lodging with William Willis, a resident of Scituate, outside Massachusetts jurisdiction. 1679: see above, "Whose Coat?" Widow: RB, 4: 71; estate: MxW 17081; Peachey's date of death was 11 May 1683; his inventory contained no real estate.

Malden, and Mystic Side who had to use the Penny Ferry or his beer shop at the Charlestown landing just beyond the Neck. For instance, Elizabeth Sprague, 26, reported Widow Anna Williams of Charlestown saying that "Harris did kiss and grope her and she was so afraid that she was forced to go out of the boat up to her knees in water and more." 1678 proved to be an *annus horribilis* for Harris and his family, as his excesses turned neighborly gossip into a welter of formal accusations: that he sold drink to an Indian, that he had propositioned and harassed young women, some of them married, and that he had shockingly abused an eleven-year-old girl.[124]

On 29 and 31 May 1678, Thomas Danforth issued a flurry of orders to the constables of Charlestown and Malden to fetch sixteen witnesses (including one from Boston) for examination at his house at 8 a.m. the following Monday. The trigger for this was the complaint by members of the Crouch-Jones family about their eleven-year-old sibling Hannah's suffering appalling abuse, and her elder sister Sarah's being propositioned.

> Hannah Crouch complained of being sick and sore, not taking any great notice at first, but she was still full of pain when making water, we asked how this came about, and she answered that ever since one night Goodman Harris in his shop cellar did so rake and abuse her that her belly was swollen up to her navel . . . her water was blood or bloody for several days. Another time she went to his house and he did take her into his bedroom, and she desired him to leave her alone and be quiet he hurt her so that he was ready to kill her and with the noise of her talking his daughter Mary in the chamber came down and prayed her father to leave the girl alone and he said he did but whip her a little and so he left.

Sarah explained why Hannah's suffering had not been more quickly examined. There was "so much sickness in Mother Crouch's house and her father Jones was sick, I did not mind her, [until] a little after, washing, I found her bloody shift." This was the time of the terrible smallpox epidemic. She and husband Thomas Jones described another incident; Harris was visiting,

> when we lived in the house bought by Goodman Pierce, Hannah came to the fire with her undercoat on, and he took her

---

124 Sprague: D & O, 3: folio 78. Indian: on 7 October 1678, three witnesses deposed that Harris had sold two quarts of hard cider to Indian John Pittime for sixpence, and that they had seen him drink it and pay. After this, Pittime "could not go for reeling and staggering." Witnesses: John Mirick, 25, Thomas Jones, 35, and Samuel Pierce, 45. MxCC D&O, 3: folio 78.

between his knees. The girl crying out, we in the other room asked what the matter was, and he said he did nothing but whip her a little.

Jonathan and William Crouch openly challenged three of Harris's adult children about his abusive reputation:

Your father hurt girls. My sister [Mary, deposed Hannah Harris] asked 'What girls?' They said 'There could be no women or girls pass over the ferry quietly for him,' and Jonathan said he saw John Harris put his hands under a woman's apron, but he do not swear it or bring another [witness] to swear it. He also said he do not have [*sic*] seduced his sister [Sarah]. They both said that John Harris dragged a woman out of the house and pulled out his members and showed them to her, and my father would have had a nurse out of the house to come home to him, saying there is no one at home.

When Thomas Jones called John Harris "a rogue," he had not only Hannah but also his wife Sarah's experiences in mind; she deposed:

I went to Goodman Harris for yeast. His wife was asleep on the bed in another room. He followed me outadoors to the corner of his yard. He told me he would give me £6 if I would show him my secret parts. I asked him was he not ashamed to ask such a question for it was a disgrace to my husband. He said I need not tell my husband. I said I would not do such a thing as that to him nor no man living. Seeing he could not obtain his end, he went his ways.

Such harassment was corroborated by Mercy Goodwin, 25: "Goodman Harris forced his hands under my coats. I asked him was he not ashamed to offer me such abuse." This had happened "a year since some time last summer." Harris was catholic in his tastes. Sarah Stowers, 22, had heard "Goodwife Williams of Boston say "Goodman Harris would &c; he said his hair was grey, but hers was too."[125]

Mary Whittemore, aged only nine or ten, also described "Goodman Harris's uncivil carriages:"

My mother was at the mill, when he came to Widow White's house where I was ironing linen. He came to me with his members and gave — — [*destroyed*] with them in an uncivil

---

[125] "Would &c:" is prim shorthand for sexual propositioning. Anne Williams was in fact a widow, possibly of Thomas Williams.

manner. I thrust him away with my hand and he came again. He told me I was such a pretty rogue it made his prick stand. I resisted him and his hat fell off. My aunt reproved me, but I told her the true occasion.

This account was questioned by Mary Wilson, 26:

At Goodman [Thomas] Shepard's house, Mary Whittemore said she never saw no such thing, but he did pull out what he had and asked her if it were not a pretty jate bone to play withal, but she then said she never see no such thing. She had heard many evil reports raised of him.

This denial was confirmed by Sarah Shepard, 27.

Defense of Harris came from his daughters, an old neighbor, and a critic of Sarah Crouch Jones. Hannah Harris, 21, and Mary Brown, 23, reported smears spread by William Crouch:

Concerning church members, he said they would take a false oath for a ha'penny. Hannah Harris asked 'What falsehood can you accuse me with?' He said 'Everyone lies for advantage' to which I answered 'Then you lie for advantage.'

Elizabeth [a misnaming for Lydia, 40?] Wood gave Harris a character reference: "She had known [him] for 23 years; for seven years she had lived in the next house and for one in his house; he never proffered any incivility in that whole time."

Mary Wilson also presented a seamier side to Sarah Jones, who

Came to my house, her husband was at [*illegible*] and she was troubled he did not come. She had a good mind to lecone? the cider at Goodman Harris's cellar. I told her she could not get in, but she knew a way to get in through the parchment window; some folks had pulled out the parchment window and gone in several times and drunk cider and there was charcoal — — [*illegible*] and could do what they would — — {*illegible*] She had seen Goodman Harris's sin and laid it on the woodpile [?].[126]

The cases involving John Harris did not come to court until 18 December 1678. The charges were "selling liquor to the Indians and lascivious practices towards sundry women at his house and elsewhere as they passed over the ferry." He was found guilty and sentenced to a £5 fine and

---

[126] All depositions are gathered in folio 78.

twenty stripes, as well as loss of his license, ten shillings costs to Constable Welch, and more to the sixteen witnesses. On 19 December 1678, Welch was ordered to take down Harris's pub sign. [127]

The exposure of serial predator John Harris by the Crouch-Jones clan and various other abused women and girls raises puzzling questions. The first, bloody, abuse of Hannah Crouch seems to have been committed in February 1678. Why was no one in authority told until the end of May? Elizabeth Welch, 42, raised this with Sarah Jones, part of whose response is illegible because of faded ink. Sarah had told Goodman—of it "two weeks after when the fame of it" began to spread. The Joneses and the Crouches may have doubted whether they would have been taken seriously. Only eight years before, Sarah Crouch, before her marriage to Thomas Jones, had been excommunicated for bearing a second bastard in two years. The first may have been fathered by Christopher Grant of Watertown. Neither the Crouch nor the Jones family was esteemed in Charlestown. Father of ten and town herdsman William Crouch had been excommunicated for habitual drunkenness in 1674. At his death from smallpox on 11 March 1678, he was worth a mere £63. Thomas Jones, like Sarah deprived of half-way membership in 1670, was described by Grant as "a dirt dauber" and may have been lame. He had been in trouble for "living from under family government," and was suspected of thieving. He died in 1679. Why little Hannah was sent back to Harris's could be excused by the family's need for beer, yeast or cider, and by the knowledge that Harris's daughter was in the house.[128]

Harris seems to have been completely reckless: his harassing Hannah in her sister's house or when his daughter was at home, or propositioning Sarah within earshot of his wife, almost beggars belief. That his harming an eleven-year-old and luring a nine- or ten-year-old did not meet with far severer penalties is a mystery. Rape of any child was a capital offense; Edward Sanders of Watertown had escaped execution by a series of legal loopholes, but nonetheless had had a fearsome punishment. Neither the Court of Assistants nor the General Court took cognizance of Harris's alleged crimes. Perhaps the Crouches' complaint was deemed too exaggerated and too late. No doctor or midwife or independent witnesses authenticated their diagnosis.[129]

---

[127]   MxCC RB, 3: 232.

[128]   Crouch: *Sex*, 41–44; Wyman 250–51; Hunnewell, vii, viii; Jones: MxCC D&O, 1: doc. 2346; 2: folios 48, 49, 53.

[129]   Sanders, Thompson: *Divided*, 186–87, 255, fn. 40.

Some witnesses, such as Paul and Mary Wilson, who questioned accounts of Harris's lubricity or the Joneses' reliability, had given evidence in the fornication scandals involving Sarah Crouch and Thomas Jones. Other doubters like Elizabeth Welch, John Whittemore, or Lydia Wood were all church members and members of the Upham clan led by the Deacon of Malden. Though two decades before, Paul Wilson had "violently solicited" Priscilla Upham against her father's will, and sung dirty songs under newly married Phineas Upham's chamber window, they were united in questioning the case against Harris.[130]

One of the last of the Harris family's many Middlesex court appearances, on 21 June 1681, elicited the following deposition from twenty-four-year-old Mary Mousall:

> Last Thursday John Harris came to our house. He asked 'What do these girls here?' I told him 'To keep me company.' He desired me to go to the other room; he would speak to me. I said he might speak here. He answered 'Little pickers have wide ears,' and went to the door and said 'I must speak with you.' When I came, he said 'Those black browed girls are clever ones for men. Some men have pleasure of their wives. My wife I had as good do against the stock.' When I see he had nothing else to say I went away to my washing.

That same evening John and Joseph were each given twenty stripes for their sexual harassment of Elizabeth Dickerman, and for possession of two barrels of strong beer in their cellar. The next morning four leading townsmen issued a complaint:

> Persons whipped last night under conviction of such wickedness were so stroked over as if they were small children; it was inferior to a schoolboy's whipping. They were whipped with no fastening, no wringing, no striving.

The tender thrashers were Constables Thomas Crosswell and Daniel Edmunds. This was the very same Crosswell whose serving maid Rebecca Lee would die as a result of the beatings she received in his household. The marriage five years later of Thomas Harris to Hephzibah Crosswell may have prompted this tempering. Soon after this escape, the Harris family moved north from Charlestown to Maine. The town, and especially its female residents, must have been greatly relieved.[131]

---

[130] *Sex*, 34–35, 84–85.

[131] Mary Moore Mousall (1657–90) was the second wife of Thomas Mousall, who was twenty-

More so than most New England townswomen, the maids and young wives of Charlestown had to be especially vigilant against sexual trespassers. Two of the five rogues examined here were transient seamen with no local responsibilities and nothing to lose. The presence of some available women in the town (like Sarah Largin, or Margaret Martin) added to the vulnerability of others. Both the mariner attacks come across as the work of frightening and unrestrained rapists, one of them further inflamed with liquor.[132]

The masters who stalked, propositioned, or raped their servants or other girls and young women were even more despicable. Peachey and Jones used their positions of power and authority to abuse maids. The lack of protection from some neighbors is alarming, especially in such a nosy, gossipy culture. John Harris was a carnal marauder: any female from nine-year-olds to grey heads excited his satyric lust. He was not unique. William Everton, another Charlestown publican, was similarly libidinous, especially when his wife, another church sister, stayed at meeting. He seems to have steered clear of serving wenches, however, preferring married women. Malden had the almost comical carpenter William Bucknam. None of these poachers was in the least subtle. They simply responded to the bidding of their hyperactive sex drives. Women could be forewarned by their approach, but their leering advances were nonetheless repellent and frightening.[133]

four years older. Stock: this may imply bestiality. Four: Joseph Lynde, Samuel Lord, Samuel Phipps, and Thomas Lord, MxCC D&O, 4: folio 93. Lee: *Sex*, 159–64. Maine:*GDMNH*, 312; Savage.

[132] See "A Damned Whore," above, and *Sex*, 182–85.

[133] Ibid., 147, 132–33.

Wealthy Women

When a woman married, her dowry came under the control of her husband. If she survived him, she would receive by law a minimum of one-third of the husband's estate for life, but his will could assign that third to other legatees at her death. These customary arrangements could be altered by prenuptial contracts, which could safeguard the woman's assets. Such agreements were most often used when women of means became betrothed. Since a young woman's father would supervise the financial bargaining in a first marriage, prenuptial contracts were commonest when widows remarried. Whether or not rich wives in fact controlled their own assets, and how wealth more generally affected their lives, is the subject of this chapter.[134]

1. Martha Rainborough Coytmore Winthrop Coggan (1617–1660)

Among the 1630s settlers in Charlestown, none was more impressively connected than Martha Rainborough Coytmore. The daughter of leading Wapping mariner and Levant merchant William Rainborough (1587–1642) and Martha Coytmore Rainborough, she was born in 1617 and brought up by her stepmother Judith (Hoxton) from the age of seven. Her father left the huge fortune of £5,500 at his death in 1642, the year the Civil War began. From her parents, Martha inherited £1,100, a dowry of mouth-watering attractiveness.[135]

Martha's two elder brothers initially followed their father's maritime profession. William Jr. came to Charlestown in the late 1630s and acquired

---

[134] Thompson, *Women in Stuart England and America*, 11, 121, 261. On specific contracts: Thompson, *Divided*, 128–29, 241, fn. 16; Thompson, *Cambridge Cameos*, 114.

[135] *ODNB*; "Origins;" Mass Archives, 27 March and 19 May 1657.

the original meeting house and its plot. He went back to England in 1642, returning briefly as a Parliamentary naval officer a year later. Like his elder brother Thomas, he converted to land warfare in 1643, and became increasingly egalitarian in both politics and religion. Thomas, equally radical, quickly rose to command a Parliamentary regiment, many of whose officers were returned New Englanders. He was an outspoken "leveller" during the post-Civil War Putney Debates among the army representatives. He was assassinated in a bungled Royalist kidnap attempt near the end of the Second Civil War on 29 October 1648. In November, he was laid to rest in the family plot at St. John's Chapel, Wapping.[136]

Martha's mother's existing connections to the Nowells, the Graveses, and the Tyngs were cemented when in 1635 Martha married her cousin Captain Thomas Coytmore, master of the *Elizabeth Bonaventure* (ca. 1612–44). The Coytmores were equally influential in East London international trade, and the matriarch Katherine Myles Gray Coytmore (1576–1659) emigrated to Charlestown and lived on there into her mid-eighties. Martha's young husband quickly became a selectman and deputy for Charlestown; he was granted choice lots, including waterside property, and five hundred acres in Charlestown Village, later Woburn. He invested in a town mill on Three-Mile Brook on Mystic Side (see Map 2) and oversaw wharf, warehouse, and porterage rates. In 1643 he returned from a hugely profitable voyage on the *Trial*, the first ocean-going vessel built in Massachusetts, to Faial in the Azores and St. Kitts in the Caribbean. Martha had a son, Thomas, in 1642, and another, William, in 1644. Fragmentary accounts suggest that she kept a shop and sold such luxuries as currants and sugar. The death of newborn William was soon followed by the shock of learning that her husband had drowned in December 1644 off the southern Spanish coast. He was only thirty-two. Nonetheless, his assets already totalled £1,266. Mr. Increase Nowell was overseer of the estate, and the selectmen quickly moved to protect Coytmore property from trespassers and filchers in the Middlesex County Court.[137]

Martha Coytmore was a grieving, but wealthy, widow of twenty-seven with a son of three. Once her mourning was over, she was unlikely to

---

[136] See "Origins." Thomas's famous speech at Putney in the fall of 1647 included the timeless egalitarian creed; "I think that the poorest he that is in England hath a life to live as the greatest he . . . Every man that is to live under a government ought first by his own consent to put himself under that government . . . I should doubt whether he was an Englishman or no that should doubt of those things." *ODNB*. W. R. D. Jones, *Thomas Rainborowe, c. 1610–48* (Woodbridge: Boydell, 2005), 4, 9, 18, 128.

[137] Appointments and grants: *MR*, 1: 332; 4,2: 306; *Possessions*: 150–51; CTR, 1: 658; MxCC D&O, 1: doc. 1730. *Trial, WJ*, 2: 92–93; shop: Mass Archives, 1644–45; drowned: *WJ*, 2: 249; assets: Mass Archives. 16 November 1647; trespass: D&O, 1: docs. 1603–05, 1695, 1704, 1719.

remain a widow for long. Her next husband was a most improbable candidate: Governor John Winthrop, at nearly sixty, was old enough to be Martha's father; furthermore he was sickly and virtually bankrupt. Martha's protectors—Nowell and probably mother-in-law Katherine Coytmore—created a trust fund for young Thomas, and the Winthrop-Coytmore prenuptial agreement was unprecedentedly approved by the General Court and copied into the Colony Records. A year after the marriage, Martha gave birth to a son, baptized on 17 December 1648 as Joshua. The baby was just over a hundred days old when his father died. The General Court, surveying the wreckage of the Winthrop estate, granted Martha £200 towards Joshua's upbringing. Alas, by 1651, both he and his stepbrother Thomas Coytmore were dead. Once again, Martha, at this point only thirty-two, was alone. However, she had her protected fortune, including property in Charlestown, worth £600, and soon asserted her claim to the remainder of her Rainborough inheritance from her father.[138]

Sure enough, Martha Rainborough Coytmore Winthrop was targeted by another widower, this time Boston's first shopkeeper, merchant Mr. John Coggan. They married in March 1652. The sixty-one-year-old groom had only been a widower for two months, and Martha was his fourth wife. Within nine months and five days she gave birth to a son, Caleb, who lived to the age of 19. Coggan's other two surviving daughters were already grown up, one a widow.[139]

Coggan assumed management of the old Coytmore estate in Charlestown. He was a busy and apparently successful merchant with two shops and several houses in Boston, a share in a large warehouse, and a valuable farm in Romney Marsh. He instituted official confirmation of 500 acres in Woburn to the late Thomas Coytmore, and elicited an order that the grant should be laid out for the benefit of the new Mistress Coggan. Martha could expect to

---

[138] Winthrop: Francis Bremer, *John Winthrop: America's Forgotten Founding Father* (New York: Oxford University Press, 2003), 376; C. G. Pestana, "Early Governors and Status," *NEQ*, 78 (2005), 533–34. Sickly: in a 1647 letter to Peter Stuyvesant of New Amsterdam, Winthrop referred to his "craziness in the head." C. Gehring, ed., *Correspondence, 1647–53, New Netherlands Document Series* (Syracuse: Syracuse University Press, 2000), 8. Martha's movable property amounted to £418, as well as considerable real estate; the boy's trust fund, at £640, represented half Thomas Coytmore's assets. Prenuptial: *MR*, 2: 232–36; wreckage: ibid., 274–75. Claim: Aspinwall, 31 October 1649, Letter of Attorney to Captain John Leverett. Governor Winthrop's son Stephen had married Martha's stepsister Judith Rainborough in 1643; they had left for England in 1645.

[139] *GMB*, 403–04; widow Mary Coggan Woody would marry as her second husband Thomas Robinson of Scituate in January 1653; her sister Elizabeth married Joseph Rock of Boston about 1651; on this connection, see "A Wild Ward."

continue living in the privileged manner to which she was accustomed.[140]

However, she and her third husband were in for some nasty shocks. On 17 March 1657 Mr. Joseph Hills of Malden drew up Martha's accounts. Much of the £620 that Martha had inherited from Thomas on 21 July 1645 had disappeared. Property had been lost, damaged or devalued; money owed to the estate had not been paid; some items were simply "wanting." Furthermore, Martha had run up large debts: an accumulated £172 (which Coggan paid) including £34 for "her son's boarding and burial." When all deductions had been made, Mistress Coggan only had about £100 left. On 13 May 1657, her husband presented these accounts along with a four-page petition to the General Court. He protested that "I should have a generous estate with her as the estate was presented" to me, but all that was left was "household stuff." Massachusetts Archives also preserve a petition from Martha. Quoting Old and New Testament precedents, she contests the £200 legacy claims made by the children of her brother-in-law William Tyng against her dwindling assets. Unless the court supported her case, "I am likely to be exposed to want . . . if God bring [me] again into widowhood, as probably He may," she pleaded. No wonder she compared herself to "Hannah, a woman of sorrowful spirit."[141]

Martha's third marriage, like her previous ones, proved short-lived. John died at the age of sixty-two on 27 April 1658, shortly after their second child Sarah, who had survived less than three months. Martha was forty. In his will, John left her the minimum "widow's thirds." The rest of his £1,339 fortune (including all the Coytmore property) went to five-year-old Caleb. Though Martha was appointed executrix, she was joined by merchants Joseph Rock (her stepson) and Joshua Scottow. Three other powerful men were appointed overseers. The appraisers soon found the estate encumbered with debts of at least £455. Settling these and complicated claims of other relatives led to seventeen years of intrafamily dispute. [142]

Martha would be spared most of this contention. On 24 October 1660, John Hull, Boston merchant, recorded two suspicious deaths. The

---

[140]   *GMB,* 401–03. *MR,* 4,1: 272, 281.

[141]   Hills, who had moved from Charlestown to Malden, was appointed in March 1648 as one of four trustees for Martha's child William Coytmore, *MR,* 2: 233. Accounts: Mass Archives, 27 March 1657; three others cosigned Hills's computations; petitions: ibid, 13 May 1657. Elizabeth Coytmore, Thomas's sister, had married William Tyng; their daughters' claim was on their uncle Thomas's estate. The General Court's answers to the petitions: *MR,* 4,1: 304, 337. The latter expressed exasperation at Martha's continued dissatisfaction after "much time spent hearing the case."

[142]   *GMB,* 404–5. Debts: after Coggan's death, Martha had insufficient movables to pay his debts, and on 12 May 1659 the General Court authorized her to sell land, *Sfk Deeds,* 3: 347.

first involved "one Mrs. Coggan, a gentlewoman that had lived in good credit and before thought to be very pious [died] not without suspicion of poison . . . Two awful strokes unto all that knew them, and no little scandal, by accident to religion and a great brand of infamy upon themselves. This is not the death of the righteous." The immediate motive for this tragic suicide was explained in a letter to Martha's former stepson, John Winthrop Jr., on 27 November 1660.

> Sir, what I wrote you, in my former, concerning Mrs. Coggan I had it from Anthony Elcock, who received it in the Bay, viz. she was discontented that she had no suitors, and that had encouraged her farmer, a mean man, to make a motion to her for marriage, which accordingly she propounded, prosecuted and proceeded in it so far that, afterwards, when she reflected what she had done, and what a change of her outward condition she was bringing herself into, she grew discontented, despaired, and took a great quantity of ratsbane, and so died: Fides sit penes authorem [The source is reliable].

Her estate was appraised at £1,030, but included Coggan's and her own real estate, presumably because main legatee Caleb was still a minor. Financial "want" had not prompted her self-destruction.[143]

Martha "despaired." Back in early 1649, after the birth of her son Joshua Winthrop, she seemed to have suffered from postpartum depression. Her sister-in-law Lucy Winthrop Downing expressed relief at the news that "she grows upwards again." In 1660 she could be excused for thinking that the hand of God was against her. Yet another husband, another child, had been taken from her. In 1659 her aged stepmother Katherine Coytmore, a rare beacon of continuity, had died. All through her life Martha had been surrounded by powerful men: her father, brothers, husbands, kinsmen, governors, entrepreneurs, merchants, mariners. She derived status and privilege from these respected figures. Yet they were always deserting her: her father and brothers off to sea. Brother William back to England from Charlestown for the Civil War. Husband Thomas drowned. Brother Thomas assassinated. Two further husbands quickly dead. In 1660 her radical brother William was on the run from Restoration vengeance in England. Only one child survived from five live births, and probably more stillbirths and miscarriages. Her choice of her last two fatherly husbands suggests a need in her for a prestigious authority figure.

---

[143] Hull, Diary, 195–96; letter: from Rev. John Davenport, G.E. MacCracken, "Early Cogans in English and American History," R, 111 (1957), 15. Estate: GMB, 403.

Without them, and without the fortune with which she had begun her adult life, Martha was exposed to both emotional and eventually financial "want." Her sense of desperation is suggested by her encouragement of her "mean" tenant. Life without companionship was not worth living. At the age of forty-three, alone, she ended it.[144]

2. SARAH HAYMAN ELSON (1642–80)

The sea was in the blood of the Hayman family, who arrived in Charlestown, probably from Bristol, after the Restoration, in 1663. Sarah was twenty-one, and fairly soon married another recent arrival, James Elson, who, like Sarah's elder brother, was a seafarer. James was also a shipbuilder, and had a yard near father John Hayman's ropewalk. Sarah's younger brother was only eleven, but he too would soon take to the water. All her in-laws came from maritime families: Thomas Berry, Hannah Trumbull and Elizabeth Allen. As well as manufacturing ropes, cordage, and cables (with the help of black and mulatto servants), Mr. Hayman (as he was always addressed) was successively chosen church member, constable, selectman, jury foreman and tithingman of Charlestown. He was also a leading initiator of the town's dry dock in the late 1670s. Sarah was entwined in a lucrative, but hazardous, employment.[145]

Just how hazardous seafaring could be was revealed to young Mistress Elson in 1678. On 20 November, Boston merchant John Hull, who had often consigned goods on Captain Elson's *Blessing* in the mid-1670s to Barbados and England, recorded "James Elson taken by the Algerines, where I lost one-eighth of my ship £114 or more." The *Blessing* had been on the final leg of its 30 November 1677 round voyage to the West Indies and Europe, returning from London to Boston. Hull recorded Elson's ransom being dispatched on 20 June 1679, but no sooner was he back home in Charlestown than he died on 18 January 1680, perhaps as a result of his "captivation."[146]

---

[144] Lucy: *WP*, 5: 97; births: Martha had had no live births between December 1652 and December 1657. Choice: The prenuptial agreement with John Winthrop may suggest an "arranged marriage," but the contract could have been agreed after espousal. Other widowers of her own age were available in Charlestown in the mid 1640s, like Robert Long, Jr., and in the early 1650s, like Richard Russell. "Mean tenant": the most likely candidate was Thomas Green of Malden, whose wife died in August 1658. However, he married another widow on 5 September 1659. MacCracken, 15, *GMB*, 403, Savage.

[145] Arrival: CTR, 3: 51. Family: Wyman, 489. Bristol: Lechford, 128. Servants: MxCC RB, 3: 121–22, Bartholomew, Indian mulatto; D&O, 3: folio 70, Domingo, Negro; 4: folio 82, John, Negro; son Samuel had a female black servant, Mall or Moll, RB, 3: 237. Dry dock: D&O, 4: folios 83, 89; *MR*, 5, 180, 230; Mass Archives: 23 February 1677; *Possessions*, 168–69.

[146] Hull, Diary, 163; Letter Book, 299, 361, 417. See "Ordeals of Captain Foster."

He was alive long enough, however, for Sarah, two of whose infants had already died, to conceive again. She was appointed executrix in James's will along with Boston merchant James Whitcomb. However, within weeks of her husband's death, she too had sickened. On 20 March 1680 she made her own will; she left gold rings to 12 relatives, silks and cash bequests to others, and £3 to Charlestown's poor. The residue went to three nieces and her father. She had lost her baby and was on the point of losing her own life. We hear no more of her, or of the Elson line. However, we continue to hear a great deal about the Elson estate.[147]

Problems with the Elson estate arose from several causes. James had made more than one will. His executor Whitcomb was dilatory, and this prevented Sarah's sole executor, her father, from proceeding with administration. Whitcomb's excuse was that Elson's account book after his captivity in Algiers was in some confusion. Hayman claimed to know nothing of his son-in-law's affairs. Though he petitioned the General Court to hasten proceedings, he was told that he should proceed by law. Accordingly, on 30 September 1680, nearly ten months after James's death, Mrs. Elson's executor sued Mr. Elson's executor, and at last accounts were finalized.[148]

Elson proved to be a wealthy young man. His estate was appraised at £1,046. He left £104 in cash, £489 of real and personal property, including a "Negro girl" and silver "plate" worth £26, a ship's hull worth £240, shares in various ships and in the dry dock, and £179 owed for work on the dock. According to James's wills of 6 June 1676, 20 October 1677, and 6 January 1680, Sarah was to inherit two-thirds of the estate, £638 after Whitcomb's adjustments. James had added requests to Sarah on 30 June 1679: to try to redeem Richard Elson and another mariner from captivity. Yet another codicil included provisions for maintaining James's stepmother, the widow Elizabeth Elson, and the disposal of his legacy to Sarah after her death.[149]

In the few weeks between James's death and Sarah's, she and her father were doubtless eager to know how much she and the child she was carrying would have to live on. When she made her will on 20 March 1680, she was presumably leaving only personal assets. The Elson wealth she

[147]   Sarah died on 28 March 1680, *Charlestown V.R.* Wills: MPR, 5: 227–36, MxCC D&O, 4: folio 89.

[148]   On the Whitcomb family in England and New England, see Savage, Brenner, *Merchants and Revolution,* 103; Thistlethwaite, *Dorset Pilgrims,* 41. Petition: D&O, 4: folio 89; as a consolation Hayman, now seventy, was excused further military service, folio 91.

[149]   Estate: Two inventories are in D&O, 4: folio 91; the estate owed £154. Adjustments: on 3 October 1680, Middlesex County Court supported Hayman's suit, and ordered Whitcomb to pay £129 he had withheld, RB, 3: 324. James's sister Thomasine had married mariner David Harris; their daughter Ann Harris would be a beneficiary after Sarah's death.

had briefly inherited was already assigned after her death. Whitcomb's accounts valued the late Sarah's assets at £638, her two-thirds. However, he debited £390 from her estate for James's niece according to James's 1677 will. In the end, this lucky girl, still underage, became the chief beneficiary of James Elson's house and household goods.[150]

Sarah Elson was thirty-eight when she died. She had been a wealthy widow for a few weeks. As a daughter of Mr. John Hayman, she probably brought a handsome dowry to her husband, and it may be that part or all of this portion made up her legacies in March 1680. However, the marital estate was not hers to dispose of. In that, she only had a life interest. Many widows received a mere third, according to the letter of the law. More generous husbands often reduced their bequests in the event of their widows remarrying. The assumption was that the husband controlled the long-term disposal of "his" family's wealth, including what his "helpmeet" had contributed.[151]

3. Margaret Lock Willoughby Hammond (CA. 1629–83)

When he died on 4 April 1671, Francis Willoughby was one of the richest men in Charlestown. His probate inventories totalled £4,813. As deputy governor of Massachusetts, he was also the most prestigious. His long and mathematically complex will of 4 June 1670 stated in one of the first items that his "loving and beloved wife" Margaret "brought a considerable estate with her . . . household goods, plate and jewels." We learn also that when he composed this document Margaret was "big with child." The baby did not survive. Though she would remarry, this seems to have been Margaret's last pregnancy. Francis had expected that she would "change her condition" but was confident that her "cordial affection . . . and natural love to her children" would never "turn to the prejudice of her little ones" after she took a new husband. He referred to Susannah, aged six, Nathaniel, about nine, and Francis Jr., about eleven. He bequeathed to her, over and above her marriage portion, "three parts and a half (or four eighths and one sixteenth of the whole) to hold and enjoy as her own proper estate *for ever* [my italics]." He underlined his trust in her by appointing her sole executrix. As a result of her husband's death at the age of 56, Margaret had become one of the richest women in Charlestown, and in theory one of its

---

[150] D&O, 4: folio 93, Whitcomb accounts, 21 June 1681.

[151] See "Sarah Symmes," above; Rodgers, passim.

most powerful and prestigious inhabitants.[152]

That inexhaustible gleaner of genealogical materials in late Victorian England, Henry FitzAlan Waters, is the source of our modest information about Mistress Margaret Willoughby's background. She was one of six children of William Lock of Wimbledon, gentleman, and Susannah, daughter of Roger Cole of St. Saviour's Southwark, who had brought to her marriage considerable property in Southwark and neighboring Lambeth. If Margaret's last pregnancy was indeed in 1670, she may have been born in the late 1620s. When and how she met Francis is not known. A bond of 12 May 1662 by Francis, undertaking that Margaret should receive a minimum of £200 if she survived him, was signed by Thomas Bragne, parson of Southwick, Hampshire. The parish is just outside the major English Channel naval base of Portsmouth. From 1652 until the end of the decade, Willoughby was the Commissioner of the Navy responsible for Portsmouth's dockyard, fitting out, hiring and manning its ships. In 1659, he was briefly Portsmouth's Member of Parliament. Bragne was married to Margaret's sister Hannah, and Francis may have met her through the Bragnes. It is also possible that before attaining gentility and moving to Wimbledon, the Lock family had lived in Willoughby's birthplace of Wapping. The only clue as to when they married is in the May 1662 will of Elizabeth Willoughby of London, Francis's mother. She frequently refers to "my daughter Margaret, my said son Francis his now wife," suggesting that the marriage may have been fairly recent. Since Margaret had two children before emigrating to Charlestown in 1662, her marriage to Francis probably took place about 1658, when she would have been in her late twenties.[153]

The tone of Francis Willoughby's will shows that their thirteen-odd years of marriage had been mutually supportive, "loving," and enriched by "cordial affection." Margaret had acquired five stepchildren, three of whom were still under fourteen. The elder of the five were in their twenties by the time Margaret arrived in Charlestown in 1662, but she would not have escaped her husband's angry frustration with eldest son Jonathan (b. 1636), who had attended Harvard between 1651 and 1654 and had married in London in 1661. This "prodigal," who had cost his father a small fortune, did return to New England, but moved to the distant frontier town of Wethersfield, Connecticut,

---

[152]   Rodgers, 3: 11–21; see above, "Godly Merchants."

[153]   Waters, *R*, 47 (1893) 417–19, 49 (1895) 146. Bernard Capp, *Cromwell's Navy* (London: Oxford University Press, 1989), 49, 144, 280–81, 290–91. Willoughby's father William had preceded him at Portsmouth from 1649 to his death in 1651. The bond was drawn up just before the Willoughbys' departure from England for Charlestown, Rodgers, 3:18. Elizabeth Willoughby will: Rodgers, 2: 130–134.

in 1664. Sarah (b. 1641) married and moved to Norwalk, Connecticut.[154]

When Margaret arrived in Charlestown in 1662, she would have been welcomed by another "stranger in the country," Francis's young cousin Lawrence Hammond (ca. 1638–99) who had been admitted an inhabitant of the town on 25 July 1661. The men's mothers were sisters, and in 1662 Jane Hammond was in Virginia. Francis's mother left Lawrence £5 that year. Hammond acted as Willoughby's agent in land purchases in 1662 and 1668, and in 1670 the ailing deputy governor appointed his cousin as his attorney. The same year Hammond witnessed Francis's will and was one of the four overseers required to "manifest affection and respect to my wife in all that assistance that she shall stand in need of, she being a stranger in the country."[155]

Initially, Hammond's assistance had to be platonic; he was married. In 1673, when one of the chimneys of the eleven-room Willoughby mansion caught fire, it was cousin Hammond who paid the relict's statutory ten-shilling fine. In 1674, however, Abigail Willett Hammond died at the age of 30, and the following year "affection and respect" promoted Hammond from cousin to husband. If our speculations are correct, Margaret would have been some years older than Lawrence. Nonetheless, as an expert accountant and diligent man of business, her new husband was invaluable in administering his late cousin's somewhat tangled assets. From 1679 to 1680, the two of them finally had to sue the even more complicated Bellingham estate for a nineteen-year-overdue debt, whose unpaid interest far exceeded the principal. Three years later, they won judgment on another longstanding loan. They were also defendants in other cases for money that Francis had owed, for instance to Parnell Nowell, John Coad, and John Hull. In November 1681, the Hammonds were sued by Margaret's stepson Nehemiah Willoughby, by now a merchant in Salem, for failing to pay the legacies of father Francis and grandmother Elizabeth to William Willoughby, who had died in 1677 of smallpox. Nehemiah was William's executor. The wealth that Margaret had inherited brought with it considerable problems.[156]

---

[154] Rodgers, 3: 11–14; A. M. McEwen, "The Campfield husband of Sarah Willoughby," *R*, 118 (1964) 296. Surviving younger children were Nehemiah (b. 1644), Jeremiah (b. 1651) and William (b. ca. 1ca. 1652). I. J. Greenwood, "Willoughby Family," *R*, 30 (1876) 51–62.

[155] Inhabitant: CTR, 1: 622. Virginia and £5: Rodgers, 2: 132. Land:*Possessions,* 155; D&O, 2: folio 53, 5 April 1670. Ailing: *MR*, 4,2: 458. Agent: Hammond also signed a £125 bond in 1668 on Willoughby's behalf, D&O, 2: folio 50. Willoughby's will awarded Hammond £40 and expenses, "provided he deal respectively with my wife and assist her about settling my estate," Rodgers, 3: 13.

[156] Chimney: CTR, 3: 140. Assets: on 16 October 1671, Margaret and another overseer, Richard

On 21 August 1680, Margaret made her will. Compared to Willoughby's it was the model of simplicity. She left half her estate to Lawrence and half to her daughter Susannah Willoughby. Her two sons had both died. Nathaniel is not mentioned in his father's will of 1670. Francis died as an adolescent in 1678; he had caught smallpox on Jenner's ship returning from London. Margaret left bequests to her sister Elizabeth Lock in England and to Hammond's eldest son Francis, embarking on a seafaring career: her one-eighth share in a sailing pink. She also remembered Charlestown's poor with an unusually generous legacy of £20. She appointed her husband her executor. She died on 2 February 1683.[157]

The widower was executor to the executrix of Willoughby's estate. Four months after Margaret's death, he had to sue neighbor Thomas Brigden for £34, which he had owed the estate for more than twelve years. On 11 December 1684, we find Hammond in the bizarre situation of suing the late Francis's estate for £200 due by the Bragne bond of 1662 to the estate of his late widow Margaret. In the same month he was judged liable for £100 borrowed by Francis way back in 1668. Margaret had also borrowed money when she was still Widow Willoughby. Hammond was dunned for that too. By 1684, three-times widower Lawrence Hammond was courting another wealthy widow, Ann, the relict of Dr. William Gerrish. He soon became entangled in the collection of Gerrish's unpaid bills, and in conflicts with outraged patients who claimed to have been overcharged. Let us hope that Ann's charms and Gerrish's £300 estate were worth all this bother.[158]

Margaret Lock Willoughby Hammond was a gentlewoman who, like Margaret Winthrop, had endured the challenge of a transatlantic voyage with small children, and settling in a strange town with a busy, often absent, husband. By 1662, Francis had been away from Charlestown for more than a decade, had witnessed the implosion of the great Cromwellian experiment he had so forcefully served, been summarily displaced by the Restoration, and returned in exile to a provincial, intolerant and paranoid colony. Many of his former friends and colleagues were gone: Increase Nowell and Robert Sedgwick dead, Nicholas Shapleigh dying, Nicholas Davison often in Maine. He found that the region's communal

---

Russell, had to sue Benjamin Shapleigh for £125 owed by his late father Nicholas, D&O, 2: folio 57. Bellingham: D&O, 4: folio 86; another loan: RB, 3: 286; *Assistants*, 1: 157. Nowell, £100: Rodgers, 3: 19; Coad, £137: *Essex CC*, 4: 401; Hull, £170: RB, 4: 93; Nehemiah, *Essex CC*, 8: 204.

[157]   Will: D&O, 4: folio 110; Francis: see "Captain Jenner's Voyages."

[158]   Brigden: RB, 4: 69; bond: RB, 4: 102; Widow: RB, 4: 93; Gerrish: RB, 4: 65, 76, 221; see Thompson, *Cambridge Cameos*, 281–284.

spirit had sadly shrunk; his philanthropy towards Harvard, for instance, was not copied by his neighbors. Clergy and legislators were narrow-minded and factious. Margaret must have needed all her "cordiality and affection" to counter such disillusionment, as would Lawrence, as he grew increasingly indignant at the presumptuous folly of "the common people" of Charlestown. Meanwhile, her resident Willoughby stepchildren were growing into adolescence and her second son dying. She must learn to manage three black servants in her large household. All these challenges confronted her without a kinship network to turn to, as she would have had in England.[159]

Yet despite her wealth and her status, we hear nothing of Mrs. Willoughby or Mrs. Hammond in the public sphere. Willoughby's will assumed that men would have to administer his estate, even though Margaret was his executrix, and that she would need male agents to organize her affairs. When she had to attend court she was always with a man: Richard Russell just after Francis's death, then Lawrence, first her spokesman and then her husband. When Willoughby was dying, it was his male cousin rather than his wife who saw to his business. It is difficult to determine whether Margaret's personality was a factor, though given the similar fates of Martha Rainborough and Sarah Hayman, it would be tempting to conclude that women's wealth was deemed far too important to be left in women's control. However, we should not forget wealthy Mistress Sarah Symmes, the intrepid business manager of the minister's family affairs; or Widow Alice Rand, running a considerable estate for forty years; or Widow Arrald Cole's eagle eye over family assets. It may well have been that our three heiresses' marriages to energetic men of business repressed their entrepreneurial drives; their very wealth conspired against their independence.

---

[159]   Harvard: Rodgers, 3: 13–14; see "Godly Merchants." Lawrence: see "Succession Crisis." Black: D&O, 3: folio 77.

Conclusion:
Gender and Fundamentalisms

The twenty women we have met cover wide ranges of age, role, status, values, and relationships. Alice Rand lived to be ninety-seven; Hannah Crouch was eleven when abused; Mary Whittemore only nine or ten when propositioned, but armed with a hot iron. Sarah Largin and Mary Robinson were troublesome teenagers. Wives like Alice Brackenbury, Mary Gould, Ursula Cole, Martha Coytmore, and Sarah Elson had to cope with their husbands' long absences, serving as their deputies in public business or having to stand by while male agents took over. Katherina Sims, the free Cuban black woman, was accidentally stranded in Virginia while her husband John was carried to Boston. She proved a forceful and effective defender of her own freedom. Mary Mansfield had to endure grinding poverty with a delusional husband; Sarah Largin suffered nearly a decade of want. Their styles and expectations were diametrically different from those of the comfortable Sarah Symmes, or the three wealthy wives, though Martha Coggan's accountant briefly terrified her with the prospect of penury.

Our widows also varied in station and authority. Arrald Cole, Alice Rand, and Katherine Coytmore all enjoyed considerable wealth and exercised control over their assets; they were matriarchs. In 1662, well-heeled and well-connected Widow Mary Newall returned to Charlestown a Baptist, and a Baptist she stayed, despite fines and communal pressure. Much more dependent were elderly women like Agnes Wadland, Mary Nash, or other widows who figure in the Charlestown welfare rolls, from Catherine Morley in 1636 to Mary Pratt in 1688.[160]

---

[160] Morley: CTR, 1: 6; Pratt: CTR, 4: 83, 89; cf. Widow Hale, CTR, 4: 16; Widow Cole, CTR, 4: 54; Widow Dady, CTR, 4: 56; CTrR, passim.

Attitudes diverged too, between the piety of Arrald Cole or Sarah Symmes and the subversive carnality of Ursula Cole or Sarah Largin. Margaret Willoughby was an ideal wife in her husband's eyes, but Thomas Jones or Henry Streeter may have had mixed feelings about their Sarahs, as would have Captain Richard Martin, mariners John Cross, Robert Manser, and Thomas Smith, or alcoholic laborer William Brown, about their free and easy wives.[161]

From our group we can construct a rough model of the different stages of women's lives in seventeenth-century Charlestown. Young girls in most families would live under their mothers' tutelage, learning increasingly complex household skills, usually including reading and sometimes writing. By the age of nine, Mary Whittemore could be entrusted with the ironing while her mother was at the mill. Little Hannah Crouch was sent to the Penny Ferry alehouse to fetch yeast. Some less fortunate girls would lose their mothers and either grow up under a stepmother, like Martha Rainborough, or else be fostered like Mary Robinson or Sarah Largin. The results in their cases were discouraging.[162]

Teenage girls and unmarried women in their early twenties would be customarily "put out" or "disposed" to work in other families as serving maids. They continued to learn the arts of housewifery in preparation for marriage. At this stage, the need for sexual purity was dinned into them; their virginity must be preserved. Plenty of predatory males circled round: mistresses' sons, like Joseph Harris, John Row or James Tufts; masters like John Jones or Thomas Peachey; foreign seamen like Peter Grant or William Morgan (Sarah Largin's hay mate); or perennial lechers like John Harris. Even privileged young women like Mary Robinson might be susceptible to passionate ardor. A few young women like Sarah Poor (Stephen Geary's lover), Sarah Largin, Sarah Crouch, or Margaret Martin reared up against the leading reins of modesty, but they were exceptional. Though the unmarried women of Middlesex County were less biddable than their elders hoped, most obeyed the demand for premarital virginity.[163]

Most were also faithful after marriage. Once Sarah Crouch, the mother of two illegitimate children, became Goodwife Jones, her availability ceased. When John Harris offered her £6 to show him her "secret parts," her response would have been the envy of the saintliest sister: "Was he

---

[161] Thompson, *Sex*, 149–52, 182–85.

[162] Education: Thompson, *Women in Stuart England and America*, 187–220.

[163] Row, Tufts, Martin: see *Sex*, 61–64, 45–53, 182–85.

not ashamed to ask such a question, for it was a disgrace to my husband . . . I would not do such a thing to him nor no man living." Arrald Cole expected her new daughter-in-law to be "modest and virtuous," imbued with spiritual piety. These early years of marriage were frequently the time that mothers-to-be turned their minds to their immortal souls, and began the arduous application process for church membership.[164]

Mature wives had exhausting domestic responsibilities: bearing, nursing, and raising children, teaching children and maids both practically and spiritually, helping married daughters and daughters-in-law. They had to feed their families. This involved cultivating the kitchen garden and orchard, milking, making beer and cider, and running the farmyard with its poultry and fattening pig. Housewives were the great preservers. Ursula Cole turned spare milk into cheese and butter. Most probate inventories had "powdering tubs" for salting meat in the cellar. Roots and fruit had to be carefully stored down there. Vinegar was increasingly used for pickling, and sugar for preserves. Keeping a household fed through the winter was an annual challenge. Sarah Symmes, merchant's daughter, kept the accounts. Alice Brackenbury ran the farm, despite the disdainful disobedience of her young sharecropper. She took her maid out with her to the fields to help clear the soil for the plow. Some better-off women were entrepreneurs: Mistresses Coytmore, Russell, Symmes, and Sprague ran shops. Mary Mansfield, at the other end of the financial scale, was eager to support herself through her needlework. Alice Rand proved a canny estate manager. As providers, preservers, preceptors, earners, and managers, wives were vital to the household economy and communal culture.[165]

Inevitably, social status made an enormous difference to women's lives, attitudes and treatment. To be addressed as "Mistress" inferred a deference and respect that would be laughably inappropriate in dealing with a goodwife. Though both were wild foster children, heiress Mary Robinson's life was almost unrecognizable in comparison to deprived Sarah Largin. Mary was put out to the elite household of Captain Lawrence Hammond and his wealthy third wife Margaret (Willoughby); despite her reputation, she was courted by both a wealthy merchant's son and the mysterious businessman John Walley. By contrast, neglected Sarah Largin

---

[164]   Crouch: see above, "A Damned Whore"; membership: "From Symmes to Morton," above.

[165]   Joan Thirsk, *Food in Early Modern England* (London: Hambledon, 2007); J. E. McWilliams, "To Forward Well-Flavored Productions: The Kitchen Garden in Early New England," *NEQ*, 77 (2004), 25–50.

hung out with randy sailors and had to make do with the disreputable pauper Henry Streeter for a husband.

Occasionally social assumptions were challenged, with shocking results. When Mistress Mansfield, deprived of her twins, defamed Mistress Russell and her esteemed husband, townspeople were aghast. They must have been equally amazed at the sight of the bare back of the daughter-in-law of an English member of Parliament being lashed with ten stripes. True, the Mansfields were town charges, yet they had betrayed their inherited position in provincial society by their improvidence and their impudence. We can similarly sense elite affront when the merchant's widow Martha Coggan entertained the prospect of marriage to a mere tenant, a mean fellow. Her realization of her gaffe, driven by loveless loneliness, resulted in her death. Social suicide triggered physical suicide. As a general rule, however, the status and wealth of parents were handed down to daughters; the size of a dowry dictated marriage choices. Sarah Crouch might have an infatuated fling with the wealthier Christopher Grant, but for a husband she had to settle for dirt dauber Thomas Jones. It would take the Streeters three generations and migration to a distant frontier to achieve gentility.[166]

Whatever her station, a woman's relations with men were meant to reflect the separation of their roles. The woman's center was the home, the man's "the world": the world of production, of business and property, of politics. This was the ideal, and sometimes, as we have seen with wealthy women, it led to wives or widows' experiencing powerlessness when their husbands were absent or no more. Other men stepped in and took over their family affairs. Martha Coggan lost hope without a husband. Even as doughty a nonconformist as Mary Gould needed a man's help to deal with her late husband's estate. Sarah Jones rejected John Harris's advances because it would disgrace her *husband*. Alice Brackenbury had to turn to male neighbors to help her deal with her opinionated young sharecropper— what did women know about men's work, farming? Alice's initial mistake had been too much feminine generosity. Early in 1681, Widow Hannah Barrett petitioned the Middlesex County Court in severe financial difficulties. Her husband had left her in comfort, but "my womanlike act, love and lenity had put power out of my hand to my son, giving away what was my own and impoverishing myself." Women, such examples suggested, simply were not emotionally equipped to deal with the world.[167]

---

[166]   Grant: Thompson, *Sex in Middlesex*, 38–39, 41–44.

[167]   Barrett: MxCC D&O, 4: folio 92.

Yet there were many exceptions to this gender demarcation: Sarah Symmes, for instance, effectively ran the family's material business, as did long-term widow Alice Rand. Dying men acknowledged the economic impetus that their wives' portions and participation had given their early enterprises. The most striking breakthrough came in religious life, where the good women in a community became the heart of church membership: the main link between family and meetinghouse, between one godly generation and the next. Despite ministerial apprehensiveness, the sisters expanded their influence. They petitioned the General Court. They voiced their doubts about infant baptism and helped found breakaway cells. A few, like Elizabeth Bowers, went to the extreme of embracing Quakerism. Yet, as some pious women questioned orthodoxy, others took it upon themselves to act as unofficial moral police, overseeing town morality and alerting the authorities to aberrant behavior: illicit sex, after-hours drinking, lying, and bad language. Through observation and conversation, the Sisters were custodians of town reputations—a powerful, worldly role.[168]

Networks were vital webs for women's lives. Kinship groups were at the centre of their gatherings. When Widow Wadland clashed with Stephen Geary, first one daughter then another rushed, menacingly, to her defence. The Crouch-Jones women linked arms to defend little Hannah from John Harris; Harris's daughters and some of their friends and neighbors united in counter-attack. Church women could add spiritual sisters to birth sisters. Women neighbors were in and out of each other's houses all the time. Elizabeth Stitson spread her suspicions of Jane Moulton among her "gossips." Captain Martin's womenfolk were exposed by nosy neighbors and sisters. William Crouch had a low opinion of such saints: "Concerning church members, he said they would take a false oath for a halfpenny." When pressed, that turned out to mean that *he* would. News traveled fast along these networks. It took less than an hour for a crowd to gather outside Peachey's locked shop when word got out that his maid, detained in there with him, was "in distress." Women without such support groups were vulnerable. Goody Peachey, new to the town, had to go down to the shop alone. Margaret Willoughby, even after a decade, was "a stranger in the land," especially in need of male assistance. For most women, however, especially in the second generation, the sense of membership in a women's world, with both its supports and its prohibitions, would reinforce their sense of belonging and empowerment.[169]

---

[168]   Bowers: Thompson, *Cambridge Cameos*, 173–81.

[169]   For English background: Bernard Capp, *When Gossips Meet: Women, Family and Neighbor-*

Networks not only increased in complexity as each generation of women married into other clans, but also expanded geographically as second- and especially third-generation daughters had to move to less crowded settlements, or even, like Sarah Largin or the Harris daughters, to different colonies. Though the sisterhood of church members grew over time in proportion to male saints, so too did status divisions, evident, for instance, in meetinghouse seating precedence so socially important to the younger generations. I have discussed in detail elsewhere other changes over time in women's roles, expectations and attitudes, and Charlestown's female population is well represented in that analysis.[170]

What was the feminine experience of Charlestown's fundamentalist religious regime like? Certainly women like Arrald Cole seem to have internalized a providential, Bible-centred and God-fearing piety. The good woman, as Mary Maples Dunn says, was equated with the good Christian. Baptist women renounced orthodox church fellowship—a giant step—because they could not wrong their consciences by having their babies baptized. Contemporaries described Margaret Willoughby and Martha Coggan as both "virtuous" and "pious," and Sarah Symmes was a role model for a whole generation of town women. Evidence from the Middlesex County Court Records supports this view that many Charlestown women were committed believers.[171]

Seventeenth-century Charlestown stiffened the backs of doubters or lukewarm Christians with savage discipline. The authorities not only brought to bear the frightening punishment of excommunication, isolating individuals from needed fellowship, but made blasphemy a capital offence. They dealt out physically brutal sentences for moral offenses: the death penalty for adultery, for instance; fierce floggings for sexual "crimes," like those inflicted on the pregnant Seaborn Batchelor, or monthly on Sarah Poor until she revealed her second baby's father; for subversive comments like Mary Mansfield's; and limitless imprisonments for "heresy." The idea of toleration was generally greeted with outrage. This was the road to perdition; just look at the chaos afflicting Interregnum England. Some offenders had to undergo humiliating shame sentences: standing in a dunce's cap and white sheet before the gender-divided congregation, or

---

hood in *Early Modern England* (London: Oxford University Press, 2003).

[170] *Women in Stuart England and America,* and *Sex.*

[171] Dunn, "Saints and Sisters," 594. Court Records: *Sex,* 196–98. Baptists: none was so challenged as English Baptist Mary Campion, who thwarted her Presbyterian husband's insistence on infant baptism by beheading her child, J. R. Ruff, *Violence in Early Modern Europe* (Cambridge: Cambridge University Press, 2002), 33.

wearing a hangman's rope and halter. The "religious police" of inquisitive neighbors, intrusive church members, constables, watchmen, meeting-house overseers, and tithingmen proved highly effective enforcers.[172]

Female modesty was stipulated through meek speech, a rigid dress code, and the requirement of an overall plainness. Attractiveness was a snare. Every girl was indoctrinated with treasuring her virginity. It was the passport to a good marriage. Unions were the result of complex negotiations. The couple themselves usually "agreed," but parents or guardians involved themselves in the financial aspects of these clan mergers. Sometimes the young and the mature might clash. Mary Robinson briefly rejected her assigned mate for a passionate intruder. Christopher Grant's parents stymied Sarah Crouch's crush on him. Martha Coytmore's marriages to men her father's age smack of external calculations rather than her own emotions. Puritan partnerships were less manipulative than some forms of arranged marriages, but they were a far cry from modern love matches.[173]

Some wives endured stunted or conflicted marriages. We will soon meet poor Sarah Lowden, terrified to go home because of her husband John's drunken brutality. Rebecca Trerice could not bear to live under the same roof as Master Nicholas. Alice Brackenbury was humiliated by her absent husband's negligence regarding his sharecropping deal. Widow Nash's daughter was deserted by her improvident husband, and then accused of witchcraft. The wives of John Harris, Thomas Peachey, and William Everton had to endure the opprobrium surrounding their knavish mates. The Martin household was certainly fractious, and probably violent. The aptly named Crosswell women flogged maidservant Beck Lee mercilessly. Despite Puritan ideals of female spirituality and companionate marriage, the sexist assumptions of Old England could prove deepseated. The elites' responses to Mistress Hutchinson, to Quaker missionaries, and to Baptist sisters revealed their prejudices against "weaker vessels." To such authoritarian notables, wives should be obedient, modest, and, above all, quiet.[174]

---

[172] *Sex*, Ch. 11.

[173] Ibid., 132–33, 191–92. J. Kamensky, "Talk like a Man," *Gender and History*, 8 (1996), 22–47.

[174] Puritan idealization: N. Z. Davis, *Society and Culture in Early Modern France* (Cambridge: Polity, 1987), 90; A. Fletcher, *Gender, Sex and Subordination in England 1500–1800* (New Haven: Yale University Press, 1995), 54, 173, 198, 363; S. Mendelson and P. Crawford, *Women in Early Modern England* (Oxford: Clarendon Press, 1998), 31, 33, 36–39, 180–85, 334, 389–401; R. L. Greaves, "Role of Women in Early English Nonconformity," *Church History*, 52 (1983), 299–311; Suzanne Trill, "Religion and the Construction of Feminity," in H. Wilcox, ed., *Women and Literature in Britain 1500–1700* (Cambridge: Cambridge University Press, 1996),

Despite these similarities with other fundamentalist societies, there were countervailing forces that mollified oppression. The painstakingly assembled defenses of individual rights in the English common and statute laws mitigated the power of religious decrees. Popular opinion rebelled against capital sentences for adultery or Quaker blasphemy. The documented rights of a black woman were respected by the court. The culture of discipline imposed social restraint, reducing vengeful violence associated with family honor and shame. Arbitration and legal settlements were preferred over duels and vendettas. Masculine brutality and bragging were condemned; the thuggish aggression of foreign seamen was jarringly alien. Young militiamen letting rip after training day found themselves in court. Charlestown women also benefited from the moral tone of town society.[175]

The Calvinist celebration of women's individual conscience conferred a spiritual status and a recognition of female activism. After a long struggle, Charlestown women Baptists were allowed to worship at their own church; they had won considerable lay sympathy. As Peter Lake has written,

> There can be little doubt that the Puritan view of godliness could and did create a more positive image of womankind and allow female believers to claim areas of spiritual and social space for development and exercise of their personalities. Godliness was the spur and sanction for an urgent autodidacticism leading to a sense of control over their lives, confidence in themselves, and a new level of assurance about their gender identity.

Protestant women in England, France, and New England were glorified among the martyrs of religious turmoil. However, female involvement in the movement was not confined to martyrdom.[176]

30–55. Sexist: L. Gowing, *Domestic Dangers* (Oxford: Clarendon, 1996), and *Common Bodies* (New Haven: Yale University Press, 2003); D. Purkiss, "Material Girls," in C. Brant and D. Purkiss, eds., *Women, Texts and Histories 1575–1760* (London: Routledge, 1992), 69–101; M. Ingram, "Scolding Women Cucked and Washed," in J. Kermode and G. Walker, eds., *Women, Crime and the Courts in Early Modern England* (Chapel Hill: University of North Carolina Press, 1994), 49–80.

[175] Adultery: *Sex*, 128–30; Quakers: Foster, *Long Argument*, 190–95. Discipline: R. Thompson, *Women in Stuart England and America* (London: Routledge, 1974), Ch. 11; M. Ingram, "Slander Suits in Early Modern England," in P. Coss, ed., *The Moral World of Law* (Cambridge: Cambridge University Press, 2000), 135–160; Fletcher, 111–12, 130, 150; Gowing, *Domestic Dangers*, 37.

[176] Greaves, 307–11; P. Lake, "Female Piety," *Seventeenth Century* 2 (1987), 147–49; Fletcher, Ch. 17; Davis, 92.

Potentially autocratic clerical power was counterbalanced and corralled by elected lay bodies, from grand juries up to the Governor's Council and the General Court. True, women could not vote or serve in any of these offices, but they could and did petition; when heading households, they were empowered to sue in courts, buy and sell land and administer estates. Various comments scattered through these pages suggest that they also exerted considerable informal influence in family and communal affairs.

On 5 May 1649, a large crowd of London women petitioners returned to Parliament after an initial misogynistic rebuff. "Are we Christians and yet must sit still and keep at home?" they demanded. Many Charlestown women had emigrated from dense and busy urban backgrounds: Bristol, Dunstable, Stepney, Southwark. In such neighborhoods, keeping at home was rare. In Old England and New England, women were used to being out and about: at the market, running stalls or small businesses, helping friends, family, and neighbors with nursing, child-minding, sewing, providing heating, food or drink. They assisted husbands with agricultural, commercial, or artisanal tasks—or they just went visiting. Housebound they were not. Little escaped their attention. Three published volumes of Middlesex probate records contain ample proof that the women of Charlestown, rather than being commodified, ignored, or relegated to obscurity, were generally admired and valued, and rightly so. To us, their aspirations might appear frustratingly restricted, but in fact they were on the road to emancipation, and the potential for defiance.[177]

---

[177] Mendelson and Crawford, 304; Davis, 66–67, 80, 62; Jane Cox, *Hatred Pursued Beyond the Grave* (London: Her Majesty's Stationery Office, 1993), 20–26; P. Crawford and L. Gowing, *Women's Worlds in Seventeenth-Century England* (London: Routledge, 2000), 254; Gowing, *Domestic Dangers*, 265; Fletcher, 256–63.

Part 7

Violence

Introduction

Though pride was a sin for the Puritans, they nonetheless prided themselves on their culture of discipline. This emphasized theocentricity, hard
work, frugality, prudence, self-control, neighborliness, and "holy watchfulness." Where differences arose they should be settled by prayerful arbitration and concessive conciliation. No saint in unresolved conflict
could participate in the Lord's Supper. Infractions should be remorsefully
confessed. Compensation should be gracefully paid. Those in authority—
especially ministers, godly magistrates, masters, mistresses or parents—
should be unquestioningly obeyed. In this pious, purposeful, cooperative,
and committed culture, peace, calm, selflessness, and providential success
would prevail.[1]

    Experiments in the culture of discipline had been tried in old Eng-
land in the sixteenth and early seventeenth centuries, but the surrounding national culture had been hostile and invasive. Some early emigrants
had belonged to godly cells and conventicles, like John Cotton's in Boston, Lincolnshire. Those in Zechariah Symmes's company probably had
similar experiences of meeting, praying, fasting, meditating, and giving
thanks together. They secluded themselves from the beer-swilling, foul-
mouthed, bawdy, idle, improvident, fornicating, violent, abusive mass of
fellow countrymen whose ideal society was a "Merry England" where guts
could be stuffed without effort, insults and grudges paid off with fists or

---

[1]   William Hunt, *The Puritan Moment* (Cambridge: Harvard University Press, 1983), 79–84,
140–55, 166, 179; Keith Wrightson, "Puritan Reformation of Manners," (PhD. diss., Cambridge
University, 1973). Roger Thompson, "'Holy Watchfulness' and Communal Conformism," *NEQ*,
56 (1983), 504–22. Richard P. Gildrie, *The Profane, The Civil, and the Godly* (University Park:
Pennsylvania State University Press, 1994), 1–27. Infractions: e.g., Solomon Phipps's self-flagellating acknowledgement of his "folly and sin in words and actions" against fellow church member
John Fowle on 4 August 1688, and his "endeavouring to excuse and justify" himself to conciliators, Hunnewell, ix.

clubs or knives or swords, and where pagan anniversaries like carnival or May Day could be celebrated without restraint or thought for the morrow. This traditional culture, centred on the alehouse rather than God's house, was what Puritans called "the world," the pit of the godless. Their attempts to supplant it were interpreted by traditional authorities as attempts to overthrow them. Many early emigrants to Massachusetts left the old country because their leaders had been silenced or were on the run. They were God's "saving remnant" who would impose His culture of discipline in the New World.[2]

Predictably, such utopian ambitions collided with the realities of human nature and the stresses of survival. Not all arrivals were saints; not all saints were agreed. At the very first Court of Assistants, held at Charlestown on 25 August 1630, justices were appointed to deal with "abuses . . . and punish offenders." Ten days later, they had their first two cases— theft and fraud—to adjudicate. Many Charlestown inhabitants shared the values of the godly experiment; despite uninitiated and hostile visitors to the port, it proved to be more law-abiding and orderly than Wapping or Southwark. Nonetheless, controversy, bad behavior, negligence, and jealousy did erupt, and all too often these involved violence.[3]

Violence came in many forms. It could be verbal; it could be physical. Both can be subdivided. Verbal abuse could consist of angry shouting matches, blood-curdling threats, or insidious slanders. Physical abuse could be spontaneous fisticuffs, grabbing of hair or neckcloths, threatening or wounding with weapons, even murder. It could be orchestrated and planned; it could be drunken; it could be sexual or racist; it could be committed by enraged individuals, groups, families, or gangs; it could even be organized war.[4]

I have identified sixty-four cases of various kinds of abusive behavior involving Charlestown people in the thirty-four years of the Middlesex County Court Records between 1649 and 1686. Vandalism, riot and mutiny, and symbolic violence (like Christopher Goodwin's smashing and

---

[2] Thompson, *Divided*, 27–31. On other factors in what Norbert Elias has termed "the civilizing process" in early modern Europe, see Julius R. Ruff, *Violence in Early Modern Europe* (Cambridge: Cambridge University Press, 2002), 3–4, 8–9, 74, 110, 126. S. Hindle, "Keeping the Public Peace," in P. Griffiths, A. Fox, and J. R. Ruff, eds., *The Experience of Authority in Early Modern England* (Basingstoke: Palgrave Macmillan, 1996), Ch. 7. On reformed towns and parishes in England, see Barry Levy, *Town Born* (Philadelphia: University of Pennsylvania Press, 2009), 17–34.

[3] Court: Edmund S. Morgan, ed., *The Founding of Massachusetts* (Indianapolis: Bobbs-Merrill, 1964), 391–94. Law-abiding: Thompson, *Sex*, 193–4.

[4] Every able-bodied male Charlestown resident over 16 served in the militia and had weapons at home; see Ruff, *Violence*, 45.

overturning of baptismal vessels in the meetinghouse) were rare—nine incidents in all, averaging about two per decade. There were only seven reported cases of domestic physical abuse inflicted on wives, children or servants. Verbal outbursts, including slanders, threats, and abuse of officials were commonest: twenty-six over the three and a half decades. Next in number were physical assaults, mainly against neighbors or law enforcers, totaling 20. The 1660s was the decade with the most cases: twenty-four cases of all types of violence, including eleven verbal and seven physical attacks. The 1650s had fifteen cases (eight verbal, four physical), the 1670s thirteen (four verbal, five physical), and the 1680–86 period nine (three of each). Speculation about causes of crests and troughs in current crime figures is fraught with difficulty; how much more so for the distant past.[5]

Some festive days could trigger explosions of violence. After militia training days, a holiday spirit prevailed and plentiful drink was available. College Quarter Days had an end-of-term unruliness, and commencements at Harvard attracted large crowds from surrounding towns. Some young people furtively celebrated old English holidays like the Twelve Days of Christmas, May Day, and Bonfire Night on 5 November. We have seen a group of tipsy young militiamen creating mayhem at Ursula Cole's; Paul Wilson orchestrated rowdy and destructive outbursts on both May Day and November 5. Some Charlestown men were involved in a drunken riot at Harvard's 1670 commencement. Most of this group violence involved over-liquored young men.[6]

Where most people were toughened from childhood by hard physical labor, where literacy was generally basic and much conversation forcefully direct, where housing and domestic life were crowded and devoid of much privacy, where feelings had to be repressed, and where dangerous implements were all around, violence was probably nearer the surface. A recent authority concludes that "violence was part of the discourse of early modern interpersonal relations." Where farming was mixed, involving both crops and livestock, and dependent on neighborly cooperation; where, in the second generation, accessible land was becoming increasingly expensive, the younger generation increasingly numerous, and the divide between rich and poor increasingly wide, the triggers for conflict

---

[5]   CTR adds six more cases to these totals: four in the late 1660s, and two in the early 1670s. It was rare for town meetings or selectmen to deal with cases of violence; this was the responsibility of the Commissioners for Small Causes, few of whose records have survived. Other incidents may have gone unreported.

[6]   Militia: Thompson, *Sex*, 94–96; Quarter Days: Thompson, *Cambridge Cameos*, 81–86; Commencement: MxCC D&O, 2: folio 56; Wilson: Thompson, *Sex*, 35, RB, 1: 274.

similarly grew, and with them, the spill over into violence—the do-it-yourself solution to frustrating problems. Even courts often dealt savagely with offenders. For those unwilling or unable to pay fines, bloody whippings on bare backs were the usual alternative. Constables and jailers were ordered that the lash must be "well laid on." As well as its whipping post, Charlestown had its stocks, and after 1680, its cage. Reform through violence was the nostrum of the age.[7]

We have already encountered examples of violence in previous sections: women and children being sexually abused, for instance; fights about ownership of property, like the Sheppie-Cole canoe or the ship seized by Captain Walker; or land disputes, like the Guppie-Blanchard saga or Lowden's wall. Some physical conflicts involved assertions of rights, such as fights over the Stinted Common, the mutiny against the capricious Captain Martin, or the armed rising against the Dominion of New England. We have heard some violent words too: Widow Wadland and her kin screaming at Stephen Geary, the Rocks' outrage at Mary Robinson and John Walley, Symmes's scoffing disdain for Thomas Gould, or Ursula Cole's outbursts against officious constables. These provide a background.

Here we will foreground attempts at conciliation after fights, the effects of alcohol on levels of violence, the buildup and background to physical assaults, domestic abuse, revenge attacks, violent servants, and racial hostility culminating in war.

---

[7] Ruff, *Violence*, 2; Thompson, *Divided*, Ch. 7; Thompson, *Cambridge Cameos*, 105–10, 145–48, 161–66, 205–12, 235–38, 309–13. Cage: RB, 3: 319, 15 June 1680. The first of twenty-six tasks of town constables was "to whip and punish any that are to be punished." *MR*, 4,1: 324.

Communal Conciliation, 1650

On 25 March 1650 (considered the first day of the new year in the seventeenth century), a summons was served on John Goble, son of Thomas and Alice Goble of Charlestown, to answer the complaint of Richard Temple for defamation for saying Temple was a lying rascal. Behind this formal court action lay the failure of a concerted effort at preventive conciliation.

The evidence for communal attempts to end the conflict comes from a later deposition of husbandman William Baker, aged about 52, who had been in Charlestown since 1633. He had served twice as a selectman, and had only weeks before acquired three quarters of a cow common from Thomas Goble. His testimony is undated, but Temple's bill of charges refers to his costs when two witnesses "did attend an arbitration between them" on 24 March (1650). This would place Baker's recollection in the year 1652; it reads as follows:

> Upon a difference which was between Thomas Goble and Richard Temple about a goose this winter will be three winters [1649/50] upon the apprehension of wrongs that Thomas Goble and his wife had done to the said Richard Temple, the elders of Charlestown church did send for Thomas Goble and his wife home to Mr. Symmes's house together with Richard Temple and those that were witnesses of his side, namely Goodman Grissell of Charlestown, Goodman Killick and his man. There was also in presence Mr. Increase Nowell with the three elders of Charlestown, Mr. Russell beside some others. In which debate about the difference between Goodman Temple and Goodman Goble, Goodman Temple did affirm that Goodman Goble struck him when he was down all along

with his face to the ground. Mr. Symmes then demanded of him how he did know Thomas Goble struck, and when that he saw him. He answered No I saw him not but I felt him. Mr. Symmes asked Daniel Houchin which was then by whether he saw Goodman Goble strike him. He answered No. Mr. Symmes again asked Goodman Temple why say you he struck you when neither you yourself nor your witness saw him. Goodman Temple replied as before. Mr. Symmes, seeing his irrational answers, replied upon him It is just as when children are at hot cockles [a blindfolded player lies down and then has to guess who hit him] and he that lies down rises up and upon conjecture accuses one for striking him but indeed knows not whether he did or not.[8]

The attempts to end the feud between Temple and Goble involved the elite of the town. The three elders were ministers Zechariah Symmes and Thomas Allen, and the lay ruling elder Mr. John Green, responsible for church discipline. Increase Nowell was a founding assistant of both company and colony and had served as ruling elder; Mr. Richard Russell was a long-serving deputy to the General Court who would become an assistant in 1659. The "others" may have included town selectmen.

Their failure led to the summons next day, and to three cases before the County Court on 2 April 1650. The first was Temple's suit against Thomas, Alice, and John Goble for breach of the peace and trespass. Since the trespass was judged "under [the minimum] 40 shillings, the action was [ruled] out of court and the plaintiff to allow the defendants costs of 10 shillings." The Gobles' gloating was short-lived. In Temple's suit against John Goble for defamation, Samuel Pierce testified that John Goble indeed had said that Temple was a lying rascal, and John Grey testified the same. The jury found for the plaintiff damages of 20 shillings with costs of 15/10d.[9]

The source of animosity became much clearer when the court moved on from civil actions to criminal prosecutions. The three Gobles were presented for a riot against Temple. In these very early days of the Court Records, the depositions were sometimes entered in the Record Book rather than being filed separately. Francis Grissell [Griswold] testified that he had seen John Goble and Temple fighting. The father "did stoop to give some advantage" and Grissell said "two against one was not fair and went between them to still them," but John "remained pulling and

---

8   MxCC D&O, 1: docs 92, 93, 94. Cow common: *Possessions*, 112.

9   MxCC RB, 1: 5, 2 April 1650.

his father came still to pluck and help him and Goble's wife and daughter also coming, Temple forbad them coming on his land and Goble's wife took hold of the goose . . . it was her son's goose and they got it from Temple and John Goble ran away with it." Crucially, however, Grissell "saw no blows given."

Daniel Houchin fleshed out the details: John had come "about the Creek and Temple warned him to keep off the land." He offered that if John "would go to Kilcop's house, if the goose were his he should have it." However, John advanced on Temple "and did strike him and then his father came and both fell on him and hauled Temple down so that he cried out Murder." Temple did not hit Goble. Houchin had changed his evidence since being cross-examined by Symmes about actually seeing Temple being struck.

Temple deposed that John "professed that he would have my blood but he would have the goose." His father "laid violent hands" on Temple, and having got him down gave him two blows. Temple cried out murder when he was crushed to the earth. Grissell came and said "Fie! Fie! What, two on one." At the end of the scrum, Thomas Goble said to Temple: "If my son die within a year and a day, I will arraign you at the Bar for it."

Temple then took his oath "that he is afraid that John Goble and his father in the woods may endanger his life." They were bound in £20 to keep the peace. The court found them guilty of riot and fined the father twenty shillings, and the son forty. They were released from their bond on 1 October 1650.[10]

The vendetta continued, however. The rest of Baker's testimony explains its persistence:

> Now in the beginning of June 1651 Richard Temple entreated me to help him weed his corn which [*illegible*] Goodman Mead, Richard Kettle's son and servant at which time discussing about differences between Goodman Goble and Goodman Temple and in special about Goodman Temple's oath taken in court formerly against Goodman Goble then I said to Goodman Temple he had no more reason for his oath aforesaid at Mr. Symmes's than one of those boys who wrought by us. Goodman Temple replied Why say you so. I answered repeating the agitation at Mr. Symmes's and with Mr. Symmes's answer to him. Richard Temple replied: the sundry oaths in

---

10   Ibid., 11–12, 14.

court were equivalent to his, neither that although he had not witness to prove he struck him then yet I do not say but that he might strike me at some other time.

On 5 October 1652, Temple sued the Goble parents for defamation "in saying that he had taken a false oath." Temple's alleged admission to Baker is highly ambiguous; all he seems to concede is that he had no witness to the blows (except Houchin). Goble acknowledged uttering the words, but was unable to get the legally required corroboration for Baker's allegations. The court awarded Temple £4 damages and costs of £1-8-2d. Thereafter the conflict was stilled.[11]

The depredations of a wandering goose had set off two and a half years of intense hostility. Temple's warning the Goble clan off his land suggests that trouble may have been brewing before. He seems to have been genuinely scared of Goble vengeance. On the other side, Thomas Goble suspected Temple of violent (or perhaps supernatural?) recriminations against his son.

Why the initial, time-consuming, and ultimately frustrated elite involvement? One reason may have been that Thomas Goble and his wife were both long-standing church members. Temple had only arrived in Charlestown about 1646, and did not apply for colony freemanship (for which church membership was a prerequisite) until 1672. Serious charges against saints, quarrels between saints, or even quarrels between fellow townspeople could best be handled informally in a spirit of godly reconciliation. Feuds could insidiously poison communal relations beyond the two families. Court actions between neighbors were rare and unseemly. Nonetheless, the £20 bond restored the peace. There were no more fisticuffs or blood. Legal orders with serious financial sanctions replaced assertions of clan honor.[12]

Symmes's role, at least in Baker's account, was dominant. His tone seems to have been deeply skeptical of Temple's version. If someone was being hit while held face down, it defied belief that he would not know

---

[11] Ibid., 27.

[12] *GM*, 3: 81–83 has a sketch of the Gobles. John's brother Daniel and nephew Stephen (son of his brother Thomas) were executed in September 1676 for the murder of three friendly Indian women. Late in 1659, Thomas Goble Jr. witnessed another fight between neighbors near the Neck; see "Mass Violence." "James Davis gave sundry blows to Thomas Mousall [who stood] by his pales keeping him off with his hands. Father [Barnabas] Davis took Mousall by the collar or hair. I perceive Father Davis was in drink . . . He said 'Let them alone.'" The fighters were both sixteen-year-olds. Mousall was son of a Deacon; the Davises were not church members, and as we saw in "Sharecropping Conflicts," selfishly untrustworthy. Their assaults cost them thirty-one shillings, MxCC RB, 1: 196, 27 December 1659.

who was slugging him. The "hot cockles" analogy to boys' games seems gratuitously insulting. We can only infer that the conciliators did not trust Temple's word; like Goble, they considered him "a lying rascal." Baker's allegation of Temple's subsequent false oath in court stoked this doubt. However, Symmes's hectoring, legalistic attitude is reminiscent of his later bullying contretemps with Thomas Gould, the Baptist. In explaining her long silence before accusing Jane Moulton of fraudulent accusation of rape, Elizabeth Stitson cited the disadvantage of a non-member's evidence against a member's. Nonetheless, the court accepted Temple's allegation that he had been defamed, and agreed that the Gobles were indeed a violent threat.[13]

By the mid-1650s, Temple had taken his family out of Charlestown and moved to Concord. By 1657, when he died, Thomas Goble lived there too.

---

[13]   Gould: see above "Thomas Gould and the Baptist Debates"; Stitson: see "Young Women Abused."

Fosket Follies, 1663

The contrast between a culture of discipline and a do-it-yourself vengefulness imported from the Old World is illustrated by the defamation suit
of John Mousall v. John Fosket and Thomas Tyrrell of 16 June 1663. The
case arose from Tyrrell's attempts to make "love to [court] the maidservant
[Mary Nicholls, 21, at church-meeting time] without orderly leave." Fosket,
aged twenty-seven, had arrived in Charlestown only five years before. He
was probably a former servant of John Mousall, and had recently married
Elizabeth, the adopted daughter of Robert Leach. On 15 June he berated
Elizabeth Richardson Mousall, 28, with exceeding her authority since Mary
Nichols was simply house-sitting. He called Elizabeth "base jade . . . whore . .
. he was in debt to her but he would be even with her." Her husband John, 32,
came home to this fracas, confronted Fosket, and "put him out and threw
him down in the yard," while a servant restrained Tyrrell. This prompted
Fosket to besmirch Mousall as a "Rogue and beastly Rascall" who had exposed his erections beside Fosket's bed, to various maids, and two or three
times recently to Goodman Bullard. He taunted Mousall to come out "and
he would thrash his coat so as he never was so thrashed in his life." For this
unseemly outburst, and for physical threats with his "great stick" and an iron
peel (shovel), Fosket was fined £2. Tyrrell was penalized £5 according to
ordinance; both had to pledge £10 bonds for good behavior. John Mousall
subsequently sued Fosket for his battery and slander.[14]

---

[14]   Elizabeth Fosket (1642–82) was the daughter of William and Elizabeth Powell. Her mother
had died when she was two, *R*, 86 (1932), 349; *Connecticut Nutmegger*, 27 (1994), 219–20. Fosket
(misnamed Fosdick): *Sex*, 175–76; MxCC RB, 1: 286, 291. I can discover nothing about Tyrrell.
The events discussed here are based on depositions and orders filed in MxCC D&O, 1: Folio 34,
docs. 2292–2304, 2311, 2337–2357. "Whore" and "jade" were commonly used terms of abuse
against women in England: L. Gowing, *Domestic Dangers*, Ch. 1. "Beastly" may imply either sodomy or bestiality, *Sex*, 72–74. Mousall's manhandling implies that Fosket's voice was stronger
than his physique.

Tyrrell was employed by Fosket's father-in-law, Robert Leach. Elizabeth Mousall had recently inherited £84 from her father, Samuel Richardson of Woburn. What Fosket owed her, and his grounds (if any) for alleging her whorishness and baseness are unknown. However, a prosecution more than two decades before may help to corroborate Fosket's charges against Mousall. On 10 October 1641, the Quarterly Court of Assistants "censured John Mousall to be whipped for attempting to abuse a boy." Mousall would have been 14 or 15 at this time, having arrived in Charlestown in 1630 with his wealthy carpenter father Ralph (ca. 1603–57). If, indeed, a cloud of rumor and innuendo hung over John Mousall's name, Fosket may have been voicing commonly held suspicions of the late deacon's son.[15]

The Mousalls' troubles re-erupted ten weeks later, between 2 and 3 p.m. on 26 August 1663. On 1 September Edward Wright, 36, a shoemaker, and Return Waite, 23, a tailor,

> were sitting in the shop at Boston at work. Seeing Paul Wilson [a Mousall servant over from Charlestown] go by they called to him and enquired concerning the hurt done to John Mousall of Charlestown. He said it was very true and he could prove there was one that belonged to the house [there] when the hurt was done. A chest had been broken open in which he [Mousall] had writings; if none were left he should lose £40; their bed was cut, their bedding, apparel, linen and wool, and curtains; they had not a rag to put on but was on their backs. Several other mischiefs were done which we could not believe unless we saw them. Three or four men were examined, altogether.

Fosket was the immediate suspect. He and his father-in-law Robert Leach had to enter bonds of £20 each for Fosket's court appearance to answer charges about "wrong done to the goods of John Mousall" on 26 August.[16]

Apart from "being even," Ursula Cole, 30, suggested another motive. Fosket's friend Thomas Tyrrell was at her house and asked "had she any acquaintance with Goodwife Mousall. I said I did." Tyrrell told her that

---

[15] Inherit: Rodgers, 1: 315. Prosecution: *MR*, 1: 343. *WJ*, 2: 38, reports magistrates in 1641 discussing capital punishment for the rape of a young girl, comparing it to sodomy and bestiality. Mousall family: *GMB*, 1309–1312; Ralph left £873. Age: John was said to be seventy-four in 1703, but old age was frequently exaggerated by a few years. Another John Mussel, aged fifteen, was listed on the *Elizabeth* on 9 April 1635, Hotten, 54; however, "no records for this passenger have been found in New England," *GM*, 5: 201.

[16] Writings: probably deeds, mortgages, loan receipts; possibly Thomas Tyrrell's book (see below).

Elizabeth Mousall "had a book of his and could I get it from her . . . The title was *The Expert Midwife*. I said it was hard coming by such a book . . . He swore he would have it or break up all the books in John Mousall's house. He would have it if it were in the house or else he would lose his life or Goodwife Mousall should lose hers."[17]

For the prime suspects to escape severe punishment for this unprecedented vandalism, alibis were essential. The Leach family seems to have gathered every sighting of Fosket and Tyrrell in order to rule them out. The patriarch Robert, 57, swore that Tyrrell "was not ten poles [55 yards] from our house until he went to the meadow about 2 o'clock." Fosket was gone from the house only about half an hour between 11 a.m. and noon to fetch a pair of haypoles in the marsh. Otherwise, he too was about the place until two o'clock. This was corroborated by Goodwife Mary Leach, by Tyrrell himself, and by another servant John Guy. After 2 p.m. a flock of witnesses from young servants to middle-aged landowners testified to having seen Fosket haying out at Winter's Hill towards Mr. Winthrop's Farm (Ten Hills), and later at the Neck. They were quite specific: "the day Captain Pierce set sail out of the harbour at Boston." When Joseph Batchelor, 17, met Fosket going out haying, he asked "what a clock it was. [I] said about two."[18]

John Mousall was suspicious of these clan-orchestrated alibis. He asked John Call the day after the mischief "if I told Goodman Leach's folks anything he had told me the day before?" Call denied it. Despite Leach's assurance that Tyrrell "was not from his house," Mousall "would not believe him or any of his house." A witness confirmed that Fosket's morning alibi was false, but he was covered for the crucial period of 2–3 p.m.[19]

The case for the prosecution contained some contradictory evidence. Baker John Call, 27, had been at Mousall's on the day of the attack. After seeing Fosket and Guy and Tyrrell going out to their meadow "with instruments to make hay," he had gone to Mousall's to borrow something. "I

---

[17] This could have been one of the four editions of Nicholas Culpeper's *A Directory for Midwives*, first published in 1651; a second part appeared in 1662. Such medico-pornographic books are discussed in Roger Thompson, *Unfit for Modest Ears* (London: Macmillan, 1979), 161–64; they are known to have been in New England by this time: *Sex*, 85–86, 87. Deacon Ralph Mousall's probate inventory of 30 May 1657 included books valued at £1-10-0. Samuel Richardson's of 29 March 1658 listed 14 books and two bibles valued at £2-10-0, Rodgers, 1: 287, 313. Tyrrell's final imprecations seem a bit extreme even for so prized a book.

[18] Witnesses: John Palmer, John Call, John Wayte, John Sprague, William Crouch, Josiah Woods, Nathaniel Dawdy, Joseph Grindle. The sightings were on or around the road out to Medford.

[19] Test. John Palmer, Mx CC D&O, 1: doc. 2347. He had waited from 9 to 11 a.m. for Fosket to return to Leach's from his errands.

rapped once or twice on the house but there came no answer, so I rapped again and called if anyone was in. Then John Mousall came to the door and spoke . . . His door had been flung [broken] open twice and he suspected John Guy and Thomas Jones. He tarried in his house to watch . . . [Call could] see no hurt done . . . nothing was amiss with the beds which stood nigh the door." Fosket latched on to this evidence. Mousall "was in the house the same time the mischief was done . . . This whole affair was one of Goodman Mousall's own lies." It was "like picking his house [of his own] money."[20]

After the vandalism, Goody Mousall joined in the hunt. She hurried out to her husband beyond Leach's. "Have you been there yet?" she asked. "Aye," he replied, "but there's nothing to be done, for they [the suspects] had made a stir so soon that there was still one body or another that cleared them . . . Goodman Jones took Tom Jones's part . . . Goodman Call cleared John Fosket." Josiah Wood told them that "he wondered that they had laid it to their charge" when a witness ignorant of the attack had seen Fosket, Guy and Tyrrell "a mile off and going to work."

Charlestown magistrate Richard Russell had to try to make sense of this bizarre situation. As well as binding Foskett and Tyrrell to appear, he also issued an arrest warrant for John Guy and Thomas Jones, suspected "for thievish intentions and [responsible for] the house having been rifled, divers goods abused, cut, removed and some things carried out of the house." Meanwhile, Fosket took the counter-offensive; he sued Mousall "for defamation of his good name by saying 'Thou art a thief.'" Goody Mousall was also required to appear.

Frustratingly, the court records for 6 October 1663 have no sign of these prosecutions and actions being tried, except that Mousall's suit against Fosket for the July slander and assault was withdrawn. We will never know who stole and slashed. Perhaps Russell had dealt with the vandalism as a "small cause" on his own authority. Perhaps he had managed to reconcile the principals and warn out the hangers-on. John Guy soon departed for Casco Bay, where he became a tenant farmer (and part-time fisherman?) for the next twelve years. Thomas Tyrrell, perhaps reunited with his *Expert Midwife*, drops from view. Thomas Jones was already in debt, and would soon be in all kinds of trouble over his passion for Sarah Crouch. He would be sent to cool his ardor in Barbados. John Fosket's life with his growing family and construction business was interrupted by

---

20 Jones, 18, was a recently arrived servant of William Crouch, who gave Fosket an alibi; Guy was employed by Robert Leach.

service in King Philip's War (1675–76). At his death in 1689 he left a modest £160 to his second wife Hannah and four surviving children.[21]

The Mousalls are not recorded as having any more children after Elizabeth in 1659, when John was thirty and Elizabeth twenty-four. They had further contretemps with ten neighbors in the 1680s over rights to their woodlot. John also served in King Philip's War, and after 1674 on petty and grand juries. He was not admitted to full church membership until his late sixties, in 1696. Was there a continuing communal suspicion of his sexual orientation so noisily broadcast by John Fosket? People in Boston were eager to hear all about his and Elizabeth's misfortunes. Was his wife a grinding creditor, a malicious gossip, "a base jade," and a relentless enemy? The savage confrontation of June 1663 and the house-trashing two months later exposed raw nerves and violence close to the surface of town life. Fosket was unusually volatile. As he ranted against the Mousalls, a neighbor "asked him if he was mad, and told him he acted more like a child than a man." This local incredulity suggests the gulf between indigenous restraint and the do-it-yourself honor-and-shame culture of "being even" which fired newcomer Fosket. Tyrrell could be similarly wild, talking about recovering his dirty book or losing his life. Nevertheless, Fosket's outburst exploded an official taboo, and gave a revealing flash of a seamier, though rare, side of Charlestown life.[22]

---

[21] Guy: Savage; Jones: *Sex*, 42–44, 168–70. Fosket: Wyman, 360; Frothingham, 185. In 1672 Fosket was granted permission to cart twenty loads of stone from the quarry on the common; the next year he was licensed to cut eighty boults of cedar. In 1681, he was involved in a fight at the quarry attempting to stop removal of stone. He had a lime kiln on the common, CTR, 3: 134,144; 4: 27, 47.

[22] Mousall woodlot, see above, "Common Rights." Volatile: in 1667, Fosket was reported for refusing to pay his church rate; he may have been a Baptist sympathizer, MxCC D&O, 2: folio 43; two years later, he was convicted of stealing fallen timber, CTR, 3: 103; in 1672 he was fined for abusing the town hog reeves, CTR, 3: 135. Cf. the 1681 quarry fight, CTR, 4: 27. Dirty books: on adolescent fascination with such reading matter, see Thompson, *Sex*, 85–87. Rare: only two Middlesex cases of the capital crime of sodomy are recorded in either *Assistants*, or MxCC *Records*; on this and related topics, see *Sex*, 72–74.

A Mason's Revenge:
Welch v. Goodwin, 1672

Boundary disputes were not the only cause of occupational conflict. Craftsmen could also lapse into vengeful violence against competitors. Such seems to have been the cause of an attack on 25 July 1672. At 8 a.m. on Monday 29 July, Mr. Thomas Danforth examined seventeen-year-old Thomas Welch Jr., who complained that the younger Christopher Goodwin, 25, had assaulted him four days before. The most detailed account came from Thomas's mother Elizabeth, 40, who had had twelve children, five of whom had died. Thomas was her eldest boy.

> Her son was in the highway with the team [of horses or oxen] when Christopher Goodwin came running towards him with his fist bent and struck him on the breast so as she even heard the noise as though the wind had been beaten out of his body . . . and gave him a kick in the belly of which her son complained sorely and was restless in the night and doth yet complain of the grief and pain from the blow lighting on the bottom of his belly. John Bicknell said Beat him blind, and the worst he could do against Welsh was too little, and if it were his case he knew what he would do, and many other provoking and reproachful terms.

Thomas's own account added that Goodwin had "threatened him to strike his teeth down his throat." Four other witnesses were present. Jacob Indian, servant to Sergeant Thomas Welch, swore "he saw the blows given." Goodwin denied the allegations; he "gave no blow nor touched Thomas with fist or foot." John Bicknell "saw no blow and heard no words." Danforth took £10 bonds from both Goodwin and Bicknell to keep the peace and to appear at the next court. The outcome of that case is not known.[23]

The Goodwin family had a reputation for outbursts and sexual assaults. In 1663, Christopher Goodwin, Sr. (ca. 1617–82), a mason, had dashed the christening vessels to the meetinghouse floor in protest against infant baptism. Twice in 1665 he was prosecuted for sexual offenses. In June, the grand jury presentment cited "uncivil carriages against the wife of Thomas Pierce and some others." On 7 August, the court heard father Christopher's confession of a far more heinous offense:

> On 2 August 1665 he took Anna, the daughter of Goodman [John?] Fowle, aged about two and a half, and set her upon the bench, and took up her coats, and put himself into a preparation to commit evil with her, calling it a foolish temptation and that the child is clear . . . Present [in court] his wife and son.

The shame would afflict all family members. The father had never been admitted to church membership. Now, they were cold-shouldered by the Baptist group.[24]

Seven years elapsed between this disgraceful time and the brutal attack on young Welch, which must have exploded after a period of tense hostility. There is no specific recorded wrong committed by Welsh against Goodwin, but Bicknell's vengeful urgings show that this was a settling of grudges. It is possible that the rivalry arose from work. Christopher, like his father, was a mason. So were Bicknell and Welch. Young Thomas may have been an apprentice of the famous Charlestown Stonecutter, known only by the style of his gravestone carving. They may have quarreled about the touchy issue of access to stone, or workmanship, or competition for stonecutting and building jobs. Goodwin's threat to "strike [Welch's] teeth down his throat" hints at verbal insults as a trigger, though a kick in the groin could be payback for some sexual slander. Goodwin had married Mercy Crouch in 1672; she was the younger sister of the notorious Sarah Crouch. Mercy had recently given evidence in the lurid paternity case

---

[23] MxCC D&O, 2: folio 60. Two other witnesses were William Brown and William Crouch, both brothers-in-law of Goodwin. Brown was also a surety for the £10 bonds.

[24] Ibid., 2: folios 38, 39. RB, 1: 287. Goodwin failed to appear to answer the first complaint, and was therefore also charged with contempt. His wife was a church member. See above, "Thomas Gould and the Baptist Debates." John Bicknell (ca. 1649–79) was the son of William Bicknell, brickmaker; he was brought up by his stepmother Martha Metcalf Smythe Bicknell, and after his father's death in 1659, by his stepfather, Nathaniel Stow of Concord. John married Sarah Wheate of Concord in 1675, Wyman, .

involving Sarah's first bastard. She deposed that suspect Christopher Grant had also made indecent advances to her, and when she repulsed him had called her "a dirty slut." Thomas may have been requoting. Whatever the cause, Goodwin might easily have killed his victim.[25]

Violence continued to dog the Goodwins. In the early 1680s, Christopher's brother John moved to Boston. In 1688 four of his children were "bewitched" by Mary Glover, their Irish washerwoman. Several ministers, including Charles Morton, intervened as the horrifying torments increased. Both Cotton Mather and the father left vivid accounts of the supernatural violence suffered by the children, especially the eldest, thirteen-year-old Martha. Even when the "witch" was executed on 16 November 1688, the fits continued. The Goodwin family must have felt haunted.[26]

The younger Christopher had seen violence and suffering as a soldier in King Philip's War. In 1690, he became involved as a bystander when he heard maidservant Rebecca Lee being violently beaten in the Crosswells' house. Here he was on the side of the victim, who subsequently died. He lived on to 1703 with his second wife, the widow Joanna (Long) Johnson, and left a very modest £103. At regular intervals in his fifty-six years he had inflicted or encountered violence. In the face-to-face communities of early New England, it was an inevitable fact of life.[27]

---

[25] Crouch case: Thompson, *Sex*, 43–44. Access: see above, "Fosket Follies" about a fight at the quarry in 1681. Work: Goodwin and Bicknell masons were partners in constructing Zechariah Symmes's stone tomb in 1673. CTR, 3: 140, 141; Bicknell's elder brother Samuel, also a mason, was a neighbor of the Goodwins and shared land. They jointly repaired the Townhouse chimneys in 1681, CTrR, 3: 54v, B(7)r. Charlestown Stonecutter: R. L. Tucker, "Lamson Family Gravestone Carvers," *Markers*, 10 (1993), 152–55.

[26] Hall, *Witch-Hunting*, 265–79.

[27] Crosswell: Thompson, *Sex*, 160–62.

Unneighborly Carriages:
Smith v. Frost, 1673

7 October 1673 was Court Day in Charlestown, but about noon some very discourteous behavior was taking place on the boundary line between the lands of Abraham and Martha Smith and Joseph and Hannah Frost, and in the adjacent lane. Two accounts give strikingly opposed views of what went on that day. First, the deposition of Joseph, written in his own hand with highly idiosyncratic spelling (here modernized):

> I was standing in my door and saw Goody Smith and her servant boy Humphrey Bradshaw with their dog hunting one of my hogs up and down the field, and into the yard and along the rail, which made him hang himself by the yoke between two rails and then they set the dog on him. I went and entreated them to let my hog alone, but they would not. I did take hold of him by the hide standing in the highway looking to loosen him but could not. Goody Smith's hogs in the highway came running about me as if they would eat me up. I took a small bough and beat them from me being unwilling to be devoured by a company of swine. Goody Smith was exceedingly enraged and they still did what they could to kill my hog with her servant and the dog, throwing stones at him, and I not willing to let my hog be killed did beat off their dog. Her anger turned upon me and she threw stones at me with all her might and then took up a post about four feet long and of great weight in a violent manner and darted it at my head, saying "You Devil! I'll brain you!" I was forced to defend myself as well as I could although I did receive

damage by it and was wounded. Still she threw stones at me until I went from her.

Joseph's account was delivered at sunset on 12 October to Mr. Thomas Danforth, in answer to a complaint already lodged by Martha "that you haven't carried yourself neighborly towards her, but have beaten and wronged her." Her slant was as follows:

> I saw Joseph Frost take up a stick about the size of a wrist. I thought he came to strike Humphrey Bradshaw, the boy, so I stood before the boy and Joseph struck me from the lane. He beat me on the head, it amazed [stunned] me and brought me almost to the ground. He dealt me several other blows. He is so ready to quarrel with us I am in fear of my life. Three or four times my husband have gone to him about it hoping he might consider of it and give satisfaction for the several blows. He bade me prove it. [I said] I could by some [witnesses] and prove him a liar. Therefore, please take some course with him, for if some had not come up the lane I had suffered some mischief by breaking my bones or something else as bad or worse. The next day after, Joseph's wife riding past said "You have got a good mow now; much good may you do with it." My husband heard these words to me.

Abraham Smith, Sambo Negro, twelve-year-old John Whittemore, and William Bond Jr. all corroborated the fact that Joseph had struck the first blow. Sambo, with load-bearing experience, described the stick as "bigger round than a burthen pole." Bond, called in to Smith's on his way home, was shown her arms, "black and blue in two or three places." Another witness saw the bruising a week later. No wonder! Frost had smashed at her, wielding the stick with two hands. Three witnesses stated "the dog was a pole [5½ yards] behind her in the Indian stalks and not on the hog."

Frost wrote an answer to these accusations:

> I am wronged. My hitting her on the head is absolutely false, as is [her being] amazed and stunded [sic]. She nearly killed me with a post. I would not have hit her arm if she was not grabbing my hog's leg. It is no small grief to me to be the cause of trouble and contention. I have . . . been to them to end the strife between us. They would not [let me] take two faithful honest witnesses with me when I went to offer reasonable

satisfaction for any wrong. They held me to unreasonable terms, always resolved to go to the extremes of law against me. I have and do suffer fear of the future; therefore I have removed from them and left all that I had whatsoever it doth cost me. Being persecuted in one place, I do go to another.

Two Frost witnesses emphasized the Smiths' adamant attitude. Joseph could not "wrong his conscience" by admitting all their charges.[28]

The jury, familiar with the characters and reputations of the two sets of neighbors, decided that both Joseph and Martha were to blame. They sentenced Joseph to a hefty £5 fine, and Martha to £2. A year later, each petitioned the court for abatement. Martha expressed herself as "very sorry for any offence that I have given either God or man and promise[d] to be more careful in time to come." Her husband was informed that her fine (to be paid by him) was cut to ten shillings. Joseph professed himself humbled, suppliant, "beseechful," as well as "necessitous." He escaped with an admonition.[29]

Swine in neighbors' crops was one of the commonest causes of interfamilial violence. Even though it had the required yoke round its shoulders, this marauder had managed to wriggle under the boundary rail to gorge on Smith's vital winter feed. It is clear that this was not the first dispute. Goodwife Frost's jibe about "a good mow" suggests that there had been a previous quarrel about hay bounds. The fast and furious ferocity of the battle derived from accumulated anger. It was fortunate that no one was killed, not even the hog. Bystanders curtailed the frenzy. Even after tempers had cooled, each party blamed the other, rationalizing their own excesses. They might have been describing two different incidents.[30]

Both contestants shared similarities. They were close in age: Joseph thirty-three and Martha thirty-five. The Frosts had three young children, the Smiths two. Both were church members, and both had come to Charlestown from neighboring Cambridge. With "tools in the shop," Frost appears to have been an artisan. His wife Hannah, who rubbed salt into Martha's wound, was the daughter of Rev. John Miller, minister of Dorchester. Smith was probably a husbandman. Martha's only previous

---

[28] MxCC D&O, 3: folio 62. Frost remained in Charlestown, but may have moved to another dwelling.

[29] Folio 67, 7 September 1674. RB, 3: 81, 98, 108.

[30] Hogs: e.g., Thompson, *Cambridge Cameos,* 105–10, 309–12; Thompson, *Divided We Stand,* 84–87, 180–82. Fast: Abraham Smith witnessed the violence, but did not have time to intervene.

brush with authority had occurred a year before: she had been "censured with public admonition" on 6 October 1672 by the church "for her sin of lying." What had prompted this severe and unusual humiliation is not known. It adds irony to her throwing "liar" in Frost's face. Frost came from a distinguished but impoverished family. His father, Edmund, had been the ruling elder of the Cambridge church from 1636 to his death in 1672. He had been largely dependent on his quarterly stipend. In 1672, he left only £118 (£88 real estate) between his widow and eight adult offspring.[31]

This was not the last time Frost would be involved in a violent incident and be called a liar. On 11 April 1682, he lodged a complaint against Patrick Mark, who leased 20 acres of pasture and meadow from James Russell, "out by the Rocks."

> He made a violent assault upon me with a rock and called me liar and thief. 'I swear thou devilish rogue I'll end your days!' Then he grabs me by the throat and the neckcloth. He first asked me if I had not taken away stones he had dug, I said I had not. Then he said I had wronged him and his children and made it my work to do him mischief. It was my wicked base doing to bring out his children about their follies last year, and I should smart for it.

Frost certainly seemed to have a provocative streak. Mark would later be involved in opposition to the privatization of the Stinted Common, but was not otherwise known for his violence. Like most New Englanders, however, he did not quickly forget a wrong or drop a grudge. At this point Frost seemed to be serving as the town's messenger and may have told on the Mark children in that capacity, or as a member of the petty jury. Something in his personality betrayed a shiftiness that made people mad. Towards the end of his life he moved out of Charlestown and joined his brother James in Billerica. When he died in 1692 his assets totalled £192,

---

[31]   Martha: Wyman, 874; admonition: Hunnewell, viii; a "Sister Smith" was one of the gossiping snoopers whom Goody Martin detested. Martha was a possible candidate among several, Thompson, *Sex,* 184. Edmund: *GM,* 3: 593–97; Rodgers, 3: 138–42; Thompson, *Cambridge Cameos,* 7–8. When the two Cromwellian regicides Major-General Goffe and Major-General Whalley visited Frost in Cambridge on 23 August 1660, before escaping to the Connecticut Valley, they were "received with great kindness and love. [One commented] I would prefer to be with this saint in his poor cottage, than any prince I know of."

with £127 real estate. Materially he had done better than his father, but had inherited less of his saintliness.[32]

Any conflict between neighbors was cause for concern in the town, but violence between two church members, sister and brother in Christ, was particularly disturbing. They were expected to lead exemplary, loving lives, not to "brain" and "amaze" each other. Such expectations probably explain attempts on both sides to repair relations before the lay authorities became involved. The mutual distrust proved too deep, however. Frost would have witnessed Sister Smith's church trial and voted for her conviction; "once a liar, always a liar" was a common belief. For her part, Martha found Joseph "so ready to quarrel." Only removal and eventual joint repentance restored the peace.

---

[32] Complaint: D&O, 4: folio 99; lease: *Andros Tracts*, 1: 97; "Rocks:" D&O, 5: folio 122, see Map 2, "Landscape" and "The Stinted Common." The town treasury records list payments to Mark's wife Sarah around 1670; by 1681, their four surviving children were all teenagers, though the precise follies they committed are not known. CTrR, 40R, 43A, r.

Seadogs' Land War:
Martin v. Waffe, 1676

On the night of 23 June 1676, during the dying days of King Philip's War, people at Captain Richard Martin's in Charlestown were suddenly alarmed by the sensation of axe blows to the cornerpost of the house. A daughter ran into the room and told her father that "Tom Waffe was cutting down their house. Mr. Martin spoke to him out of the window and Waffe said he would cut as much of his [Martin's] flesh if he had him there, and with a great many unhandsome words and like a mad man railed at Mr. Martin." This was the account given by Samuel Ballatt, 38, a shipbuilder, who happened to be at the house pressuring Martin to pay the £61 he still owed for his ship *Blossom* that Ballatt had built about 1670. Miriam Draper, 54, of Roxbury, who was staying in "a little house of Richard Martin's," added to the unhandsome words: Waffe said "he would run a spit through Mr. Martin then and many other times." Mary Ford, 35, had heard Waffe call for an axe the day before and had threatened to "chop Martin's boy down" if he interfered. No wonder that Captain Martin was "put in fear of his life," as well as "his house being weakened."[33]

Miriam Draper's evidence suggests that this was no sudden conflict, but rather had been building up over time. The source of Waffe's rage was his conviction that Martin had encroached on his family's property. One witness, mariner Inigo Potter, 40, supported this contention. "The

---

[33] Depositions in this case are in MxCC D&O, 3: Folios 72–73; Ballatt's case against Martin for final settlement is in the same, Folio 76, Dec. 1677, and D&O, 4: Folio 83, 8 Dec. 1677, 2 Oct. 1679; the total cost of the 182-ton ship was £743-16-0. See above, "Captain Martin's Day in Court." James Draper and his family had been warned out of Charlestown on 3 April 1676; the town was desperately trying to cope with a flood of war refugees. "Fear": £100 attachment against Waffe, 5 July 1676.

passage between Widow Bell's house and the [Martin] fence was wider six years agone than now, I being then a tenant." However, revered deacon William Stitson, 75, negated Potter's recollection. "About 1670, with other selectmen of Charlestown, I was called to view the setting up of Richard Martin's front fence. I saw the workmen pluck up the corner-post and put a new one in the same place. This was next to Widow Bell's house."[34]

The defendant, Thomas Waffe, did not appear at the 3 October 1676 court at Cambridge. He had appointed as his attorneys Andrew Robinson and Samuel Bicknell, both of Charlestown. In the first action, the jury awarded Martin £1 damages and costs against Waffe for "cutting down his house and threatening him." Waffe's attorneys lost his counterclaim against Martin "for trespass by setting a fence and drain on plaintiff's land." More costs were forfeited.[35]

What lay behind all this accumulated violence, claim, and counterclaim? Relationships will shed some light. Thomas Waffe was a 30-year-old mariner who would take command of the sloop *Swan* in 1680. His parents were John (ca. 1620–ca. 1651) and Katherine Waffe (1623–92). His father had died when Thomas was only about six years old, and his mother, still in her twenties and with three young children, soon married Abraham Bell, 31, a waterman who had recently arrived in Charlestown from New Haven. They had five more children. On the last day of 1662, Abraham was cast away in his lighter coming in to Pullen Point. His body was found four days later and buried on 7 January 1663. He left the modest estate of £154. Katherine Waffe Bell did not remarry. John Waffe, Thomas's elder brother, was apprenticed at this time as a teenager to Captain John Trumbull, and subsequently moved to England. Trumbull's daughter Elizabeth (1641–89) had married Captain Richard Martin (1632–94) in about 1660. Thomas Waffe may have been affected by the early death of his father, his mother's remarriage, and his growing up under a "stranger" stepfather in a household of younger stepsiblings. His mother's sudden second widowhood may have induced powerful protective feelings in her oldest son living at home. When his mother later complained of neighbors' intrusions, Thomas would have felt, as the leading male of the Waffe-Bell clan, a legal and emotional duty to act for his extended family interests.[36]

---

[34] Potter had been in the crew of an earlier *Blossom* in 1662; its skipper was Martin's father-in-law, John Trumbull. *Essex CC*, 2: 331.

[35] MxCC RB, 3: 147.

[36] Estate: Rodgers, 2: 138–41. Waffe-Bell: Wyman, 985; Trumbull-Martin: Wyman, 658.

By the time Thomas Waffe took an axe to Martin's house, he had married a woman called Alice and moved to Boston. His sister had married Andrew Robinson in 1674 and his stepsister Hannah Bell had married bricklayer/mason Samuel Bicknell in 1669. This close relationship explains their appointment as Thomas's attorneys. Thomas's mother was fifty-three years old by 1676, and though her assets had been pretty meager, "by her great pains and labor in bringing up the eight children" fathered by her two husbands, she had managed to hold on to the family house and land in Charlestown. At this time, however, Katherine "being now well stricken in years," and her children "now arrived at men's and women's estate," had agreed to divide up the family assets, with £60 to Katherine as her widow's "thirds," a double portion to John as the eldest son, and equal portions to the rest. Middlesex County Court would shortly nominate a high-powered committee to administer the land sale and financial division.[37]

These circumstances help to explain the timing of Waffe's acting on the simmering anger at long-perceived land filching by his defenseless mother's neighbors. The Waffe-Bell clan would want *all* its land entire before a sale. Any buyer would need to feel confident about the precise bounds. A major result of King Philip's War was the destruction of frontier settlements and the closing of the "safety valve" for the land-hungry third generation then maturing. The value of land in the older, safer settlements would inevitably rise and clan control of holdings would need watchful assertiveness. Waffe's axe was a peculiarly potent weapon to stake the family's claims.[38]

More personal factors were involved, however. Waffe's animus against Martin is tangible; the hacked house is a poor substitute for what Waffe would have liked to do to Martin himself. There may have been professional bad blood between the well-endowed Martin-Trumbull clan and the stretched Waffe-Bells. Trumbull's training of John Waffe may have created interfamily problems. Thomas Waffe was a highly ambitious young seaman who would in a few years seek his fortune from wrecks of Spanish ships in the Caribbean, and would have to grapple with buccaneers on his ship. He could be excused for envying the less demanding life of a transatlantic skipper of ampler means.[39]

Certainly the Martins were hardly the neighbors Widow Bell would have chosen. The adolescent racket and sexual shenanigans of the two

---

[37] Rodgers, 2: 140–41. Bicknell's brother John helped provoke Christopher Goodwin's attack on Thomas Welch Jr. in 1672, see above, "A Mason's Revenge."

[38] Frontier: Thompson, *Cambridge Cameos*, 169–70, and below, "Mass Violence."

[39] Buccaneers: MxCC D&O, 4: Folio 112, 1683–84.

daughters, Elizabeth and Margaret, were the talk of the town. Their mother was deeply suspect for entertaining privateers and visiting seamen when her husband was away. Margaret and her mother fought like wildcats, and the women had a reputation for talking dirty, missing church, and whorish promiscuity, the mother's going back many years. The Martin house in the later 1670s seemed to many in Charlestown little better than a bordello.[40]

Betty Martin, who had had to be married off to a mere seaman at the age of 16, recognized that their critics and enemies in Charlestown were "the people of God . . . the [church] members." This mutual hostility probably lay behind Mrs. Martin's losing a contest about meetinghouse seating—a hugely sensitive issue reflecting communal reputation and rank—and being humiliated by banishment to the gallery six years earlier. One of these people of God was Widow Katherine Bell. She had become a church member as Katherine Waffe in 1645, though neither of her husbands was admitted. She had triumphantly defended her daughter Mary's reputation against her master, the lecherous Captain John Jones, in 1671. She was the type of neighbor on whom the Martin women had heaped "scorn and reproach." One of the most detailed and damning depositions against the Martins when they challenged town gossip was sworn by Hannah, the wife of Henry Salter, a Waffe stalwart. The year Widow Bell finally sold up was the same year that the Martin women were exposed in the court.[41]

Seafarers were renowned for their passions afloat and especially ashore. Martin was a skipper unloved by his crew, untrustworthy and ungenerous. Waffe's direct action with an axe may well have been the culmination of years of fruitless requests. It was a gesture of frustration, far more intense and dramatic than the throwing down of fences. The Shylockian threat to slash away flesh indicated both Waffe's wrath and the worth he attached to his loss. The piece of land in conflict was probably small, but the psychological value and importance of bounds, titles and ownership were paramount. "Meum et tuum," the Latin for property, "mine and thine," depended on the recognition and acceptance of dividing lines; where those divisions were disputed, between neighbors as between nations, war could result.[42]

---

[40]   Thompson, *Sex*, 182–85.

[41]   Ibid; Jones: MxCC D&O, 2: Folio 57, 16 Oct. 1671.

[42]   Martin: MxCC D&O, 2: Folios 43, 51, and above, "The Sea."

Drink and Violence

Puritans were not teetotalers. Alcohol was often the safest beverage. It had medicinal qualities in an age before painkilling drugs or anaesthesia. Children would routinely drink small beer, and many Charlestown orchards contributed to the hard cider pressed every fall. During the latter part of our period, wine imported from Madeira, Spain and the Canaries, "strong waters" from the Netherlands, and brandy from France were supplemented by rum from the West Indies.[43]

Retailers were meant to be licensed annually; they had explicit orders against selling alcohol to children, servants, or Native Americans. In the ordinance they must prevent excessive habitual drinking, drunkenness, gambling, and after-hours imbibing. Sometimes aged, impoverished, or disabled people were issued licenses, as a way of keeping them off the relief rolls. They were less likely to enforce regulations stringently. A few innkeepers, like John Harris or William Everton, were totally unsuitable. For other poor people, a little illicit provision of home-brewed liquor could help balance inadequate budgets. In all, twenty-eight people, including an African American, were convicted of illegal liquor sales between 1650 and 1686. Fourteen of these were presented during the 1680s. One way or another, anyone determined to get drunk could get drink.[44]

Drink does not make everyone violent. It can induce sleepiness, amorousness, jollity, melancholy, paralysis, or nausea. However, for some it can dangerously lower the inhibitions against violence in word, deed, or both. Of thirty cases of convicted drunkenness in Charlestown in the 36

---

[43] W. J. Rorabaugh, *The Alcoholic Republic: An American Tradition* (New York: Oxford University Press, 1979) has excellent background.

[44] Orders: see MxCC RB, 1: 49; Harris: see above, "Young Women Abused;" Everton: Thompson, *Sex,* 147, 198. On 5 June 1684, Coniungo, a free black man, was charged with selling beer at half price to seamen, MxCC D&O, 4: folio 107.

years from 1650 to 1686, five involving British residents led to abusive behavior. Eleven Native Americans, whose tolerance seems to have been lower than whites, all became belligerent and violent. The worst decade for cases of drunkenness was the 1670s, when eight people were convicted, two for violent behavior. Among the resident alcoholics, loneliness was a common problem. One such we meet now.[45]

1. Alexander Stewart

In 1652, more than five hundred Scottish prisoners of war, captured after the Battles of Dunbar and Worcester, were transported to Massachusetts as servants. Several from the *Sarah and John* were employed in Charlestown households, and their immediate impact has been described as "violent." Nicholas Wallace, for instance, was sued in 1655 for seducing a serving maid and forced by the court to marry her. Soap boiler John Roy, "overcome with temptation," was convicted of premarital fornication in 1663. Henry Marre was accused of physically abusing a four-year-old boy "in his great passion." Passion and physical violence were also vented against masters, wives, and those in authority. The staid long-term residents of Charlestown must have felt like the Romans during the Barbarian Invasions.[46]

Alexander Stewart, another Charlestown Scot, was soon in trouble with the authorities. On 28 December 1656, during the traditional Twelve Days of Christmas (one of those pagan festivities loathed by the Puritans), he was charged with "Affront to the Constable of Charlestown, giving him the lie." Trouble with constables often erupted when they went round the pubs at the 9 p.m. curfew to speed late drinkers homeward. Stewart was fined six shillings and eight pence. His calling the constable a liar was a fairly typical piece of Caledonian belligerence.[47]

A tailor by trade, Stewart elected to stay in Charlestown even when many of his countrymen returned home in 1660 after the Restoration of King Charles II, for whom they had been campaigning when captured by

---

[45]   Mrs. Joanna Davison, widow of Nicholas from 1664 to 1675, was excommunicated on 10 August 1673 for persistent and scandalous drunkenness; she was restored just before her second marriage, on 20 December 1674, Hunnewell, viii. William Brown, estranged husband of Elizabeth, was warned about frequenting "ordinaries" (pubs), CTR, 3: 125, 24 April 1671. On Indians and liquor, see Thompson, *Cambridge Cameos*, 235–38.

[46]   MxCC RB, 1: 87, 90; Thompson, *Sex*, 106, 221, fn. 57. The Scots had been supporting Charles II's attempt to recover the throne.

[47]   RB, 1: 169.

Cromwell's troops. In 1662 he married nineteen-year-old Hannah Templar, who had arrived in Charlestown from Yarmouth on Cape Cod in 1660 with her grandparents, tanner Richard and Ann Pritchard, and her parents Richard and Hannah Pritchard Templar. In 1665 James, their first child to survive, was born.[48]

The following year Stewart got into a fight in which he was nearly blinded. Richard Rosmorgan deposed on 18 December 1666 that in company with his future brother-in-law John Walker, he:

> met Alexander Stewart who asked John Walker when he would have mended his oven. Walker answered he knew no oven he had. Stewart said his father's oven. Walker answered he could not tell. Stewart called him "Jackanapes," he would kick his breech and ran after him to strike him. Walker said to him "Come" he was prepared for him. Walker struck him two blows but with what he knows not, but he saw Stewart fall.

James Davis, also present at this confrontation, added:

> Stewart followed Walker to the Templars' log pile . . . Walker said he did it in his own defence. He would do it again.

Stewart had to be taken to Dr. Chickering, who found "some hazard of his eye . . . but no symptoms that the wound is mortal. It could not be [inflicted] with a fist." This contradicted Walker's own evidence: Stewart had said to him "Will you not speak to me and lifted up his hand as if to strike him, upon which [Walker] defended himself and struck him with his hand."[49]

Walker's weapon emerged in the formal complaint by Stewart's father-in-law Richard Templar and Constable Thomas Hett: on Tuesday 27 November 1666 in the evening, "John Walker wounded Alexander Stewart in his face near the eye with a lathing hammer." Mending (or not mending) an oven, and wielding a hammer used for nailing laths to battens, points to Walker's being a tiler or a plasterer. Exactly one year later, on 27 November 1667, each combatant was required to enter £30 bond to accept the award of "loving friends Thomas Welch and Solomon Phipps (with the help of Thomas Hett if needed)" of compensation from Walker

---

48 Wyman, 901.

49 Depositions: MxCC D&O, 2: folio 41; Rosmorgan had been charged with premarital fornication with Hopestill Mirick on 21 March 1666, folio 40; Walker married Hannah Mirick in 1672, Wyman, 676. Hannah had been convicted of fornication with another man in 1670, folio 53, Hunnewell, vii.

who had "inconsiderately struck a blow or blows very prejudicial to Alexander Stewart." The award must be decided within 14 days.[50]

Presumably there had been disagreement about whether Walker had acted in self-defense, as he claimed. Stewart had an aggressive reputation. He was a Scot. He may have been almost incomprehensible. Two witnesses cited his bellicosity. On the other hand, Walker's response was both provocative and disproportionate; he could have blinded or even killed his assailant. The arbitration seems to have settled the matter.

By 1674, the Stewarts had five children. Margaret, born in August of that year, was the last. Her mother Hannah died ten days later, on 21 August 1674. Thereafter Alexander went to pieces. On 30 March, he was charged with receiving stolen goods, along with other clothworkers. The next year Stewart received a formal warning about his behavior. On 14 July 1676, Samuel Dowse reported:

> I was commanded by the constable to go with him to the house of Alexander Stewart, who called the constable a young jackanapes and turbulent fellow. The constable warned Stewart that his house was a suspected house, he had information he kept drunken company and followed disorderly courses concerning his drinking.

This warning was ignored. On 19 December 1676, after a cloud of witnesses reported seeing Stewart "several times disturbed with drink . . . he could hardly cross the street . . . he reeled to and fro . . . he staggered back against Mrs. Nowell's pales . . . he reeled back from his door," Thomas Danforth issued an arrest warrant. What worried the selectmen as much as Stewart's careering from the alehouse to his house via collisions with people's fences was the effects on his young family, especially eight-year-old John, who "greatly suffers from his father's neglect." Deacon Ludkin added Stewart's "neglect of his calling and of God." His sottishness had persisted "notwithstanding good counsel given him." For "excessive drinking and misspence of time," he was fined six shillings and eightpence.[51]

Controversy dogged Stewart's last years. In 1684 he was involved in a family spat about Richard Pritchard's estate; Stewart was sued for £10, and

---

[50] Loss of RB 2 denies us reports of the court's decisions; however, folio 44 reveals that Stewart had brought an action for damages against Walker on 14 February 1667.

[51] Stolen: D&O, 3: folio 70; the thief was Bartholomew Indian, and the owner Mr. James Elson. Tailor Thomas Peachey was another recipient. Warning and arrest: folio 73. Dowse would succeed as constable in 1677. Cloud: Aaron Ludkin, Hannah Baxter, Joseph Lamson, Thomas Lord, Thomas Rand. Sentence: RB, 3: 161.

lost. By then he had had to sell his house. In 1685 he was sued for withholding £5-2-0 for the board and lodging of his apprentice son Samuel,
aged 13, from his master. Again he lost. In the spring of 1686 he died. The
circumstances were mysterious, so a coroner's jury was summoned on 9
May 1686. However, the political crisis of the end of the Old Charter government prevented the recording of their verdict. Stewart's Charlestown
life had emerged from obscurity, exuded pugnacity, experienced adversity,
and expired in uncertainty.[52]

2. John Lowden (1641–78)

We have already met Ursula Cole's nephew John Lowden as a drinker and
a fighter. At 10:30 p.m. on 4 July 1667, his shilling reminded his aunt where
she had secreted her bottle of strong waters. Before the night was out, John
had rudely rebuffed the constable's summons, truculently refused to say
how many men were boozing in his house at the Neck (close to the Penny
Ferry alehouse), struck one of the watch, and grabbed the constable by
the throat. After he had sobered up, craven apologies, along with £1-10-0
to the constable and watch, probably reduced his sentence. Thereafter, he
seems to have reformed for a while. That year he was admonished by the
church and then pardoned after confession. In 1668, he took the Half-Way
Covenant when his wife became a full member of the church.[53]

That late night of drinking, din, and desperado happened when John
was twenty-six. A hatter by trade, he had been married for five years to Sarah
Stevenson or Stimpson, one of the six daughters of humble shoemaker
Andrew and Jane Stevenson of Cambridge. John and Sarah had two sons.
The second was named after John's father Richard, a shipwright. Richard
(1613–1700) had been a diligent citizen of Charlestown since the 1640s.
In 1642, four years after arrival, he was admitted a church member and
freeman, and thereafter he proved indispensable in a wide range of practical tasks for the town: building or mending gates, bridges, fences, extensions, and highways, carting, surveying, collecting money, arbitrating disputes, and administering probate estates. He was sergeant of the militia,
an unprecedented four-time constable, and a tithingman. Though never a
selectman, he was a public-spirited neighbor for more than 50 years. He
had married Mary Cole at the end of the 1630s. John was their oldest child.

---

[52]   D&O, 4: folio 108, transcribed in Rodgers, 2: 565–66. Samuel: D&O, 5: folio 114. Coroner:
ibid., folio 124.

[53]   See above, "Ursula Cole: Unorthodox Alewife"; D&O, 2: folio 43. Hunnewell, vi.

Richard left an estate of £381 when he died at the age of eighty-seven. It is hard to believe that eldest son John was not a grave disappointment to his father, especially after the revelations of December 1674.[54]

John Lowden's brother-in-law Peter Frothingham was thirty-eight, five years older than John. He had married John's sister Mary in 1665, when she was about twenty. About 8 p.m. on 2 December 1674, Peter deposed,

> Going past Lowden's house I heard his wife in the highway crying in a lamentable manner and I then asked what was the matter. She was afraid that her husband when at home in his drink would knock her on the head. I went to the door he being in the house and asked him if he were not ashamed to abuse his wife so as he did. I thought it would be better for him to be in his bed. Upon this he came out in a great rage and did abuse me both with his tongue and his hands.

Sixteen-year-old Zechariah Brigden saw what happened to Peter

> in the highway, [with John] throwing him down in the stones, striking him, threatening what he would do if in this house, railing on him "Liar," "Devilish Liar!" Peter went away to drive home his cart. Lowden followed him, took hold, and pulled him out of his cart, struck him on the breast and kept him down on the ground. Goodman Swetzer's servant took him off.

Constable Fowle, 36, was summoned.

> I found his wife at a neighbour's. She said she was even glad when he was so drunk she could crawl to bed. She was in a neighbour's chimney corner with a great swelling over her eye. She said her husband did it. I met him in the highway and asked him why he would offer abuse to his wife. He said it was a lie. I was a lying fellow to say so. Peter Frothingham was about to speak to Lowden [when] he lifted up his hand and struck him with many reviling words.

Two "next neighbors," brothers Nathaniel Frothingham, 32, and Samuel, 25, reported

> observing his bad carriages, [coming] home late at night frequently, and much in drink and so intragged therewith he is

---

54 Stevenson: *Cambridge Cameos*, 129–34. Lowden: Wyman, 632–33; "Lowden's Wall" above.

a disturbance to his neighbours. His wife is forced to fly out of the house and go for shelter to neighbours' houses fearing the rage of her husband. She had come to our houses several times. She was afraid he would knock her on the head when he comes home in his drunken fit.

Fowle summoned two watchmen, Thomas White, 39, and Stephen Waters, 32, and

charged us to assist him in taking Lowden to Mr. Russell. Lowden refusing for a while, and after seemed willing, but desired us to let him go to his shop for his hats a boiling that would be spoiled else. The constable said we would stay [wait] a quarter of an hour. The constable asked his wife whether Lowden had hats a boiling, but she said no. Whereupon we charged Lowden with a lie, but he put it off with some equivocation. We were unsatisfied. He told us we were all liars, with many railing speeches.

At the court on 15 December 1674, Lowden was fined £5 and required to enter a £20 bond for good behavior.[55]

However much he had reformed in 1667, Lowden had plainly reverted. By now, six children had been born; the youngest was just over a year old. His drinking, disturbance, and wife-abuse had been going on for some time. On 27 July 1674 the Charlestown church admonished him again for "the scandalous sin of drunkenness." Poor Sarah Lowden was plainly terrified of her husband "knocking her on the head" with a tool, stick, or club, as he had on 2 December. Her Frothingham in-laws provided refuges for her when she fled from John's drunken rages, and Peter intervened on her behalf, to his considerable cost. In all nine witnesses came forward to corroborate Lowden's persistent and excessive alcohol abuse and the uncontrolled violence it unleashed—Sarah "was afraid for her life," said one.[56]

Not only was Lowden making his wife's life "lamentable," he was also ruining his family's livelihood. In April 1675 he petitioned for relief because of "the poor estate that now I stand in." He was also isolated. On 10 January 1675 he was found incorrigible by the church and excommunicated. He

---

[55] MxCC D&O, 3: folio 66; RB, 3: 113. Intragged: not known to *OED*, but its meaning seems obvious. On 6 April 1675 the fine was reduced to £1 in cash, and he was released from his bond, ibid., 118, 120.

[56] Witnesses: as well as those named: Joseph Dowse, 20, Ruth Frothingham. Admonition: Hunnewell, 8. Wife-abuse: cf. Laura Gowing, *Domestic Dangers*, 206–31.

remained ostracized for more than three years. Hammond recorded his death on 4 April 1678 during the smallpox epidemic. He was only thirty-seven.[57]

Alcohol had ruined Lowden's life. It released anger and violence of appalling ferocity: against authority figures, against any critics, and particularly against his wife. He may have been reacting to the good citizenship of his righteous father. With his modest £150 in assets, he may have envied his younger brother James, a successful wheelwright with his eye on a wealthy widow. He may have inherited a Cole gene from his mother Mary. His uncle John had a violent streak. At least Sarah Lowden was able to make a new life for herself back in Cambridge with widower James Kibby, whom she married in 1679. Between them they had eleven children.

Alcohol abuse and its resultant human and familial tragedies were a problem for the authorities and residents of early Charlestown, but on a very minor scale compared with later generations. Where women and children were at risk, "holy watchfulness" was a positive good, rather than merely inquisitive eavesdropping. Neighbors and kinsfolk intervened to protect the vulnerable from the wrath of intoxicated men. Sarah's or Hannah's lament it may have been; *Angela's Ashes* it was not.[58]

---

[57] Excommunication: ibid. Estate: D&O, 3: folio 69. Hammond, Diary, 170.

[58] See Thompson, *Sex*, index: s.v. "drink and drunkenness."

Violent Servants

Scottish servants had no monopoly on violence. Although servants were generally the least visible town residents, sometimes they found themselves in the unwelcome spotlight of the Middlesex County Court. As well as the other two classic adolescent misdemeanors, fornication and theft, violence towards masters and mistresses was an occasional household nightmare. Employers were unlikely to report such behavior if they could avoid it, since it reflected poorly on their authority. However, some simply could not bear the aggravation any longer, and appealed to town or county officials for support.[59]

The best-documented servile truculence was that of John Salter (1656–1700), son of the negligent, hard-drinking Henry and his busybody wife, Sister Hannah. John was sent off to the household of William Eager in neighboring Cambridge at the age of twelve. In 1673, having already

---

[59] On fornicating servants: Thompson, *Sex*, 19–33; Charlestown cases: MxCC RB, 1: 57, 20 June 1654, Elizabeth Harnice and John Morrice; 83, 20 December 1654, Nicholas Wallace and Jane Lindes; 146, 6 October 1656, Samuel Tingley and Mary Deane; 233, 25 June 1661, Mary Edwards and Samuel Starr; 285, 16 June 1663, John Roy and Elizabeth Phipps; 296, 6 October 1663, Seaborn Cromwell and Robert Parris. D & O, 2: folio 39, 7 June 1665, William Brown and Elizabeth Down; folio 40, 21 March 1666, Richard Rosmorgan and Hopestill Mirick; folio 48, 6 October 1668, Zechariah Hill and Deborah Norton; folio 51, 6 April 1669, Thomas Deane and Elizabeth Burrage; folio 58, 10 June 1671, Thomas Jones and Sarah Crouch; folio 62, 8 October 1673, Zechariah Crisp and Mary Stanwood; RB, 3: 114, 15 December 1674, Samuel Eaton and Elizabeth Cole; D&O, 3: folio 77, 14 March 1677, Henry Beresford and Hannah Lathrop; RB, 4: 44, 20 June 1682, Stephen Geary and Sarah Poor; 74, 23 October 1682, William Johnson and Sarah Burrage; 152, 7 April 1685, Samuel Allen and Elizabeth —; 214, 15 December 1685, Ebenezer Austin and Thankful Benjamin; D&O, 4: folio 94, 20 June 1681, John Thompson and Sarah Winton; 105, 7 December 1683, Daniel Payne and Bethia Blanchard. On theft, see "Adolescent Port Life" and RB, 1: 254, 1 April 1662, Thomas Wasse, John Lathrop and John Chadwick steal provisions from Thomas Brigden on the Sabbath; D & O, 2; folio 56, 9 March 1671, Thomas Slade and Nicholas King steal from John Knight; D & O, 4: folio 89, 29 January 1680, three black servants steal from James Davis; RB, 4: 25, 20 December 1681, Honor Hall steals £3-12-3 from Elizabeth Martin; 32, 4 April 1682, Elizabeth Coulter steals gold from same.

lied, stolen, and absconded, he attacked his dame and threw her in the fire. For this, he was sentenced to twenty lashes, imprisonment, and double remuneration for lost time. Attacks on women were particularly contemptible. Meanwhile, John's elder brother Henry, sent off to Andover, had to be put in a leg-lock for absconding from both work and prison. By the time these boys were "disposed of," the harm had been done.[60]

Two servants, William Whitt in 1668 and Arthur Hindes in 1681, were presented for insubordination. Whitt was complained of by innkeeper Widow Long "for breach of the peace and other mutinous practices." The constable was "empowered to break open any chest, trunk, or box belonging to him and take notice of any indenture between him and his mistress for service for sundry years." He may well have been trying to shorten his contract. Hindes had abused "his master [another innkeeper] Richard Stowers, with blows and words, cursing and swearing." No other depositions have survived.[61]

The behavior of two servants to outsiders suggests potential aggression within households. On 17 March 1669, William West, servant to Thomas Brigden (one of whose servants had stolen from him seven years before) was remanded to Cambridge prison charged with "cruel striking of an Indian." Examined by Richard Russell about the wounding of Will Indian, dwelling at Thomas Gould's Ten Hills Farm, West claimed that Will had "taken up a haypole and struck him about the head, whereupon West struck two or three blows about the head and shoulders from which [Will's head] swelled exceedingly so that he is under the care of Doctor Chickering in a dangerous posture." The deposition of an "Indian squaw" makes it clear that West had provoked the Indian, and that the staff West used was about three inches in diameter. West confessed, but neither the court's sentence nor the Indian's fate is known. This servant seems to have come close to murder.[62]

Drink fueled the second incident. Two watchmen, one Thomas Peachey, recounted the events of about 7 p.m. on 7 May 1673.

> The constable commanded our attendance. We saw Henry Trussell, servant to Samuel Ballatt, distempered with drink going to his lodging. So soon as he was within the door, he

---

[60] See "Ursula Cole;" RB, 3: 106; D&O, 3: folio 67. Cf. Jerathmeel Bowers, stepbrother of Benanuel, whose incorrigible behavior at Deacon Howe's in Watertown included calling his mistress "an ordinary [public-house] whore, a burnt-tail [gonorrhean] bitch and hopping toad." Thompson, *Sex*, 106.

[61] D&O, 2: folio 45; D&O, 4: folio 95.

[62] D&O, 2: folio 51.

threatened the constable, and with his stick struck the constable. The constable commanded Peachey to lay hold on him, but before he could, he struck said Peachey a grievous blow on the arm as may be plainly seen.

Shipwright Ballatt, himself a victim of violent attack two years previously, had to enter bond for his employee's good behavior. Of the ill-behaved Trussell, no more is heard.[63]

All of these violent servants, apart from Salter, were strangers to Charlestown and probably recently arrived in the colony. Rather than helping and learning, they brought misery to their employers and mayhem to the community. Most of them quickly moved on; we doubt they were missed.[64]

---

[63] D&O, 3: folio 62. Ballatt later helped build the dry dock, *Possessions*, 168–69. His servant Hercules would be the leader of a black thieving ring in 1680, RB, 3: 312; Stephen Geary also worked for him, see "Whose Herbs?" In 1671, he had been heaved into the river by Captain Samuel Hayman, after an unspecified dispute. CTrR, 45 v.

[64] Cf. Thompson, *Sex*, index s.v. "Servants."

Mass Violence: Metacom's or King Philip's War, 1675–76

War legitimizes violence. It overrides the moral inhibition and the physical revulsion against killing, maltreating, insulting, and openly hating other human beings. It lumps variegated individuals into an undifferentiated "enemy." It feeds paranoia, disgust, irrationality and credulity. Sudden wild misperceptions and false generalizations take decades to correct (if ever). By dehumanizing the "Other," war creates "conditions for guilt-free massacre." All these responses plumed during the bitter and bloody conflict known for centuries as King Philip's War, and recently renamed Metacom's War. It would hardly be an exaggeration to describe this Anglo-Native American carnage as a genocidal war. Many white settlers applauded mindless, causeless murders of unarmed, helpless "enemies." White heroes were emphatically not the conciliators, or the protectors of friendly Indians, as Daniel Gookin, Thomas Danforth, or John Eliot had been, but the bloodthirsty hunters of red people, *any* red people, as with Samuel Moseley or the Goble boys. On the other side, former captive Mary Rowlandson described a sagamore boasting that "the Indians would drive all the English into the sea," a praying Indian who wore a necklace made of white people's fingers, and the bloodcurdling whoops of glee as scalping parties returned to their camps with trophies. This was a war to the death, which Metacom came close to winning.[65]

---

[65] Troy Duster, "Conditions for Guilt-Free Massacre," in N. Sanford & C. Comstock, *Sanctions for Evil* (San Francisco: San Francisco State University Press, 1970), Ch. 3. Still a good narrative account of war strategies, actions, and theatres, though racially embarrassing, is Douglas E. Leach, *Flintlock and Tomahawk* (New York: Norton, 1966). For perceptive updates: James Drake, *King Philip's War* (Amherst: University of Massachusetts Press, 1998); Jill Lepore, *The Name of War* (New York: Viking, 1999); Jenny H. Pulsipher, "Massacre at Hurtleberry Hill," *WMQ*, 53 (1996), 459–86, and "Our Sages are Sageles," ibid., 58 (2001), 431–48; John Wood Sweet, "The

When Captain John Smith sailed into the mouth of the Charles River in 1614, he found "numerous Indians . . . great troops of well-proportioned people." Within five years their numbers had plummeted. This was mainly a result of a decimating plague of unfamiliar European diseases transmitted by immune fishermen and traders to the vulnerable Natives, but also compounded by an attack on the Massachusetts Indian federation by Micmacs from eastern Maine. The great Pawtucket chief in Massachusetts, Nanepashemet, was killed. Leadership of the remnants passed to his widow, known as Squaw Sachem, based in Medford near Mystic Ponds, and to his friendly son known as John Sagamore of Winnisimmet, just across the Mystic River (modern-day Chelsea). In 1630 John warned Charlestown of a plot by Narragansetts to the south and "all around about us to the eastward in all places, to cut off the English." The settlers quickly set about fortifying the town. This sowed the seed among the whites of fear and suspicion of Native Americans.[66]

In 1639, in the wake of the Pequot War, and following local complaints, Charlestown thought it prudent to conclude a formal agreement with Squaw Sachem and her second husband, the shaman Webcomit. In exchange for twenty-one coats, nineteen fathoms of wampum, three bushels of corn, and the promise of two more coats per year, the Indians conveyed all their land within the Charlestown lines to the town. However, Squaw Sachem "reserved the [Mystic Ponds] land for her life to plant and hunt upon," with reversion after her death to various leading townsmen. Edginess about Indian intentions and eagerness for Indian land were two enduring themes of colonial Anglo-Native relations.[67]

Apart from the Mystic Ponds village, I have not found evidence of Indian presence in Charlestown before the 1660s. What meetings there

---

Indians' New England," ibid., 732–39. *The Narrative of the Captivity and Restoration of Mrs. Mary Rowlandson* was first published in Boston in 1682; see C. H. Lincoln, ed., *Narratives of the Indian Wars* (New York: Scribners, 1913), a long excerpt in John Demos, ed., *Remarkable Providences* (New York: Braziller, 1972), 285–310, and in its entirety, Neal Salisbury, ed., *The Sovereignty and Goodness of God* (Boston: Bedford/St. Martin's, 1997).

[66] "Early Records of Charlestown," Alexander Young, ed., *Chronicles of the First Planters of the Colony of Massachusetts* (Baltimore: Genealogical Publishing, 1975), 371, 377; references to "the north side of the Charles River, full of Indians, called Aberginians" are much exaggerated. Earlier Native American sites at Water Street and Town Dock, both seasonal fishing and hunting camps, have more recently been uncovered during the "Big Dig" around Interstate 93. A. E-H. Lewis, ed., *Highway to the Past* (Boston: Massachusetts Historical Commission, 2001), 4–14.

[67] Pequot: few Charlestown residents saw active service during the 1637 War; Barnabas Davis, GM, 2: 286–93 had prior connections with Connecticut, the colony most heavily involved. See "Travails and Travels" above. Another veteran, Thomas Hale, only arrived in Charlestown from Connecticut in 1659. Agreement: Mx D, 1: 157; MxCC D&O, 1: doc. 1940; *Sfk Deeds*, 1: 43; CTR, 1A: 79, 81. All town beneficiaries of the reversion gave up their gifts to Charlestown, except Edward Gibbons, whose share was sold by his son to Joshua Scottow in 1657. *Sfk Deeds*, 8: 465.

were involved the fur trade in the river valleys to the north and down east. The probate inventory of Merrimack Valley trader John Cromwell, married a little tardily to Charlestown's Seaborn Batchelor, provides a fascinating window on the trade. We have already encountered one of Cromwell's customers, Joshua Tidd, embroiled in the beaver trade with Indians in the Kennebec Valley in Maine. The violence here was between white competitors, rather than with Native American trappers.[68]

The main indication of the Indian presence in Charlestown after the 1660s arises from some Indians' apparent propensity to acquire grog illegally, and then to engage in drunken fights. The authorities seem to have been keener to nail the suppliers than the brawling boozers. However, there was consternation when a befuddled Joseph Indian was found frozen to death on the Stinted Common on 18 January 1672. Some of these Native Americans had come to the Charlestown market to sell artefacts, skins, fruit, vegetables, or game. Their takings were not always taken home, but stayed in the purses of town tapsters.[69]

Other Native American visitors sought casual farm work, especially at busy planting or harvesting seasons. Hard-pressed farmers sometimes took on Indian workers on a year-round basis. In 1669, Thomas Gould, in and out of prison because of his Baptist beliefs, had Will Indian living at Ten Hills Farm. In a fight with a white servant, Will was struck on the head with a heavy staff and severely injured. Bartholomew Indian, servant to John Bacon, enlisted a black servant to keep watch while he broke into James Elson's store during a church service. He stole money, bolts of cloth, 90 lbs of sugar and other luxury items, which he sold to various white residents. One believed his story "that he had liberty to send small ventures to sea for which he had returns."[70]

---

[68]   Rodgers, 2: 58–66. Cromwell's trading goods included twenty-seven dozen knives, twenty-two dozen awls, pipes and rings, cloth, canvas, molasses, fish, tobacco and salt. He had considerable amounts of wampum and £82 worth of furs when he died suddenly in 1661. He appeared to be owed £214 by Indian trappers in undelivered furs. Among Cromwell's customers were Captain Francis Norton, who had fetched beaver from the trader's post at Nacooc near Chelmsford, Richard Russell, Joshua Tidd, and Richard Sprague. Numerous account items cover "victuals and lodging for an Indian," sent down to the Bay with pelts. Tidd: see "Cutting Each Other's Throats for Beaver," above.

[69]   Joseph: D & O, 2: folio 59. Suppliers: Joshua Edmunds, ibid., folio 43, 19 September 1667; William Brown and wife Elizabeth, ibid., folio 60, 6 April 1671, D & O, 3: folio 67, 14 July 1674, RB, 4: 45, 20 June 1682, D & O, 4: folio 99, 3 April 1682; John Harris, RB, 3: 232, 7 October 1678; John and Samuel Gould, RB, 4: 29, 4 April 1682; Rebecca Lee, ibid., 116, 17 June 1684; Mary Trumbull, ibid.; Coniugo [free] Negro, D&O, 4: folio 107, 5 June 1684.

[70]   Will: see above, "Violent Servants;" Bartholomew: RB, 3: 121; D&O, 3: folio 70. On Indian farm labor: Thompson, *Divided,* 149–50, 155.

In the late 1670s and the 1680s, more Indian servants were hired by the year. Some enjoyed the shelter, the victuals, and the relative leisure of the winter months only to melt away with the last of the snow. John Fosket's Indian Sam from Martha's Vineyard had a four-year contract like a European indentured servant; Sam repaid his master's redeeming him from prison by bolting. Another covenant between a white resident and a Native American was sealed on 7 April 1663, when Jethro, at that time a trusted Indian, contracted in writing before witnesses with John Smith to repay £15 worth of pork, coats, and other goods he had borrowed. He was later handed in as a traitor by his own son. Though there developed an element of economic interdependency between the two races, nonetheless there remained suspicion on the part of white Charlestowners, who associated Native Americans with drunkenness, thieving, irresponsibility, and untrustworthiness. Among the Indians, English disease, violence, land grabs, and sharp practice sowed similar frustrations which in 1675 would flare into war under an inspirational leader.[71]

Though Charlestown quickly lost its frontier status and eased its population pressures as daughter towns like Woburn and Malden were founded to the north and northeast, a steady trickle of younger-generation townspeople migrated to frontier towns closer to Native American tribal areas. Some went to the Merrimack-Nashua Valley towns of Haverhill, Dunstable, Chelmsford, Andover, Salisbury, Groton, and Lancaster, where fur trading might supplement frontier farming. Others were drawn to the farming potential of inland towns beyond the initial Middlesex settlements: Sudbury, Marlborough, Concord, Topsfield, Reading, Billerica, and Stow. The price all these venturers paid for more available land and income was greater vulnerability. Their settlements formed "the outer ring of the frontier."[72]

---

[71] Sam: D&O, 5: folio 127, 4 August 1686; other bolters: RB, 3: 204; 4: 74, 80; D&O, 4: folios 102, 105. Jethro: D&O, 1: doc. 2197; Pulsipher, "Our Sages are Sageles," 436, 443. Interdependence: cf. James Drake's covalence theory, *King Philip's War*, passim, and Sweet, "Indians' New England," 737–39.

[72] Many accurate dates of migration cannot be recovered. Haverhill: John Johnson, 1674; Dunstable: William Symmes; Chelmsford: Samuel Adams, Abraham and Pelatiah Whittemore, John Largin, 1674; Andover: Henry Salter Jr.; Salisbury: Joseph Stowers, 1668; Groton: John Cole Jr., Samuel and Mary (Waters) Davis, 1667; Lancaster: Thomas and Mary (Brazier) Wilder, 1659, Lawrence Waters, Rebecca (Waters) Whitcomb, John Roper, 1658; Sudbury: Joseph and Elizabeth (Maynard) Graves, 1666, Joseph Green (later to Stow), Mary Green Stevens, before 1658, (later to Stow), John White before 1663; Marlborough: Jonathon Johnson, 1663, Elizabeth Larkin, 1666, Mary (Shapleigh) Knight; Concord: Mary (Hadlock) Draper, after 1653; Topsfield: Phillip Knight, after 1656; Reading: Thomas Cutler, 1674, Nathaniel Goodwin, John Gould; Billerica: William Baker. Other emigrants who found themselves in harm's way: William Palmer, Stonington, Connecticut, 1653; John Mansfield Jr., Windsor, Connecticut; Elizabeth (Griswold) Palmer, and Rev. Zechariah Symmes Jr., Rehoboth, Massachusetts. Outer ring: Leach, 168.

Though King Philip's War broke out forty miles to the south in June of 1675, it spread like wildfire over much of New England. Middlesex County was in the most danger in early 1676, though Lancaster had been raided on 22 August 1675 by a band of Nipmucs led by One-Eyed John, and eight settlers had died. It was attacked again and destroyed on 10 February 1676. Some twenty hostages were captured, and at least fifty inhabitants were killed or wounded. Groton was torched on 13 March. On 18 March, Chelmsford, Andover and Haverhill were under threat. Marlborough was laid waste on 26 March. Billerica and Woburn, on Charlestown's border, were both harried. Terror stalked the county.[73]

Most Charlestown militiamen were in a large company commanded by Captain John Cutler; his son John was lieutenant and the ensign was John Call. Thirty-nine soldiers were paid a total of £30-8-0 in late July 1676, and a further twenty-nine were granted land rights at a tract called "Narraganset No. 2," now Westminster, Massachusetts, 50 miles west-northwest of Charlestown. These troops were mainly deployed to transport supplies to frontier garrisons. However, on 21 April 1676, they saw unexpected action. They were returning from what was left of Marlborough when Sudbury was suddenly attacked by about five hundred Indians. Cutler's men barely escaped encirclement. Meanwhile, messengers raced east for help. Gookin reported their reception:

> As these tidings came to Charlestown just at the beginning of
> the Lecture there, [he and Danforth] were then hearing the
> Lecture Sermon, and being acquainted therewith, they with-
> drew out of the meeting house and immediately gave orders
> for a party of horses belonging to Captain Prentice's Troop,
> under conduct of Corporal [Solomon] Phipps, and the Indian
> Company under Captain [Samuel] Hunting to march away
> for the relief of Sudbury.

Phipps's cavalrymen reached Sudbury before Hunting's infantry. They were briefly trapped by the enemy, but rescued by reinforcements from Brookfield. There was horrific carnage at Sudbury, especially in the fight for Green Hill. Hunting's Indians daringly scouted the battlefield west of the town the next morning. They found that "a large number of English bodies lay strewn over the ground where they had fallen." No Charlestown men were among the corpses.[74]

---

[73]   Leach, 157–59.

[74]   G. M. Bodge, *Soldiers of King Philip's War* (Baltimore: Genealogical Publishing, 1967), 283–87, 418. Westminster land was not assigned until 1728 and the lots laid out in 1733. Sudbury

Meanwhile, at least three young Charlestown soldiers were fighting in the Connecticut Valley. Thomas Chapman, 27, William Jamison, 20, and Joseph Lamson, 18, were militiamen under the command of a former Cromwellian sergeant: William Turner, whom we have already met as a Baptist who had fled persecution in Restoration England and joined the Gould conventicle in 1665. Though Turner's offer of professional help had been initially disdained, his value and experience were recognized during the desperate winter of 1675–76, and he raised a company. From mid-March 1676 they formed part of the defense of the Upper Connecticut Valley, where large bands of Indian warriors had been looting and burning river towns like Deerfield, and taking cattle and hostages from towns downstream. In mid-May, an escaped soldier brought news of unguarded Indian camps round Peskeompscut Falls, above Hatfield. They were celebrating their triumphs, and feasting on fish, meat, and milk from captured cattle. At dawn on 19 May, about 150 English fell upon the sleeping encampment along the riverbank, massacring at least a hundred men, women and children. However, their firing alerted other groups of Indian fighters camped nearby, and Turner's company and the local volunteers were cut off. At least forty Englishmen were killed, including Captain Turner, but the rest, including the Charlestown militiamen, managed to fight their way back to Hatfield. After the final English victory in the war and King Philip's death on 12 August 1676, the falls close to the Vermont line were renamed Turners Falls.[75]

We learn nothing of these violent and bloody encounters from the Charlestown town records. Back on the coast, the impact of the war involved suffering of two different kinds. The first to figure in the records was the arrival of refugees from devastated frontier towns. Many of these grieving, penniless victims were those relatives who had headed north and west in search of prosperity after the 1650s. Their birthplace offered a safe, if increasingly crowded, haven. Many refugees were elderly or infirm, or

---

fight: Leach, 172–74; Gookin: *R*, 7 (1853) 222; carnage: returning warriors told their hostage Mrs. Rowlandson that they had killed two English captains and nearly a hundred soldiers, Demos, 300.

[75] Leach, 200–5. Chapman (1649–87) was a ship's carpenter who had arrived in Charlestown with his brother William in late December 1669 and married Sarah Mirick in 1675. He later worked on the dry dock, and sailed on William Marshall's *Success*, 1683–85, CTR, 3: 106; Wyman, 201; "Failure in *Success*" above. He drowned in the dock on 22 October 1687. William Jamison (ca. 1645–1714), newly arrived in Charlestown, possibly from Scotland, was a tailor; he married Sarah Price of Salem in 1677 and became a church member in 1681 and constable in 1687. Wyman 548, CTR, 3: 197. Lamson (1658–1722), later a famous stonecutter, was a son of William of Ipswich and lived for a time in Malden, but witnessed Alexander Stewart's frequent bouts of drunkenness in Charlestown, Wyman, 694. See "Drink and Violence" and "Introduction."

women with young children. All were traumatized. As Indian attacks on Middlesex County came closer and closer (Sudbury is only twenty miles west of Charlestown, Woburn on its border), the pressure on food, accommodation, and services mounted. With its fishing and trading links down east, Charlestown was also a refuge for displaced Mainers.[76]

The first refugees arrived on 8 February 1676 from Mendon, followed on 6 March by two "distrest" families from Casco Bay, Maine. Two weeks later nine families—thirty-six men, women and children—were listed with their places of asylum, often with kinfolk. They had fled from Groton, Sudbury, Lancaster, Cambridge Village (Nonantum), and Woburn. Nineteen more families were granted cow commons on 3 April to graze what livestock they had rescued, and thirty acres of town arable land were set aside for them to raise crops. By the end of the month, another fifteen families from nine different towns had arrived. In all, forty fleeing families had descended on the town by the end of the war, numbering well over a hundred new mouths to feed. On 6 June 1676, Thomas Welch was ordered by the selectmen to hire or impress labor "to help the helpless." This included Charlestown households whose menfolk had gone off to the war.[77]

The second ordeal recorded in the town books was that inevitable by-product of war: higher taxes. As early as 20 November 1675, a huge hike in both "country" (colony) and town rates was announced. On 12 June 1676, the General Court ordered a levy of ten times the usual rate. The Charlestown Treasury Book is full of war disbursements for the town defenses and the militia. These burdens descended just as townspeople were confronting the influx of refugees, with depleted manpower. Charlestown may have escaped torch and tomahawk, but it experienced severe material strain. Hardly surprising, then, that the town was seriously behind in its rate payments to Massachusetts Treasurer John Hull.[78]

The brutality attendant on war was brought home to Charlestown by three events away from the fighting. Two involved deaths of Indian non-combatants. The notorious thief and troublemaker John Largin, brother of the "damned whore" Sarah, was involved in the first incident. Warned

---

[76]   Maine: Leach, 94; Charles E. Clark, *The Eastern Frontier* (Hanover, NH: University Press of New England, 1983), 33, 67, 113.

[77]   CTR, 3: 185–93. Refugees: see Appendix. When a food relief ship arrived from Dublin in 1676, more than two thousand Massachusetts people were judged eligible because of hunger, Leach, 247.

[78]   Hike: colony to £617, sixfold increase, and town £205, fourfold. CTR, 3: 182, 192; CTrR, 3: 60v; 4: 3r. Shortfall: £80, CTR, 3: 192. On war costs: Thompson, *Divided We Stand*, 153; Leach, 109–11, 244. The total cost to the United Colonies was computed at around £100,000.

out of Charlestown in December 1674, he seems to have washed up at the frontier town of Chelmsford, near Wamesit, home of a band of friendly Indians at the junction of the Concord and Merrimack Rivers. In September 1675 a settler's haystack caught fire and Indian arson was suspected. Forty militiamen were sent to escort thirty Wamesits to Charlestown for questioning. At the Court of Assistants, one was found guilty and sentenced to be sold into slavery. Two other Indians arrested in Chelmsford were convicted of spying and similarly sentenced. As the acquitted Indians went through Woburn on their return, they had to pass the town band on its training day. Though the militiamen were ordered to ground their arms, a shot rang out and a Wamesit fell dead. The culprit was a soldier called Knight, who was probably a kinsman, possibly a son, of John Knight of Charlestown. He pleaded an accident, and was (contentiously) acquitted. In Leach's account:

> The surviving Indians resumed their residence at Wamesit on the Merrimack River. Soon [early November] a barn fire of mysterious origin was attributed to Wamesit Indians, whereupon [15 November] a gang of Chelmsford men set out to take the law into their own hands. Arriving at the Indian village, they called to the natives to come out from their wigwams. The Indians, not expecting any harm, stepped forth. There was a blast of gunfire, and an Indian boy dropped dead, while four or five others, including the boy's mother were wounded.

One of two shooters was John Largin. He was charged with murder, but, again, the jury balked at conviction. He was referred to the County Court on a lesser charge of wounding, but no record of a verdict survives. This was a cold-blooded massacre by a lynch mob of vigilantes. Jury reactions to both outrages against the Wamesits reflect the powerful racial hostility among the Massachusetts populace.[79]

The second bloodletting involving people associated with Charlestown took place at the time Metacom was being hunted down forty miles to the south in early August 1676. A patrol of Concord horsemen at Hurtleberry Hill rode past a group of six berry-picking Indian women and children from a camp of friendly Indian refugees across the Charles at

---

[79] Largin: see "A Damned Whore," above. Woburn: Pulsipher, "Massacre," 474; Knight: Wyman, 591; Rodgers, 3: 244–46; contentiously: the bench disagreed with the jury verdict, and several times required them to reconsider; they refused to budge, Leach, 149. Chelmsford: Leach, 149–50. Trials: *MR*, 5: 57–8; *Assistants*, 1: 57.

Cambridge Village (Nonantum). Four militiamen, two born in Charlestown, broke away from the patrol, returned to the berry pickers, and, without provocation, killed them; "some were shot through, others had their brains beaten out with hatchets," according to Daniel Gookin. On 11 August, Daniel Goble (whose family had been involved in a violent confrontation in Charlestown 20 years before when he was nine), his nephew Stephen, Nathaniel Wilder (a refugee from Lancaster), and Daniel Hoar were committed to Boston prison. They were tried on 4 September 1676 and sentenced to death. The Gobles were executed on 21 and 26 September; Wilder and Hoar, who seem to have been accessories, had their sentences commuted to the payment of compensation to the two bereaved Native American husbands. This attack was another premeditated slaying of innocents, reflecting a strain of settler frenzy demanding nothing less than extermination.[80]

The third event heightening the war's horrors was the arrival in Charlestown of Mrs. Mary Rowlandson and what was left of her family. Rowlandson had been ransomed on 2 May 1676, through the mediation of John Hoar among others, after her kidnapping at Lancaster on 10 February 1676. She and her minister husband were guests of the Shepherds for 11 weeks, five days less than the period of her captivity. She relished the kindnesses "of many tender-hearted friends in the town." We know what horrors and deprivations she would have described because they have been preserved in her famous *Narrative*, published in 1682. Her account could not but have inflamed the sense of hate-filled revulsion against Native Americans already seething in many white hearts.[81]

Distrust of Indians is reflected in the postwar rebuilding and strength-

---

[80] Pulsipher, "Massacre," 459–64. Gobles: see above "Community Conciliation," and *GM,* 3: 81–83. Wilder had been born to an elite Charlestown family in 1655, shortly before they moved to Lancaster, Wyman, 1030; M. H. Wilder, *Book of Wilders* (privately printed), 12–17, 78. Hoar: from November 1675, Daniel's father John had protected fifty-eight local Nashoba Indians in Concord by building them a protected encampment in the town and providing them with work. This was at the behest of colony authorities. Some of his neighbors opposed this humane treatment and called in "Indian hater" Captain Samuel Moseley, who hauled the inmates off to Boston, and thence to the appalling conditions of Deer Island. Leach, 150; Pulsipher, "Massacre," 470.

[81] Lincoln, ed., *Narratives of the Indian Wars;* excerpted in Demos, ed., *Remarkable Providences,* 285–311. Mrs. Rowlandson's description of her captors typify many white attitudes: savage, brutish, barbarous, merciless, hellish, black, hideous, whooping, inhuman, pagan, unstable, like mad men, wolves, hell-hounds. She described victims "knockt on the head" with hatchets, their bodies stripped naked and desecrated, their bowels split open, their heads scalped. She listed treacheries committed by praying Indians against whites. Yet she also recorded acts of kindness by her and her daughter's captors, the bravery and solace of friendly Indian envoys—"Though they [Tom Dublet and Peter Indian] were Indians, I took them by the hand and burst out into tears"—and her admiration for Native Americans' wilderness skills as well as their ability to live off the land and to survive harrowing hardships.

ening of Charlestown's fortifications at the Neck after 1677 attacks on in-shore vessels. The general jumpiness resulted in the tragic death of John Dexter. Probably mistaken for an Indian, he was shot in the night by Captain Samuel Hunting in 1677. This was a bitter irony, because Hunting (1644–1701) was an exception to the lynch mob mentality. Only recently arrived in Charlestown from his birthplace of Dedham, this sea captain assumed command of a company of "praying Indians" (Native Americans who had converted to Christianity) in the dark days of 1675. On 21 April 1676, he led his company in the dash out to Sudbury where they fought and scouted with conspicuous bravery. In mid-August 1676 they were dispatched to Mount Wachusett (Princeton, central Massachusetts), to destroy Indian provisions and round up pockets of resistance. Hunting was a rarity, however. The popular hero was the vigilante boss Samuel Moseley. He symbolized the belief that the only good Indian was a dead Indian. Neither optimism about Anglo-Indian relations nor proposals for racial harmony by Gookin or Eliot would survive this bloody confrontation of 1675–76. The evil genie of race hatred could not be stuffed back into its bottle.[82]

All Charlestown's inhabitants experienced the horrors of organized violence in this war. Many able-bodied men felt it directly through their involvement in skirmishes or full-scale battles at Sudbury or Turners Falls. Their patrols and provisioning expeditions took them to torched and pillaged garrisons in frontier towns. All townspeople would have an indirect sense of the traumas of sinister sounds in the night, dawn attacks, flaming arrows into thatch, haystacks, or shingles, lead shot thudding into clapboards, shadowy figures in the woods, discovering scalped corpses or dismembered livestock, crops burning in the fields or barns, hearing the screams of the kidnapped or dying. All this would pour from the mouths of the dozens of refugees in the town. It would reinforce the mood of murderous hatred against all Indians, praying as well as preying.[83]

---

[82] Fortifications: CTR, 3: 209; Pulsipher, "Massacre," 476. Hunting: Dexter death, Hammond, Diary, 169, 4 December 1677. *Assistants*, 1: 114. *National Genealogical Society Quarterly*, 78 (1990), 85–97; Pulsipher, 468. Moseley: Pulsipher, 466–76; Leach, 148, 150, 153, 162; Thompson, *Cambridge Cameos*, 171–72. Gookin and Eliot: ibid., 167–72.

[83] Rowlandson, in Demos, *Remarkable Providences*, 286–88. Margaret Ellen Newell records mass slave auctions of hundreds of captured Narragensett and Wampanoag Indians in 1676 and 1677. Other prisoners were assigned to towns damaged in the war. "The Changing Nature of Indian Slavery in New England, 1670–1720," in C. G. Calloway and N. Salisbury, eds., *Reinterpreting New England Indians and the Colonial Experience* (Boston: Colonial Society of Massachusetts, 2003), 106–36.

Post-traumatic stress disorder was not a phrase that tripped off Puritan tongues. For the Puritans, the atrocities and sufferings of war (followed by the smallpox epidemic of 1677–78) were signs of God's anger at the "Creolian degeneracy" of the people of New England, especially the "rising generation," reviled with such relish in the sermons and writings of Increase Mather and his colleagues. Thanks to their agitation, this equation of war and epidemic with divine punishment prompted the campaign for self-flagellation and self-improvement culminating in the Great Reform Synod of 1679. Mrs. Rowlandson's *Narrative,* probably circulated in manuscript before its publication in 1682, aided and abetted this movement. Her (clerically fostered) account is studded with scriptural commentary and divinely ordained providences. Even her captivity is seen as providential: after a comfortable life in Lancaster, "the Lord had His time to scourge and chasten me." Yet another white reverse calls to mind God's words in Psalms 81:13–14: *Oh that My people had heeded Me and walked in My ways, I should soon have subdued their enemies.* Only when the English recognized their powerlessness would God intervene: *Help Lord, or we perish!* Rowlandson glossed this cry for help: "When the Lord brought His people to this, that they saw no help in any thing but Himself, then He takes the quarrel into His own hands. And though they [Metacom's warriors] had made a pit, in their own imaginations, as deep as hell for the Christians that summer (1676), yet the Lord hurled themselves into it." Never mind the Matherians' critic, William Hubbard, who more plausibly blamed English defeats on "contempt of our enemies." The "wrath of God" reading of the terrible events of 1675–78 provided a much-needed cathartic stimulus for a stunned and struggling people. Reformation was a form of exorcism.[84]

APPENDIX
REFUGEES IN CHARLESTOWN, 1676

CTR, 3: 183, 8 February 1676: Daniel Lovett and wife [Joanna (Blott), daughter of former Charlestown church member] from Mendon, driven out by the Indian War. [2 in party]

187, 6 March 1676: Joseph Ingersoll, house carpenter, wife and two children from [Falmouth] Casco Bay. [4]
John Rider, husbandman, wife and one child, [Falmouth] Casco Bay. [3]

---

[84] Ibid., 295, 305, passim; Foster, *Long Argument,* 218–230.

20 March 1676: Widow [Mary Axtell] Maynard and two grandchildren from Sudbury lodge with William Bullard, along with [her daughter] the wife of Daniel Hudson from Concord. [4]

Goodwife [Elizabeth, wife of William] Robinson and two children from Cambridge Village, and Goodwife [Hannah, wife of John] Wilder and three children at her father's Edward Brasier. [7]

188. Father [James] Thompson of Woburn to Corporal [Thomas] White's. [1]

Mansfield's house let to Goodwife [wife of John of Lancaster, killed 1676] Roper. [1]

Goodman [Thomas] Tarbell [from Groton] at John Baxter's. [1]

Lawrence Waters and wife, Samuel Waters, wife and two children from Lancaster at Stephen Waters's. [6]

Jacob Waters and wife at John Mousall's. [2]

Samuel Davis, wife and five children from Groton at [brother-in-law] William Ridland's. [7]

Josiah Whitcomb, wife [Rebecca Waters] and two children from Lancaster at John Cogan's. [4]

Mrs. Phillips, widow of Mr.[George?] Phillips, to Goodwife Hale's. [1]

189. 3 April 1676, Cow Common Grants:

Thomas Tarbell Jr. [with wife and four children?] at [brother-in-law] Samuel Leman's. [6?]

William Longley [father of Ann Tarbell] and family from Groton at Increase Turner's. [5?]

John Whitcomb [brother of Josiah, with wife and three children?] from Lancaster at Thomas Adams's. [5?]

190. Old Goodman Bairstow of Watertown at William Dady's. [1]

Joseph Parker of Dunstable exposed to destruction [with wife and four children?] at Mr. Trumbull's. [6?]

Moses Newton of Marlborough, house burnt down [with wife and two children?] at [stepfather] John Penticost's. [5?]

John Wilder [see family above, 188] at [father-in-law] Brazier's. [1]

Jonathan Johnson from Marlborough [with wife and four children?] at his father William Johnson's. [6?]

Thomas Stevens of Sudbury [with wife Mary (Green) and five children] at brother-in-law Jacob Green's. [7?]

John Houghton from Lancaster [with wife and three children?]. [5?]

John Green Jr. from Sudbury. [1]

191. 26 April 1676, Persons coming to Charlestown.

From Groton: Cornelius Church and wife at John Baxter's. [2]

From Marlborough: Deacon [William] Ward at Samuel Ward's. [1]

From Watertown: James Treadway and wife at [brother-in-law] Henry Balcomb's. [2]

From Lancaster: John Houghton and family at Samuel Bicknell's. [See above, 190]

From Chelmsford: James Richardson and family at John Trumbull's. [4+]

From Lancaster: Joseph Waters at John Patefield's. [1]

From Lancaster: James Sawyer at John Cutler's. [1]

From Groton: Ensign Lawrence at Mr. Henry Phillips's. [1]

From Cambridge Village: Isaac Bacon at John Burr's. [1]

From Cambridge: William Munro, wife and family at [brother-in-law] Samuel Frothingham's. [8]

From Groton: James Knapp at Widow Bennett's house. [3]

From Chelmsford: John Waldo and wife. [2]

[From Chelmsford] Lt. Thomas Henchman and family. [4?]

192. 6 November 1676: Zechariah Sawtell [from Groton with wife and three children?] to be town bellman from 7 November to 30 April 1677. [5?]

Probable Totals:
Families: 40; Persons: 126.

Anger Management, Communal and Divine

Cuffing, lashing, punching, grabbing, kicking, hammering, clubbing, burning, screaming, cursing, wounding, bewitching, murdering, massacring: from these accounts of rage, thuggery, threats, scapegoating, getting even, and grudge-settling, Charlestown appears a brutal place. Certainly there were families and individuals with violent reputations: the Gobles, the Davises, the Goodwins, the Largins, the Salters, John Lowden, John Fosket. Often beneath these outbursts lay deeper problems: Lowden's alcoholism and falling short of his parents' expectations, the family shame at Father Goodwin's pedophilia and carnality, Stewart's alien origins, grinding Largin penury, and Fosket indebtedness. Targets for assaults were sometimes social suspects or outcasts such as victim of homophobia John Mousall, untrustworthy neighbors Richard Temple or Martha Smith, or the promiscuous Martin women.

In several cases, it is clear that incidents were the culmination of long periods of tension. Fosket had previously been a Mousall servant and owed the family money. Thomas Tyrell had been caught with a valued illicit book that had been confiscated. He wanted it back. Goodwin and Bicknell were settling scores with Thomas Welch, a competitor. Widow Bell had been contesting bounds with the Martins for years. Similarly, the Smiths had long been claiming the disputed mowing with the Frosts; and was this the first Frost hog to wriggle under the fence? Whoever trashed Mousall's house was venting well-matured revenge. The fifteen months of warfare against Metacom's federation lowered the inhibitions against racial violence, lending sanction to Largin's and the Gobles' homicides.

Sometimes, though, we get the impression that, whatever the cause, combatants simply hated each other's guts. The Gobles loathed Temple. The Smiths and the Frosts could not stand each other. The Frothinghams feared and detested John Lowden. There was no love lost between the Bells and the Martins. This dislike ran in clans, who rushed to the support of their members—most notably the Leach family shielding John Fosket and Thomas Tyrell. The Bells spoke up for Thomas Waffe; the Frothinghams risked injury for sister-in-law Sarah Lowden. Even Stewart's in-laws, the Templars, came to his defence. Widow Wadland had had similar support from her relatives in her spat with Stephen Geary. The hatred erupted in screaming home truths at offenders, like Geary's sexual irresponsibility, or the Smiths' greed for land. It also prompted physical fury like Goodwin's frenzied attack on Welch, Temple's near-suffocation at the Gobles' hands, Sister Smith's black and blue arms, or Stewart's hammered eye-socket. Waffe would have attacked Martin with his axe if he had had the chance. In all these battles, one of the combatants might well have been killed.

Such attacks were exceptional, according to surviving records. The horrified responses of witnesses tend to confirm their rarity. Yet we should ask how common less severe physical or verbal abuse was in early Charlestown. The short answer is that then, as with similar incidents now, we do not know. The reasons for our ignorance are, however, different. In the present day we do not know because, apart from isolated public disturbances, like political or industrial protests, gang- or drug-related street battles, or weekend binge drinking, private brutality *is* private. Appalling cases of child cruelty, sexual abuse, emotional blackmail, pedophile seduction, internet suicide groups, or spousal assaults are often only discovered after months or years in our domestically insulated and isolated spaces.

Such privacy was unknown in seventeenth-century Charlestown. People were rarely alone. Neighbors, kinsfolk, passers-by, servants, children, officials were always popping in, or peering in (like baker John Call at the Mousalls') or listening in. Living spaces were cramped and crowded; often the only privacy from servants or children, even in bed, was provided by drawing the bed-curtains. Furthermore, communities, as we have seen, were minutely regulated, and if rules and conventions left loopholes, rumor and gossip filled the gaps. Minding one's business included minding everyone else's. It is unlikely that these incidents of extreme violence represented the tip of an iceberg; they *were* the iceberg.[85]

---

[85] D. Wootton, "Never Knowingly Naked," *London Review of Books,* 15 April 2004, 26–27; Gowing, *Common Bodies.* Regulated: see above "Town Government."

In seventeenth-century England, a much consulted counsellor bewailed "the unspeakable tyrannies of hard-hearted yoke-fellows." The only specific example of spousal abuse in the records of Charlestown is John Lowden, though we have suggested a few other unsatisfactory unions. While manners among many townspeople were probably rougher than nowadays, and the treatment of dependants, especially children and servants, included corporal punishment, it was conventionally mild correction compared to the lashings meted out to criminals. We cannot be certain whether slapping or shouting were accepted as part of daily life, because such behavior would have gone unremarked. However, there is evidence that excesses were quickly spotted and checked.[86]

The other early antidote to physical or verbal abuse was the internalized culture of discipline. Calvin's Geneva and the Elizabethan homilies might condemn wife-beating, but far more influential were the positive calls for loving neighborliness, companionate marriage, individual self-control, considered speech, hard work, moderation, and trustworthiness. This was not just a recommended lifestyle; this was the Puritan interpretation of God's command. Falling short resulted not just in guilt, but in divine punishment, like plagues of locusts, or blasted wheat, or smallpox epidemics, or Indian attacks, or lost ships, or royal threats to Puritan independence. Such sanctions concentrated minds, restrained fists, and swallowed back threats and curses. Charlestown might be a comparatively cosmopolitan port, but its settled population was predominantly God-fearing and temperate. Threatening and ill-behaved visitors were shockingly out of place.[87]

Nevertheless, as we are about to see, the culture of discipline did not prohibit all violence. Defiance of papist tyranny was doing God's work; as with the godless Native Americans, violence against evil was considered a positive duty.

---

[86] Counsellor: Richard Napier; see Michael MacDonald, *Mystical Bedlam* (Cambridge: Cambridge University Press, 1983), 103; on domestic violence in England: Fletcher, *Gender, Sex and Subordination,* 192–223; Gowing, *Domestic Dangers,* 206–31. Unsatisfactory: see above, "Women: Conclusion." Corporal punishment: cf. the complaint against the constables that the Harrises, guilty of "such wickedness" against several women, were "so stroked over as if they were small children; it was inferior to a schoolboy's whipping . . . " See above, "Young Women Abused." Excesses: Thompson, *Sex,* 159–62; *Cambridge Cameos,* 47–54.

[87] See above, "Young Women Abused," "Whose Coat?" and "Violent Servants."

Part 8

Defiance

Chronology of the Glorious Revolution

1660

25 MAY: Charles II returns to England: the Restoration.

Enumeration (Navigation) Act.

1662

JUNE: Arrival of the King's Letter confirming 1629 Charter, requiring toleration of Protestants, judicial proceedings "In His Majesty's Name," and property-based franchise.

1663

Staple (Navigation) Act.

1664–66

King's Commissioners in New England and New York.

1667

Second Anglo-Dutch War (began 1664) ends disastrously.

1673

Plantation Duty (Navigation) Act.

1675–76

MAY TO AUGUST: King Philip's (Metacom's) War.

1676

10 JUNE: Edward Randolph arrives in Boston on his first inspection; stays 6 weeks.

1677

27 JULY: Lords of Trade in London decide 1629 Massachusetts charter must be amended.

1678

16 MAY: Lords of Trade to seek writ against 1629 Charter.

1678–81

"Popish Plot" or the Exclusion Crisis (exclusion of the Catholic James from royal succession) in England.

1680–82

34 out of 36 ships charged with smuggling by Randolph as New England Customs Collector acquitted by Massachusetts juries.

1681

Charles II prorogues his last Parliament, and rules thereafter without a legislature, financially dependent on Louis XIV, the Catholic absolute monarch of France. English dissenters persecuted.

1683

OCTOBER: London loses its charter. Randolph in Boston with royal command: compromise on charter, or lose it. Compromise rejected by "die-hard" faction.

1684

23 OCTOBER: Massachusetts Charter of 1629 vacated (revoked) in London.

1685

6 FEBRUARY: Charles II dies; James II, his Roman Catholic brother, succeeds.
29 SEPTEMBER: James II refuses assembly in planned royal regime in Massachusetts.

1686

12 MAY: Last election in Massachusetts under the 1629 charter.

17 MAY: Joseph Dudley reads his newly arrived royal commission as president of the interim Council of New England.

18 DECEMBER: Sir Edmund Andros takes over as governor-general of the Dominion of New England. T. Graves appointed royal judge; L. Hammond militia captain.

1687

4 APRIL: James's first Declaration of Indulgence tolerating Roman Catholics and dissenters, published in Boston in August.

MAY: Maypole erected and cut down in Charlestown. Fighting between sailors of H.M.S. *Kingfisher* and Charlestown inhabitants.

19 JULY: British Sailor found dead; watch attacked.

2 SEPTEMBER: Rev. Charles Morton's Charlestown lecture against persecution charged with sedition.

1688

16 MARCH: Order given for only one annual town meeting to elect selectmen.

30 MARCH: Increase Mather escapes to London to petition James II.

25 APRIL: Second Declaration of Indulgence.

15 MAY: Great guns moved from Charlestown to Boston.

General invalidation of land titles without new fees and patents.

November: Andros leads 300 troops against Maine Indians.

5 NOVEMBER: William of Orange lands at Torbay with army from Holland.

23 DECEMBER: James II flees to France. Glorious Revolution in England.

1689

FEBRUARY: Rumors about William's invasion reach New England.

MARCH: Andros returns to Boston at end of month.

4 APRIL: News of William's Hague Declaration and "happy change in England" arrives in Boston.

18 APRIL: Glorious Revolution in Boston. Andros and company captured and imprisoned; Declaration of Gentlemen and Merchants; Council for Safety in charge.

1 MAY: John Winslow brings confirmation of Glorious Revolution in England.

2 MAY: Council calls town representatives to a 9 May meeting in Boston.

21 MAY: Charlestown inhabitants' declaration for continuation of Council.

22 MAY: Election of town representatives to convention.

24 MAY: Convention confirms 1686 governor and assistants; to govern with advice of town representatives until will of the monarchs is known. Richard Sprague plus twelve Andros collaborators tell convention that

they expect fair treatment, as was promised to Andros when he surrendered.

14 JUNE: Council orders continuance of militia officers in post in 1686.

17, 19 JUNE: Charlestown Town Meeting elects and confirms town officials.

3 JULY: New Charlestown militia officers confirmed.

12 JULY: Two-thirds of Charlestown militia company renominate old officers; not approved, but 1686 officers are reinstated.

13 AUGUST: Charlestown town meeting insists Samuel Phipps, M.A., should serve as constable.

21 SEPTEMBER: Graves letter to James Russell against Middlesex County Court as "pretended court."

23 SEPTEMBER: Charlestown Town Meeting reports Graves and allies for "sedition." They are put under house arrest.

4 OCTOBER: Sprague expelled from convention for contempt.

6 OCTOBER: Sprague, Hammond, and Cutler dismissed from militia posts.

OCTOBER/NOVEMBER: Graves and eleven allies write to William and Mary about rashness in Massachusetts "pretended government" and their hope for royal settlement of the colony. Counter-address defends old charter government, and charges Graves et al. as Andros collaborators.

1 DECEMBER: Royal confirmation of temporary government until new arrangements arrives.

DECEMBER: J. Cutler Jr. fined £20 for seditious libel against legality of Middlesex Court.

DECEMBER?: Hammond and Cutler Sr. submit, after King's confirmation of temporary Massachusetts government arrives.

1690

24 JANUARY: Convention now called General Court.

25 JANUARY: Gentlemen and merchants of Boston and adjacent towns write to king, requesting royal governor and council with elected assembly.

10 FEBRUARY: Andros and Dominion officials sent back to London.

12 FEBRUARY: General Court expands freemanship to ratepaying small property owners; 917 new freemen in next two months.

February to June: Smallpox in Boston; assembly meets in Charlestown.

3 MARCH: Sprague elected chairman of Charlestown board of selectmen, Hammond Clerk of Writs.

13 MARCH: Cutler Jr. submits, with intercession from Rev. Charles Morton.

22 MARCH: Great guns to be returned to Charlestown from Boston.

22 MAY: News of successful and lucrative campaign against French in Nova Scotia.

28 MAY: Election under old charter procedure of governor, council and assembly.

9 AUGUST: Phipps expedition against Quebec sails.

NOVEMBER: News of defeat of New England expedition against Quebec.

22 NOVEMBER: Third address to the crown from notables in Boston, Charlestown and neighbors about French and Indian attacks, colonial disunity, fiscal and economic pressures; address seeks help and settlement. Later published in London, with Hammond note. Anti-notable "Publicans" respond with political satire.

1691

5 FEBRUARY: Hammond refuses summons for contempt before General Court; arrest ordered.

19 MAY: Trumbull and Reid sentenced by "pretended court." "Pretended marshal" illegally seizes property (Hammond).

20 MAY: "Pretended elections" (Hammond).

8 JUNE: First draft of new Massachusetts Charter.

19 JUNE: J. Cutler Jr. fined £20 for reproachful words against authority. Dec. appeal allowed.

7 OCTOBER: New charter sealed and patented in London.

22 OCTOBER: Charlestown has levied 20 rates towards French and Indian War; General Court orders four more to be collected. Constables refuse.

11 DECEMBER: General Court appoints 7 new rate assessors.

16 DECEMBER: General Court appoints Marshall Samuel Gookin collector.

1692

22 JANUARY: News of new charter received.

4 MAY: Election of Council.

14 MAY: New charter arrives with royal governor Sir William Phips and leading negotiator Increase Mather.

Dominion and Revolution, 1686–92

5 May 1660 marked an ominous providence. Charles II stepped ashore at Dover, and the Stuart monarchy was restored after eleven years of Puritan Commonwealth and Protectorate. A shudder of apprehension must have passed through every Puritan heart when the news reached Massachusetts. It was justified. For the next twenty-six years, the colonists of Massachusetts fended off increasingly determined royal attacks on their virtual independence and un-English politico-religious proclivities. All this while, they prayed and fasted with growing desperation for their Lord to deliver them. Then on 17 May 1686, Joseph Dudley read his commission as president of the interim Royal Council for New England and announced "more immediate dependence on the crown" to the newly elected General Court in Boston, and the First (1629) Charter era of Massachusetts history was over. As Samuel Sewall said to his stunned colleagues: "The foundations being destroyed, what can the righteous do?" Little wonder that the marshal-general was weeping and "many shed tears in prayer and at parting." This was a divine judgement of devastating ferocity.[1]

FACTIONS

Back in June 1676, newly arrived royal agent Edward Randolph had met with Massachusetts governor John Leverett and five other members of the colony council. Since he had a letter from the king to read out, he doffed his hat and three assistants followed his deferential example to the crown; the governor and two other colleagues remained covered. This

---

[1] Sewall, *Diary*, 113,115. R. N. Toppan, ed., "Dudley Records," 2 *MHSP,* 13 (1899), 222–98.

response encapsulated the problem of fending off royal "encroachments": deepening disagreements among colonists about the best tactics for doing so and even the advisability thereof. One group, known as "the faction," non-compromising resisters to the last ditch, regarded the 1629 Charter and the constitution built upon it as sacred and non-negotiable. They celebrated the crises from which God had rescued them: during the 1630s when the threatening Archbishop Laud had been distracted by the Scots; the 1660s, when war in Europe had diverted royal administrators; and the 1670s, when a series of plots and crises over a Catholic succession paralyzed Whitehall. The Almighty would always save His chosen people, argued these diehards. In Charlestown, Mr. Samuel Nowell, "a late factious preacher" turned assistant from 1680, Mr. James Russell, a council member from 1682, and selectman Captain John Phillips lent their considerable reputations to this point of view.[2]

By contrast, "the moderates" or conciliators proposed, probably accurately, that some concession to royal demands, like genuine acceptance of parliamentary trade regulations, or modest expansion of the franchise and of toleration, would have mollified the Lords of Trade and conserved the essential elements of the 1629 Charter. Among this group in Charlestown could be counted leaders such as Captains Lawrence Hammond and Richard Sprague, John Cutler Sr. and Jr., and Dr. Thomas Graves.[3]

---

[2] Hat honor (protocol): M. G. Hall, *Edward Randolph* (New York: Norton, 1969), 21. Phillips, on 17 June 1686, "had very close discourse with the President to persuade him not to accept" the royal commission, Sewall, *Diary*, 114. Four days later, Nowell "prayed that God would pardon each magistrate's and deputy's sin [in conceding] . . . and thanked God for our hithertos of mercy 56 years . . . and for what we might expect from sundry of those now set over us," ibid. See also his letter to John Richards, 28 March 1683, in M. G. Hall, L. H. Leder, and M. G. Kammen, eds., *The Glorious Revolution in America* (Chapel Hill: University of North Carolina Press, 1964), 22–23; Nowell topped the assistants' poll in 1686, Mass Archives, 13 April 1686. On his career as preacher and leader of resistance, see Sibley, *Harvard Graduates*, 1: 335–42; *ODNB; ANB*. His election sermon *Abraham in Arms* (Boston: Green, 1678) specifically challenged the royalist belief in the divine right of kings. God "hath set rulers their bounds and by His law hath determined the people's liberty and property." On Russell, see below. In December 1686, Charlestown-born John Gould, now lieutenant of Topsfield train band, was in the dock for refusing at a "riotous muster" to own the new government, and "offering his troops to support the old" 1629 regime, D. S. Lovejoy, *The Glorious Revolution in America* (New York: Harper, 1974), 182. The royal takeover of New Hampshire in 1679, and the arbitrary and venal regime of first royal governor Edward Cranfield, had been a stiffener to the resistance of the diehards, "Samuel Sewall Letter-Book," 6 *MHSC*, 1 (1886), 24; Lovejoy, 150–53.

[3] Lovejoy, 145–54; Hall, *Randolph*, 126. Connecticut and Rhode Island eventually recovered their original charters by imitating the flexible willow rather than the unbending oak. Hammond was a recent convert. On 19 December 1683 he had arrived in Portsmouth, New Hampshire, after an atrocious journey, to help his "factional" brother-in-law, Rev. Joshua Moodey, thwart customs collector Edward Randolph's attempts to seize a vessel in Piscataqua. Randolph implied that Hammond was courting popularity in Massachusetts, where he planned to run for an assistant-

A few positively welcomed the royal embrace. They were usually recent arrivals in Massachusetts who had emigrated in order to exploit the assets of New England within the English Atlantic economy. In Charlestown, the most obvious of these transplants was Charles Lidgett, who had acquired the adjacent Winthrop Ten Hills Farm estate with part of the fortune inherited from his mast-trading father in 1677. His town house and business were in Boston, his commercial partners were mainly in England, and his family had come to Massachusetts from royalist Barbados. Lidgett was an Anglican and died in London in 1698. For him and his like, the sooner the crown took over this eccentric anomaly called Massachusetts, the better.[4]

DOMINION

The shell-shocked diehards could only vow to maintain as many of the good old ways as possible, to afford minimal compliance with the new authorities, and to pray for a rapid end to this harsh judgment of God. Samuel Nowell had already argued that any compliance was "worse than to be passive only . . . to pull down the house ourselves." This surly mood typified the depression of the bitter-enders. The end for them had indeed been bitter. The moderates found themselves in a dilemma between popular opposition and their sense of responsibility and allegiance to the English crown. Some of them, like Thomas Graves, had already tussled with the "commonality" and their rash and ignorant inconsistency, and had little hesitation in accepting royal office. The militia officers, nominated by their men under the old government, would have had to sacrifice their commissions otherwise, as did Sewall in Boston. Captains Sprague and Hammond and Lieutenant Cutler stayed on, as officers of the new regime. Graves accepted appointment as a judge. Presuming that the traditional New England Way had gone for ever, reliant on the Atlantic connection for their businesses, they collaborated.[5]

---

ship in 1684. N. Bouton, ed., *The Provincial Papers of New Hampshire* (Concord, NH: Jenks, 1867), 1: 492.

[4]   R. S. Dunn, *Puritans and Yankees* (New York: Norton, 1971), 203; Bailyn, *Merchants,* 131–33, 193–96. On 3 September 1686, Sewall recorded Lidgett and other royalists who had "come in a coach from Roxbury about 9 o'clock or past, singing as they come, being inflamed with drink. At Justice Morgan's they stop and drink healths, curse, swear, talk profanely and bawdily to the great disturbance of the town and grief of good people. Such high-handed wickedness has hardly been heard of before in Boston," *Diary,* 121. The 920 acres of Ten Hills were confirmed to Lidgett by the Andros council on 10 August 1687, R. N. Toppan, ed., "Andros Records," *American Antiquarian Society Proceedings,* 13 (1899–1900), 474.

[5]   Nowell: Hall, *Randolph,* 78; Graves: see above, "Succession Crisis;" commissions: Lovejoy, 218.

Insider Dudley's seven-month regime was flexible and sensitive, but the arrival of soldier and former New York governor Sir Edmund Andros with a group of military and legal henchmen in late December 1686 brought in a brutal, arbitrary, corrupt, alien, and confrontational culture. 1687 would demonstrate to the people of Charlestown what Stuart dominion signified. The hallowed "rights of Englishmen," not to mention the privileges of saints and charter rights, would be crushed under the heels of the greedy and ungodly bullies who served a dictatorial Catholic monarch. As a new official informed a protesting minister: "You have no further privileges saving to be exempted from being sold as slaves."[6]

This clash of cultures quickly prompted outrageous vulgarities against the respectable mores of Charlestown in the spring of 1687. In May some seamen from HMS *Kingfisher* erected in Market Square a maypole, hated symbol of bawdy folk "merriment." In a riot between affronted citizens and jolly Jack-tars, Constable Timothy Phillips "commanded the King's Peace in the King's name." The response of the frigate's skipper was to grab Phillips's staff and take a swing at him. On 19 May, a British soldier was buried. Joseph Phipps of Charlestown ostentatiously kept his hat on during the Church of England service, and "a disturbance ensued." That night, the phallic totem was cut down. Sewall heard that Joseph's brother, Mr. Samuel Phipps, Harvard graduate, schoolmaster, and selectman, had encouraged the watch to perform this operation. In response, an even larger pole was set up with a garland upon it. Constable Phillips, meanwhile, was summoned before Governor Andros and bound to answer in court in December.[7]

Charlestown constables deserved danger money in this tense atmosphere. They had to confront a gang of thugs from Boston who attacked the meetinghouse and "riotously pulled down whole church windows." On 19 July 1687, one of the crew of the *Kingfisher* was found dead. His shipmates and the crew of her sister ship HMS *Rose*, the frigate that had brought Randolph from London with Dudley's commission on 13 May 1686, went on the rampage in Charlestown. According to Constables Nathaniel Adams, Samuel Hunting Jr., and Luke Perkins, Surgeon Edward Biggs and Unton Dearing of the *Rose* with Thomas Richards of Boston and four others at 10 p.m. near the landing place "in a warlike manner with swords drawn and staves in a riotous manner assaulted the constables and

---

[6]   Hall, *Randolph*, 108. Slaves: John West to Rev. John Wise, Viola Barnes, *Dominion of New England* (New York: Ungar, 1960), 88.

[7]   Sewall, *Diary*, 140; Frothingham, 221.

wounded them." Then a rock was thrown at Adams's house, smashing a window and showering a sleeping child with glass. The most alarming outcome of this bloody fracas was Andros's response when the constables sought his advice about violent servicemen. "He fell into a great rage, and did curse us, saying 'Damn you, you deserve to be indicted,' and called us ill names, and threatened to send us to jail. Addressing Timothy Phillips, Andros said: 'Look to yourself and have a care, for you are marked men—never come to trouble me more with such stories.'" [8]

Verbal and physical assaults like these on elected officials doing their jobs no doubt contributed to Rev. Charles Morton's lecture topic on Friday 2 September 1687. He declared that "persecution was come amongst us and settled amongst us, but he bid them to have courage; he hoped it would not last long." Royalist sympathizer Dr. John Clark reported Morton's sedition to Andros. The minister was examined before the Council of 24 September and bound to appear for trial at the Superior Court in Charlestown in December. Eventually, on 31 January 1688 this "chief promoter of rebellion," in Randolph's words, was acquitted in Boston on legal technicalities, despite royal efforts to pack the jury. The prosecutor claimed "that there were not honest men enough in Middlesex to make a jury to serve their turns." With town meetings discouraged, and after 16 March 1688 forbidden, the Puritan churches had become the sole institutions of communal solidarity. [9]

Arbitrary executive interference with legal process was a major complaint of town merchant, selectman, ensign, deputy, and commissioner for small causes Joseph Lynde:

> After judgments obtained for small wrongs done him, triable by your own laws before a justice of peace from whom they allowed no appeals in such cases, he was forced out of his county by a writ of false judgment; and although at the first superior court in Suffolk [Boston], the thing was so far opposed by judge Stoughton as illegal . . . yet the next term by judge Dudley and judge Palmer, said Lynde was forced to answer [before a jury] of non-residents there. I mention not my damage though it is great. [10]

---

[8]   Ibid., 220–21; MxCC D&O, 5: folio 126, 20 July 1687.

[9]   Sewall, *Diary*, 155, 162; Frothingham, 221–23. Jury: one was not a householder; many lacked estate or credit; several were "strangers," one, "a bitter enemy," coming from the far side of Connecticut, two hundred miles from Charlestown, W. H. Whitemore, ed., *The Andros Tracts,* 1 (Boston: Prince Society, 1888), 112.

[10]   Deposition 14 January 1690, about events of 1687–88, Frothingham, 219–220.

Another act of "petty tyranny" was specifically minuted in the otherwise sparse selectmen's records on 15 May 1688. "Mr. Bantam, his Majesty's gunner of the port or block house at Boston, did on the 9th day of this month carry away the great guns from the battery in this town . . . with a quantity of shot appertaining to them." This ordnance was Charlestown property. It was taken without prior warning or town permission. Peremptory force had replaced consultation and consent. [11]

However, these individual shows of executive potency were symptomatic of a more seismic shift resulting from the revocation of all colonial safeguards, titles and freedoms. People in Massachusetts, said Samuel Nowell, were "no better than slaves." Moderate Lawrence Hammond commented on this new world of prerogative and power to the privacy of his diary:

> These changes befell us: great and manifold oppressions by fines, imprisonments, illegal and arbitrary prosecutions . . . excessive charges in all lawsuits . . . claiming in the name of the King all our lands, especially such lands as were not under personal or particular improvements and the same . . . given to such [Andros cronies] who would . . . pay yearly acknowledgments [quitrents] and the large fees stated . . . Men were made offenders for a word &c.[12]

Among the "arbitrary prosecutions" Hammond bemoaned, those most oppressive to the merchants, shippers and seafarers of Charlestown were in the new Admiralty Courts. Unlike the pre-Dominion hearings of alleged breaches of the complex regulations of the Navigation Acts, these prosecutions were no longer decided by juries (which almost invariably acquitted their fellow colonists). Edward Randolph, as Collector of Customs, had torn his hair in frustration at the blatant partisanship of admiralty verdicts in the early 1680s. No more! The kind of interloping and smuggling committed by Captain Thomas Jenner was effectively eradicated by the new prerogative courts. After three decades of evasion, deceit, and culpable negligence, the Acts of Trade were effectively enforced.[13]

For Randolph and for Andros's henchmen, "a group of abject persons fetched from New York," like the bloodsucking John West, Secretary and Registrar of the Dominion, the maxim of a Renaissance cleric applied:

---

[11] CTR, 4: 88.

[12] Nowell: Petition to James II, 2 July 1688, 4MHSC, 8 (1868), 700–1; Hammond, Diary, 149–50.

[13] Hall, *Randolph*, 9–10, 19–21, 57, 101–2; Barnes, *Dominion*, 169.

"The good Lord has given us the Papacy, *let us now enjoy it!*" Dominion offices, like prerogative appointments throughout England and its nascent empire, were "offices of profit." West paid Randolph £150 per year for his dual appointment, and according to Randolph, made £300 to £400 per year out of fees alone, not to mention bribes.[14]

A petition by Charlestown shipwright Samuel Ballatt (1637–1708) reveals the exorbitance of charges. Ballatt had invested a considerable amount of capital in the construction of Charlestown's dry dock in 1679. His fees for confirming his joint ownership in this and other real estate were over £50, a small fortune. Similarly, Mr. James Russell had to pay three pence per acre for a new royal patent for Long Island, Casco Bay, Maine. If he refused, it would be granted to collaborator John Usher, Treasurer of the Dominion and brother-in-law of Charles Lidgett. The diarist Samuel Sewall left a vivid account of his angst when a writ of intrusion was served on him; this would have been Russell's fate if he had not stumped up.[15]

These opportunities for bureaucratic plunder arose because all titles to land were deemed to be revoked by the loss of the 1629 Charter. Where freeholds represented most of the wealth of all families and the capital springboard for the rising generation, loss of ownership was a terrifying threat. After the fall of the Andros regime, Joseph Lynde, a considerable landowner born and bred in Charlestown, recounted an interview with the new governor in 1687. Sir Edmund inquired of Lynde:

> What title he had to his lands, who showed him many deeds
> . . . and particularly for land that . . . would quickly be given
> [taken] away from him if he did not obtain a [new] patent for
> it . . . He further inquired how the title was derived and said
> Lynde told him [part by purchase, part as marriage portion,
> part as inheritance from his father, town grants and purchase
> from natives]. And, he said, my title was nothing worth if that
> were all. At another time after showing him an Indian deed
> for land, he said, their hand was no more worth than a scratch
> with a bear's paw, undervaluing all my titles, though every
> way legal under our former charter government. I then peti-
> tioned for a patent of my whole estate, but Mr. West, deputy
> secretary, told me I must have so many patents as there were

---

[14]   Hall, *Randolph*, 109; West: Hall, Leder and Kammen, 32.

[15]   Ballatt: Mass Archives, 12 June 1679, MxCC D&O, 4: folio 89, Frothingham 220; Russell, ibid., 219; a Writ of Intrusion was later served in 1688. Sewall: *Diary*, 172. It was computed that at the rates charged, "all the money in the country would not suffice to patent the lands therein contained." Hall, Leder and Kammen, 35–36.

counties that I had parcels of land in, if not towns. Finding
the thing so chargeable and difficult, I delayed, upon which
I had a writ of intrusion served on me in the beginning of
the summer 1688 . . . for some land . . . possessed, enclosed
and improved for about fifty years. [Reluctantly, Lynde then
resorted to bribery. He gave the Attorney General £3, with
a promise of £10 more, for a new land patent for 49 acres of
land in Charlestown that would otherwise have been given
to a Quaker ally of Andros]. The attorney general asked said
Lynde what he would do about the rest of his land, telling him
the said Lynde that he would meet with the like trouble about
all the rest of his lands that he possessed, and were it not for
the governor going to New York at this time, there would be a
writ of intrusion against every man in the colony of any considerable estate, or as many [writs] as a cart could hold . . . [16]

As well as these threatened grabs of family lands, Charlestown was
also in danger of losing its treasured Stinted Common, so recently assigned to individual proprietors as their personal holdings. Royalist merchant and officer of the Dominion Colonel Charles Lidgett owned the Ten
Hills estate adjoining the common. In 1687 he petitioned the governor
for a grant of the common. Although the "particular proprietors" protested against the expropriation of their new freeholds, on 1 August 1687
Lynde lost "about seven acres in the same common field or pasture [that]
the governor gave unto Mr. Charles Lidgett [as did] divers of my neighbours . . . " Lidgett had already acquired "waste lands" belonging to the
town, but the 1,760 acres of pasture would give him extortionate control
over Charlestown's grazing needs. When the former owners pulled up surveyors' stakes and continued to cut wood, Lidgett prosecuted them for
trespass, and elicited a writ of intrusion against Russell and Lynde in early
summer 1688. James Russell had to buy a new patent for a threatened
twenty acres that had been in his family for fifty years. Charlestown inhabitants presented a remonstrance against these outrages, claiming that
the town had been damaged to the tune of £20 by legal fees alone. Nonetheless, the Court granted Lidgett the land without a hearing, prompting
the comment "Oh wonderful justice!" For their effrontery, some of the
remonstrants were imprisoned. Perhaps Paul Wilson now saw the irony
of his threat, in the recent town struggle over the division of the Stinted

---

[16]   Frothingham, 219; Hall, Leder, and Kammen, 33–34. On the Dominion land system, see
Barnes, *Dominion*, Ch. 8. A pamphleteer described highwaymen as "honest robbers" compared
to fee-charging lawyers, ibid., 111.

Common, to go to England and appeal directly to "Good King James" to save the interest in Charlestown's common land for all townspeople.[17]

GLORIOUS REVOLUTION

By the spring of 1689, the angry, autocratic Andros and his voracious cronies had succeeded where Puritan prayer and negotiation had previously failed. Charlestown, like the vast majority of Massachusetts, had been united. On 18 April, after rumors of a successful Protestant invasion of England, and dawn reports in Boston of disturbances in Charlestown, moderate and sometime collaborator Captain Richard Sprague led Charlestown's B Company across the Charles to join the quickly commandeered spontaneous mass uprising. One of the first arrests was of Lidgett. Hundreds of supporters of the "Glorious Revolution" descended on Charlestown "out of the country." Unable to board the ferry, there they had to stay. Their presence helped induce Andros and his clique, holed up in the Castle just off the Boston shoreline, to surrender.[18]

Three Charlestown grandees, James Russell, Richard Sprague and John Phillips, were quickly coopted to the Revolutionary Council for Safety, which took over temporary control of Massachusetts until the wishes of the new monarchs William and Mary were known. John Call and John Fowle were among the 66 representatives from 44 towns who attended a meeting in Boston on 9 May that recommended that the last elected governor, deputy governor, and assistants should resume the offices taken away in May 1686. The more cautious Council proposed that the towns should elect representatives to express their wishes at a meeting on 22 May 1689. Call and Fowle, possibly chosen by an enlarged electorate based on property, returned on that date with a unanimous expression of Charlestown's wishes. Rejoicing in God's blessing of William of Orange's invasion of England, they desired the continuation of the Council for Safety, and recommended its settlement of the militia to maintain order, "until it shall please God, in his abundant mercy towards us, to settle us under such a government as shall be ... correspondent with the wisdom of the government of England." Charlestown's Declaration, unlike other towns', made no mention of regular colony

---

[17]   Frothingham, 217–19; Sewall, *Diary,* 146–47,16 August 1687; *Andros Tracts,* 1: 97–98, 153–54; Russell: ibid, 3: 97–98. Wilson: see above, "Common Rights." For a similar land grab in neighboring Cambridge, see Hall, Leder and Kammen, 29–30.

[18]   On the revolution in Britain: Steve Pincus, *1688: The First Modern Revolution* (New Haven: Yale University Press, 2009). Richard R. Johnson, *Adjustment to Empire* (Leicester: Leicester University Press, 1981), 89; Barnes, *Dominion,* 237–40; *Andros Tracts,* 1: 77–79.

assemblies of town representatives, or of a restoration of traditional town government. This moderate preference for remaining on a temporary revolutionary footing until the royal will was known was signed on behalf of the town by Lawrence Hammond, Jacob Green, and John Cutler, Sr.[19]

On 24 May 1689, however, Charlestown's moderation was overruled by a large majority of representatives from more populist rural areas who favored reinstating the Council of 1686 elected under the 1629 Charter. The moderates did succeed in adding a rider to this policy: "They do not intend an Assumption of [1629] Charter Government," but only an interim administration until direction arrived from England. While many representatives hankered after a unilateral resumption of the old constitution, the moderates tried to convince them that such a restoration should depend on the grant of the monarch, whose predecessor had engineered its revocation. Since William and Mary had promised restoration of revoked English charters, patience in Massachusetts might well be rewarded. Such arguments were only partially successful. On 7 June 1689, the representatives, calling themselves "The Convention" and "pressured from below," strong-armed the Council "by virtue of the authority devolved on you by us the representatives . . . to accept government according to our [1629] charter rules . . . until further orders from England." The government of the colony, according to this Declaration, derived from the people.[20]

DIVISIONS

Not only did Massachusetts people "rise [on 18 April 1689] as one man," in Lawrence Hammond's words, but their unanimity ensured a bloodless revolution. Yet however righteous their cause, unity in tearing off a

---

[19] Frothingham, 223–24. Three anonymous broadsides written between 10 and 24 May 1689 about the best way forward were published by R. C. Simmons, "Massachusetts Revolution of 1689," *Journal of American Studies*, 2 (1968), 2–12. Ensign John Call (1635–97), a baker, son of Thomas, selectman 1681–87, had been one of the managers of the Stinted Common; he had fought as a lieutenant in King Philip's War (Bodge, 286), and would command the Middlesex Regiment in Quebec in 1690. W. K. Watkins, *Soldiers in the Expedition to Canada in 1690* (Boston: privately printed, 1898), 27. John Fowle (1637–1711), a tanner, son of George, was town constable in 1689 and later militia captain. On Hammond and Cutler, see below. Green (1625–1701) son of the ruling elder, was a wealthy merchant, selectman 1668–72, deputy 1676–78. Franchise: Johnson, *Adjustment,* 102 and footnote 75. Other towns: Lynn, Salisbury, Woburn in R. E. Moody & R. C. Simmons, eds., *The Glorious Revolution in Massachusetts* (Boston: CSMP, 1988). 361, 362, 370.

[20] 42 towns favored resumption. Frothingham, 224; Johnson, *Adjustment,* 106–7, 119. English charters: Lovejoy, 279; in fact, as early as 26 February 1689, an Order in Council had been issued for a new charter for Massachusetts, Hall, *Randolph,* 124. Council proceedings: Moody and Simmons, 82–83, 90–91; for arguments in favor of continuing the Council for Safety, ibid., 359–60.

bunch of bloated leeches could not long disguise a major fault line in the colony, and especially in Charlestown. Added to prior divides between diehard Charter defenders and moderate compromisers was the inevitable suspicion of post-revolutionary resisters against collaborators. Compared to the terrors of other regime changes in history, the reaction of the Massachusetts resisters was remarkably mild. Randolph might write from "the common gaol, New Algiers," but his letters went out, and so, eventually, did he and his Dominion colleagues, shipped off to England in February 1690.[21]

Disagreement was signaled by defeat of the Charlestown proposal to retain the Council for Safety as an obviously interim stand-in, and further underlined on the following day. Richard Sprague and twelve other notables who had served the Dominion in military or civil capacities reminded the Council of the promises made when Andros surrendered to the rebels that none of his Massachusetts officials would be victimized. That reassurance was needed by some of the richest men in the colony suggests that "dissatisfactions . . . disputatiousness or arguments" were threatening "good treatment" and "public tranquillity." To these men, who thought of themselves as the natural and permanent ruling class, the reminder was a warning against the pretensions of "the rabble spirited by the faction."[22]

Charlestown did not have long to wait for this divisiveness to affect town affairs. On 17 June 1689, the town held its first traditional town meeting since 1686. Officials were elected to hold office until the usual election day in March 1690. There must have been some opposition to this gathering, because two days later the selectmen ordered inscription in the town book of the Convention's declaration authorizing town elections and empowering elected town officials. We shall see that one of the elected constables objected to serving, but the antipathy went further than the personal. Some moderates or collaborators in the town, calling themselves "divers thinking men," rejected resumption of 1629 charter powers without royal permission. They regarded elections as invalid. Appointments made by James II or his officials, to which oaths had been sworn, should remain in force until replaced or confirmed by the new monarchs. Prerogative trumped popular consent.[23]

Confrontation burst into the open on 2 July 1689. A special parade at 8 a.m. was requested by over forty militiamen of Charlestown's First

---

[21] Hammond, Diary, 150; Randolph: Hall, Leder, and Kammen, 63.

[22] Moody and Simmons, 84, 88, 98; Johnson, *Adjustment*, 172.

[23] CTR, 4: 92. Moody and Simmons, 359–60; Frothingham, 224.

Company. Two weeks previously, the (restored 1686) Council had ordered that surviving military officers in post in 1686 should continue, unless they were deemed unsuitable because of age, removal elsewhere or "other just exception against them (to be judged of by the government)." Vacancies could be filled by elected nominees approved by the Council. At the parade, the commanding officer, Captain Lawrence Hammond, appeared and asked what the soldiers wanted. They replied that "the Act or Order of the Council would inform him." Since the captain was only fifty years old, and still lived in the town, some of them plainly took "just exception against" him. After a very tense standoff, a militiaman asked: "If he were to continue as captain, by what commission would he hold his place, whether by Sir Edmund's or his former commission received before 1686?" The captain replied that he "came not there to answer their impertinent questions." Only vacancies could be replaced. The reply was that they "would not be debarred of their liberty." At this, Hammond, who must have got wind of the mood, announced he "would have no hand" in illegal elections. He handed a letter of resignation to his ensign, John Call, and left the field. His letter spoke movingly of the company's mutual love and affection during the twenty years he had led them. "But now observing a discontented, factious, censorious, unreasonable and mutinous spirit to spread among us, and the old peaceable, rulable, genuine spirit to languish . . . I do hereby declare myself to be free and discharged from that place and office." He signed himself "Your true friend, lover and fellow in arms, L. Hammond."[24]

Some sympathetic militiamen followed Hammond off the training ground, but the majority of the forty-two on parade went ahead with nominating replacements: former Lieutenant John Phillips as captain, John Call as lieutenant, and Samuel Kettle as ensign. The next day the Convention confirmed them. A week later, however, Hammond supporters, claiming two-thirds support, nominated an alternative list: Hammond as captain, Nathaniel Dowse for lieutenant, and Nathaniel Rand as ensign. The representatives in convention refused to accept these nominations, but on 4 July 1689 reaffirmed those in commissions on 12 May 1686. Hammond was therefore back in command, but any idea that he served under a royal commission through Andros had been firmly scotched.[25]

---

[24] Moody and Simmons, 97, 99–100, 14 June 1689; Frothingham, 225–26. Normally, "careful culture of a deferential relationship between officers and men was not only a military courtesy, but a social imperative." R. P. Gildrie, *The Profane, the Civil, and the Godly* (University Park: Pennsylvania State University Press, 1994), 123–27.

[25] Ibid.; T. H. Breen, *Puritans and Adventurers* (New York: Oxford University Press, 1980), 97–98; Moody & Simmons, 118, 132–33; Phillips had just been appointed commander-in-chief of

This saga encapsulates the issues dividing both Charlestown and the colony. The soldier's question about Hammond's commission was highly pertinent. Hammond had been a collaborator; he had accepted Andros's commission as militia captain, unlike Samuel Sewall, who had resigned. If Hammond continued to command as holder of the king's commission, rather than as the train band's 1668 nominee confirmed by the General Court, then the critical militiamen and likewise, perhaps, the Convention, justly objected against him. The liberty the soldiers demanded represented that spirit of consultation and consent that was the polar opposite to royal prerogative and rule from above. Hammond highlighted a kind of parent-child relationship based on love and obedience. To him, the questioners were nothing but factious and mutinous. His letter of resignation is reminiscent of his description of the supporters of Rev. Daniel Russell against his favorite Thomas Shepard III. They had been "too undeliberate, over-hasty, and precipitate in their motives." They had refused to hearken to their betters.[26]

LEGITIMACY

To the critical militiamen, Hammond was a Stuart stooge. Their replacement, John Phillips, had been a bitter opponent of the Dominion. He was

---

the Lower Middlesex Regiment with the rank of major, ibid., 111, 120–21. Call: see above in this chapter. Kettle (1642–94), son of selectman and ensign Richard Kettle (1614–80), a potter and former militia drummer, was Call's brother-in-law. He had a black servant, Reuben. He served as trial juror in 1676 and 1680, constable in 1682, and selectman in 1687 and 1692. He was entrusted with the guardianship of two young wards in the 1680s, MxCC RB, 4: 74, 212, and was nominated for a deaconship in 1694 but died before taking office. Hunnewell, ix. On the Rand family, see "Widows." Nathaniel (1636–96), a woodworker, was a militia sergeant and had served in King Philip's War. He had amassed a £556 fortune by his death, £490 of it real estate. His house and adjacent grounds were valued at a substantial £120. He had served as a trial juror in 1675, 1680, and 1682, and often did fencing repairs for the town. He had a Native American woman as a servant in 1684, MxCC D&O, 4: folio 107. He was elected selectman between 1680 and 1683, and 1689 and 1691. Nathaniel Dowse (1658–1719) was a glazier. He too had served in King Philip's War. His father Lawrence (ca. 1615–92), three times selectman in the 1670s, had married Nathaniel Rand's elder sister Margery ca. 1645 as his second wife. Young Dowse would have to wait until his father died before assuming town office; in 1696 he was elected town clerk, and six years later treasurer. Why so young a man should have been nominated as lieutenant is a mystery. He may have distinguished himself in the war; he may have been a protégé of Hammond. He was related by marriage to Samuel Allen, briefly royal governor of New Hampshire, 1698–99. Allen's widow Elizabeth (Dowse) lived in land occupied by Nathaniel. M. E. Hollick, "English Origins of Elizabeth Dowse," R, 162 (2008), 164–73; W. B. H. Dowse, *Lawrence Dowse* (Boston: privately printed, 1926). Both Rand and Dowse signed the 22 November 1690 opposition Address to their Dread Sovereign from the gentlemen and merchants of Boston and Charlestown; see below.

[26] The Convention may have accepted the new list because of resignations. See above, "Succession Crisis."

an early member of the Council for Safety and a recruiter assistant in the reseated charter council. Their assertion of "liberty" reflected the rising demand for broadening and secularizing the franchise and for "the voice of the people" to be heard. As a pamphleteer put it, the popular uprising which started and sustained the Glorious Revolution demonstrated that "the Sword [lay] in every man's hands." Despite his eventual and compromised reinstatement, Captain Lawrence Hammond's authority had suffered; witness his unavailing attempts to impress men for the French and Indian War in late August 1689. His "children" had grown up.[27]

Meanwhile, another member of "the better sort" found himself cut down to size. At the 17 June 1689 town meeting, one of the elected constables was Mr. Samuel Phipps, M.A. (1651–1725). He ran a school in the town and had been registrar of Middlesex deeds. He had served as town treasurer in 1686, selectman in 1687 and town clerk in 1688. His brother Joseph had caused a riot by refusing hat honor at an Anglican funeral, and his brother-in-law, Constable Timothy Phillips, had had a bruising confrontation with the captain of HMS *Kingfisher* in May 1687. Samuel had subsequently engineered the felling of the first offensive maypole. The Phippses were a leading town family; Samuel's father Solomon (1619–71), a successful carpenter, had been a busy town and county official.[28]

Mr. Phipps was outraged that as "a person so qualified and improved" as he should demean himself as a gatherer of taxes and chaser of drunks. He appealed to the Council, who sympathized, and told Charlestown to pick someone more menial. On 13 August 1689 a special town meeting was called to respond to the government. They adamantly rejected the Council's order. They presented a series of arguments, precedents, corrections, necessities, and laws. Their long and cogent petition had two major political and social assertions. The first concerned equality:

> We judge it unreasonable and neighbouring upon oppression to impose all burdensome, unprofitable and difficult offices upon men of the lower rank in the town; while others, who are, or would be esteemed, some of the first in the town, shall bear no burden, when no law or just reason can excuse them.

The second affirmed a preference for freely elected over appointed office:

---

[27] Phillips: Moody and Simmons, 54, 393; Sewall, *Diary*, 114. Hammond had also been appointed Clerk of the Dominion Middlesex Court, Frothingham, 224. Franchise: Moody & Simmons, 95; Lovejoy, 280; Breen, 94, 95–96, 236.

[28] Wyman, 749; Frothingham, 177, 179.

> We cannot yet believe that the honoured Convention . . . will
> debar us of our just liberties allowed us by law, especially
> when arbitrary government hath been so lately condemned,
> and do hope . . . our adhering to our first choice [is seen as] an
> innocent pleading and maintaining our said liberties.

To people of Phipps's assumed superiority, the ideas propounded by "the inhabitants of Charlestown," especially about liberty and equality of civic obligations, were irritatingly undeferential. Taken with the crew opposing privatization of the Stinted Common and felling of owners' timber, the plebeian lead in the rising against the Dominion, their riotous insistence on the continued imprisonment of its officials, and the recent mutiny of the militiamen, it appeared that "not knowing one's place" threatened the very structure of town society. Certainly, townspeople were in a very different mood than when they had obediently accepted the elite's "Declaration" opposing readoption of the 1629 charter government back in May 1689. Sir Edmund Andros may have been right when he cursed James II's Massachusetts subjects as "a factious rabble."[29]

Despite James II's flight across the Channel to France at Christmastime 1688, no official word had reached Massachusetts about the new government's intentions by the fall of 1689. Would William and Mary restore the old 1629 Charter? Would they condemn colonists who had rebelled against a royal government? Would they regard members of interim authorities as overreaching usurpers? Massachusetts waited in a political vacuum, increasingly desperate for directions and a sense of constitutional authenticity. Alas, William and Mary had far more pressing business, with negotiating a far-reaching constitutional settlement in Britain, James's threatening invasion of Catholic Ireland, and war against the might of France.[30]

Meanwhile, the "legal/illegal" Convention felt that they had to maintain law and order (as with town government and militia commissions) and to levy taxes to pay for defense against French and Indian attacks. On 4 July 1689, the Convention had ordered that court sittings should be resumed. Charlestown old-charter magistrate James Russell accordingly set a session of the Middlesex County Court for early October. On 21 September, he received a letter sent to all members of the bench from his neighbor Thomas

---

[29] Frothingham, 221. The town petition was also scathing with regard to Phipps's previous "pretence of applying himself to the ministry" to escape constable's office, and his "instructing one or two youths in a private way in his house" as sufficient exemption. Public education had all but collapsed under the Dominion because of shortage of funds. Barnes, *Dominion*, 131.

[30] Moody and Simmons, 9–10; Lovejoy, 279; R. C. Simmons, "Massachusetts Charter of 1691," in H. C. Allen and R. Thompson, eds., *Contrast and Connection* (London: Bell, 1976), 71.

Graves, Esq., who termed himself "Judge of their Majesties' inferior Court of Pleas, and one of their Majesties' Justices of the Peace within the County of Middlesex." Graves had been a commissioner for small causes in 1677, 1684 and 1685, but had never sat on the County Court bench under the 1629 Charter. He had been appointed a judge by Andros and assumed that his position could not be "legally vacated or superseded" until royal instructions arrived. He therefore perceived James Russell and fellow judges as "pretended magistrates" of a "pretended court of judicature not having any authority from our Sovereign Lord and Lady . . . Therefore I must, on their Majesties' behalf, warn you that you presume not to assemble at Cambridge."[31]

It rapidly emerged that Graves spoke for a group of Charlestown grandees who had similar views and similar appointments. Captain Lawrence Hammond was a Dominion company commander; his opposite number as Dominion commanding officer of B Company, Captain Richard Sprague, was Charlestown's elected deputy to the Convention meeting of 5 June 1689. Other members were Andros-commissioned lieutenant John Cutler Sr. and his son John Jr., a leading voice against the generality in the Stinted Commons conflict. This group of sometime moderates displayed what were already in England being called "Tantivy" or anti-populist "Tory" tendencies.[32]

---

[31] Taxes: Treasurer Phillips was ordered by the Council of 6 September 1689 "to give forth his warrants." However, according to Randolph "The people deny their power to raise money." Moody and Simmons, 156; Hall, Leder, and Kammen, 65. Graves letter: Frothingham, 229.

[32] Johnson, *Adjustment,* 186, 208, 280–88. "Tantivy": see *The Humble Address of the Publicans of New England* (London: 1691), 15 and *OED.* The most sophisticated early spokesman of New England Toryism was Gershom Bulkeley (ca. 1636–1713), authoritarian son of the authoritarian Rev. Peter Bulkeley of Concord, Massachusetts. He was a year ahead of Thomas Graves at Harvard (1655) and was similarly a fellow and tutor. After 16 years as a minister in Connecticut and brave service in King Philip's War, he, again like Graves, took up medicine. Based at Hartford, he practiced the new "scientific" approach throughout the Connecticut Valley. When the colony was annexed to the Dominion in October 1687, Bulkeley was appointed as a justice of the peace, yet again like Graves. The Glorious Revolution in Connecticut was commandeered by land speculator "Black James" Fitch, and charter government was unilaterally resumed. Outraged by this "great land pirate . . . this acquisitive and assertive yankee," Bulkeley resorted to political polemics in defence of "principled royalism" against demagogic mob rule. *The People's Right to Election* (1689) depicted resumption of the royally vacated charter as "Illegal, needless, unprofitable, very criminal, dangerous and hurtful to us . . . lawless usurpation and tyranny . . . rebellion and treason." Such sentiments drew sympathetic response from Graves in his *Letter from a Friend in the Bay to Mr. Gershom Bulkeley,* which attacked the "Faction's" malicious fearmongering to provoke "the fury of the mobile" and likened Andros's arrest to Brutus's betrayal of Caesar. Bulkeley's Tory manifesto *Will and Doom* (which could be paraphrased as "Might is Right") followed in 1692. He traced "the root of all bitterness" to "the churlish drug of levelling" in the 1640s, and "the unhappy rebellion in England against the noble prince" Charles I by "the faction and fag-end Commons and the Oliverian republic that [did] animate the mobile." He was scathing about the cynical manipulation of the "silly . . . deceived . . . rustical . . . deluded people" by New England rabble-rousers and the reign of terror against opponents obedient to the

This grandiose challenge to the authority of the Convention and to magistrates Russell and Phillips created a sense of shock in the town. Two days later, on 23 September 1689, a special town meeting witnessed heated claims that produced a vote to send a formal complaint about the five colleagues' "seditious writing" and "misdemeanours" at the meeting. Next day Graves and company were summoned before the Council. Despite being upbraided by Governor Bradstreet, Graves reiterated his position that as an officer of the crown, he could not recognize governor or council or convention as lawful authority until "they have commission from their sacred Majesties."[33]

Graves, Hammond, and the Cutlers, suspected of sedition, were required to enter £100 bonds. Refusing to be bound to appear at the County Court or to go to Cambridge jail, they were eventually placed under house arrest. Sprague was still a deputy. However, when the Convention met on 4 October 1689, they immediately moved to exclude him because of "his contemptuous carriage against this government." He was representative of "the many ill-willers to the peace of this colony who walk at large." Four days later he, Hammond, and Cutler were dismissed for the same reason "from their several military offices." The effect of these draconian measures was electric. Charlestown became "the most ill-affected, distracted and divided town in the country" as some supported the detainees. These supporters came from both Charlestown "and several towns thereabouts."[34]

Who these people were is revealed by the twelve signatories of a letter from "Inhabitants in Charlestown" sent to William III in the fall of 1689.

---

crown and the constitution. Bulkeley and his colleagues were smeared as "Jacobites (supporters of James II) and Papists." "They dress us in bears' skins . . . and sport themselves in baiting us." "We are sheep for the slaughter before absolute [popular] power." Bulkeley's philosophy entailed belief in divine approbation of kingship, veneration of the royal prerogative, obedience to the patriarchal monarch's commands, and return to social order through deference to the better sort. Without dutiful acceptance of authority, the "mobile" was prey either to anarchy or the tyranny of demagogues. "To sit still and be quiet," passive obedience and non-resistance, must be the patient response to disagreeable royal edicts. The alternative was "slavery . . . routs and riots, folly and error." *People's Right: Andros Tracts*, 2: 84–100; *Will and Doom*: A. Heimert and A. Delbanco, eds., *Puritanism in America* (Cambridge, Mass.: Harvard University Press, 1985), 351–58. Bulkeley: T. W. Jodziewicz, *ANB*; Fitch: B. P. Stark, ibid; J. M. Poteet, "More Yankee than Puritan," *R*, 133 (1979), 102–107. On early Toryism, recent contributions include G. Burgess, "Royalism and Liberty of Conscience," in J. Morrow and J. Scott, eds., *Liberty, Authority, Formality: Essays in Honour of Colin Davis* (Exeter: Academic Imprint, 2008), 11–28; W. Lamont, "Authority and Liberty: Hobbes and the Sects," ibid., 28–44.

[33] Frothingham, 229–30.

[34] Moody and Simmons, 165, has a Council order for 16 October indicating that Hammond, Sprague and Cutler had just lost their commissions; 159, 161. By 8 November Joseph Lynde had been confirmed as captain, Samuel Hayman as lieutenant, and Timothy Phillips as ensign, ibid., 171. Randolph's comment on division: Hall, Leder & Kammen, 65.

The letter lamented "the great disorder and confusion" caused "by rash and inconsiderate [ill-considered] actions and designs of a disaffected prevailing party amongst us." A curious rewriting of spring events followed:

> Upon strange and groundless pretences [this rash majority] did in April seize and imprison the governor . . . and other principal officers . . . and thereby wholly subvert and overthrow the government established by your Majesty's predecessor . . . and setting up and placing instead thereof several scenes and representations of government and jurisdiction. [Critics, like Graves and company, suffered] great hardships and inconvenience for maintaining and asserting your Majesty's right and sovereignty here (which by many is too much disregarded) and refusing to comply with their exorbitant, irregular and arbitrary actings and proceedings. [Despite] our considerable damage, [our] hearts [remain] full of duty and loyalty to your Majesty.

They therefore "humbly implored" the King "to settle such form and method of government" in the colony, to "heal our breaches and compose our disorders."[35]

Richard Sprague, a signatory, had apparently forgotten that he had led Charlestown's B Company across the ferry to add its firepower to the April uprising, and that he had quickly joined the Council for Safety and accepted the Convention on 29 May. John Cutler Jr. and Thomas Graves (first signer and probable author) were two other predictable Charlestown names. Less expected signatories were three ringleaders in the battle against dividing the Stinted Common in 1686. They may have anticipated restitution of commons rights to all under the new monarchs. Two petitioners from neighboring towns had rather sullied backgrounds, as did Jerathmeel Bowers. John Jackson had been a Cambridge selectman, but two others have left little trace.[36]

---

[35] Frothingham 230–31; Moody and Simmons, 400–02; I prefer the former's dating of this letter to the fall of 1689, rather than the latter's January 1690; the letter seems to predate the royal declaration, which arrived in early December.

[36] Dr. Richard Hooper (died 1690), a former ship's surgeon, had arrived in Cambridge, having briefly perched in Newbury, Hampton, and Woburn; in 1685 he had been found out trying to cheat a youth in a horse sale, Thompson, *Cambridge Cameos,* 295–97. Timothy Hawkins, aged about fifty, came from Watertown; he and his father both had drinking problems, Thompson, *Divided,* 159. Thomas Welch Jr. (1655–1700/03), a stonecutter, Samuel Whittemore (1647–1728), a wheelwright, and William Richardson had all vigorously opposed privatizing the Stinted Common, and had taken wood from it; see above, "Common Rights." It is ironic that fellow signatory

This address to the Crown by a town group at odds with the majority would have exacerbated the delicate task of the colonial agents in London who were seeking restoration of the old 1629 Charter. It advertised colonial division and gave heart to English imperial officials bent on asserting royal control over Atlantic trade and defense. By appealing to the crown over the people, the signatories behaved "in good Tory fashion." Graves and company bridled at the prospect of decisions based on popular or demagogic whims rather than the experienced judgment of the better sort.[37]

The "Charter Party" supporting the temporary government and hoping for its permanence quickly responded to "these scurvy flashes and reflections," the expected sabotage of former collaborators who had "laboured under infamy." Their "Vindication" disparaged most of Graves's colleagues as "a lewd, sorry, shabby and obscure crew," including "scum [of] Watertown and Cambridge." They assumed "Bowers" was the Quaker Benanuel, "one of Sir Edmund's setters [who] begged of him his neighbors' lands," especially parcels of the Stinted Common. Jackson had a Dominion commission as a captain, and other signers had deserted the New England Way for the newly imported Church of England. Was this the best Graves, Sprague, and Cutler could come up with?[38]

Along with vindication and appeal went counter-attack. The Middlesex County Court convicted John Cutler Jr. (who had fancied himself a legal authority in the Battle of the Stinted Common) of seditious libel for de-

---

John Cutler, Jr. had been their bitter opponent in the confrontation over commons timber. Jerathmeel Bowers (1650–1721) had lived with an abusive stepfather in Cambridge; his stepbrother Benanuel was a troublesome Quaker who lived in Charlestown on the Cambridge line. Jerathmeel had taken part in a riot at Harvard in 1670 and been flogged as a disobedient servant. He was initially warned out of Chelmsford, but seems to have settled there later, *Cambridge Cameos*, 64, 174–75. John Jackson (1645–1709) of Cambridge was selectman in 1675, *Cambridge Cameos*, 183–88. Of Andrew Mitchell, in Charlestown 1688–95, and John Robinson, little is known.

[37] Lovejoy, 324, 344.

[38] Frothingham, 232. Charlestown's minister, Charles Morton, still smarting from his treatment under Andros's "late usurping government," also entered the fray in the fall of 1689. His *Appeal to the Men of New England* was bitingly dismissive of Graves and company as "abettors of treason . . . a late gang of money-catchers . . . ridiculous blades of Charlestown." His numerous sallies were all phrased as questions: "Whether it be not the special privilege of Charlestown church and town to be furnished with deacons and captains which publish Remonstrances against the present government, and berogue the deserving gentlemen in whose hands it is? And whether those fellows (to retort the phrase upon them they so saucily use to the gentlemen in authority) could propose anything by their late mutinies and factions than by putting the country into flame? Whether those men who now show themselves violent against our return in any sort to our charters, are not therein declared enemies to the glorious designs of the greatest prince of the world? Whether it would not be a fine spot of work, when we have given to Sir Edmund Andros and his creatures the affront of dismissing them from the government, and we every hour look for a confirmation and approbation from England of what we have done, yet to restore them to their former places?" *Andros Tracts*, 3: 189–208.

claring the court "pretended." He was fined the huge sum of £20. His ally Captain Lawrence Hammond had also incurred official wrath by withholding county records because he believed the temporary regime unauthorized. The tense antagonism of the latter months of 1689 was somewhat relieved in early December, when word at last arrived from the crown confirming the current regime until permanent arrangements were concluded.[39]

Royal affirmation produced two rapid if ambiguous expiations "for the faults you judge we have committed." Hammond and Lt. John Cutler Sr. explicitly cited His Majesty's empowerment of the interim government as cause that they "cheerfully submit." They referred to the prior months as the "vacancy . . . of authority," and requested release from three months' house arrest and withdrawal of "further prosecution." They blamed their unpopular reputations "on this hour [time] and hurry of temptation and distraction" and pledged "the promoting the weal and prosperity of our country both in Church and State."[40]

The conciliatory promises of these two did not prevent eight of their fellow townsmen from putting their names to an address to William III on 25 January 1690, the day after the Convention had reassumed the 1629 title of the "General Court." They bemoaned the "very broken and unsteady posture" of Massachusetts and Maine as a result of "eruptions." They actually requested royal commissioners to "view the state of this poor land," and humbly implored a continuation of a Dominion-style governor-general over "these little provinces," with an assembly chosen not by church members alone, but by "freeholders and inhabitants." Along with usual suspects Sprague and Graves, two signers were John Cutler (who may have been the son) and his younger brother Timothy (1653–94), like his father a blacksmith, who had served as an ensign in King Philip's War. Other town signatories were Nathaniel Dowse and Nathaniel Rand, lieutenant and ensign under Hammond in 1689, gunsmith Daniel Smith (1641–1707), Jerathmeel Bowers, and Charles Lidgett of Ten Hills. The preference for combining colonies probably derived from fears about defense against Indians by land and French pirates and privateers by sea. Though the address was not seditious, it was the work of a minority (mainly mercantile) lobby whose interests were at variance with those of the majority of the General Court who had appointed colonial agents to Whitehall. It painted an unhelpful picture of the government of the colony

---

[39] Moody and Simmons, 173–78; Frothingham, 234. Richard Sprague, also charged, was acquitted.

[40] Frothingham, 234; probably written in December 1689. Cutler was a deacon of the Charlestown church.

and its competence, especially as Sir William Phips's 600-man expedition against French bases in Nova Scotia was in preparation for its departure on 22 April 1690. Three weeks after the address, the General Court did open up the Massachusetts franchise, and at least 917 non-church members attained the new property-based freemanship in March and April 1690. None of the addressers was elected to the Massachusetts Council under the new suffrage.[41]

On 11 March 1690, the General Court was meeting in Charlestown to avoid smallpox in Boston. They received a letter from Rev. Charles Morton endorsing a petition from the younger John Cutler pleading for remission of his £20 fine for sedition—"a great hole in a small estate"—in exchange for the dropping of his appeal. Morton's letter was persuasively worded. Cutler had "never joined with any petition against the present government . . . he [had] adventured far in the country's service . . . he will quietly attend his own business . . . and as to the public, he will not meddle further." It worked! Both Cutlers were (for the time being) in the clear.[42]

Meanwhile, on 3 March 1690 Charlestown had a town meeting to choose officers for the year. Elected chairman of the board of selectmen was Richard Sprague, with fellow addresser Nathaniel Rand as a colleague. Lawrence Hammond was chosen as clerk of the writs; this outstanding penman was duly confirmed by the Middlesex County Court on 11 March. Some critics of the interim Old Charter regime were not without support at home. However, other pre-Dominion fixtures were noticeably out of favor: Hammond as selectman, Graves as deputy. Sprague, of course, had been expelled from the General Court.[43]

WAR

Like the rest of New England, Charlestown was much concerned with the French and Indian threats from Maine, especially to its interests in the fish-

---

[41] Dowse and Rand may have signed as proxies for Hammond, likewise the Cutler boys for their father. On Smith, see "Whose Herbs?" above. Address: Moody & Simmons, 405–7, 409–11; the great majority of the forty-five addressers were Boston merchants. Agents: Rev. Increase Mather was already in London, as we have seen; he was joined by Elisha Cooke and Thomas Oakes, who sailed to London on 10 February 1690. Franchise: the suffrage was now to be based on payment of at least four shillings in a single rate, or real estate worth at least £6 per annum. See 1658 Tax List, "Numbers." Breen, *Puritans and Adventurers*, 94, 95–96, 236. James Russell and John Phillips both polled highly.

[42] Charlestown: Moody and Simmons, 206, 12 February 1690; letter: ibid., 222–23; Frothingham, 234–35. However, the conviction still stood.

[43] Hammond, Diary, 152. Former selectmen James Russell and John Phillips were now both assistants.

ing and timber industries and the coasting trade. As early as 6 July 1689, "a watch and ward [was ordered] to be kept up at the [Charlestown] Neck causeway to examine all Indians travelling to or from the town [and] to search their baskets or other carriage for [gun]powder, or ammunition." The strategy of the interim government was threefold: to secure New England's northeastern frontiers from raids on often isolated settlements, to capture and despoil French bases both in Nova Scotia and in Quebec, and to cooperate with other colonies through confederation. This voluntary alternative to enforced Dominion combination was what had been used before.[44]

Militiamen from Charlestown were recruited for the 400-strong frontier protection force along the Merrimack and Piscataqua Rivers, and for the two anti-French expeditions. The first, in May 1690, was led by famous wreck-hunter and future governor Sir William Phips. It captured Port Royal in Nova Scotia, took possession of the seacoast, and returned to the Charles River with French prisoners, and, far more financially important, plunder which was auctioned off to reward backers and volunteers. This success led to a far more ambitious confederated project: on 9 August 1690 over 2,000 troops sailed in a thirty-two-vessel fleet under Phipps's command for Quebec. This too was expected to be self-financing through booty, but the hope was in vain. Hammond recorded in his diary in early November 1690: "The first vessel returned from Quebec, bring[ing] news of our defeat there, all returning home, many dead and more sick of smallpox, fevers and fluxes, besides some slain by the enemy; like to be a great mortality." The "great mortality" of between 300 and 400 men, which arose from routs by French and Indians near Quebec, from terrible storms, from camp fever and disease brought back to the Bay, was only the most tangible and tragic result of this "humbling stroke." Two other reverses followed: the loss of the interim government's reputation and authority, especially in England, and, in the absence of the spoils of war, financial collapse. Its impact on Charlestown became most explosive in 1691.[45]

"The miserable and distressed condition . . . within New England" as a result of the Quebec catastrophe soon prompted another "opposi-

---

[44] Frothingham, 236; Moody and Simmons, 123–24; the Convention expressed alarm about the unusually heavy resort of Indians to both Charlestown and Boston on 6 July 1689.

[45] Hammond, Diary, 155; Thomas Hutchinson, *History of Massachusetts Bay*, ed. L. S. Mayo (Cambridge: Harvard University Press, 1936), I, 335–341; Watkins, *Soldiers in the Expedition to Canada*, 2–31; John Call captained the Middlesex Regiment; Charlestown schoolmaster John Emerson served as a chaplain. One of the vessels belonged to Andrew Belcher. Moody and Simmons, 247, 269. The Convention "hoped to recommend themselves to the king's favour and obtain the establishment of government," Hutchinson, 337.

tion" address to the king from "gentry, merchants and others . . . in Boston, Charlestown and places adjacent." The covering letter indicates that Charlestown Tories Hammond, Graves, and Sprague were leading activists in this enterprise. The signatures of Dowse, Rand, Timothy Cutler, and John Cutler Jr. appeared near the top of the sixty names; all the Charlestown names were included among the thirty-one petitioners in the published version. After the expected introduction of royalist servility, prostration, and apology, the addressers poured out their woes and frustrations: the rapine and cruelty of the French and Indians against the divided former Dominion, the Quebec disaster (launched "by those who pretend to govern . . . without your Royal Command or order") leaving Massachusetts "(as we conjecture) in further arrears of at least £50,000," Jacob Leisler's demagogic usurpation in New York (and, by implication, similar "want of government settled by Your Majesty" in Massachusetts). They concluded with humble supplication to their "DREAD SOVEREIGN" to be taken "into your immediate care and protection." [46]

In irreverent response, *The Humble Address of the Publicans of New England* satirized the grandees' Address on the grounds that it never specified which "Dread Sovereign" was intended. Since its Tantivy or Tory authors were plainly "scared out of [their] wits" by "fear of a commonwealth" and sought "to invent a perfect perpetual tyranny" like the Dominion, they might well have had James II in mind![47]

One other "outrage" in 1690 made a deep impression on Hammond. Five days after the Quebec expedition had sailed, on 14 August 1690, he recorded interim government coercion reminiscent of Andros, and potentially incriminating to his former supporters. At the departure of

---

[46] The published version of the address, printed in London, has a letter dated Charlestown, 22 November 1690, signed "L.H.": presumably Lawrence Hammond. It was in Whitehall on 9 April 1691. Moody and Simmons, 415–18; Frothingham, 232–33. A list of estates of signatories was sent to London. Apart from Sprague with £6,000 and Graves with £2,000, the other Charlestown names, Hammond £500, Cutler £500, Dowse and Rand £200, were among the financial minnows compared with Edward Shippen and Nicholas Paige, worth £12,000 each. Moody and Simmons, 480–81.

[47] Frothingham 233; *The Humble Address of the Publicans of New England*, London, 1691. The Boston Athenaeum has an original copy. R. R. Johnson, "The Humble Address . . . A Reassessment," *NEQ*, 51 (1978), 241–49, argues convincingly that the satire was written in England, probably by Morton's pupil Daniel Defoe, at the behest of Massachusetts agent Increase Mather. "Publican" referred to a tax-gatherer or tax-farmer, and by extension a despoiler of the public. The author ascribes such qualities to the opposition to the Charter government by consent. Hammond is mentioned by name, only to be derisively dismissed, 29. The "Address" is also in *Andros Tracts*, 2: 231–69. The General Court sent a more dignified response to the original Address, requesting the monarchs to restore their charter rights; however, this was not sent until 14 October 1691, Moody and Simmons, 327.

a private envoy to Governor Francis Nicholson of Virginia, previously Andros's deputy in the Dominion, "a great quantity of letters to him and others seized without a warrant, from some in Boston, were opened and read in the Council, and some kept, and so me redelivered to the messenger, and suffered to depart the next day. Some have been called to account for what they writ, and others expect the like. How congruous this is to the obtaining the Charter, they have been suing for, and how acceptable it will be to his Majesty the world may judge." Who could guess what sedition might be unearthed in opposition letters to the royalist governor of a royal colony? Who but favourites of the mob would stoop to opening gentlemen's private correspondence?[48]

During the year 1691, the "disaffected" better sort of Charlestown had individual brushes with authority, before a group revolt by the Board of Selectmen in the fall. The first confrontation involved Hammond. The submission he had made in December 1689 had not endured. Despite two General Court orders, he had still not handed over Middlesex County records in his keeping. On 4 February 1691 he was summoned before the General Court. He, "peremptorily denying to appear," was ordered to be arrested. Although the General Court records are thereafter silent about him, his diary has no more entries until May 13. In subsequent entries he refers to official institutions as "pretended." Thus, on 19 May 1691, the "pretended court in this county" convicted unlicensed liquor sellers, and the "pretended Marshall takes them under custody." On the next day: "Pretended election in Boston." It transpired that the marshal lacked the necessary written court orders, and so the two grog merchants "were advised [no doubt by Hammond or another opponent] to return home." The furious marshal Samuel Gookin returned to Charlestown and "brake open" three houses in search for the escapees. When his warrant was demanded, "he said he was the king's officer . . . he could break open any house or all the houses in the town, if he saw meet." Just as a private letter was no longer sacred, an Englishman's home was no longer his castle, or so Hammond believed.[49]

At this time, Hammond heard from Sprague about treasonable remarks he had heard in a Boston pub, George Monk's Blue Anchor. Their populist neighbor Mr. Andrew Belcher had told the company that the jury that had convicted Jacob Leisler, leader of the mass revolution in New

---

[48]   Hammond, Diary, 155.

[49]   Moody and Simmons, 212, 287, 296; Hammond, "Diary," 156–57. On Gookin, see Thompson, *Cambridge Cameos*, 229–34.

York, and Judge Joseph Dudley (a former senior Dominion official, and a Massachusetts man), who had sentenced him, all deserved to be hanged themselves. Hammond and Sprague were clearly seething at the breakdown of due deference and social respect. Chaos and anarchy seemed all too imminent, in this atmosphere of "ungovernableness" where "every man [fancied himself] a governor."[50]

The hot-headed anchorsmith John Cutler, Jr., rescued from a large fine by the good offices of his minister, Rev. Charles Morton, on 13 March 1690, could not keep his opinions to himself, as he had promised. On 19 June 1691, he was convicted before the Middlesex County Court "for reproachful words by him uttered against the present authority," which he too probably regarded as "pretended." He was fined £20. The Court of Assistants, however, later allowed his appeal.[51]

THE COST

Charlestown's John Phillips was saddled with the thankless office of colony treasurer in the interim administration. Even before the Dominion, public finances had been worrisome. Sir William Berkeley had rightly predicted in 1676 that "New England would not recover in twenty years from King Philip's War." Now, after little more than a decade, another far more costly war was upon them. Andros had had to spend his last months in power in a winter campaign in Maine trying to secure the Dominion's northeastern frontier. The threat continued. By late summer 1689, Phillips was having to spend on average more than £100 per day. Maine continued to drain Massachusetts resources in the 1690s, but the coup de grâce to colony finances was delivered by the crippling Quebec calamity.[52]

At the Treasurer's increasingly desperate behest, the General Court was forced to adopt increasingly desperate measures. Even before defeat was announced, the report of a committee for the public's £50,000 debt, including merchants like James Russell and Joseph Lynde, had prompted on 25 October 1690 a tax of ten "country rates"; a shilling-per-head poll rate

---

[50] Belcher (1647–1717) was son of a Cambridge innkeeper, and nephew of deputy governor Thomas Danforth, a diehard Charter man. Belcher was a sea captain and merchant who had recently moved to Charlestown, where he had been Richard Russell's apprentice from 1659 to 1661. He would become a Massachusetts councillor and "the greatest merchant of his day in New England." He was an early member of the Council for Safety and frequently served on General Court committees concerned with trade and finance. Moody & Simmons, passim. Lovejoy, 351, 352; Leisler: ibid., 251–56, 274–78, 294–302.

[51] *Assistants,* 1: 355, 359, 22 September 1691; Moody and Simmons, 223, footnote 2.

[52] Finances: Johnson, *Adjustment,* 129; Barnes, *Dominion,* 81–93. Berkeley: Hall, *Randolph,* 29.

followed on November 5, and another twenty country rates the next day. This made a total of thirty-seven rates in the preceding 18 months, compared with the usual second-generation levy of one rate a year (amounting to £56 in 1688). The same November 6, Charlestown's Andrew Belcher was put on a committee of merchants to procure a loan to the colony of £3,000 or £4,000. A month later came the dangerous gamble of introducing paper money; initially £7,000 was printed, but by the following May 1691 nearly £40,000 was in circulation, heavily discounted.[53]

On 6 February 1691, at a special emergency session, the General Court set colony taxes at the astronomical level of £8,000 per year for the next four years. By 17 April this had had to be raised (thanks to inflation and demands on the treasury) to £24,000 by 1 April 1692. In the face of these unprecedented demands Treasurer Phillips found himself bombarded with complaints, cries of poverty, pleas for delays, scary shortfalls, and effective bankruptcy of the colony. An embargo on all shipping because of war privateering, and the insistent demands from English merchants owed some £40,000 by their Massachusetts partners (not to mention Tory subversion) brought the Charlestown authorities to breaking point. On 21 October 1691, the town selectmen and constables (responsible for tax collecting) were summoned to the General Court to explain overdue rates. They claimed "that they had made [assigned to each ratepayer] the twenty rates, and were enjoined to make the other [ten] by the latter end of next week." On 11 December 1691, only two selectmen from Charlestown appeared by order before the General Court. They produced four lists of assessments for the twenty single rates of the town's proportion of the £24,000 levy, but reported that the three town constables "refused to receive the other four." The Court resolved on decisive (and exemplary) action. Accusing the selectmen, led by Sprague and Rand, of refusal or neglect to discharge their trust, they appointed seven other leading citizens to make the assessment. They appointed the colony marshal, Samuel Gookin, already a proven strong man, as collector, and added deputy Joseph Lynde to the seven assessors. Effective local government by consent was near the point of collapse. When Tories now spoke of "pretended" authority, it had a subtly different meaning to its previous "lack of constitutionality" definition. Now, ironically from these former collaborators with Stuart despotism, "pretended" smacked of "arbitrary." One 1691

53   Moody and Simmons, 277–78, 280, 283, 284; Hall, Leder and Kammen, 55; Breen, *Puritans and Adventurers,* 103; Andros had levied £4428 in rates and direct taxes in 1687 and 1688, Johnson, *Adjustment,* 75, 76; Charlestown's 1688 "country rate:" CTR, 4: 88; on 1691 levies, Johnson, 197–98; Hutchinson, *History,* I, 340–41.

pamphleteer blamed this slide towards "Hobbes his State of Nature" on those disaffected scoffers: "were not people's heads idly bewhizzed with conceits that we have no magistrates, no government."[54]

PROVINCE

The new charter for the Royal Province of Massachusetts, after delays, amendments and laborious negotiations, had been sealed and patented in London on 7 October 1691. Increase Mather and his fellow agents had done their utmost to salvage as much as they could of the old charter, but there were many changes imposing greater imperial control and reducing the theocratic tendencies of the old regime. The governor would no longer be elected, but appointed by the crown. The Council—the old Assistants— would continue to be elected (by the deputies rather than the freemen) but the governor had veto power on Council membership. Mather was allowed by the Lords of Trade to nominate the first Council. Out of 21 Massachusetts nominees, four were from Charlestown: former assistants James Russell and John Phillips, and former Deputies Joseph Lynde and Samuel Hayman. The Andros associates Sprague, Hammond, Cutler, and Graves were nowhere to be seen.[55]

Sir William Phips and Increase Mather arrived with the new charter on the evening of Saturday, 14 May 1692. On the Monday, two companies in arms from Charlestown accompanied Phips to the Boston Townhouse,

---

[54] Moody and Simmons, 332, 337–40; a week after Charlestown selectmen were effectively replaced, onetime resident and signer of opposition complaints Jerathmeel Bowers, now selectman of impoverished frontier Chelmsford, was imprisoned for neglecting the assessment. In 1692 Charlestown selectmen petitioned the General Court complaining that their tax assessment was higher than its usual equal. Watertown, Mass Archives, 1 November 1692. Pamphleteer: Cotton Mather, *Some Considerations on the Bills of Credit . . . addressed unto the Worshipful John Phillips, Esq* (Boston: Harris, 1691), reprinted in A. M. Davis, ed., *Tracts relating to the Currency of Massachusetts Bay* (Boston: Houghton Mifflin, 1902), 13–21; Hobbes quote, 16. Mather, a theoretical enthusiast for paper money, recalled previous discussions with Phillips about the nature of money, 15. He was the Treasurer's son-in-law. Breen, *Puritans and Adventurers*, 103–5. Thomas Hobbes's imagined "state of nature" in *Leviathan* (1651) was a selfish anarchy of "all against all", in which "force and fraud were the cardinal virtues," and life was "solitary, poor, nasty, brutish, and short."

[55] Simmons, "Massachusetts Charter of 1691;" Johnson, *Adjustment*, Chs. 3, 4. Agents Cooke and Oakes, both diehards, withdrew from negotiations in 1691 when Mather realised that the 1629 Charter would never be restored. Ibid., 227–29. Hammond moved to Boston on 20 July 1692, Diary, 163. On Lynde, see Frothingham, 219, and above, land titles invalidated; Hayman (ca. 1640–1712) was a sea captain sailing to the West Indies, son of ropemaker John Hayman (ca. 1611–86) who had come to Charlestown in 1663 and was one of the investors in the dry dock in 1677. By marriage he was connected with the Lynde, Shepard and Trumbull families. Wyman, 489. See above, "Wealthy Women."

where his commission was read. Not a moment too soon, a semblance of order and legality had been restored. Two weeks later, at Charlestown's first election of deputies under the new charter and with the 1690 franchise, Thomas Graves, conspicuous by his absence since November 1690, was quickly trying to boss his fellow citizens. He questioned the qualifications of some who proposed to vote, but the town refused to interfere. Then, when he proposed public voting, as in England, Rev. Charles Morton vehemently inveighed against it as "prophane and wicked, &c." However, according to Hammond, the two representatives were elected (by secret ballot) by only a minority; forty voters refused to vote "by papers," and "divers freeholders were not warned to the meeting, so that it was judged (by the disaffected) an illegal choice." The double overruling of Judge Graves, M. A. in the Charlestown town meeting did not bode well for political deference in the future.[56]

From Deference to Defiance

This new independence of mind had been signalled for more than a decade. The same leaders, Graves and Hammond, had clashed bitterly with the "rash and unreasonable" majority of church members in 1678 over the choice of a new minister. Again, they had encountered unbending resistance. The contretemps over the Stinted Common and the privatization of shared town assets in 1686 had pitted privileged inhabitants against less well-endowed younger families. Here, too, the excluded refused to take the decisions of proprietors lying down. They organized protests, petitions and demonstrations. One of their main targets was another neighbor who fancied himself more highly than they did, John Cutler Jr. A change was taking place in the political atmosphere.[57]

The first half century of town records gives the impression that the people of Charlestown were pretty biddable. Town meetings were less frequent; selectmen were entrusted with greater discretion; the same group of wealthy, educated public-spirited men was re-elected to the board and to other powerful positions year after year. Several of these leaders of the first generation had been men of outstanding caliber and broad experience: Increase Nowell, Richard Russell, Francis Willoughby, Francis Norton, or Robert Sedgwick. However, unlike select vestries in some English parishes, the town executive never became self-perpetuating. Re-election

---

[56]   Hammond, Diary, 161, 164, 1 June 1692.

[57]   See above, "Succession Crisis" and "Common Rights."

must be earned by acceptable performance. Yet that ready acceptance had waned with a new generation before the Glorious Revolution and its aftermath of popular assertiveness: "mutinies," bitter town divisions over the legitimacy of the interim government, demands for franchise reform, and tax strikes against war costs. The original covenantal, consensual decision-making had been undermined.

We have encountered several factors contributing to this subsidence of deference. The mood among transatlantic Puritans after the triumphant 1660 restoration of the monarchy and its score-settling cavaliers was one of desolation and apprehension. Why had God punished their cause? How far were their leaders responsible? How would He protect their independence? How should they assuage His anger? More mundanely, how should they respond to the king and to his sceptical, determined, and imperialist officials?

The next quarter century of fending off, evading, sweet-talking, double-talking, ignoring, disobeying, and time-buying ended in another disaster. Church reforms, such as the Half-Way Covenant, or campaigns against the heretical Baptists, had not placated the Almighty. The beloved old charter was revoked; "the foundations" of the godly experiment were, in Samuel Sewall's words, "destroyed."

The post-Restoration colony's tactics and its collapsing foundations incurred collateral damage that shook traditional consensuality and deference. A major casualty was ruling-class unanimity. In Charlestown, as elsewhere, several influential figures with experience of republican England were highly critical of the intolerance and persecution in Massachusetts. Godly merchants could not bite their tongues when they heard their pastor hectoring and insulting Baptists or scrupulous opponents of the Half-Way Covenant. Others lower down the pecking order needed little prompting to add their criticisms. Charlestown people would have quickly heard about the bitter face-off between Boston churches, and the paralyzing animosity between magistrates and deputies in the early 1670s. Bloodthirsty threats of assassination against Indian protectors Gookin and Danforth in neighboring Cambridge spread like wildfire.

Such contention among their "betters" became a frequent feature in second-generation Charlestown life. Mr. James Russell opposed Captain Lawrence Hammond and Dr. Thomas Graves in the church succession crisis of 1678. He was joined by Captain John Phillips in supporting popular opinion during the Dominion and after the Revolution. Disputes at the top fostered factionalism below. Partisanship was the termite nest undermining respect. The defiance of the dispossessed against privileged proprietors of the Stinted Common demonstrated a disrespect for property rights justified when the town's moral economy was spurned.

To zealots like Increase Mather or Charlestown's Thomas Shepard, Jr., the causes of divine displeasure evidenced by royal interference, Indian attacks, and the smallpox epidemic were all too obvious. The flouting of the culture of discipline by the younger generation and the neglect of patriarchal control merited every adverse providence. In Charlestown, prenuptial and extramarital pregnancies were on the increase from the 1670s. Mothers were less trustworthy in naming fathers, and fathers less ready to accept public responsibility. The town's reputation was something of an embarrassment to its primmer residents.[58]

More generally, the ministers harked back to a imagined golden age. They preached continuity; what they got was change. Mores changed not only in the sexual attitudes and manners of some of the young, but also in the wider horizons and resulting skepticism of their parents and the increasing social gulfs arising from economic opportunities. Skepticism and new opportunities produced alternative viewpoints. Alternatives reduce unquestioning deference; if thwarted, they induce defiance.[59]

Yet despite all the jeremiad sermons and uplifting reforms in the 1679 Synod, despite watchful tithingmen in neighborhoods and monitors in the meetinghouse, the blows continued. Colonial rulers fought over whether to appease or oppose the crown. The English administration lost patience and Massachusetts lost its charter.

The upheavals, domestic and imperial, during and after the Dominion have been closely examined. It remains to consider the permanence of the changes in Charlestown. Did popular resentments and reactions of the post-Restoration decades take root?

Two areas were permanently changed. The aura and long experience of Rev. Charles Morton enabled him to introduce a Presbyterian element into the Charlestown church that opened up widespread "professing" membership, and put an end to any remaining jealousies between non-members and members. Without the general alarms of the late 1680s, he would have encountered more concerted opposition. As it was, Morton's energetic advocacy of the anti-absolutist cause came from an expert on the injustices of the later Stuart monarchy.

A second related source of change that further transformed Charlestown from a covenanted community of the godly elect to an elective civil

---

58 Thompson, *Sex in Middlesex*, 11–23, 276–79.

59 Lovejoy, *Glorious Revolution*, 376–77.

parish or precinct was the 1689 secularization of the franchise, confirmed by the new charter of 1691. As we have just seen, when Dr. Graves, overwatchful against vulgar or common intruders, cast doubt on the eligibility of some would-be voters, he was again rebuffed.[60]

This rejection was the last that we hear of the self-important Graves in Charlestown. Like the other "Tory", Hammond, he withdrew to Boston, joining others of his persuasion. Another anti-populist who disappeared from the Charlestown records was John Cutler, Jr. He re-emerged as a minor official only late in 1695. Neither of Hammond's loyal lieutenants, Nathaniel Dowse and Nathaniel Rand, held office for several years after the Revolution. In April 1694 Dowse was appointed to the thankless town treasurership. The only old notable to retain a town position was Captain Richard Sprague. In 1693 and 1694 he was elected the town's representative to the general assembly.[61]

Otherwise, the management of the prudentials of the town was entrusted by the freeholders to those who had supported populist measures: James Russell, John Phillips, John Call, Samuel Kettle, Samuel Hayman, and other recent proponents of the rights of Englishmen.[62] The old gang had been unceremoniously dumped. These changes were no flashes in the pan; popular defiance of the domineering Dominion and the dominance of snobbish notables produced a permanent shift in the life of the town. Post-Dominion Charlestown, like the colony as a whole, had become a more secular, questioning community, jealous of its citizens' rights. Such watchfulness would prove essential in the coming century, as Charlestown experienced its fourth alteration: enveloping imperial control, with British officials, customs collectors, revenue officers, and Royal Navy patrols. That change would not prove permanent, but that is another story.

---

[60] J. M. Sosin, *English America and the Revolution of 1688* (Lincoln: University of Nebraska Press, 1982), 221, 230.

[61] CTR, 3: 108–35.

[62] The 1692 first selectman, Nathaniel Carey, merchant-mariner son of James, was forced to leave his post when his wife was accused of witchcraft by the undeferential young women of Salem; see Frothingham, 237–39.

Part 9

Epilogue

Three Towns, Three Experiments: Charlestown, Watertown, and Cambridge

The three founding towns on the north bank of the Charles River that I have been studying for the last seventeen years each can be summed up in a thematic phrase. Watertown's is "Divided We Stand"; Cambridge's "Hope Deferred." Charlestown's has been "From Deference to Defiance." The three towns can also be typified in other ways, based on geography, economy, and society.

Watertown was "a plantation for husbandmen principally." Although it had the first bridge over the Charles, and thriving agriculture-based industries such as malting, fulling, and tanning, its upstream location and predominantly agrarian economy contributed to its sense of "bounded localism" and isolation. This inward-looking parochialism contributed to its factional town politics and seesawing partisanship.

The hopes at Cambridge's founding were ambitious. The merchants who settled there in the 1630s planned a river harbor, shipbuilding yards, and profitable commerce. Harvard College would make the town a famous theological and intellectual center, rivaling old Cambridge as one of the hubs of the Calvinist International. With its domain on both sides of the Charles, and reaching up to the Shawsheen, it would support a growing population with ample resources. None of this happened. Cambridge merchants quickly realized that they could not compete with Boston or Charlestown, and moved downstream with their investment capital. By 1670, Harvard was on the brink of collapse, and the town's heyday as a founding religious center had passed. The great reforming synods of the 1660s and 1670s convened at Boston. Publication would migrate across the river as well, to the center of colonial bookselling. A sense of dismemberment gripped the squeezed town center as outskirts sought independence: first Billerica, then the South Side (Newton), and then "the Farms" at Lexington. Each time, the town's land resources, tax base, and personnel were weakened. Cambridge was in danger of declining into another agrarian backwater. History would show, however, that Cambridge's hopes were only deferred; they escaped extinction.

Deference in early Charlestown was not hard to find. In 1640, Thomas Moulton, a farmer and fisherman in his fifties, was frustrated by the evasions and partiality of the Charlestown magistrate regarding a longstanding boundary dispute with an influential neighbor. At friends' he let fly "misbeseeming words of injustice against Mr. Nowell." Despite the righteousness of his cause, he quickly abased himself with copious apologies to the worshipful judge. Such first-generation responses were routine. They derived from a mixture of fear, respect, trust, and submission. One's betters knew best. This mindset lay behind the relinquishment of day-to-day political power by the town meeting to the selectmen, or the collapse of criticism of General Court persecution of Rev. John Wheelwright. However, diffidence did not last. Gradually, in a whole range of issues, questioning and direct opposition reared up. By 1672, Charlestown's minister, delivering the prestigious election sermon to the General Court, bemoaned the insubordination of the laity, exacerbated by the weak will of the magistracy. From old-style "determined steersmen," they had shrivelled into "man-pleasing, temporising, humorizing [gluttons for] popularity." Who were the masters now?

Though Charlestown was peninsular—almost an island—it was far less isolated than upstream Watertown. The haven looking across Boston Harbor to the ocean beyond was defined by its wide horizons and its cosmopolitanism. Its inhabitants knew ports all over the Atlantic, either personally or vicariously. It entertained, albeit sometimes grudgingly, visitors from far and wide. As the major outlet of Middlesex County, it acquired an unenviable reputation for vice and indiscipline. Its residents and their friends appeared in the courts more regularly that its neighbors'. As well as these declining standards, Charlestown experienced other disappointments. Initially envisioned as the colony capital, it ultimately lost out to Boston; by 1690 it was commercially and culturally trailing its Suffolk rival. After 1660, the "new merchants" and the new capital settled on the southern lip of the Charles.

The initial impression of these three neighbors is of how different they were despite their close proximity. Watertown's English origins were centered on the River Stour between Essex and Suffolk. Its leaders were on the whole unremarkable. Its ministers were faithful pastors and committed teachers, but none was in the first rank. After the rapid departure of Sir Richard Saltonstall, the town lacked a resident magistrate for most of the seventeenth century. Executive responsibility devolved upon groups of yeomen, craftsmen, and professionals, "the middling sort," who would have been churchwardens, vestrymen, overseers of the poor, or constables in their English parishes. They were competent and usually public-spirited, but they lacked the natural majesty of a knight, a squire, or a justice of the peace. They were not "worshipful."

The results of this power vacuum at the top were manifold. Watertown, unrestrained and well-endowed, distributed some 20,000 acres of its 24,500-acre domain in a helter-skelter six years, 1636 through 1642. The town also permitted early dispersal of its population, begetting a variety of centers and interest groups. From these decisions and from its truncated hierarchy arose its defining feature: popular and partisan insistence on executive accountability. At least once a decade, and almost annually in the turbulent 1680s, the board of selectmen would find itself unceremoniously dumped, and its critics in power. Sometimes the cause was perceived corruption or partiality; at others, complacency or incompetence earned their just desserts. In 1647, non-freemen displaced privileged freemen and undid their injustices. Most often, these divisions revolved around the allocation of land, but other issues like the siting of a new meetinghouse, allowing remote groups to secede, or rationing of other agricultural resources could also spark explosions. Though Watertown had its fair share of poor families, it had very few who left estates of more than £600; during each decade from 1650 to 1690, the majority of decedents owned property of between £100 and £300 in value. Much of this wealth was in land, as we would expect from "a plantation of husbandmen principally."[1]

Cambridge immigrants, by contrast, came from a wider watershed. Not only did groups derive from the Colne Valley in northern Essex, but Yorkshire, Tyneside, Norfolk, and London also contributed. Spared some of the shock of the new by the pioneering work of previous settlers, the mixed bag of replacements was united in its devotion to the Rev. Thomas Shepard, harried out of England by Archbishop Laud. This charismatic preacher, soul doctor, and preserver of orthodoxy was soon joined by the Rev. Henry Dunster at Harvard, sited at Cambridge thanks to its pastor's defense of the New England Way. The synod to counter antinomianism

---

[1] Thompson, *Divided*, 252, fns. 18, 22.

convened there, and the orthodox dogma of the Massachusetts churches was hammered out in the Cambridge Platform. Pastor and president were succeeded by the "matchless" Jonathan Mitchell, champion of the Half-Way Covenant in the 1660s. Influential ministerial voices provided the elite leadership for the first two generations.

Promising secular leaders, though, did not establish their authority in the early years. Men like Harlakenden, Pelham, the Cookes, or Collins moved out of town, returned to England, or died. It was not until the 1650s that two men of stature took the reins: homegrown Thomas Danforth and newly arrived Daniel Gookin. Danforth, elected a magistrate from 1659 to 1678 and deputy governor from 1679 to 1686, was the recorder of Middlesex County, the indomitable and legible writer of thousands of official documents. He was a leading defender of the first charter against royal encroachment, and a friend to the praying Indians. Gookin arrived in Cambridge in 1647, and was an assistant from 1652 to 1686. He was both a military commander and the Superintendent of the Indians. Both these second-generation men proved active and efficient town leaders and disciplinarians, though they lacked the inherent authority of a Nowell or a Russell. Many neighbors had seen young Thomas grow through adolescence to manhood; others recoiled from his relentless ambition to build a great estate in and around the town. Gookin had two suspicious streaks: he was Irish, and had arrived from Virginia. The pair's heroic defense of the friendly Indians against popular genocidal bloodlust during King Philip's War led to death threats and a loss of authority. Nevertheless, their meticulous commitment ensured a steadying of the town in the second and third generations.

Beneath these two colony officers was a cadre of selectmen and deacons drawn from the wealthier farmers and craftsmen. This elite was wealthier than Watertown's; between 1649 and 1699 three Cambridge residents left more than £1,000; nine bequeathed estates valued between £999 and £500. As daughter settlements separated, Cambridge boards became increasingly alarmed at the decline of resources, especially timber. However prudent their rationing appeared, they did not get their own way without a struggle. Town meetings dropped selectmen wholesale on seven occasions when the inhabitants detected self-serving behavior, overreaching, elitism, or negligence. When the Seven satisfied their demanding constituents, however, they were regularly reelected. The 1680s witnessed an alarming surge in factionalism, like Watertown's, and extra-legal demonstrations reminiscent of Charlestown's commoners' protests. Despite this neighborly convergence, Cambridge had never been as seemingly passive as early Charlestown; paradoxically, it never managed to match the haven town's profitable bustle.[2]

Charlestown's busyness derived from its metropolitan origins. The 1630s immigrants from London and Bristol were dominated by merchants; seafarers; fish, fur and lumber traders; shipbuilders; distributors; retailers; and commercial agents. Plenty of farmers and artisans came too, and everyone had to pitch in during the first years' battle for survival. The early tone was set by founder Increase Nowell. The permanent administrator of the whole colony, Nowell was one of Massachusetts's few "Gents." The seventeenth-century definition of a gentleman was that you knew one when you saw one. The gentleman had a natural authority derived from birth, education, experience, wealth, and public service. If you failed to recognize a gentleman and show him proper respect, you would very quickly regret your oversight. Enforcement was immediate and punitive. Nowell had City experience and Puritan connections; he would prove a strenuous maintainer of the New England Way against any diluters or polluters of its purity.

Nowell's successor Richard Russell was similarly genteel and well connected, with a wealthy wife, the sheriff of Bristol for his father-in-law, and a close kinsman a London merchant and leading radical politician. After a dazzling career in Cromwellian England, a colleague on the bench until his early death was Francis Willoughby, shipbuilder, merchant, and administrator. These magistrates and their merchant partners were the elite of Charlestown, regularly reelected to town offices. Russell had seen Charles I's autocracy in action in 1630s Bristol; Willoughby had suffered from his son's supporters after the Restoration. They, and their colleagues familiar with English affairs, were more inclined to toleration in the second generation. This set them on a collision course with the zealous Zechary Symmes, whose detonations subsequently failed to flatten dissidents. Such elite divisions encouraged popular defiance.

Charlestown probate inventories from 1650 to 1686 reveal some enormous fortunes. Russell (£3,505) and Willoughby (£4,813) were among eleven residents who left estates over £1,000. This was mercantile wealth, as was that of most of the twenty-two decedents worth between £999 and £500. At the bottom of the scale were thirty-five people leaving less than £100, often a lot less; many others had too little to be inventorized. The

---

2   Cambridge estates: Thompson, *Cambridge Cameos*, 28–29; one of the inventories greater than £1,000 was that of Thomas Danforth. 1680s: ibid., 38–43.

port's social ladder stretched far longer than its neighbors' and hierarchy was consequently more pronounced.[3]

Despite its wide horizons and the dangers of the deep, Charlestown enjoyed surprising social stability. Among families who moved to the town between 1629 and 1686, eighty remained there for twenty years or more until the patriarch's death. Of course, a proportion of these would have been away on voyages for considerable periods, but to Charlestown they returned, in Charlestown they retired. Of 148 family heads whose life spans are recorded, twenty lived beyond their eightieth birthdays, forty-two to over seventy, and a grand total of a hundred to sixty or more. The seafaring town was inevitably more mobile than its neighbors, but it retained a solid core.[4]

Our tracing of the breakdown of deference during the last two decades of our period has mapped many arenas and many causes. The most striking confrontations pitted increasingly large groups of Charlestown citizens against an elite faction that disdained the opinions and interests of the populace, whom they dubbed "the mobile," the non-abbreviated forerunner of the mob. Their plumped-up satisfaction at being "so qualified and improved," that paralleled their courtierly kowtowing to royal authority, to their "dread sovereign," would have made the flesh of Nowell or Russell creep. These "grandees" were ill at ease with their neighbors, and vice versa. Their mannered Tory superiority invited popular defiance. Ironically, neither divided Watertown nor disappointed Cambridge were so riven in the aftermath of royal intervention in the late 1680s.

The distinctiveness of these close Middlesex neighbors should not blind us to their underlying similarities, not least those derived from shared English institutions, procedures, and national culture. All were settled by "companies" with lay or clerical leaders and binding tendrils of kinship. Family continued to be a cohesive force in all three towns. We have seen its effectiveness in Charlestown's transatlantic trade networks. On a local scale, the clan linked arms to defend threatened members in all three communities. Some networks were kept busy if they were related to the inevitable problem families each town endured. For every Watertown Knapp or Grant, there was a Cambridge Bowers or Gibson or Healey. We have encountered at least a dozen persistent troublers of Charlestown.

A critical mass of families, problematic or cooperative, tended to be socially stable and often long-living. Though groups might move out to

---

[3]   Rodgers, 1–3: passim, and MW, 1676–86, at MA.

[4]   Residence dates and life spans from Wyman, *GMB,* and *GM.*

daughter settlements like Malden or Woburn, Waltham, Lexington, or Newton, and every town had its "perchers," ex-servants or late arrivals gathering strength for frontier settlement, a solid core remained over the generations in the original setting. They often kept in contact with distant relatives. Even in Charlestown, social ties and continuity prevailed. In all three places, family names and land ownership persisted into the nineteenth century.[5]

Whatever their alternative sources of income, the economic basis of each community was sustainable mixed husbandry. Maintaining the crucial balance between cereals, timber, and livestock required constant close control and prudent rationing of resources. The town as a political-economic unit depended on wide participation in administration and services as well as strict adherence to a culture of discipline and compromise. Good neighborliness was not voluntary.

All the north-bank founders had to adapt to the changes and challenges an unpredictable new world thrust upon them. While the expanse of "free" land, even in cribbed Cambridge and Charlestown, brought freehold ownership to first-generation and many second-generation farmers inured to uncertain English tenancies, shortage of hands in the New World limited most families' ambitions to the husbandry of their own household workforce. Both transplanted religion and politics enjoyed release, from corrupt, unaccountable, and punitive hierarchies and from the luxurious, immoral and "Catholicized" tone set by the royal court that seeped downward to pollute the whole nation. Suddenly, persecuted hot Protestant cells found themselves in control in their new settlements. Similarly, towns were freed from royal and magnatial control, and had to take over their own management. Each year their freemen unprecedentedly *elected* their own governors, magistrates, and deputies.

This heady revolution came with a multitude of challenges: climate, "wilderness," supplies, local populations, foreign competitors. After survival came the questions. What precise church organization and religious practice should be adopted? How would power be shared? How should freedom and order be balanced? Each community had to confront these overarching issues, as well as myriad local problems. Their responses were inevitably somewhat shaped by their old-country experiences. Nonetheless, Watertown, Cambridge and Charlestown were part of a multifarious "Great Experiment," in the long run just as influential as better-publicized concurrent experiments in Britain.

---

[5] See Peter Tufts' 1818 "Plan of the Peninsula of Charlestown" reproduced in Wyman and Frothingham.

For the experimenters on the Charles's north bank, their efforts, their lapses, their successes, and their failures were all part of the divine plan. Providence had led them across the Atlantic, and providence was the force shaping their destinies in Middlesex County. With the interpretative help of their Bibles, their consciences, and their ministers, they were led to understand and subject themselves to God's purpose. Despite some terrible reverses, sufferings, and punishments, the godly were implacable and dauntless. They learned their lessons, reformed, and soldiered on. What else could a chosen people do?

Index

For the reader's convenience, some entries have been aggregated under the broader headings of "offices and officers," "trades, professions, and employment," and "ships." Localities are listed under the country, the state, or "Charlestown." The given names of Indians and Negroes, most of whom did not have formal surnames (although they appeared in some records as "John Indian" or "John Negro"), are listed under "Indians" or "Negroes."

   Boldface page numbers indicate that the person or topic is the main subject of that chapter.

alehouses, 11, 19n, 137, 140, 210, 424, 436, 464, 465
Alewife Brook, 97, 103
alewives, xxvii, **357–63**
Alexander
 William, Earl of Stirling, 166n
Algeria, 244
 Algiers, 152n, 244, 416, 417
Allen
 _____, 50
 Captain, 50
 Ann (Sadler) (Harvard), 21
 Daniel, 250, 250n
 Elizabeth, 416
 Elizabeth (Dowse), 508n
 J., 58, 59, 60, 67, 73, 149
 James, 230–31, 317, 317n, 322n
 John, 211n, 305
 Joanna (Sedgwick), 205
 Rebecca, 210, 211n
 Samuel, 469n, 508n
 Thomas, 21, 96, 198, 205, 208, 234, 264, 265, 265n, 272n, 278, 293, 294n, 305n, 330, 366, 440
 Walter, 49, 62
 William, 208n
allotters, 9, **67**, 286, 296
Ambrose
 Henry, 171, 171n, 172
Anabaptists, 272, 274, 289, 294, 294n, 308, 352
anchorsmiths, 11, 150, 520
Anderson
 John, 170
 Robert Charles, xxvi, 369
Andros
 Sir Edmund, 133, 377, 492, 493, 494, 498n, 499, 500, 501, 502, 503, 504, 506, 507, 508, 510, 511, 511n, 512n, 514, 514n, 518, 518n, 519, 520, 521n, 522
Angier
 Ephraim, 206, 206n, 209
Anglo-Dutch Wars
 First (1652–54), 15, 153, 167, 200
 Second (1664–67), 200, 250n, 334, 491
 Third (1672–74), 376, 381
Antinomian Crisis and antinomianism, xxvii, 263, **283–93**, 285n, 295, 296, 324, 331, 334, 349, 529
anti-Semitism, 254
apprentices, 23, 143, 166, 202, 206, 252, 375, 404, 450, 465, 520n
Arbella, 15, 21, 45
arbitration, 81, 105, 110, 116–17, 119, 120, 133, 175, 185, 256, 366, 404, 435, 439, 464, 465
arbitrators, 78, 120, 156, 378, 384, 465
archaeological finds, xxiv, 213n, 214, 214n, 215

Archbold, Mr., 35
Arrabella, 37, 39
Arrowsic Island, 168 (map), 175, 177n, 178, 179
Artillery Company, 271, 279
artisans, 3, 14, 19, 32n, 47, 78, 82, 97, 101, 111, 121, 126, 135, 139, 142, 144, 146, 219, 240, 289, 378, 396, 431, 454, 531
Ashley River, 223
Aspinwall
 William, 159, 160, 192, 195, 196, 286, 289
Assembly of Divines, Westminster, 306
assessors, 177n, 495, 521
assistants, 79, 165, 178n, 206n, 253, 275, 277, 279, 304, 310, 310n, 314, 315n, 317, 319, 320, 320n, 440, 493, 496, 497, 497n–498n, 504, 509, 516n, 522, 530
Atherton Associates, 320
Atlantic Ocean, xxiv, 4–5, 11, 37, 53, 54, 140, 152 (map), 153, 156, 161, 162, 168, 170, 217, 218, 220, 224, 237, 238, 244, 255, 256, 264, 322, 384, 498, 514, 530, 534
Attwood
 Phillip, 51, 64, 65, 109n
Atwater
 Joshua, 203, 399
auditors, 35, 88, 196, 271, 319
Austin
 Ebenezer, 469n
 Richard, 50, 74, 75, 138, 138n
Avery
 John, 377n, 378n
Aylesbury, Mr., 274
Azores, xxiv, 17, 151, 152 (map), 170, 217, 218, 412

B
Babb
 Captain, 35
Bachiller
 Stephen, 183n
Bacon
 Daniel Jr., 403, 404
 Francis, 287
 Isaac, 484
 Susan, 403–04
Bahamas, 152 (map), 217, 218, 220, 221, 225, 227, 238
Bailyn
 Bernard, 200
Bairstow
 Goodman, 483
Baker
 Alice (Hickman), 349
 Humphrey, 21, 349
 Joseph, 208, 208n
 Sarah, 8n, 21, 349–50
 Thomas, 145

William, 51, 59, 64, 67, 70, 72, 286, 287, 288, 289, 296n, **439–43**, 446, 475n
bakers, 11, 28, 221, 486, 505n
Balcomb
  Henry, 62, 484
Ball
  John, 117
ballads, 210–11
Ballatt
  Anna, 393
  Samuel, 61, 62, 73, 77, 150, 232, 232n, 233, 239, 240n, 391n, 392n, 457, 447n, 470, 471, 471n, 502
Balliol College, Oxford, 183
Banfield
  Elizabeth, 231
Bantam, Mr., 501
Baptists, 264, 277, 279, **294–312**
Barbados, 7n, 31, 106n, 152 (map), 155, 155n, 156n, 159, 160, 170, 170n, 197, 198, 203, 204, 211n, 217, 218, 221, 221n, 222, 223, 223n, 224, 225, 226, 226n, 227, 233, 234, 238, 246n, 249, 250n, 276n, 382, 383, 383n, 402n, 416, 447, 498
  Bridgetown, 224, 225
Barbary pirates, 153, 244, 244n, 255, 257–58
Barber
  Thomas, 64, 74, 76, 132n
Barlow
  Edward, 38n
Barnes
  Agnes (Bent), 113, 113n
  John, 113n
  Richard, 113
Barney
  Sister, 355
  Jacob, 355
barns, xxiv, 101, 104, 108, 112, 121, 122, 373, 374, 375, 397, 479, 481
barrels, inspectors of (viewers of pipestaves), **68**
Barrett
  Hannah, 426
  James, 51, 62, 65, 69, 70, 118, 172
  Steven, 71, 132n
  William, 359, 360, 360, 360n
Barron
  John, 222n
Bartholomew
  William, 201
bastard (illegitimate) children, *see* illegitimate (bastard) children
Batchelor
  Agnes (Wadland) (Gillingham), 390, 392
  Joseph, 77, 138, 138n, 141, 390, 446
  Seaborn, 392, 396, 428, 474
  William, 50

Bates
  Edward, 115n
  Susan, 114, 115n
battery gunners, **75**, 224, 501
Battle of Bunker Hill, xxiv, xxv, 212n
Baxter
  Hannah, 464n
  John, 16, 50, 74, 483, 484
Bay Colony, 35, 213
Bayley
  Jean de, 163n
  John, **163–67**, 163n
  Robert, 38
B Company, 504, 511, 513
Beale
  Martha, 399
  William, 202, 203
bear-baitings, 19
beaver pelts, 42, 153, 161, 164, **174–79**, 400, 474, 474n
Beecher
  Christian, 14
  Thomas, 14, 27, 57, 58, 59, 67, 68, 149, 256
beer, 142, 175, 408, 409, 425
  drinking, 207, 209–10, 361, 362, 435, 461
  for sailors on ships, 218, 219, 220
  selling, 208, 358, 359, 359n, 361, 363, 405, 461, 461n
  unlicensed sales of, 287, 362, 363, 378n, 461, 519
Belcher
  Andrew, 61, 517n, 519, 520n, 521
Bell
  Abraham, 49, 150, 155, 171, 190n, 402n, 458, 486
  Dorothy, 231n
  Hannah, 459
  Katherine (Waffe), 231n, 401, 402n, 458, 459, 460, 485, 486
  Mary, 401, 402, 402n
Bellingham
  Richard, 305, 311, 420
bellringers and bellmen, 69, **76**, 335n, 391, 484
bells, 98, 384
Belvill
  Christopher, 50
Bendall
  Freegrace, 383
Benjamin
  family, 209
  A., 64, 77
  John, 209, 209n
  Joshua, 206, 207, 207n, 208n, 209n, 210
  Thankful, 469n
Bennett
  Widow, 484

Bennett *cont.*
George F., 154n
John, 133, 134, 134n, 136n, 154
Bent
Agnes, 113, 114
John, 113, 114
Berbean
John, 51
Beresford
Henry, 469n
Berkeley
Isaac, 163, 164, 166, 167
Sir William, **163–68**, 166n, 520
Bermuda, 152 (map), 164n, 221, 221n
Berry
Thomas, 416
bestiality, 410n, 444n, 445n
Betts
John, 62, 65, 73, 239, 240
Bible, xxvii, 267, 301, 387, 299, 305, 357, 428,
482, 538
Bicknald/Bicknell
Alice, 192
G., 50
Hannah (Bell), 459
John, 192, 449, 450, 450n, 451n, 459n, 485
Martha Metcalf Smythe, 450n
Samuel, 451n, 458, 459, 484
Sarah (Wheate), 450n
William, 450n
Bickner
Samuel, 215
Big Dig project, xxiii, xxiv, 96n, 212, 473n
Biggs
Edward, 499
Biknall
G., 50
Bissell
Stephen, 150, 214, 214n, 215, **238–41**,
239n, 240n
Black
Daniel, 103n
blacks. *See also* Negroes
as a foreman, 245
free blacks, xxvii, 39, **382–84**, 382n, 423,
430, 461, 461n, 474n
as servants, 36, 48n, 197, 206n, 266, 266n,
318n, 383, 383n, 384n, 416, 416n, 417,
422, 469n, 471n, 474, 508n
slander about "black" illegitimate child,
379–80
blacksmiths, 27, 32, 45, 138, 150, 197, 201,
515
Blanchard
family, xxiv, **113–20**, 143, 438
Agnes (Bent) (Barnes), 113, 113n
Bethia, 118, 469n

George, 71, 77, 113, 114n, 115, **116–18**,
116n, 117n
Hannah, 115, 115n, 118, 118n
Hannah (Shepard), 118n
John, 51
Joseph, 62, 117, 118, 118n
Mary, 114, 115–16, 115n
Mary Sweetzer, 117
Nathaniel, 41n, 115
Rachel, 118n
Samuel, 62, 71, 114, 116, 116n, 117, 118–19
Sarah, 115n
Susan (Bates), 114, 115n
Thomas Jr., 115n
Thomas Sr., 41n, 113, 113n, 114–15, 114n,
115n, 116
Blanchard Farm, 70, 115, 118
Blancher
George, 51
Nathaniel, 51
Samuel, 51
Blaney
J., 149
blasphemy, 299, 301n, 302, 428, 430
Blessing, 34n, 35, 416
Block Island, 175n
Blossom, 16, 154, 155, 232, 232n, 233–34, 236,
237n, 257, 457, 458n
Blott
Joanna, 482
Blue Anchor pub, Boston, 519
Blunt
S., 64, 77, 150
boatmen, 10, 11, 219, 239
boatswains (bosuns), xxvii–xxviii, 37, 39,
218, 234, 235, 250, 250n, 251, 251n, 252,
252n, 253, 254
Bockholdt
John, 294
Bohemia Company, 221
Bond
William Jr., 453
bondsmen, 78, 120, 173n
Bonfire Night, 437
Book of Possessions, xxvi, 46, 63, 96, 127, 397
Book of Sports (James I), 54, 323, 323n
booksellers, 183, 198n, 201, 340n, 530
bookselling, 198n, 201, 340n, 530
Boston, *see under* Massachusetts
Boston Ferry, 98
Boston Harbor, 164, 187, 190, 220, 296, 353,
357, 446, 530
Boston Latin School, 233n
Boston Post, xxv
Boston Public Library, xxvi
bosuns, *see* boatswains

Boulter
  Nathaniel, 194n
boundary disputes, 58n, 81, 83, 101, 120,
    121–24, 125–26, 135, 363, 449, 452,
    454, 530
boundary lines, 99 (map), 116, 142, 143, 288
boundsmen, **68–69**, 83, 83n
Bourne
  family, 16
  Nehemiah, 13, 272n
  Robert, 13
Bow
  Alex, 50
Bowers
  family, 351
  Ambrose, 185
  Benanuel, 51, 113, 126, 126n, 127, 134,
    134n, 143, 295n, 306, 321n, 353, 353n,
    357, 470n, 514, 514n, 532
  Elizabeth, 427
  Jerathmeel, 470n, 513, 513n–514n, 515,
    522n
Boyle
  Robert, 325n, 326
Brackenbury
  Alice (Brackenbury), **107–11**, 142, 242,
    423, 425, 429
  Anne, 107, 242, 243n, 348
  Mary, 107, 184
  Samuel, 107, 108, 110, 111n
  William 50, 58, 59, 61, 67, 71, **107–11**,
    108n, 242, 242, 429
Bradford
  family, 177
  William, 178
Bradly, Mr., 49
Bradshaw
  Humphrey, 452, 453
Bradstreet
  Simon, 237n, 277, 512
Bragne
  Hannah (Lock), 419
  Thomas, 419, 421
branding punishment for burglary, 375n
brandy, 218, 221, 375n, 461
Branson
  Ann (Shapleigh), 31, 32n
  Henry, 31, 32n
Brasier/Brazier
  Edward, 72, 131, 483
  G., 50
  Hannah, 483
  Mary, 475n
Brattle
  Thomas, 60, 327
  William, 327
braziers, 365, 371

brazilletto wood, 216, 217, 217n, 218, 218n,
    221, 22n, 226, 256
Breed
  Ebenezer, 213
Brenner
  Robert, 166
breweries, 19
brewers, 11, 20n, 22, 38, 79, 159, 193, 201,
    221, 317n
brewhouses, 19, 100 (map), 101, 160, 197,
    198, 205, 229
bricklayers, 219, 459
brickmakers, 9, 27, 403n, 450n
Bridge/Bridges
  Matthew, 376n
  Robert, 35
  W., 68
Brigden
  Thomas, 28, 49, 62, 63, 68, 70, 74, 75, 76,
    224, 421, 469n, 470
  Thomas, Jr., 49, 68, 75, 172n
  Zechariah, 466
Briggs
  John, 234, 234n, 235, 235n
  Peter, 373
Bright
  Henry, 5n
Brinsley
  Alexander, 345, 345n
Bristol Merchant Adventurers Society, 6, 52,
    53, 166
Broadmead Church of Christ, Bristol,
    England, 395n
Brooks
  Sister, 356
  C., 71
brothels, xxvii, 11, 12, 19, 208n, 248
Broughton
  family, 183
  Mr., 51
    mill of, 51
  Thomas, **102–06**
Brown
  Abraham, 245
  Elizabeth, 462n, 474n
  G., 51
  Hugh, 159
  James, 32n, 51, 64, 286, 287, 288, 288n,
    289, 314, 315, 315n
  Joseph, 314
  Mary, 406, 407
  Richard, 22n
  Samuel, 234n
  W. Jr., 64
  William, 63, 138, 141n, 184, 185n, 229,
    252n, 314, 424, 450n, 462n, 469n, 474n

fur trade, xxiv, 53, 153, 160, **174–79**, 178n, 196, 255, 474, 475
gambling houses, 19
inns, xxiv, 9n, 11, 19, 210, 378, 380, 380
ironworks, 22, 160, 161, 172, 197, 198n, 201, 202, 203
mast trade, 10, 37n, 204, 383, 498
mills, xxiv, 19, 41n, 51, 79, 94 (map), 98, **102–06**, 160, 246, 330, 359, 360–61, 374, 375, 406, 412, 424
quarries, 81, 126, 127n, 129, 448n, 451n
ropewalks, xxiv, 369, 416
shops, xxiv, 12, 21, 79, 156, 161, 162, 176, 180, 197, 206, 209, 350, 375, 386, 388, 403–04, 405, 412, 413, 425, 427, 454, 467
sugar mills, 246
tanneries, 12, 41n, 239
taverns and public houses (pubs), xxvii, 12, 19, 80, 94 (map), 96, 100 (map), 118, 119, 191, 200n, 201, 207n, 209, **213–14**, 213n, 215, 229, 255, 267, 384n, 408, 462, 462n, 470n, 519
Three Cranes Tavern, 80, 94 (map), 96, 100 (map), 119, 200n, 201, **213–14**, 213n, 215, 229, 384n
tide mills, 41n, 79, 98, 160
timber industry, 124, 516
timber trade, xxiv, 121, 145, 154, 157, 167, 187, 218, 226, 358, 533
Tufts Mill, 104n
watermills, 79, 83n, 99 (map), 101n
windmills, xxiv, 79, 94 (map), 98
butchers, 19, 21, 32n, 198, 202, 221, 303
Butler
    Daniel, 199, 203
Buttolph
    Thomas, 309n

C

Cabot
    John, 5
cage, for punishment, 266, 428
Call
    J. Jr., 69
    John, 50, 61, 64, 65, 70, 73, 266n, 446, 446n, 447, 476, 486, 504, 505n, 507, 508n, 517n, 526
    Thomas, 28, 46n, 64, 69, 505n
Calvert
    Cecilius, 2nd Baron Baltimore, 376, 379n
Calvin
    John, 305, 487
Calvinism, 13, 54, 270, 285n, 294, 323, 430, 529
Cambridge Platform, 272, 295, 306, 530
Camden
    William, 287

camp fever, 517
Campfield
    Sarah (Willoughby), 419, 419n
Campion
    Mary, 428n
Canada Company, 166n
Canary Islands, 37n, 152n, 157, 160, 343, 461
Cane
    Jonathan, 375, 376n
Cape Cod, 152 (map), 181, 463
Capon
    James, 63, 136n
captivity
    among Indians, 472, 480, 480n, 482
    among pirates, 244, 244n, 245–46, 248, 318n, 416, 417
    of indentured servants, 38, 38n
Carey
    family, 6, 24
    Mr., 49
    James, 6, 24, 26, 60, 62, 63, 77, 150, 344n, 526
    Jonathan, 130n
    Nathaniel, 61, 63, 526
Caribbean, xxiv, 3, 17, 53, 151, 152 (map), 157, 159, 170n, 177, 200, 224, 246n, 249, 255, 257, 272, 384, 412, 459
Carmes, 208, 208n
Carolina, 152 (map), 223, 223n, 224, 225, 225n, 226, 257
Caron
    Joseph, 174
carpenters and woodworkers, xxvii, 11, 23, 28, 31, 32, 33, 80, 83, 84, 111, 117, 122, 138, 142, **149–50**, 171, 172, 176, 180, 189n, 202, 214, 215, 218, 219, 221, 232, 234, 242, 243, 249n, 252, 300n, 344n, 375, 378, 390, 391, 391n, 396, 410, 445, 477n, 482, 508n, 509
Carr
    Edward, 46n, 62
Carrington
    Edward, 50, 61, 62, 64, 65, 67, 70, 75, 77, 286, 287, 287n, 288, 289, 359, 360, 360n
    Elizabeth, 289, 349, 373
Carter
    Widow, 50
    Caleb, 71, 74, 130n
    Hannah (Long) (Cookery), 41n
    J., 63, 64, 72, 73
    Samuel, 41n, 50, 62, 64, 72, 74, 150
    T. Jr., 64, 65, 72
    Thomas, 50, 61, 62, 63, 64, 65, 70, 71, 72, 130n, 288n
    Thomas Sr., 77, 138
Cartwright
    Peter, 380

Casco Bay, 177, 179, 183, 186, 402n, 447, 478, 502

Cases of Conscience (Mather), 329

Catholicism, xxiii, 13, 30, 137, 258, 283, 284, 492, 493, 497, 499, 510, 533

caulkers, 10

caulking, 218, 219n, 238n, 369n

census, xxv

census takers, 144

Century of Town Life, A (Hunnewell), xxv

Chaderton
Laurence, 323, 323n

Chadwell
T., 62

Chadwick
John, 469n

Chalkley
Elizabeth, 18, 373, 375, 376, 379, 381
Robert, 18, 51, 62, 63, 64, 65, 70, 72, 358, 373, 373n, 374, 375, 376n, 381, 403

Chamberlain
John, 63, 134

chandlers, 26, 35, 218, 221

Chapman
Charles, 224
Sarah (Mirick), 477n
Thomas, 77, 150, 477, 477n
William, 477n

Chapman, 161, 197

Charles I, 6, 46, 53, 141, 166n, 275, 326, 511n, 531

Charles II, 58n, 141, 224, 276, 277, 310, 317n, 326, 334, 462, 491, 492, 496

Charles River, xxiv, 7, 54, 93, 94 (map), 96, 99 (map), 151, 169, 213, 328, 365, 473, 473n, 517, 529, 534

Charlestown, xxiii, xxiv, xxivn, xxv, xxvn, xxvi, xxvii, xxviii, xxix, 3, 4, 5, 6, 7, 9, 10, 10n, 13, 14, 15, 16, 16n, 17, 17n, 18, 18n, 20, 21, 22, 23, 24, 25n, 27, 29, 31, 32, 32n, 35, 36, 36n, 39, 39n, 40, 40n, 41, 45n, 46, 46n, 47, 47n, 48, 49, 51, 52, 53, 54, 57, 78, 79, 80, 80n, 83, 84, 86, 87, 87n, 93, 94 (map), 95, 95n, 96n, 98, 98n, 100 (map), 101, 102, 103, 103n, 105, 106, 106n, 107, 108, 108n, 110, 112, 114, 116, 117, 118, 119, 120, 121, 122n, 124, 125, 126, 128, 129, 130, 131, 133, 134, 135, 136, 137, 138, 140, 140n, 141, 142, 143, 144, 146, 149, 152 (map), 153, 154, 155, 155n, 156, 157, 158, 159, 160, 161, 162, 162n, 163, 164, 164n, 165, 166, 167, 168, 169, 169n, 170, 170n, 171, 171n, 172, 175, 176, 176n, 177, 178, 178n, 180, 182, 183, 185n, 186, 187, 188, 188n, 189, 189n, 190, 191, 192, 193, 193n, 195, 197, 197n, 198, 199, 200n, 201, 202, 205,
206n, 207, 207n, 208, 208n, 209, 209n, 210, 211, 211n, 212, 212n, 213, 213n, 215, 216, 216n, 219, 219n, 220, 220n, 223, 223n, 224, 225, 226, 228, 229, 230, 231, 233n, 235n, 236, 237, 238, 239, 240, 242, 243, 245, 246, 247, 248, 248n, 249, 249n, 252, 253, 253n, 256, 257, 258, 258n, 263, 264, 265, 266, 267, 268, 271, 272, 272n, 274, 275, 276, 278, 279, 280, 281, 283, 286, 287, 288, 288n, 289, 289n, 290, 291, 292, 293, 295, 296, 296n, 297, 301, 302, 303, 304, 304n, 306, 307, 307n, 309, 309n, 310, 311, 313, 314, 315, 317, 317n, 318, 318n, 319, 320, 320n, 321, 321n, 322, 323, 324, 325, 326, 327, 328, 329, 329n, 330, 333, 334, 341, 342, 343, 344, 345, 345n, 347, 348, 348n, 349, 350, 351, 351n, 352, 352n, 353, 353n, 354, 354n, 355, 357, 357n, 358, 362, 363, 364, 365, 366, 367, 367n, 368, 369, 372, 372n, 373, 373n, 375, 375n, 376n, 377, 381, 382n, 383, 383n, 384, 384n, 385, 386, 387, 388, 389, 390, 392, 393, 394, 395, 395n, 396, 397, 398, 399, 400, 400n, 401, 402, 403, 403n, 404, 405, 408, 409, 410, 411, 412, 413, 414n, 415, 416, 416n, 417, 418, 419, 419n, 420, 421, 422, 423, 424, 428, 430, 431, 436, 436n, 437, 438, 439, 442, 443, 444, 445, 447, 448, 450, 452, 454, 454n, 455, 457, 457n, 458, 459, 460, 461, 462, 463, 465, 467, 468, 471, 473, 473n, 474, 475, 476, 477, 477n, 478, 479, 480, 480n, 481, 482, 484, 485, 486, 487, 493, 494, 495, 497, 497n, 498, 499, 500, 500n, 501, 502, 503, 504, 505, 506, 508, 508n, 509, 510, 511, 512, 513, 514n, 515n, 516, 517, 517n, 518, 518n, 519, 520, 520n, 521, 522, 522n, 523, 524, 525, 526, 529, 530, 530, 531, 532, 533

Back Lane, 96

battery, 81, 84, 94 (map), 100 (map), 101, 501

Book of Possessions, xxvi, 46, 63, 96, 127, 397

Bow Street, 96
boundary lines, 99 (map), 116, 142, 143, 288

Breed's Hill, xxiv, 94 (map), 96

Bunker Hill, xxiii, xxiv, 94 (map)

burying grounds, xiv, xxivn, 44, 94 (map), 98, 192, 267, 329

City Square, 96n, 212, 213n, 214n

common (Stinted Common), xxv, 47n, 70, 71, 72, 73, 79, 81n, 83, 88, 93, 95, 95n, 97, 110, **124–41**, 127n, 128n, 139n, 143, 145, 208, 254, 258, 300, 397, 430, 438, 445, 448, 456n, 474, 503, 505n, 510, 511, 513, 513n 514, 523, 533

Chaucer
  Geoffrey, 19, 218n
cheesemakers, xxvii, 357, 358, 425
Cheever
  Ezekiel, 73, 233n, 368
Chesapeake, xxiv, 3, 6, 41n, 57, 159, 161, 257, 383n
Chickering
  Elizabeth, 320n
  John, 60, 69, 360, 463, 470
Child
  Ephraim, 200
  John, 204
  Sir Josiah, 204
Childe
  John, 198
  Robert, 272, 274, 275, 279
Childe Petition, 164n
children
  as apprentices, 23, 143, 166, 202, 206, 252, 375, 404, 450, 465, 520n
  beer drinking by, 461
  debates over baptism of, **294–312**
  foster care for, xxviii, 78, 371, 373, 379, 381, 389, 396, 424, 425
  guardians for, 113, 115n, 211n, 385, 387, 389, 429, 508n
  illegitimate (bastard), 247, 367, 374, 375, 379, 393, 393n, 396, 399, 408, 434, 451
  rape of, 399, 408, 445n, 190
  sexual abuse of, 423
  as wards, **485–88**, 508n
  witchcraft and, 329
chimney-sweeps, **69**
Chin
  George, 402
China, 340n
Christianity. *See* church
Christmas, 193, 437, 462
Church
  Cornelius, 484
church, **261–335**. *See also* Baptists; ministers; preachers
  absence from services in, 296, 304, 304n, 309n, 354–55
  Antinomian Crisis and, **283–93**, 324
  conflicts in England affecting, 310–11
  confession and, 263, 265n, 304, 331, 332, 333, 334, 435, 465
  Congregationalist beliefs and, 22, 183, 272, 287, 289, 304, 306, 307, 309, 347, 351, 352
  continuity in, 335
  conversions and, 263, 264, 265n, 270–71, 274, 279n, 280, 282, 282n, 284–85, 285n, 344, 481, 497

excommunication and, 31, 267, 290, 292, 296, 297, 298, 300, 303, 304, 308, 341, 341, 351, 352, 355, 408, 428, 462n, 467
godly merchants and, 263, **269–82**, 524
Gould and debates about baptism in, **294–312**
Half-Way Covenant and, 200, 278n, 301, 308, 311, 317, 317n, 321, 322, 324, 328, 331, 334, 347, 387, 408, 465, 524, 530
hostility between members of different churches and, 311
Hutchinson's exile and, 289, **290–92**, 349
membership in, xxv, xxvii, 7n, 22n, 31, 35, 39, 45n, 47n, 79, 141, 144, 164n, 167n, 170, 171n, 176, 189n, 190, 195, 209, 211n, 229n, 242, 243n, 248, 256, 263, 264, 265, 265n, 266, 267, 271, 279, 284, 288, 288n, 289, 290, 292, 296, 298, 300n, 301, 302, 302n, 303, 304n, 306, 307, 309n, 311, 315, 317n, 318, 318n, 319, 321, 322, 328, 331–32, 333, 334, 345, 346, 347, 351, 353, 354, 356n, 373, 387, 397, 398, 400, 401n, 407, 408, 409, 416, 425, 427–28, 429, 435n, 442, 442n, 443, 448, 450, 450n, 454, 456, 460, 465, 477n, 482, 515, 516, 523, 525
membership requirements and, 265n, 321, 322, 328, 331–32, 333, 334, 347, 425, 427–28, 525
Morton's influence on, **325–30**
New England Way and, 265n, 313, 324, 328, 498, 514, 529, 531
praying Indians and, 472, 480n, 481, 532
Presbyterian beliefs and, 202, 306, 326, 328, 428n, 525
profession and, 329, 331–32, 411, 525
punishment for offenses against, 211n, 264, 266, 267, 284, 292, 296, 301, 311, 341, 352, 355, 428
ruling elders in, xxix, 22n, 265, 298, 388, 440, 455, 505n
sermons and, 308, 313, 314, 315, 497n, 512
succession crisis over replacement for Rev. Shepard in, **313–21**
Symmes's influence on, **322–25**
vergers in, **76**, 144, 265, 335n, 386
women's lives and, 428–31
women's nonconformist activities and, 352–56
church staff
  bellmen, 335n
  churchwardens, 354n, 523
  vergers, 144, 265, 335n, 386
cider, 220, 238–39, 258, 405n, 407, 408, 425, 461
circumcision, 301
Civil War, 15, 30, 35, 46, 124n, 202, 207n, 224, 275, 325, 364, 411, 412, 415

Compendium Physicae (Morton), 326
conciliation, 84, 127, 144, 165, 165n, 276, 281, 284, 355, 435, 435n, **439–43**, 472, 497, 515
Concord River, 479
confession, 263, 265n, 304, 331, 332, 333, 334, 435, 465
Confession of Faith, 304
Congregationalism, 22, 183, 272, 287, 289, 304, 306, 307, 309, 347, 351, 352
Connecticut, 35, 87, 103, 136n, 159, 320, 330, 398n, 473n, 497n, 500n, 511n
  Hartford, 31, 34, 176, 248, 283, 315n, 319n
  New Haven, 167n, 193, 265, 458
  New London, 314
  Norwalk, 398, 419
  Saybrook, 34n
  Stonington, 475n
  Wethersfield, 419
  Windsor, 5, 34, 34n, 177n, 215n, 239, 240, 241n, 475n
Connecticut River, 33, 34, 157, 239, 241n, 309, 376
Connecticut Valley, 33, 106, 170, 283, 455n, 477, 511n
constables, xxviii, xxiv, 42, 48n, 51, **61–63**, 79, 81, 82, 83, 84, 87n, 116, 117, 118, 120, 133, 176, 209, 229, 240, 286, 289n, 301, 309, 318n, 320n, 355, 356, 359, 360, 361, 362, 366, 367, 373, 385, 388, 396, 402, 403n, 405, 408, 409, 416, 429, 438, 438n, 462, 463, 464, 464n, 465, 466, 467, 470, 471, 477n, 487n, 494, 495, 499–500, 505n, 506, 508n, 509, 510n, 521, 529
Constitution, xxiii
consumption, 21
contracts, 163, 171, 213n, 267n, 470, 475
  farming and, 107–10, 188
  house construction and, 214–15
  merchants and, 34, 222, 232, 242, 271
  prenuptial, 411, 413, 416n
  ship crews and, 242, 253
  shipbuilding and, 232, 232n, 239–40, 240n, 241
  town employees and, 80, 378
Convers
  family, 253
  Ann (Long), 211n, 254n
  Edward, 58, 59, 64, 67, 103, 103n, 105
  James, 211n
  Josiah, 103n
  Rebecca, 254n
  Sarah, 210, 211n
conversions, 263, 264, 265n, 270–71, 274, 279n, 280, 282, 282n, 284–85, 285n, 344, 481, 497
Cook
  R., 64, 70
Cooke
  Elisha, 237n, 516n, 522n
  G., 51

Joseph, 530
  Richard, 51, 61
  Samuel, 530
Cookery
  Mr., 50
  Hannah (Long), 41n
Cooper
  family, 367n
  Anthony Ashley, 1st Earl of Shaftesbury, 225n, 226, 227
  Richard, 367
  Thomas, 14
coopers, 10, 17, 22, 27, 28, 50, 171, 202, 220, 224, 228, 304n, 317n, 318, 353, 373
Copernicus, Nicolaus, 326
Coppin
  Thomas, 194, 194n, 195
Corbett
  Elizabeth, 6
Corbin
  John, 207, 207n, 210
cordwainers, 32n, 396
corn, 43, 44, 109, 114, 115, 116, 118, 119, 120, 178, 220, 266, 441, 473
coroner's juries, 375n, 465
corsairs, 153, 242, 244, 234, 255
Cory
  Thomas, 51
cottagers, 3
Cotton
  Captain, 252
  John, 54, 265n, 270, 281, 284, 285, 286, 289, 290, 291, 333, 435
Coulter
  Elizabeth, 469n
Council of Assistants, Mass., 305
Council for New England, 125, 133, 178, 182, 182n, 183, 183n, 492, 496
Council for Plantations, 225n
Council of the North, 364
Council for Safety, 493, 494, 504, 505, 505n, 507, 509, 511n, 512, 513, 512n, 516, 519, 520n, 522
Council of State, 30, 167, 224n
Courser
  Her, 50
  William, 372
Court of Assistants, 79, 110, 133, 135, 216n, 224n, 253, 254n, 304, 309n, 318n, 398, 408, 436, 445, 479, 520
courtship, 360n, 389
Coventry, Mr., 34
cow commons, 83, 97, 122n, 125, 125n, 126, 126n, 127, 127n, 128, 128, 130, 130n, 131, 135, 137, 139, 197, 199n, 266, 335, 363, 397, 439, 478, 483
Cox
  Margaret, 344

customs collectors, 380, 492, 497n, 501, 526
customs commissioners, 166
customs officers, 219, 222
customs searchers, 161, 222
customs on shipments, 217, 221, 222, 380
Cutler
  Goodman, 32
  John, 16, 51, 58, 60, 61, 62, 65, 69, 70, 73,
    77, 131, 133, 134, 136, 138, 140, 315n,
    316, 317n, 360n, 476, 484, 515, 515n
  John Jr., 60, 62, 65, 77, 124, 127n, 131–32,
    133, 138, 138n, 150, 494, 495, 497, 511,
    512, 513, 513n, 514, 515, 515n, 516,
    516n, 518, 520, 522, 526
  John Sr., 266n, 494, 497, 498, 505, 511, 512,
    512n, 515, 515n, 516, 516n, 518n, 522
  Mehitabel (Nowell) (Hilton), 16
  Nathaniel, 16
  Robert, 27, 50, 59, 61, 139n, 150, 266n
  Thomas, 65, 69, 77, 475n
  Timothy, 369, 515, 516n, 518
Cutter
  G., 51
  W., 68

D
Dade/Dady
  Widow, 395n
  N., 62, 72
  William, 50, 60, 62, 63, 65, 67, 70, 72, 74,
    77, 198, 202, 303, 360, 483
Damariscove Island, 182
damnified goods, cullers of, 77
Damon
  J., 74, 76
Dana
  R. H., 151
Danforth
  Samuel, 208, 208n, 305n, 306–07
  Thomas, 67, 88, 113, 116, 125, 127, 128n,
    131n, 135, 184, 197, 207, 230, 305, 317,
    321n, 344n, 360, 361, 369, 391, 393, 405,
    449, 453, 464, 472, 476, 520n, 524, 530, 531n
Dastin
  Josiah, 9
  Lydia, 9
Datini
  Prato Francesco di Marco, 269
D'Aulnay
  Charles de Menou, 162, 163, 163n, 164,
    165, 165n, 167, 168 (map)
Davenport
  John, 167n, 311, 415n
Davis
  family, 485
  Barnabas, 6, 23, 26, 33–35, 33n, 50, 65,
    106, 442n, 473n

Barnabas Jr., 367n
H., 63, 64
Hopewell, 136, 137n
James, 442n, 463, 469n
John, 68, 153n
Mary (Waters), 475n
Nathaniel, 63, 64, 132n
Nicholas, 17, 27
Patience, 34, 108, 367n
Samuel, 50, 107–12, 109n, 145, 475n, 483
Davison
  family, 16
  Joanna (Miller), 16n, 462n
  Nicholas, 16n, 23, 24, 27, 50, 59, 60, 145,
    150, 421, 462n
Davison Company, 255
Dawdy
  Nathaniel, 446n
"Dayly Observations" (Willoughby), 284
Deacon
  Joseph, 257, **382–84**, 382n, 383n, 384n
  Rachel, 382, 382n, 383, 384
deacons, 9, 16, 103, 104, 105, 131, 137, 138,
    162n, 176, 202, 223n, 248, 265, 266n,
    286, 298, 304n, 314, 316, 317, 317n,
    318n, 349, 351, 365, 398, 400n, 409,
    442n, 445, 446n, 458, 464, 470n, 484,
    508n, 514n, 515n, 532
Dean/Deane
  Mary, 469n
  Thomas, 198n, 200, 202, 469n
Dearing
  Union, 499
debts, 115n, 117, 117n, 119, 119n, 155, 156n,
    161, 176n, 192, 198, 198n, 199, 201–05,
    226n, 232, 233, 240, 241, 279–80, 281,
    282, 350, 353n, 358, 358n, 363, 367, 369,
    370, 378, 379, 398n, 400, 414, 414n, 420,
    444, 447, 485, 520
Declaration of Gentlemen and Merchants, 493
Declaration of the Hague, 493
Declaration of Indulgence, 310, 326, 493
deeds, 445n, 502, 509
Deer Island, 187, 480n
defamation, 138, 243, 348, 367, 379, 386, 388,
    401–02, 402n, 426, 439, 440, 442, 443,
    444–48
Defence, 213, 353
Defoe
  Daniel, 326, 518n
Delaware, 152 (map), 196, 202, 250n, 377
  Broadkill Hundred, 377
  Cape Henlopen, 380
  Kent and Sussex Counties in, 376–77
  Lewes, 376, 377
Delaware River, 160, 376, 377n, 381n
Democratic Party, xxv

Denton

Dr., 400n

deputies, xxvii, 9, 39, 39n, **57–58**, 79–80, 84, 88, 125, 161, 162n, 165, 178n, 233, 271, 275, 279, 290, 311, 317n, 319, 320n, 388, 412, 423, 440, 497n, 500, 505n, 511, 512, 516, 521, 522, 523, 524, 533

deputy governors, Massachusetts, 16, 21, 88, 113, 127, 197, 220, 276–77, 285, 319, 355, 360, 391, 397n, 418, 420, 520n, 530

deputy husbands, 111

deputy secretaries, 204, 378, 502, 504

Descartes

René, 326

Dexter

John, 65, 71, 481

Richard, 51, 62, 65, 72

Dickens

Charles, 370

Dickerman

Elizabeth, 399, 404, 409

discipline, 436, 440, 444, 487

diseases

camp fever, 517

Indians and, 473, 475

scurvy, 45, 219n, 242, 514

smallpox, 47, 48, 111n, 121, 154, 206n, 209, 220, 223n, 240n, 249, 265, 281, 308n, 313, 314, 334, 394, 405, 408, 420, 421, 468, 482, 487, 516, 517, 525

Dissenting Academy, 326

Dixon

William, 127n

dockers, 11

docks, xxiv, 79, 96, 98, 100 (map), 218n, 239, 240, 240n, 241, 318n, 320, 416, 417, 471n, 473n, 477, 502, 522n

doctors and physicians, xxvii, xxviii, 7, 17, 27, 30, 88, 111, 189, 189n, 209, 233n, 250n, 266, 272, 274, 275, 279, 307, 319, 321, 360, 400n, 408, 463, 470, 497, 500, 513n, 524, 526

Dolphin, 7n, 244, 247

Dominican Republic, 272

Dominion of New England, 39, 236, 277, 326, 328, 334, 438, 492, 494, **498–504**, 506, 508, 510, 510n, 511, 511n, 514, 517, 518, 519, 520, 524, 525, 526

Dorchester Company, 5, 182, 225n

Douro River, 219

Douse

Lawyer, 49

Down

Elizabeth, 469n

Downing

John, 49

Lucy Winthrop, 415

dowries, 143, 166n, 350, 411, 418, 426

Dowse

Elizabeth, 508n

Joseph, 64, 69, 467n

Lawrence, 60, 61, 62, 63, 64, 65, 66, 69, 70, 71, 72, 76, 77, 396, 397, 508n

Margery (Rand), 396, 508n

Nathaniel, 69, 507, 508n, 515, 516n, 518, 518n, 526

Samuel, 62, 74, 77, 464, 464n

Drake

Francis

Draper

James, 457n

Mary (Hadlock), 475n

Matthew, xxv

Miriam, 457

drapers, 6, 7n, 26, 52, 166, 196, 202–03, 353

Drapers' Company, 166, 202, 203

Drapier

G., 49

Drayson

Stephen, 234, 234n

dried fish, 5–6, 76, 151, 157, 159, 160, 161, 196, 219, 220

Drinker

Edward, 62, 63, 64, 70, 303, 304, 307, 309, 310, 353n, 354, 462

John, 49

N., 64

Phillip, 28, 68

drinking. *See* alcohol use; drunkenness

drivers of commons, 83n

drownings, 15, 17, 22, 119, 151, 153, 154, 155, 402n, 412, 415, 477n

drunkenness, xxvii, xxviii, 12, 19, 138, 140, 182, 225, 229, 287, 369, 378n, 403, 404n, 408n, 429, 437, **461–68**, 462n, 474, 475, 477n

Dryden

family, 291n

dry docks, xxiv, 79, 98, 218n, 239, 240, 240n, 241, 318n, 320, 416, 417, 471n, 477, 502, 522n

Dublet

Tom, 480n

Dudley

Joseph, 492, 496, 499, 500, 519

Thomas, 178n, 291, 291n, 324

Dummer

Richard, 214

Dunn

Mary Maples, 356, 428

Dunnington

Arrald, 17, **342–46**, 344n, 357, 422, 423, 424, 425, 428

Edward, 344

Margaret (Cox), 344

Harbord/Harbertt/Herbert
  Henry, 50, 65, 67, 70, 72
Hardee
  William, 230
Harlakenden
  Roger, 530
Harnice
  Elizabeth, 469n
Harrington
  Mr., 50
  Richard, 63, 64, **171–73**, 171n
Harris
  family, 15, 427, 428
  Ann, 417n
  Anna, 317n, 401n
  David, 417n
  Elizabeth, 400n, 401n
  Hannah, 406, 407
  Hephzibah (Crosswell), 409
  John, 50, 68, 191, 208, 210, 399, **404–09**, 405n, 410, 424, 426, 427, 429, 461, 474n, 487n
  Jonathan, 406
  Joseph, **206–10**, 207n, 208n, 424
  Mary, 208
  Thomas, 68, 208, 400n, 409
  Thomasine (Elson), 417n
  William, 15, 16
Hart
  John, 198
Harvard
  Ann (Sadler), 21, 23
  John, 21, 23, 24, 27, 54, 144, 264, 265, 325
  Katherine (Rogers), 21
  Robert, 21
Harvard College, 18n, 21, 40, 81, 103, 110, 111, 113, 153, 178n, 233n, 276, 276n, 280, 295, 307, 314–15, 314n, 317n, 319, 320, 326, 327, 330, 352, 419, 437, 511n, 514n, 529, 529
Harvard Square, Cambridge, Massachusetts, 96
Harvard University, 7n
Harwood
  family, 297n
  Abiah/Abiel, 352, 353, 356
  Elizabeth, 352n
  George, 352n
  Henry, 352n
  John, 352n
  Mary, 296, 351, 352, 352n, 353, 356, 423, 426
  Nathaniel, 352, 352n
hatters, 19, 32n, 360n, 465
Haverland
  William, 38
Hawkins
  A., 64
  Elizabeth, 178

Jane (Charter), 22
John, 227
Robert, 98
Thomas, 17, 22, 27, 53, 119, 149, 153, 164, 165, 168, 178, 258n
Timothy, 513n
Hawthorne
  Nathaniel, 339
Haxton
  James, 230
Hayden
  Hannah Maynard, 211n
  James, 18n, 50, 65, 150, 155n, 191, 211n
  John, **210–11**, 211n
Hayes
  Sylvester, 206, 207, 209, 209n, 210, 361n
haygrounds, 95n, 97, 104, 121
Hayman/Heyman
  family, 16, 416
  John, 60, 62, 69, 77, 309, 315n, 318, 319, 320, 369, 402, 416, 417, 417n, 418, 522n
  N., 62
  Samuel, 58, 61, 416n, 471n, 512n, 522, 522n, 526
  Sarah, **416–18**, 422
Haynes
  Mehitabel, 320n
Hazzard
  Elizabeth (Kelly), 395n
heads of households, **49–51**
Hearsy
  William, 37n
Henchman
  Thomas, 484
Henry VIII, 141
Hepburn
  Anna, 41n, 318n
  George, 17, 27, 50, 189n, 318n
  Hannah, 17
herdsmen, **66–67**, 83, 83n, 124, 137, 138, 144, 408
Hett
  Thomas, 49, 46, 62, 64, 65, 68, 463
Heyman see Hayman/Heyman
Hibbins
  William, 17
Hickman
  Alice, 349
Higginson
  Francis, 14, 15, 16, 344, 345n
  John, 305, 305n, 306
Hildrick
  R., 70, 72
Hill
  Widow, 209
  Abraham, 46n, 64, 235n
  Isaac, 137

Hill *cont.*
  Jacob, 57, 59, 64, 67, 212, 235, 235n
  Richard, 162n
  Valentine, 160
  Zechariah, 469n
Hills
  Abraham, 211, 211n
  Hannah (Stowers), 211n
  Joseph, 46n, 96, 100 (map), 114, 115, 150,
    414, 414n
  Rebecca, 349
  Sarah, 349
Hilton
  family, 16
  John, 234n
  Lydia (Maynard) (Hale), 249
  Mary, 249
  Mehitabel (Nowell), 16, 249
  Nowell, 16, 150, 154, 251, 252, 253, 253n
  William, 149, 223n, 249
Hinckley
  family, 177
Hindes
  Arthur, 470
Hispaniola, 164n, 272, 273, 274
History of Charlestown (Frothingham), xxv
History of New England (Hubbard), 297
Hoar/Hoare
  Daniel, 480, 480n
  John, 480, 480n
  Leonard, 314n
Hobart
  Gershom, 315, 315n
  Jeremiah, 145
  Peter, 315n
  Susannah (Graves), 315n
Hocking
  John, 179, 179n
Hodges
  family, 23, 46, 383n
  Humphrey, 383, 383n
  John, 16, 24, 27, 53, 149, 256, 383n, 397
  Mary (Miller), 16, 16n
Hog Island, Casco Bay, 177, 317n
hog reeves, **63–64**, 81, 81n, 83n, 97, 448n
Holden
  Richard, 31
holidays, 437
Holland. *See* Netherlands
Hollar
  Wenceslaus, 11
Holyoke
  Eleazer, 35
homosexuality, 138–39, 485
Honduras, 33n
honor killings, 340, 340n, 430

Hooker
  Thomas, 33–34, 35, 87, 283
Hopewell, 156
Hopkins
  James, 29, 54
  Matthew, 30
horses, 83, 93, 106n, 118, 127, 143, 156n, 157,
  160, 197, 198, 203, 204, 219, 246–47,
  248, 249, 249n, 359, 449, 476, 513n
Horseshoe tavern, Boston, 207n
Horton
  Thomas, 49
Hose *see* House/Hose
Hosseini
  Khaled, 340n
hostlers, 38
Houchin
  Daniel, 440, 441, 442
Houghton
  Elinor (Newman), 193
  John, 483, 484
  Mary, 22, 193n
  Nicholas, 193, 193n
  Robert, 22, 53, 159, 160, 161n, 166, 193,
    194n, 195, 196, 197, 199
House/Hose
  Samuel, 211n
  Sarah, 210, 211n
House of Correction, 374, 375n
House of Representatives, Massachusetts, xxv
houses
  cost of building new, 214
  dimensions of, 214
  gardens with, 41, 101, 142, 199, 275, 390,
    391–92, 397, 425
  Great House, xxiii, xxiv, 4, 15n, 94 (map),
    96, 96n, 194n, **212–14**
  Long's new house, **214–15**, 214n, 215n
  round houses, 214, 214n
  tax list (1658) information on, **49–51**
  timber needed for, 214n
  Wadland's garden and, **390–94**
  widow's walk on, 214, 215, 241
  windows in, 214, 215, 407
Houte
  Rombout van den, 19
Howard
  Mary, 121–22, 139n, 352n
  Nathaniel, 70, 72, 122n
  Sarah, 122, 356
Howe
  Deacon, 470
Howes
  Elizabeth, 14n
Hoxton
  Judith, 411

leather dressers and processors, 19, 150
leather sealers, **74**, 144
Lechford
    Thomas, 34, 35, 159, 400, 401
Lee
    Rebecca, 399, 409, 429, 451, 474n
    Samuel, 71, 325, 326n
Leeward Islands, 151, 246
Leffingwell
    Hannah, 239
leg-locks, 470
Leisler
    Jacob, 518, 519
Leman
    Samuel, 64, 150, 483
Levant, 7n, 15, 166, 411
Levant Company, 52, 166, 227
Leverett
    John, 169n, 170, 205, 272, 272n, 311, 317,
      327, 385, 413n, 496
Lewis
    John, 46n
libel, **210–11**, 494, 495, 514
licenses, 79, 276n
    for alcohol and beer selling, 225n, 208, 287,
      362, 378n, 363, 408, 461
    of inns, 9n
    for quarries, 126
    relief rolls and, 461
    for retailers, 461
    for schoolmasters, 73, 328
    of taverns, 207, 213, 213n, 408
    for trade with Indians, 177, 177n, 179
    for wood-cutting, 138, 448n
Lidget/Lidgett
    Charles, 126n, 134n, 135, 383, 498, 498n,
      502, 503, 504, 515
    Peter, 37n, 198, 200, 202, 309n, 311n, 383,
      383n
lightermen, 11, 150, 171, 187
Lillie
    Samuel, 224
Lindes
    Jane, 469n
Line
    Thomas, 51
Lion's Whelp, 4
Littell
    Thomas, 51
Lloyd
    Edward, 220n
Lock
    Elizabeth, 421
    Hannah, 419
    Margaret, 21, **418–22**, 420n, 422
    Susannah (Cole), 419
    William, 17, 419

Locke
    John, 326
Logick System, A (Morton), 326
London Committee of Safety, 166
London Company of Skinners, 174
Long
    family, 9, 16, 213, 253, 348, 382n
    Mrs., 119
    Widow, 470
    Abigail (Symmes), 195
    Ann, 211n, 254n
    Deborah, 213
    Elizabeth, 213
    Elizabeth (Hawkins), 178
    Hannah, 41n
    Joanna, 451
    John, 9n, 50, 60, 149, 195, 197, 198, 198n,
      200n, 201, 205, 223n
    Mary, 211n
    Mary (Burr), 214
    Michael, 76, 171–72, 190n
    Mych, 49
    Nathaniel, 178
    Robert, 8, 9n, 24, 27, 50, 59, 64, 67, 81n,
      173n, 200, 200n, 213, 213n, 214n, 215,
      229
    Robert Jr., 416n
    Samuel, 213
    Sarah (Tidd), 176, 214, 422
    Zachery/Zechariah/Zechary, 49, 62, 77,
      138, 149, 176, 213, 214–15, 239, 247,
      258
Long Island, Casco Bay, Maine, 502
Long Island Sound, 283
Longley
    William, 483
Long Swamp, 43
Lord
    Alice (Rand), 41n
    Samuel, 62, 64, 65, 410n
    Thomas, 41n, 62, 64, 65, 69, 71, 73, 74, 75,
      76, 77, 410n, 464n
Lords of Trade, 492, 497, 522
Lothrop, *see* Lathrop/Lothrop
Louis XIV, 492
Lovells Island, 187, 188, 188n, 190
Lovett
    Daniel, 482
    Joanna (Blott), 482
Lowden
    James, 62, 63, 65, 71, 72, 73, 77, **122–23**,
      127n, 139n, 143, 191, 361, 438, 468
    John, 359, 360, 360n, 361, 404n, **465–68**,
      429, 485, 486, 487
    Mary, 466
    Mary (Cole), 343, 345, 357, 357n, 465
    Mary (Howard), 122, 139n

Mary (Shard) (Gove), 41n, **364–71**, 369n,
371, 423, 425, 426, 428
Mapes
W., 66
maps, xxv, xxvn, 94 (map), 99 (map), 100
(map), 152 (map), 168 (map), 376n
Marable
J., 65
Marble
Gershom, 251n
March
Goodwife, 360, 402
John, 17, 27, 51, 64, 69, 70, 72
Rebecca, 17
mariners, 13, 14, 16, 17, 18, 18n, 21, 24, 26,
27, 40, 48, 101, 135, 154, 155, 161, 165,
175, 176n, 184, 187, 190, 190n, 200n,
211n, 212n, 215, 223, 224, 229n, 243,
244, 247, 248, 249, 251, 253, 253n, 255,
256, 303, 317n, 344, 345, 352, 353, 354n,
360n, 372n, 383n, 384, 388, 388n, 390,
393, 394, 402n, 403n, 410, 411, 415, 417,
417n, 424, 457, 458, 526n
Mark
Nathaniel, 134
Patrick, 70, 71, 129, 132n, 134, 134n, 138,
455, 456n
Sarah, 456n
Marlborough Arms tavern, Boston, 207n
Marr/Marre
_____ (Wallace), 36n
Henry, 36n, 462
marriages, 5, 7n, 8n, 9, 9n, 15, 16, 16n, 17,
18n, 21, 21n, 22, 22n, 23, 29, 29n, 31,
36n, 39, 41, 41n, 95, 106n, 107–08, 110,
113, 113n, 114, 115n, 118, 118n, 121,
127n, 136, 136n, 137, 137n, 138, 139n,
159, 162n, 167, 170n, 176, 177, 178, 184,
187, 192, 193, 193n, 195, 199, 203, 204,
205, 207n, 211n, 214, 216n, 223, 223n,
228, 229n, 230n, 239, 242, 248, 249,
253, 254, 257, 265, 274, 276, 287, 296,
304n, 307, 315n, 317n, 319, 319n, 320,
320n, 324, 325, 332, 340, 344, 345, 347,
349, 350, 350n, 351n, 352, 352n, 353,
354, 356, 357, 362n, 364–65, 365n, 368,
369, 372, 375, 378n, 381, 382n, 383n,
384, 384n, 385, 386, 387, 388, 389, 390,
394, 395, 396, 397, 397n, 398, 398n, 399,
400n, 402n, 404, 405, 408, 409, 410, 412,
413, 413n, 414, 414n, 415, 416, 417n,
419, 420, 422, 428, 429, 444, 450, 450n,
458, 459, 460, 462n, 463, 463n, 465, 466,
468, 474, 477n, 487, 502, 508n, 522n
Cole's letter on, 342–44, 346
courtship before, 360n, 389
dowries in, 143, 166n, 350, 411, 418, 426

early age of, 48
free black woman Katherina's kidnapping
and, **382–84**, 423
with Indians, 396, 480
magistrates and, 267n, 328
prenuptial agreements in, 411, 413, 416n
remarriage by widows, 395n, 396, 411
women as deputy husbands in, 111
women's lives and, 424–25
Marshall
Henry, 251, 253
Mary (Hilton), 249
William, xxvii, 149, **249–59**, 249n, 253n,
477n
William Jr., 150, 253, 253n
marshalls, 233, 235
Martin
family, 485, 486
Benjamin, 234, 235
Elizabeth, 460, 469n
Elizabeth (Trumbull), 24, 232, 248, 267n,
458, 460
J., 63, 149
Margaret, 348, 410, 424, 455n, 460
Richard, xxvii, 16, 24, 118, 123, 149, 154,
156, **232–37**, 232n, 234n, 235n, 237n,
238, 243, 243n, 248, 256, 257, 424, 427,
429, 438, **457–60**, 457n, 486
martyrdom, 30, 430
Mary I, 30
Mary, 160
Mary and Elizabeth, 229, 230, 231
Mary and John, 5, 317n
Maryland, 376, 377n
Mason
Anne (Greene), 194, 194n, 195
Arthur, 382n
John, 183n, 194, 194n, 195
Rachel, 382n
masons, 9, 27, 81, 126, 215, 301, 329, 329n,
450, 451n, 459
Massachusetts, xxiii, xxiv, xxv, 3, 5, 13, 16, 17,
22, 30, 31, 32, 34n, 35, 36, 39, 40, 41, 42,
42n, 47, 52, 79, 84, 87, 93, 95, 135, 137,
138, 151, 152 (map), 153, 159, 161, 162,
163, 165, 170, 175, 177, 178n, 179, 182,
183n, 186, 187, 195n, 197, 201, 202, 205,
212, 219n, 239, 242, 243, 247, 259, 264,
268, 270, 271, 272, 274, 376, 376n, 277,
278, 283, 285n, 292–93, 294, 295, 303,
310, 311, 313, 317n, 321, 321n, 322, 323,
326, 328, 329, 330, 341, 345n, 352n, 354,
358, 365, 366, 370, 381, 404n, 412, 414,
418, 436, 462, 473, 478, 478n, 479, 492,
494, 495, 496, 497n, 498, 501, 504, 505,
505n, 506, 510, 515, 516, 518, 518n, 520,
520n, 521, 522, 524, 525, 530

Massachusetts *cont.*

Andover, 470, 475, 475n, 476

Arlington, 103

Barnstable, 388n

Billerica, 231n, 288, 296n, 351n, 455, 475, 475n, 476, 530

Boston, xxiv, xxvi, xxvii, 3, 7n, 13, 15, 16, 33, 34, 34n, 41n, 45, 45n, 46, 48n, 68, 94 (map), 98, 104, 105, 110, 118, 119, 149, 150, 151, 158, 159, 160, 162, 163, 163n, 164, 164n, 165, 166, 166n, 168, 169, 169n, 170n, 171n, 175, 175n, 176n, 177n, 178, 178n, 180, 183, 184, 187, 191, 192, 195n, 196, 198, 199n, 200, 201, 202, 203, 204, 206, 207, 207n, 208, 208n, 209, 210, 211n, 212n, 213, 216n, 217, 218, 219, 220, 220n, 221, 222, 223, 223n, 224, 224n, 225, 226, 229n, 231, 231n, 233, 233n, 234, 236, 237n, 238, 242, 244, 248, 249n, 250, 250n, 252, 254, 255, 258, 263, 264, 270, 275n, 278n, 279n, 284, 285, 286n, 287, 288, 289, 290, 291, 292, 296, 300, 303, 305, 309, 309n, 310, 311, 312, 314, 316, 317, 321, 328, 329, 331, 333, 345n, 348n, 353, 354, 355, 356, 358n, 362, 363, 365, 365n, 371, 372, 373, 374, 382n, 383, 383n, 384, 384n, 385, 386, 387, 388, 389, 397n, 401, 402n, 405, 406, 413, 413n, 414, 416, 417, 423, 445, 446, 448, 451, 459, 473n, 480, 480n, 491, 492, 493, 494, 495, 498, 498n, 499, 500, 501, 504, 508n, 516, 516n, 517, 517n, 519, 522, 522n, 524, 526, 529, 530

Bradford, 315, 315n

Braintree, 41n, 42, 114, 115, 233, 233n, 318n, 365

Cambridge, 27, 41n, 52, 70, 72, 85n, 88, 99 (map), 103, 104, 104n, 125, 127, 127n, 133, 135–36, 143, 155, 169, 169n, 202, 206n, 210, 211n, 232, 236n, 266, 266n, 295, 304, 306, 313, 316, 317, 317n, 320n, 359–60, 362, 367n, 374, 375, 375n, 376n, 383n, 393n, 395n, 454, 455, 455n, 458, 465, 468, 469, 470, 378, 484, 504n, 511, 512, 513, 513n, 514, 514n, 520n, 524, 529–30, 529, 530–31, 531n, 532, 533

Cambridge Village, 478, 480, 483, 484

Capanagassett, 175, 176n

Cape Ann, 4, 5, 7, 182

Charlestown, *see* Charlestown

Chelmsford, 103n, 176, 215n, 474n, 475, 475n, 476, 479, 484, 514n, 522n

Concord, 9n, 41n, 106, 135, 352n, 443, 450n, 475, 475n, 479, 480n, 483, 511n

Dedham, 41n, 481

Deerfield, 477

Deer Island, 187, 480n

Dorchester, 5, 34n, 177, 177n, 178, 214, 454

Dunstable, 42n

Duxbury, 43

Everett, 93, 99 (map)

Gloucester, 5, 182

Green Hill, 476

Groton, 110, 315n, 362, 475, 475n, 476, 478, 483, 484

Hadley, 30

Hampton, 513n

Hatfield, 476

Haverhill, 383n, 475, 475n, 476

Hingham, 4, 42, 189n, 190, 247, 315n, 318n

Hull, 187, 288

Hurtleberry Hill, 479

Ipswich, 30, 41n, 165n, 182, 201, 244, 396, 477n

Lancaster, 475, 475n, 476, 478, 480, 480n, 482, 483, 484

Lovells Island, 187, 188, 188n, 190, 357

Lynn, 41n, 305n, 354n, 367, 396n, 505n

Malden, 4, 32, 39, 46, 47n, 69, 93, 95, 98, 99 (map), 103, 108, 108n, 111, 114, 118, 119, 121, 142n, 150, 187, 216n, 235n, 246, 247, 288, 289, 303, 349, 351, 396, 400n, 405, 409, 410, 414, 414n, 416n, 475, 477n, 533

Marblehead, 159, 176n, 182, 235, 235n, 246, 383n

Marlborough, 276, 475, 475n, 476, 483, 484

Martha's Vineyard, 475

Medfield, 321n

Medford, 7, 35, 93, 95n, 98, 99 (map), 103, 104, 105, 114, 115, 115n, 120, 145, 296, 446n, 473

Mendon, 127n, 478, 482

Menotomy, 72

Nantasket, 187, 188, 189n, 190

Narraganset, 476

Naumkeag, 4

Newbury, 7, 7n, 182, 209n, 214, 288, 513n

Newton, 530, 533

Newtown (now Cambridge), 283

Nonantum, 478, 480

Peskeompscut Falls, 476

Princeton, 481

Reading, 98, 112, 309n, 475, 475n

Rehoboth, 190n, 475n

Romney Marsh, 231n, 413

Rowley, 314n

Roxbury, 208n, 354n, 396, 457, 498n

Salem, xxiv, 3, 4, 7n, 14, 30, 165n, 168, 178n, 182, 184, 213, 231n, 235, 235n, 288, 314, 329, 381n, 420, 477, 477n, 526n

Salisbury, 475, 475n, 505n

Saugus, 160, 172n, 203

Scituate, 22, 104, 211n, 404n, 413n
Somerville, xxiv, xxv, xxvn, xxvi, 93, 125
Stoneham, 93
Stow, 475, 475n
Sudbury, 114, 140n, 475, 475n, 476, 478, 481, 483
Topsfield, 330n, 350, 475, 475n, 497n
Turners Falls, 310, 477, 481
Waltham, 533
Wamesit, 479
Watertown, 22n, 31, 32, 35, 39n, 52, 85n, 95n, 135, 175n, 198n, 201, 207n, 209, 210, 239, 295, 316, 317, 376n, 408, 470n, 483, 484, 513n, 514, 529, 530–31, 530, 532, 533
Wenham, 30
Wessaguscassett, 42
Westminster, 476, 476n
Weymouth, 41n, 42, 43, 44, 115, 115n, 177, 178n
Woburn, 9, 36n, 46, 95, 95n, 98, 99 (map), 103, 103n, 105n, 115n, 142n, 162n, 211n, 215, 238, 239, 254n, 288, 288n, 289, 291, 291n, 304, 307, 308, 309, 345, 351n, 356, 357n, 402, 403, 403n, 412, 413, 445, 475, 476, 478, 479, 483, 513n, 533
York County, 186
Massachusetts Bay Company, xxiv, 4, 7, 21, 22, 35, 95, 144, 159, 161, 162n, 170, 174, 174n, 212–13, 212n, 286, 352n
Massachusetts Charter, 135, 174, 178n, 253, 310, 315n, 355, 465, 491, 492, 494, 495, 496, 497, 502, 505, 505n, 506, 510, 511, 514, 516, 518n, 519, 520n, 522n
Massachusetts Historical Society, xxv
Massachusetts House of Representatives, xxv
mast makers, 150, 219, 232
mast trade, 37n, 204, 383, 498
mast yards, 10
Mather
    Cotton, 186, 245, 248, 314, 315, 318, 328, 330, 451
    Increase, 88, 311, 317, 317n, 329, 482, 493, 495, 516n, 518n, 522, 522n, 525
    Richard, 7n
Matthews
    Marmaduke, 47n, 288, 289, 291n, 349, 351
Maverick
    Anna (Harris), 317n, 401n
    Elias, 315, 316, 317n, 320, 321, 400, 401n
    John, 317n
    Samuel, 163, 164, 317n
May Day, 436, 437
Mayhew
    Thomas, 153n
Maynard
    Elizabeth, 475n
    Lydia, 249
    Mary Axtell, 483

mayors, xxv, 354n
maypoles, 493, 499, 509
Mead
    Goodman, 441
    N., 65
measurers of boards, **75–76**
measurers of salt, **76**
medicine chests, 220
Mediterranean Sea, 6, 11, 17, 52, 53, 145, 152 (map), 153, 157, 159, 166, 181
Meech
    John, 5n
meetinghouses, xxiv, 15, 31n, 78, 79, 81, 84, 88, 94 (map), 96, 140, 176, 205, 211n, 213, 215n, 224, 265, 266–67, 266n, 284, 295, 310, 318n, 319, 334n–335n, 351, 368, 385, 399, 427, 428, 429, 437, 450, 460, 499, 525, 529
Mehta
    Deepa, 340n
Mellins
    Elizabeth, 247
Mellows
    Abraham, 64, 286
    Edward, 59, 61, 67, 68, 286, 287, 288, 289
    Hannah, 288
    Oliver, 287
Melvin
    John, 136, 136n
membership, church, *see* church, membership in
Memorable Providences (Mather), 330
Menotomy Bridge, 95n, 98
Menotomy Ferry, 98
Menotomy River, 93, 97, 103
merchants and retailers, xxv, 4, 6, 7n, 8n, 9, 11, 12, 13, 14, 14n, 16, 16n, 21, 21n, 22, 26, 27, 35, 37n, 39, 40, 42, 48, 52, 80, 84, 85, 101, 104, 106, 106n, 121, 135, 138, 145, **150**, 151, 154, 155, 158, 159, 160, 161, 161n, 162, 163, 163n, 164, 164n, 165, 166, 167, 168, 169, 169n, 170n, 177, 179, 180, 181, 183, 183n, 184, 185n, 187, 192, 193, 196, 197n, 198, 199n, 200, 201, 202, 203, 204, 206n, 210, 211n, 213, 215, 216n, 219, 220n, 222, 223n, 224, 225, 226n, 227, 229n, 240, 242, 245, 247, 250, 255, 256, 257, 258, 263, 268, **269–82**, 271n, 288–89, 291, 293, 303, 304n, 309, 311, 314, 316, 317n, 318n, 345n, 351, 352, 352n, 353, 354n, 355, 358n, 363, 365, 378, 380, 382n, 383, 385, 387, 388, 388n, 391n, 399, 411, 413, 414, 415, 417, 420, 425, 426, 494, 500, 501, 503, 505n, 516n, 517, 519, 520, 520n, 521, 524, 526n, 529, 530, 531
Merrick
    Joseph, 75

Newell *cont.*
Hannah (Larkin), 354
John, 7n, 50, 61, 62, 63, 129, 130, 304n, 353, 354n
Jonathan, 304n, 353–54
Joseph, 7n
Mary, 304n, 354n
Mary (Pitt), 6, 7n, 24, 26, 258, 303, 304n, 351, 353–55, 354n
Roger, 354n
William, 304n, 354n
New England, 3, 6, 7n, 13, 15, 17, 22, 23, 30, 31, 32, 33, 34, 35, 36, 37, 38, 39, 39n, 42, 44, 46n, 47, 48, 53, 54, 84, 85, 86, 87, 104n, 106, 113, 114, 133, 141, 155, 155n, 158, 160, 161, 162, 164n, 167, 168, 172n, 173, 174, 178, 178n, 183n, 186, 193, 196n, 198, 200, 201–02, 212, 216n, 217, 218, 223n, 235n, 236, 240, 248, 249, 253, 265n, 273, 274, 275, 283, 292, 294, 295, 296, 304, 306, 307, 317n, 324, 326, 333, 343, 345n, 347, 353n, 355, 365, 370, 376n, 381, 384, 388, 410, 412, 430, 432, 438, 446n, 451, 455, 476, 482, 491, 492, 493, 495, 498, 513n, 516, 517, 520
New England Congregationalism, 304
New England Merchant, 153
New England Way, 265n, 313, 324, 328, 498, 514, 529, 531
Newfoundland, 4, 152 (map), 156, 160, 162n, 167, 181, 183n, 225, 354n
New(h)all
family, 354n
New Hampshire, 168 (map), 183n, 194, 289, 320n, 326n, 497n, 508n
Dover, 137
Great Bay, 194n
Hampton, 365, 369
Little Harbor, 195n
Odiorne's Point, 179n, 195
Portsmouth, 154n, 183n, 194, 276, 497n
Rye, 179n, 194
Strawberry Bank, 183n
New Jersey, 250n, 381, 381n
New Salem, 381, 381n
Upland County, 381
Newman, Elinor, 193
New Netherland, 250n, 272, 307n, 376
New Providence, 217, 217, 218n, 220, 221, 221n, 225, 226
Newton
Sir Isaac, 326
Moses, 483
New York, 250n, 376, 377n, 378, 491, 499, 501, 503, 518, 519
New Amsterdam, 9, 157, 167, 217n, 413n

Nicholls
Mary, 444
Randall, 49, 59, 60, 61, 62, 67, 59, 150, 309
Nicholson
Francis, 518
Noah's Ark tavern, Boston, 207
Noddle's Island, 115, 164n, 231n, 296, 309, 311, 353
nonconformists, 8, 13, 20, 53, 205, 283, 310, 326, 349, 352, 354, 426
Norden
Nathaniel, 246
North Africa, 152 (map), 244
North Atlantic, 4–5, 53, 152 (map), 162, 220
North Carolina
Cape Fear, 152n, 223
Curratuck, 229, 229n
North Church, Boston, 311, 317, 321
North Company, 317n
Norton
C., 50
Deborah, 469n
Elizabeth, 195
Francis, 9n, 22, 23, 27, 50, 53, 57, 58, 59, 60, 61, 73, 83n, 84, 145, 150, 158, 160, 169n, 170n, 173n, **192–205**, 193n, 194n, 197n, 198n, 258, 279, 282, 474n, 523
George, 194, 195
John, 192
Mary (Houghton), 22, 193, 193n, 197, 198–99
Richard, 194
Robert, 194
Walter, 194, 195
notaries, 34, 159, 160, 192, 195, 286, 400, 401
Nova Scotia, 16, 152 (map), 156, 164, 166n, 167, 168 (map), 170n, 272, 495, 516
Port Royal, 162, 163n, 166n, 168 (map), 517
Nowell
family, 16, 23, 24n, 106, 412
Mrs., 464
Mistress, 50
Alexander, 14
Increase, 14–15, 23, 27, 45, 54, 58, 59, 63, 67, 79, 81, 86, 95n, 96, 103n, 144, 158, 265, 282, 291, 291n, 293, 333, 401, 412, 413, 421, 439, 440, 523, 530, 531
Mehitabel, 16, 249
Parnell (Coytmore), 15, 104, 104n, 420
Samuel, 80, 87, 104, 104n, 131n, 315, 315n, 497, 497n, 498, 501
Nowell Farm, 99 (map), 104, 104n, 106
Noyes
family, 114
Joseph, 196, 199, 204
Peter, 114

nurses, 78, 117n, 358, 363, 406, 431
Nutt
 Miles, 49
Nye
 Phillip, 309
Nylander
 Robert, xxv

O

Oakes
 Thomas, 516n, 522
 Urian, 313, 316, 317n
oakum, 218n, 368, 369n, 371
officers and offices, **57–77**
 arbitrators, 78, 120, 156, 378, 384, 465
 assessors, 177n, 495, 521
 assistants, 79, 165, 178n, 206n, 253, 275,
  277, 279, 304, 310, 310n, 314, 315n, 317,
  319, 320, 320n, 440, 493, 496, 497, 497n–
  498n, 504, 509, 516n, 522, 530
 battery gunners, **75**, 224, 501
 bellringers and bellmen, 69, **76**, 335n, 391,
  484
 bondsmen, 78, 120, 173n
 boundsmen, **68–69**, 83, 83n
 chimney-sweeps, **69**
 clerks of market, **74**
 Clerk of Writs, 63, 494
 collector of fines, 144
 commissioners, **73**, 88, 164n, 166, 176, 192,
  199, 199n, 205, 213n, 275, 388, 500
 commissioners for small causes, 39n, **77**, 131,
  132, 190, 195, 235n, 319, 437n, 500, 51
 constables, xxviii, xxiv, 42, 48n, 51, **61–63**,
  79, 81, 82, 83, 84, 87n, 116, 117, 118, 120,
  133, 176, 209, 225, 229n, 240, 286, 289n,
  301, 309, 318n, 320n, 355, 356, 359, 360,
  361, 362, 366, 367, 373, 385, 388, 396,
  402, 403n, 405, 408, 409, 416, 429, 438,
  438n, 462, 463, 464, 464n, 465, 466, 467,
  470, 471, 477n, 487n, 494, 495, 499–500,
  505n, 506, 508n, 509, 510n, 521, 529
 Court of Assistants, 79, 110, 133, 135,
  216n, 224n, 254n, 304, 309n, 318n, 398,
  408, 436, 445, 479, 520
 cullers of bricks, **77**
 cullers of damnified goods, **77**
 cullers of dried fish, **76**
 deputies, xxvii, 9, 39, 39n, **57–58**, 79–80,
  84, 88, 125, 161, 162n, 165, 178n, 233,
  271, 275, 279, 290, 311, 317n, 319, 320n,
  388, 412, 423, 440, 497n, 500, 505n, 511,
  512, 516, 521, 522, 523, 524, 533
 deputy secretaries, 204, 378, 502, 504
 drivers of commons, 83n
 fence viewers, **69–71**, 81, 83n, 97, 118, 120
 ferrymen, **68**, 150, 191, 208, 211n, 309, 317n
 field drivers, **71–73**, 83, 97

fire wardens, **75**
General Court, xxvii, 31, 41, 42, 47, 47n,
 79, 82, 84, 95n, 125, 129, 130, 131, 141,
 161, 164, 165, 170n, 177, 177n, 185, 186,
 195, 199, 210, 211n, 243, 271–72, 275,
 277, 278, 285, 286, 287, 288, 289, 289n,
 290, 294, 294n, 304, 309, 309n, 313, 324,
 330, 349, 352–53, 367, 388, 408, 413,
 414, 414n, 417, 427, 431, 440, 478, 494,
 495, 496, 508, 515, 516, 518n, 519, 520,
 520n, 521, 522n, 530
grand jury, 176, 228, 229n, 296, 304, 354n,
 355, 374, 450
gravediggers, **74**, 101
herdsmen, **66–67**, 83, 83n, 124, 137, 138,
 144, 408
hog reeves, **63–64**, 81, 81n, 83n, 97, 448n
jailers, 438
judges, 166, 388, 492, 498, 500, 511, 519,
 523, 530
justices of the peace, 500, 511, 511n, 529
land allotters, 9, **67**, 286, 296
magistrates, xxvi, xxvii, 6, 79, 80n, 81, 84,
 87, 119, 122n, 133, 156n, 169, 172, 173,
 175, 179, 186, 207, 208n, 209, 228, 230,
 267n, 292, 302, 304n, 305, 308, 309n,
 311, 313, 317, 321n, 328, 339, 340, 344,
 351, 360, 362, 369, 377, 377n–378n, 385,
 393n, 435, 445n, 447, 497n, 510, 511,
 512, 522, 524, 530, 529, 530, 531, 533
marshalls, 233, 235
mayors, xxv, 354n
measurers of boards, **75–76**
measurers of salt, **76**,
packers of flesh, **75**
pound keepers, **75**, 80, 83, 139
rate commissioners, **73**, 88, 176, 388
recorders, 63, 321n, 530
registrar of deeds, 509
schoolmasters, 47, **73**, 84, 86, 188n, 233n,
 328, 368, 370, 499, 517n
sealers of leather, **74**, 144
sealers of weights and measures, 74, 83n
selectmen, xxix, 6, 39n, 42, 46, 57, **58–61**,
 68, 69, 80, 80n, 81, 83n, 86, 88, 95, 97,
 98, 101, 116, 117, 118, 120, 121, 123,
 123n, 124, 125, 126, 127, 128, 129, 131,
 132, 144, 161, 162n, 170n, 176, 177n,
 195, 208, 208n, 209, 211n, 215n, 223,
 266, 267n, 272n, 279, 286, 288n, 296,
 300n, 302, 303, 309, 314, 315, 317n,
 318n, 319, 320n, 335n, 362, 368, 369,
 375, 376n, 388, 390, 390n, 393, 395, 397,
 398, 400n, 404, 412, 416, 437n, 439, 440,
 458, 464, 465, 478, 493, 494, 497, 499,
 500, 501, 505n, 506, 508n, 509, 513,
 514n, 516, 516n, 519, 521, 522n, 523,
 526n, 530, 529, 530

officers and offices *cont.*

shepherds, 97, 136, 137n

sheriffs, 182, 380

surveyors, 4, 7, 9, 45n, 103, 116, 120,
128–29, 110, 139, 143, 144, 201, 222,
286, 289, 351n, 377, 503

surveyors of highways, **64–65**, 80, 83, 98,
122, 123, 286

surveyors of woodlots, 83n

tithingmen, 47, **77**, 79, 392, 392n, 416, 429,
465, 525

town clerks, xxv, xxvi, 6, 7, **63**, 82, 128, 129,
132, 304n, 319, 320n, 353, 375, 508n, 509

town criers and messengers, **69**, 144, 391,
455, 476

treasurers, 42, **76**, 82, 84, 110, 133, 206n,
272, 279, 316, 320n, 352n, 478, 502,
508n, 509, 511n, 520, 521, 522n, 526

tree wardens, **65–66**, 81, 126, 129, 139, 139n

vergers, **76**, 144, 265, 335n, 386

viewers of pipestaves (inspectors of barrels),
68

wheat pricers, **77**

Offspring

Charles, 9n

Olbon

Elizabeth, 189n

Old North Church, Boston, 304n

Old South Church (Third Church), Boston,
278, 311, 317, 356, 387

Oliver

family, 209n

Joanna, 7n, 209n

John, 7n, 209n

orchards, 115, 197, 363, 375n, 397, 425, 461

Orton

T., 69, 76, 150

Osborne

Sarah, 304n, 349, 351, 351n, 357

Thomas, 46n, 50, 66, 298, 302, 303, 304,
304n, 310n, 351, 351n, 354

Owen

John, 309

oxen, 83, 103, 104, 105n, 108–09, 114n, 115,
116, 117n, 119, 449

Oxenbridge

Frances (Woodward), 21n–22n

John, 22n, 311

Oxonian Sparkles, 325n

P

packers of flesh, **75**

Paige

Nicholas, 518n

Paine

family, 30, 46

Steven, 62, 65, 70, 132n

painters, 219

Palgrave

Richard, 17, 27

Palmer

Abraham, 5n, 18, 45, 57, 58, 59, 63, 67, 68,
150, 155, 212

Elizabeth (Griswold), 475n

John, 50, 62, 64, 65, 70, 71, 72, 446n, 500

W., 58, 59, 61, 67, 68, 72, 94 (map), 100
(map)

Walter, 5n, 45, 96, 212

William, 475n

Parke

Mr., 198n, 203

Joseph, 215n, 483

Parker

James, 50, 103n, 104n, 215n, 483

Parris

John, 163

Robert, 397n, 469n

Pate

William, 204

Patefield

John, 50, 484

Patsill

William, 192

Patterson

Edward, 189n

Faith, 188, 189n

James, 231n

Pattison

John, 230, 231n

paupers, 84, 340, 367, 377, 426

Payne

Daniel, 469n

Edward, 18, 18n, 27, 149

Margery (Fell), 18n

Steven, 51, 65, 70, 71, 77

Peachey/Peachie

Goody, 427

Elizabeth, 210, 211n

Mary (Robinson), 404, 410

Thomas, 64, 211n, 229, 229n, 230n, 403,
404n, 410, 424, 429, 464n, 470–71

Pead

William, 204

Pearce

Thomas, 50

Peat

William, 204

Pelham

Herbert, 530

Nathaniel, 153n

Penhallow

Samuel, 326, 326n

Pennington

Isaac, 20

for sedition, 516
of servants, 399, 487, 514n
for sexual offenses, 339, 340, 362, 390, 403, 428, 487n
on ships, xxvii, 234
for slander, 379, 380
stocks and leg-locks for, 378, 438, 470
for theft, 375n
for town-regulation transgressions, 81, 83, 88, 203, 209, 304, 404, 448n, 501
for trespassing, 137n
for unlicensed wood-cutting, 31n, 126, 128, 132, 133, 138, 139
for vandalism, 446
for violence, 438, 438n, 454
whipping and flogging as, xxvii, xxviii, 7, 209, 234, 266, 371, 374, 383n, 393, 397n, 401, 409, 426, 428, 438, 438n, 445, 487n, 470, 487, 514n
Purchase
family, 183
Puritans, 3, 5, 7, 8, 8n, 9, 9n, 13, 14, 20, 23, 24, 29, 30, 33n, 35, 41, 54, 84, 135, 137, 164n, 176, 183, 200, 236n, 263, 265n, 273, 282, 283, 285, 301, 306, 323, 326, 341, 363, 429, 430, 435, 482, 487, 524
Purkiss
Diane, xxvi
Putney Debates, 15, 412, 412n

Q

Quakers and Quakerism, 285n, 289, 295n, 296n, 304n, 307n, 308, 313, 321n, 324, 347, 351, 254n, 355, 357–58, 373n, 378, 381, 383n, 427, 429, 430, 503, 514, 514n
Quarles
Francis, 287
quarries, 81, 126, 127n, 129, 448n, 451n
Quebec, 495, 504n, 517, 518, 520
Queens' College, Cambridge, 325

R

Rainborough
family, 15, 16, 46
Judith, 16n, 413n
Judith (Hoxton), 411
Martha, 15, 16n, 244, **411–16**, 416n, 413n, 414n, 422, 424, 429
Martha Coytmore, 411, 412
Thomas, 15, 412, 412n, 413, 415
William, 15, 27, 205, 244, 411, 415
William Jr., 15, 411–12
Raleigh
Walter, 227
Ramsbottom
Mary Macmanus, 264, 330, 331, 332, 334, 347

Rand
Alice, 41n, **395–97**, 396n, 397, 397n, 398, 422, 423, 425, 427
Alice Jr., 396
Elizabeth, 396
J., 63
Margery, 396, 508n
Mary, 5n
Nathaniel, 61, 64, 65, 69, 70, 71, 122, 123, 396, 397n, 507, 508n, 515, 516, 516n, 518, 518n, 521, 526
Robert, 62, 395, 395n, 396n, 397
S., 70
Sarah (Eddenden), 397n
Susanna, 396
T. Jr., 74, 77
Thomas, 49, 60, 62, 63, 65, 66, 69, 70, 71, 72, 202, 396, 397n, 464n
William, 396n, 397
Randall
Giles, 285n
Randolph
Edward, 237n, 247, 259, 310, 314n, 491, 492, 496, 497n, 499, 500, 501, 502, 506, 511
Ranters, 15, 285n
rape, 190, 208, 340, 383n, 399, 400, 403–04, 408, 410, 443, 445n
rate assessors, 177n, 495, 521
rate commissioners, **73**, 88, 176, 388
rattlesnakes, 213n
Rawson
Edward, 317, 344n
Read
D., 71
Samuel, 64, 124n, 127n, 128n
reading skills, 344n, 392
recorders, 63, 321n, 530
Records of the Governor and Company of Massachusetts Bay, xxv
Redmayne
John, 194n
registrar of deeds, 509
Relief, 249
religion. *See* Baptists; Catholicism; church; Congregationalism; Presbyterianism; Protestantism; Quakers and Quakerism
Remington
Daniel, 383, 383n
John, 383n
retailers. *See* merchants and retailers
Return, 246
Rhode Island, 34n, 177, 289, 292, 320, 497n
Block Island, 175n
Newport, 307
Providence, 265, 288
Rice
Hannah, 137

Sarah, 6
Sarah Champney, 355–56
T., 61, 62
William, 51
Rutherford
James, 251n
Rutter
family, 114n
Ryall
J., 62, 65, 77

S
Sadler
Ann, 21, 23
Saffin
Elizabeth Lidgett, 126n
Sagadahock, 175, 178, 179, 181
Sagamore
John, 473
sailmakers, 11, 221
sailors, 11, 12, 16, 19–20, 81, 151, 157, 210,
234–35, 267, 275, 426, 493
St. George
Sir Richard, 193
St. Kitts, 151, 152 (map), 412
St. Saviour's church, Southwark, London, 18,
19, 20, 21, 21n, 23, 325, 349, 418
St. Stephen
Sir Charles, 167n
Salisbury
N., 68
Sally
Anna (Hepburn), 41n, 318n
Manus, 64, 318n, 397, 402n
Rebecca, 401, 402n
Sarah, 402n
Salmon
John, 221n
salt
manufacture of, 106n, 212n
measurers of, 76
shipments of, 167n, 184, 221, 276n, 474n
Salter
family, 485
Hannah, 358, 359, 359n, 360n, 391n, 403,
460, 469
Henry, 51, 69, 150, 223, 358, 359, 359n,
360n, 403, 404n, 460, 469, 470, 485
Henry, Jr., 470, 475n
John, 469–70, 471, 485
Saltonstall
Muriel (Gurdon), 30
Richard, 33, 34, 34n, 35, 529
salt works, 212n
salvatory box, 220
Sampson
Consider, 399

Sandemans (importers), 219n
Sanders
Edward, 408
Sanderson
Robert, 366
Sanford
Henry, 249n, 254, 254n
Sarah and John, 36, 36n, 462
Sargent
Sarah, 349
William, 32n
Saugus Ironworks, 160, 172, 198n, 201, 202,
203
Savage
James, 369, 388
Thomas, 198n, 201, 345, 345n
sawmills, 53, 154n, 319n
Sawtell
Zechariah, 76, 484
Sawyer
James, 484
Scarlet Letter, The (Hawthorne), 339
schoolmasters, 47, 73, 84, 86, 188n, 233n, 328,
368, 370, 499, 509, 517n
schools, 40, 81, 98, 129, 233n, 276, 509
scientific method, 327
Scientific Revolution, 325
Sconce (Fort) Point, 6, 7
Scooly
J., 65
Scotland, 41, 124n, 152 (map), 170, 229, 230,
238, 477n
Scottish prisoners of war, 36–40, 231n, 462
Scottish settlers, 23, 190n, 229n, 230, 235,
257, 339n, 350n, 462–65, 469, 477n, 497
Scott
Mr., 51
John, 49, 62, 64
Scottow
Joshua, 414, 473n
scriveners, 344n, 364, 369, 370
scurvy, 45, 219n, 242, 514
sea, 147–259. See also fishermen and seamen;
fishing industry; ships
adolescent port life and, 206–11
challenges of, 151–57
coasting and inshore fishing and, 238–41
collisions and, 155–56
crews and, xxvii, xxix, 39, 42, 153, 156–57,
161, 165, 172–73, 175, 182, 208, 218–20,
222–24, 229, 230, 231, 232–35, 235n,
236, 243, 243n, 245–47, 248, 249–54,
250n, 256–57, 275, 348, 363, 377, 380,
383, 390, 460, 499
death at sea, 154–55
drowning and, 15, 17, 22, 151, 153, 154,
155, 402n, 412, 477n

sexual abuse
foreign seamen and, 402–03
rape and, 190, 208, 340, 383n, 399, 400,
403–04, 408, 410, 443, 445n
of young women, **399–410**
sexual behavior
Cole's brushes with authority over, **357–63**
fornication cases and, 118, 224, 361n, 362,
374, 397n, 409, 435, 462, 463n, 469,
469n
homosexuality and, 138–39, 485
servants and, 214n, 380, 396, 399, 404, 444,
445, 469, 469n
Streeter's experiences and, **372–80,**
Shakespeare
William, 23, 198
Shapleigh/Shapley
family, 297n
Captain, 49
Abiah/Abiel (Harwood), 352, 353, 356
Alexander, 7n
Ann, 31, 32n
Benjamin, 420n
Joseph, 352, 356
Mary, 475n
Nicholas, 7, 7n, 26, 49, 63, 150, 223n, 420n,
421
Shard
Humphrey, 365
Mary, 365
sharecropping, **107–12**, 142, 145, 425, 426,
429
Sharpe
Elizabeth, 396n
Mary, 5, 5n
Susanna, 396n
Sheafe
W., 150
Shepard
family, 522n
Hannah, 118n
Hannah (Blanchard), 118n
Ralph, 51, 119n
Samuel, 314n, 319
Sarah, 407
Thomas, 50, 54, 63, 65, 71, 77, 117, 236n,
265, 266n, 267, 280, 285n, 289, 297, 300,
301, 305n, 306, 307, 308, 407, 529
Thomas Jr., 118n, 264, 313–314, 314n, 316,
321, 323, 333, 358, 525
Thomas Sr., 278, 314n
Thomas III, 265, **314–18**, 321, 321n, 330,
333, 508
Shepherd
family, 480
Francis, 138
John, 138

shepherds, 97, 136, 137n
Sheppie
Elizabeth, 210, 211n, 402n
Hannah, 210
Thomas, 49, 134n, 150, 185, 185n, **187–91**,
255, 256, 345n, 357, 358n, 438
sheriffs, 180, 182, 203, 304n, 353, 355, 380,
533
Sherman
Goody, 165n
Elizabeth, 387
John, 198n, 201, 316, 317
shipbuilders and shipwrights, xxiv, 9, 10, 11,
13, 15, 16–17, 27, 121, 122, 145, **149–50**,
161, 168, 170n, 211n, 215, 223, 232, 274,
275, 276n, 345, 358n, 391n, 392n, 416,
457, 465n, 471n, 502, 511, 531
shipmasters. *See* sea captains
Shippie
T., 76
T. Sr., 76
Shippen
Edward, 518n
ships
Accadia, 167, 170n
Adventure, 275
Arbella, 15, 21, 45
Arrabella, 37, 39
Blessing, 34n, 35, 416
Blossom, 16, 154, 155, 232, 232n, 233–34,
236, 237n, 257, 457, 458n
Chapman, 161, 197
Constitution, xxiii
Defence, 213, 353
Dolphin, 7n, 244, 247
Elizabeth Bonaventure, 412
Expedition, 239, 241
Gilbert, 159
Gillyflower, 163, 164, 165
Griffin, 8, 13, 290, 324, 349
Hopewell, 156
John, 170
John and Kathleen, 402n
John and Sarah, 214
John and Thomas, 216–25, 217n, 221n, 227
Jonathan, 113, 114n
Kingfisher, 493, 499, 509
Lion's Whelp, 4
Lyon, 6
Mary, 160
Mary and Elizabeth, 229, 230, 231
Mary and John, 5, 317n
Naseby, 276
New England Merchant, 153
Planter, 161
Relief, 249
Return, 246

ships *cont.*
Richard, 161
Rose, 499
Sarah and John, 36, 36n, 462
Seafort, 151
Sparrow, 42
Success, 249–54, 477n
Susan and Ellen, 365
Swallow, 175
Swan, 153, 246n, 458
Trade Increase, 170n
Trial, 412
Tryal, 151
Unity, 170, 173
shipwrecks, 7, 17, 42, 151, 153, 155–156,
155n, 236, 237n, 281, 333, 459, 517
Shipwrights' Company, 11
shoemakers, 27, 28, 38, 136, 144, 175, 202,
308, 375, 396, 445, 465
shopkeepers, 21, 156, 197, 206, 412
shops, xxiv, 12, 21, 79, 156, 161, 162, 176,
180, 197, 206, 209, 350, 375, 386, 388,
403–04, 405, 412, 413, 425, 427, 454, 467
shoremen, 159, 160
Shrimpton
family, 309, 353
Elinor, 371
Henry, 231n, 309n
Jonathan, 309
Samuel, 309, 311n
Shute
Rachel (Deacon), 382
William, 382
Sibley
J., 64, 69
Sierestad, Asne, 340n
Simpson
J., 62, 64
Sims
John, 383, 383n, 384, 384n, 423
Katherina, xxvii, **382–84**, 423
skinners, 174, 174n, 203
skippers. *See* sea captains
Slade
Thomas, 362n, 469n
slander, 243, 386, 379–80, 436, 437, 444, 447, 450
slaughtermen, 11
slavery, 499, 501, 512
Indians in, 479, 481n
pirate captives in, 244, 245
slaves. *See* Negroes
slave trade, 162n, 203, 216, 221–22, 226, 227,
227n, 256, 382, 383–84, 383n, 384n
Slocum
Joshua, 151
Small
Francis, 194n

smallpox, 47, 48, 111n, 121, 154, 206n, 209,
220, 223n, 240n, 249, 265, 281, 308n,
313, 314, 334, 394, 405, 408, 420, 421,
468, 482, 487, 516, 517, 525
Smith/Smyth(e)
family, 393
Sister, 243n, 348
Abraham, 51, 64, 65, 70, 71, 72, **452–54**,
454n, 485, 486
Daniel, 62, 390, 391–92, 515
Elizabeth (Wadland), 390
Henry, 377n–378n
John, 49, 62, 64, 65, 70, 150, 117, 117n,
171, 172, 178, 202, 215, 232, 243, 344,
358n, 473, 475
John Jr., 118
Martha, **452–56**, 455n, 485, 486
Matthew, 10n, 28, 49, 66, 69, 72, 73, 74, 76, 144
Michael, 51, 111, 398, 398n
Nathaniel, **111–12**, 289
Rachel (Blanchard), 118n
Sir Thomas, 141
Thomas, 14, 64, 424
W., 66, 69
smuggling, 53, 220, 227, 259, 492, 501
Snelling
George, 20
soap boilers, 36n, 462
social status of women, 425–26
sodomy, 444n, 445n, 448n
Soley
Matthew, 149, 154, 155n, 229
Somerset
John, 230, 231
Somers Island, 7n
Sowers
Hannah, 210, 211n
Spain, xxiv, 6, 15, 17, 53, 152 (map), 157, 160,
167, 200, 412
Bilbao, 170, 173, 196, 198, 245
Cadiz, 22, 151, 152 (map)
Madeira, 461
Sparrow, 42
Spencer
Mr., 50
Ambrose, 374n
spinners, 366
spiritists, 285, 286n
sponsors, 4, 42
Spot Pond, 99 (map), 136, 139n
Sprague
family, 158
Alice, 5
Elizabeth, 405
Joan, 289
Joan (Warren), 5, 39
Joanna, 349

Trade Increase, 170n
trades, professions, and employment
  accountants, 233, 319, 420, 423
  agents, 3, 53, 54, 156, 158, 159, 168, 170n,
    176, 178n, 189n, 196, 247, 274, 277, 310,
    384n, 420, 422, 423, 496, 514, 515, 518n,
    522, 531
  alewives, xxvii, **357–63**
  anchorsmiths, 11, 150, 520
  apprentices, 23, 143, 166, 202, 206, 252,
    375, 404, 450, 465, 520n
  artisans, 3, 14, 19, 32n, 47, 78, 82, 97, 101,
    111, 121, 126, 135, 139, 142, 144, 146,
    219, 240, 289, 378, 396, 431, 454, 531
  auditors, 35, 88, 196, 271, 319
  bakers, 11, 28, 221, 486, 505n
  bellringers and bellmen, 69, **76**, 335n, 391,
    484
  blacksmiths, 27, 32, 45, 138, 150, 197, 201,
    515
  boatmen, 10, 11, 219, 239
  boatswains (bosuns), xxvii–xxviii, 37, 39,
    218, 234, 235, 250, 250n, 251, 251n, 252,
    252n, 253, 254
  booksellers, 183, 198n, 201, 340n, 530
  braziers, 365, 371
  brewers, 11, 20n, 22, 38, 79, 159, 193, 201,
    221, 317n
  bricklayers, 219, 459
  brickmakers, 9, 27, 403n, 450n
  butchers, 19, 21, 32n, 198, 202, 221, 303
  carpenters and woodworkers, xxvii, 11, 23,
    28, 31, 32, 33, 80, 83, 84, 111, 117, 122,
    138, 142, **149–50**, 171, 172, 176, 180,
    189n, 202, 214, 215, 218, 219, 221, 232,
    234, 242, 243, 249n, 252, 300n, 344n,
    375, 378, 390, 391, 391n, 396, 410, 445,
    477n, 482, 508n, 509
  caulkers, 10
  census takers, 144
  chandlers, 26, 35, 218, 221
  cheesemakers, xxvii, 357, 358, 425
  clothiers, 365, 371
  clothworkers, 170n, 193n, 203, 464
  coal merchants, 11, 11n, 236n
  coopers, 10, 17, 22, 27, 28, 50, 171, 202,
    220, 224, 228, 304n, 317n, 318, 353, 373
  cordwainers, 32n, 396
  cottagers, 3
  craftsmen, xxix, 79, 84, 136, 172, 218, 239,
    265, 266, 270, 302, **449–51**, 529, 530
  dockers, 11
  doctors and physicians, xxvii, xxviii, 7, 17,
    27, 30, 88, 111, 189, 189n, 209, 233n,
    250n, 266, 272, 274, 275, 279, 307, 319,
    321, 360, 400n, 408, 463, 470, 497, 500,
    513n, 524, 526

drapers, 6, 7n, 26, 52, 166, 196, 202–03,
  353
dyers, 19
farmers, 4, 48, 78, 83, 93, 101, 103, 115,
  116, 146, 196n, 213, 240, 289, 296, 351,
  397, 398, 400, 415, 425, 426, 474, 518,
  530, 530, 531, 533
feltmakers, 19, 20
ferrymen, **68**, 150, 191, 208, 211n, 309,
  317n
fishermen and seamen, 48, **150**, 151, 154,
  155, 155n, 159, 160, 165, 174, 176n,
  181–86, 185n, 187, 189, 190, 203, 210,
  211n, 240n, 246, 255, 276, 283, 320, 328,
  345n, 357, 358, 362, 383n, 400, 447, 473,
  473n, 530
fishmongers, fish dealers, and fish merchants, 159, 160, 161, 161n, 183n, 185n,
  200, 221, 531
fish traders, 159, 160, 161, 162, 196, 274,
  320, 531
fullers, 4, 21, 26, 52
fur traders, 176, 177, 178n, 255
glaziers, 32n, 84, 289, 508n
glovers, 17, 27, 313, 318n
goldsmiths, 364, 366, 370
gunners, **75**, 84, 220, 224, 501
gunsmiths, 390, 515
haberdashers, 192, 193
hatters, 19, 32n, 360n, 465
hostlers, 38
husbandmen, 3, 4, 106, 192, 296n, 439,
  454n, 482, 529, 529
innkeepers, 9, 24, 27, 201, 206n, 365n, 378,
  461, 470, 520n
ironmongers, 161, 202
joiners, 28, 41, 138, 202
laborers, 3, 39, 210, 220, 221, 424
leather dressers and processors, 19, 150
lightermen, 11, 150, 171, 187
maltsters, 9, 26, 79, 162n, 202, 223n
mariners, 13, 14, 16, 17, 18, 18n, 21, 24, 26,
  27, 40, 48, 101, 135, 154, 155, 161, 165,
  175, 176n, 184, 187, 190, 190n, 200n,
  211n, 212n, 215, 223, 224, 229n, 243,
  244, 247, 248, 249, 251, 253, 253n, 255,
  256, 303, 317n, 344, 345, 352, 353, 354n,
  360n, 372n, 383n, 384, 388, 388n, 390,
  393, 394, 402n, 403n, 410, 411, 415, 417,
  417n, 424, 457, 458, 526n
masons, 9, 27, 81, 126, 215, 301, 329, 329n,
  450, 451n, 459
mast makers, 150, 219, 232
merchants and retailers, xxv, 4, 6, 7n, 8n, 9,
  11, 12, 13, 14, 14n, 16, 16n, 21, 21n, 22,
  26, 27, 35, 37n, 39, 40, 42, 48, 52, 80, 84,
  85, 101, 104, 106, 106n, 121, 135, 138,

145, **150**, 151, 154, 155, 158, 159, 160,
161, 161n, 162, 163, 163n, 164, 164n,
165, 166, 167, 168, 169, 169n, 170n, 177,
179, 180, 181, 183, 183n, 184, 185n, 187,
192, 193, 196, 197n, 198, 199n, 200, 201,
202, 203, 204, 206n, 210, 211n, 213, 215,
216n, 219, 220n, 222, 223n, 224, 225,
226n, 227, 229n, 240, 242, 245, 247, 250,
255, 256, 257, 258, 263, 268, **269–82**,
271n, 288–89, 291, 293, 303, 304n, 309,
311, 314, 316, 317n, 318n, 345n, 351n,
352, 352n, 353, 354n, 355, 358n, 363,
365, 378, 380, 382n, 383, 385, 387, 388,
388n, 391n, 399, 411, 413, 414, 415, 417,
420, 425, 426, 494, 500, 501, 503, 505n,
516n, 517, 519, 520, 520n, 521, 524,
526n, 529, 530, 531
midwives, xxvi, 78, 267, 393, 393n, 396,
446, 446n
millers, 36, 51, 79, 98, 106, 360
ministers, xxvii, xxix, 5, 5n, 8, 8n, 9, 9n,
13, 14, 21, 22, 22n, 23, 24, 26, 27, 29, 30,
34, 41n, 47, 47n, 48n, 54, 81, 84, 86, 87,
87n, 95n, 96, 102, 103, 104, 105, 110,
114, 142, 145, 164n, 167n, 173, 182, 183,
183n, 186, 198, 201, 205, 208n, 211n,
213, 214, 215, 233, 226, 233, 257, 263,
264–65, 266n, 267, 272n, 280, 283, 284,
285, 286n, 287, 288, 288n, 289, 290, 291,
293, 294n, 295, 296, 297, 298, 301, 303,
304, 305, 305n, 306, 307, 308, 309, 310,
311, 313, 314, 314n, 315, 315n, 316, 317,
317n, 318, 319n, 320, 321, 321n, 322,
323, 324, 325, 326, 326n, 328, 329, 330,
331, 333, 334, 334n, 335, 340, 344, 347,
349, 350, 350n, 351, 355, 356, 365, 366,
367, 373n, 384, 388, 388n, 415n, 422,
435, 440, 451, 454, 475n, 480, 493, 495,
497, 499, 499n, 500, 508, 511n, 514n,
516, 516n, 520, 523, 525, 530, 529, 530,
531, 534
notaries, 34, 159, 160, 192, 195, 286, 400,
401
nurses, 358, 406
oakum pickers, 368, 369n, 371
painters, 219
pilots, 15, 218, 236, 401n
potters, 10, 28, 307, 508n
preachers, 8, 8n, 13, 14n, 20, 24, 32n, 54,
181, 186, 263, 265, 270, 281, 284, 285n,
286, 295, 315, 318, 323, 325, 329, 341,
355, 497, 497n, 531n
printers, 359
publicans, 211n, 309, 410, 495, 518n
retailers, 6, 531
ropemakers, 11, 218, 221, 318n, 522n
sailmakers, 11, 221

schoolmasters, 47, **73**, 84, 86, 188n, 233n,
328, 368, 370, 499, 509, 517n
scriveners, 344n, 364, 369, 370
sea captains (skippers, shipmasters), xxviii,
9, 15, 16, 17, 18n, 21, 37, 39, 53, **149**,
153, 155, 156, 159, 161, 162, 163n, 165,
168, 169, 170, 170n, 176, 178, 184, 199,
213, 214, 216, 216n, 221, 221n, 222, 223,
224, 229, 231n, 234, 236, 237, 238n, 240,
241–48, **249–54**, 256, 257–58, 263, 293,
306, 318n, 382n, 383, 384, 402n, 458n,
459, 460, 481, 499, 520, 522n
seamstresses, 366, 369
shepherds 97, 136, 137n
shipbuilders and shipwrights, 9, 10, 11, 13,
15, 16–17, 27, 121, 122, 145, **149–50**,
161, 168, 170n, 211n, 215, 223, 232, 274,
275, 276n, 345, 358n, 391n, 392n, 416,
457, 465n, 471n, 502, 511, 531
shoemakers, 27, 28, 38, 136, 144, 175, 202,
308, 375, 396, 445, 465
shopkeepers, 21, 156, 197, 206, 412
skinners, 174, 174n, 203
slaughtermen, 11
soap boilers, 36n, 462
spinners, 366
stavenders, 220
stonecutters, xxiv, xxiv, 127n, 450, 466n,
513n
sugar merchants, 11, 160, 197, 201, 203,
205
surgeons, 22, 27, 234, 499, 513n
surveyors, 4, 7, 9, 45n, 103, 116, 120,
128–29, 110, 139, 143, 144, 201, 222,
286, 289, 351n, 377, 503
surveyors of highways, 64–65, 80, 83, 98,
122, 123, 286
surveyors of woodlots, 83n
tailors, 27, 28, 136, 136n, 177, 208n, 211n,
229, 239, 294, 312, 351n, 359, 365, 366,
404, 445, 462, 464n, 477n
tanners, 11, 240, 463, 505n
tilemakers, 28
tobacconists, 11
trappers, 160, 174, 176, 177, 178, 474, 474n
turners, 7, 26, 161, 219, 289
victuallers, 11, 28, 38, 257, 382
vintners, 199, 203
wagon-makers, 296
washerwomen, 329, 451
watchmen, 76, 78, 169, 221, 358, 360, 404,
429, 467, 470
watermen, 38, 42, 155, 357, 402n, 458
weavers, 18, 19
whalers, 151
wheelwrights, 122, 127n, 137, 296, 373,
375, 468, 513n

trades, professions, and employment *cont.*
  woodcorders, 75, 76
  yeomen, 3, 4, 26, 84, 106, 107, 193n, 529
train bands, xxix, 47, 81, 272, 497n, 508
transatlantic trade, 4, 5–6, 7, 15, 16, 17, 20,
    22, 23, 33, 35, 53, 152 (map), 157, 158,
    159–62, 166, 196, 198, 200, 205, 216n,
    217n, 223, 242, 244–45, 249–53, 310,
    384, 388, 421, 459, 534
trappers, 160, 174, 176, 177, 178, 474, 474n
Treadway
  James, 484
treasurers, 42, **76**, 82, 84, 110, 133, 206n, 272,
    279, 316, 320n, 352n, 478, 502, 508n,
    509, 511n, 520, 521, 522n, 526
treaties, 162, 219, 377n
Treaty of Saint-Germain-en-Laye, 162
Treaty of Westminster, 377n
Treble
  John, 400, 401n
tree wardens, **65–66**, 81, 126, 129, 139, 139n
Trelawney
  Robert, 183, 183n, 256
Trerice
  Elizabeth, 21n
  Hannah (Lynde), 162n, 223n
  John, 21, 162n, 223n
  Nicholas, 17, 21, 24–25, 27, 49, 53, 153,
    158, 159, 161–62, 162n, 163, 165, 228,
    256, 384, 429
  Rebecca, 21n, 49, 223n, 384
  Rebecca (Hurlston), 21, 22, 150, 161–62,
    223n, 429
  Sarah, 21n
trespassing, 65, 97, 105, 116, 117, 122, 124, 133,
    135, 137n, 300n, 401, 412, 440, 458, 503
Trial, 412
Trumbull
  Mr., 51
  family, 24, 459, 522n
  Elizabeth, 24, 232, 458
  Elizabeth (King), 23
  Hannah, 416
  John, 16, 23, 24, 27, 41n, 49, 155–56, 156n,
    173, 176, 232n, 234n, 235n, 256, 258,
    263, 264, 306–07, 310n, 458, 458n, 459,
    483, 484
  John T., 483, 495
  Mary, 474n
  T., 62, 65, 149
Trussell
  Henry, 470, 471
Tryal, 151
Tuck
  T., 149
Tuffnal
  Richard, 22

Tufts, xxiii
  James, 396, 424
  Peter, 32n, 51, 60, 61, 62, 66, 67, 68, 70, 71,
    77, 106n
Tufts Mill, 104n
Tufts University, xxiv
Turkey, 166, 244, 245
Turkey Company, 166
Turks (pirates), 315n
Turner
  Increase, 483
  J., 63
  Thomas, 202
  William, 303, 303n, 304, 304n, 305, 306,
    308, 309, 309n, 310n, 477
turners, 7, 26, 161, 219, 289
Tuttle
  W., 64
Twelve Days of Christmas, 437, 462
Tyne River, 236n
Tyng
  family, 412
  Anne, 307
  Edward, 199n, 317
  Elizabeth (Coytmore), 414n
  William, 15, 414, 414n
Tyrrell/Tyrell
  Thomas, **444–48**, 444n, 445n, 446n, 485,
    486, 496

U

Underhill
  Captain, 161
United Colonies, 478n
Unity, 170, 173
Upham
  family, 409
  John, 103, 109n
  Phineas, 409
  Priscilla, 409
Usher
  family, 16
  Captain, 49
  Elizabeth (Symmes), 201
  Hezekiah, 201
  John, 309n, 311n, 502

V

vandalism, xxvii, 138, 436, 445–46, 447
Vane
  Henry, 286, 289, 290
Vassall
  John, 13
  Samuel, 13
  William, 13
Venner
  Thomas, 242

vergers, **76**, 144, 265, 335n, 386
Vermont, 477
Verney
    Sir Ralph, 400n
victuallers, 11, 28, 38, 257, 382
viewers of pipestaves (inspectors of barrels), **68**
Vine
    William, 63, 150, 392n
vintners, 199, 203
violence, 79, 84, 143, 145, **433–87**
    anger resulting in, **485–87**
    against children, 437, 438
    communal conciliation to end, **439–43**
    competition among craftsmen and, **449–51**
    culture of discipline and, 487
    defamation suit against Foskett and,
        444–48
    disputes between neighbors and, **452–56**
    drinking and, **461–68**
    festive days and, 437
    forms of, 436
    general causes of, 255–56
    housing disputes and, **457–60**
    against Indians, 470, 474, 475, 478–80, 524
    King Philip's War and, **472–84**
    land disputes and, 437, 438
    men and, 24, 117, 120, 171, 189, 209, 285,
        361–62, 378n, 430, 437
    number of cases of, in Charlestown,
        436–37, 437n
    prevalence of, **255–59**
    punishment for, 438, 438n, 454
    against seamen, xxvii–xxviii, xxix, 255–56
    against servants, 429, 437, 451, 452, 453,
        474, 514n
    by servants, 438, **469–71**
    against women, 340, 340n, **390–94**, 394,
        399, 403–04, 409, 437, 438
Virginia, 7n, 16, 17, 33, 152 (map), 153, 156n,
    159, 162n, 170n, 223, 229, 229n, 238,
    257, 265, 319, 319n, 377n, 382, 383,
    383n, 420, 423, 518, 530
    Lower Norfolk County, 319n
Virginia Company, 14
Vyall
    John, 207, 207n, 208

W
Wade
    Jonathan, 46n
Wadham College, Oxford, 325
Wadland
    Agnes, **390–94**, 391n, 423, 427, 438, 486
    Amos, 390, 391
    Crispin, 150, 390, 390n, 391
    Crispin Jr., 150, 390, 391
    Elizabeth, 390

Waffe
    Alice, 459
    John, 402n, 458, 459
    Katherine, 231n, 401, 402n, 458, 459, 460, 485
    Thomas, 123, 149, 153, 231, 255, 256, 258n,
        402n, **457–60**, 457n, 486
    Thomas Jr., 402n
wagon-makers, 296
Waite/Wayte
    John, 62, 446n
    Mary, 349
    Return, 445
Waldo
    John, 484
Wales, 5
Walford
    Thomas, 45, 45n
Walker
    Anna, 170
    Augustine, 41n, 149, 155n, **169–73**, 173n,
        197, 238n, 248, 254, 256, 257, 258
    Hannah (Mirick), 463n
    John, 399, 438, 463–64, 463, 464n
    Mary, 173
    Nathaniel, 377n
Wallace
    Widow, 36n
    John, 36n
    Nathaniel, 177n
    Nicholas, 36n, 462, 469n
Walley
    John, 385, 386, 387, 388, 389, 425, 438
    Thomas, 388n
    William, 149, 154
Wallis
    Nicholas, 49
walls, 10, **121–24**, 143
Walton
    George, 194n
wampum, 177, 473, 474n
Wapping Dock, 96, 98, 100 (map)
Wapping Dock Bridge, 98
Ward
    Mr., 235n
    Samuel, 50, 60, 62, 70, 72, 318, 319, 484
    William, 484
wardens, 127n, 202, 325
    church, 354n, 523
    fire, **75**
    tree, **65–66**, 81, 126, 129, 139, 139n
wards, **485–88**, 508n
Wardwell
    William, 207, 207n
warehouses, xxiv, 98, 101, 162, 171, 171n, 197,
    217, 219, 252, 402n, 412, 413
Warham
    John, 34

Woody
   Mary (Coggan), 387, 387n, 413n
Woolrich/Woolrych
   J., 57, 58, 67
Woory
   R., 62, 150
World War II, 151
wrecks, 7, 17, 42, 151, 153, 155–156, 155n,
      236, 237n, 281, 333, 459, 517
Wren
   Christopher, 325n
Wright
   Edward, 445
Wyer
   Edward, 50
   Edward Jr., 133, 136n

Wyeth
   family, 367n
   G., 51
   Robert, 367
Wyllie
   John, 234
Wyllys
   Mehitabel, 319n, 320, 320n
Wyman
   John, 105n
   Thomas Bellows, xxv, xxvi

Y
yeomen, 3, 4, 26, 84, 106, 107, 193n, 529
Young
   Anne, 203n

CPSIA information can be obtained at www.ICGtesting.com
Printed in the USA
BVOW070605171211

278569BV00003B/1/P